ARTIFICIAL INTELLIGENCE

CRITICAL CONCEPTS

ARTIFICIAL INTELLIGENCE

Critical Concepts

Edited by Ronald Chrisley
Editorial Assistant: Sander Begeer

Volume I

London and New York

First published 2000
by Routledge
11 New Fetter Lane, London EC4P 4EE

Simultaneously published in the USA and Canada
by Routledge
29 West 35th Street, New York, NY 10001

Routledge is an imprint of the Taylor & Francis Group

Typeset in Times by RefineCatch Limited, Bungay, Suffolk
Printed and bound in Great Britain by
TJ International Ltd, Padstow, Cornwall

British Library Cataloguing in Publication Data
A catalogue record for this book is available from the British Library

Library of Congress Cataloging in Publication Data
Artificial intelligence: critical concepts/edited by Ronald Chrisley with Sander Begeer.
p. cm.
Includes bibliographical references.
ISBN 0–415–19331–1 (set)—ISBN 0–415–19332–X (v. 1)—ISBN 0–415–19333–8 (v. 2)
—ISBN 0–415–19334–6 (v. 3) —ISBN 0–415–19335–4 (v. 4)
1. Artificial intelligence.   I. Chrisley, Ronald.   II. Begeer, Sander.

Q335.5.A7825 2000
006.3—dc21   00–062568

ISBN 0–415–19331–1 (set)
ISBN 0–415–19332–X (volume 1)

CONTENTS

CONTENTS

CONTENTS

CONTENTS

CONTENTS

CONTENTS

CONTENTS

CONTENTS

CONTENTS

ACKNOWLEDGEMENTS

The publishers would like to thank the following for permission to reprint their material:

Ablex Publishing Corporation for permission to reprint Fodor, J. "Modules, Frames, Fridgeons, Sleeping Dogs, and the Music of the Spheres", in Pylyshyn, Z. W. (ed), *The Robot's Dilemma: The Frame Problem in Artificial Intelligence*, 1987, pp. 139–149.

Academic Press for permission to reprint Husbands, P., Harvey, I. Cliff, D. and Miller, G. "Artificial Evolution: A New Path for Artificial Intelligence?", in *Brain and Cognition*, 34, 130–159. Copyright © 1997 by Academic Press. All rights of reproduction in any form reserved.

American Association for Artificial Intelligence for permission to reprint Glymour, C., Ford, K. M., and Hayes, P. J. "The Prehistory of Android Epistemology", in Ford, K.M., Glymour C. and Hayes, P.J. (eds) *Android Epistemology*, pp. 3–21 and Armer, P. "Attitudes Toward Intelligent Machines", in Edward A. Feigenbaum and Julian Feldman (eds) *Computers and Thought*, 1962, pp. 389–406 and LaChat, M.R. "Artificial Intelligence and Ethics: An Exercise in the Moral Imagination", in *The AI Magazine*, 7(2) 1986: 70–79.

American Psychological Association for permission to reprint Neisser, U., Boodoo, G., Bouchard, T. J., Jr., Boykin, A. W., Brody, N., Ceci, S. J. Halpern, D. F., Loehlin, J. C., Perloff, R., Sternberg, R. J. and Urbina, S. "Intelligence: Knowns and Unknowns", *American Psychologist*, 51, 1996: 77–101.

The Annals of the New York Academy of Sciences for permission to reprint Pagels, H. "Panel Discussion: Has Artificial Intelligence Research Illuminated Human Thinking?", in Pagels, H. *Computer Culture: The Scientific, Intellectual and Social Impact of the Computer*, 1984, pp. 138–60.

Association for Computing Machinery for permission to reprint Newell, A. and Simon, H. "Computer Science as Empirical Inquiry Symbols and Search

ACKNOWLEDGEMENTS

The Tenth Turing Lecture", in *Communications of the Association for Computing Machinery*, 19, March 1976: 105–32. © 1976, Association for Computing Machinery.

Basic Books for permission to reprint Crevier, D. "The Tree of Knowledge", in Crevier, D. *AI: The Tumultuous History of the Search for Artificial Intelligence*, 1993, pp. 145–63 and Hofstadter, D. R., "Waking Up from the Boolean Dream, or, Subcognition as Computation", in Hofstader, D. R. *Metamagical Themas: Questing for the Essence of Mind and Pattern*, 1985, pp. 631–65.

California Institute of Technology for permission to reprint Von Neumann, J. "The General and Logical Theory of Automata", in Jeffress, L.A. (ed.) *Cerebral Mechanisms in Behavior*, 1951.

Cambridge University Press for permission to reprint Smolensky, P. "Connectionism and the Foundations of AI", in Partridge, D. *The Foundations of Artificial Intelligence*, 1990, pp. 306–27; Dennett, D.C. "Why not the Whole Iguana?", in *Behavioral & Brain Sciences*, 1, 1978: 103–104; Schank, R.C. "What is AI, Anyway?", in Partridge, D. and Wilks, Y (eds) *The Foundations of Artificial Intelligence: A Sourcebook*, 1990, pp. 3–13; Suchman, L.A. and Trigg, R.H. "Artificial Intelligence as Craftwork", in Chaiklin, S. and Lave, J. (eds) *Understanding Practice: Perspectives on Activity and Context*, pp. 144–78; Winograd, T. "Thinking machines: Can there be? Are we?", in Partridge, D. and Wilks, Y. (eds) *The Foundations of Artificial Intelligence: A Sourcebook*, 1990, pp. 167–89; Dennett, D. "Cognitive Wheels: The Frame Problem of AI; in Hookway, C. (ed.) *Minds, Machines & Evolution: Philosophical Studies*, 1984, pp. 129–51; Woolgar, S. "Why not a Sociology of Machines?", in *The Case of Sociology and Artificial Intelligence Sociology*, 19(4), 1985: 557–72 and Descartes, R. "Discourse on Method", part 5, in Cottingham, J., Stoothoft, R. and Murdoch, D. (trans.) *The Philosophical Writings of Descartes*, 1985, pp. 131–41.

The Controller of HMSO for permission to reprint McCarthy, J. "Programs with Common Sense (with discussion)", in *Proceedings of the Symposium on the Mechanization of Thought Processes*, National Physical Laboratory, pp. 75–93, © Crown Copyright 1958 and Selfridge, O.G. "Pandemonium: A Paradigm for Learning", *Mechanization of Thought Processes*, 1959, pp. 511–31, © Crown Copyright 1959. Reproduced by permission of the Controller of HMSO.

Daedalus, Journal of the American Academy of Arts and Sciences for permission to reprint McCarthy, J. "Mathematical Logic in Artificial Intelligence", in *Daedalus: Journal of the American Academy of Arts and Sciences*, 117(1), Winter 1988: 297–311; Waltz, D.L. "The Prospects for Building Truly Intelligent Machines", in *Daedalus: Journal of the American Academy of Arts and Sciences*, 117(1), and Agre, P. (1988) "The Soul Gained and Lost: Artificial Intelligence as a Philosophical Project", in *Daedalus: Journal of the American Academy of Arts and Sciences*, 117(1), winter 1988: 1–21.

Elsevier Science for permission to reprint Margaret A. Boden "Creativity and Artificial Intelligence", in *Artificial Intelligence*, 103(1–2) 1998: 347–56; Bobrow, D.G. and Hayes, P.J. (eds) "Artificial Intelligence – Where are We?", in *Artificial Intelligence*, 25, 1985: 375–415; Smith, B.C. "The Owl and the Electric Encyclopedia", in *Artificial Intelligence*, 47, 1991: 251–88 and McCarthy, J. "Review of 'Artificial Intelligence: A General Survey' by Professor Sir James Lighthill", *Artificial Intelligence*, 5(3) 1974: 317–22; Rosenbloom, P.S. Laird, J. E., Newell, A. and McCarl, R.A. "Preliminary Analysis of the Soar Architecture as Basis for General Intelligence", in *Artificial Intelligence*, 47, 1991: 289–325; Beer, R. "A Dynamical Systems Perspective on Agent-Environment Interaction", *Artificial Intelligence*, 72(1–2), 1995: 173–215; Lenat, D. and Feigenbaum, E. "On the Thresholds of Knowledge", in *Artificial Intelligence*, 47(1–3) 1991: 185–250 and Kirsh D. "Today the Earwig, Tomorrow Man?", in *Artificial Intelligence*, 47(1–3), 1991: 161–84; Bechtel, W., "Consciousness: Perspectives from Symbolic and Connectionist AI.", in *Neuropsychologia*, 33, 1994: 1075–1086 and Lighthill, J. "Artificial Intelligence, A General Survey", in *Artificial Intelligence: A Paper Symposium*, 1972: 1–22.

Guildford Publications Inc. for permission to reprint excerpts from Bateson, G. "The Cybernetics of 'Self'", in *Psychiatry*, 34(1) 1971: 1–18.

Hackett Publishing for permission to reprint Leibniz, G. "The Monadology", in Cahn, S. M. (ed.) *Classics of Western Philosophy*, (3rd ed.) 1977, pp. 604–13.

Harcourt Brace and Co. for permission to reprint Miller, G.A., Galanter, E. and Pribram, K.H. "The Simulation of Psychological Processes", in Miller, G.A., Galanter, E. and Pribram, K.H., *Plans and the Structure of Behaviour*, 1960, pp. 41–57.

HarperCollins Publishers Ltd. for permission to reprint Hobbes, T. "Reason and Science", in Plamenatz, J. (ed.) *Leviathan*, chapter 5, pp. 81–87.

Herbert, A. Simon for permission to reproduce Newell, A., Shaw, J.C. and Simon, H. "Report on a General Problem-Solving Program", in *Proceedings of the International Conference on Information Processing*, 1960, pp. 256–64.

IEEE for permission to reprint Minsky, M. "Steps Toward Artificial Intelligence", in *Proceedings of the IRE*, 49, 1, January 1961: 8–30. © 1961 IRE (now IEEE).

Johns Hopkins University Press for permission to reprint Wright, I.P., Sloman, A. and Beaudoin L.P. "Towards a Design-Based Analysis of Emotional

Episodes (with commentaries)", in *Philosophy, Psychiatry and Psychology*, 3(2) 1996: 101–26 and Fryer, D.M. and Marshall, J.C. "The Motives of Jacques de Vaucanson", in *Technology and Culture*, 20: 257–69.

John Wiley & Sons, Inc. for permission to reprint Fogel, L.J., Owens, A.J. and Walsh, M.J., "Introduction", in Fogel, L.J., Owens, A.J. and Walsh, M.J. *Artificial Intelligence through Simulated Evolution*, pp. 1–10; Newell, A., "Intellectual Issues in the History of Artificial Intelligence", in Machlup, F. and Mansfield, U. *The Study of Information – Interdisciplinary Messages*, 1983, pp. 187–227 and Torrance, S. "Ethics, Mind and Artifice", in Gill, K.S. (ed.), *Artificial Intelligence for Society*, 1986, pp. 55–72. Reproduced by permission of John Wiley and Sons Ltd.

Kluwer Academic Publishers for permission to reprint Copeland, B.J. and Proudfoot, D. "On Alan Turing's Anticipation of Connectionism", in *Synthese*, 108, 1996: 361–77.

Massachusetts Institute of Technology, Centre for Advanced Engineering Study for permission to reprint Steels, L. "The Artificial Life Roots of Artificial Intelligence", in Langton, C.G. *Artificial Life, An Overview*, 1996, pp. 75–110.

The family of Mrs. Warren McCulloch and MIT Press for permission to reprint McCulloch, W.S. and Pitts, W.H. "A logical Calculus of the Ideas Immanent in Nervous Activity", in McCulloch, W.S. *Embodiments of Mind*, 1943 pp. 19–40.

Macmillan Press Ltd for permission to reprint Leibniz, G. "Preface to the General Science", in Wiener, P. (ed.) Leibniz Selections, 1951, pp. 15–17.

MIT Press for permission to reprint Edwards, P.N. "The Machine in the Middle: Cybernetic Psychology and World War II", in Edwards, P. *The Closed World*, 1996, pp. 174–207; excerpts from Minsky, M. "The Society of Mind" in Winston, P. H. (eds) 1990 *Artificial Intelligence at MIT, Expanding Frontiers*, 1: 244–69; Brooks, R. A. "Intelligence Without Reason", MIT AI Lab Memo 1293, April 1991, Reprinted in *Proceedings of 12th International Joint Conference on Artificial Intelligence*, Sydney, Australia, 1991, pp. 569–595; Heims, S.J. "Describing 'Embodiments of Mind': McCulloch and His Cohorts", in *Constructing a Social Science for Post War America: The Cybernetics Group 1946–1953*, 1991, pp. 31–52 and Minsky, M. "Logical vs. Analogical or Symbolic vs. Connectionist or Neat vs. Scruffy", in Winston, P.H. and Shellard, S.A. (eds) *Artificial Intelligence at MIT, Expanding Frontiers*, 1990, 1: 218–44; Dreyfus, H. "Introduction to the MIT Press Edition", in Dreyfus, H. *What Computers Still Can't Do*, 1992, pp. 1–67; Haugeland, J. "Introduction", in *Artificial Intelligence: The Very Idea*, 1985, pp. 2–12 and Simon, H. "Understanding the Natural and the Artificial World", in Simon, H. *Sciences of the Artificial*, 1969, pp. 1–24.

The National Computing Centre Ltd. for permission to reprint Simons, G. "Towards Electronic Computers", in *Evolution of the Intelligent Machines: A popular history of AI*, 1988, pp. 53–63.

Open Court Publishing Co. for permission to reprint La Mettrie, J. O. de, "The Man-Machine", in La Mettrie, J. O. de, *Man a Machine*, pp. 85–149.

Oxford University Press for permission to reprint Turing, A.M., "Computing Machinery and Intelligence", in *Mind*, 236: Oct. 1950, 433–60 and Whitby, B. "The Turing Test: AI's biggest blind alley?", in Millican, P. and Clark A. *Machines and Thought: The Legacy of Alan Turing*, pp. 53–62.

Pamela McCorduck for permission to reprint McCorduck, P. "Robotics and General Intelligence", in McCorduck, P. *Machines Who Think: A Personal Inquiry into the History and Prospects of Artificial Intelligence*, 1979, pp. 209–239.

Perseus Books for permission to reprint Gardner, H., "Artificial Intelligence: The Expert Tool" in Gardner, H. *The Mind's New Science*, 1985, pp. 138–181.

Princeton University Press for permission to reprint Ashby, W. R. "Design for an Intelligence-Amplifier", in Shannon, C.E. and McCarthy, J. (eds), *Automata Studies*, 1956 and Lucas, J.R. "Minds, Machines and Godel: A Retrospect", in Millican, P.J.R. and Clark, A. *Machines and Thought: The Legacy of Alan Turing*, 1996, pp. 103–124.

Professor John McCarthy for permission to reprint McCarthy, J., Minsky, M.L., Rochester, I.B.M. and Shannon, C.E. "A Proposal for the Dartmouth Summer Research Project on Artificial Intelligence", 1955.

Psychological Review for permission to reprint Rosenblatt, F. "The Perceptron: A Probabilistic Model for Information Storage and Organization in the Brain", in *Psychological Review*, 65(6), 1958: 386–408.

Rand Organization for permission to reprint Dreyfus, H., "Alchemy and Artificial Intelligence", in *Rand Organization Internal Report*, 1965.

Springer-Verlag Ltd for permission to reprint Cordeschi, R., "The Discovery of the Artificial. Some Protocybernetic Developments 1930–1940", in *AI & Society*, 1991, pp. 218–38 and Laufer, R. "The Social Acceptability of AI Systems: Legitimacy Epistemology and Marketing", *AI and Society*, 6, 1992: 197–220.

The Stanford Electronic Humanities Review for permission to reprint Mazlish, B., "The Man-Machine and Artificial Intelligence' in *The Stanford Electronic Humanities Review*, 4(2) 1995 Constructions of the Mind: 21–45.

Taylor and Francis for permission to reprint Cohen, J., "Theory of Robots in the Seventeenth and Eighteenth Centuries", in Cohen, J, *Human Robots in*

Myth and Antiquity, 1965, pp. 68–80; Aizawa, K., "Connectionism and Artificial Intelligence, History and Philosophical Interpretation", in *Journal of Experimental and Theoretical Artificial Intelligence*, 4, 1992; Boden, M. "Horses of a Different Color?", Ramsey, W.H., Stich, S.P., and Rumelhart, D.E. *Philosophy and Connectionist Theory*, pp. 3–20 and Adam, A. "The Knowing Subject in AI", in Adam, A. *Artificial Knowing, Gender and the Thinking Machine*, 1998, pp. 69–99.

The University of Chicago Press for permission to reprint Rosenbleuth, A., Wiener, N. and Bigelow, J., "Behavior, Purpose and Teleology" in *Philosophy of Science*, 10, 1943: 18–24.

The University of North Carolina Press for permission to reprint Bolter, J.D. "Artificial Intelligence", in Bolter, J.D., *Turing's Man: Western Culture in the Computer Age*, 1984, pp. 189–213.

W. H. Freeman and Company for permission to reprint Weizenbaum, J. "Artificial Intelligence", in Weizenbaum, J. *Computer Power and Human Reasoning: From Judgment to Calculation*, 1976, pp. 202–28. © 1976 by W. H. Freeman and Company. Used with permission.

Yale University Press for permission to reprint Mazlish, B. "Babbage, Huxley and Butler", in Mazlish, B. *The Fourth Discontinuity*, 1993, pp. 130–55.

The publishers have made very effort to contact authors/copyright holders of works reprinted in *Artificial Intelligence: Critical Concepts*. This has not been possible in every case, however, and we would welcome correspondence from those individuals/companies we have been unable to trace.

Chronological Table of Reprinted Articles and Chapters

Date	Author	Article/Chapter	References	Vol.	Chap.
1935	Thomas Ross	Machines That Think – A further statement	Psychological Review XLII, 387–93.	I	16
1937	Thomas Ross	The Synthesis of Intelligence – Its implications	Psychological Review XLII, 185–9.	I	17
1942	Ada Lovelace	Translator's Notes (Excerpts) for L.F. Menabrea's Memoir	R. Taylor (ed.), *Sketch of the Analytical Engine Invented by Charles Babbage*, L.F. Menabrea with Notes upon the Memoir by the Translator, 1942, pp. 245–58 and 284.	I	12
1943	Arturo Rosenblueth, Norbert Wiener and Julian Bigelow	Behavior, Purpose and Teleology	*Philosophy of Science*, 10, 18–24.	I	19
1950	A.M. Turing	Computing Machinery and Intelligence	*Mind* LIX(236): 433–60.	II	25
1951	G. Leibniz	Preface to The General Science	P. Wiener (ed.), *Leibniz Selections*, Macmillan Press Ltd, 1951, pp. 12–17.	I	8
1951	John von Neumann	The General and Logical theory of Automata	L.A. Jeffress (ed.) *Cerebral Mechanisms in Behavior*, Hixon Symposium Hafner Publishing, 1951, pp. 1–41.	I	22
1953	J.O. de La Mettrie	Man a Machine	G.C. Bussey (ed.), *Man a Machine*, 1747, French text with English translation of *L'homme machine*, 149, Open Court, 1953, pp. 85–55.	I	11
1955	J. McCarthy, M.L. Minsky, N. Rochester and C.E. Shannon	A Proposal for the Dartmouth Summer Research Project on Artificial Intelligence	J. McCarthy, M.L. Minsky, N. Rochester and C.E. Shannon, A Proposal for the Dartmouth Summer Research Project on Artifical Intelligence.	II	26
1956	W. Ross Ashby	Design for an Intelligence-Amplifier	C.E. Shannon and J. McCarthy (eds), *Automata Studies*, Princeton University Press, pp. 215–33.	III	52

Year	Author	Title			Source
1958	John McCarthy	Programs with Common Sense	II	27	*Proceedings of the Symposium on the Mechanization of Thought Processes*, National Physical Laboratory/HMSO, pp. 77–91.
1958	F. Rosenblatt	The Perceptron: A probabilistic model for information storage and organization in the brain	II	39	*Psychological Review* 65(6): 386–408.
1959	O.G. Selfridge	Pandemonium: A paradigm for learning	II	40	*Proceedings of the Symposium on Mechanisation of Thought Processes*, HMSO, pp. 513–31.
1960	A. Newell, J.C. Shaw and H. Simon	Report on a General Problem-Solving Program	II	28	*Proceedings of the International Conference on Information Processing*, UNISCO House, Paris, France, pp. 256–64.
1960	G.A. Miller, E. Galanter and K.H. Pribram	The Simulation of Psychological Processes	II	29	G.A. Miller, E. Galanter and K.H. Pribram, *Plans and the Structure of Behavior*, Harcourt Brace, pp. 41–57.
1961	Marvin Minsky	Steps Toward Artificial Intelligence	II	30	*Proceedings of the IRE* 49(1): 8–30.
1962	Paul Armer	Attitudes Toward Intelligent Machines	IV	79	E.A. Feigenbaum and J. Feldman (eds) *Computers and Thought*, McGraw-Hill, pp. 389–406.
1962	T. Hobbes	*Leviathan*, Chapter 5 'Of Reason and Science'	I	7	J. Plamenatz (ed.), *Leviathan*, HarperCollins Publishers Ltd, 1962, pp. 81–7.
1965	J. Cohen	Theory of Robots in the Seventeenth and Eighteenth Centuries	I	5	J. Cohen, *Human Robots in Myth and Antiquity*, Taylor & Francis, 1965, pp. 68–80.
1965	Hubert L. Dreyfus	Alchemy and Artificial Intelligence	III	59	*Rand Organization*, pp. 1–90.
1965	Warren S. McCulloch and Walter H. Pitts	A Logical Calculus of the Ideas Immanent in Nervous Activity	I	20	W.S. McCulloch, *Embodiments of Mind*, MIT Press, 1965, pp. 19–39.
1966	L.J. Fogel, A.J. Owens and M.J. Walsh	Introduction to *Artificial Intelligence Through Simulated Evolution*	III	54	L.J. Fogel, A.J. Owens and M.J. Walsh, *Artificial Intelligence Through Simulated Evolution*, John Wiley & Sons, pp. 1–10.
1969	H. Simon	Understanding the Natural and the Artificial World	IV	70	H. Simon, *Sciences of the Artificial*, MIT Press, pp. 1–24.

Chronological continued

Date	Author	Article/Chapter	References	Vol.	Chap.
1971	Gregory Bateson	Epistemology and Ontology. Excerpt from "The Cybernetics of 'Self': A Theory of Alcoholism"	*Psychiatry* 34(1): 1–18	III	48
1972	James Lighthill	Artificial Intelligence: A General Survey	*Artificial Intelligence: A Paper Symposium*, Elsevier Science, pp. 1–21.	III	62
1974	John McCarthy	Review of "Artificial Intelligence: A General Survey"	*Artificial Intelligence* 5(3): 317–22.	III	63
1976	Allen Newell and Herbert A. Simon	Computer Science as Empirical Enquiry: Symbols and search	*Communications of the Association for Computing Machinery* 19: 105–32.	II	31
1976	Joseph Weizenbaum	Artificial Intelligence	J. Weizenbaum, *Computer Power and Human Reasoning: From Judgment to Calculation*, W.H. Freeman, pp. 202–28.	III	56
1977	G. Leibniz	*Monadology*	S.M. Cahn (ed.), *Classics of Western Philosophy* (3rd edn), Hackett Publishing, 1977, pp. 604–13.	I	9
1978	Daniel C. Dennett	Why Not the Whole Iguana?	*Behavioral and Brain Sciences* 1: 103–4.	III	46
1979	David M. Fryer and John C. Marshall	The Motives of Jacques de Vaucanson	*Technology and Culture* 20, 1979: 257–69.	I	10
1979	P. McCorduck	Robotics and General Intelligence	P. McCorduck *Machines Who Think: A Personal Inquiry into the History and Prospects of Artificial Intelligence*, W.H. Freeman, 1979, pp. 209–37.	I	23
1981	Ned Block	Psychologism and Behaviorism	*Philosophical Review* 90: 5–43.	IV	72
1983	Allen Newell	Intellectual Issues in the History of Artificial Intelligence	F. Machlup and U. Mansfield, *The Study of Information – Interdisciplinary Messages*, John Wiley & Sons, 1983, pp. 187–227.	I	1
1984	J.D. Bolter	Artificial Intelligence	J.D. Bolter, *Turing's Man: Western Culture in the Computer Age*, University of North Carolina Press, pp. 189–213.	IV	83

Year	Author	Title	Source	Part	Page
1984	Daniel Dennett	Cognitive Wheels: the frame problem of AI	C. Hookway (ed.), *Minds, Machines & Evolution: Philosophical Studies*, Cambridge University Press, pp. 129–51.	III	64
1984	Heinz R. Pagels	Panel Discussion: Has artificial intelligence research illuminated human thinking?	H. Pagels, *Computer Culture: The Scientific, Intellectual and Social Impact of the Computer*, Annals of the New York Academy of Sciences, pp. 138–60.	III	57
1985	Daniel G. Bobrow and Patrick J. Hayes (eds)	Artificial Intelligence – Where Are We?	*Artificial Intelligence* 25: 375–415.	II	32
1985	R. Descartes	Part Five of *Discourse on the Method*	J. Cottingham, R. Stoothoff and D. Murdoch (Trans.) *The Philosophical Writings of Descartes*, Cambridge University Press, 1985, pp. 131–41.	I	6
1985	H. Gardner	Artificial Intelligence: The Expert Tool	H. Gardner, *The Mind's New Science*, Perseus Books, 1985, pp. 131–81.	I	2
1985	John Haugeland	Introduction to *Artificial Intelligence: The Very Idea*	J. Haugeland, *Artificial Intelligence: The Very Idea*, MIT Press, pp. 2–12.	IV	66
1985	D.R. Hofstadter	Waking Up from the Boolean Dream, or, Subcognition as Computation	D.R. Hofstadter, *Metamagical Themas: Questing for the Essence of Mind and Pattern*, Basic Books, pp. 631–65.	II	42
1985	Steve Woolgar	Why Not a Sociology of Machines? The Case of Sociology and Artificial Intelligence	*Sociology* 19(4): 557–72.	IV	81
1986	Michael R. LaChat	Artificial Intelligence and Ethics: An exercise in the moral imagination	*The AI Magazine* 7(2): 70–79.	IV	78
1986	Steve Torrance	Ethics, Mind and Artifice	K.S. Gill (ed.), *Artificial Intelligence for Society*, John Wiley & Sons, pp. 55–72	IV	77
1987	Jerry A. Fodor	Modules, Frames, Fridgeons, Sleeping Dogs, and the Music of the Spheres	Z.W. Pylyshyn (ed.), *The Robot's Dilemma: The Frame Problem in Artificial Intelligence*, Ablex Publishing, pp. 139–49.	III	65

Chronological continued

Date	Author	Article/Chapter	References	Vol.	Chap.
1988	John McCarthy	Mathematical Logic in Artificial Intelligence	*Daedalus: Journal of the American Academy of Arts and Sciences* 117(1): 297–311.	II	34
1988	G. Simons	Towards Electronic Computers	*Evolution of the Intelligent Machines: A popular history of AI*, 1988, pp. 53–64. NCC Publications, Manchester	I	14
1988	David L. Waltz	The Prospects for Building Truly Intelligent Machines	*Daedalus: Journal of the American Academy of Arts and Sciences* 117(1): 191–212.	II	43
1990	Marvin Minsky	Excerpts from *The Society of Mind*	P.H. Winston and S.A. Shellard (eds), *Artificial Intelligence at MIT, Expanding Frontiers* Vol. 1, MIT Press, pp. 244–69.	II	33
1990	Marvin Minsky	Logical vs. Analogical or Symbolic vs. Connectionist or Neat vs. Scruffy	P.H. Winston and S.A. Shellard (eds), *Artificial Intelligence at MIT, Expanding Frontiers*, Vol. 1, MIT Press, pp. 218–43.	II	45
1990	Roger C. Schank	What is AI, Anyway?	D. Partridge and Y. Wilks (eds), *The Foundations of Artificial Intelligence: A Sourcebook*, Cambridge University Press, pp. 3–13.	IV	67
1990	Paul Smolensky	Connectionism and the Foundations of AI	D. Partridge and Y. Wilks (eds) *The Foundations of Artificial Intelligence: A Sourcebook*, Cambridge University Press, pp. 306–26.	II	44
1990	Terry Winograd	Thinking Machines: Can There Be? Are We?	D. Partridge and Y. Wilks (eds), *The Foundations of Artificial Intelligence: A Sourcebook*, Cambridge University Press, pp. 167–89.	III	60
1991	Margaret A. Boden	Horses of a Different Color?	Ramsey, W.H., Stich, S.P., and Rumelhart, D.E., *Philosophy and Connectionist Theory*, Taylor & Francis, 1991, pp. 3–19.	II	41

Chronological continued

Date	Author	Article/Chapter	References	Vol.	Chap.
1993	Bruce Mazlish	Babbage, Huxley and Butler	B. Mazlish, *The Fourth Discontinuity*, Yale University Press, 1993, pp. 130–55.	I	13
1993	Lucy A. Suchman and Randall H. Trigg	Artificial Intelligence as Craftwork	S. Chaiklin and J. Lave (eds), *Understanding Practice: Perspectives on Activity and Context*, Cambridge University Press, pp. 144–78.	IV	68
1994	William Bechtel	Consciousness: Perspectives from Symbolic and Connectionist AI	*Neuropsychologia* 33: 1075–86.	IV	74
1995	Philip E. Agre	The Soul Gained and Lost: Artificial intelligence as a philosophical project	*Stanford Humanities Review* 4(2), 1995: 1–19.	IV	69
1995	Randall D. Beer	A Dynamical Systems Perspective on Agent-Environment Interaction	*Artificial Intelligence* 72(1–2): 173–215.	III	53
1995	Clark Glymour, Kenneth M. Ford and Patrick J. Hayes	The Prehistory of Android Epistemology	K.M. Ford, C. Glymour and P.J. Hayes (eds), *Android Epistemology*, American Association for Artificial Intelligence/MIT Press, 1995, pp. 3–21.	I	3
1995	Bruce Mazlish	The Man-machine and Artificial Intelligence	*Stanford Electronic Humanities Review* 4(2), 1995: 21–45.	I	4
1996	B. Jack Copeland and Diane Proudfoot	On Alan Turing's Anticipation of Connectionism	*Synthese* 108, 1996: 361–77.	II	38
1996	P.N. Edwards	The Machine in the Middle: Cybernetic psychology and World War II	P. Edwards, *The Closed World*, MIT Press, 1996, pp. 175–207.	I	18
1996	J.R. Lucas	Minds, Machines and Gödel: A retrospect	P.J.R. Millican and A. Clark, *Machines and Thought: The Legacy of Alan Turing*, Princeton University Press, pp. 103–24.	III	58

Year	Author	Title	Publication		
1996	U. Neisser, G. Boodoo, T.J. Bouchard Jr., A.W. Boykin, N. Brody, S.J. Ceci, D.F. Halpern, J.C. Loehlin, R. Perloff, R.J. Sternberg and S. Urbina	Intelligence: Knowns and unknowns	*American Psychologist* 51: 77–101	IV	71
1996	Luc Steels	The Artificial Life Roots of Artificial Intelligence	C.G. Langton, *Artificial Life, An Overview,* Massachusetts Institute of Technology Centre for Advanced Engineering, pp. 75–110.	III	47
1996	Blay Whitby	The Turing Test: AI's biggest blind alley?	P. Millican and A. Clark (eds), *Machines and Thought: The Legacy of Alan Turing,* Oxford University Press, pp. 53–62.	IV	73
1996	Ian P. Wright, Aaron Sloman and Luc Beaudoin	Towards a Design-Based Analysis of Emotional Episodes	*Philosophy Psychiatry and Psychology* 3(2): 101–26.	IV	75
1997	P. Husbands, I. Harvey, D. Cliff and G. Miller	Artificial Evolution: A new path for artificial intelligence?	*Brain and Cognition* 34: 130–59.	III	55
1998	A. Adam	The Knowing Subject in AI	A. Adam, *Artificial Knowing, Gender and the Thinking Machine,* Routledge, pp. 69–98.	IV	82
1998	Margaret A. Boden	Creativity and Artificial Intelligence	*Artificial Intelligence* 103(1–2): 347–56.	IV	76

PREFACE

This reference work is intended to assist those who wish to chart the history of the concept of artificial intelligence. It is not in itself, then, a history, although here and there its compilation did require taking a stand on issues of historical contention. Nor is it concerned exclusively with the academic and industrial research field known as Artificial Intelligence (or, more familiarly, "AI"), although the contributions of that field loom large in the substance of this set. What is included here are the texts which either exemplify or document the milestones in the development of the concept of an intelligent artifact, a concept which predates the field of AI by several centuries (if not millennia). The set omits much (though not all) of the personal, political, and economic detail that is necessary for a complete understanding of the field of AI. But much, if not all, of what is included here is of direct relevance to understanding not only artificial intelligence in general, but the field of AI in particular. We humans thought about the possibility of intelligent artefacts centuries before we tried to build them, and tried to build them centuries before the digital computer and "AI" appeared. It is evident that this thinking and groundwork pre-shaped, to a great extent, the engineering attempts at artificial intelligence of the latter half of the twentieth century through to the present.

Although the set begins with a section entitled "General Historical Context" this is slightly misleading, as many of the papers in the subsequent sections were chosen for their attention to locating the issues with respect to preceding thinkers and ideas. In all subsections, the papers are arranged in chronological order of their content.

Volume II, and Part I of Volume III cover the three main approaches to artificial intelligence being pursued today. Or rather, they cover two approaches and a third catchall confederation of diverse, but related, work. Since all of these share most of the same historical legacy, it was always going to be a bit arbitrary to draw a line between the general historical context and that for each of the approaches. A cut-off point of 1950 (the date of Turing's "Computing Machinery and Intelligence") was chosen as the watershed: if a piece was written before 1950 (or primarily about a time before 1950), it is in the general historical section (Part I, if its temporal compass was on the span of centuries, Part II if its remit was more focused). Pieces concerned with matters after 1950 are in whichever of Volumes II, III or IV is most appropriate: Volume II and Part 1 of Volume III for the various approaches, Part II of Volume III for works that argue against the possibility of building intelligent artefacts, Volume IV, Part I for papers relevant to the concept of artificial intelligence itself, and Volume IV, Part II for items that attempt to broaden the scope of the discussion of intelligent artefacts.

Obviously, this set is primarily the work of others, rather than my own. Thus I thank all of the living authors for their contributions, and especially those authors who offered suggestions and advice. Special thanks go to my editorial assistant, Sander Begeer, without whom the project would never have been completed, and who played an active role in giving the set its final structure and composition. Frances Parkes, Paula White, Natalie Foster and the other staff at Routledge/Taylor & Francis provided enthusiasm and encouragement, and are to be thanked for their patience when deadlines were not met again and again. The University of Sussex and the School of Cognitive and Computing Sciences (COGS) went to great lengths to provide me with the resources necessary for completing a work of this magnitude. Of particular help was the assistance provided by Mark Clark of the Research Grants Office, and Richard Coates, the Dean of COGS. Numerous other people contributed suggestions, answered queries, or provided stimulating discussions, including, but not limited to: Alan Bundy, Michele Carenini, Karine Chemla, Andy Clark, Song De, Ron Eglash, James Fetzer, Lee Giles, Steven Harnad, David Israel, James Kerr, John Laird, Seppo Linnainmaa, Chris Malcolm, Jose Negrete Martinez, Maurizio Matteuzzi, Hank Mishkoff, John Moffett, Kane Oliver, Derek Partridge, Stuart Russell, Erik Sandewall, Matthias Scheutz, Michael Schroeder, Terry Sejnowski, Jouko Seppänen, Noel Sharkey, Jörg Siekmann, Mark Steedman, Josefa Toribio, Achille Varzi, Mike Wheeler, and Tom Ziemke. Apologies to those who assisted but whom I have failed to mention here. Finally, warm thanks goes to Sibel Kulaçoğlu whose unflinching emotional support and exuberance were a constant source of inspiration.

GENERAL INTRODUCTION
The concept of artificial intelligence

Ronald Chrisley

And if a bird can talk, who once was a dinosaur
And a dog can dream; should it be implausible
That a man might supervise
The construction of light?
Adrian Belew

When attempting to characterise a concept of anything, one might well ask "which concept?" or "whose concept?" Even as rarefied a concept as that of artificial intelligence varies with cultural and intellectual context. In this set, the activities of the field of AI loom large because the emphasis is on the concept of artificial intelligence from the perspectives of those we might call the *practitioners* of artificial intelligence: those who have actually attempted to create an intelligent artefact. This is not to say that all included writers are practitioners; but those who are not do pick up the intellectual agenda of the practitioners before and after them. Thus, there is only marginal discussion of the concept of artificial intelligence as employed by myth makers, theologians, politicians, poets, playwrights, satirists, writers and filmmakers.

Even with this clarification, some might require further preliminaries. Those of a philosophical bent might wonder at the very possibility of charting the "development of a concept". For example, the creation stories and mythologies of many cultures speak of an intelligent agent, God, creating another intelligent agent, a human, out of artifice (that is, not through child-birth). Surely this is a different concept of artificial intelligence than the one being employed in research today! Thus, there is not one concept which is developing or changing, but rather a temporal succession of any number of different concepts. One might think that moving from one to the other, as this set does again and again, is just a chronic case of changing the subject.

There are two ways to reply to this. My preferred way is to go against current philosophical views and claim that concepts, like objects, are not individuated solely by their intrinsic properties. Just as an object might

1

change its colour or shape and still remain the same object, so also might a concept undergo change to its modal, logical or epistemological properties and still remain the same concept. As in the case of objects, what glues the different concept-stages together over time is a notion of continuity – spatio-temporal continuity in the case of objects, and conceptual continuity in the case of concepts. Part of the function of reference works such as this one is to provide the materials required to determine the existence or absence of conceptual continuity between the concepts of different times and contexts.

The foregoing is an unorthodox and as yet unelaborated view, so for those who require more secure foundations, there is another reply, based on Putnam's view of natural kind terms (see the Block paper Article 7 in Volume IV). To concede that there are many concepts of artificial intelligence expressed by the items in this set is not to say that they are all talking about different topics. Concepts are on the Fregean level of *sense*; what unites the talk here is sameness of *reference*. The ancients had a concept of gold which differs from ours considerably (for one thing, it did not involve the notion of atomic number). Yet when they said things about gold using their concept of gold, they were saying things about the very same stuff that we make claims about when we use our concept of gold. The same goes for artificial intelligence. It must be admitted that since Putnam's point was made for the case of natural kind terms, this line of reasoning only applies if a case can be made for "artificial intelligence" being a natural kind term (a suspect assumption perhaps, given the usual opposition between what is natural and what is artificial), or if Putnam's argument can be extended to cover more than just natural kind terms. But these philosophical niceties take us too far afield.

Another conceptual difficulty concerns the natural/artificial distinction itself. That it is crucial to the concept of artificial intelligence is without doubt: for example, the distinction is required in order to prevent sexual reproduction from being classified as achieving artificial intelligence (although perhaps an investigation, informed by theories of gender politics and power, into why such an exclusion is seen to be of paramount import-ance, is called for here). Yet most of the participants in the field of artificial intelligence today are naturalists: they join with Boyle in rejecting the Aristotelian distinction between natural and artificial; they think that there is no special dualism between humans and animals, mind and matter; there is no supernatural soul. Yet if humans are natural, then surely artefact construction is itself a natural activity. And so the distinction between artificial and natural intelligence seems to be an untenable, arbitrary one, on which nothing can hinge.

This may be the case, but it works in favour of artificial intelligence research, not against it. It is only the critic of the possibility of artificial intelligence that needs to make a sharp, principled distinction between it and natural intelligence, so that the former, and not the latter, can be shown to be impossible. For the naturalist, artificial intelligence vs. natural intelligence becomes natural intelligence brought about in a (particular) new way vs. natural intelligence brought about the traditional way.

Perhaps a more serious difficulty with the concept of artificial intelligence is an apparent contradiction in the very notion. On this view, "artificial intelligence" is an oxymoron, since intelligence implies, and artefactuality is inconsistent with, autonomy. Take the latter point first: Aristotle made the point that an artefact is defined in terms of the purpose or function that it is intended to have. If it does not have an intended function, then (at least for Aristotle), it is not an artefact. Contrast this with our notion of thinking, as expressed by Morris:

> Something whose "success" is too closely dependent upon the inter-vention of a designer or supervisor does not count as a thinker, because it is not responsible for what it does . . . The notion of responsibility used here . . . is meant just to capture whatever is required to make sense of the idea that a person is the doer of her deeds. Someone who is responsible in this sense is not always to be praised or blamed for what is done – if praise or blame is due at all. But, where praise or blame is due, the doer of a deed should get it, unless there is some other person to whom it can be passed. And we cannot make sense of a person being a responsible subject in this sense, if she could never be properly praised or blamed.
>
> (Morris 1992: 206)

So for an artefact to be truly thinking, it must be that it itself, and not its designer, is responsible for its actions. And yet inasmuch as it is itself respon-sible, it is to the same degree difficult to talk of it being an artefact, with a pre-given function or purpose. For responsibility seems to require the ability to determine one's own purposes and goals. In this respect, this conceptual conundrum reflects the centuries-old debate concerning the problem of evil. If God created us (if we are artefacts), then He is responsible for what we do (an untenable conclusion, since some of the things we do are evil, and yet God is omnibenevolent). If we are to be given responsibility for our actions (if we are to be thinkers), then it must be that we are not God's artefacts, we are not his creations (which violates the Judaeo–Christian view of God a sole creator of "all that is, seen and unseen").

A technical response to this situation would be to notice that Morris only speaks of thinking, not intelligence. This leaves room for the possibility of a kind of non-autonomous intelligence that is less than thinking, but which does not contradict artefactuality. This is cold comfort, however, to the majority of the people interested in achieving artificial intelligence; for them, nothing less than a fully autonomous, thinking artefact will do. Another option is to reject the Aristotelian idea that an artefact must have a designer-intended purpose or function, thus leaving room for artefacts which are autonomous, independent of us, and thus candidates for true intelligence. But now we no longer have a handle on what makes something an artefact. Simply being the end product of causal sequences which we initiate is not sufficient, since that would include natural childbearing. But at this point the dialectic returns to familiar ground, and we are back at the end of the discussion on the artificial/natural distinction. It may be that no such distinction is necessary to *do* artificial intelligence, but recognising that the distinction is arbitrary may change one's view of the origins of the concept of artificial intelligence, and one's expectations for its future course.

Reference

Morris, M. (1992) *The Good and the True*. Oxford: Oxford University Press.

Part I

GENERAL HISTORICAL CONTEXT: OVERVIEWS

INTRODUCTION

The Development of the Concept of Artificial Intelligence—Historical Overviews and Milestones

Ronald Chrisley

1 Overview

It is fitting to place Newell's article at the beginning of this set, given the large influence it exerted on the conception of this reference work. It is no coincidence that the kind of enquiry in which Newell was engaged is a paradigmatic example of the kind of activity for which this set is meant to provide resources. His paper is an attempt to chart the history of the field of AI, and the organisation which he prefers – not by theories, methodologies, paradigms, tasks, nor cognitive functions, but instead by examining the intellectual issues involved – has substantial overlap with the approach taken in compiling this set. However, given that his interest is the field of AI, several of the issues he mentions are not so much conceptual as they are technological. That is, their impact on the concept of artificial intelligence is indirect, mediated by an implicit premiss: that intelligence is constituted by whatever techniques turn out to be necessary for workers in the field of artificial intelligence to synthesise it. Despite his intellectual ambitions, it must be noted that Newell reveals an engineering bias when he deems the philosophy of mind to be a peripheral matter, and that it is technological advances alone, and not conceptual developments, which allowed "serious" artificial intelligence to be done.

Understanding Gardner's approach is assisted by keeping in mind that this account was intended to situate the field of AI within a larger picture of cognitive science, "the mind's new science". While in some respects insightful, the account is nevertheless often derivative, relying heavily on McCorduck's *Machines Who Think*. Yet this, combined with the fact that it has been widely read, in fact makes it an important inclusion in the set in that it provides a concise summary of what has come to be the received history of artificial intelligence within the fields of AI and cognitive science themselves. Thus, emphasis is placed on Dartmouth, but that meeting is viewed as the culmination of an intellectual strand beginning in the seventeenth century with Descartes and Vaucanson, winding through Babbage, Boole, Whitehead & Russell, Shannon, Turing, McCulloch and Pitts, Wiener and von Neumann. The emphasis here is on the development and formalisation of logic on the one hand, and machines which can mechanise these logical norms and transitions on the other. The contribution of the Dartmouth participants is then, broadly, the joint application of these two ideas to the task of creating an intelligent machine.

As is common to many of the accounts, not only of the 1950s and 1960s in particular but of the entire history of artificial intelligence in general, a contrast is made between two approaches, which differ mainly in the extent to which they are guided by considerations of neurophysiological verisimilitude. Gardner opposes one pair with another: Newell and Simon vs. McCulloch and Pitts (contrast Boden's assessment of the latter pair, as mentioned below in the discussion on their article "A Logical Calculus of the Ideas Immanent in Nervous Activity"). The difference is the level at which similarity to human intelligence should be pursued: is it at a low, structural level, thus requiring detailed understanding of the brain; or is it at a higher, behavioural/functional level, which may be implemented in machines in a way quite different from how it is in the brain? From what Gardner says, one might be tempted to define the field of AI (as opposed to other fields trying to achieve artificial intelligence, such as cybernetics) as those researchers who took the latter approach. But the fact is that there were/are some cyberneticists who, like Newell and Simon, favoured a more abstract approach, sometimes on a level higher even than the Dartmouth group and their descendants.

The truth is that it is difficult to state a conceptual distinction between the two groups unless one looks ahead to the two conceptual developments in the field of AI which Gardner documents. After detailing some programs that were considered major advances in the field, and before concluding with discussions of the four early critics of AI (Weizenbaum, Dreyfus, Lighthill and Searle), he highlights (1) a move from general to more domain specific systems; and (2) a move from procedural to declarative knowledge. Both of these changes made what was previously an implicit assumption into a central explicit doctrine: that intelligence is primarily a matter of *knowledge*. It is this focus on knowledge which is taken to be characteristic of the orthodoxy in the field of AI. Note that move 2 prevents a trivialisation of the claim that intelligence is knowledge. Almost anyone could agree with that claim if they were allowed to expand arbitrarily the extension of "knowledge"; but the focus on declarative knowledge renders those parts of life which can only be understood in terms of "knowing how" as peripheral to intelligence and thus AI.

The first sentence of the Glymour, Ford and Hayes' overview, which equates artificial intelligence with android *epistemology*, makes it clear that they share the epistemic view of intelligence. This view suggests that the historical development of our understanding of the *objects of knowledge* is foundational for the development of the concept of artificial intelligence. Accordingly, Glymour et al. start with the logic, epistemology and metaphysics of Plato and Aristotle, and follow a thread of logic and its mechanisation through Lull, Pascal, Leibniz, and Bacon. A brief hiccup comes with Descartes' dualism. Though foreshadowing the hardware/software distinction, it nevertheless defies the possibility of the reduction of the mental to the physical. The logico–mechanical line continues to develop, however, via Hobbes, Kant, Boole, Frege and Russell. Form Frege on, the intellectual dependence is consolidated into a genealogy where the teacher/father passes the torch on to the student/son, who in turn becomes a teacher: Frege begat Carnap, Carnap begat Simon and Pitts and Hempel, Hempel begat Massey begat Buchanan (begat Mycin?). Like Gardner, Glymour et al. make a neurophysiological/non-neurophysiological distinction between two approaches to artificial intelligence, "connectionist vs. symbolic". They trace the origin of what they take to be the central connectionist view (Hebbian learning at a synapse) back to the nineteenth century psychologists such as Brucke and especially Freud, and leave the story there.

Mazlish is not just interested in the development of the concept of artificial intelligence, nor just the development of automata, but mainly in the effect that these have had on humanity's conception of itself. The paper of his which has been included here was adapted from chapter three of his book *The Fourth Discontinuity* for inclusion in a special edition of *The Stanford Humanities Review* entitled *Constructions of the Mind: Artificial Intelligence and the Humanities* (which also contains the article from Agre and many other articles that would have made excellent inclusions in this set). Mazlish's claim is that artificial intelligence has made humanity rethink its place in the cosmos in as profound a way as did the rejection of a geo-centric astronomy and the adoption of an evolutionary biology. The article included here documents an aspect of the development of the concept of artificial intelligence that is otherwise intentionally neglected in this set: the concept's role in myth, fiction and the arts. That said, there are some notable omissions in his story. In focusing on automata, he neglects the roots of the concept of artificial intelligence in the Judeo–Christian scriptures and ancient myth. In addition to his observations concerning golems, one can go further to note that the move from "emeth" to "meth" is a case of symbol manipulation *par excellence*, with the role of "truth" (the meaning of "emeth") being crucial to the operation of the golem: an idea which was to remain a central aspect of at least logic-based artificial intelligence work in modern times. The significance of the golem is further heightened when one learns that more than one famous pioneer in the field of AI claimed to be heirs to the Rabbi Loew tradition. Lastly, Fritz Lang's film *Metropolis*, which features the famous robot Maria, is notably absent from Mazlish's comparative discussion.

2 Focus

The earliest scientific attempts at creating artificial intelligence focused on the concept of autonomy. Cohen locates the beginning of the epoch of modern automata with Descartes, while simultaneously linking Descartes' ideas with those that came before (e.g. Thales, Galen) and after (e.g. Leibniz, La Mettrie, Freud). If the rumours are true, then Descartes was one of that very rare company, a philosopher of artificial intelligence who actually tried to build an intelligent artefact. Nonetheless, it is his thinking, rather than his *Francine*, which has had monumental impact on the concept and practice of artificial intelligence. Despite being famous for embracing a dualist view of reality which places the mind outside of the physical sphere, his otherwise mechanistic view of nature played a crucial role in expanding the possibilities for artificial intelligence. This expansion began when La Mettrie extended Descartes' mechanistic view of animals to humanity itself. Cohen points out that what was important here was the fact that La Mettrie was "the first to state the problem of mind in terms of physics", and not La Mettrie's proof itself, which was merely "a statement of empirical correlation between physiological and psychical events". Crucial here, too, is mention of Vartanian's analysis of *L'Homme-Machine*, which locates the chief limitation of La Mettrie's model in its "insensitivity to duration". Vartanian's assertion that temporality is, by contrast, essential to human experience will be echoed (almost certainly unknowingly) centuries later in the dynamicist challenge to the symbolic approach to artificial intelligence (Volume III, Part II).

Cohen next focuses on contemporary critiques of Descartes, such as Cyrano de Bergerac's *Estate et empires de la lune*, which is striking in its similarity to modern thought experiments in this area, which often make use of a "Martian" perspective or some such. Giles Morfouace de Beaumont is mentioned for his attack on dualism and his defence of animals saying "who could endow a machine with the sensitive soul of a beast or with power of reproduction?" His contemporary, Father G. H. Bougeant argued that animals have language and can understand each other well, even if we cannot understand them. Spinoza (satirically) wrote that the golem "has as much life as any other human being, if one accepts the new viewpoint that the relation between body and mind is so loose that it can in a moment be lifted and replaced". This could be seen as a precursor to Wittgenstein's behaviourist/anti-dualist arguments. England's Lord Chief Justice Sir Matthew Hale was a severe critic of Cartesian reductionism which he claimed "renders living creatures merely mechanisms or 'Artificial Engins'". Coleridge's attack on

Descartes was unknowingly ironic: Coleridge argued that Descartes' dualism made as much sense as saying that one's feelings could be put in spatial relation to one another, and yet Descartes explicitly claimed that the mind was not spatial. But these last two make it clear how Descartes' literal limitation of the mechanical view to the case of animals has often been set aside, with the effect that at times Descartes was seen as a threat to dualism, not an adherent of it.

Cohen concludes with a discussion of what he takes to be Descartes' most important contribution: "his great faith in the mathematical method". Descartes' influence on science is put in comparison to Hobbes, eight years his senior, and Leibniz. Their faith in mathematics led to the first "robot-mathematician" by Pascal, and had Leibniz, having read about Lull's *Ars Magna*, "dream of a machine that could calculate so well as to be able to derive a complete mathematical system of the universe". Cohen notes Leibniz' view that the art of thinking would come to perfection through an analysis of games, a view which continues to play a crucial role in the field of artificial intelligence.

What Descartes says at the end of Part Five of the *Discourse on the Method* is striking in its relevance to the development of the concept of artificial intelligence. He considers the question of how we could tell from the behaviour of an automaton that it is not a real man (and therefore, not really intelligent). Descartes offers two behavioural limitations of automata: (1) an automaton would be unable to produce different arrangements of words that are meaningful and appropriate; and (2) an automaton would only be able to imitate our behaviour in a fixed number of ways, since our reason is a "universal instrument" while an automaton must have a different organ for each purpose. Although Descartes relied on the implication of the form: "failure to match human behaviour means an automaton is not intelligent" (lacks reason), it is not unfair to suppose that the same reasoning would have led him to assent to the converse: "if something is behaviourally equivalent to a human, it must possess reason". Although Descartes was not restricting his attention to linguistic behaviour, his emphasis on language as being a stumbling block for mechanised reason makes it reasonable to see the Turing Test, which does restrict its attention to linguistic behaviour, as a descendant of Descartes' thinking. For if the only obstacle to producing a reasoning automation is its inability to use language flexibly, meaningfully and appropriately, then surely creating a machine which passes the Turing Test is sufficient for creating an artefact which truly thinks. Of course, the linguistic limitation was not the only obstacle Descartes mentioned: there was also the matter of universality to be overcome. Thus, Descartes' experience with automata anticipates the more modern experience of interacting with Weizenbaum's Eliza program: initial fascination, but eventual disillusionment as it is realised that Eliza can only cope with a limited number of situations, pre-anticipated by her programmer. As with the linguistic case, this does not seem to be limited reasoning, but no reasoning at all. But this issue, too, was explicitly addressed by Turing in his results concerning universal machines (namely, that there exist machines which can be programmed to simulate any other machine) and the Church–Turing thesis (that for any effective procedure there is a Turing machine which can compute it). The upshot of Turing's work here is: Descartes was wrong; there are mechanisms which can act as "universal instruments". Although these foundational notions in artificial intelligence contradict Descartes' conclusions, they give his work a fundamental role by accepting his framing of the issues – in particular, the idea that the essence of reason is seen only in diverse linguistic behaviour. This assumption, and the questioning of it, is a dichotomy which would go on to generate many of the branches in the concept of, and work in, artificial intelligence.

A tantalising reference to a lost section of his *Treatise on Man* hints at another point of connection between Descartes' thinking and artificial intelligence. It might be thought that dualism would be a hindrance to artificial intelligence, since after the engineering work in the physical realm is completed, one would still have to bring about the mental substance that is necessary for true mentality and reason. But here Descartes speaks precisely of the *creation* of the soul, over and above the arrangement of matter. The fact that Descartes doubtlessly has *divine* creative powers in mind not withstanding, his remark leads us to question: what is it about the dualistic picture that supposedly prevents artifice? Cannot the mental realm also be manipulated? If there is causal interaction between the physical and mental realms, as Descartes maintained, then why should there be any obstacle to creating and shaping the mental substance in a manner necessary and sufficient for reason? In this respect, Descartes' comment that reason "cannot be in any way derived from the potentiality of matter" seems misplaced, if understood in an unrestricted form. The happiest reconciliation of his views may be this: while material configurations cannot *constitute* reason, they can *give rise to* it. Fortunately, all that is required of the material-trafficking artificial intelligence practitioner is the latter.

Of final interest is Descartes' use of the analogy of the helmsman in the ship, the very analogy which Wiener would use when coining the term "cybernetics" some three hundred years later. At various times, including the present, it has been fashionable to label traditional, symbolic artificial intelligence "Cartesian", and therefore reject it in favour of a more cybernetic view, one which sees control theory and dynamics rather than computation as crucial for understanding intelligence and cognition. But notice here that Descartes is rejecting the cybernetic analogy, not in favour of a more detached, symbolic, dualistic, representational picture, but rather in favour of a view that sees mind and body even more tightly coupled than a helmsman is with his ship. To be fair, Descartes does restrict his remarks here to "movement, feelings and appetites", leaving open the possibility that reason or intelligence proper is, by contrast, of a detached nature. Despite the popularity of this interpretation, it is not one explicitly supported in this passage.

One can distinguish two ways in which one might help bring about artificial mentality. The first involves primarily engineering breakthroughs that result in mechanisms which are more mind-like. The second, more conceptual way attempts to create mind-like artefacts not so much by making machines more like minds, but rendering minds to be more easily understood as machines. Hobbes makes this latter kind of contribution to artificial intelligence. The focus of interest of Western scientific culture had been reduced from mentality in general to the particular case of reason centuries, perhaps millennia, before Hobbes. Already in Plato we find a distinction between *logos* (reason) and *dianoia* (perceiving, contemplating, realising or recognising), and Aristotle distinguishes *noesis*, the process of understanding, from *nous* (related to the Greek word for seeing), an abstract ability to think (cf. Vroon 1980, chapter 2). But Hobbes further assisted the enterprise of artificial intelligence by in turn reducing reasoning to something more mechanically, indeed computationally, tractable: "Reason . . . is nothing but reckoning". This view of reason as calculation has in recent times been frequently criticised as being too idealised, too "perfect" to apply to human cognition (although it is interesting to note that most critics have retained Hobbes' equation of reasoning and computation, and have instead questioned the focus on pure reason). The inference usually drawn is that artefacts built on the foundation of Hobbesian reason will either be so different from the familiar form of human intelligence that they will not be recognisable as intelligent, or (more frequently) that such machines will be too brittle to cope with the real, messy, unreasonable world. But the target of such objections is not Hobbesian reason: Hobbes spends much of Chapter V making it clear how reason and the capacity for error ("absurdity") go hand in hand (thus anticipating similar, recent conclusions in the philosophy of cognitive science concerning the necessity, for true representational capacities, to be capable of misrepresenting) (e.g., Fodor 1984). So reason, although reckoning, is not merely applying inference rules to a database of strings which encode knowledge. Rather, it is a family of capacities which (in addition) compensate for the eight kinds of "absurdity" which Hobbes delineates. In this sense, Hobbes was much more radical than is typically acknowledged, since he was suggesting that all of reason (including the processes of concept-formation, error-detection and compensation, etc.), not just the syntactic move from premises to conclusion, can be understood as reckoning. Put another way, reasoning is but reckoning, but reckoning is more than blind syntactic symbol manipulation. Nevertheless, it is not this Hobbes, but Hobbes as usually interpreted, who had a monumental impact on the concept of artificial intelligence.

Hobbes is also of note for making an explicit connection between artificiality and Plato's individual/republic analogy. He opens *Leviathan* with:

"By art is created that great Leviathan, called a Commonwealth or State – (in Latin, Civitas) which is but an artificial man". Here we have an intellectual precursor to an idea expressed in Turing's 1950 paper, and Minsky's "Society of Mind" (see the introductions to Volume II, Part I sections 1 and 2 respectively).

Leibniz' *Preface* is included primarily because it is one of the locations of his famous *calculemus* (i.e. "let us calculate") line, which also appears in modified form, e.g. in his *Dissertio de Arte Combinatoria* of 1666: if controversies were to arise, "there would be no more need of disputation between two philosophers than between two accountants. For it would suffice to take their pencils in their hands, and say to each other: Let us calculate." Although in the included passage the emphasis is on scientific rather than philosophical problems, the upshot is the same: the idea of reasoning and problem solving through mechanical computation. Although this idea is a vital ingredient for what is to come, on its own it envisions more a kind of prosthesis to enhance our own intelligence (see the inclusion from Ashby in Volume III, Part I) than an autonomous intelligent artefact. Note the qualification that immediately follows the slogan: "I still add: *in so far as the reasoning allows on the given facts*" (original emphasis). This concession was not to express itself in modern work as an acknowledgement of any fundamental limitation of the symbolic approach as much as it was to be manifested in two imperatives: to find an appropriate knowledge representation formalism; and later to ensure that enough knowledge was encoded in the system being constructed (cf. the inclusion from Lenat and Feigenbaum in Volume II, Part I).

There is much of interest in Leibniz' *Monadology* as well. The similarities between section 17 and Searle's Chinese Room thought experiment cannot be ignored. Whereas Descartes and Turing used external behaviour as evidence for the presence of mind, and Wittgenstein made such behaviour criterial for mentality, both Leibniz and Searle accept the possibility of behaviour which is intelligent-like, but move inside the purportedly intelligent system to find that, at least in cases of certain kinds of mechanism, there is, in fact, nobody home. Of course, there are important differences between Leibniz' mill and Searle's Chinese Room: Searle is not attacking the possibility of a machine having a mind (since he concedes, in a way Leibniz (predating La Mettrie) could not, that humans are machines), but only that certain kinds of mechanism – namely programs operating on symbols – are not sufficient for mentality. Furthermore, Leibniz uses external perception to see that there is nothing more than mechanism, and therefore no mentality, in the mill. Searle does not beg the question in this way – he does not appeal to external sense, but to introspection. Searle is not introspectively aware of any understanding of Chinese going on, so there is no understanding of Chinese going on. But it is interesting that Searle's conclusions to the effect that understanding is some sort of biological secretion fit in well with

Leibniz' conclusion that mind (perception) must itself be a simple substance, rather than a compound of non-mental substances or mechanism.

More troubling are the difficulties that Leibniz' metaphysics, based on monads, gets him into, especially in sections 17, 18 and 64. Every simple substance constitutes/is constituted by perceptions, and the self-sufficiency of these simple substances makes them incorporeal automata. This is troubling for understanding the development of the concept of artificial intelligence, for we now see the notion of an automaton extended beyond the idea of physical mechanism to include "divine" or "natural" machines. It might seem a strange development indeed that forces a man of Leibniz' day to use "divine" and "natural" as synonyms: but it is the logical consequence of viewing nature as the product of divine art. Here, as in Genesis, the parallel made between man's artifice and God's artifice threatens an elimination of the natural/artificial distinction, thus trivialising the concept of artificial intelligence itself (see the General Introduction). However, even stranger is the reason that Leibniz gives for the inferiority of artificial (that is, man-made) automata: they are not sufficiently mechanical! Natural automata are machines which are made of smaller machines, which are in turn made of smaller machines, *ad infinitum*. It is notable that Leibniz' does not conclude that man-made automata are therefore barred from being intelligent – the possibility is left open for them to be intelligent, even if inferior to us in that or other respects. Although we now believe that the mechanism of natural systems does bottom out in simple, non-mechanical substances, Leibniz' point can be rephrased to retain relevance: only automata which are hierarchical, exhibiting mechanical complexity on a variety of scales, will be fluid and adaptive enough to rival human/biological intelligence. But Leibniz' original objection to man-made automata was not this contingent: by declaring that natural automata were decomposable into machines *ad infinitum*, Leibniz was forever placing the sophistication of natural automata out of the reach of man's artifice, which must begin somewhere, with simple, non-mechanical substances. But Leibniz does not consider the possibility that man might start with what God has provided: simple biological machines, be they cells or chemicals. As long as each level of organisation built from these components is itself machinelike, then a man-made artefact could have the infinitistic mechanical structure Leibniz takes to be characteristic of natural automata. Would we withhold the label "man-made" from such devices simply because they got a head start from God's mechanical engineering? We do not require a carpenter to have created the wood she carves in order to say that her chair is man-made. So it seems that Leibniz' prohibition of sophisticated man-made automata turns out to be a contingent one after all.

Fryer and Marshall attempt to redress what they take to be an inaccuracy in the historical record: the labelling of Jacques de Vaucanson as a mere toy maker and entertainer. They persuasively argue that Vaucanson's aim was to understand behaviour by simulating (or even re-creating) it in automata. Their conclusions imply that Vaucanson may have been the first to pursue artificial intelligence not as an end in itself, but as a means to further understanding natural intelligence – an approach which would later be enshrined as a principal methodology of cognitive science.

Given what is said above concerning Cohen's paper, let alone what is said in Cohen's paper itself and in the historical overviews, nothing more needs to be said here concerning the selection from La Mettrie, except that the work is somewhat frustrating in the current context. A connection is never explored between man being a machine and the fact that machines are built by man, to yield the question: could an artificial man-machine be created by humans? That work was left to the many thinkers that were influenced by La Mettrie.

Until Babbage, the conceptual developments in artificial intelligence were far outstripping the technology necessary to attempt their realisation. L. F. Menabrea, originally a military engineering officer but later a general and Prime Minister of Italy, heard a description of the Analytical Engine by Babbage in 1840. He summarised Babbage's ideas in a paper, Babbage being too concerned with the developments of his engines to publish any proper descriptions of them himself. Of interest to the concerns here is Menabrea's distinction between two aspects of intelligence: the mechanical, and the domain of reasoning or understanding – a conceptual move which, given the mechanistic view of calculation that Babbage presented to Menabrea, gives up on the Hobbesian ideal of reasoning as calculation and instead focuses on the residue of intellect which *can* be so understood. But it is not Menabrea's main text that is included here. Countess Ada Lovelace (daughter of Lord Byron, and namesake of the US Department of Defence programming language ADA) translated the paper and extensively annotated it, providing us with the best contemporary account – an account that even Babbage recognised to be clearer than his own. It is these notes (in fact, only Note A and part of Note G), rather than the description of the machine itself, that have most relevance to the development of the concept of artificial intelligence. In Note A, Lovelace makes two important conceptual points. First, she makes a distinction between an operator and that which is operated on; next she makes the point that the objects of operators need not be numerical, but anything which can be formalised:

> The operating mechanism can even be thrown into action independently of any object to operate upon . . . Again, it might act upon other things besides *number*, were objects found whose mutual fundamental relations could be expressed by those of the abstract science of operations, and which should be also susceptible of adaptations to the action of the operating notation and mechanism of the engine. (original emphasis)

Lovelace then offers music composition as an example of such a non-numerical case of computation.

Compare (Newell 1980: 137):

> The mathematicians and engineers then [in the 1950s] responsible for computers insisted that computers only processed *numbers* – that the great thing was that instructions could be translated into numbers. On the contrary, we [Newell and Simon] argued, the great thing was that computers could take instructions and it was incidental, though useful, that they dealt with numbers. (original emphasis)

Together, these two points yield a distinction which would reappear in symbolic artificial intelligence in various forms: the program/data distinction, the heuristic/search method distinction, the knowledge/inference engine distinction (see the quote from Davis in the discussion of Crevier's paper, below), etc.

Lovelace follows Leibniz in thinking of the machine as a kind of intelligence prosthesis, but with a twist; the very same processes (and this could only be meant in a rather sophisticated notion of functional identity of processes) "pass through" our brains and that go through the Analyser:

> It were much to be desired, that when mathematical processes pass through the human brain instead of through the medium of inanimate mechanism, it were equally a necessity of things that the reasonings connected with *operations* should hold the same just place as a clear and well-defined branch of the subject of analysis, a fundamental but yet independent ingredient in the science, which they must do in studying the engine.

The suggestion is that because the Analytical Engine "cannot be confounded with other considerations", it will be able to reason more clearly and successfully than we do.

The section of Note G that is included is the source of the (in)famous "Lady Lovelace's Objection" (to use Turing's appellation) to artificial intelligence: that a computer could never think because it could never originate anything. Of course, as Hartree, Turing and some others admit, this is not what Lovelace actually said; she was speaking only of the Analytical Engine. But even this more modest (and surely correct) claim is in tension with what she says in Note A. There she takes great pains to say how much an advance the Analytical Engine is over the Difference Engine, but in doing so seems to suggest that the Analytical Engine can do more than what is allowed by Note G:

> ... it is scarcely necessary to point out, for instance, that while the Difference Engine can merely *tabulate*, and is incapable of *developing*,

17

the Analytical Engine can *either tabulate or develope.* (original emphasis)

We may say most aptly, that the Analytical Engine *weaves algebraical patterns* just as the Jacquard-loom weaves flowers and leaves. Here, it seems to us, resides much more of originality than the Difference Engine can be fairly entitled to claim. (original emphasis)

Further commentary on and context for Babbage is provided by Mazlish, who compares and contrasts him with his contemporaries: not only Huxley and Butler as stated in the title, but also lesser known figures. For example, in Carlyle we can perhaps see the first conscious acknowledgement of the "second way" of pursuing the goal of machines which are like humans, that of making humans more machinelike. It is usually thought that Babbage's contribution to artificial intelligence was clearly of the other, technological sort. But the case is not so clear-cut. That Babbage's work was a milestone in the development of computers is without question, and it is not in dispute that advances in computation led to drastic changes in the concept of artificial intelligence. But did Babbage's work have a more direct effect on the concept? Given Lady Lovelace's comments, it might be presumed that Babbage had no such pretensions, although it must be admitted that Mazlish notes the aspects of Babbage's work that suggest otherwise. Regardless of whether Babbage was explicitly concerned with making machines more like humans, it seems that he was also concerned with rendering humans, even God, as machinelike calculators. Furthermore, in Babbage we see a nexus in history: the culmination of historical strands such as the entertaining automata of the eighteenth century, a Leibnizian focus on games, a Cartesian emphasis of mathematics, as well as the first instance of what was to become a defining aspect of work in artificial intelligence: funding by the military.

Simons documents the developments, initiated by Babbage, that would provide the technology essential for the modern, scientific approach to artificial intelligence: the electronic computer. He also discusses Alan Turing, whose importance to artificial intelligence is profound and multifaceted, tracing his ideas back to his influences: La Mettrie and Butler via Brewster, as well as Beutell and Hilbert. Perhaps his discussion relies heavily on Hodges' biography of Turing, but it is none the worse for that.

Cordeschi looks for the roots of the background assumptions of modern artificial intelligence (what he calls the "culture of the artificial") in the pre-cybernetics period of 1930–1940. Of interest is a concession he makes early on, to the effect that if one sees artificial intelligence as primarily an engineering enterprise, then his analysis does not apply; instead, "artificial" just means "inorganic" in the pre-cybernetic and cybernetic periods, while it just means "computational" in artificial intelligence research after that – what Cordeschi calls "cognitive AI". Cordeschi makes his case by looking at the "robot approach" of Hull, which was, in essence, a synthetic approach to verifying behaviourism. But this was no simplistic, ideological behaviourism – Hull was willing to allow all manner of internal states, self-modification, and memory to play a role in his proposed machines. In this he was directly opposing McDougall, who claimed that it was the inability of machines to modify their behaviour on the basis of memory which established the non-mechanical nature of mind. Cordeschi looks at Hull's proposed circuits in some detail, following his work through to the distinction eventually made between merely purposive behaviour and the class of truly mental behaviours involving plans. It was this latter kind of behaviour which he hoped to explain with the concept of "ultra-automaticity": a response anticipatory mechanism. Comparisons and contrasts are also made with Hull's methodology and the influential work of Craik. Cordeschi leaves us with "the fateful word" being uttered in 1943: surely he means the word "feedback", and chooses 1943 because it is the year in which Rosenblueth, Wiener and Bigelow published their seminal paper.

The work of Ross is another topic covered by Cordeschi, in the context of the refinements to Hull's methodology that also included the work of Walter and Ashby. Ross' designs, like those of the others just mentioned, is noteworthy in that they are examples of modern, scientific, but in some sense *non-computational* attempts to construct artificial intelligence. The first of the two papers from Ross merely describes such a machine; the second paper does this also, but in addition makes a point which would later become a key component of the concept of artificial intelligence: the idea that an intelligent machine need not resemble the mechanism underlying human or animal intelligence. This would be embellished later by Armer (Volume IV, Part II) and others in the flight analogy argument for artificial intelligence, and would also be reflected in the philosophical literature as the multiple-realisability of functional states.

Although most histories of the field of artificial intelligence emphasise the Dartmouth conference of 1956, there were several earlier meetings that played a critical role in the evolution of the concept of artificial intelligence, including the 1942 Cerebral Inhibition Meeting, the ten Macy Conferences held between 1946 and 1953, and the Hixon Symposium held in 1948. Edwards' contribution covers the highlights of these meetings with regard to artificial intelligence, including discussions of McCulloch, Pitts, Wiener, Rosenblueth, von Neumann, von Foerster, Shannon, and several others. However, his intention in this selection, as in the book from which it is taken, is not just to relay these events, but to establish the claim that the military backdrop of the research in this period is inseparable from the content of the research itself, that the concept of intelligence and the methodologies proposed for its synthesis were heavily influenced by the militaristic surround – economic and otherwise – of the researchers involved. This provides a counterpoint to the account, in (Dreyfus and Dreyfus 1988), of the rise of artificial intelligence in the 1950s and 1960s, an account which emphasises the (primarily US) military sponsorship of symbolic artificial intelligence over non-symbolic, neo-cybernetic approaches such as Rosenblatt's Perceptron work.

Discussed in the Edwards paper, and mentioned at the very end of the Cordeschi's discussion is the seminal 1943 paper by Rosenblueth, Wiener and Bigelow. This was the written version of a presentation by Rosenblueth which instigated the post-war series of conferences on cybernetics and from which the field of cybernetics eventually evolved. The paper had two goals. The first was to define behaviouristic study, which was done in a way that opposed such study to functionalism. The main contribution here was to provide a behavioural taxonomy, but even this was enough to have a lasting conceptual and methodological influence – for one thing, the taxonomy was so constructed as to be applicable to both organisms and machines. But one cybernetic generalisation that this taxonomy suggests – "all purposeful behaviour may be considered to require negative feedback" – is problematic. Feedback systems, *a fortiori* negative feedback systems, are only a subclass of purposive systems. The paper appears to transcend the traditional question of artificial intelligence by turning the tables and claiming that machines can do things that people cannot – until it is made clear that this is only meant in an uncontentious way, such as "having electrical output". The paper is more even-handed than much of the work, either supporting or oppositional, that followed; the authors allow for the possibility that one might later need different means of studying organisms and machines. It is noted that functional study reveals deep differences between organisms and machines: there are no wheels in organisms, they have a uniform distribution of energy, and use spatial rather than temporal multiplication. The taxonomy offered would allow one to see the similarities.

But even more revealing of the differences between these cyberneticians and the symbolists to follow was the role of the machine in their work. Rosenblueth et al. admit that their focus on synthesis of intelligence in non-protein materials is merely a practical matter, and might change: "the ultimate model of a cat is of course another cat". Thus the "behaviourist" cyberneticists were not as opposed to multiple-realisability as some functionalist critiques have made them out to be. In fact, it was the symbolists who placed significance on one particular way of achieving intelligent behaviour: programming a digital computer. True, it was acknowledged that this computer could be realised in any substrate, but this does not change the fact that the symbolists were in fact more restrictive than their behavioural cousins.

The second aim of the Rosenblueth, Wiener and Bigelow paper was to stress the importance of the concept of purpose. Their largely philosophical remarks here explain, to a much greater extent than does the part of the paper dealing with the first aim, why the paper appeared in a philosophy journal. Their analysis is that previous thinkers were rightly distrustful of the problematic notion of a final cause, but these thinkers made the mistake of throwing out the notion of purpose as well. It is argued that the notion of purpose is not opposed to determinism; causality is concerned with functional relationships, while teleology is only concerned with behaviour. Perhaps this, more than anything else, was the most important conceptual contribution of the paper: a further insight into how the normativity of intelligence could be realised in the meaninglessness of the mechanical.

Boden has more than once made the point that McCulloch and Pitts' paper "A Logical Calculus of Ideas Immanent in Nervous Activity" started the field of artificial intelligence. She does this by arguing for it in her entry "Artificial Intelligence" in the *Routledge Encyclopaedia of Philosophy*, and also by including the paper as the first entry in her collection *The Philosophy of Artificial Intelligence*. Her main contention is that it "integrated three powerful ideas of the early twentieth century: propositional logic, the neuron theory of Charles Sherrington, and Turing computability". With regard to the latter, Boden notes that McCulloch and Pitts showed that "every net computes a function that is computable by a Turing machine", and that "their work inspired early efforts in both classical and connectionist AI because they appealed to logic and Turing computability, but described the implementation of these notions as a network of abstractly defined 'neurons' passing messages to their neighbours" (which makes it all the more noteworthy that McCulloch and Pitts do not cite Turing in their list of references). Boden's assessment of how their paper made the field of artificial intelligence possible is tripartite: it resulted in von Neumann's choice of binary arithmetic in designing the digital computer; it reminded researchers of the Hobbesian insight that calculation could underlie all reasoning, not just mathematics; and it launched the computational study of neural networks.

The Heims' paper breaks with the rest of the set in being primarily biographical, focusing on the work and persons of McCulloch and Pitts; this, together with its absence of the political slant of the Edwards' piece makes it a balancing complement to that account.

Although the official 1951 publication date puts it after the watershed of 1950 which is being employed to divide the early and modern sections of this set, von Neumann's paper is merely a slightly edited version of one presented at the Hixon Symposium in 1948 which, together with the content of the paper, warrants putting it here. Von Neumann's primary interest is in exploring how biology might help us understand automata; the converse is a secondary interest. He begins with a discussion of the relative merits of analogue vs. digital machines. Although he notes that "the first well-integrated, large computing machine ever made was an analogy machine, V. Bush's Differential Analyzer", he goes on to show, in a manner quite different from Turing's universality-based arguments for the same conclusion, the advantages of digital computers. In particular, the noise-related error of analogue computers grows much more quickly as the number of components increases than does the round-off error of digital computers. Next, he compares biological systems with (digital) computers; admitting that the nervous system is partly analogue, he restricts his attention to the digital aspect. Although the neuron itself is not purely digital, he notes that the same goes for components in digital machines; what matters is whether a component's *function* is to be digital. Von Neumann then realises that this means that one must employ intentional terms just to make the analogue/digital distinction. This has substantial implications for those who would wish to use computation and artificial intelligence as a way of understanding intentionality. If even digitality is, as Brian Cantwell Smith puts it, a "post-intentional" notion (Smith 1995), then how can one appeal to digitality to explain intentionality (as does, e.g., Dretske 1980) in a non-circular manner?

Another interesting notion that von Neumann expresses in this paper, but which should probably receive further consideration, is his notion of a switching organ. What is important is not the idea of the organ itself, which is just a black box which is capable of causing several stimuli of the same kind as the ones which initiated it. Rather, the insight is in the conclusion that von Neumann draws: the energy of the organ must derive not from the original stimulus, but from an independent source. This concept might be of use in drawing the representational/non-representational distinction.

Next comes a comparison between the sizes of organisms and the computing elements of the day, with von Neumann concluding that the large size and unreliability of vacuum tubes was what was then limiting the size and power of artificial automata. Given the vast improvements in hardware since 1948, only the third of von Neumann's limitations on "current" technology is still applicable: the lack of a logical theory of automata. In a move that is in stark contrast with his foregoing adumbration of digitality, and indeed his intellectual image as being a kind of "Mr. Digital", von Neumann argued that formal logic "is one of the technically most refractory parts of mathematics", because it deals with rigid, all-or-none concepts, thus cutting it off from the "best cultivated portions of mathematics". The theory of automata, he maintained, is currently a chapter in formal logic: it is combinatorial rather than analytical. It needs to change so that it is not binary, all-or-nothing. In particular, the actual time it takes to perform a computation must be taken into account. In this regard von Neumann was flying in the face of what has become a Turing machine orthodoxy, and presages the criticisms of the dynamicists (such as van Gelder 1998). The new logic of automata should also incorporate the probability, however slight, of an operation failing, rather than assuming perfect compliance. This issue illustrates why there is a need for such a theory in order to construct more complex automata. Unlike in nature, with digital computer design and construction we have to stop errors immediately. This is because we are more "scared" of errors, because of our ignorance of how to handle them (lack of a theory). Similarly, most of our diagnostic tools assume only one component is faulty – another example of how our ignorance limits our ability. One can see the connectionist emphasis on robustness and analogue systems as responding to this consideration, but not in the way von Neumann recommended – he would have criticised such work for its lack of theoretical foundations.

Von Neumann states the main result of the McCulloch–Pitts theory: any functioning which can be defined unambiguously in a finite number of words can be realised by a neural network. But he identifies two problems with this: (1) will the network be of practical size?; and (2) can every mode of behaviour be put unambiguously into words? The latter in effect challenges the Church–Turing thesis and the role it has played in justifying unquestioned faith in approaches to artificial intelligence based on the digital computer. Von Neumann's objection is that although words can capture any "special phase" of any behaviour, he thinks it unlikely that this could be done for any general concept, such as "analogy". Instead of capturing the behaviour in words, he suggests – in a way that recalls Rosenblueth, Wiener and Bigelow's comment that the best model of a cat is another cat – that "it is possible that the connection pattern of the brain itself is the simplest logical expression or definition of this principle [the general concept of analogy]". Here we have a von Neumann who is quite at odds with the symbolic, digital computation approach to artificial intelligence. But since he does not want to abandon logical theory altogether, he phrases his conclusion as a call for logic to undergo a "pseudomorphosis" to neurology.

The last portion of the paper is a fascinating discussion of the possibilities of self-reproducing automata, a notion of von Neumann's that has had lasting effect in several fields. It is in this section that the paper's first reference to Turing is made, building on his theory of automata. A transcription of the discussion that followed the paper's presentation has also been included.

From the start, it was obvious that something would have to be included from McCorduck's famous personal history of the field of artificial intelligence. The difficulty was in deciding which chapter to include, since almost every chapter is highly relevant and revealing. Much the same could be said concerning Crevier's more recent history of the field. Although McCorduck's discussion of the Dartmouth conference is extensive, it was decided that since Dartmouth is discussed elsewhere (e.g. in Gardner's overview), her chapter that covered the period from Dartmouth to the end of the 1960s would be included (further coverage of the early years of modern artificial intelligence is provided in other papers in the set – e.g. Brooks' paper, Article 1 in Volume III). At this point the goal of artificial intelligence was still a kind of universal, Leibnizian intelligence, as witnessed in Newell and Simon's General Problem Solver program and McCarthy's concentration on common sense reasoning. McCorduck covers this, but also documents the dissatisfaction which would eventually lead research away from small general intelligence programs toward large, knowledge-based approaches, shunning toy domains in favour of real-world tasks such as robotics (e.g. the Shakey project).

However, it was not robot controllers, but expert systems which were to demonstrate the successes of the knowledge-based approach. And, as Crevier (quoting Simon) says at the outset, it was not only the dissatisfaction with general approaches, but also advances in hardware which led to the rise of expert systems in the late 1960s, 1970s and 1980s: DENDRAL, MYCIN, TEIRESIAS and XCON. The key idea here was that the knowledge in a system, and the operations that organised and exploited that knowledge, could be kept distinct. This, following Lovelace, was a unification of von Neumann's separation of program and data, with the idea that computers are symbol processors, not number-crunchers. Randall Davis' choice of the term "inference engine" is revealed to be an acknowledgement of this Babbagean legacy: "And knowing about Babbage, I figured inference engine was in the right spirit. It would orient them toward thinking of a machine because it was an engine, but orient them toward thinking of a machine that was doing inference, not arithmetic." Crevier's list of six advantages of expert systems is succinct and persuasive: they facilitate explanation and therefore user confidence, they allow for dynamic reordering of knowledge elements, they allow several alternatives to be considered, they are easily modifiable, they are semantically transparent, and they are robust – "one can usually remove any single rule without grossly affecting program performance" – a desideratum that would haunt workers in traditional artificial intelligence when the connectionists wielded it against them soon after.

References

Boden, M. A. (1998) "Artificial Intelligence", in E. Craik (ed.), *Routledge Encyclopaedia of Philosophy*, London: Routledge.

Boden, M. A. (1990) *The Philosophy of Artificial Intelligence*, Oxford: Oxford University Press.

Dretske, F. (1981) *Knowledge and the Flow of Information*, Cambridge: MIT Press.

Dreyfus, H. L. and Dreyfus, S. E. (1988) "Making a Mind versus Modeling the Brain: Artificial Intelligence back at a branch point", *Daedalus, Journal of the American Academy of Arts and Sciences* 117(1): 15–44.

Fodor, J. A. (1984) "Semantics, Wisconsin Style", *Synthese* 59: 231–50.

Newell, A. (1980) "Physical Symbol Systems", *Cognitive Science* 4: 135–83.

Smith, B. C. (1995) *On the Origin of Objects*, Cambridge: MIT Press.

van Gelder, T. (1998) "The Dynamical Hypothesis in Cognitive Science", *Behavioral and Brain Sciences* 21: 615–28.

Vroon, P. A. (1980) *Intelligence: on Myths and Measurement*, Amsterdam: North-Holland.

1

INTELLECTUAL ISSUES IN THE HISTORY OF ARTIFICIAL INTELLIGENCE

Allen Newell

Source: F. Machlup and U. Mansfield, *The Study of Information—Interdisciplinary Messages*, John Wiley & Sons, 1983, pp. 187–227.

Science is the quintessential historical enterprise, though it strives to produce at each moment a science that is ahistorical. With a passion bordering on compulsion, it heeds the admonition that to ignore the past is to be doomed to repeat it. Science has built its main reward system around discovering and inventing, notions that are historical to the core. Thus, writing about science in the historical voice comes naturally to the scientist.

Ultimately, we will get real histories of artificial intelligence (henceforth, AI), written with as much objectivity as the historians of science can muster. That time has certainly not come. We must be content for a while with connections recorded in prefaces, introductions, citations, and acknowledgements—the web that scientists weave in their self-conscious attempt to make their science into a coherent historical edifice. So far, only a few pieces, such as *Machines Who Think*, provide anything beyond that, and they still have no deliberate historiographic pretensions. [McCorduck, 1979.]

This essay contributes some historical notes on AI. I was induced to put them together originally in response to a request by some of our graduate students in computer science for a bit more historical perspective than is usual in their substantive fare. It is to be viewed as grist for the historian's mill but certainly not as serious history itself. The attempt to define and document all of what I put forward is beyond my resources for the moment. This essay's claim to accuracy, such as it is, rests on my having been a participant or an observer during much of the period. As is well known to historians, the accuracy of the participant-observer is at least tinged with bias, if not steeped in it. The situation is worse than that; I am not just a participant but a partisan in some of the history here, including parts still ongoing. Reader beware.

How is the history of a science to be written?

Human endeavors are indefinitely complex. Thus, to write history requires adopting some view that provides simplification and homogenization. The standard frame for the history of science is in terms of important scientific events and discoveries, linked to and by scientists who were responsible for them. This assumes that scientific events declare themselves, so to speak. In many respects this works, but it does so best when the present speaks clearly about what concepts have won out in the end, so that we can work backward through the chain of antecedents, adding only a few dead-ending branches to flesh out the story.

With fields in an early state—and AI is certainly one—critical events do not declare themselves so clearly. Additional frameworks are then useful. Obvious ones of general applicability are proposed theories and research methodologies; neither is very satisfactory for AI. The theoretical ideas put forth have, especially when successful, been embedded in computer systems (usually just as programs but sometimes including special hardware). Often, the systems speak louder than the commentary. Indeed, a common complaint of outsiders (and some insiders) is that there is no theory in AI worthy of the name. Whether true or not, such a perception argues against taking theories as the unit in terms of which history is to be written. As for research methodology, AI as a whole is founded on some striking methodological innovations, namely, using programs, program designs, and programming languages as experimental vehicles. However, little additional methodological innovation has occurred within the field since its inception, which makes for lean history.

Similarly, the more sophisticated units of historical analysis, such as the *paradigms* of Kuhn or the *research programmes* of Lakatos, provide too coarse a grain, [Kuhn, 1962; Lakatos, 1970]. It can be argued that AI has developed and maintained a single paradigm over its short lifetime, or at most two. Similarly, it has contained at most a small handful of research programmes. But units of analysis work best with enough instances for comparative analysis or for patterns to emerge. There are certainly too few paradigms for an internal history of AI. The same is probably still true of research programmes as well, though it would be of interest to attempt such a description of AI.

Useful frameworks for historical analysis can often be based on the organization of subject matter in a field. AI proceeds in large part by tackling one task after another, initially with programs that can accomplish them crudely, followed gradually by successive refinements. Game-playing, theorem-proving, medical diagnosis—each provides a single developmental strand that can be tracked. Thus, a history of AI as a whole could be written in terms of the geography of tasks successfully performed by AI systems. Almost orthogonal to this task-dimension is that of the intellectual functions necessary for an intelligent system—representation, problem-solving methods, recognition, knowledge acquisition, and so forth—what can be termed the physiology of intelligent systems. All these functions are required in any intellectual endeavor of sufficient scope, though they can be realized in vastly different ways (i.e., by different anatomies), and tasks can be found that highlight a single function, especially for purposes of analysis. Thus, a history can also be written that follows the path of increased understanding of each function and how to mechanize it. Both of these structural features of AI, and perhaps especially their matrix, provide potentially fruitful frameworks for a history. Their drawback is just the opposite from the ones mentioned earlier, namely, they lead to histories that are almost entirely internal, shedding little light on connections between AI and neighboring disciplines.

I settle on another choice, which I will call *intellectual issues*. It is a sociological fact of life that community endeavors seem to polarize around issues—fluoridation versus ban fluoridation, liberal versus conservative. Such polarizing issues are not limited to the purely political and social arena but characterize scientific endeavors as well—heliocentrism versus geocentrism, nature versus nurture. Intellectual issues are usually posed as dichotomies, though occasionally three or more positions manage to hold the stage, as in the tussle between capitalism, socialism, and communism. Intellectual issues are to be distinguished from issues in the real world of action. No matter how complex and ramifying the issues of individual freedom and state control that lie behind a fluoridation campaign, the passage or defeat of an ordinance banning fluoridation is a concrete act and is properly dichotomous. But with nature versus nurture, the dichotomy is all in the eye of the beholder, and the real situation is much more complex (as is pointed out and nauseum). The tendency to polarization arises from the way people prefer to formulate intellectual issues.

Scientifically, intellectual issues have a dubious status at best. This is true even when they do not have all the emotional overtones of the previous examples. Almost always, they are defined only vaguely, and their clarity seldom improves with time and discussion. Thus, they are often an annoyance to scientists just because of their sloganeering character. Some time ago, in a conference commentary entitled You Can't Play Twenty Questions with Nature and Win, I myself complained of the tendency of cognitive psychology to use dichotomies as substitutes for theories (e.g., serial versus parallel processing, single-trial versus continuous learning). [Newell, 1973*b*.]

Intellectual issues surely play a heuristic role in scientific activity. However, I do not know how to characterize it, nor am I aware of any serious attempts to determine it, though some might exist. Of course, large numbers of scientists write about issues in one way or another, and almost all scientists of an era can recognize and comment on the issues of the day. Were this not true, they could hardly be the issues of the particular scientific day. From a historical and social standpoint, of course, intellectual issues have a perfectly objective reality. They are raised by the historical participants themselves, and both the existence of intellectual issues and the activity associated with them can be traced. They enter the historical stream at some point and eventually leave at some other.

Whether intellectual issues make a useful framework for a scientific history seems to me an entirely open question. Such a history does not at all substitute for histories based on events and discoveries, laid down within a framework drawn from the substantive structure of a field. Still, ever since that earlier paper in 1973. I have been fascinated with the role of intellectual issues. Recently, I even tried summarizing a conference entirely in terms of dichotomies. [Newell, 1980a.] Withal, I try it here.

The intellectual issues

I will actually do the following: I will identify, out of my own experience and acquaintance with the field, all of the intellectual issues that I believe have had some prominence at one time or another. Although I will take the field of AI as having its official start in the mid-1950s, the relevant intellectual issues extend back much earlier. We surely need to know what issues were extant at its birth. I will attempt to put a date both on the start of an issue and on its termination. Both dates will be highly approximate, if not downright speculative. However, bounding the issues in time is important; some issues have definitely gone away and some have come and gone more than once, though transformed each time. I will also discuss some of the major features of the scientific scene that are associated with a given issue. I will often talk as if an issue caused this or that. This is in general illegitimate. At best, an issue is a publicly available indicator of a complex of varying beliefs in many scientists that have led to some result. Still, the attribution of causation is too convenient a linguistic practice to forego.

Table 1 lays out the entire list of intellectual issues. In addition to the short title of the issue, expressed as a dichotomy, there is an indication of an important consequence, although this latter statement is necessarily much abbreviated. The issues are ordered vertically by date of birth and within that by what makes historical sense. All those born at the same time are indented together, so time also moves from left to right across the figure; except that all the issues on hand when AI begins in 1955 are blocked together at the top. Issues that show up more than once are multiply represented in the table, according to the date of rebirth, and labeled #1, #2, and so forth. When the ending date is not shown (as in *Reason versus Emotion and Feeling #1: 1870–*), then the issue still continues into the present.

Table 1 The intellectual issues of AI

1640–1945	Mechanism versus teleology: settled with cybernetics
1800–1920	Natural biology versus vitalism: establishes the body as a machine
1870–	Reason versus emotion and feeling #1: separates machines from men
1870–1910	Philosophy versus the science of mind: separates psychology from philosophy
1910–1945	Logic versus psychologic: separates logic from psychology
1940–1970	Analog versus digital: creates computer science
1955–1965	Symbols versus numbers: isolates AI within computer science
1955–	Symbolic versus continuous systems: splits AI from cybernetics
1955–1965	Problem-solving versus recognition #1: splits AI from pattern recognition
1955–1965	Psychology versus neurophysiology #1: splits AI from cybernetics
1955–1965	Performance versus learning #1: splits AI from pattern recognition
1955–1965	Serial versus parallel #1: coordinate with above four issues
1955–1965	Heuristics versus algorithms: isolates AI within computer science
1955–1985	Interpretation versus compilation: isolates AI within computer science
1955–	Simulation versus engineering analysis: divides AI
1960–	Replacing versus helping humans: isolates AI
1960–	Epistemology versus heuristics: divides AI (minor): connects with philosophy
1965–1980	Search versus knowledge: apparent paradigm shift within AI
1965–1975	power versus generality: shift of tasks of interest
1965–	Competence versus performance: splits linguistics from AI and psychology
1965–1975	Memory versus processing: splits cognitive psychology from AI
1965–1975	Problem-solving versus recognition #2: recognition rejoins AI via robotics
1965–1975	Syntax versus semantics: linguistics from AI
1965–	Theorem-proving versus problem-solving: divides AI
1965–	Engineering versus science; divides computer science, including AI
1970–1980	Language versus tasks: natural language becomes central
1970–1980	Procedural versus declarative representation #1: shift from theorem-proving
1970–1980	Frames versus atoms: shift to holistic representations
1970–	Reason versus emotion and feeling #2: splits AI from philosophy of mind
1975–	Toy versus real tasks: shift to applications
1975–	Serial versus parallel #2: distributed AI (Hearsay-like systems)
1975–	Performance versus learning #2: resurgence (production systems)
1975–	Psychology versus neuroscience #2: new link to neuroscience
1980–	Serial versus parallel #3: new attempt at neural systems
1980–	Problem-solving versus recognition #3: return of robotics
1980–	Procedural versus declarative representation #2: PROLOG

The issues are discussed in historical order, that is, according to their order in the table. This has the advantage of putting together all those issues that were animating a given period. It has the disadvantage of mixing up lots of different concepts. However, since one of the outcomes of this exercise is to reveal that many different conceptual issues coexisted at any one time, it seems better to retain the purely historical order.

Mechanism versus teleology: 1640–1945

We can start with the issue of whether mechanisms were essentially without purpose. This is of course the Cartesian split between mind and matter, so we can take Descartes as the starting point. It is an issue that can not be defined until the notion of mechanism is established. It is and remains a central issue for AI, for the background of disbelief in AI rests precisely with this issue. Nevertheless, I place the ending of the issue with the emergence of cybernetics in the late 1940s. If a specific event is needed, it is the paper by Rosenblueth, Wiener, and Bigelow, which puts forth the cybernetic thesis that purpose could be formed in machines by feedback. [Rosenblueth, Wiener, and Bigelow, 1943.] The instant rise to prominence of cybernetics occurred because of the universal perception of the importance of this thesis. (However, the later demise of cybernetics in the United States had nothing whatsoever to do with any change of opinion on this issue.) AI has added the weight of numbers and variety to the evidence, but it has not provided any qualitatively different argument. In fact, from the beginning, the issue has never been unsettled within AI as a field. This is why I characterize the issue as vanishing with cybernetics. It does remain a live issue, of course, in the wider intellectual world, both scientific and nonscientific, including many segments of cognitive science. Above all, this issue keeps AI in perpetual confrontation with its environment.

Intelligence presupposes purpose, since the only way to demonstrate intelligence is by accomplishing tasks of increasing difficulty. But the relation is more complex the other way around. While purpose could hardly be detected in a device with no intelligence, that is, with no ability at all to link means to ends, no implication follows about the upper reaches of intelligence. Animals, for instance, are obviously purposive yet exhibit strong limits on their intelligence. Thus, settling the question of artificial purpose does not settle the question of artificial intelligence. The continuation of this basic controversy throughout the entire history of AI over whether intelligence can be exhibited by machines confirms this separation. Yet, historically it is not right to posit a separate issue of mechanism versus intelligence to contrast with mechanism versus teleology. No such distinction ever surfaced. Instead, there is an underlying concern about the aspects of mentality that can be exhibited by machines. This shows itself at each historical moment by denying to machines those mental abilities that seem problematic at the time.

Thus, the argument moves from purpose in the 1940s to intelligence in the 1950s. With the initial progress primarily in problem-solving, we occasionally heard in the 1960s statements that machines might solve problems but they could never really learn. Thus, the basic issue simply endures, undergoing continuous transformation.

Natural biology versus vitalism: 1800–1920

A critical issue for AI that had come and gone long before AI really began is the issue of vitalism—do living things constitute a special category of entities in the world, inherently distinct from inanimate physical objects. As long as this issue was unsettled, the question of whether the mind of man was mechanical (i.e., nonspecial) was moot. It is difficult to conceive of concluding that the animate world does not generally obey the laws of the physical world but that the mind is an exception and is entirely mechanical. Thus, only if vitalism has been laid to rest for our bodies can the issue be joined about our minds.

The vitalist controversy has a long and well-chronicled history. Retrospectively, it appears as an inexorable, losing battle to find something special about the living, though the issue was joined again and again. Organic matter was just a different kind of matter from inorganic matter—an issue laid to rest finally with the synthesis of urea, an indisputably organic material, from inorganic components in 1828 by Wohler. Organisms had their own inherent internal heat—an issue laid to rest in the work of Bernard by the mid-1800s. For our purposes, the starting and ending dates of the issue are not critical. Vitalism's last champion may be taken to be the embryologist Hans Driesch at the turn of the century, who proposed that organisms develop only by virtue of nonmaterial vital principles, called *entelechies*. [Driesch, 1914.] Issues almost never die, of course, as the continued existence of the Flat Earth Society should remind us. Nevertheless, no substantial intellectual energy has been focused on vitalism in more than fifty years. That the human body is a physical machine, operating according to understood physical laws and mechanisms, sets the stage for considering the mechanistic nature of thought and intelligence.

Reason versus emotion and feeling #1: 1870–

The basic separation of the heart from the head occurred long ago and is a fundamental part of Christian folk psychology. It is background. What concerns us is the ascription of reason (cold logic) to machines and the belief that a machine could have no heart—no feelings or emotions—to ever conflict with its reason. I do not seem to find any good way to fix the initiation of this issue. The striking characteristic of the golem of Rabbi Loew in 1580 seemed to have been literal-mindedness, not heartlessness. And

31

nineteenth-century artificial humans seemed to combine all the human attributes, as did, for instance, Frankenstein's constructed monster. [Shelley, 1818.] But by the twentieth century, certainly in *R.U.R* (*Rossum's Universal Robots*), we clearly have the intelligent robot, who is without soul, hence, without emotions or independently felt wants. [Capek, 1923.] So I have split the latter two dates and taken 1870 as the start.

The relevance of this for AI is in providing a basis for separating machines from humans that is different from the issue of purpose. Although a birth-right issue of AI, it does not play a major role. That the issue is there can be seen clearly enough in the paper on "Hot Cognition" by Abelson, which put forth some proposals on how to move machine intelligence in the direction of having affect. [Abelson, 1963.] The lack of prominence stems in part, no doubt, from the strong engineering-orientation of AI, which emphasizes use-ful mental functions (e.g., problem-solving and learning). In agreement with this, Abelson is one of the few social psychologists associated with AI, and the paper was given at a psychology conference. Thus, this issue remains in the background, waiting to become prominent at some future time.

Philosophy versus the science of mind: 1870–1910

For science as a whole, the separation from philosophy and the acceptance of empiricism as a fundamental tenet occurred centuries ago. For psychology, this occurred very recently, in the last decades of the nineteenth century. Indeed, psychology celebrates the establishment of the first experimental laboratory (Wundt's in Leipzig) in 1879. It was not an especially difficult passage for psychology, given the rest of science as a model. It can be con-sidered complete by the rise of behaviorism, say, by Watson's classic paper. [Watson, 1913.] Thus, this issue emerged and vanished before AI began. The residue was a continuing tradition in philosophy concerned with mind, which was completely distinct from work in psychology and, even more so, from technology. This issue ensured that when AI did emerge, which happened instantly on computers becoming sufficiently powerful,[1] it would be without more than peripheral involvement of the philosophy of mind.

Logic versus psychologic: 1910–1945

We continue to lay out the issues—and their resolutions—that were in effect at the birth of AI. This issue concerns whether symbolic logic was to be taken as revealing how humans think or whether humans use some sort of unique "psychologic." It surely started out with logic identified with thought, as Boole's classic monograph entitled *The Laws of Thought* testifies. [Boole, 1854.] But logic was rapidly transformed from an explication of the possible varieties of thinking to a device for probing the foundations of mathematics. We can take the *Principia Mathematica* of Whitehead and Russell as marking the completion of this transformation. [Whitehead and Russell, 1910–1913.] The effect was to separate logic from psychology (and also from the philosophy of mind, although that is a more complex story).

Modern logic, of course, was integrally involved in the development of the digital computer, and, thus, it enters into the history of AI. But logic did not enter AI at all as the logic of thought; that separation remained. Logic was part of the underlying technology of making mechanisms do things. In fact, it was precisely the split of logic from thought that set logic on the path to becoming a science of meaningless tokens manipulated according to formal rules, which, in turn, permitted the full mechanization of logic.

Thus the issue was really settled by 1910, and the status in the first half of the century was that psychologic was not a significant item on the agenda of any science. This, of course, was due to behaviorism's restriction of psychology's agenda. I have placed a date of 1945 for the ending of this issue; this is really an ending of the phase of separating logic from thought. The nerve-net model of McCulloch and Pitts can be used to mark this, along with the work of Turing on which it depended. [Turing, 1936; McCulloch and Pitts, 1943.] They attempted to show that physical systems that echo the structure of the brain could perform all computations, which is to say, all logical functions. Whether this is seen as saying more about the brain or more about logic can be argued; in either case, it brought them back into intimate contact. We might think that the ending of one phase of the issue (the stable separation of logic from thought) should initiate a new phase, namely, a new controversy over the exact nature of the connection. But it did not happen that way. Rather, the issue was not discussed, and basic questions about the mechanization of mind took the form of other issues. The reason that happened cannot be explored here. In part, it comes from the shift with AI from the characterization of the brain in computational terms to the digital computer, where logic played a completely technical and engineering role in describing sequential and combinational logic circuits.

Analog versus digital: 1940–1970

When computers were first developed in the 1940s, they were divided into two large families. Analog computers represented quantities by continuous physical variables, such as current or voltage; they were fast, operated simultaneously, and had inherently limited accuracy. Digital computers represented quantities by discrete states; they were slow, operated serially, and had inherently unlimited accuracy. There was a certain amount of skirmishing about which type of computer was better for which type of job. But the technical opinion-leaders maintained a view of parity between the two families—each for its own proper niche. Inevitably, there arose hybrid computers, which claimed to have the best of both worlds: digital control and memory coupled with analog speed and convenience.

It was all over by 1970. The field of computers came to mean exclusively digital computers. Analog systems faded to become a small subpart of electrical engineering. The finish was spelled not just by the increased speed and cost-efficiency of digital systems, but by the discovery of the Fast Fourier Transform, which created the field of digital signal processing and thus penetrated the major bastion of analog computation. The transformation of the field is so complete that many young computer scientists hardly know what analog computers are.

The main significance of this issue, with its resolution, was to help create the discipline of computer science and separate it from electrical engineering. Its effect on AI lies mostly in the loss of an analytical point of view, in which the contrast between analog and digital computation is taken as the starting point for asking what sort of information-processing the nervous system does. An admirable example of this point of view can be seen in the notes for von Neumann's Silliman Lectures, published posthumously. [von Neumann, 1958.] This style of analysis belongs to the world of cybernetics and not to that of AI. I doubt if many young AI scientists have read von Neumann's little book, though it was highly regarded at the time, and von Neumann was one of the towering intellects of the computer field.

Symbols versus numbers: 1955–1965

We now come to the first of the issues that characterizes AI itself, as opposed to the background against which it emerged. The digital-computer field defined computers as machines that manipulated numbers. The great thing was, its adherents said, that everything could be encoded into numbers, even instructions. In contrast, scientists in AI saw computers as machines that manipulated symbols. The great thing was, they said, that everything could be encoded into symbols, even numbers. The standard measure of a computation at the time was the number of multiplications it required. Researchers in AI were proud of the fact that there were no multiplications at all in their programs, though these programs were complex enough to prove theorems or play games. The issue was actively pursued as a struggle over how the computer was to be viewed. However, it was joined in an asymmetric way. The bulk of the computer field, and all its responsible opinion-leaders, simply adopted the view that computers are number manipulators. There was no attempt to argue against the view that computers are symbol manipulators. It was just ignored, and the standard interpretation maintained. Researchers in AI, on the other hand, were actively engaged in promoting the new view, considering the standard one to be a radical misreading of the nature of the computer and one that provided a significant barrier to the view that computers could be intelligent.

The result of this clash of views was to isolate AI within computer science. AI remained a part of computer science, but one with a special point of view that made it somewhat suspect, indeed somewhat radical. This isolation is important historically, for it has affected the professional and disciplinary organization of the two fields. It derives ultimately, no doubt, from a basic divergence of views about whether computers can or cannot exhibit intelligence. This overarching issue, of course, continued to be important on its own, as witnessed by the debates that occurred throughout the 1950s on whether machines could think. But the more specific issues that it spawned also had independent lives.

The issue of symbols versus numbers did not arise until after the first AI programs came into existence, circa 1955. Before that time, programs were classified as numerical versus nonnumerical. This latter class was a miscellany of all the things that processed data types other than numbers—expressions, images, text, and so forth.[2] This included the few game-playing and logic programs but much else as well. The symbols-versus-numbers issue emerged only when a positive alternative became formulated, that is, symbolic manipulation. This was not a synonym for nonnumerical processing, for it laid the groundwork for the separation of image- and text-processing from AI. Indeed, the work on machine translation, which started in the early 1950s, was initially considered as one strand in the development of intelligence on machines. [Locke and Booth, 1957.] But that effort became concerned with text and not symbols and developed its own identity as computational linguistics. (All of this, of course, was before text processing in its current meaning emerged—an event that bore no significant relation to the development of computational linguistics.)

I have placed the ending of this issue at about 1965, although I do not have a significant marker event for its demise. The issue is certainly not alive now and has not been for a long time. In part, this is due to the prominence of many nonnumerical data types in computer science generally, such as text and graphics. These make the characterization of computers as number manipulators no longer ring true. In part, it is due to the shift within theoretical computer science to algebraic and logical formalisms, with the concurrent retreat of numerical analysis from its early dominant role. In part, of course, it is due to the success of AI itself and the demonstrations it brought forward of the symbolic character of computation. It is tempting to say that the cause was simply the growth of scientific understanding—but such reasons do not fare well in historical accounts. In any event, my recollection is that the symbols/numbers issue was no longer prominent by the late 1960s, though a little historical digging might place it five years later.

Symbolic versus continuous systems: 1955–

An important characterization of a science, or an approach within a science, is the class of systems it uses to construct its theories. Classical physics, for instance, viewed systems as being described by systems of differential equations. Given a new phenomenon to be explained, a physicist automatically, without a thought, used differential equations to construct his or her theory of that phenomenon. Mathematical psychology in the 1950s and 1960s could be characterized by its acceptance of Markov processes as the class of systems within which to seek theories of particular phenomena.

The issue is within what class of systems should a description of intelligent systems be sought. On one side were those who, following the lead of physical science and engineering, adopted sets of continuous variables as the underlying state descriptions. They adopted a range of devices for expressing the laws—differential equations, excitatory and inhibitory networks, statistical and probabilistic systems. Although there were important differences between these types of laws, they all shared the use of continuous variables. The other side adopted the programming system itself as the way to describe intelligent systems. This has come to be better described as the class of symbolic system, that is, systems whose state is characterized by a set of symbols and their associated data structures. But initially, it was simply the acceptance of programs per se as the theoretical medium.

Adopting a class of systems has a profound influence on the course of a science. Alternative theories that are expressed within the same class are comparable in many ways, but theories expressed in different classes of systems are almost totally incomparable. Even more, the scientist's intuitions are tied strongly to the class of systems he or she adopts—what is important, what problems can be solved, what possibilities exist for theoretical extension, and so forth. Thus, the major historical effect of this issue in the 1960s was the rather complete separation of those who thought in terms of continuous systems from those who thought in terms of programming systems. The former were the cyberneticians and engineers concerned with pattern recognition; the latter became the AI community. The separation has been strongly institutionalized. The continuous-system folk ended up in electrical-engineering departments; the AI folk ended up in computer-science departments. (It must be remembered that initially computer-science departments were almost exclusively focused on software systems and almost all concern with hardware systems was in electrical-engineering departments.)

I believe this issue largely explains one peculiar aspect of the organization of the science devoted to understanding intelligence: By almost any account, pattern recognition and AI should be a single field, whereas they are almost entirely distinct. By now, in fact, due to another important historical twist, many people in computer science work in pattern recognition. But if such people also know traditional pattern recognition, they are seen as interdisciplinary.

Another interesting implication is buried here. The issue is not properly dichotomous, for there exist other classes of systems within which to search for intelligent systems. One obvious candidate is logic.[3] Were there not scientists who believed that logic was the appropriate class of systems? And if not, why not? First, by logical systems is meant the class of systems that do logical operations, such as AND, OR, NOT, and so forth.[4] This is the class corresponding to the logic level in the hierarchy of computer structures. The logic level is located between the circuit level and the program (symbol) level. All three levels are equally comprehensive and provide three possibilities for ways of describing intelligent systems. Indeed, circuit and program levels correspond exactly to the continuous and symbol positions of the issue under discussion. Now, in fact, in the early days, there were attempts to build logic machines and discuss the behavior of systems directly in terms of logic circuits. The classical neural networks of McCulloch and Pitts were an effort at modeling the neural system at the logic level. [McCulloch and Pitts, 1943.] But all these efforts rapidly died out and were all but gone by the mid-1960s. My own guess about why this happened is that the hierarchy of computer levels indicated quite clearly what to do with a logic level—namely, compose a higher level system. But this implied simply reproducing existing program-level systems, at least without some new organizational ideas at the program level. But the logic level provided no such ideas, nor could it. Thus, there was nowhere to go. In fact, the history of these efforts seems quite obscure, and tracing the demise of logic as a system language for intelligent systems would be a substantial, though rewarding, undertaking.

Problem-solving versus recognition #1: 1955–1965

An interesting issue grew up in association with the continuous/symbolic split. Those thinking within the framework of continuous systems concentrated on pattern recognition as the key type of task for machines to do—character recognition, speech recognition, and visual-pattern recognition. They also often concentrated on learning (as noted in the following paragraphs), but it was almost always a recognition capability that was being learned. The Perceptron of Rosenblatt can be taken as paradigmatic here. [Rosenblatt, 1958.] Contrariwise, those thinking within the framework of symbolic systems concentrated on problem-solving as the key type of task for machines to do—game-playing, theorem-proving, and puzzle-solving.

This separation of tasks reinforced the split between these groups. To the AI community, the intellectual depth of the tasks performed by the pattern-recognition systems seemed relatively trivial compared with the problem-solving tasks done by the programming systems. But just because of that, a myth grew up that it was relatively easy to automate man's higher reasoning functions but very difficult to automate those functions man shared with the rest of the animal kingdom and performed well automatically, for example, recognition. Thus, work on recognition was at the foundation of the problem of intelligence, whereas work on problem-solving was an add-on.

The symbolic/continuous split and the problem-solving/recognition split are organically related. Each task is the one most easily approached in terms

37

of the class of systems adopted. However, that does not make the two intellectual issues the same. Scientists can hold quite different attitudes about the two splits, and the two issues can become uncoupled in a different era under different conditions. Both these issues emerged in the late 1950s concurrently with the birth of AI. By 1965 the two fields of AI and pattern recognition had separated rather completely and taken up distinct, relatively permanent institutional roles. The conflict could be considered to have reached a resolution. However, it was to become unstuck again almost immediately.

Psychology versus neurophysiology #1: 1955–1965

Strongly coordinated with the issues of symbolic versus continuous systems and problem-solving versus recognition was another, conceptually distinct issue, namely, whether AI would look to psychology or to neurophysiology for inspiration. That human intelligence was to be both guide and goad to engineering intelligent systems was clear. However, this did not discriminate between psychology and neurophysiology. As is well known, these two disciplines speak with entirely separate, though not necessarily contradictory, voices. In general, those concerned with continuous systems and pattern recognition looked to neurophysiology; those concerned with symbolic systems and problem-solving (i.e., AI) looked to psychology. Evidence of the exclusive attention of early AI to psychology (in contradistinction to biology) is amply provided by the two major sets of readings of those years. [Feigenbaum and Feldman, 1963; Minsky, 1968.] By 1965, this issue was no longer a live one, and the cast for AI was set.

The split between neurophysiology and psychology did not dictate the split between symbolic and continuous systems; if anything, it was the other way around. Neurophysiology, of course, was linked to continuous variables, with its signals, networks, and geometry. But experimental psychology was not linked at all to symbolic systems. The dominant class of systems in psychology at the time was that of stimulus/response (S/R) systems, an abstract form of inhibition-and-excitation network. The only alternatives were the continuous fields of Gestalt theory or the pseudo-hydraulic systems of Freudian psychology (both only vaguely defined, though that is irrelevant here). In fact, the class of symbolic systems was discovered within AI and imported into psychology. [Newell and Simon, 1976a; Newell, 1980b.] Thus, the choice of psychology by AI was made because the class of systems that AI took to work with, that is, programming systems, led to psychologically, not physiologically, revealing tasks.

Neurophysiology played a key role in keeping continuous systems from suffering the same fate as logic systems. Whereas with logic systems there was nowhere to go except toward program-like organizations, with continuous systems there was the brain to model. We need not demand an answer to what the higher organization would be, we could just take as guide the brain as revealed in current neurophysiological work. It is true, of course, that in the late 1940s and early 1950s, the discrete approximation to the nervous system (neurons as digital threshold devices) promised to provide neurophysiological inspiration for the class of logic systems. But under a barrage of criticism, even the engineers came to accept the nervous system as too complex to be modeled by logic-level systems, which is to say, its continuities had to be taken seriously. Thus, without any source of inspiration, logic-level systems faded away as a separate language for modeling intelligence, but continuous systems remained.

Performance versus learning #1: 1955–1965

Yet another issue can be identified that is coordinated with the issue of symbolic versus continuous systems. AI concentrated on creating performance systems, that is, systems that performed some task demanding intelligence. Cybernetics and pattern-recognition research concentrated on creating systems that learned. Indeed, another subfield grew up that called itself self-organizing systems. [Yovits, Jacobi, and Goldstein, 1962.] In practice, self-organizing systems largely overlapped with the work in pattern recognition and it had common roots in cybernetics. But self-organizing systems took the problem of learning as the central focus rather than the problem of recognition. For instance, within self-organizing systems, there was considerable interest in embryology, even though it had little to do with recognition at the time.

Through the early 1960s, all the researchers concerned with mechanistic approaches to mental functions knew about each other's work and attended the same conferences. It was one big, somewhat chaotic, scientific happening. The four issues I have identified—continuous versus symbolic systems, problem-solving versus recognition, psychology versus neurophysiology, and performance versus learning—provided a large space within which the total field sorted itself out. Workers of a wide combination of persuasions on these issues could be identified. Until the mid-1950s, the central focus had been dominated by cybernetics, which had a position on two of the issues—using continuous systems and orientation toward neurophysiology—but no strong position on the other two. For instance, cybernetics did not concern itself with problem-solving at all. The emergence of programs as a medium of exploration activated all four of these issues, which then gradually led to the emergence of a single composite issue defined by a coordination of all four dimensions. This process was essentially complete by 1965, although I do not have any marker event. Certainly by 1971, at the second International Joint Conference on Artificial Intelligence in London, it was decided that henceforth the conference would not accept pure pattern-recognition papers, an act which already reflected an existing state of affairs.

Serial versus parallel #1: 1955–1965

It is worth noting for future reference that most pattern-recognition and self-organizing systems were highly parallel network structures. Many, but not all, were modeled after neurophysiological structures. Most symbolic-performance systems were serial programs. Thus, the contrast between serial and parallel (especially highly parallel) systems was explicit during the first decade of AI. The contrast was coordinated with the other four issues I have just discussed. However, I do not recollect it playing nearly as active a role as any of the other four, so I have simply added it on as a comment.

Heuristics versus algorithms: 1955–1965

These issues were not the only ones that emerged in the first decade of AI's existence, nor the most important. A candidate for the most important initial issue was AI's development of heuristic programs in contradistinction to algorithms. Algorithms were taken to be programs that guaranteed that they would solve a problem or solve it within given time bounds. Good programs were algorithmic, and if not, the fault lay with the programmer, who had failed to analyze his or her problem sufficiently—to know what the program should do to solve this problem. Heuristic programs, on the other hand, were programs that operated by means of heuristic rules of thumb—approximate, partial knowledge that might aid in the discovery of the solution but could not guarantee to do so. The distinction implied that intelligent problem-solving could be attained by heuristic programs. For a short while, one name for the field of AI was heuristic programming, reflecting, in part, a coordin-ation with such subfields as linear programming and dynamic programming (which were also just then emerging).

An important effect of this issue was to isolate AI within computer science but along a different dimension than the issue of symbols versus numbers. Heuristic programming indicates a commitment to a different course than finding the best engineering solution or mathematical analysis of a problem. According to the standard engineering ethos, the proper use of the computer requires the engineer or analyst to exert his or her best intellectual efforts studying the problem, find the best solution possible, and then program that solution. Providing a program with some half-baked, unanalyzed rules seemed odd at best and irrational, or even frivolous, at worst. A good example of this tension can be found in the work of Wang, whose theorem-proving program performed much better than the LOGIC THEORIST. [Newell, Shaw, and Simon, 1957; Wang, 1960.] The thrust of Wang's position was that much better theorem-provers could be built if appropriate results in mathematical logic were exploited. The defense by the AI community stressed finding how humans would solve such problems, in effect denying that the fullest analysis of experimental tasks was the object of the investigation. Another important example was the MACSYMA project to construct an effective computer system for physicists and engineers to do symbolic manipulation of mathematical expressions. Although this work grew out of two prior efforts in AI, it was cast by its leaders as "not part of AI," but, rather, as part of an area of computer science called symbolic manipulation, which took a thoroughgoing engineering and analytical attitude. [Slagle, 1963; Moses, 1967.]

I have put the demise of the issue at the mid-1960s; the issue gradually ceased to be discussed, though the distinction continues to be made in textbooks and introductory treatments. Once the field was underway, with lots of AI systems to provide examples, the point at issue became transparent. Moreover, the distinction has difficulty in being transformed into a technical one, because it is tied to features external to the procedure itself, namely, to the problem that is supposed to be solved and the state of knowledge of the user of the procedure.

Interpretation versus compilation: 1955–1985

A third issue served to separate AI from the rest of computer science, in addition to the issues of symbols versus numbers and heuristics versus algorithms. AI programs were developed in list-processing languages, which were interpretive, whereas the mainstream of language development was moving irrevocably toward the use of compilers. Prior to the mid-1950s, programming languages beyond assemblers were interpretive. The major turning point in compilers, FORTRAN, was developed in the mid-1950s,[5] and it determined the direction of programming-language development (though, of course, not without some controversy). Speed of execution was the consideration uppermost in the minds of the programming fraternity. In contrast, AI took the interpretive character of its languages seriously and declared them to be necessary for attaining intelligent systems. This was epitomized by the use of full recursion, but it penetrated throughout the entire philosophy of language design, with the attractive idea of putting intelligence into the interpreter.

This separation of AI programming from mainline high-level language programming, which started immediately at the birth of AI, has persisted to the present. Its effects go much deeper than might be imagined. This separation has played a major role in determining the heavy AI involvement in interactive programming, which contrasts with the minimal involvement of the central programming-languages, with their adherence to the compile-and-run operating philosophy. Just for fun, I have indicated the end of this issue in 1985, on the assumption that the coming generation of powerful personal computers will finally force all languages to come to terms with full dynamic capabilities in order to permit interactive programming. But this is pure conjecture, and the separation may now be wide enough to require a generation to heal.

The grounds for this issue can be traced to demands for efficiency on the one hand versus demands for flexibility on the other; perhaps the issue should have been so labeled. For instance, the main programming community in the late 1950s also had a strong negative reaction to list-processing, because of its giving up half the memory just to link the actual data together. But, although the general efficiency issue was always on the surface of discussions, the total situation seems better described in terms of distinct structural alternatives, that is, interpreters versus compilers, list structures versus arrays, and recursion versus iteration.

Simulation versus engineering analysis: 1955–

One issue that surfaced right from the start of AI was whether to make machines be intelligent by simulating human intelligence or by relying on engineering analysis of the task. Those who were primarily trying to understand human intelligence inclined naturally to the simulation view; those who were primarily engineers inclined to the pure task-analysis view. The principle was frequently invoked that we do not build a flying machine by simulating bird flight. On the simulation side, there was more than one position. The majority took the view that casual observation and casual introspection was the appropriate approach—that is, the human was a source of good ideas, not of detail. A few, usually with strong psychological interests or affiliations, took the view that actual experimental data on humans should be examined.

This issue seems never to have produced any important crises or changes of direction in the field; however, it has probably decreased the amount of mutual understanding. There seems to be little movement in a scientist's position on this issue. Each investigator finds his or her niche and stays there, understanding only superficially how those with different approaches operate. The position adopted probably reflects fairly deep attitudes, such as determine whether a scientist goes into an engineering discipline or a social/behavioral discipline in the first place. This is to be contrasted with many fields where methods are effectively neutral means to ends, to be used by all scientists as the science demands. There is little indication of diminution of this issue over the years, although starting in the 1970s, there has been some increase in the general use of protocols to aid the design of AI systems, even when there is no psychological interest.

This completes the set of new issues that arose coincident with the birth of AI. Five of them—symbolic versus continuous systems, problem-solving versus recognition, psychology versus neurophysiology, performance versus learning, and serial versus parallel—separated AI from other endeavors to mechanize intelligence. But the goal of mechanizing intelligence bound all of these enterprises together and distinguished them from the greater part of computer science, whose goal was performing tasks in the service of mankind. Three issues—symbols versus numbers, heuristics versus algorithms, and interpreters versus compilers—clustered together to make AI into a relatively isolated and idiosyncratic part of computer science. Finally one—simulation versus engineering—was purely internal to AI itself.

Replacing versus helping humans: 1960–

An issue that surfaced about five years after the beginning of AI was whether the proper objective was to construct systems that replace humans entirely or to augment the human use of computers. The fundamentally ethical dimension of this issue is evident. Yet, it was not overtly presented as an issue of social ethics but, rather, as a matter of individual preference. An investigator would simply go on record one way or another, in the prefaces of his or her papers, so to speak. Yet, there was often an overtone, if not of ethical superiority, of concordance with the highest ideals in the field. Those whose inclinations were toward AI did not so much meet this issue head on as ignore it. Indeed, it was perfectly possible to take the view that work in AI constituted the necessary exploration for man/computer symbiosis. [Licklider, 1960.]

A relatively weak issue such as this could not really become established unless man/machine cooperation offered technical possibilities and challenges as exciting as constructing intelligent machines. Thus, the beginning of this issue coincides with the appearance of interesting interactive systems, such as SKETCHPAD, which had an immense influence on the field. [Sutherland, 1963.]

Artificial intelligence scientists have had a relatively large involvement in the development of user/computer interaction throughout the history of computer science; for example, in time-sharing in the 1960s and 1970s, in making languages interactive in the 1970s, and in developing personal machines in the early 1980s. One explicit justification given for this involvement was that AI itself needed much better programming tools to create intelligent programs—a reason quite independent of the issue presented here. However, it is not possible to untangle the relations between them without some rather careful historical analysis.

Many of those who opted for working in user/computer cooperation tended not to become part of AI as the latter gradually evolved into a field. However, as I have already noted, it was entirely possible to work in both AI and user/computer cooperation. Still, the net result was an additional factor of separation between those in AI and those in neighboring parts of computer science.

Epistemology versus heuristics: 1960–

It is easy to distinguish the knowledge that an intelligent agent has from the procedures that might be necessary to put that knowledge to work to exhibit the intelligence in action.[6] The initial period in AI was devoted almost exclusively to bringing into existence modes of heuristic processing worthy of consideration. In 1959. John McCarthy initiated a research position that distinguished such study sharply from the study of appropriate logical formalisms to represent the full range of knowledge necessary for intelligent behavior. [McCarthy, 1959.] This study was clearly that of epistemology—the study of the nature of knowledge. It bore kinship with the subfield of philosophy by the same name, although, as with so many other potential connections of AI and philosophy, the orientation of the two fields is highly divergent, although the domain of interest is nominally the same.

There has been little controversy over this issue, although the two poles led to radically different distributions of research effort. Work on epistemology within AI has remained extremely limited throughout, although recently there has been a substantial increase. [D. G. Bobrow, 1980.]

Search versus knowledge: 1965–1980

In the first years of AI, through the early 1960s, AI programs were characterized simply as highly complex programs, without any particular notion of common structure. For instance, the field was also called *complex information processing* as well as *heuristic programming*. By 1965, however, it had become clear that the main AI programs used the same fundamental technique, which became known as *heuristic search*. [Newell and Ernst, 1965.] This involves the formulation of the problem to be solved as combinatorial search, with the heuristics cast in specific roles to guide the search, such as the selection of which step to take next, evaluation of a new state in the space, comparison of the present state to the posited goal-state, and so on. As the scope of AI programs seemed to narrow, there arose a belief in some AI scientists that the essence of intelligence lay not in search, but in large amounts of highly specific knowledge, or *expertise*. This issue was well enough established by the mid-1970s to occasion the declaration that a paradigm shift in AI had already occurred, the original paradigm having been heuristic search with little knowledge of the task domain and the new paradigm being knowledge-intensive programs. [Goldstein and Papert, 1977.]

It may be doubted that these changes amounted to an actual paradigm *shift*. What clearly did happen was a major expansion of AI research to explore systems that included substantial domain-specific knowledge. The subfield currently called expert systems, which includes many of the attempts at constructing applied AI systems, emerged in the mid-1970s in part as a result of this emphasis. However, it became clear that heuristic search invariably continued to show up in these programs. Whenever it did not, the problems being solved by the AI system were extremely easy relative to the knowledge put into the system.

It is useful to see that two types of searches are involved in intelligence. The first is the search of the problem space, that is, heuristic search, which is combinatorial. The second is the search of the system's memory for knowledge to be used to guide the heuristic search. This memory search is through a pre-existing structure that has been constructed especially for the purpose of being searched rapidly; it need not be combinatorial. Both types of searches are required of an intelligent system, and the issue of search versus knowledge helped to move the field to a full consideration of both types. The net result was not so much a shift in the paradigm as a broadening of the whole field. This had become clear enough to the field so that by 1980 the issue can be declared moot.

Power versus generality: 1965–1975

Another way to characterize the major early AI programs is that they took a single well-defined difficult task requiring intelligence and demonstrated that a machine could perform it. Theorem-proving, chess and checkers playing, symbolic integration, IQ-analogy tasks, and such management-science tasks as assembly-line balancing—all these fit this description. Again, there was a reaction to this. Although AI could do these sorts of tasks, it could not do the wide range of presumably trivial tasks we refer to as having common sense. The need was for generality in AI programs, not power.

This call had been issued early enough. [McCarthy, 1959.] However, it was really not until the mid-1960s that a significant shift occurred in the field toward the generality and commonsense side. This gave rise to using small constructed puzzles and artificial problems to illustrate various components of everyday reasoning. A typical example was the monkey-and-bananas task, patterned after simple tasks solved by Köhler's chimpanzee, Sultan. Whereas such problems would have seemed insignificant in the early years, they now became useful, because the goal of research was no longer power, but understanding how commonsense reasoning could occur.

By 1975, this shift had run its course, and new concerns for working with relatively large-scale real problems took over with the development of expert systems already mentioned. As could have been expected, the end of this period of emphasis did not mean a shift back to the original issue. Although expert systems tackled real problems and, hence, were obviously powerful, they did not achieve their power by the heuristic-search techniques of the early years; instead they used large amounts of domain-specific knowledge (coupled, sometimes, with modest search).

However, as is usual in the history of science, work on powerful AI programs never stopped; it only diminished and moved out of the limelight. By 1975, highly successful chess programs emerged, built on heuristic-search principles, with an emphasis on large amounts of search—a million positions per move in tournament play—and good engineering. Thus, intellectual issues shift the balance of what gets worked on but rarely shut off alternative emphases entirely.

Competence versus performance: 1965–

The Chomskian revolution in linguistics also started in the late 1950s. It was, along with AI, just one of many similar and interrelated developments in engineering, systems, and operational analysis. Although each of these developments had a particularly intense significance for some particular field, for example, linguistics or computer science, they all formed a common interdisciplinary flux. Gradually, these activities sorted themselves into separate subfields or disciplines, developing opposing positions on the issues previously laid out, as we have seen for AI vis-à-vis cybernetics and pattern recognition.

In many ways, linguistics was a special case. It was already a well-formed discipline, and the revolution was at the heart of the discipline, not in some peripheral aspect that could have split off and aligned with other intellectual endeavors. Furthermore, only very few linguistics participated in the general flux that was occurring in the world of engineering and applied mathematics. Linguistics was culturally and organizationally quite distinct, having strong roots in the humanities. In fact, it probably made an immense difference that Noam Chomsky became affiliated with the Massachusetts Institute of Technology (MIT).

It was not until the mid-1960s that issues emerged that determined relations between linguistics and other subfields and disciplines. A principal issue was the distinction between competence and performance, which was moved to a central position in the new linguistics by Chomsky. [Chomsky, 1965.] Linguistic competence was the general knowledge a speaker had of the language, in particular, of the generative grammar of the language. Performance was the actual production of utterances, which could be affected by many additional factors, such as cognitive limits, states of stress, or even deliberate modifications for effect. The distinction made useful operational sense for linguistics, because there were two sources of evidence about human-language capabilities, the actual utterance and the judgment of grammatically—a sort of recall/recognition difference, although that analogy was never exploited.

This distinction might seem innocuous from the standpoint of science history, that is, purely technical. In fact, it served to separate quite radically the sciences concerned primarily with performance, namely AI, computational linguistics, cognitive psychology, and psycholinguistics, from linguistics proper. Linguistics itself declared that it was not interested in performance. More cautiously said, competence issues were to have absolute priority on the research agenda. But the effect was the same: Work in any of the performance fields was basically irrelevant to the development of linguistics. There could be a flow from linguistics to these other fields, and, indeed, there was an immense flow to psycholinguistics, but there could not be any significant flow in the other direction.[7]

A more effective field-splitter would be hard to find. It has remained in effect ever since, with the competence/performance distinction being extended to other domains of mentality. This has certainly not been the only significant cause of the separateness of AI from linguistics. There are important isolating differences in method, style of research, and attitudes toward evidence. Many of these other issues share substance with the competence/performance distinction and affect the separation between psychology and linguistics much more than that between AI and linguistics. Thus, perhaps these issues can be left to one side.

Memory versus processing: 1965–1975

During the immediate postwar decades, the mainstream of individual human psychology was strongly influenced by the general ferment of engineering, system, and operational ideas (as I have previously termed it). This involved human factors and information theory in the early 1950s; and signal detection theory, control theory, game theory, and AI in the mid-1950s. As with linguistics in the period of 1955–1965, all these ideas and fields seemed to mix while matters sorted themselves out. By the mid-1960s, psychology had focused on memory as the central construct in its view of man as an information processor. Short-term memory and the visual iconic store combined to provide an exciting picture of the interior block-diagram of the human mental apparatus (what would now be called the architecture). This settled what the main lines of investigation would be for the field; the marker event for this conviction is Neisser's book, *Cognitive Psychology*. [Neisser, 1967.]

This settlement is important for the history of AI, because AI's influence on psychology in the 1955–1965 period was primarily in the area of problem-solving and concept formation. With psychology opting for memory structure, psychology and AI went fundamentally separate ways. Although the work on problem-solving remained a common concern, it was a sufficiently minor area in psychology, so that it exerted only a modest integrating effect. AI itself during this period had little interest in memory structure at the block-diagram level. Psychologically relevant research on memory by AI researchers did exist but moved out of AI into psychology; for example, the work on EPAM (Elementary Perceiver and Memorizer). [Simon and Feigenbaum, 1964.]

47

In the second half of the 1960s came another major advance in cognitive psychology, namely, the discoveries of how to infer basic processes from reaction times. [Neisser, 1963; Sternberg, 1966.] This insight promised even greater ability to dissect human cognitive processes and confirmed the basic choice of psychology to analyze the block-diagram level of cognition. This insight also broadened the analysis from just memory structure to the stages of information-processing. In this respect, it might seem better to call the issue under discussion one of system levels: AI focusing on the symbolic level and psychology focusing on the architecture,[8] that is, the equivalent of the register-transfer level. However, the concern with memory so dominates the years prior to 1965, when this issue was being sorted out, that it seems preferable to label it memory versus processing.

Long-term memory has been absent from the previous account. During this period, AI was certainly concerned about the structure of long-term memory, under the rubric of semantic memory. This would seem to provide common ground with psychology, yet initially it did not do so to any great extent. Two factors seem to account for this. First, in psychology, the new results, hence the excitement, all involved short-term memories. The established theory of learning, interference theory, against which these new ideas about memory made headway, assumed a single memory, which was in essence long-term memory. Second, the memory that psychology considered was episodic—learning what happened during an episode, such as learning what familiar items were presented at a trial. This stood in marked contrast with semantic memory, which appeared to be a timeless organization of knowledge. Only gradually did the psychologically relevant work on semantic memory by a few investigators capture any significant attention within cognitive psychology. The seminal publication of Anderson and Bower's *Human Associative Memory* can be taken as a marker of the beginning of this attention. [Anderson and Bower, 1973.]

Problem-solving versus recognition #2: 1965–1975

In 1965, AI took back the problem of recognition that had become the intellectual property of the pattern-recognition community. This can be marked rather precisely by the work of Roberts on the recognition of three-dimensional polyhedra. [Roberts, 1965.] The essential features were two: First, recognition was articulated, that is, the scene had to be decomposed or segmented into subparts, each of which might need to be recognized to be a different thing. Thus, the result of recognition was a description of a scene rather than just an identification of an object. But a description is a symbolic structure that has to be constructed, and such processes were quite outside the scope of the pattern-recognition techniques of the time, though exactly of the sort provided by AI. Second, a major source of knowledge for making such recognitions came from adopting a model of the situation (e.g., it

48

consists only of polyhedra). This made recognition processes strongly infer-ential, again fitting in well with work in AI, but not with work in pattern recognition.

By the late 1960s, work on vision was going on throughout AI, but the transformation went further than just vision. Three laboratories (at MIT, Stanford, and the Stanford Research Institute) started major efforts in robot-ics. Vision was to be coupled with arms and motion and in at least one AI center (Stanford), with speech. The entire enterprise was radically different in its focus and problems from the research in pattern recognition that was still going on in parallel in departments and research centers of electrical engin-eering. In fact, there was little actual controversy to speak of. Both groups simply did their thing. But likewise, there was no substantial rapprochement.

Syntax versus semantics: 1965–1975

The Chomskian revolution in linguistics was strongly based on theory. Built around the notions of generative and transformational grammar, it posited three distinct components (or modules) for phonology, syntax, and seman-tics, each with its own grammar. The initial emphasis was on syntax, with work on semantics much less well developed.[9] Despite cautions from the competence/performance distinction, the inference was clear from both the theory and practice of linguistics—syntactic processing should occur in a separate module independently of semantic processing. Indeed, what computational linguistics there was in association with the new linguistics involved the construction of programs for syntactic parsing.

In the late 1960s, a reaction to linguistics arose from within the AI and computational linguistics communities. It took the form of denying the sep-aration of syntax and semantics in the actual processing of language. The initial analysis of an utterance by the hearer was as much a question of semantics as of syntax. Language required an integrated analysis by the hearer and, hence, by the theorist. This reaction can be marked by the work of Quillian, whose introduction of semantic nets was a device to show how semantic processing could occur directly on the surface structure of the utterance (though presumably in conjunction with syntax). [Quillian, 1968.]

This reaction was grounded more broadly in the assertion of the import-ance of processing considerations in understanding language, the very thing denied by the competence/performance distinction. It sought to put process-ing considerations into the mainstream of linguistic studies, the latter being owned, so to speak, by the linguistics community. One result, as might have been expected, was to compound the separation between linguistics, on the one hand, and computational linguistics and AI, on the other. Another was to create a stronger independent stream of work on language in AI with its own basis.

Theorem-proving versus problem-solving: 1965–

Theorem-proving tasks have always been included in the zoo of tasks studied by AI, although the attention these tasks received initially was sporadic. However, some logicians and mathematicians worked on theorem-proving in logic, not just as another task, but as the fundamental formalism for understanding reasoning and inference. In the last half of the 1960s, with the development of a logical formalism called resolution, this work in theorem-proving took center stage in AI. [Robinson, 1965.] It seemed for a time that theorem-proving engines would sit at the heart of any general AI system. Not only was their power extended rapidly during this period, but a substantial amount of mathematical analysis was carried out on the nature of theorem proving in the predicate calculus. Even further, theorem-proving programs were extended to handle an increasing range of tasks, for example, question-answering, robot-planning, and program-synthesis.

A consequence of this success and viewpoint was that theorem-proving was taken to be a fundamental category of activity distinct from other problem-solving, with its own methods and style of progress. A good indicator of this is Nilsson's AI textbook, which divides all problem-solving methods of AI into three parts: state-space search, problem-reduction (i.e., subgoals), and predicate-calculus theorem-proving. [Nilsson, 1971.] It is not clear whether this issue has been laid to rest by now or not. As recounted in the following section, under the procedural/declarative issue, theorem-proving has become much less central to AI since the mid-1970s. But theorem-proving and problem-solving still remain distinct research strands.

Engineering versus science: 1965–

Computer science is torn by a fundamental uncertainty over whether it is an engineering or science discipline. There is no doubt about the engineering side; computer science designs and creates artifacts all the time. The doubt exists on the nature of the science involved. Computer science certainly studies intellectual domains that are not part of other disciplines. The question is whether or not they have the character of a science. However, the dichotomy need not be accepted: A third alternative is that the unique intellectual domain of computer science is part of mathematics. Computer science would then join other engineering specialties, such as control theory and information theory, which have their own characteristic mathematical development.

Much rests on the putative outcome of this issue: What should computer science be like in the future? Should departments of computer science be part of the college of engineering or the college of arts and sciences? What status should be accorded to various subdisciplines in computer science? Can a thesis involve just a design? And more. The start of this issue coincides with the creation of departments of computer science in the mid-1960s, which served to raise all these questions. Whether the issue will ever be laid to rest is unclear, but it is certainly unlikely while the whole field grows dynamically, with a continuing flood of new and destabilizing notions.

Artificial intelligence participates along with the rest of computer science in the uncertainties over whether it is an engineering or science discipline. However, the issue for AI has its own special flavor. AI participates with many disciplines outside computer science in the attempt to understand the nature of mind and intelligent behavior. This is an externally grounded scientific and philosophic goal, which is clearly not engineering. Thus, the nature of the science for AI is not really in doubt as it is for the rest of computer science. However, this does not end the matter, for interactions occur with other issues. For instance, to the extent that we are oriented toward helping humans rather than replacing them, we may not wish to accept the understanding of the nature of mind as a scientific goal, but only as a heuristic device.

The orientation toward engineering or science can have major consequences for how a field devotes its energies. Currently, for example, an important divergence exists in the subfield of computer vision. Should the nature of the environment be studied to discover what can be inferred from the optic array (a scientific activity); or should experimental vision systems be constructed to analyze the data they generate within the framework of the system (an engineering activity)? That both activities are legitimate is not in question; which activity gets the lion's share of attention is in dispute. And there is some indication that an important determiner is the basic engineering/science orientation of a given investigator.

Language versus tasks: 1970–1980

The 1970s saw the emergence of concerted efforts within AI to produce programs that understand natural language, amounting to the formation of a subfield, lying partly in AI and partly in computational linguistics. The key markers are the works of Woods and Winograd. [Woods, 1970; T. Winograd, 1971]. This issue had been building for some time, as we saw in the issue of syntax versus semantics.

The emergence of such a subfield is in itself not surprising. Natural language is clearly an important, even uniquely important, mental capability. In addition to AI, there existed another relevant field, computational linguistics, concerned generally with the application of computers to linguistics. Neither is it surprising that this subfield had almost no representation from linguistics, although, of course, linguistics was of obvious central relevance.[10] The syntax/semantics issue, which had reinforced the separation of linguistics from AI, was a primary substantive plank in the programme of the new subfield.

What is interesting was the creation of another attitude within a part of AI, which can be captured by the issue of language versus tasks. Studying the understanding of language was seen as a sufficient context for investigating the nature of common sense. An important discovery was how much knowledge and inference appeared to be required to understand even the simplest sentences or short stories. Thus, the very act of understanding such stories involved commonsense reasoning and, with it, the essence of general human intelligence. Programs could be interesting as AI research, so the attitude went, without doing any other task in addition to understanding the presented language input. The effect of this strategic position was to separate the work in natural-language processing from the tradition in AI of posing tasks for programs to do, where the difficulty could be assessed. The issue did not occasion much discussion, although its effects were real enough. The issue was masked by the fact that understanding by itself was a difficult enough task for AI research to make progress on. No one could object (and no one did) to not adding what seemed like an irrelevant second difficult task for the system, which would simply burden the research endeavor.

Procedural versus declarative representation #1: 1970–1980

Recall that resolution theorem-proving flourished in the late 1960s and bid fair to become the engine at the center of all reasoning. In fact, it took only a few years for the approach to come up against its limitations. Despite increases in power, relative to prior efforts, theorem provers were unable to handle any but trivial tasks. Getting from logic to real mathematics—seen always as a major necessary hurdle—seemed as far away as ever.

The reaction to this state of affairs became known as the procedural/declarative controversy. Theorem provers were organized as a large homogeneous database of declarative statements (clauses in resolution), over which an inference engine worked to produce new true statements to add to the database. This was the essence of a declarative representation of knowledge and its attractions were many. Its difficulty lay in the costs of processing. The inference engine treated all expressions in the database alike or, more precisely, without regard for their semantics. There also seemed no way for a theorem prover to be given information about how to solve problems. These two features added up to a major combinatorial explosion. The remedy—the procedural side of the issue—lay (so it was claimed) in encoding information about the task in procedures. Then knowledge would be associated directly with the procedures that were to apply it; indeed, the procedures would embody the knowledge and, thus, not have to be interpreted by another inference engine. This would permit the appropriate guidance for problem-solving and, thus, keep the combinatorial explosion under control.

There are irremediable flaws in both sides of the argument whether knowledge should be coded in procedural or declarative form, just as there are irremediable flaws in both sides of the argument whether a program is heuristic or algorithmic. Both procedural and declarative representations are necessary to make any computation at all happen. In consequence, arguments over the issue were largely inconclusive, although they produced the closest thing to a public issue-controversy in AI's short history. However, the effect on the course of AI research was enormous. First, work on theorem-proving shrank to a trickle, with what remained mostly devoted to nonresolution theorem-proving. Second, so-called planning languages emerged as a result—PLANNER, QA4, CONNIVER, POPLAR, and so forth. [Bobrow and Raphael, 1974.] These programming-language systems were intended to provide a vehicle for writing the sorts of domain-dependent, procedure-oriented theorem provers called for in the debate. While that did not quite happen, these languages in themselves provided a major conceptual advance in the field. The effects of this issue had about run their course by 1980.

Frames versus atoms: 1970–1980

In a paper that circulated widely before it was published in the mid-1970s, Marvin Minsky raised the issue about the size of representational units in an intelligent system. [Minsky, 1975.] Knowledge should be represented in *frames*, which are substantial collections of integrated knowledge about the world, rather than in small atoms or fragments. The basic issue is as old as the atomistic associationism of British empiricism and the countering complaints of the Gestaltists. How are the conflicting requirements for units of thought and contextual dependence to be reconciled?

This issue had hardly surfaced at all in the first decade of AI. List structures, the basic representational medium, were in themselves neither atomistic nor wholistic but adaptable to whatever representational constructs the designer had in mind.[11] But the coming to prominence of resolution-theorem-proving in the late 1960s brought with it as a side effect the *clause* as the unit of representation. The clause was a primitive assertion that could not be broken down into a conjunction of other assertions—primitive predicates P, negations of primitive predicates $\sim P$, disjunctions P or Q, implications P implies Q, and so forth. The total knowledge of the system was to be represented as the conjunction of clauses—that is, to use the old Gestaltist phrase, as an *And-sum* of separate bits of knowledge.

Thus, the issue of size of representational unit grew out of the same ground as the procedural versus declarative controversy, and, indeed, it was articulated by the same group at MIT who had made most of the latter issue. As is always the case, concern was, in fact, widespread but had been subordinated to other concerns. [Abelson, 1973; Norman, 1973; Schank, 1973.] Minsky was the first one to give clear voice to the concern. The effect of the paper was dramatic, despite the fact that the paper itself was entirely speculative and discursive. Throughout AI, the concept of the frame as the appropriate data structure was widely embraced. By 1980, frame systems were an established part of AI, and a very substantial fraction of the work in knowledge representation was involved in such systems.

Much follows on this development (in conjunction with the procedural/declarative issue)—the rise of substantial research effort in knowledge representation and the strengthening of renewed ties with philosophy. [Brachman and Smith, 1980.] These efforts conjoin with those of AI epistemology, discussed earlier. They raise some new issues, such as the relation of philosophic work on meaning to directly inspired computational models. But these issues have not yet jelled enough to be included in their own right.

Reason versus emotion and feeling #2: 1970–

Philosophy has a long-standing concern with the mechanization of mind. Indeed, under the rubric of the mind/body problem, it can be said almost to own the problem, it having been bequeathed to philosophy by Descartes. In its genesis, AI had very little involvement with philosophy, beyond the background awareness that comes from participation in the general intellectual culture. No philosophers of mind were involved and no technical philosophical issues were dealt with. a glance at the content of the two fields provides one obvious clue. The phenomena attended to in philosophy are sensations as subjective experiences—*raw feels*, to use a bit of philosophic jargon. A typical article is entitled "The Feelings of Robots." [Ziff, 1959.] Thus, though AI and philosophy of mind ostensibly deal with the same problem, in fact they go after largely distinct phenomena.[12]

The issue has not been especially active, but it has been raised. [Gunderson, 1971.] It is argued that performance functions (i.e., those functions AI currently deals with, called *program-receptive* functions) can be mechanized; but that sentient functions (i.e., feelings, called *program-resistant* functions) cannot. Whether this will ever grow to a substantial controversy is hard to tell at this point. It is certainly available as a reserve position that can serve to separate AI from the philosophy of mind. It adds to the general background concern, discussed in the first occurrence of this issue, of the absence of emotion and feeling in the development of intelligent systems.

Toy versus real tasks: 1975–

As noted in the power/generality issue, the field took a shift in the mid-1960s away from powerful programs toward programs that could exhibit common sense. Further, as noted in the language/tasks issue, this line further transmuted to being concerned with understanding via the understanding of natural language. Concomitantly, programs were often built to work on small simple illustrative tasks or environments, usually puzzles or made-up situations.

By the mid-1970s some systems had been developed that worked with real tasks that had substantial intellectual content, to judge from their role in the real world. The initial such system can be taken to be DENDRAL, which determined the structural formula for chemical molecules, given the data on the mass spectrogram.[13] [Lindsay, Buchanan, Feigenbaum, and Lederberg, 1980.] DENDRAL began in the late 1960s and grew in power throughout the early 1970s. It was joined in the mid-1970s by several systems that performed competently in real medical-diagnosis tasks, of which MYCIN was the paradigm. [Shortliffe, 1974.] This was the immediate locus of expert systems, which, as previously noted, grew up as part of the general emphasis on knowledge in contrast to search. With it grew an attitude that AI in general should no longer work on small illustrative, artificial tasks but that it was time to work on real tasks. The simple artificial tasks came to be called toy tasks, not just because the term conveys the contrast between childish and grown-up pursuits, but also because stacking children's blocks had become a favorite illustrative task environment.

The tension between basic research and application exists in all sciences at all times. Sciences sometimes build institutional structures to contain the tension. As we saw in the issue of science versus engineering, computer science has kept its basic and applied components mixed together in a single discipline, thus exacerbating the tension. The tension was, in fact, especially severe for AI during the decade of the 1970s. The climate in Washington was not benign for basic research in general, and there was sustained pressure from AI's primary government funding agency (DARPA—Defense Advanced Research Projects Agency) to make AI pay off. That said, however, the distinction between toy versus real tasks is not solely the distinction between basic and applied research. Tasks taken from the real world and performed by intelligent humans as part of their working lives carry a prima facie guarantee of demanding appropriate intelligent activity by systems that would perform them. It can be argued that such tasks are the appropriate ones for AI to work on, even if the goal is basic research. Thus, the toy-versus-real-tasks issue stands ambiguously for both meanings—basic versus applied and irrelevant versus relevant basic science.

Serial versus parallel #2: 1975–

By the mid-1970s, computer science had for some time been seriously exploring multiprogramming and multiprocessing. These provided the groundwork for considering parallel systems for doing AI. A major instigation occurred with the development of the Hearsay-II model of speech understanding. [Lesser and Erman, 1977.] Hearsay-II comprised a number of knowledge sources (acoustic, phonetic, phonological, lexical, syntactic, semantic, and pragmatic), each working concurrently and independently off a common blackboard that contained the current working state about the utterance and each contributing their bit to the evolving recognition and reacting to the bits provided by the others.

The Hearsay-II structure was certainly a parallel one, but it was at a level of parallelism quite different from earlier network models, namely, a modest number (tens) of functionally specialized processes. Furthermore, individual processes remained fundamentally symbolic (even though lots of signal-processing was inherent in the speech-recognition task). Hearsay-II was only one of several efforts to pursue the notion that an intelligent system should be thought of in terms of communicating subprocesses rather than as an individual serial machine. A metaphor arose for thinking about an intelligent system—the scientific community metaphor—which took the operation of science, with its notion of cooperation, publication, experiment, criticism, education, and so forth, as the appropriate model for intelligent activity. Gradually, a group of people emerged interested in working on distributed AI.

Performance versus learning #2: 1975–

As noted earlier, learning was generally associated with work on pattern recognition. With the split between problem-solving and recognition, work on learning within AI declined. As always, it never stopped entirely. Indeed, such is the basic fascination with learning processes, and with the belief that they hold the key to intelligence, that each learning program that was constructed received substantial attention.[14] [Samuel, 1959; D. A. Waterman, 1970; Winston, 1970; Sussman, 1975.] However, each learning system was relatively idiosyncratic, with its own interesting lessons, so that the whole did not add up to a coherent effort for the field.

A reversal of this state of affairs developed by the late 1970s. It was triggered by the spread of a class of programming systems, called production, or rule-based systems, which are used for both constructing expert systems and analyzing human cognition. [Waterman and Hayes-Roth, 1978.] To appreciate their role in the resurgence of work on learning, we must take a step back. To create a learning system requires solving two research problems. First, a space of potential performance programs must be created, in which learning will constitute moving from one program to another, searching for programs with better performance. If the space of programs is too vast and irregular, then learning is, in effect, automatic programming, and it becomes extremely difficult. If the space is too limited, then learning is easy, but the performance programs are of little significance. Determining the right space is, thus, a critical research activity. Second, given the space, it is still necessary to design an interesting learning system, for the space only lays out the possibilities. Thus, inventing the learning system is also a critical research activity.

A major reason why early AI learning-systems seemed so idiosyncratic was that each made unique choices on both these dimensions. Most important, doing research on learning was doing a double task and taking a double risk.

A production system is composed entirely of a set of *if-then* rules (if such and such conditions hold, then execute such and such actions). At each instant, the rules that hold are recognized, and a single rule is selected to execute. In such a system, the natural space of performance programs consists of subsets of if-then rules, and the primitive act of learning is to add a new rule to the existing set (or sometimes to modify an existing rule in some simple way, such as by adding another condition). This space of performance programs is neither too limited nor too open, since it is easy to restrict the rules to be learned to a special class. As a consequence, the first research choice is essentially made for the researcher, who can then concentrate on constructing an interesting learning program. Moreover, learning programs will have much in common, since they now use similar spaces of performance programs. Indeed, this is just what happened in the late 1970s as researchers began to construct a wide variety of small learning systems, all built around variants of the production-system formalism. [Michalski, Carbonell, and Mitchell, 1983.] It must be realized, of course, that such focusing of effort does not remove the collective risk. If production systems are the wrong program organization to be exploring, then the entire field is moving down an unproductive path.

Psychology versus neuroscience #2: 1975–

AI would appear to be at the mercy of the immense gulf that continues to separate psychology and the biology of the brain. As each field continues to progress—which both do dramatically—hopes continually spring up for new bridging connections. No doubt at some point the permanent bridge will be built. So far, although each increment of progress seems real, the gap remains disappointingly large.

It is possible that AI has a major contribution to make to this by exploring basic computational structures at a level that makes contact with neural systems. In the early instance of psychology versus neurophysiology (which was before the term *neuroscience* had been coined), that possibility seemed quite remote. The theoretical structures that did make contact with neurophysiology were remote from the computational structures that preoccupied AI researchers. Then the split occurred, with pattern recognition all but moving out of computer science.

In the mid-1970s, a new attempt began to connect AI with neuroscience, initiated by the work of David Marr. [Marr, 1976.] The emphasis remained on vision, as it had been in the earlier period. But the new effort was explicitly computational, focusing on algorithms that could perform various low-level vision functions, such as stereopsis. Although Marr's effort was new in many ways, and based on specific technical achievements, most of the global issues of the earlier time reappeared. This work has now expanded to a larger group, which calls its work, among other things, the new connectionism, and promises to be a substantial subfield again, this time within AI.

Serial versus parallel #3: 1980–

The new wave of neuroscience-inspired AI contains, of course, a commitment to highly parallel network structures. The issue of serial versus parallel merits a separate entry here to maintain a clear contrast with the distributed AI effort, which defined the second wave of concern with parallel systems. In this third phase, the degree of parallelism is in the millions, and computing elements in the network have modest powers; in particular, they are not computers with their own local symbols. In the new structures, computation must be shared right down to the roots, so to speak. The interaction cannot be limited to communicating results of significant computations. Furthermore, the communication media between elements are continuous signals, and not just bits. However, unlike the earlier work, these new computational systems are not to be viewed as neural nets; that is, the nodes of the network are not to be put in one-to-one correspondence with neurons, but, rather, with physiological subsystems of mostly unspecified character.

Problem-solving versus recognition #3: 1980–

Robotics has returned to AI after having left it for most of the 1970s. Perhaps it is unfortunate to call the issue problem-solving versus recognition, since recognition is only one aspect of robotics. The main sources of the new wave of effort are external to AI—industrial robotics plus the concern of the decline in American productivity and the trade position of the United States vis-à-vis Japan and West Germany. The initial growth of industrial robotics took place largely outside of AI as a strictly engineering endeavor. As a result, the initial growth tended to minimize the intelligence involved, for example, sensory-motor coordination. One component of the new association of robotics with AI is the coupling of significant amounts of vision with manipulators, reflecting the continued advance of vision capabilities in AI throughout the 1970s. (Touch and kinesthetic sensing is increasingly important, too, but this does not build so strongly on prior progress in AI.) Importantly, along with industrially motivated aspects, there is also a revival of basic research in manipulation and movement in space and over real terrains.

It might seem that this is just another purely technical progression. But with it has returned, as night follows day, the question of the relation of AI and robotics as disciplines, just as the question was raised in the issue of problem-solving versus recognition during the late 1960s. Is robotics a central part of AI or only an applied domain? Do graduate students in AI have to understand the underlying science of mechanics and generalized coordinate systems that are inherent in understanding manipulation and motion? Or is that irrelevant to intelligence? Cases can be made either way. [Nilsson, 1982.]

Procedural versus declarative representation #2: 1980–

In the late 1970s, a new programming system called PROLOG emerged, based on resolution-theorem-proving and constituting, in effect, a continuation of the effort to show that declarative formulations can be effective. [Kowalski, 1979.] The effort is based primarily in Europe, and it is a vigorous movement. The attack is not occurring at the level of planning languages, but at the level of LISP itself. Over the years, LISP has established itself as the lingua franca of the AI community. Even though various other programming systems exist, for example, rule-based systems of various flavors, practically everyone builds systems within a LISP programming environment. The planning languages (PLANNER, CONNIVER, etc.), which showed how to effect another level of system organization above LISP, have not proved highly effective as a replacement, and they receive only modest use. As already noted, their contribution has been primarily conceptual. Thus, although the original attack on theorem-proving was in terms of the planner languages, the modern counterattack is at the level of LISP. By being centered in Europe, with very little attention paid currently to PROLOG in the major AI centers in the United States, the issue takes on additional coordinated dimensions. The outcome is far from clear at this juncture.

Discussion

It should be clear by now why I entered the caveats about historical accuracy at the beginning. Each of the issues raises serious problems of characterization and historical grounding. No attempt has been made to define an intellectual issue, so that some modestly objective way could be found to generate a complete set of issues, for example, by placing a grid over the literature of the field. Several additional issues might well have emerged, and some of those presented here might not have made the grade. Thus, the population of issues exhibited must be taken, not just with a pinch of salt, but soaked in a barrel of brine. Similar concerns attend dating the issues and my interpretation of them; nevertheless, some comments about the total picture seem worthwhile.

What is missing?

I do know why some issues did not make it. Three examples will illustrate some reasons. The first is the broad but fundamental issue of the ethical use of technology and the dehumanization of people by reduction to mechanism. This issue engages all of technology and science. It seems particularly acute for AI, perhaps, because the nature of mind seems so close to the quick. But the history of science reminds us easily enough that at various stages astronomy, biology, and physics have seemed special targets for concern. There has been continued and explicit discussion of these issues in connection with AI. [Taube, 1961; Weizenbaum, 1976; McCorduck, 1979.] I have not included them in the list of intellectual issues because they do not, in general, seem to affect the course of the science. Where some aspect does seem to do so, as in the issue of helping humans or replacing them, it has been included. However, the broader issue certainly provides a thematic background against which all work goes on in the field, increasing its ambiguity, and the broader issue undoubtedly enters into individual decisions about whether to work in the field and what topics to select.

The second example involves Hubert Dreyfus, who has been a persistent and vocal critic of AI. [Dreyfus, 1972.] He has certainly become an issue for the field; however, this does not necessarily produce an intellectual issue. Dreyfus's central intellectual objection, as I understand him, is that the analysis of the context of human action into discrete elements is doomed to failure. This objection is grounded in phenomenological philosophy. Unfortunately, this appears to be a nonissue as far as AI is concerned. The answers, refutations, and analyses that have been forthcoming to Dreyfus's writings have simply not engaged this issue—which, indeed, would be a novel issue if it were to come to the fore.

The third example involves the imagery controversy, which has been exceedingly lively in cognitive psychology. [Kosslyn, Pinker, Smith, and Shwartz, 1979.] The controversy is over the nature of the representations used by humans in imagining scenes and reasoning about them. There is no doubt about its relevance to AI—the alternatives are a classical dichotomy between propositional (symbolic?) representations and analog ones. Thus, at heart, it is a variant of the issue of analog-versus-digital representation, which has received mention. But for reasons that are quite obscure to me, the imagery issue has received hardly any interest in the AI community, except where that community also participates in cognitive psychology. As things stand at the moment, this would be an issue for cognitive science, but it is not one for AI.

Though enumerating intellectual issues exposes a certain amount of the history of a field, even if only from particular viewpoints, some important parts can be missed. These seem to be endeavors that were noncontroversial or where the controversies were merely of the standard sort—of what progress had been made, what subfields should get resources, and so forth. Thus, work on program synthesis and verification goes unnoticed. Also, the major effort in the 1970s to construct speech-understanding systems is barely noticed. Perhaps this is not a valid point about the basic historical scheme but reflects only the unevenness of my process of generating issues. Certainly, there were issues in speech-recognition research both in the 1960s, when Bell Laboratories decided to abandon speech recognition as an inappropriate task, and in the 1970s, when a substantial effort sponsored by DARPA to construct speech-understanding systems was dominated by AI considerations over speech-science considerations. Perhaps intellectual issues are generated from all scientific efforts in proportion to the number of scientists involved in them (or to their square?); all we need to do is look for them.

Characteristics of the history

Turning to what is revealed in Table 1, the most striking feature, to me at least, is how many issues there are. Looked at in any fashion—number active at one time (fifteen on average) or total number of issues during AI's quarter-century lifespan (about thirty)—it seems to me like a lot of issues. Unfortunately, similar profiles do not exist for other fields (or I do not know of them). Perhaps the situation in AI is typical, either of all fields at all times or of all fields when they are getting started. In fact, I suspect it is due to the interdisciplinary soup out of which AI emerged. [See my paper "Reflections on the Structure of an Interdiscipline" in this volume.] Many other related fields were being defined during the same post-World-War-II era—cybernetics, operations research, management science, information theory, control theory, pattern recognition, computer science, and general systems theory. Even so, I do not see any easy way of pinning down a correct interpretation of why there are so many issues.

Issues are not independent; they come in clusters, which are coordinated. Researchers tend to fall into two classes, corresponding to one pole or another on all issues in the cluster. Clusters that occur in this history are as follows (where polarities of subissues have been reoriented, if necessary, to make them all line up together, corresponding to the superordinate issue):

AI versus Cybernetics

  Symbolic versus continuous systems
  Problem-solving versus recognition
  Psychology versus neuroscience
  Performance versus learning
  Serial versus parallel

AI versus Computer Science

  Symbols versus numbers
  Heuristics versus algorithms
  Interpretation versus compilation
  Replacing versus helping humans
  Problem-solving versus theorem-proving

Problem-Solving versus Knowledge Search

Heuristics versus epistemology
Search versus knowledge
Power versus generality
Processing versus memory

Linguistics versus AI and Cognitive Psychology

Competence versus performance
Syntax versus semantics

Engineering versus Science

Engineering analysis versus simulation
Engineering versus science
Real versus toy tasks

Wholes versus Atoms

Procedural versus declarative representation
Frames versus atoms

A cluster might seem to define a single underlying issue, which can then replace component issues. However, the fact that issues are coordinated does not make them identical. Some scientists can always be found who are aligned in nonstandard patterns. In fact, some of the clusters seem much more consistent than others. Thus, the multiplicity of issues keeps the scientific scene complex, even though, because of clustering, it appears that it should be clear and simple. In fact, many of the groupings are more easily labeled by how they separate fields than by any coherent underlying conceptual issue.

Clustering of issues does seem to be a common occurrence; for instance, a standard advanced text on learning in psychology begins with a list of seven dichotomous issues that characterize learning theories. [Hilgard and Bower, 1948 and 1975, pp. 8–13.] The first three—peripheral versus central, habits versus cognitive structures, and trial-and-error versus insight—form a coordinated cluster that characterizes stimulus/response theories versus cognitive theories (to which could even be added tough-minded versus tender-minded, the contrast William James used to distinguish the two main types of psychologists). One possible source for such coordinated clusters is the attempt to find multiple reasons to distinguish one approach from another. The approach comes first and the issues follow afterward. Then the issues take on an autonomous intellectual life and what starts as rationalization ends up as analysis.

A major role of the issues here seems to be to carve up the total scientific field into disciplines. AI computer science, logic, cybernetics, pattern recognition, linguistics, and cognitive psychology—all these seem to be discriminated in part by their position on these various issues. The issues, of course, only serve as intermediaries for intellectual positions that derive from many circumstances of history, methodological possibilities, and specific scientific and technical ideas. Still, they seem to summarize a good deal of what keeps the different fields apart, even though the fields have a common scientific domain.

Is the large burst of issues that occurred at the birth of AI just an artifact of my intent to gather issues for AI? If the period just before AI began, say from 1940–1955, were examined carefully, would many more issues be added? The relevant question should probably be taken with respect to some other field as a base. Would a burst like this be found for cybernetics, which started in 1940–1945? My own suspicion is yes, but I have not tried to verify it.

Perhaps then the situation of AI could turn out to be typical. We would find a plethora of issues in any science if we would but look and count; the list from Hilgard and Bower might serve as a positive indicator. However, before rushing to embrace this view, some counterevidence should be examined. An interesting phenomenon in this same postwar period was the emergence of several one-theorem fields. Game theory, information theory, linear programming, and (later) dynamic programming—all had a single strong result around which the field grew.[15] Certainly, each also provided a novel formulation, which amounted to a class of systems to be used to theorize about some field. But initially there was only one striking theorem to justify the entire field. It gave these fields a curious flavor. My personal recollection is that all these fields, while exciting, profound, and (sometimes) controversial, had none of the complexity of issues that we find in Table 1.

Intellectual issues and progress

There is a natural temptation to use the history of intellectual issues to measure progress, once it has been explicitly laid out. It is true that some issues have vanished from the scene, such as symbols versus numbers; that seems, perhaps, like progress. It is also true that other issues seem to recur, such as problem-solving versus recognition; that seems, perhaps, like lack of progress. Neither interpretation is correct, I think. Rather, the progress of science is to be measured by the accumulation of theories, data, and techniques, along with the ability they provide to predict, explain, and control. This story is not to be told in terms of such intellectual issues as populate this paper. It requires attention to the detailed content, assertions, and practice of the science itself. True, at the more aggregate level of the *paradigms* of Kuhn or the *programmes* of Lakatos, whole bodies of theory and data can become irrelevant with a shift in paradigm or programme. But on the scale of the twenty-five years of AI research (1955–1980), the story is one of accumulation and assimilation, not one of shift and abandonment. It is not even one of settling scientific questions for good.

What then is the role of intellectual issues in the progression of science? To echo my earlier disclaimer, I can only conjecture. Intellectual issues seem to me more like generalized motivators. They evoke strong enough passions to provide the springs to action, but they are vague enough so that they do not get in the way of specific work. They can be used to convey a feeling of coherence among investigations in their early stages, before it is known exactly what the investigations will yield.

Evidence for this is that issues do not really go away; they return and return again. Repetition is abundant in Table 1. The model that suggests itself immediately is the spiral—each return constitutes a refined version of the issue. Though the issues are certainly not identical each time, it seems difficult to construe the changes as any sort of progressive refinement; some seem more like wandering (e.g., the serial/parallel issue). A more plausible explanation (to me) is that intellectual issues reflect perennial unanswerable questions about the structure of nature—continuity/discontinuity, stasis/change, essence/accident, autonomy/dependence, and so forth. Whenever in the course of science one of these can be recognized in the ongoing stream of work, an appropriate intellectual issue will be instantiated, to operate as a high-level organizing principle for a while. To be sure, this picture does not capture all that seems to be represented in our population of intellectual issues. But it seems substantially better than viewing science as progressively resolving such issues.

Conclusion

Putting to one side questions about the accuracy of the particular set of issues displayed in Table 1, of what use is a history of a scientific field in terms of intellectual issues? To repeat once more: It cannot substitute for a substantive history in terms of concepts, theories, and data; however, it does seem to capture some of the flavor of the field in an era. It is clearly a component of the paradigm of a field or of research programmes within a field. And, let us confess it, intellectual issues have a certain spiciness about them that makes them fun to talk and write about. Perhaps it is the sense of touching fundamental issues. But perhaps it also echoes Bertrand Russell's famous aphorism that dealing with intellectual issues has all the advantages of theft over honest toil.

I thank Elaine Kant and Stu Card for comments on an earlier draft and Paul Birkel and Marc Donner for leading me to write the paper. Note: This research was sponsored in part by the Defense Advanced Research Projects Agency (DOD), ARPA Order No. 3597, monitored by the Air Force Avionics Laboratory under Contract F33615-78-C-1551. The views and conclusions contained in the paper are those of the author and should not be interpreted as representing the official policies, either expressed or implied, of the Defense Advanced Research Projects Agency or the United States government.

Notes

1 A case can be made that serious AI started as soon as computers attained 4K of random-access primary memory.
2 The concept of data type did not arrive in clear form until much later.
3 In fact, there are additional possibilities. [Newell, 1970.]
4 It might also mean the class of theorem-proving systems using logical calculi; but this is really a subclass of symbol systems.
5 In fact, the first report of FORTRAN at a scientific meeting occurred at the same session as the first report of a list-processing language. [Backus et al., 1957; Newell and Shaw, 1957.]
6 Said this way, the connection of this issue to the competence/performance issue discussed later would seem to be overwhelming. However, the research programmes associated with the two issues have never made common cause.
7 This is not the whole story of the relations of linguistics with other fields; for example, there have been important contacts with logic and philosophy.
8 Although the term *architecture* is just now coming into common use in psychology.
9 There was work on phonology, but the domain lay outside the range of interest of AI and, in fact, of psychology as well.
10 Among the contributors to the first conference on Theoretical Issues in Natural Language Processing, a series that became the forum for this subfield, I can identify only one mainstream linguist. [Schank and Nash-Webber, 1975.]
11 This is because list structures approximate general symbolic systems. The neutrality is easily confirmed in the continued and universal use of list-processing languages to realize systems of all kinds along this dimension.
12 Another example is the problem of induction, where philosophy is concerned with the certainty of induction and AI is concerned with performing the inductions. [Newell, 1973c.]
13 The other system often mentioned similarly is MACSYMA, the highly sophisticated program at the Massachusetts Institute of Technology for doing symbolic mathematics. As mentioned earlier, it had deliberately removed itself from being an AI program.
14 Some other systems were built, which might have been viewed as learning systems, but, instead, were taken simply to be performance programs in specialized task environments, for example, induction programs.
15 Another field, general systems theory, also had a single idea around which to build—that there are common laws across all levels of systems from the atomic through cellular through societal through astronomical. But there was no central result available, only the system view, and this field has been markedly less successful than others in its growth and health.

References

Abelson, Robert P., "Computer Simulation of 'Hot' Cognition," in Tompkins, Silvan S., and Messick, Samuel, eds., *Computer Simulation and Personality: Frontier of Psychological Theory* (New York: Wiley, 1963), pp. 277–298.

Abelson, Robert P., "The Structure of Belief Systems," in Schank, Roger C., and Colby, Kenneth M., eds., *Computer Models of Thought and Language* (San Francisco: W. H. Freeman, 1973), pp. 287–339.

Anderson, John R., and Bower, Gordon H., *Human Associateive Memory* (Washington, D.C.: V. H. Winston, 1973).

Backus, John, et al., "The FORTRAN Automatic Coding System," in *Proceedings of the Western Joint Computer Conference*, sponsored by the Institute of Radio Engineers, the American Institute of Electrical Engineers, and the Association for Computing Machinery and held [in Los Angeles] Feb. 26–28, 1957; pp. 188–198.

Bobrow, Daniel G., ed., Special Issue on Non-Monotonic Logic, *Artificial Intelligence*, vol. 13 (Apr. 1980), pp. 1–172.

Bobrow, Daniel G., and Raphael, Bertram, "New Programming Languages for Artificial Intelligence Research," in *ACM Computing Surveys*, vol. 6 (Sept. 1974), pp. 153–174.

Boole, George, *An Investigation of the Laws of Thought, on which are Founded the Mathematical Theories of Logic and Probabilities* (London: Walton and Maberly, 1854. Republished as vol. 2 of George Boole's *Collected Logical Works*, Chicago: Open Court, 1916; New York: Dover ed., 1961).

Brachman, Ronald, J., and Smith, Brian C., eds., Special Issue on Knowledge Representation, *SIGART Newsletter*, vol. 70 (Feb. 1980), pp. 1–138.

Čapek, Karel, *R. U. R.* (*Rossum's Universal Robots*) (Garden City, N.Y.: Doubleday, Page and Co., 1923).

Chomsky, Noam, *Aspects of the Theory of Syntax* (Cambridge, Mass.: MIT Press, 1965).

Dreyfus, Hubert L., *What Computers Can't Do: A Critique of Artificial Reason* (New York: Harper and Row, 1972; rev. paperback ed., 1979).

Driesch, Hans, *The History and Theory of Vitalism* (London: Macmillan, 1914). Translated from the German.

Feigenbaum, Edward A., and Feldman, Julian, eds., *Computers and Thought* (New York: McGraw-Hill, 1963).

Goldstein, Ira, and Papert, Seymour, "Artificial Intelligence, Language, and the Study of Knowledge," in *Cognitive Science*, vol. 1 (Jan. 1977), pp. 84–124.

Gunderson, Keith, *Mentality and Machines* (Garden City, N.Y.: Doubleday, 1971).

Hilgard, Ernest R., and Bower, Gordon H., *Theories of Learning* (New York: Appleton-Century-Crofts, 1948; 4th ed., 1975).

Kosslyn, Stephen M.; Pinker, Steven; Smith, George E.; and Shwartz, Steven P., "On the Demystification of Mental Imagery" [with peer commentaries], in *Behavioral and Brain Sciences*, vol. 2 (Dec. 1979), pp. 535–581.

Kowalski, Robert, *Logic for Problem Solving* (New York: North-Holland, 1979).

Kuhn, Thomas, S., *The Structure of Scientific Revolutions* (Chicago: University of Chicago Press, 1962; 2nd enlarged ed., 1970).

Lakatos, Imre, "Falsification and the Methodology of Scientific Research Programmes," in Lakatos, Imre, and Musgrave, Alan, eds., *Criticism and the Growth of Knowledge*, proceedings of the International Colloquium in the Philosophy of Science, London, 1965 (Cambridge: Cambridge University Press, 1970), vol. 4, pp. 91–195.

Lesser, Victor, and Erman, Lee, "A Retrospective View of the Hearsay-II Architecture," in *Proceedings of the Fifth International Joint Conference on Artificial*

Intelligence (Cambridge, Mass.: MIT Artificial Intelligence Laboratory, 1977), pp. 790–800.

Licklider, J. C. R., "Man-Computer Symbiosis," in *IRE Transactions on Human Factors in Electronics*, vol. HFE-1 (1960), pp. 4–11.

Lindsay, Robert; Buchanan, Bruce; Feigenbaum, Edward A.; and Lederberg, Joshua, *Applications of Artificial Intelligence for Organic Chemistry: The DENDRAL Project* (New York: McGraw-Hill, 1980).

Locke, William Nash, and Booth, A. Donald, eds., *Machine Translation of Languages: Fourteen Essays* (Cambridge, Mass., and New York: Technology Press of MIT and Wiley, 1957).

Marr, David C., "Early Processing of Visual Information," in *Philosophical Transactions of the Royal Society of London*, vol. 275 (1976), pp. 483–534.

McCarthy, John, "Programs with Common Sense," in *Mechanization of Thought Processes* (London: HMSO, 1959).

McCorduck, Pamela, *Machines Who Think: A Personal Inquiry into the History and Prospects of Artificial Intelligence* (San Francisco: W. H. Freeman, 1979).

McCulloch, Warren S., and Pitts, Walter H., "A Logical Calculus of the Ideas Immanent in Nervous Activity," in *Bulletin of Mathematical Biphysics*, vol.5 (1943), pp. 115–133.

Michalski, Ryszard S.; Carbonell, Jaime; and Mitchell, Tom, eds., *Machine Learning—An Artificial Intelligence Approach* (Palo Alto, Calif.: Tioga Press, 1983).

Minsky, Marvin L., ed., *Semantic Information Processing* (Cambridge, Mass.: MIT Press, 1968).

Minsky, Marvin L., "A Framework for Representing Knowledge," in Winston, Patrick H., ed., *The Psychology of Computer Vision* (New York: McGraw-Hill, 1975), pp. 211–277.

Moses, Joel, "Symbolic Integration" (Ph.D. diss., Massachusetts Institute of Technology, 1967).

Neisser, Ulric, "Decision-time without Reaction-time: Experiments in Visual Scaning," in *American Journal of Psychology*, vol. 76 (Sept. 1963), pp. 376–385.

Neisser, Ulric, *Cognitive Psychology* (New York: Appleton-Century-Crofts, 1967).

Neumann, John von, *The Computer and the Brain* (New Haven, Conn.: Yale University Press, 1958).

Newell, Allen, "Remarks on the Relationship Between Artificial Intelligence and Cognitive Psychology," in Banerji, Ranan B., and Mesarović, Mihajlo D., eds., *Theoretical Approaches to Non-Numerical Problem Solving*, proceedings of the Fourth Systems Symposium, held [at Case Western Reserve University] 1968 (New York: Springer-Verlag, 1970), pp. 363–400.

Newell, Allen, "You Can't Play Twenty Questions With Nature and Win: Projective Comments on the Papers of this Symposium," in Chase, William G., ed., *Visual Information Processing*, proceedings of the Eighth Annual Carnegie Symposium on Cognition, held [at Carnegie-Mellon University, Pittsburgh] May 19, 1972 (New York: Academic Press, 1973*h*), pp. 283–310.

Newell, Allen, "Artificial Intelligence and the Concept of Mind," in Schank, Roger C., and Colby, Kenneth M., eds., *Computer Models of Thought and Language* (San Francisco: W. H. Freeman, 1973*c*), pp. 1–60.

Newell, Allen, "One Final Word," in Tuma, David T., and Reif, F., eds., *Problem Solving and Education: Issues in Teaching and Research*, proceedings of a conference held [at Carnegie-Mellon University, Pittsburgh] Oct. 9–10, 1978 (Hillsdale, N.J.: Lawrence Eribaum, 1980*a*), pp. 175–189.

Newell, Allen, "Physical Symbol Systems," in *Cognitive Science*, vol. 4 (Apr./June 1980*b*), pp. 135–183.

Newell, Allen, and Ernst, George, "The Search for Generality," in Kalenich,

Newell, Allen, and Shaw, John C., "Programming the Logic Theory Machine," in *Proceedings of the Western Joint Computer Conference*, sponsored by the Institute of Radio Engineers, the American Institute of Electrical Engineers, and the Association for Computing Machinery and held [in Los Angeles] Feb. 26–28, 1957, pp. 230–240.

Newell, Allen; Shaw, John C.; and Simon, Herbert A., "Empirical Explorations of the Logic Theory Machine: A Case Study in Heuristics," in *Proceedings of the Western Joint Computer Conference*, sponsored by the Institute of Radio Engineers, the American Institute of Electrical Engineers, and the Association for Computing Machinery and held [in Los Angeles] Feb. 26–28, 1957, pp. 218–230.

Newell, Allen, and Simon, Herbert A., "Computer Science as Empirical Inquiry: Symbols and Search" [the 1976 ACM Turing Award Lecture]; in *Communications of the ACM*, vol. 19 (Mar. 1976*a*), pp. 113–126.

Nilsson, Nils J., *Problem Solving Methods in Artificial Intelligence* (New York: McGraw-Hill, 1971).

Nilsson, Nils J., "Artificial Intelligence: Engineering, Science or Slogan?" in *AI Magazine*, vol. 3 (Jan. 1982), pp. 2–9.

Norman, Donald A., "Memory, Knowledge, and the Answering of Questions," in Solso, Robert L., ed., *Contemporary Issues in Cognitive Psychology: The Loyola Symposium on Cognitive Psychology* [Chicago] 1972 (Washington, D.C.: Winston, 1973), pp. 135–165.

Quillian, M. Ross, "Semantic Memory," in Minsky, Marvin L., ed., *Semantic Information Processing* (Cambridge, Mass.: MIT Press, 1968), pp. 216–270.

Roberts, Lawrence G., "Machine Perception of Three-Dimensional Solids," in Tippett, James T., et al., eds., *Optical and Electro-Optical Information Processing.* Symposium on Optical and Electro-Optical Information Processing Technology [Boston] 1964 (Cambridge, Mass.: MIT Press, 1965), pp. 159–197.

Robinson, Alan J., "A Machine-Oriented Logic Based on the Resolution Principle," in *Journal of the Association for Computing Machinery*, vol. 12 (Jan. 1965), pp. 23–41.

Rosenblatt, Frank, "The Perceptron: A Probabilistic Model for Information Storage and Organization in the Brain," in *Psychological Review*, vol. 65 (Nov. 1958), pp. 386–408.

Rosenblueth, Arturo; Wiener, Norbert; and Bigelow, Julian, "Behavior, Purpose and Teleology," in *Philosophy of Science*, vol. 10 (Jan. 1943), pp. 18–24.

Samuel, Arthur L., "Some Studies in Machine Learning Using the Game of Checkers," in *IBM Journal of Research and Development*, vol. 3 (July 1959), pp. 210–229.

Schank, Roger C., "Identification of Conceptualizations Underlying Natural Language," in Schank, Roger C., and Colby, Kenneth M., eds., *Computer Models of Thought and Language* (San Francisco: W. H. Freeman, 1973), pp. 187–247.

Schank, Roger C., and Nash-Webber, Bonnie, eds., *Theoretical Issues in Natural Language Processing*, proceedings of the first conference on Theoretical Issues in

Natural Language Processing (prepared by Bolt, Beranek and Newman, Inc., Cambridge, Mass, 1975).

Shelley, Mary Wollstonecraft, *Frankenstein; or The Modern Prometheus* (1818 text), ed. James Rieger (Indianapolis: Bobbs-Merrill, 1974).

Shortliffe, Edward H., "MYCIN: A Rule-Based Computer Program for Advising Physicians Regarding Antimicrobial Therapy Selection" (Ph.D. diss., Stanford University, 1974).

Simon, Herbert A., and Feigenbaum, Edward A., "An Information-Processing Theory of Some Effects of Similarity, Familiarization, and Meaningfulness in Verbal Learning," in *Journal of Verbal Learning and Verbal Behavior*, vol. 3 (Oct. 1964), pp. 385–396.

Slagle, James R., "A Heuristic Program that Solves Symbolic Integration Problems in Freshman Calculus," in Feigenbaum, Edward A., and Feldman, Julian, eds., *Computers and Thought* (New York: McGraw-Hill, 1963), pp. 191–203.

Sternberg, Saul, "High-Speed Scanning in Human Memory," in *Science*, vol. 153 (5 Aug., 1966), pp. 652–654.

Sussman, Gerald Jay, *A Computer Model of Skill Acquisition* (New York: American Elsevier, 1975).

Sutherland, Ivan E., "SKETCHPAD: A Man-Machine Graphical Communication System," in *AFIPS Conference Proceedings, Vol. 23: 1963 Spring Joint Computer Conference*, organized by the American Federation of Information Processing Societies and held [in Detroit] May 1963 (Washington, D.C.: Spartan Books, 1963), pp. 329–346.

Taube, Mortimer, *Computers and Common Sense: The Myth of Thinking Machines* (New York: Columbia University Press, 1961).

Turing, Alan M., "On Computable Numbers, with an Application to the Entscheidungsproblem," in *Proceedings of the London Mathematical Society*, vol. 42, no. 2 (1936), pp. 230–265.

Wang, Hao, "Toward Mechanical Mathematics," in *IBM Journal of Research and Development*, vol. 4 (Jan. 1960), pp. 2–22.

Waterman, Donald A. "Generalization Learning Techniques for Automating the Learning of Heuristics," in *Artificial Intelligence*, vol. 1 (spring 1970), pp. 121–170.

Waterman, Donald A., and Hayes-Roth, Frederick, eds., *Pattern-Directed Inference Systems*. Report of a Workshop on P-D I Systems [Honolulu] 1977 (New York: Academic Press, 1978).

Watson, John B., "Psychology as the Behaviorist Views it," in *Psychological Review*, vol. 20 (Mar. 1913), pp. 158–177.

Weizenbaum, Joseph, *Computer Power and Human Reason: From Judgment to Calculation* (San Francisco: W. H. Freeman, 1976).

Whitehead, Alfred North, and Russell, Bertrand, *Principia Mathematica* (Cambridge: Cambridge University Press, 1910–1913; 2nd ed. 1925–1927; paperback ed. 1962).

Winograd, Terry, "Procedures as a Representation for Data in a Computer Program for Understanding Natural Language" (Ph.D. diss., Massachusetts Institute of Technology, 1971).

Winston, Patrick H., "Learning Structural Descriptions from Examples" (Ph.D. diss., Massachusetts Institute of Technology, 1970).

Woods, William A., "Transition Network Grammars for Natural Language Analysis," in *Communications of the ACM*, vol. 13 (Oct. 1970), pp. 591–606.

Yovits, Marshall C.; Jacobi, George T.; and Goldstein, Gordon D., eds., *Self-Organizing Systems*, proceedings of a Conference on Self-Organizing Systems [Chicago] 1962 (Washington, D.C.: Spartan, 1962).

Ziff, Paul, "The Feelings of Robots," in *Analysis*, vol. 19 (Jan. 1959), pp. 64–68.

2

ARTIFICIAL INTELLIGENCE

The expert tool

H. Gardner

Source: H. Gardner, *The Mind's New Science*, Perseus Books, 1985, pp. 131–81.

> I am prepared to go so far as to say that within a few years, if
> there remain any philosophers who are not familiar with some
> of the main developments in artificial intelligence, it will be fair
> to accuse them of professional incompetence, and that to teach
> courses in philosophy of mind, epistemology . . . without dis-
> cussing . . . aspects of artificial intelligence will be as irrespon-
> sible as giving a course in physics which includes no quantum
> theory.
>
> (Aaron Sloman)

The summer of 1956 at Dartmouth

In the summer of 1956, a group of ten young scholars trained in mathematics and logic gathered on the campus of Dartmouth College in Hanover,
New Hampshire. Their purpose: to confer about the possibilities of producing computer programs that could "behave" or "think" intelligently. As
they had declared in their grant application to the Rockefeller Foundation:
"The study is to proceed on the basis of the conjecture that every aspect of
learning or any other feature of intelligence can in principle be so precisely
described that a machine can be made to simulate it"[1] (McCorduck 1979,
p. 93).

Of the numerous scholars who attended parts of the summer institute,
four in particular came to play crucial roles in the development of a new field
called artificial intelligence. First of all, there was John McCarthy, then an
assistant professor of mathematics at Dartmouth and eventually the founder
and first director of the A.I. labs at both the Massachusetts Institute of
Technology (1957) and Stanford University (1963). McCarthy was the major
organizer of the institute and the coiner (according to most accounts) of the
term *artificial intelligence*. The remaining three leading figures were Marvin

Minsky, then a Junior Fellow in mathematics and neurology at Harvard and eventually the director of the Artificial Intelligence Laboratory at M.I.T.; and Herbert Simon and Allen Newell, then at the Rand Corporation in Santa Monica and also at Carnegie Institute of Technology (now Carnegie-Mellon University) in Pittsburgh, where they have remained until this day.

The summer at Dartmouth gave these and other scholars a chance to exchange views and to arrange to collaborate on future work. Various authorities during the 1940s and early 1950s had expressed the belief that computers should be able to carry out processes resembling human thinking, and it was the job of the present assemblage to put these promises to the test. Alex Bernstein, then a programmer for International Business Machines in New York City, talked about the chess-playing program on which he was working. Arthur Samuel, also of the I.B.M. Corporation, discussed a program that played checkers. Newell and Simon described a program that they had devised to solve theorems in logic. Nathan Rochester of I.B.M. in Poughkeepsie described work on programming a model of neural networks, while Marvin Minsky discussed the use of computers to prove Euclidean theorems.

The meeting at Dartmouth did not fulfill everyone's expectations: there was more competition and less free exchange among the scholars than the planners had wished. Nonetheless, the summer institute is considered pivotal in the history of the cognitive sciences, in general, and in the field of artificial intelligence, in particular. The reason is, I think, chiefly symbolic. The previous decade had seen the brilliant ideas of an older generation—Norbert Wiener, John von Neumann, Warren McCulloch, Alan Turing—all point toward the development of electronic computers which could carry out functions normally associated with the human brain. This senior group had anticipated developments but were uncertain whether they themselves would have the opportunity to explore the promised land.

At Dartmouth, members of a younger generation, who had grown up in an atmosphere seeded with these seminal ideas, were now ready (and in some cases, beyond mere readiness) to devise the machines and write the programs that could do what von Neumann and Wiener had speculated about. These younger scholars were attracted by powerful (if still vague and poorly understood) notions: data being processed by a program and then becoming part of the program in itself; the use of computers to process symbols rather than simply to "crunch numbers"; the proclivity of new languages for bringing out unsuspected potentials in the machine's hardware; the role of computers in testing scientific theories. Perhaps conducted in isolation, the meeting might not have had much of an impact. But it came just weeks before the meeting at M.I.T. (see pages 28–29), where some of the same participants, and such formidable figures from neighboring fields as Noam Chomsky in linguistics and George Miller in psychology, were presenting their own ideas to the emerging world of cognitive science, And, finally, it was the time as well of key publications—not only Simon and Newell's Logic Theorist and Marvin Minsky's widely circulated "Steps toward Artificial Intelligence" (1963), but also important monographs by Bruner, Chomsky, Lévi-Strauss, Piaget, and many other scholars of a cognitive bent. While no single event can lay claim to signaling the "birth" of all of cognitive science, the workshop at Dartmouth is the chief contender within the field of artificial intelligence.

The ideas of artificial intelligence

Since the Dartmouth meeting, artificial intelligence has had a brief but stormy history. Part of the storm swirls around definitions. Nearly all authorities agree that artificial intelligence seeks to produce, on a computer, a pattern of output that would be considered intelligent if displayed by human beings. Most authorities see the computer program as a test of a particular theory of how a cognitive process might work. But thereafter consensus falters. Some definitions stress the devising of programs; others focus on programming languages; others encompass the mechanical hardware and the human conceptual component, as well as the software. Some practitioners want to simulate human thought processes exactly, while others are content with any program that leads to intelligent consequences.

Authorities also disagree on how literally to take the thinking metaphor. Some researchers take what has come to be termed the "weak view," where the devising of "intelligent" programs is simply a means of testing theories about how human beings might carry out cognitive operations. Others, however, put forth much more forceful claims about their field. According to the view of "strong AI," as phrased by philosopher John Searle, "the appropriately programmed computer really *is* a mind, in the sense that computers given the right programs can be literally said to understand and have other cognitive states. In strong AI, because the programmed computer has cognitive states, the programs are not merely tools that enable us to test psychological explanations; rather the programs are themselves the explanations" (1980, p. 417). I shall consider the merits of weak and strong A.I. at the conclusion of this chapter.

But while the tension between weak and strong claims is one of the most momentous debates, it is by no means the only one. As Robert Wilensky, a leading artificial intelligence researcher, recently commented, "Artificial intelligence is a field renowned for its lack of consensus on fundamental issues" (1983, p. *xii*). Indeed, in a recent capsule history of artificial intelligence, Allen Newell (1983) was able to single out no fewer than three dozen issues that have at times divided the field. While some of these are quite technical, and others of only transient interest, two of them seem to me of particular note. The first is the tension between "generalists" and "experts"—a tension recalling the dialectic between the modular and the central-processing perspectives in contemporary psychology. Generalists believe in overarching programs (or families of programs) that can be applied to most any manner of problem: experts place their faith in programs that contain much detailed knowledge about a specific domain but prove relatively restricted in their applicability. A second tension has to do with the scientific status of the field. While some of the founders were prepared to make strong claims for scientific importance (and, indeed, see A.I. as replacing epistemological pursuits), more skeptical commentators have wondered whether artificial intelligence deserves to be considered a scientific discipline at all. From their point of view, A.I. is simply a form of applied engineering—even gimmickry—with no real standing as a theoretically based scientific discipline. To be sure, similar skeptical challenges have been leveled at other of the cognitive sciences; but perhaps because of the dramatic promise of a "thinking machine," the battles about the scientific status of A.I. have been particularly vehement.

In this chapter, I shall observe the wide swings of mood and the diverse viewpoints that have characterized the leading practitioners and commentators during the first three decades of A.I. It is not possible, of course, to touch on every strand of artificial intelligence; for example, except incidentally, I shall not discuss work on robots, retrieving information from data bases, planning optimal combinations or optimal schedules, simulating organizational activities, or writing programs that write programs, even though each of these areas is becoming part of standard reviews of artificial intelligence (Nilsson 1980; Waldrop 1984a, 1984c; Winston 1977). But I will touch on those lines of work that seem to me to be most relevant to human psychology and, at the conclusion of this chapter, attempt to situate the field of A.I. within the broader framework of cognitive science.

The dream of artificial intelligence

A.I. may have a short history, but the dream of a mechanical mind goes back a long time. Early intimations can be discerned in the work of René Descartes, who was interested in automata that could simulate the human body (he was skeptical about simulating the mind). Whether or not inspired by Descartes, thinkers within the French tradition seem to have been the first to pursue the idea of a machine that can reason. In Paris in 1747, a French physician named Julian Offray de la Mettrie published his book *L'Homme Machine*, in which he argued that "the human body is a machine that winds up its own springs" (quoted in McCorduck 1979, p. 36), and that the brain, as the organ of thought, was subject to study and duplication. As he put it, "thought is so little incompatible with organized matter, that it seems to be one of its properties on a par with electricity, the faculty of motion, and impenetrability" (quoted in Lowry 1971, p. 42).

Pursuing such a train of thought on a more practical level was the craftsman Jacques de Vaucanson, a builder of automata who thrilled Europe during the early part of the eighteenth century with mechanical flute players, ducks, and tabor-pipe players. In a lengthy accompanying document, Vaucanson indicated how each part of the flute player was in fact modeled after comparable components of the human model. According to the historian of psychology John Marshall, Vaucanson "was concerned to formulate and validate—in the most precise and formal language available to him—a theory of the German flute player" (Fryer and Marshall 1979, p. 261).

The scene now shifts to nineteenth-century England, to investigators who pursued the mechanization of thought in ways much closer to our own. One such character was the brilliant and prescient Cambridge mathematician Charles Babbage who devoted many years to devising an automatic table calculator which could carry out the complicated computations needed for navigation and ballistics. Unfortunately the machine that he designed would have required the production of thousands of precision parts; and while scientists of today think that Babbage's machine would have worked, the British government withdrew its support after investing the then large sum of seventeen thousand pounds. Meanwhile, inspired by his collaboration with one Lady Lovelace, Babbage became even more grandiose, conceiving of a machine that could tabulate any function whatever and could, in principle, play chess (McCorduck 1979, pp. 25–27). This "difference machine" (as it was called) was based on the difference tables of the squares of numbers. It would use punched cards of the sort hitherto used to control special weaving looms: there were operation cards, which directed the operations to be performed, and variable cards, which determined the particular variables on which the operations were to be performed (Dorf 1974). Any arithmetic problem could be set; and, provided that the proper cranks were turned, the right answer should issue forth.

While Babbage was attempting to implement his ambitious mechanical aspirations, another British mathematician, George Boole of Queens College Cork, was involved in a different but equally momentous undertaking: that is, to figure out the basic laws of thought and to found them on principles of logic. In order to eliminate the ambiguities of natural language (which had dominated logic since the time Aristotle had studied the syllogism), Boole used a set of arbitrary symbols (a, b, x, y, and so on) to stand for components of thought. As he put it, "a successful attempt to express logical propositions by symbols, the laws of whose combinations should be founded upon the laws of the mental processes which they represent, would, so far, be a step toward the philosophical language" (quoted in Hilton 1963, p. 163). These symbolic elements could be combined or dissociated through operations like adding, subtracting, or multiplying, so as to form new expressions, or new conceptions, involving the same elements. These procedures amounted to a kind of "mental algebra," where reasoning could be carried out in abstract positive or negative terms, unsullied by the particular associations tied to specific contents. And these operations were termed by Boole the "laws of thought." Most important for the future, Boole observed that his logic was a two-valued or true-false system. Any logical expression, no matter how complex, could be expressed either as 1 (standing for "all," or "true"), or as 0 (standing for "nothing," or "false"). The idea that all human reason could be reduced to a series of yes or no discussions was to prove central for the philosophy and the science of the twentieth century.

The significance of Boole's work was finally appreciated a half-century later by Alfred North Whitehead and Bertrand Russell when they produced their *Principia Mathematica* (1910–13). The goal of this work, as I have noted, was to demonstrate that the roots of mathematics lie in the basic laws of logic. Whitehead and Russell relied heavily on the formalism pioneered by Boole. Russell went so far as to declare in his ascetic manner, "Pure mathematics was discovered by Boole in a work he called 'The Laws of Thought'" (quoted in Halacy 1962, p. 106).

The cluster of ideas represented by Babbage's calculating machines, Boole's laws of thought, and Whitehead and Russell's decisive demonstrations were eventually to be integrated by scholars in the 1930s and 1940s. Their work culminated in the first computers and, eventually, the first programs that can be said to display intelligence.

Realizing the dream

Many individuals set the groundwork for the mid-century explosion which led to Dartmouth and its aftermath. Of tremendous significance was the work of the M.I.T. mathematician Claude Shannon. In 1938, Shannon published "A Symbolic Analysis of Relay and Switching Circuits"—possibly the most important, and also the most famous, master's thesis of the century. In this work, Shannon showed that relay and switching circuits of the type found in an electronic machine could be expressed in terms of equations of a Boolean sort: for the true-false system could parallel "on-off switches," or closed and open states of a circuit. Indeed, any operations that could be described in a finite set of steps could be carried out by such "switching" relays. Shannon's work laid the groundwork for the construction of machines that carried out truth-logic operations, and also suggested new ways in which the circuits could be designed and simplified. At a theoretical level, he also indicated that the programming of a computer (laying out a set of coded instructions to be precisely followed) ought to be thought of as a problem of formal logic rather than of arithmetic, an insight that grew out of Boole's work. In one swoop, Shannon had injected a subject of purely academic interest into the world of practical machinery, including the newly emerging computing machines.

Shannon's insights did not occur in an intellectual vacuum. Alan Turing was then putting forth his idea (1936) that any explicitly stated computational task could be performed by a machine in possession of an appropriate finite set of instructions. He was demonstrating that, in principle, there was only one kind of computer (though, of course, there could be many models built in many ways); and he was beginning to think about the central issues of artificial intelligence: the relationship between human thought and machine thought. This concern manifested itself some time later in the famous Turing test, where a skeptic was challenged to distinguish the answers of a human respondent from those put forth by a computer (see page 17). Vannevar Bush, an engineer at M.I.T., who had suggested to the young Claude Shannon that he explore the analogy between electrical network theory and the propositional calculus, was beginning to build machines that could solve differential equations. Also at this time, as I mentioned earlier, Warren McCulloch and Walter Pitts (1943) were developing their ideas about neural networks, specifically that anything that can be exhaustively and unambiguously put into words can be realized by a suitable finite network of neurons; thus, the brain can be construed as a machine in a more precise way than before and, indeed, be thought of as a Turing machine (McCorduck 1979, p. 15). And Norbert Wiener was weaving together the strands of cybernetics, a new interdisciplinary field which investigated feedback mechanisms in organic matter and in automata.

Finally, there was John von Neumann, in touch with all of these veins of thought, and with perhaps the most sustained interest in the theory of computing machines. He is generally credited with developing the idea of a stored program, where the operations of the computer can be directed or controlled by means of a program or a set of instructions, housed in the computer's internal memory. (It was thus no longer necessary to reprogram for each new task.) He demonstrated how binary logic and arithmetic could work together in forming stored programs. One can encode instructions to the machine in the same language as that used for the data it processes, and thus mix instructions and data in the program and store both in the computers. These conceptual breakthroughs opened the way for adjuncts to programming—such as *assemblers*, which can cull together subroutines into the main program, and *compilers*, which can translate from one language (usually a high-level programming language which is convenient to use) to a more basic language, reflected in the actual electromechanical operations of the computers. finally, von Neumann pursued with special vigor the analogies (and disanalogies) between the brain and computing machines.

It is not entirely clear whether von Neumann appreciated the potential of programs to attack and solve problems of intellectual depth. Yet he was certainly aware of the nexus of issues in this area and if he had not died of cancer while still relatively young, he might well have become the major figure in the history of artificial intelligence. But this role was shared by four scholars at the Dartmouth meeting in 1956: Herbert Simon and Allen Newell, Marvin Minsky, and John McCarthy.

The programs of the Dartmouth tetrad

Programs for problems: Allen Newell and Herbert Simon

While all the scholars at Dartmouth were actively engaged in thinking about thinking machines, only the team of Newell and Simon had already demonstrated that these ideas "in the air" could be implemented. Their first program, Logic Theorist (LT), could actually prove theorems taken from Whitehead and Russell's *Principia*.

Confident that their discovery marks an important point in the intellectual history of science in this century, Newell and Simon have described their progress in detail. In 1952 the two men had met at the Rand Corporation and had been impressed by the fact that the new electronic computers were more than simply "number crunchers" and could, in fact, manipulate all manners of symbols. Working with Cliff Shaw, a colleague at Rand, Newell and Simon began to explore the kinds of symbol-manipulation task that might be solved by a computer. Among other things, they considered the playing of chess and the solving of geometrical problems and arrived almost as an afterthought at the proof of logical theorems.

Newell and Simon knew it would be difficult to write programs capable of complex forms of information processing directly in the language of computers. What they needed was a "higher-level" language, one more congenial to the human programmer, which could then automatically be translated into the "machine language" of the computer. In 1955 the Newell team began to devise such "information processing languages" (IPL) or "list processing languages." On 15 December of that year, Simon simulated "by hand" a proof from Whitehead and Russell's *Principia*; moreover, the hand simulation was carried out in such detail that his colleagues agreed that the procedure could actually be carried out on an early computer called (after von Neumann) the Johnniac. Simon told his class in mathematical modeling, "Over Christmas Allen Newell and I invented a thinking machine" (quoted in McCorduck 1979, p. 116). And in August 1956, the Logic Theorist program actually produced on Rand's Johnniac computer the first complete proof of a theorem (Whitehead and Russell's theorem 2.01).

List processing was a technique developed to answer the problem of allocating storage in a limited computer memory. Until that time, the allocation of space had been prescribed at the beginning of a program run. But the Logic Theorist ate up memory so rapidly and unpredictably that users could not afford to allocate memory storage permanently. Shaw and Newell solved the problem by labeling each area of storage, having the machine maintain an updated list (including lists of lists) of all available spaces, and simply making the storage space available as needed.

In addition to solving the space-allocation problem, this method of list processing allowed the programmers to create data structures to store information in a way that was readily accessible and that, not coincidentally, may have borne a resemblance to human thought processes.

How does the computer program Logic Theorist actually work? This program discovers proofs for theorems in symbolic logic, of the kind originally presented in Whitehead and Russell's *Principia Mathematica*. The program contains the basic rules of operation—a list of axioms and previously proved theorems. The program then receives a new logical expression and is instructed to discover a proof. From that point on, the program runs through all the operations of which it is capable in an effort to find a proof. If it finds one, the proof is printed out on a long strip of paper. If not, it declares it cannot solve the problem and ceases its operations.

The demonstration that the Logic Theorist could prove theorems was itself remarkable. It actually succeeded in proving thirty-eight of the first fifty-two theorems in chapter 2 of the *Principia*. About half of the proofs were accomplished in less than a minute each; most of the remainder took from one to five minutes; a few took fifteen to forty-five minutes; there was a strong relation between the number of items in the logical expression and the length of the proofs. It turned out that one proof was more elegant than Whitehead and Russell's attempt of fifty years before—as Simon informed Bertrand Russell, who was delighted by this ironic twist. However, the *Journal of Symbolic Logic* declined to publish an article co-authored by the Logic Theorist in which this proof was reported (McCorduck 1979, p. 142).

It was still possible that this demonstration—although intriguing to engineers or logicians—could fall outside the purview of scientists interested in the operation of the human mind. But Newell, Simon, and their colleague Cliff Shaw stressed that they were demonstrating not merely thinking of a generic sort but, rather, *thinking of the kind in which humans engage*. After all, Logic Theorist could in principle have worked by brute force (like the proverbial monkey at the typewriter); but in that case, it would have taken hundreds or even thousands of years to carry out what it actually achieved in a few minutes. Instead, however, LT worked by procedures that, according to the Newell team, were analogous to those used by human problem solvers. Among the methods used by LT are substitution of one kind of expression for another; a detachment method, where the program works backward from something that has already been proved to something that needs to be proved; and a syllogistic form of reasoning, where if "*a* implies *b*" is true, and "*b* implies *c*" is true, then "*a* implies *c*" is also true.

In a further effort to underscore parallels between human and machine problem solving, Newell and Simon performed various experiments with their program. They showed that, if they removed the record of previous theorems (on which solutions to new theorems were constructed), the Logic Theorist could not solve problems it had previously handled in ten seconds. This was perhaps the first attempt ever to perform an experiment with a computer to see if it "responds" in the way that human beings do.

Trying to portray their demonstration in the proper light, the Newell team also stressed the resemblance between human and machine problem solving. They based this claim on some protocols they had gathered on human subjects engaged in the same tasks. In both humans and computing machines, the team found certain staples of human problem solving. For example, they reported certain moments of apparent insight as well as a reliance on an executive process that coordinates the elementary operations of LT (for example, substitution, detaching) and selects the subproblem and theorems upon which the methods operate. In conclusion, they located their work centrally within the new cognitive vogue:

> We do not believe that this functional equivalence between brains and computers implies any structural equivalence at a more minute anatomic level (for example, equivalence of neurons with circuits). Discovering what neural mechanisms realize these information processing functions in the human brain is a task for another level of theory construction. Our theory is a theory of the information processes involved in problem-solving and not a theory of neural or electronic mechanisms for information processing.
>
> (Newell, Shaw, and Simon 1964, p. 352)

These remarks can be seen as directed at those—for instance, the McCulloch circle—who looked for the secret of the computer's operations (and of thinking in general) in an understanding of how neural circuitry works. The Simon and Newell group bet that this analogy was not helpful, and that it would be more profitable to conceptualize problem solving at a much more macroscopic level. For twenty-five years, this "dry" view has carried the day: as we shall see, it is only in the last few years that an approach that pays closer attention to what is known about the nervous system has begun to gain support within the artificial intelligence community.

By devising and running Logic Theorist, Newell and Simon showed that A.I. was a possibility, if not a reality. While all claims before had, in a sense, been handwaving, two key demonstrations had now been made: (1) computers could engage in behavior that, if exhibited by humans, would unambiguously be considered intelligent; (2) the steps through which the programs pass in the course of proving theorems bear a non-trivial resemblance to the steps observed in human problem solving.

But Newell, Simon, and their colleagues were soon after even bigger game. Their most ambitious project was the devising of the General Problem Solver (GPS), a program whose methods (at least in principle) could be utilized for all manner of problem solving (Newell and Simon 1972). The General Problem Solver was capable of such apparently diverse tasks as solving theorems, playing chess, or solving such puzzles as the missionary-cannibal conundrum, the tower of Hanoi, and cryptarithmetic—a fiendish mind bender where letters stand for numbers and the sums or products of words yield yet other words. But GPS did not just attempt to solve these problems in the most efficient way. Rather, it sought to mimic the processes used by normal human subjects in tackling such problems. Thus, a very important part of this research enterprise was the collection of protocols that recorded the introspections and notations of subjects engaged in problem solving.

The methods used by the General Problem Solver can be readily described. In *means-ends analysis,* one first states the desired form of the solution of a problem, and then compares one's present place in the process of problem solution with the final goal desired. If these two instances coincide, then the problem has been solved. If not, the solver (human or mechanical) clarifies the difference and searches for methods to reduce the difference between where one is and where one wants to go.

The art in the General Problem Solver lies in the methods of reducing this distance. A table is set up that associates the system's goals with operators that may be of use in achieving them. Once the difference has been computed between the present situation and the goal, the system then selects on operator associated with that difference and tests whether the operator is applicable to the current situation. If it can be applied, and if it produces a result that is closer to the desired end state, it is repeated again. If it proves inapplicable, then the system generates a subgoal, whose aim is to reduce the difference between the current situation and the situation where the operator can be applied. This procedure is simply repeated until the goal is achieved or it has been demonstrated that it cannot be achieved with the information given, or with the operators available in the program.

The General Problem Solver also exhibited other features designed to facilitate problem solving. It was possible to decompose the program into subproblems which could be tackled one at a time. It was possible to ignore some of the complicating factors in a situation in order to arrive at a plan of attack. It was possible to omit certain details of a problem as well. For example, in solving a problem in the propositional calculus, the machine can decide to ignore differences among the logical connectives and the order of symbols, only taking into account what the symbols are and how they have been grouped.

While the General Problem Solver was eventually abandoned because its generality was not as great as its creators had wished, and because the field of artificial intelligence moved in different directions, the program can be regarded as the first to simulate a spectrum of human symbolic behavior. GPS also occupied a major role in Simon and Newell's thinking about the enterprise in which they were engaged. As they conceived it, all intelligence involves the use and manipulation of various symbol systems, such as those featured in mathematics or logic. In the past, such manipulation had been done only by the human being within the confines of his own head, or with paper and pencil, but, with the advent of the digital computer, symbol manipulation has become the province of electronic machinery as well. On the Newell-Simon account, the computer is a physical symbol system like the human brain and exhibits many of the same properties as the human being whose behavior it has now been programmed to simulate.

Just as the cell doctrine has proved central in biology, and germ theory is pivotal in the area of disease, so the concept of *physical symbol system* is deemed by Simon and Newell and their colleagues at Carnegie-Mellon as the core doctrine in the area of computer science. Proceeding in Boolean spirit, the job of the theorist is to identify that set of processes which operates on symbolic expressions in order to produce other expressions that create, modify, reproduce, and/or transform symbolic structures. A physical symbol system is necessary and sufficient to carry out intelligent actions; and, conversely, any system that exhibits general intelligence will prove upon analysis to be a physical symbol system. Such a system consists of a control, a memory, a set of operations, and input and output: its input consists of objects in certain locations; its processes are operations upon the input; its output is the modification or re-creation of objects in certain locations.

A key notion in the Newell-Simon scheme is the production system, in which an operation will be carried out if a certain specific condition is met. Programs consist of long sequences of such production systems operating on the data base. As described by the theorists, the production system is kind of a computational stimulus-response link; so long as the stimuli (or conditions) are appropriate, the response (or production) will be executed. In the course of developing the General Problem Solver, Simon and Newell had propounded a perspective on artificial intelligence, a theory of thinking, and an agenda for future research.

The vision of Newell and Simon was formidable. From their perspective, the profound similarities between the human mind engaged in solving a problem, and the computer programmed to solve the same problem, far overrode differences in hardware (an electronic machine versus a parcel of neural tissue). Both are simply systems that process information over time, proceeding in a more or less logical order. Moreover, to the extent that the steps noted by an introspecting individual paralleled the lines of a computer program, one was no longer simply engaging in weak A.I.: it made sense to think of this man-made physical symbol system as actually engaging in problem solving.

Critics of the Newell-Simon effort brought up a number of issues. First of all, all the information in the computer program had been placed inside the program by humans: thus, to put it colloquially, the problem solver was only doing what it was programmed to do. For instance, it was Newell and Simon who structured the problems given to the program and, in some cases, determined the order in which they were presented. Use of terms like insight was but a misleading metaphor. To Newell and Simon, this criticism appears anachronistic: so long as the program was not simply engaging in rote repetition of steps but actually used rules to solve problems to which it had not previously been exposed, its behavior was as "intelligent" as that of a human being. Simply old-fashioned habits of thought induced critics to withhold the term *intelligent*. Indeed, it was necessary to think of humans as being programmed with rules, just like computers. Not all scholars were convinced by this "democratic response."

Another line of criticism centered on certain differences between human beings and computer programs. For example, human beings can improvise shortcuts or heuristics, whereas computers will repeat the same processes unless they can be programmed to learn from earlier efforts. Recognizing this limitation in the General Problem Solver, Newell and Simon set out to devise programs capable of learning.

A final line of criticism involves the kinds of problem posed to the General Problem Solver. Despite its ambitious name, the problems were all puzzles or logical challenges: these lend themselves to expression in symbolic forms, which in turn can be operated upon. This restriction to "closed" questions was essential since GPS could tackle only mathematical-logical problems. Clearly, many problems confronted by humans (such as finding one's way about a forest or learning to master a dance) are not readily expressed in symbolic logic. Here we encounter a revealing instance of how notions of "thinking" or "problem solving" may be artificially constrained by the programs that currently exist.

Some of these criticisms pertain to other efforts in artificial intelligence as well, but each separate line of inquiry deserves consideration on its own merits. Let me therefore turn more briefly to what other principal investigators were doing in the first decade or so following the Dartmouth conference.

Marvin Minsky and his students

Marvin Minsky at M.I.T. has not been as active a contributor to the published literature as Newell and Simon, nor is a single line of work particularly associated with his own laboratory. But as a seminal thinker about artificial intelligence, who had arrived independently at some of Newell and Simon's ideas, and as a mentor of an active cadre of talented students, he played a significant role in the progress wrought by artificial intelligence in the 1960s (and thereafter).

Under his inspiration, Minsky's students have led artificial intelligence in directions other than those explored by Newell and Simon. One student, T. G. Evans, devised a program in the late 1960s which solved analogies of a visual sort (1968). Expressed anthropomorphically, the program was shown a pair of figures that bore some relation to one another, and was asked to select another set of figures from a set that completed the visual analogy. Thus, for example, the program is shown "A is to B" and must then pick that picture out of five which indicates the relations that obtain between "C" and "D."

It must be noted that the program does not solve the visual analogy by use of perceptual "pick-up" mechanisms (of the sort humans might use), but converts the description into symbolic forms of the sort that would be used in a numerical analogy problem. The program accomplishes the analogy by describing both A and B as figures, and then characterizing the difference between the descriptions (in terms like *inside, above, left of, rotated,* or *reflected*); next, it applies the identified difference as a transformation rule to C, in order to arrive at a pattern having the same description as one of the five candidate numbered patterns (Boden 1977). Evan's program performs this task at the level of a high school sophomore. To program at that level, Evans had to build one of the most complex programs that had ever been written. The machine had about a million bits of memory, and the program had to use every bit of it.

Another individual working in Minsky's laboratory, Daniel Bobrow, adapted the work on problem solving to a linguistic domain (1968). Bobrow's STUDENT program was designed to solve the kinds of algebra problem which youngsters encounter in high school mathematics books. As an example, one of the problems posed in Bobrow's thesis went like this:

> The gas consumption of my car is 15 miles per gallon. The distance between Boston and New York is 250 miles. What is the number of gallons of gas used on a trip between New York and Boston?
>
> (Bernstein 1981, p. 113)

As described by Marvin Minsky, the program assumed that every sentence is an equation; it was given knowledge about certain words to help it locate the equation. For example, the word *is* was coded to mean equal amounts, on both sides of an equation. *Per* meant division. The program was driven by these desired meanings to analyze the syntax. In Minsky's words:

> From the mathematical word "per" in that first sentence's "miles per gallon," it can tell that the number 15 would be obtained by dividing a certain number x of miles, by some other number, y, of gallons. Other than that, it hasn't the slightest idea what miles or gallons are, or, for that matter, what cars are. The second sentence appears to say that something else equals two hundred and fifty miles—hence the phrase "the distance between" is a good candidate to be x. The third sentence asks something about a number of gallons—so that phrase of "gas to be used on a trip" is a candidate to be y. So it proposes one equation: $x = 250$, and another equation, $x/y = 15$. Then the mathematical part of the program can easily find that $y = 250/15$.
>
> (Bernstein 1981, p. 113)

STUDENT illustrates well the powers that were being exhibited by programs in the mid-1960s, as well as certain limitations for which they were criticized. That the programmers were extremely clever, and that the machines could often carry out feats that, if executed by human beings, would unquestionably be considered intelligent, was difficult to dispute (though certainly some critics did [see Arnheim 1969; Dreyfus 1972]). And yet it seemed equally clear that the procedures used were often completely at variance with those ordinarily used by ordinary people. Faced with the preceding problem, a flesh-and-blood student would think about the nature of an automobile trip, the geographic locations of New York and Boston, and what happens when you are using up gas on such a trip. Indeed, the student would almost have to look through these particularities in order to figure out just what the actual mileage per gallon should be (even as he might hazard a plausible guess based simply on his own "real world" experience).

In the case of the computer, however, the procedure was almost the exact opposite. The computer had no idea what the problem was about, and would have performed in exactly the same way had the issue been pennies for peanuts or millions for missiles. The computer's knowledge was purely syntactic. The program is designed to expect certain statements about equalities and to draw the most probable inference about which entities in the problem are likely to constitute the principal components of an equation. It becomes a relatively trivial matter to confuse the program—for example, by including the word *is* in a context where it does not denote an equation but rather forms part of a relative clause or an incidental remark. Similarly, one can wreak havoc by injecting the word *per* as part of an expression, such as *per* capita or *per* chance. The human subject will sometimes be fooled by some extraneous fact which looks relevant (for example, the cost of the gas). The computer's difficulty is that it cannot look through the particular way in which it has been programmed in order to pick up the actual reference of a word or a number. Having no insight about the subject matter of a problem, the computer is consigned to make blunders that, in human beings, would never happen or would be considered extremely stupid.

Indeed, the computer resembles a human being who is asked to solve an algebra problem in a foreign language, of which one knows but a few words: faced with such an enigma, both computer and foreigner gravitate to the few numbers each recognizes, and make the best guess about the mathematical operations that should be carried out on those numbers. While the problems selected by Minsky and students span a wider gamut than those tackled by GPS, they are always reformulated as symbolic expressions of a canonical sort. Nonetheless, it must be stressed that, as with the Newell-Simon efforts, the programs worked. The kinds of exercise expressed in ordinary language, over which schoolchildren have struggled for generations, could be solved by a mechanical process.

Lists and logics: John McCarthy

While the Simon and Minsky laboratories were busily engaged in fashioning demonstration programs, John McCarthy—first at M.I.T., later at Stanford—was engaged in less flashy but equally important endeavors. One of his major accomplishments was to design LISP (for "*list p*rocessing"), the computer language that became most widely used in the field of artificial intelligence (McCarthy et al. 1962; Foster 1967).

As I have indicated with respect to Newell and Simon's early work, it was important for workers to have a language in which they could think readily about problem solving, and one that mimicked closely the kinds of mental step through which a human problem solver putatively passes. LISP and LISP-like "higher-order" languages came to be considered the mathematics of artificial intelligence, the precise and unambiguous argot in which theories are cast (see also Boden 1977 and Winston 1977). The language is basically concerned with the presentation and manipulation of lists, of items on lists, and of lists of lists, each of which can be named. Both programs and data are structured as lists. LISP's power derives from the fact that it is a recursive programming language, one well suited to the description and manipulation of structures and sets of structures. As a recursive language, it is hierarchical and can be described (and can operate) at several levels of detail. LISP is also very flexible: the program can move among levels that are nested within one another, can refer to and operate upon itself as often as necessary, and can automatically reallocate bits of memory. For these and other reasons, LISP and its descendants have continued to be used by most cognitively oriented workers in the computer sciences.

But McCarthy is more than a mere inventor of a useful language. He also has had strong ideas about the goals of artificial intelligence and how they can best be achieved. McCarthy believes that the route to making machines intelligent is through a rigorous formal approach in which the acts that make up intelligence are reduced to a set of logical relationships or axioms that can be expressed precisely in mathematical terms. With Patrick Hayes, then of Edinburgh University, McCarthy wrote a seminal article in 1969, in which he argued for the use of a formal predicate calculus substrate embedded within a system designed for understanding language (McCarthy and Hayes 1969). He called for the formalization of concepts like *causality, ability*, and *knowledge*. If such an approach were to be adopted, it would prove possible to use theorem-proving techniques that are not dependent on the details of particular domains. McCarthy's system was based upon a faith in the consistency of a belief system and upon a view that all knowledge is (or can be) thought of in purely logical terms. As we shall see, these assumptions have had relatively few proponents in recent years. Still, McCarthy has adhered to the general program. He has been designing a nonconventional modification of standard logic in order to model common-sense reasoning, and his former associate Hayes (1982) has been trying to formulate in logical terms the thinking processes of "naive physics"—the physics of the man in the street. McCarthy stands as an extreme proponent of one point of view in artificial intelligence—a man who holds high standards for the field and is less willing than others to bend to the practical or to the particular.

Other programming milestones

While mainstream scholars in the 1960s were either pursuing logical problem solving or theorizing about the proper course of artificial intelligence, certain other work undertaken during that era held considerable implications for the future. One such line was carried out by Edward Feigenbaum, an early student of Simon's. In collaboration with Joshua Lederberg, a Nobel Laureate in genetics at Stanford, Feigenbaum decided to analyze data from a mass spectrograph (Feigenbaum, Buchanan, and Lederberg 1971). The result was a program named DENDRAL which was designed to figure out (on the basis of a vast amount of data from mass spectrographs) which organic compound was being analyzed. After processing the relevant data, the program formulated hypotheses about the compound's molecular structure and then tested those hypotheses by way of further predictions. The ultimate output was a list of possible molecular compounds ranked in terms of decreasing plausibility. DENDRAL's performance compared favorably with that of expert chemists (Boden 1977).

As a program, DENDRAL departed from Simon and Newell's classical model in two ways. First of all, DENDRAL made use of considerable stored knowledge about chemicals. It was predicated on the assumption that experts have a great deal of knowledge and as much of it as possible ought to be possessed by any program that purports to behave intelligently. Second, if seemingly at odds with this assumption, was the decision not to try to emulate the ways in which human beings would solve the problem. Feigenbaum was explicitly interested in top-flight performance, and not particularly intent on mimicking the way that a human being would operate when confronted with the same closetful of information. Here we see an early sign of the sharp cleavage that was to ensue between simulation of human behavior and cultivation of intelligent performances by whatever means.

Two other investigative lines in the 1960s attempted to enter into a seemingly elusive area of human performance: meaningful conversation between individuals. In view of Turing's famous challenge (see pages 17–18), this was a tempting goal to pursue. Kenneth Colby, a psychiatrist then working at Stanford, and Joseph Weizenbaum of M.I.T. both wrote programs that modeled two-person dialogues. In Colby's case, he was interested in psychiatric disorders and so produced a program whose answers might be given by a paranoid personality with a particular obsession about the Mafia:

Why are you in the hospital?
I SHOULDN'T BE HERE.
Who brought you here?
THE POLICE.
What trouble did you have with the police?
COPS DON'T DO THEIR JOB.
What do they do instead?
COPS ARREST THE WRONG PEOPLE.
Are you Italian?
MY BACKGROUND IS BRITISH BUT I WAS BORN IN THIS
COUNTRY.
Do you know any Italian crooks?
I TRY TO AVOID THE UNDERWORLD.

(Boden 1977, pp. 100–1; see also Colby 1975)

Weizenbaum sought to reproduce the behavior of a Rogerian therapist, who assumes a nondirective stance toward clients:

Men are all alike.
IN WHAT WAY?
They're always bugging us about something or other.
CAN YOU THINK OF A SPECIFIC EXAMPLE?
Well, my boyfriend made me come here.
YOUR BOYFRIEND MADE YOU COME HERE.
He says I'm depressed much of the time.
I AM SORRY TO HEAR THAT YOU ARE DEPRESSED.
It's true. I am unhappy.
DO YOU THINK COMING HERE WILL HELP YOU NOT TO
BE UNHAPPY?
I need some help, that much seems certain.
WHAT WOULD IT MEAN TO YOU IF YOU GOT SOME
HELP?
Perhaps I could learn to get along with my mother.
TELL ME MORE ABOUT YOUR FAMILY.

(Boden 1977, pp. 106–7; see also Weizenbaum 1966)

Both of the programs were disguised with sufficient artfulness that they might, for a time, fool an unsuspecting person conversing with the computer or a naïve witness of an interchange. Yet both devisers concede that anyone who knew the design of the program, or was able to make the correct inference, could readily unmask (or "defrock") the program. The reason is that, as in the case of Bobrow's STUDENT program, the programs do not in any interesting sense understand the words being used but are simply constructed in such a way that certain key words will trigger fixed responses. For example,

Weizenbaum's ELIZA depends on pattern-matching techniques. Each sentence in the input text is scanned for key words like *I, you, like, and father:* if one of these words is found, the sentence is transformed according to a rule associated with that word. In contrast, if no such key word is found in the input text, ELIZA responds with a content-free formula, such as "WHY DO YOU THINK THAT?" or with a neutral referral to some earlier remark. There are some other fiendish features. For example, suppose that in the absence of a recognizable key phrase, a decision is made to revert to an earlier topic: the program is so devised that it will return to a topic that had been prefixed by the term *mine* on the not unreasonable assumption that such topics are likely to be "charged" for the conversant.

It should be noted, not entirely parenthetically, that while the Colby and the Weizenbaum research programs were developed in similar fashions, and indeed initially involved some collaboration, the two men have evolved diametrically opposed attitudes toward artificial intelligence. They also have engaged in a heated personal dispute. Weizenbaum, it seems, became disaffected with the whole field of artificial intelligence: he was appalled that some individuals in the clinical professions and in the mass media took his rather whimsical demonstrations as a serious therapeutic tool which might actually be used with disturbed human beings. Colby, on the other hand, is a "true believer," who feels that computers have an important role to play in research about mental illness and possibly in its treatment as well. The issues between these two individuals run deep and touch on the humanistic aspect of the use of computers—a theme that has come up repeatedly in recent debates about the value, and the values, of artificial intelligence.

The phenomenal SHRDLU

While the Weizenbaum and Colby programs make no pretense of actually understanding the utterances to which they are responding (being "dumbly" keyed instead to certain triggering phrases), a different story concerns a program devised around 1970 by an M.I.T. doctoral student, Terry Winograd. Called SHRDLU (after the seventh through the twelfth most frequent letters in a printer's array), this program operates in a way remote from those I have so far described. Rather than being a general problem solver, or a responding mechanism simply activated by key words, SHRDLU purports to be an understanding expert—albeit one working in a very limited domain. Winograd designed for his program a make-believe world of simple blocks which could (if they really existed) be piled and stacked in various ways: his program is sufficiently sophisticated in its linguistic knowledge that it can carry out a complex set of instructions. Moreover, SHRDLU issues signs that these instructions are, in fact, understood—one of the clearest signs of that understanding being that the program asks for clarification in cases where instructions are ambiguous.

What does SHRDLU do? Briefly, it replies to questions about its block world as posed by an interviewer, executes commands on the simulated objects in the block world, and reports the results. Sometimes these are simple actions like *grasp*, *move*, *or put*; while at other times, they are actions at a higher level of abstraction, like *stack* and *clear top*. Before *stack* can be handled, for example, the tops of both objects that will form the stack must be cleared. The program searches for actions that will achieve each subgoal and for sets of preconditions for each action in turn. This task may involve the construction of a sequence of actions from the goal state back to the state in which all the preconditions of the action necessary to initiate the chain have been satisfied.

Let us eavesdrop on some sample snatches of SHRDLU's expertise:

Pick up a big red block.
OK

. . .

Find a block which is taller than one you are holding and put it into the box.

. . .

OK
What does the box contain?
THE BLUE PYRAMID AND THE BLUE BOX.
What is the pyramid supported by?
THE BOX

. . .

Can a pyramid be supported by a block?
YES

. . .

Will you please stack up both of the red blocks and either a green cube or a pyramid?
OK
Which cube is sitting on the table?
THE LARGE GREEN ONE WHICH SUPPORTS THE RED PYRAMID.
Is there a large block behind a pyramid?
YES, THREE OF THEM: A LARGE RED ONE, A LARGE GREEN CUBE AND THE BLUE ONE.

. . .

When did you pick up [the green pyramid]?
WHILE I WAS STACKING UP THE RED CUBE, A LARGE RED BLOCK, AND A LARGE GREEN CUBE.
Why?
TO GET RID OF IT.
Why did you do that?

TO CLEAN OFF THE RED CUBE.

. . .

Put the blue pyramid on the block in the box.
OK

. . .

Thank you.
YOU'RE WELCOME.
(Winograd 1972, quoted in Boden 1977, pp. 115–22)

Compared with the level of understanding exhibited by other programs, SHRDLU was a major breakthrough. To be sure, its simulated world was small, and the number of actions it could carry out and of questions it could answer, extremely limited. Still, within its particular universe, the program performed in a plausible way, "perceiving" distinctions and "acting out" commands, as if to suggest that it actually understood what was being asked of it. (Whether it can be said to *really* understand is a question of tremendous controversy, as we shall shortly see.)

Winograd's program was more sophisticated than its predecessors owing to its use of a series of expert parsers or specialists: a syntactic specialist which segments the sentence into meaningful word groups; a sentence specialist which determines how the objects described by a noun group relate to the action described by a verb group; and a scenario specialist which understands how individual scenes relate to one another and to the sequential story they must collectively tell. For example, in the block world situation, the scenario specialist must handle pronoun references (no mean task) and the temporal sequence of all actions performed. In addition to these experts which can flexibly interact with one another and share information, the program also has belief systems, knowledge about problem solving (such as the mechanisms of deduction), and specialists that detect whether an utterance is question, command, or comment.

SHRDLU was, for its time, a stunning demonstration of apparent language production and understanding capacities. Yet, according to Daniel Dennett (1978), one of its chief contributions lay in another sphere. Specifically, the SHRDLU experiment explored some of the extensive demands imposed on any system that undertakes to follow directions, plan changes in the world, and then keep track of them. While the ways in which these tasks are done may not simulate the way that a real person would work in a real block world, the procedures devised by Winograd were ingenious and at least suggested the kinds of problem that would have to be confronted by any system seeking truly to understand, rather than simply to mimic understanding.

Certain limitations should be noted, however. SHRDLU does not have adequate semantic information to appreciate the differences in meaning between function words like *and*, *the*, and *but*. More tellingly, SHRDLU lacks any ability to learn to perform better. Its knowledge suffices for it to know why it does what it does but not enough for it to remember what has gone wrong when a failure occurs, or to learn from error to make more appropriate responses in the future. A later block-world program, designed by Gerald Sussman (1975) and called HACKER, showed that such learning was, in fact, possible.

Winograd's program came into being at a crucial moment in the history of artificial intelligence. There were furious debates going on about that time, both within the artificial intelligence community and between it and its severest critics. In many ways, the Winograd program spoke to these debates, even if it did not singlehandedly resolve them.

Pivotal issues

The need for expert systems

First, debates within the A.I. community. The 1960s were a time of excitement about general problem solving. Led by the redoubtable Newell and Simon, the search was on for programs that could, at least in principle, deal with every manner of material. But by the late 1960s, the limitations of these programs, which had to be couched in highly general terms, were becoming increasingly evident.

About this time, Edward Feigenbaum returned to Carnegie, his alma mater, to deliver a talk to an audience that included Newell, Simon, and other leading cognitive scientists. Feigenbaum threw out a challenge to his former teachers: "You people are working on toy problems. Chess and logic are toy problems. If you solve them, you'll have solved toy problems. And that's all you'll have done. Get out into the real world and solve real-world problems" (Feigenbaum and McCorduck 1983, p. 63). Feigenbaum had brought along information about DENDRAL, his expert system which incorporated massive amounts of specific knowledge about organic compounds. While DENDRAL was achieving impressive successes, it initially met a skeptical audience. As Joel Moses of M.I.T. has commented:

> The word you look for and you hardly ever see in the early AI literature is the word knowledge. They didn't believe you have to know anything, you could always rework it all . . . In fact 1967 is the turning point in my mind when there was enough feeling that the old ideas of general principles had to go . . . I came up with an argument for what I called the primacy of expertise, and at the time I called the other guys the generalists.
>
> (Quoted in McCorduck 1979, pp. 228–29)

Moses noted Allen Newell's intense objections to his approach:

He called my position the big-switch theory, the idea being that you have all these experts working for you and when you have a problem, you decide which expert to call in to solve the problem. That's not AI, you see ... I think what finally broke Newell's position was Winograd.

(Quoted in McCorduck 1979, p. 229)

And, indeed, shortly after Winograd's program had been completed, even the leaders of the old guard, like Marvin Minsky and Allan Newell, became convinced of the limitations of generalist programs and of the need for systems possessing considerable specialized or expert knowledge. Yet analogous issues were to return in other guises: for example, the question whether there should be a general language for all artificial intelligence programs or many specifically crafted tongues.

Procedural versus declarative representation

As for the preferred manner of programming, there was at the same time a vigorous battle between scholars who favoured *declarative representation*—knowledge coded essentially as a set of stored facts or declarations—and those who favored *procedural representation*—knowledge coded as a set of procedures or actions to be carried out. In the early 1970s, the respective camps were sharply divided, with those wedded to LISP typically veering in favor of declarative knowledge. In their view, declarative languages are easy for people to understand and use. Moreover, such programs are economical, since a bit of information has to be stored only once and can then be tapped at will. Declarativists felt that intelligence rests on a highly general set of procedures which can be used widely, coupled with a set of specific facts useful for describing particular knowledge domains; they were not convinced that knowledge of a subject matter is necessarily bound up with the procedures entailed in its use in one or another context.

In a manner reminiscent of the functionalists in psychology, the proceduralists felt that human intelligence is best thought of as a set of activities that individuals know how to do; whatever knowledge is necessary can be embedded in the actual procedures for accomplishing things. Many things that we do know how to do are best viewed as procedures; and, indeed, it is difficult to describe them formally in a declarative way. For example, if one wants to build a robot to manipulate a simple world, one does it most naturally by describing these manipulations as procedural programs. Procedural representation has the additional advantages of allowing ready use of higher-order (second-level) control information or knowledge of where one routine in a program has to be triggered by another, and being applicable across several domains (Boden 1977; Cohen 1977; Newell 1983; Winograd 1975).

The debate about procedural versus declarative representation has become somewhat muted in the last several years. There is now increasing recognition that not all computing functions lend themselves better to one mode of representation than to another; and that, in fact, some problems are better handled by one approach, other problems by its rival. Initially Winograd had been a chief proponent of procedural systems; but he himself wrote a paper describing the advantages of these two different modes and, more recently, has collaborated with Daniel Bobrow in devising several Knowledge Representational Languages which incorporate both procedural and declarative components (Bobrow and Winograd 1977).

The three sharpest cuts

Also in the early 1970s, at the same time that these intramural debates were going on among scholars generally in sympathy with the goals of artificial intelligence and at odds only about the optimal means, far more critical examinations of artificial intelligence were also afoot. Joseph Weizenbaum (1976), an early practitioner who had devised the seductive ELIZA, launched a strong attack on A.I. enthusiasts. In his view, many of their claims were excessive, wholly out of line with what had actually been achieved. Moreover, he was critical of the future aspirations of artificial intelligence; he believed that many of the tasks now being assigned to machines has best be left to human beings ("Render unto Johnniac . . ."), and that a dangerous confusion was taking place regarding what was properly the realm of humans and what ought to be ceded to machines. People are entities that are wholly different from machines; such uniquely human experiences as love and morality must remain sacrosanct.

In an even more wide-ranging attack on artificial intelligence, Hubert Dreyfus, a phenomenologically oriented philosopher at the University of California in Berkeley, had published in 1972 a critical book called *What Computers Can't Do: A Critique of Artificial Reason*. Dreyfus made much in this book of the fundamental differences between human beings and computers: he claimed that, unlike computers, human beings have a fringe consciousness; a tolerance for ambiguity; a body that organizes and unifies one's experience of objects and subjective impressions; the potential for boredom, fatigue, or loss of drive; and clear purposes and needs that organize one's situation.

According to the tale Dreyfus spins, after an initial run of apparent successes, artificial intelligence had bogged down because it had no way of coming to grips with these fundamental differences between human beings and machines. It was wedded to the notion that all human behavior—including all intelligence—can be formally described by logical rules. But human life is only as orderly as necessary; it is never completely rule-governed: life is what humans make it and nothing else. Since a computer is not involved ("engaged") in a situation, since it has no needs or wants or purposes, it must treat all facts as equally relevant at all times: it cannot make the kinds of discrimination and evaluation that are the stuff of human life and make it meaningful.

Weizenbaum's book was greeted critically, but with a modicum of respect, by his colleagues in artificial intelligence; on the other hand, hardly any computer scientist had a good word to say about Dreyfus's harsh verdict. Clashes of personality and even charges of intellectual incompetence came to dominate the debate. Regrettably, there was little serious discussion between critics and enthusiasts about the issues raised—possibly because of the different value systems involved. If one believes (with Weizenbaum) that there are certain areas where computers should not be used, this is an ethical, or perhaps a religious, judgment; and if one believes (with Dreyfus) in a phenomenological approach to understanding, where the feelings of the experiencing human body are central, one is committed to an epistemological tradition foreign to virtually everyone in the world of computer science and artificial intelligence.

(I ought to point out that Dreyfus's book went into a second edition in 1979, and that he feels that certain trends in artificial intelligence—for example, the adoption of organizing schemas or frames—go some distance toward incorporating the human approach to experience. As for the computer science community, at least a minority now feels that Dreyfus has raised issues that deserve to be addressed seriously. Nonetheless, Dreyfus's next book is tentatively entitled *Putting Computers in Their Place*.)

Perhaps most disturbing to A.I. workers was the negative review given to their field by a supposedly disinterested English observer, Sir James Lighthill, who had been requested by his government's Science Research Council to evaluate the state of the art in British artificial intelligence. Lighthill found relatively little to admire and wrote disparagingly about the distance between initial expectations and actual achievements in the first twenty years:

> Most workers in AI research and in related fields confess to a pronounced feeling of disappointment in what has been achieved in the last 25 years. Workers entered the field around 1950, and even around 1960, with high hopes that are very far from being realized in 1972. In no part of the field have the discoveries made so far produced the major impact that was then promised . . . In the meantime, claims and predictions regarding the potential results of AI research had been publicized which went even farther than the expectations of the majority of workers in the field, whose embarrassments have been added to by the lamentable failure of such inflated predictions.
>
> (1972, p. 17; see also Lighthill et al. 1973)

Lighthill went on to comment:

When able and respected scientists write in letters to the present author that AI, the major goal of computing science, represents "another step in the general process of evolution"; that possibilities in the 1980s include an all-purpose intelligence on a human-scale knowledge base; that awe-inspiring possibilities suggest themselves based on machine intelligence exceeding human intelligence by the year 2000 [one has the right to be skeptical].

(1972, p. 17)

There was one bright note in Lighthill's deflationary document. He singled out for special approval Winograd's thesis: in his view, SHRDLU succeeded by using principles that suggest genuine knowledge and sensitivity to the demands of natural language within a limited universe of discourse. That Lighthill was able to make this distinction indicates that he was not bent on dismissing all of artificial intelligence equally, and also points once again to the special contribution made by this one dissertation which appeared in the early 1970s.

Indeed, it seems fair to say that artificial intelligence has bounced back from these knocks of the early 1970s and has had some singular successes during the late 1970s and early 1980s. As Margaret Boden, a philosopher sympathetic to A.I., has declared:

Suffice it to say that programs already exist that can do things—or, at the very least, appear to be beginning to do—which ill-informed critics have asserted *a priori* to be impossible. Examples include: perceiving in a holistic as opposed to an atomistic way; using language creatively; translating sensibly from one language to another by way of a language-neutral semantic representation; planning acts in a broad and sketchy fashion, the details being decided only in execution; distinguishing between different species of emotional reaction according to the psychological context of the subject.

(Boden 1981, p. 33)

Even as the sights have been lowered from the "absurd overoptimism" of the 1950s, the actual achievements by certain workers are notable and have convinced most observers outside of the field itself that the experiments are at least interesting and should be taken seriously.

Innovations in the 1970s

While the critics of A.I. were not easily silenced, there were, by general consensus, a new burst of energy and several significant achievements in the field in the early 1970s. This second wave is epitomized by Winograd's SHRDLU, the shift from generalist to expert knowledge systems, and the fusion of features of declarative and procedural approaches. At this time, there was another vital, though rather controversial trend: the increasing use of a top-down approach to the understanding of language and other cognitive domains.

As exemplified in the work of Roger Schank and his colleagues at Yale University (Schank 1972; Schank and Abelson 1977), an "understanding" mechanism has several expectations of what a text is like in general; it also incorporates a core set of knowledge structures about details of the subject matter under discussion. These structures are built in as part of a prior knowledge base; they can then be brought to bear upon a particular text in an effort to comprehend how that text resembles, but also how it differs from, other instances of its genre. In the best-known formulation, Schank has introduced the notion of a *script*—the canonical set of events one can expect in an often encountered setting, such as a meal at a restaurant or a visit to a doctor's office. The script then allows one to make sense of different meals, ranging from a snack at McDonald's to a banquet at Maxim's; or of a series of visits to different medical specialists. Such a structured framework allows the "understander" to deal expeditiously with a variety of otherwise difficult-to-assimilate texts (much as Frederic Bartlett's story schemas allowed his subjects to make sense of an otherwise mysterious ghost story).

Another influential top-down approach is Marvin Minsky's (1975) notion of a *frame*: an expected structure of knowledge about a domain that consists of a core and a set of slots. Each slot corresponds to some aspect of the domain being modeled by the frame. In a frame, a description is created and then maintained by substituting observed for predicted values. Thus, for example, when a robot enters a room through a doorway, it activates a "room frame" which leads into working memory and arouses a number of expectations about what might be seen next in a typical room. If the robot then perceives a rectangular form, this form, in the context of a room frame, might suggest a window. The slots include those at a top level—fixed parameters representing things that are *always* true about a proposed situation (like a room having four walls). Lower levels have many terminals—slots that must be filled with specific instances of data: for example, objects, like a window, that one is more or less likely to encounter in a room. It is assumed that individuals possess many hundreds of organizing and interpreting frames, and that combinations of these frames will be invoked in any reasonably complex situation.

Pluralisms

Minsky has also put forth an intriguing conception about how the mind works, leading to novel proposals about how computer programs should be crafted. Rather than believing in a simple general processor or central processor, through which all information must be passed, or in an organized or unified mind that oversees all activity, Minsky now views mental activity as consisting of many agents, each of which is a specialist of some sort. According to this "society of minds" view, the mind consists of several dozen processing centers, or "agents," which can handle different types of knowledge simultaneously. Each of the local agents has a function, which is called upon in certain circumstances, and each has access to other agents. The agents communicate by emitting excitation and inhibition rather than by transmitting symbolic expressions. They can also censor information, much like a Freudian superego. Under this scheme, some parts of the mind know certain things, while other parts know things about the former. In fact, knowledge about *which* agents can know or accomplish which things becomes a crucial component of this new way of thinking about the mind (Minsky 1979, 1982).

Minsky's idea of a frame and his "society of minds" metaphor are not in themselves theories which can be subjected to clear-cut scientific tests, but are better thought of as organizing frameworks (frames, if you will) which lead to the devising of programs that perform more effectively and model human behavioral activity more faithfully. In that sense, his ideas can be seen as reactions: reactions against those approaches that fail to build in prior knowledge or expectations, and as well against those approaches that feature detailed knowledge of a specific area but have absolutely no generality or connection to any other domain. The ultimate impact of Minsky's new ideas on artificial intelligence is not yet known.

With these widespread shifts in how the knowledge base is conceptualized, there has also been increasing dissatisfaction with the kind of computer that usually serves the A.I. researcher: the serial digital "von Neumann" computer. Scholars like Minsky himself, and younger ones like Geoffrey Hinton and James Anderson (1981), raise an intriguing possibility: since the brain is itself a parallel rather than a serial mechanism, with millions of neural events occurring simultaneously, the simulation of human activities ought to be carried out by computers that also operate in parallel fashion. The brain is an apparatus that learns, that executes many special-purpose activities, and that has information dispersed throughout large reverberating circuits. Hinton, Anderson, and their colleagues call for a computer that more closely parallels the operation of the human brain, and for programs that feature many cooperating individual agents. Most of these efforts thus far involve the simulation of visual processing—an area well enough understood in neurophysiological terms to permit a plausible anatomical simulation. A growing number of experts speculate that the next innovative wave of artificial intelligence will utilize "parallel kinds" of architecture for information processing (Feigenbaum and McCorduck 1983). I shall take a look at some of these ideas about "non-von Neumann" style computing in the discussion of visual perception in chapter 10.

Understanding of language

In addition to this influx of new ways of thinking, there have also been impressive achievements in some of the specific subject areas of artificial intelligence—achievements that reflect new concepts and can be said to atone for the contrived performances of the earlier generation of programs. In the area of language, for example, Roger Schank and his colleagues at Yale University, as well as his students who have now moved to other research centers, have produced programs that give précis of stories, skim newspaper articles, and answer questions and draw inferences about plot, character, and motivation in stories (Schank and Abelson 1977; Wilensky 1983).

Schank's claims about his programs, as well as his more general theories of language, have generated much controversy. He traces the failure of early language programs to their narrow focus on grammar and calls for programs that truly "understand the language," or at least parts of it. But many critics feel that *understanding* is being used in an illegitimate sense. I shall review this line of criticism when I come to John Searle's general skepticism about machines engaging in any kind of "intentional" behavior. There has also been debate about Schank's characterization of language. He maintains that everything we can talk or think about boils down to a small group of basic conceptual elements, and goes so far as to declare just what those elements are and how they work, thus doing apparent violence to subtleties of meaning. For instance, he claims that all the verbs of everyday speech can be analyzed in terms of twelve primitive actions (for example, move, ingest, grasp), which concern the handling, movement or transference of things, abstract relationships, and ideas. Schank provides no theoretical justification for his list but puts forth many examples of how one can analyze verbs in light of these primitive cores. Upon these verbs one should be able to construct a general understanding of language, one focusing almost entirely on semantics, to the exclusion of syntactic factors.

Schank's linguistic formulations have not convinced those who work in the Chomskian tradition of linguistic processing. From their perspective, Schank has created a set of *ad hoc* mechanisms which, however successful in certain limited circumstances, are completely unprincipled. There is no systematic criterion for determining when a particular script should be activated, or a theoretically motivated reason to choose one particular conceptualization of a verb over another. For example, why analyze eating in terms of ingesting, rather than including the muscular movements, thoughts, and reactions of an agent who is eating food? Or why invoke a script of a doctor's office rather than an office in general, or an oral surgeon's in particular, when going to a dentist? To such critics, there is no point in proceeding with the task of language understanding until one has a viable theory of the structure of language—a theory that includes the various aspects of language, including syntax, and can be applied to any kind of linguistic input (Dresher and Hornstein 1976).

Though many observers would agree on the theoretical limitations of Schank's pursuit, the fact that his programs work reasonably well at their appointed task cannot be readily dismissed. Moreover, many scholars believe that Schank has hit upon the level of generalization that may be appropriate for the creation of an "understanding system." He focuses on units of meanings, not individual words; uses words to retrieve expectations rather than to craft sentences; and focuses on semantics rather than on syntax. Just as the top-down approach has helped to rejuvenate cognitive psychology, Schank's strategic "bets" have proved surprisingly successful, at least up to now.

While the prospect of a program that understands natural language as human beings do still seems far off, there have been significant advances in other aspects of natural-language competence. Some approaches, such as those of William Woods (1975) and Ross Quillian (1968), follow the road of semantics; while others, such as those of Mitchell Marcus (1979), prefer the trail of syntax. Raj Reddy's HEARSAY (Reddy et al. 1973) program addresses the problem of understanding speech by drawing on several kinds of knowledge—semantic, pragmatic, syntactic, lexical, phonemic, and phonetic—and analyzing the signal at a variety of levels from the single-sound segment to the complete phrase. Each knowledge source takes a look at the hypothesis generated by all the others (and "displayed" on a central blackboard) and then makes a "best" guess about what has been said. While this system certainly lacks elegance, or the tightness of a theoretically motivated approach, it exploits that quality of piecing together bits of evidence that may be involved in understanding speech under less than optimal circumstances.

Perception

There has been analogous, and perhaps more unambiguous, progress in the area of visual perception. Around 1960 a brief flurry of excitement surrounded PERCEPTRON, a mechanism designed by Cornell's Frank Rosenblatt for the purpose of recognizing letters (and other patterns) placed in front of its "eyes." PERCEPTRON consisted of a grid of four-hundred photocells, corresponding to neurons in the retina; these cells were connected to associator elements, whose function was to collect electrical impulses produced by the photocells; connections were made randomly, because it seemed the best way to mimic the brain (Bernstein 1981; Dreyfus 1972). (When random wiring did not work, PERCEPTRON was rewired in a more deliberate way, which improved its performance in pattern recognition.) Another set of components entailed response units: an associator would produce a signal only if the stimulus was above a certain threshold.

Marvin Minsky and Seymour Papert at M.I.T. believed that the machine was built upon erroneous concepts, and that it was more profitable to find the principles that will make a machine learn than to build one in the hope that it just might work. As they saw it, it was necessary to build some prior structure in the machine and to provide the system with informative feedback about successes or failures. Minsky and Papert eventually published a book in which they demonstrated conclusively the limitations of PERCEP-TRON theory (1968). For a while their critique put a damper on the field, because A.I. workers drew the conclusion that nothing further could be accomplished in the area of form recognition using systems based on the model of neural networks.

However, at M.I.T. by the early 1970s, more impressive efforts had been launched in the area of visual perception. Patrick Winston's program (which seems to have escaped an acronymic fate) was able to learn how to distinguish those block configurations that were arches from those that were not. The program learned to recognize tables, arches, pedestals, and arcades by being shown examples and counterexamples of each. The program searched for those differences between positive and negative instances which affected proper identification. A tentatively posited concept was then enriched by analyses of subsequent instances. While (like SHRDLU) the Winston program worked only in a very narrow domain it made use of deep insights about how shapes can be juxtaposed.

Building on several other lines of work (Clowes 1971; Roberts 1965), David Waltz (1975) at M.I.T. devised a program capable of analyzing an entire graphic scene. Not only could it contrive a three-dimensional descrip tion of objects in a drawn scene, but it was also able to recognize two different pictures as being representations of the same scene. Waltz exploited an empirical discovery: if you can label the elements of which an image is constituted, you can so constrain the physically possible scenes that, in most cases, there is but a single interpretation of the scene. In fact, it was even possible to resolve ambiguity in the figure. As Patrick Winston declared:

> Waltz' work on understanding scenes surprised everyone. Previously it was believed that only a program with a complicated control structure and lots of explicit reasoning power could hope to analyze complicated scenes. Now we know that understanding the constraints the real world imposes at junctions is enough to make things much simpler. A table which contains a list of the few thousand physically possible ways that edges come together and a simple matching program are all that is required ... It is just a matter of executing a very simple constraint-dependent iterative process that successively throws away incompatible line arrangement combinations.
>
> (1977, p. 227)

Even more impressive accomplishments in the area of visual perception came from another M.I.T. researcher, David Marr, who took upon himself the task of modeling the early phases of the perception of objects and scenes. Marr was impressed by Chomsky's theoretical approach to what a language is and how any organism can learn a language; accordingly, Marr pondered what is involved in *any* artificial-intelligence program and in *any* visual system as well as the actual details involved in recognizing a complex scene in the real world. And while he did not himself work directly with the visual nervous system, he designed his programs to be consistent with the processes known to characterize the visual system. Marr's sophistication in formulating the problem as well as certain striking results won him widespread admiration before his untimely death at the age of thirty-five in 1980. I shall take a closer look at Marr's accomplishments (Marr 1982) when I focus in chapter 10 on the issue of how one recognizes an object.

Of course, many other researchers and programmers could be mentioned: both those involved in "mainline" work in language, visual perception, and problem solving; and those tilling peripheral soils, such as Christopher Longuet-Higgins's (1979) work in the recognition of musical keys or Richard Young's (1974) work simulating children's cognitive processes on Piaget-type tasks. There are also under way promising new efforts, whose overall impact cannot yet be judged. For example, Douglas Lenat (1976; 1984) has developed an approach to heuristic reasoning as a supplementary means for solving problems and even for finding new heuristics. In any event, the general point should be clear: there has been a second burst of energy in the field of artificial intelligence since the crisis of the early 1970s. If the accomplishments are not yet up to human snuff, they can no longer be readily dismissed as resting on superficial procedures or depending on cheap tricks, but are clearly addressing central issues in human intelligent behavior.

The Chinese room

Nonetheless, not all observers are convinced of the ultimate worth of artificial intelligence. In what may well be the most searching critique of it yet, the Berkeley philosopher of language John Searle has written an article entitled "Minds, Brains, and Programs" (1980). Because Searle's article was published in a journal of open peer commentary, where it generated several dozen responses from sympathetic as well as angered critics, the issues involved in the debate have become well known and, in a sense, serve as a capsule summary of the principal themes in contemporary artificial intelligence.

Searle begins by excluding from his critique the claim of weak or cautious A.I.: that is, that artificial intelligence can illuminate the processes of human behavior. He has no problem (at least as far as his article is concerned) with this variant of A.I., where the computer serves as a tool for the study of mind, allowing hypotheses to be rigorously tested. Searle's quarrel lies with the claim of strong A.I., that the appropriately programmed computer really is a mind and can be said literally to understand and to experience other cognitive states. While few scholars hold the "strong" view as baldly as does Searle's hypothetical target, the vehemence of certain responses to Searle's critique confirm that he struck a raw nerve.

Searle's conundrum

To combat the strong view of A.I., Searle introduces his provocative Chinese room example. Suppose, he says, that an individual (in this case, Searle) is locked in a room and given a large batch of Chinese writing. Suppose that he knows no Chinese writing and may not even be able to discriminate Chinese from other kinds of squiggles. Suppose next that he is given a second set of Chinese characters together with a set of rules for collating the second batch with the first. The rules are in English and are therefore understood by Searle. The rules teach him to correlate one set of formal symbols with another set. This process is repeated with other materials so that the speaker becomes accomplished at correlating the characters with one another and, hence, can always provide the "right" set of characters when given an initiating set. Then, to complicate the situation further, suppose that the speaker is also given questions and answers in English, which he is also able to handle. The speaker is then faced with the following situation:

> Suppose also that after a while I get so good at following the instructions for manipulating the Chinese symbols and the programmers get so good at writing the programs that from the external point of view—that is, from the point of view of somebody outside the room in which I am locked—my answers to the questions are absolutely indistinguishable from those of native Chinese speakers. Nobody just looking at my answers can tell that I don't speak a word of Chinese. Let us also suppose that my answers to the English questions are, as they no doubt would be, indistinguishable from those of other native English speakers, for the simple reason that I am a native English speaker. From the external point of view—from the point of view of someone reading my "answers"—the answers to the Chinese questions and the English questions are equally good. But in the Chinese case, unlike the English case, I produce the answers by manipulating uninterpreted formal symbols. As far as the Chinese is concerned, I simply behave like a computer: I perform computational operations on formally specific elements. For the purposes of the Chinese, I am simply an instantiation of the computer program.
> (Quoted in Hofstadter and Dennett 1981, p. 33)

Searle's argument is more complex and subtle than this single quotation reveals, but its general tenor can be grasped. He believes that the Turing test is no test whatsoever of whether a computer program has a mind or is anything like a human being, because humanlike performance can be faked by any individual or machine that has been supplied with a set of formal rules to follow under specific circumstances. So long as one is simply following rules—so long as one is engaged in syntactic operations—one cannot be said to truly understand. And the computer is a machine *par excellence* for formal operations, unencumbered by any semantic knowledge, by any knowledge of the real world, or by any intention to achieve certain effects by its specific response. Therefore, it is a fundamentally different kind of entity from a human being who understands the semantic content of an utterance, and has his own purposes for communicating. Conclusion: the program of strong A.I. is bankrupt.

Counterattacks

Knowing that his argument will not go unchallenged, Searle himself anticipates the major counterarguments. He reviews the Berkeley or "systems reply": the claim that while the individual in the room may not understand the story, he is part of a whole system—ledger, paper, data banks, and so on; and the system itself understands. Searle's response is that the individual could memorize or internalize all the materials in the system (for example, memorize the rules in the ledger and the data lists of Chinese symbols and do all calculations in his head) and still would not understand.

A second response is the robot response of the Yale Contingent. According to this line of argument, a computer could be put inside a robot, and the robot could walk around and do all the sorts of things that real people do; being thus in touch with the real world, such a robot would really understand. But Searle says that, while this reply tacitly agrees that understanding is more than formal symbol manipulation, it still fails to make its case—because Searle could, unbeknownst to himself, actually become the robot. For example, the Chinese symbols might actually come to him from a television camera attached to the robot: thus, the Searle-robot would appear to be perceiving. Analogously, the symbols that he is issuing forth could make motors move the robots, arms, and legs: thus, the Searle-robot would act. In either case, however, Searle would actually be making all of the formal manipulations of symbols by himself and still would know nothing of what is going on. In one sense, he would be the homunculus of the robot but would remain in total ignorance of the Chinese meanings.

A third line of argument, traced this time to Berkeley and M.I.T., is the brain-simulator reply. This response suggests another scenario: a program now simulates the actual sequence of neuron firings at the synapses of the brain in a native Chinese speaker when he is engaged in, for example, story understanding or question answering. The machine now taking in stories simulates the formal structure of actual Chinese brains in processing the stories, and gives out Chinese answers as output. Searle says that even creeping up this close to the operation of the brain still does not suffice to produce understanding. Instead, he says, imagine that rather than a mono-lingual man being in a room shuffling symbols, the man is equipped with an elaborate set of water pipes with valves connected to them. When the man receives the symbols, he looks them up in the program and then determines which valves to turn on and off. Each water connection corresponds to a synapse in the Chinese brain, and the whole system is so rigged that eventually Chinese answers pop out. Now, points out Searle, the man does not understand Chinese, nor do the water pipes. The problem with the brain simulator is that it is simulating the wrong things about the brain. Searle indicates that

> as long as it simulates only the formal structure of the sequence of neuron firings at the synapses, it won't have simulated what matters about the brain, namely its causal properties, its ability to produce intentional states . . . That the formal properties are not sufficient for all the causal properties is shown by the water pipe example: we can have all the formal properties carved off *from* the relevant neuro-biological causal properties.
>
> (Quoted in Hofstadter and Dennett 1981, p. 340)

Searle goes on to list other replies, and combinations of replies, and responds to them in similar fashion, but it is in his response to the brain simulator reply that he tips his hand. He believes understanding is a property that comes from a certain kind of machine only—a machine like the human brain which is capable of certain processes, such as having and realizing intentions. As he says, it is not because I am an instantiation of a computer program that I am able to understand English; but, as far as we know, "it is because I am a certain sort of organism with a certain biological (i.e., chem-ical and physical) structure, and this structure, under certain conditions, is causally capable of producing perception, action, understanding, learning, and other intentional phenomena" (quoted in Hofstadter and Dennett 1981, p. 344).

In the journal, respondents attacked Searle's argument at every point. Some, steadfastly embracing positions Searle has already attacked, said that he had misunderstood them, or that when properly pursued, particular responses could indeed accomplish what Searle denied. Other critics accused him of being a mystic, antiscientific, antitechnological, or just another philosopher gone bad. Much was made about the caricature embodied in his single fake Chinese speaker. Respondents claimed that Searle's example is just not plausible: in order to be able to carry off the behavior successfully, the man or the system would need to achieve genuine understanding, or what we would unhesitatingly call genuine understanding were it to be found in a human being. There are orders of magnitude Searle ignored (for example, the effort it would take to anticipate and translate all possible messages) and only this sleight-of-hand allows him to make his case. Searle has also been accused of confusing levels: it is the person who understands, and not the brain; and similarly, it is the computer as a whole that understands, and not the program.

To my mind, when Searle remains on his own ground—in putting forth the example of the man equipped with a set of formal rules for responding in Chinese—he is convincing. While I would not join Searle in ruling out the possibility of any machine's understanding a natural language, I certainly feel that the word *understand* has been unduly stretched in the case of the Chinese room problem in its various manifestations.

It is Searle's positive explanation of why the rest of us understand, when he speaks about the intentionality of the brain, that can be legitimately attacked. The whole notion of the brain as a causal system that displays intentionality is obscure and difficult to understand, let alone to lay out coolly like a computer program. Zenon Pylyshyn, a computer scientist from the University of Western Ontario, scores telling points: "What Searle wants to claim is that only systems that are equivalent to humans . . . can have intentionality. His thesis thus hangs on the assumption that intentionality is tied very closely to specific material properties—indeed, that it is literally *caused* by them." Pylyshyn wonders whether Searle is proposing that intentionality is a substance secreted by the brain (1980*a*), and then poses this puzzle:

> [Suppose] if more and more of the cells in your brain were to be replaced by integrated circuit chips, programmed in such a way as to keep the input-out *function* of each unit identical to that of the unit being replaced, you would in all likelihood just keep right on speaking exactly as you are doing now except that you would eventually stop *meaning* anything by it. What we outside observers might take to be words would become for you just certain noises that circuits caused you to make.
>
> (p. 442)

Searle's argument, it seems to me, loses its force if, by definition, only human brain or brainlike mechanisms can exhibit properties of intentionality, understanding, and the like. If this is true by definition, then there is no point to the controversy. If, on the other hand, Searle allows (as he must) that nonprotoplasmic entities can also possess the "milk of human intentionality," he must explain what it takes to be intentional, to possess understanding, and the like. Such explanation is going to be difficult to provide, because we have no idea how the causal properties of protoplasm allow individuals to think; and, for all we know, the process is as odd as one of those Searle so effectively ridicules.

In an effort to address these concerns, Searle has written a book on *Intentionality* which he defines as the property of mental states and events by which they are directed at objects and states of affairs in the world. Intentional states include beliefs, fears, desires, and intentions (1983*a*, p. 1). In the book, he declares:

> My own speculation, and at the present state of our knowledge of neurophysiology it can only be a speculation, is that if we come to understand the operation of the brain in producing Intentionality, it is likely to be on principles that are quite different from those we now employ, as different as the principles of quantum mechanics are from the principles of Newtonian mechanics; but any principles, to give us an adequate account of the brain, will have to recognize the reality of, and explain the causal capacities of, the Intentionality of the brain.
>
> (p. 272)

Indeed, Searle seems to believe that, to do cognitive studies, one needs only two levels of explanation—the level of intentionality (a plain English discussion of the organism's wishes, beliefs, and so on)—and a neurophysiological explanation of what the brain does in realizing these intentional states. He finds no need for a level of symbolic representation, which dominates work throughout the cognitive sciences (1983*b*). To the extent that these lines of argument sound like mere handwaving, Searle's positive assertions about intentionality have little force. To the extent that he can specify just what he means, and show that intentionality is not in principle restricted to organic brains, a genuine scientific issue will have been joined. Thereafter, researchers in artificial intelligence can try to simulate the very behavior that Searle believes lies beyond their explanatory scope.

It is possible, however, that the issues between Searle and his critics—and perhaps even between those in sympathy and those out of sympathy with A.I.—transcend questions of a scientific nature. In an angry critique of the Searle paper, computer scientist Douglas Hofstadter makes the following conjecture:

> This religious diatribe against AI, masquerading as a serious scientific argument, is one of the wrongest, most infuriating articles I have ever read in my life . . . I know that this journal is not the place for philosophical and religious commentary, yet it seems to me that what Searle and I have is, at the deepest level, a religious disagreement and I doubt that anything I say could ever change his mind. He insists on things he calls "causal intentional properties" which seem to vanish as soon as you analyze them, find rules for them, or simulate them.

But what those things are, other than epiphenomena, or innocently emergent qualities I don't know.

(Quoted in Searle 1980, p. 434)

If Hofstadter is right about the underlying reasons for the disagreement, then there is no way in which either side can convince the other. At stake is a matter of faith, in which reason will not even be considered relevant by either side.

Critics and defenders: the debate continues

Whatever the merit of Searle's arguments, they do not question the legitimacy of most current work in artificial intelligence; in fact, as he indicates, he has no qualms about accepting the utility of A.I. as an aid in conceptualizing and testing theories of human intelligence. But, as we have seen, some critics challenge A.I. at an even more fundamental level. As one example, Joseph Weizenbaum (1976), raises ethical questions about whether A.I. should be allowed to impinge on territory that has hitherto been restricted to human beings, such as issues of justice or love.

Another line of criticism suggests that efforts to simulate human intelligence are perfectly valid, but that most of the A.I. community has heretofore used superficial models which do not approach the core of human thought processes. Initially, this line of criticism came from those in the camp of transformational linguistics, like Elan Dresher, Norbert Hornstein (Dresher and Hornstein 1976), and Kenneth Wexler (1978). From their perspective, rather than trying to build upon deep principles of language (or whatever area happens to be modeled), artificial intelligence is simply a practical, trial-and-error pursuit and is unlikely ever to come up with anything that has generality and explanatory power. For instance, as they see it, Schank's program is too vague and unspecified, and there are no algorithms for determining the "primitive verb" or the script that is relevant to a given linguistic string. In contrast, Winograd's program is criticized for being too specifically tied to a given "micro-world" and thus being inapplicable to any new specimen of language. According to this "purist" philosophy, scientists ought to be spending their time analyzing systems in themselves, studying competent human beings, or fashioning theoretical explanations of what intelligence or competence amounts to: theories that can stand up to the standards of the "hard" sciences. Perhaps, once the *real* operative principles are understood— as they are beginning to be understood in the area of syntactic processing—it should be relatively trivial to program the computer to carry out these operations. In the next chapter, I shall examine this transformationalist vision of acceptable explanatory models in cognitive science.

These critics are arguing that artificial intelligence has not yet attained the standing of a genuine scientific endeavor. Instead, it is just a convenient tool whose operating principles are of scant theoretical interest– views that have been recently echoed by some of the most active workers in artificial intelligence. Terry Winograd, once the darling of the A.I. community, has been pondering the limitations of computer-based understanding and has moved away from simulation experiments. He and Daniel Bobrow declare:

> Current systems, even the best ones, often resemble a house of cards ... The result is an extremely fragile structure which may reach impressive heights, but collapses immediately if swayed in the slightest from the specific domain (often even the specific examples) for which it was built.
>
> (Bobrow and Winograd 1977, p. 4)

Schank has conceded the difficulties involved in devising systems without having good models, and has newly acknowledged the philosophical nature of many problems:

> AI is very hard. What is the nature of knowledge? How do you abstract from existing knowledge to more general knowledge? How do you modify knowledge when you fail? Are there principles of problem solving that are independent of domain? How do goals and plans relate to understanding? The computer is a way of testing out ideas. But first, we need to understand what we're supposed to be building models of.
>
> (Quoted in Waldrop 1984*a*, p. 805)

Workers like John McCarthy (1984) have been pondering what Daniel Dennett (1983) terms the "smoking gun" problem of artificial intelligence: how a program can decide which of the unexpected features in a situation can be ignored. (For example, if it is to resemble human intelligence, a frame of a boat trip should ignore the fact that the oars on a rowboat are blue rather than green but dare not ignore the fact that one of the oarlocks is broken.) John Seely Brown and Kurt van Lehn, researchers at Xerox PARC in Palo Alto, admit that most current A.I. work fails to meet traditional criteria of scientific theories, and decry the absence of "competitive argumentation" whereby the power of one simulation can be rigorously compared with the power of another. By such comparison, it is possible to indicate *why* one accepts some computational principles, while rejecting others. In lieu of such argumentation, these authors wryly suggest, artificial intelligence theories have stood on the toes rather than on the shoulders of their predecessors (van Lehn, Seely Brown, and Greeno 1982).

The realization that one's chosen discipline may not have been operating in a scientifically impeccable manner is not in itself an instant panacea, but it is an important first step—may be the most important step in the maturing of a discipline. A second valuable trend, in my view, has been the growing number of workers in A.I. who seek systems reflecting the deep principles at work in a particular domain of knowledge. Spurning both the search for the most general properties of problem solving (which proved elusive with the General Problem Solver) and the interest in those expert systems that perform well simply by drawing with brute force on massive amounts of stored knowledge, these researchers take seriously the principles that appear to be at work in the only other intelligent system we know—the human being. I shall examine some of their promising efforts in the latter chapters of this book.

It is possible, of course, as a result of a careful study of different areas, we will discover that the deepest principles do indeed operate across areas, and that we will ultimately require a general knowledge base or problem solver rather than a host of separate experts. As I suggested with respect to the work of John Anderson (1983) in cognitive psychology, such a dream may still materialize, but the likelihood seems small.

My own analysis suggests that, after a period of excessive claims and sometimes superficial demonstrations, artificial intelligence has advanced to a more measured view of itself and has, in the process, attained a set of reasonably solid accomplishments. This maturing process has involved a recognition that the practice of A.I. entails deep philosophical issues which cannot be ignored or minimized. Involved as well has been a recognition that there are limits to what can be explained by current A.I. methods and that even whole areas of study may lie outside of artificial intelligence, at least now and perhaps permanently. It is important to have genuine demonstrations and not just verbal descriptions of possible programs: this insistence has been among the greatest contributions of Newell and Simon. But it is equally important that these demonstrations reflect robust principles and are not just fragile constructions with limited application.

Given my own view that the future of cognitive science lies in the study and elucidation of particular domains of knowledge, I believe that the field will achieve scientific status when it freshly illuminates the domains and knowledge systems with which it is concerned. As the psychologist John Marshall declares:

> I just don't care what members of the AI community think about the ontological status of their creations. What I do care about is whether anyone can produce principled, revealing accounts of, say, the perception of tonal music . . ., the properties of stereo vision . . ., and the parsing of natural language sentences. Everyone that I know who tinkers around with computers does so because he has an attractive theory of some psychological capacity and wishes to explore certain consequences of the theory algorithmically.
>
> (1980, p. 436)

Christopher Longuet-Higgins makes the same general point in a somewhat different way:

> It is perhaps time that the title "artificial intelligence" were replaced by something more modest and less provisional ... Might one suggest, with due deference to the psychological community, that "theoretical psychology" is really the right heading under which to classify artificial intelligence studies of perception and cognition ... The task of the theoretician is to formulate hypotheses and to elicit their logical implications as carefully as he can, with due attention to matters of internal consistency and predictive power; the duty of the experimenter is to confront the predictions of a theory with firm and relevant observations, and to suggest points at which the theory needs modifying in order to bring it into line with experiment—if that is indeed possible. The time has now come, it seems, when the task of theory construction is altogether too intricate to be consigned to spare moments away from the laboratory; it is at least as much of a discipline as good experimentation.
>
> (1981, p. 200)

Marshall and Longuet-Higgins are pointing to the increasingly close ties being forged between experimental cognitive psychology and artificial intelligence. Psychologists can benefit from the careful simulations made by A.I. researchers, and can put their own typically informal models to rigorous tests; A.I. scientists can determine whether their hypothesized models of human behavior are actually realized by the subjects about whom they have been speculating. It seems plausible to me that parts of psychology and parts of computer science will simply merge into a single discipline or, as I suggested in the previous chapter, that they will form the central core of a newly forged cognitive science.

Of course, there may well be areas of computer science, as well as of psychology, that do not take part in this merger. This would be quite proper. The idea that artificial intelligence must be able to handle all psychological (or all philosophical) issues, or it will be unable to handle any of them, must be exorcised. Similarly, there is no more reason for us to think of humans as being completely identical to computers than for us to cling to the notion that there are no useful resemblances or parallels between these two kinds of (potentially) thoughtful entity.

Nonetheless, the issue of the actual degree of similarity between humans and computers cannot be permanently ignored. One of the principal findings of recent artificial intelligence is that the digital serial von Neumann computer seems in many ways an inadequate model of human cognition. To the extent that this finding is reinforced—and much of the research in the latter part of this book can be cited as supporting evidence—then we will have

111

confirmation of the computational paradox. Artificial intelligence has demonstrated that the computer can be a useful tool for studying cognition and that it serves as a reasonable model for some human thought processes. But whether it is the best model for the most important processes is still very much an open question.

Artificial intelligence and cognitive psychology may well merge as the central components of a new cognitive science, but they cannot in themselves constitute the field. Philosophy will remain a source of important questions, a repository of invaluable reflections on those questions, and a valuable critic of cognitive scientific practices. But an equally important partner in this newly fashioned line of inquiry will be those disciplines that take as their appointed task the analysis of particular domains of cognition. Of the various disciplines that must assume this burden, linguistics is, by all accounts, the discipline that has accomplished the most and is thus most centrally involved in cognitive science. Moreover, and perhaps for this reason, other disciplines look to linguistics as a possible model of how to study a particular domain and to apply the powerful (and perhaps too powerful) tools of the psychologist and the computer scientist. Because of the intrinsic importance of language among the human cognitive faculties, because of linguistics' role as a possible model for domain-specific studies, and because of the tremendous strides made in linguistics over the past few decades, it is appropriate to turn now to the scientific study of language.

Note

1 This historical sketch follows the account given by Pamela McCorduck (1979), a historian of artificial intelligence.

3

THE PREHISTORY OF ANDROID EPISTEMOLOGY

Clark Glymour, Kenneth M. Ford and Patrick J. Hayes

Source: K.M. Ford, C. Glymour and P.J. Hayes (eds), *Android Epistemology*, American Association for Artificial Intelligence/MIT Press, 1995, pp. 3–21.

Contemporary artificial intelligence (AI) can be viewed as essays in the epistemology of androids, an exploration of the principles underlying the cognitive behavior of any possible kind of mechanical agents. Occasional hyperbole and flimflam aside, artificial intelligence is a wonderful subject, full of new ideas and possibilities, unfettered by tradition or concern (other than inspirational) for the accidents of human constitution, but disciplined by the limits of mechanical computation. More than other new sciences, AI and philosophy have things to say to one another: any attempt to create and understand minds must be of philosophical interest. In fact, AI is philosophy, conducted by novel means. That AI emerges from ideas of computer science is, of course, a familiar observation. The central insights of Babbage, Turing, von Neumann and other pioneers on how a machine might actually be built that could manipulate and be influenced by symbols are widely recognized. But for all the novelty, many of the central ideas that animate artificial intelligence, and even particular techniques and themes prominent in contemporary practice, have a long philosophical ancestry. In fact, the sources of key assumptions and insights underlying much of AI—such as that the mind is computational, that computational devices can be a simulacrum of the mind, the fundamental idea that machines can "calculate" with symbols for things other than numbers, and that there is a plethora of possible artificial minds yet to be invented—are deeply embedded in the history of philosophy. This background includes the history of logic, the emergence of combinatorics, the merging and separating of theories of deduction and computation from psychological theories, the formation of the first program for a possible cognitive agent, characteristic designs of programs for machine learning, characterizations of conditions for causal inference, and no doubt a good deal more. In addition to any list of ideas, there is what might best be characterized as an attitude towards machinery. AI has an engineer's respect for things that work and a pragmatic willingness to try anything that will produce the results needed. In the spirit of medieval astronomy, it wants only to save the phenomena, not to hypothesize psychological truth. While important parts of modern science have emerged from trying to understand machines—thermodynamics and steam engines, for example—the direct intellectual merging of philosophy and engineering seems strange, even rather outrageous, in our modern academic culture. But many earlier philosophers seem to have had a similar kind of affection and respect for machinery. This eassy attempts briefly to survey some of the philosophical sources of contemporary ideas about artificial intelligence. More extended treatments can be found in Glymour (1992) and in Haugeland (1985).

Back to the Greeks: Plato and Aristotle

According to both Plato and Aristotle, the objects of knowledge have a special *formal structure*. The sort of thing a person may know is that one thing or kind of property is a *finite combination* of other things or kinds of properties. Man is a combination of *rational* and *animal*. *Triangle* is a combination of *closed*, *rectilinear*, *figure*, and *three-sided*. Plato and Aristotle differed about the metaphysics, of course. For Plato these combinations are ideal objects or forms; for Aristotle they are essential attributes of concrete objects. For both philosophers, however, all knowledge consists of knowing such combinations of forms or essential attributes of a thing or kind. For example, according to Plato, knowledge of virtue is knowledge of which simple forms are combined into the form of virtue. Any AI knowledge engineer will recognize the idea and be attracted by its computational virtues. The anticipations are, however, more detailed. In the *Meno*, Socrates and Meno search for an answer to the question "What is virtue?" Socratic method is to collect positive and negative examples and to search for hypotheses that cover the positive and exclude the negative. In the course of the dialogue, Meno points out through a question the first theorem of computational learning theory: how will they know when they have found the correct answer? Meno's point, of course, is that they cannot, solely on the basis of a finite sample, decide the truth of a contingent, universal claim by any rule that will yield the truth in all logically possible circumstances consistent with the sample. Socrates' response to Meno is that the process of discovery is what is now called in artificial intelligence *explanation-based reasoning*. Everyone, according to Plato, already knows implicitly at birth all of the laws of forms. The process we think of as empirical discovery is simply a matter of realizing which formal truth, or consequence of laws of forms, applies to a particular set of cases and adding that truth to one's explicit knowledge.

114

The conjunctive view of the objects of knowledge suggests questions about combinations of properties. Ultimately, on either the Platonic or Aristotelian view, any kind of property that can be the object of scientific knowledge can be analyzed into a combination of simple properties that cannot be further analyzed. The number of distinct kinds that can be the objects of knowledge then consists of the number of distinct combinations of these simple properties, whatever they are. What is the number of pairs of distinct properties if there are n properties altogether? What is the number of triples of distinct properties if there are n properties altogether? What is the number of distinct combinations of any particular number m of properties drawn from n properties? How can these distinct combinations be enumerated and surveyed? If one has the Platonic-Aristotelian conception of the form of knowledge, these are fundamental questions.

In Europe, it was just such questions that gave rise to the mathematical subject of combinatorics, the study of the numbers of possible combinations satisfying given conditions. The first mathematical results of this kind in the West seem to occur in a commentary on Aristotle by Porphyry, written in the 3rd century A.D. Porphyry wished to comment on all of the similarities and difference among five Aristotelian "voices," and so he posed the problem of enumerating all the distinct pairs of things that can be obtained from a collection of five things. He observed that one might think that this number is 20, because one can choose the first thing of a pair in any of five ways, and the remaining member of the pair in four distinct ways. But Porphyry correctly argued that the number of pairings is not 20:

> Such is not the case; for though the first of the five can be paired with the remaining four, when we come to the second, one of the pairs will already have been counted; with the third, two; with the fourth, three and with the fifth, four; thus there are in all only ten differences: $4 + 3 + 2 + 1$.
>
> (cited in Edwards, 1987, p. 20)

Roughly 250 years later, Boethius wrote commentaries on Porphyry's commentary on Aristotle, and in them he provided a more general, alternative proof. But Porphyry's combinatoric result seems not to have been significantly extended until the Renaissance. Even without technical advances, however, combinatoric ideas remained important.

In the Middle Ages, the conception of the objects of knowledge as combinations of simple attributes that make up a kind or a complex property led to a conception of the method for acquiring knowledge. The method, insofar as it deserves the name, consisted of trying to "analyze" a thing into its simple properties (analysis) and then trying to put it back together by combining those properties (synthesis). Sometimes—in Renaissance chemistry, for example—"analysis" meant physically decomposing a substance into "simpler" substances, and "synthesis" meant physically reconstituting a substance of that kind, but for the most part the analysis and synthesis were purely mental.

Ramón Lull and the Infidels

After the reintroduction of classical learning into Christian Europe, one would expect that Christian intellectuals would have applied the methods they had learned from Aristotle and Plato to the study of God, and they did. God, too, had fundamental properties, and one could consider the combinations of His attributes. In the 13th century, the questions of how to enumerate, organize, and display God's attributes led to a fundamental insight, one that we nowadays take for granted. It concerns the odd life of the great Spanish philosopher, Ramón Lull, a 13th century Franciscan monk.

The notion of mechanical aids in carrying out an algorithm and the notion of an algorithm itself are ancient, perhaps prehistoric. But one of the central insights of modern computational thinking, the idea that machines can aid nonnumerical and nongeometrical reasoning through manipulating discrete symbols, first appeared in the West, as far as we know, in the writings of Ramón Lull. The source of Lull's idea lay in a traditional metaphysical view and in the slowly emerging mathematics of combinatorics. Lull's motives, however, were entirely religious.

Lull's life illustrates that a philosopher can also be a man (or woman) of action, if only bizzare action. Lull grew up in a wealthy family and passed his early adulthood in the court of James II of Spain. He spent his time with games and pleasantries and is reputed to have made great efforts to seduce the wives of other courtiers. Accounts have it that after considerable effort to seduce a particular lady, she finally let him into her chambers and revealed a withered breast. Taking this sight as a sign from God, Lull gave up the life of a courtier and joined the Franciscan order, determined that he would dedicate his life to converting Moslem civilization to Christianity, and in a curious way, philosophy gained from that dedication.

Lull moved to Majorca and spent several years mastering the Arabic language, studying and writing tracts (of which he eventually authored hundreds) against Islam and for Christianity. About 1274, Lull had a vision of the means by which Moslems could be converted to Christianity. Stimulated by the idea, he wrote another book, his *Ars Magna*. While Lull's fundamental style of thought is mystical and obscure, it contains one logical gem.

In effect, Lull's idea was that Moslems (and others) may fail to convert to Christianity because of a cognitive defect. They simply were unable to appreciate the vast array of the combinations of God's or Christ's virtues. But thanks to this vision, Lull believed that infidels could be converted if they could be brought to see the *combinations* of God's attributes. Further, he thought that a *representation* of those combinations could be effectively presented by means of appropriate machines, and that supposition was the key to his new method. Lull designed and built a series of machines to be used to present the combinations of God's virtues.

A typical Lullian machine consisted of two or more disks having a common spindle. Each disk could be rotated independently of the others. The rim of each disk was divided into sections or *camerae*, and each section bore a letter. According to the application for which the machine was intended, the letters would each have a special significance. They might denote, for example, an attribute of God. One Lullian machine, for example, has the letters "B" through "R" around the rims of an inner disk, and around the outer disk Latin words signifying attributes of God: Bonitas (B), Magnitudo (C), Eternitas (D) and so on. A Lullian machine was operated by rotating the two disks independently, much as we would a star finder or (some years ago) a circular slide rule. At any setting of the disks, *pairs* of God's attributes would be juxtaposed on the rims of the inner and outer disks. Rotating the disks would create different pairings. One would thus discover that God is Good *and* Great, Good *and* Eternal, Great *and* Eternal, and so forth. The heretic and the infidel were supposed to be brought to the True Faith by these revelations.

Lull lectured on several occasions at the University of Paris. He traveled throughout Europe attempting to raise money for missions to North Africa to convert Moslems to Christianity. He himself is reported to have made three such trips to Africa. Tradition has it that on his third trip, at the age of 83, he was stoned to death, but some biographers are so lacking in romantic sentiment that they dispute this account.

This story may seem a bizarre and slightly amusing tale of no particular philosophical significance. But buried within Lull's mysticism and his machines is the seed of a collection of powerful ideas that only began to bear fruit 350 years later, in the 17th century. One of the great ideas implicit in Lull's work is that nonmathematical reasoning can be done, or at least assisted, by a mechanical process; the other is that reasoning does not proceed by syllogism, but by combinatorics. Reasoning is the decomposition and recombination of representations. The decomposition and recombination of attributes can be represented by the decomposition and recombination of *symbols*, and that, as Lull's devices illustrate, is a process that can be made mechanical.

Computation and discovery in the 17th century: Pascal, Leibniz and Bacon

Lull's work was known even in the 17th century, when a version of his ideas was taken up by Leibniz. Interestingly, the 17th century has a hidden history that strived, but failed, to articulate a theory of reasoning that combines logic, algebra, and combinatorics.

In 1642, Blaise Pascal, the French philosopher, mathematician, and inventor, perfected what until recently had been generally thought of as the first automatic calculating machine.[1] Like Lullian machines, Pascal's machine used rotating wheels, but unlike Lull's, it actually did something—addition and subtraction—including carries or borrows. This machine, called Pascaline, seems very simple now but was a contemporary public sensation raising both excitement and fear—not unlike today's AI research program; and, skeptics might add, Pascal's machine had a defect that AI may share: it cost more to produce than people were willing to pay for it. Although the Pascaline's functionality was limited, it showed that tasks that previously might have been expected to require human attention or thought could be made fully, automatically mechanical. The process of building the calculating device seems to have had a substantial impact on Pascal's philosophical thinking. With a prescience for enduring controversy, in his *Pensées*, Pascal (1670/1932) remarked that "The arithmetical machine produces effects which approach nearer to thought than all the actions of animals." What animals have that the calculator lacked, Pascal wrote, is will.

Pascal's *Treatise of the Arithmetical Triangle*, in which the Binomial Theorem is first established, helped to make it evident that the analysis of combinations arising from the Aristotelian and Platonic traditions was an aspect of algebraic relations among numbers. Descartes' mathematical work had shown that geometry, the traditional mathematical language of the sciences, also had an algebraic side and that important geometrical properties could be characterized algebraically. By the middle and latter parts of the 17th century, algebraic relations, usually presented as geometrical statements of ratios, had become the form in which natural science expressed the laws of nature. Kepler's third law was essentially such a relation, and so was the Boyle-Mariotte law of gases, and the inverse square law of gravitation. It was only natural to suppose that the actions of the mind—thought—must also have laws that can be described by such relations, and that the combinatorics of analysis and synthesis are a hint of them. Gottfried Leibniz came to that very conclusion.

Pascal's *Treatise* was published in 1654. The next year Leibniz, then 19 years of age, published his first work, a Latin treatise on logic and combinatorics, *De Arte Combinatoria*. He did not yet know of Pascal's work, but he learned of it subsequently, and in later years when he journeyed to Paris, he tried unsuccessfully to meet with Pascal, who had retreated to religious quarters at Port Royal. Pascal had shown that the same combinatorial numbers or binomial coefficients also arise in relations between the terms of certain infinite series, and reflection on the properties of series eventually helped lead Leibniz to the discovery of the differential and integral calculus.

Leibniz's first work was really a combinatorial study of logic in the Aristotelian tradition. It is the only work on logic that Leibniz ever published. Over the course of the rest of his life, Leibniz wrote a long series of unpublished and incomplete papers on logic. They show the formation of some of the key modern ideas about deductive inference and proof, and they also show how very difficult the issues were for one of the greatest philosophers and mathematicians of the century. Leibniz's logical theory is not consistent and thorough (Leibniz had a difficult time completing anything), but it contains many ideas that were successfully elaborated in later centuries, and it also shows clearly the limitations of the Aristotelian framework.

Following tradition, Leibniz assumed that every proposition consists of a predicate applied to a subject and that in this regard the structure of language reflects the structure of the world. In the world, substances *have* attributes. But Leibniz gave this notion a twist. Substances don't, in his view, *have* attributes in the sense that one and the same substance could have an attribute or not have it. A substance *just is* a combination of attributes. You, for example, are nothing but the combination of all of the properties that you have. So there is no property that you in fact have that *you* could not have—an entity that didn't have some property you have wouldn't be you. So, finally, every property you have, you have *necessarily*. The same holds for any other substance in the world. Whatever properties a substance has, it has necessarily.

In Leibniz's theory, every concept *just is* a list or combination of primitive concepts. All true propositions are true because the list of primitive concepts of the subject term is appropriately related to the list of primitive concepts of the predicate term. Leibniz says that every true proposition is true because it is an instance of the identity $A = A$. He meant that if a proposition is true, the subject and predicate lists will be such that by eliminating irrelevant parts of one or the other, the same combination of concepts or attributes is found in the subject as is found in the predicate. So every true proposition can be given a proof. The proof of a proposition consists of the following:

1. Producing the combinations of simple concepts that are, respectively, the concept denoted by the predicate of the proposition and the concept denoted by the subject of the proposition.
2. Showing that the concept of the predicate is included in the concept of the subject, or vice-versa, according to what the proposition asserts.

Leibniz wrote extensively about these two steps. He never succeeded in making clear just how the analysis of concepts was to be obtained—of course, neither had Aristotle or the Scholastic tradition of analysis and synthesis. Leibniz envisioned the creation of an enormous dictionary or encyclopedia; his vision was ridiculed by Swift in the latter's account of Laputan scholarship and has not had a good reputation since the 18th century. In the 1950s, Bar-Hillel noted that a successful mechanical translator, in order to properly distinguish ambiguities such as "pen" in "the ink is in the pen" and "the sheep are in the pen," would have to have access to a huge

119

database of all of human knowledge. Bar-Hillel's observation was considered a *reductio ad absurdum* argument for the impossibility of machine translation. But something like Leibnizian "dictionaries" are indeed being constructed in AI and used in machine translation, albeit with a rather more complex theory of the structure of knowledge, but still based on the idea—now with the backing of 20th century logical theory—that in a computational sense a concept simply is a combination of all that is known about it, so that a suitably rich enumeration and organization of all this knowledge is sufficient to capture the concept.

If a universal dictionary could be assembled that expressed each concept in terms of the simplest concepts, Leibniz was convinced that the production of scientific knowledge would become *automatic*. He thought an *algorithm* or mechanical procedure could be found to carry out the second part of the procedure for giving proofs. The way to formulate such a procedure is to treat the problem as though it is part of *algebra*. Each simple term and each complex term should be given a letter or other symbol (Leibniz sometimes suggested using numbers as symbols for concepts), and then one would use algebraic methods to search for algebraic identities. On other occasions, he suggested representing concepts by geometrical figures, such as lines, and trying to carry out the second step of the aforementioned two-step process by geometrical procedures. The essential thing is that there is a *mathematics* of reason (in fact, that is the title of one of the logical papers Leibniz completed), and this mathematics can be carried out automatically.

Again, much current AI research, given more adequate flesh by developments in logic, is based on a modification of Leibniz's vision. One entire subfield of AI is concerned with "computational logic," a phrase that Leibniz would have understood immediately. Pascal and Leibniz would perhaps also have understood one aspect of the computational difficulties of this field. The reasoning process is indeed governed by combinatorics, quite aside from problems of undecidability. Combinatorial analysis shows that the search spaces of reasoning expand too rapidly to submit to straightforward enumeration, so the mathematics of reasoning seems to require "dictionaries" of heuristics, which are the subject of active research.

Pascal's success with calculating machines inspired Leibniz to devise his own machine, which he called the Stepped Reckoner. Although conceptually much more sophisticated than either the Calculating Clock or the Pascaline, Leibniz's Stepped Reckoner appears never to have operated properly; its manufacture was beyond machining techniques of the day. Leibniz's efforts to build a better machine led him to realize that a binary notation would permit a much simpler mechanism than required for his and Pascal's decimal-based devices. He envisioned a binary calculator that would use moving balls to represent binary digits (Leibniz, 1679).[2] As noted by Augarten (1985), the notion of binary representation had more than practical import for Leibniz. He regarded the remarkable expressiveness of binary enumeration as a sort of natural proof of the existence of God, asserting that it demonstrated that God, the omniscient *one* (1), had created everything out of *nothing* (0). Thus as did Lull and Pascal before him, Leibniz attached deep religious significance to his efforts at mechanization.

Pascaline's wheels carried numerals, and it performed arithmetic, but Leibniz saw that these machines were manipulating symbols in ways that were best understood in combinatoric terms and that there was nothing about the idea which restricted it solely to arithmetic. During the first half of this the 20th century, when the idea of mechanical arithmetic had become commonplace, this insight was still rare. An early British government report on the significance of computing machines declared that they were not worth the investment of much research effort, on the grounds that there was not a great need for more gun-aiming tables.

In 1620, Francis Bacon's *Novum Organum* sought to provide the inductive method for the new science. Bacon describes a nearly algorithmic procedure, often ridiculed by 20th century philosophers of science for whom the very idea of discovery by algorithm was anathema. Bacon's discovery procedure assumes the investigator is in search of the "form" of a phenomenon, which for Bacon, as for Aristotle and Plato, meant at least a conjunction of features essential, necessary, and sufficient for the phenomenon. The investigator should then collect positive instances of the phenomenon, forming them in a table. Again, negative instances, otherwise as like positive instances as possible, should be collected in a table. Third, a table should be formed of instances exhibiting the phenomenon in varying degrees, if the phenomenon admits of such variation. Now the investigator should find—Bacon doesn't say how—whatever combination of features is common to all positive instances, absent from all negative instances, and concommitant in degree with the degree of the phenomenon in the table of degrees.

Bacon's problem setting, and his method, were revived around the middle of this century in the study in cognitive psychology of "concept learning." Procedures proposed by Bruner, and later by Hunt, and still later by statistical concept learners, have their logical and historical roots in Bacon's new method.

The Cartesian way

René Descartes' mathematical innovations created linkages that proved essential to the very idea of a mechanics of mind. Descartes' algebraic geometry transformed aspects of the traditional geometrical formalism for the mathematical description of nature into systems of algebraic equations. With that transformation, an algebraic expression became possible for Kepler's laws, Boyle's law, and so on. The binomial theorem in turn established connections between algebra and combinatorics, the mathematics of mind.

Yet, philosophically, Descartes was unconnected with the invisible thread that bound Hobbes, Leibniz and Pascal. The Cartesian conception of mind was not, like Hobbes', of a material device that represents by physical symbols and reasons by computation. Descartes' mind, it is almost too banal to note, was of an entirely different substance than matter; Descartes' mind could exist were nothing material to exist; Descartes' mind could be influenced by material conditions, but it was not bound by and characterized by the principles that constrain matter.

This idea is tantalizingly close to the modern conception of software. Software is also immaterial and remarkably unconstrained by physical principles, yet when provided with a suitable material substrate (not a pineal gland), it can have startling material effects. The Cartesian error was only to think of it as a *substance* rather than something like a pattern or a specification. But perhaps Descartes can be forgiven—philosophers and lawyers are still not quite clear about exactly how to describe software. Fortunately, however, programmers are able to create and use it with some confidence.

For the purposes of our topic, Descartes' principal contemporary influence is on the opponents of artificial intelligence, through two ideas. First, Descartes thought of procedures, algorithms, methods, and rules as inextricable from meaning and intention. Descartes' rules for inquiry are not even approximately mechanical as are Hobbes'; instead, Descartes formulated his rules in terms for which there are only inner criteria: examine whether ideas are *clear*; examine whether ideas are *distinct* from others. It was this very subjective twist on method that irritated Descartes' materialist critics, such as Pierre Gassendi. In our century, the Cartesian view of method seems to have prompted (no doubt through more proximate sources, such as phenomenalism) Wittgenstein's argument that a purely subjective language is impossible, because extra-linguistic criteria are required to constitute correct or incorrect usage, and a language without standards of use is not a language at all. Wittgenstein's private language argument has been recast by Saul Kripke as an argument about the irreducibility of rules or algorithms to material or physical relations. Briefly, Kripke argues that rules—for example, the rule for addition—require *meanings* that somehow determine how the rules apply to a potential infinity of as yet unexamined cases. But meanings are *normative*; meanings have to do with how language ought to be used. And, to conclude the argument, norms are not part of the physical world.

The second Cartesian influence on contemporary discussions occurs through a strategy of argument that is ubiquitous in contemporary philosophical opposition to artificial intelligence. Descartes' criterion for possibility is imagination: If p is (or can be) imagined, then p is possible. Hence, if the denial of p can be imagined, then p is not necessary. In combination with some other ideas about possibility and necessity—for example, the idea that fundamental scientific identifications of properties ("water is H_2O") entail that the identity claims are necessary—the Cartesian fallacy sows considerable confusion. A well-known recent example of this confusion is Searle's Chinese room argument. Searle wants to refute the thesis that *any* physically possible system that implements a program for understanding Chinese with sufficient speed therefore understands Chinese. Searle imagines that he is placed in a room containing baskets full of Chinese symbols and a rule book (in English) for matching Chinese symbols with other Chinese symbols. People outside the room (who understand Chinese) slide questions written in Chinese under the door. In response he manipulates the symbols according to the rules in the book and answers by sliding strings of Chinese symbols back out under the door. The rule book is supposed to be analogous to the computer program, and Searle to the computer. These answers are indistinguishable from those of a native Chinese speaker, although, according to Searle, neither he nor the room nor the two of them together understand Chinese. Even if one were to (mistakenly) grant his second conclusion (that the whole system didn't understand Chinese), Searle's fantasy is only a counterexample to anything of interest to artificial intelligence if one supposes that because Searle can imagine himself running the program, that this is actually possible. But before he could generate a single output Searle-in-the-box would become bored and his Chinese friends would have long since found better things to do.

Minds and procedures: Hobbes to Kant

Thomas Hobbes, the 17th century autodidact and mathematical eccentric best known for his writings on political philosophy, also formulated a rather clear anticipation of Newell and Simon's notion of intelligence as a physical system that manipulates symbols:

> By ratiocination, I mean computation. Now to compute is either to collect the sum of many things that are added together, or to know what remains when one thing is taken out of another. Ratiocination, therefore, is the same with addition and subtraction; and if any man add multiplication and division, I will not be against it, seeing multiplication is nothing but addition of equals one to another, and division nothing but a subtraction of equals one from another, as often as is possible. So that all ratiocination is comprehended in these two operations of the mind, addition and subtraction.
>
> But how by the *ratiocination* of our mind, we add and subtract in our silent thoughts, without the use of words, it will be necessary for me to make intelligible by an example or two. If therefore a man sees something afar off and obscurely, although no appellation had yet been given to anything, he will, notwithstanding, have the same idea of that thing for which now, by imposing a name on it, we call it *body*. Again, when by coming nearer, he sees the same thing thus and

thus, now in one place and now in another, he will have a new idea thereof, namely, that for which we now call such a thing *animated*. Thirdly, when standing nearer, he perceives the figure, hears the voice, and sees other things which are signs of a rational mind, he has a third idea, though it have yet no appellation, namely, that for which we now call anything *rational*. Lastly, when, by looking fully and distinctly upon it, he conceives all that he has seen as one thing, the idea he has now is compounded of his former ideas, which are put together in the mind in the same order in which these three single names, *body, animated, rational*, are in speech compounded into this one name, *body-animated-rational*, or *man*. In like manner, of the several conceptions of *four sides*, *equality of sides*, and *right angles*, is compounded the conception of a *square*. For the mind may conceive a figure of four sides without any conception of their equality, and of that equality without conceiving a right angle; and may join together all these single conceptions into one conception or one idea of a square. And thus we see how the conceptions of the mind are compounded. Again, whosoever sees a man standing near him, conceives the whole idea of that man; and if, as he goes away, he follows him with his eyes only, he will lose the idea of those things which were signs of his being rational, whilst, nevertheless, the idea of a body-animated remains still before his eyes, so that the idea of rational is subtracted from the whole idea of man, that is to say, of body-animated-rational, and there remains that of body-animated; and a while after, at a greater distance, the idea of animated will be lost, and that of body only will remain; so that at last, when nothing at all can be seen, the whole idea will vanish out of sight. By which examples, I think, it is manifest enough what is the internal ratiocination of mind without words.

We must not therefore, think that computation, that is, ratiocination, has place only in numbers, as if man were distinguished from other living creatures (which is said to have been the opinion of Pythagoras) by nothing but the faculty of numbering; for *magnitude, body, motion, time, degrees of quality, action, conception proportion, speech* and *names* (in which all the kinds of philosophy consist) are capable of addition and subtraction.

(Hobbes, 1962, pp. 25–26)

There are several important thoughts in this passage. One is that reasoning is a psychological process, so that a theory of logical inference should be a theory of the operations of the mind. Another is that representations can have an encoding by, or be analogous to, numbers. A third is that the theory of reasoning is a theory of appropriate combinations; just what the objects are that are combined is obscure in this passage, but other passages suggest that Hobbes thought of the mind as composed of particles, and some of these particles, or collections of them, serve as symbols (or, as Hobbes would say, names) for things, and it is these physical symbols that are combined or decomposed in reasoning.

Later English writers of philosophical psychology, Locke, Hume, Mill, and Maudsley, for example, thought of the content of a theory of mind as, at least in part, a theory of mental procedures, specifically procedures in which mental objects—"ideas"—are linked or "associated." Associationist psychology typically avoided Hobbes' mechanical formulations, and his connection of procedures with algorithms and numerical encodings had no influence. Instead, mental procedures were explained in terms of "similarity" and "vivacity" and temporal proximity of occurrence of ideas.

The procedural viewpoint was given a very different turn in the closing decades of the 18th century in Kant's *Critique of Pure Reason* and his related works. As with the associationist writers who influenced him, Kant gives no hint that mental processes are computational, but he offers an original view of those processes themselves, quite unlike anything before. Kant is the modern father of the notion of top-down processing.

Kant recognized that the logical theory which he had inherited from Aristotle, and which he assumed to be sound and complete, could not account for mathematical inference. Euclid's geometrical proofs, which prove by construction the existence of objects with specified properties, cannot be turned into valid syllogistic arguments, nor can Euclid's proofs of theorems in number theory be obtained by syllogism. Yet Kant was convinced that classical mathematics and much else (including that all events are governed by causal regularities and features of Newtonian physics) is known *a priori* and not derived from inductions founded on experience. Kant's solution to the conundrum is that the content of experience is literally a *function* (in the mathematical sense) of the procedures of mind and of unknowable features of things in themselves. The difference between what is needed to obtain Euclid's proofs and what Aristotle's logic can do is built into the mind itself, not as axioms but as procedures that automatically construct the content of experience from the deliverances of sense. Things in themselves deliver, in unknowable ways, sensation, or what Kant sometimes calls the matter of experience; the "faculty of intuition" then contributes spatial and temporal features; and the "schematism of the understanding" contributes object identity, causal regularity, and the synthesis of the individual pieces into a unified experience. The faculty of intuition automatically constructs images, for example, that satisfy the requirements of Euclidean axioms, and the schematism ensures that nothing random happens in experience. Kant repeatedly remarks that the process of synthesis and the operation of the schematism are unconscious, and he observes that how the schematism works will likely remain unknown (immediately thereafter he plunges into lengthy remarks about how the schematism works).

125

The 19th century: Boole, Frege and Freud

George Boole's work can be seen as a continuation of Leibniz's vision. Boole provided an algebra of logic and considered the algebra important because it provided a method for correct reasoning. Boole, too, viewed the mathematical theory of reasoning as a description of psychological laws of nature, but he also realized the contradiction between this analysis and the obvious fact that humans make errors of reasoning.

> The truth that the ultimate laws of thought are mathematical in their form, viewed in connection with the fact of the possibility of error, establishes a ground for some remarkable conclusions. If we directed our attention to the scientific truth alone, we might be led to infer an almost exact parallelism between the intellectual operations and the movements of external nature. Suppose any one conversant with physical science, but unaccustomed to reflect upon the nature of his own faculties, to have been informed, that it had been proved, that the laws of those faculties were mathematical; it is probable that after the first feelings of incredulity had subsided, the impression would arise, that the order of thought must, *therefore*, be as necessary as that of the material universe. We know that in the realm of natural science, the absolute connection between the initial and final elements of a problem, exhibited in the mathematical form, fitly symbolizes that physical necessity which binds together effect and cause. The necessary sequence of states and conditions in the inorganic world, and the necessary connection of premises and conclusion in the processes of exact demonstration thereto applied, seem to be coordinate.
>
> Were, then, the laws of valid reasoning uniformly obeyed, a very close parallelism would exist between the operations of the intellect and those of external Nature. Subjection to laws mathematical in their form and expression, even the subjection of an absolute obedience, would stamp upon the two series one common character. The reign of necessity over the intellectual and the physical world would be alike complete and universal.
>
> But while the observation of external Nature testifies with ever-strengthening evidence to the fact, that uniformity of operation and unvarying obedience to appointed laws prevail throughout her entire domain, the slightest attention to the processes of the intellectual world reveals to us another state of things. The mathematical laws of reasoning are, properly speaking, the laws of *right* reasoning only, and their actual transgression is a perpetually recurring phenomenon. Error, which has no place in the material system, occupies a large one here. We must accept this as one of those ultimate facts, the

origin of which it lies beyond the province of science to determine. We must admit that there exist laws which even the rigor of their mathematical forms does not preserve from violation. We must ascribe to them an authority the essence of which does not consist in power, a supremacy which the analogy of the inviolable order of the natural world in no way assists us to comprehend.

(Boole, 1951, pp. 407–408)

Caught by the image of logic as the laws of reasoning akin to the law of gravitation, Boole did not try to resolve this difficulty by supposing that his was the theory of some ideal agent; he did not think that he was describing other minds than ours, imaginary minds still somehow recognizably similar to our own.

About thirty years later, Frege gave the first adequate formulation of the logic of propositions—Boole had in effect described something closer to mod 2 arithmetic—and formalized a system of logic that included both first-order logic and the quantification over properties, although the latter part of his system was, as Russell showed, not consistent. Frege insisted on separating logic from psychology, and so he did not suffer Boole's embarrassment over human error. Frege's achievement, and the logical developments of the next fifty years that extended it, at last put in place one of the principal tools for the study, among many other things, of android epistemology. Another conceptual tool arose at nearly the same time from physiology.

While the 18th and early 19th centuries witnessed thinkers such as Pascal, Leibniz, and Boole struggling to find a mechanical basis for reasoning, the end of the 19th and the beginning of the 20th century saw two remarkably different ways of reconciling psychology with the notion that reasoning is computation. Each of these lines of work leads to a branch of contemporary AI research. The "symbolic" approach to AI emphasizes structures of reasoning, while "connectionist" artificial intelligence focuses on brain-like architectures.

Prefaces to modern connectionist works usually trace the ideas back as far as Hebb's (1949) *The Organization of Behavior*; occasionally writers will note passages of William James near the turn of the century that have a connectionist flavor. But the basics of connectionist models of computation and of mind were fully developed by the late 19th century in the private views, and some of the public views, of neuropsychologists. We know of no better statement from this time than Sigmund Freud's private writings, where a great many details, including what is now called "Hebbian learning" and the "Hebbian synapse" are described. Freud was trained as a neuroanatomist by Ernst Brucke, one of Europe's leading physiologists and an uncompromising materialist. Early in the 1890s physiologists learned of synaptic junctions, and in Vienna that revelation immediately led to connectionist speculations by the senior research assistants in Brucke's laboratory, including Freud.

127

While others published similar views, Freud developed his ideas in his unpublished *Project for a Scientific Psychology*, written in 1895. Freud's theory of dreams began in that essay, and the last chapter of Freud's first book on dreams is clearly derived from it. (For a more detailed account of Freud's connection with connectionism, see Glymour, 1991).

We return now to the symbolic tradition. Kant held that the objects of experience are constructed or "synthesized," but he was not at all clear about what they are constructed from or how the details of such a construction could work. After Frege's work, a few philosophers began to have novel ideas about what a "construction" or "synthesis" might be. The three most important philosophers first influenced by Frege were Bertrand Russell, Ludwig Wittgenstein, and Rudolf Carnap. Russell had an important correspondence with Frege, and Carnap went to Jena to study with him. Frege's anti-psychologism may have had a curious and healthy effect, for Carnap especially had no hesitation in developing a mathematics of cognition that, while motivated by psychological ideas, did not pretend to describe how people actually reason. This attitude was crucial to the pragmatic approach of early work in AI.

Russell and Carnap each proposed (at about the same time) that extensions of Frege's logical theory, or Frege's logic in combination with set theory, could be used to describe the construction of physical objects from the data of sensation. Russell and Whitehead had developed techniques to carry on Frege's logicist program to reduce mathematics to logic; Russell and Carnap, independently, thought that the same techniques could be used to give an account of the possibility of knowledge of the external world.

Russell's idea was that starting with variables ranging over basic entities (the sense data) and with predicates denoting properties of sense data (such as *red*), one could then *define* terms that would denote *sets* of sense data. Physical objects would literally be sets of sense data, or sets of sets of sense data or sets of sets of sets of sense data, and so on. Similarly, higher order properties of physical objects (such as the property of being a tree) would also be appropriate sets of sense data (or sets of sets of sense data, etc.). Russell sketched these ideas in a popular book, *Our Knowledge of the External World*, but he made no attempt to describe any logical details. Meanwhile, Carnap actually produced an outline of such a system.

Carnap's book, *The Logical Structure of the World*, was published in 1928. Carnap assumed that the fundamental entities over which the variables of his system range are what he called *elementary experiences*—an elementary experience is all that appears to someone at a particular moment. In addition, he assumed one relation between elementary experiences is given in experience, namely, the relation that obtains when one recollects that two experiences are similar in some respect or other. (For example, they might both be experiences that contain a red patch somewhere.) The construction of the world begins with a finite list of pairs of elementary experiences; for each pair in the list, the person whose experiences they are recollects that the first element in the pair is in some respect similar to the second element in the pair. Qualities such as color and tone are then defined as certain sets (or sets of sets or sets of sets of sets, etc.) formed from this list. Objects are to be constructed in the same way.

One of the most remarkable things about Carnap's logical construction of the world is that it is not presented only as a collection of logical formulas that are to be applied to terms denoting elementary experiences and the relation of recollection. Carnap also described the construction as a *computational procedure*. That is, along with each logical construction he gave what he called a "fictitious procedure" that shows how to calculate a representation of the object constructed from any list of pairs of elementary experiences. The procedures are perfectly explicit, and they could be represented in any modern computer language. Carnap was the first philosopher (indeed the first person) to present a theory of the mind as a computational program. The use of logical representations immediately suggested (to Carnap anyway) that computation can be done not just on numbers, but on symbols that represent nonnumerical objects. This was really Ramón Lull's idea, and Hobbes' idea after that, but in Carnap's work it begins to look as though it might really work.

William Aspray (1981) has given a persuasive account of the origins of the theory of computation, as it emerged in this century, from philosophical issues in the foundations of mathematics rooted in the 19th century. We think it is fair to say, however, that while the development of the essentials of recursion computation theory was motivated by philosophical issues, the profession of philosophy contributed nothing to them. Gödel gave an account of his incompleteness results to the Vienna Circle, but the audience seems to have missed their import. Alonzo Church was at the center of things, but in the 30s and 40s he was in the mathematics department at Princeton, and there is no evidence that anyone in the philosophy department at the time had an inkling of the revolution going on around them.

Late in the 1920s or thereabouts, Frank Ramsey developed the idea of subjective utility theory and the theory of measurement of subjective utilities. Belatedly, Carnap approached Ramsey's conception of probability, and by the middle of the century, Carnap proposed that we think of inductive norms as the design principles for an android that would begin life with some probability distribution and carry on by conditioning on the evidence it acquired throughout life. When, early in the 1960s, electronic digital computers began to be available for research, the first expert systems for medical diagnosis used Bayesian methods much as Carnap had imagined. Whether there was any direct influence from the philosophical tradition, we do not know. Russell, too, came late in life to think of epistemology as principles of android design. His last serious work, *Human Knowledge, Its Scope and Limits*, abandons the idea of building up the world from sense data and considers especially the general knowledge of kinds and causes that systems must innately have in order to convert sensation into knowledge of the world.

Carnap had two students, Walter Pitts and Herbert Simon, who contributed directly to the formation of the subject of artificial intelligence in the middle of this century, and Simon, of course, contributed many of the leading ideas in the subject. And Carnap had another student, Carl Hempel, who contributed indirectly to the first commercial computer programs for automated scientific discovery. For all of their influence, neither Carnap nor Hempel seems to have had a glimmer of the possibilities in android epistemology, and both flatly denied—Hempel repeatedly and vehemently—the possibility of machine discovery.

Hempel's influence came through his students. One of his doctoral students at Princeton, Gerald Massey, had a doctoral student at Michigan State, Bruce Buchanan, who went to work at Stanford in what was then a very odd job: helping to design and implement programs for chemical identification with mass spectroscopy. Joshua Lederberg and others had developed algorithms for identifying the hydrocarbon compounds consistent with chemical law and a given formula, and the task was to use these algorithms as part of an inference engine. In the Dendral and Meta-Dendral programs, Hempel's theory of explanation and his instance-based approach to hypothesis confirmation were adapted and applied.

Conclusion

The history of modern computing has as a central theme the development of methods for representing information in a physical form which is both stable enough to be reliable as a memory and plastic enough to be changed mechanically. The algorithms of Pascal's and Leibniz's calculating machines were physically represented in their mechanical structure. It was not until Babbage's (1792–1871) Analytical Engine that a machine was designed that did not directly physically embody the algorithms that it could execute. Significantly, it used a punched-card technique for encoding information and algorithms which was originally developed for use in mechanical looms of the late 19th century. The engineers were beginning, quite serendipitously, to provide the ideas which could give flesh to Leibniz's vision.

AI is re-establishing the cooperation between philosophy and engineering which so motivated and enlightened Pascal and Leibniz, but now android epistemology is working with richer tools. In the centuries of philosophical discussion since Pascal and Leibniz first saw how arithmetic could be mechanized, the concept of "machine" has not been much extended beyond Pascaline. But AI is working with new kinds of machines—not just physical computing machines but also "virtual" machines which consist of software (run on other, "actual" machines) but perform real feats in the world.

Through the work of Turing's student, Robin Gandy, and others, theorists are developing new and more general formal conceptions of machines that compute.

Some of the early work in artificial intelligence seems to have taken philosophical theories more or less off the shelf, specialized them to particular tasks, and automated them, so that some of the early work in the subject has the flavor of automated philosophy of science, and even some of the more recent work in machine learning—for example, work on discovering laws and work on causal inference—bears the mark of philosophical sources. But the period is past in which android epistemology could rely substantially on independent work in philosophical logic and philosophy of science. What future development requires is not separation of labor by disciplines, but rigor and imagination, clarity of broad motive and clarity of detail, and a willingness to take off the blinkers of disciplines. Philosophy should not be just one more set of blinkers.

Notes

1 It is now clear that Pascal was preceded by the German polymath Wilhelm Schickard and his Calculating Clock. Schickard was a protege of Kepler.
2 Leibniz is often erroneously credited with inventing binary arithmetic, but its roots are much older, reaching at least back to the ancient Chinese. Binary counting systems have been found in many of the world's ethnologically oldest tribes (Phillips, 1936). It seems that ancient man was much taken with the pairwise nature of his body—two legs, arms, eyes and ears. Binary multiplication is first described in the wonderfully named manuscript "Directions for Obtaining Knowledge of All Dark Things," believed to have been written by a scribe named Ahmes in about 1650 B.C.

References

Aspray, W. (1981). *From mathematical constuctivity to computer science: Turing, Neumann, and the origins of computer science in mathematical logic.* Ann Arbor, Michigan: University Microfilms International.
Augarten, S. (1985). *Bit by Bit* London: Unwin.
Boole, G. (1951). *The Laws of Thought.* New York: Dover.
Carnap, R. (1967). *The logical structure of the world: Pseudoproblems in philosophy.* Berkeley: University of California Press. [Originally published in 1928.]
Edwards, A. (1987). *Pascal's Arithmetical Triangle.* Oxford University Press.
Gardner, M. (1968). *Logic Machines, Diagrams and Boolean Algebra.* New York: Dover.
Glymour, C. (1991). Freud's androids. In J. Neu (Ed.), *The Cambridge Companion to Freud.* Cambridge University Press.
Glymour, C. (1992). *Thinking Things Through.* Cambridge, MA: MIT Press.
Haugeland, J. (1985). *Artificial Intelligence: The Very Idea.* Cambridge, MA: MIT Press.
Hebb, D. O. (1949). *The Organization of Behavior.* New York: Wiley.

Hinton, G. E., Plaut, D. C., & Shallice, T. (1993, Oct.). Simulating brain damage. *Scientific American*, pp. 76–82.

Hobbes, T. (1962). *Body, Man and Citizen*. Collier.

Holland, J. (1975). *Adaptation in Natural and Artificial Systems*. Ann Arbor: University of Michigan Press.

Leibniz, G. W. (1679). *De progression dyadica—Pars I*, in the collection of Niedersächsische Landesbibliothek, Hanover. [Reprinted in Herrn von Leibniz, *Rechnung mit Null und Eins* (pp. 42–47). Siemens Aktiengesellschaft: Berlin.]

McGinn, C. (1982). *The Character of Mind*. Oxford University Press.

Pascal, B. (1932). *Pensées*. New York: E.P. Dutton. [Originally published in 1670.]

Phillips, E. W. (1936). Binary calculation. *Journal Inst. Actuaries*, 67, 187–221.

Russell, B. (1926). *Our Knowledge of the External World as a Field for Scientific Method in Philosophy*. London: G. Allen & Unwin.

Russell, B. (1948). *Human Knowledge: Its Scope and Limits*. New York: Simon & Schuster.

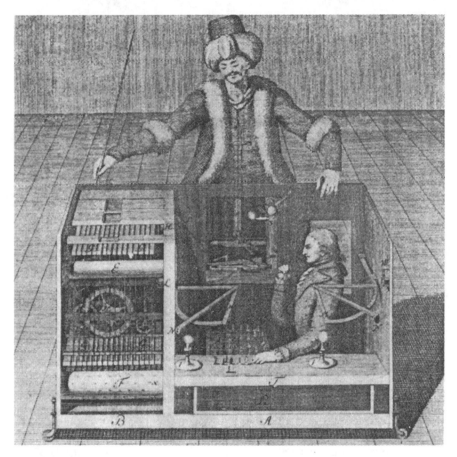

The Great Chess Automaton, 18th century, etching, from Joseph Friedrich, *Üeber Den Schachspieler Des Herrn Von Kempelen Und Dessen Nachbildung*, 1789.

4

THE MAN-MACHINE AND ARTIFICIAL INTELLIGENCE

Bruce Mazlish

Source: *Standford Electronic Humanities Review* 4(2), 1995: 21–45.

For thousands of years humans have wrestled with the question of their "human" nature. In particular, they have attempted to define themselves in relation to the animal kingdom. Yearning either to take on some of the superior attributes of other animals or to rise above their own animal nature by becoming angelic, humans have mostly sought to define themselves as a special sort of creation.

Humans have also created machines; and their new creations, in turn, have raised the question of whether animals are merely a variant of the machine and whether the machine, as a kind of monster, can turn against its creator and either "take over" or make humans over into its own image.

These concerns about man's animal and mechanical nature came forcefully together in the West in the seventeenth century and did so in terms of a debate over what was called the *animal-machine*. Were animals mere machines, and were humans the same—that is, man-machines?

René Descartes's answer, for example, was that animals *were* simply machines, and human beings, *if* one were to set aside their possession of an immaterial soul, might also simply be considered as machines. His famous dualism, however, saved human uniqueness. Michel de Montaigne and his followers took an opposite tack, often asserting the superiority of beasts over humans, vaunting the naturalness of the former. By the eighteenth century, Julien Offray de Mettrie sought to end the debate by declaring that man was a machine, no different in this respect from any other mechanical being. Needless to say, the debate has continued to rage.

In the history of mechanical contrivances, it is difficult to know how many of the automata of antiquity were constructed only in legend or by actual scientific artifice. Icarus's wings melt in the light of historical inquiry, as they were reputed to do in the myth; but was the flying automaton, attributed to a

Chinese scientist of *c.* 380 BC actually in the air for three days, as related? (The same story is told of Archytas of Tarentum.)[1] The mix of fact and fiction is a subject of critical importance for the history of science and technology; for our purposes, the aspirations of semi-mythical inventors can be as revealing as their actual embodiment in levers and gears.

Chinese and Greek traditions are especially rich on the subject of automata. Indian and, somewhat later, Arabic sources are also copious. Western-centered and limited as this article is, I am compelled to note the preeminence of Chinese science and technology in this area. Joseph Needham has made this fact evident in his monumental work, *Science and Civilization in China.*

The wealth of mechanical toys cited in ancient China is awesome. In addition to the flying machine mentioned earlier, mechanized doves and angels, fish, and dragons abounded; automated cup-bearers and wine-pourers were prominent; and hydraulically-moved boats, carrying figures of singing girls, animals, and men in motion are said to have amused the emperors. Of particular interest are the chariots that moved of themselves—*automobiles*—attributed by legend to the scientist Mo Ti in the fourth century BC. Were they actually wheelbarrows, or "pedicarts"? A mechanical man of jade is reported, as well as all kinds of wooden dolls, gold Buddhist statues, and puppet orchestras.

"What is man?" asked such automata, by their actions. "Man is the mechanician" is the most obvious answer. Are humans also machines? Needham cites a long passage, which I repeat here, that vividly gives us the flavor of automata development in China and raises the questions of humans' dual nature. The passage, from the *Lieh Tzu*, whose probable date is the third century BC, tells of how

> King Mu of Chou made a tour of inspection in the west . . . and on his return journey, before reaching China, a certain artificer, Yen Shih by name, was presented to him. The king received him and asked him what he could do. He replied that he would do anything which the king commanded, but that he had a piece of work already finished which he would like to show him. "Bring it with you tomorrow," said the king, "and we will look at it together." So next day Yen Shih appeared again and was admitted into the presence. "Who is that man accompanying you?" asked the king. "That, Sir," replied Yen Shih, "is my own handiwork. He can sing and he can act." The king stared at the figure in astonishment. It walked with rapid strides, moving its head up and down, so that anyone would have taken it for a live human being. The artificer touched its chin, and it began singing, perfectly in tune. He touched its hand, and it began posturing, keeping perfect time. It went through any number of movements that fancy might happen to dictate. The king, looking on

with his favourite concubine and other beauties, could hardly persuade himself that it was not real. As the performance was drawing to an end, the robot winked its eye and made advances to the ladies in attendance, whereupon the king became incensed and would have had Yen Shih executed on the spot had not the latter, in mortal fear, instantly taken the robot to pieces to let him see what it really was. And, indeed, it turned out to be only a construction of leather, wood, glue and lacquer, variously colored white, black, red and blue. Examining it closely, the king found all the internal organs complete—liver, gall, heart, lungs, spleen, kidneys, stomach and intestines; and over these again, muscles, bones and limbs with their joints, skin, teeth and hair, all of them artificial. Not a part but was fashioned with the utmost nicety and skill; and when it was put together again, the figure presented the same appearance as when first brought in. The king tried the effect of taking away the heart, and found that the mouth could no longer speak; he took away the liver and the eyes could no longer see; he took away the kidney and the legs lost their power of locomotion. The king was delighted. Drawing a deep breath, he exclaimed, "Can it be that human skill is on a par with that of the great Author of Nature?"

"Anyone would have taken it for a live human being"—here we have one of the key phrases. The robot makes advances to the ladies and incurs the King's wrath, presenting a sexual threat which is so prevalent, as we shall see, in fears about automata. In the sentence "Can it be that human skill is on a par with that of the great Author of Nature?" is sounded what in the West we know of as the Promethean theme.[2]

The Greeks, too, were absorbed with automata of one kind or another. The Delphic oracles spoke through a wind-operated "voice," and the god Hephaestus is said to have forged a sort of robot of bronze, named "Talos," to guard Crete. Indeed, statues and effigies were themselves god-like: that is, filled with the voices of the gods. We catch this sense of the statue as divine in the writing of Callistratus, in the fourth century AD, about an ivory and gold statue of the god Asclepius: "Shall we admit that the divine spirit descends into human bodies, there to be even defiled by passions, and nevertheless not believe it in a case where there is no attendant engendering of evil? ... for see how an image, after Art has portrayed in it a god, even passes over into the god himself! Matter though it is, it gives forth divine intelligence."[3]

A true history of automata would give all the details, and would cover the ground systematically.[4] I wish merely to highlight the topic, and to pick it up again in more modern times. Note Needham's concluding comment that when the Chinese and European traditions of mechanical toys "came together in the middle of the thirteenth century, the European tradition did not show up to much advantage. The triumphs of the European "Gadget Age" were yet to come."[5]

In the thirteenth century in Europe, for example, we find reports of exemplary mechanical doves and angels made by Villard de Honnecourt. In the fifteenth century, the mathematician and astronomer Johannes Müller constructed an eagle and a fly that astounded his contemporaries. The twentieth-century historian of science Pierre Duhem has proposed a tentative explanation: "The fly, for instance, would beat its wings by means of springs concealed within it, and make the tour of a dinner-table suspended from a hair invisible to the guests, finally approaching the hand of Regiomontanus [Müller] because of a magnet secretly held by him."[6]

In this account, Müller seems as much magician as mechanician. The connection is not accidental, according to Francis Yates and others, who posit a "Hermetic Tradition" in Renaissance science. Yates's argument, for example, is that "the Renaissance magus was the immediate ancestor of the seventeenth-century scientist." In turn, the Renaissance magus "had his roots in the Hermetic core of Renaissance Neo-Platonism."[7]

It was especially Marsilio Ficino, along with Pico della Mirandola, who revived and carried forward the Hermetic tradition into the Renaissance. Ficino translated the collection of treatises that supposedly were written by Hermes Trismegistus, whom he believed to have been a real Egyptian priest and who gave an account, like Moses, of man and the cosmos. In the Hermetic story of creation, however, man is given permission by the Father not only to dominate over the animals, but also to share in the demiurgic powers: that is, to create and animate artificial beings, as we would call them, or, in my terms, machines. Thus, in the Hermetic *Asclepius*, as Yates informs us, "The Egyptian priests . . . are presented as knowing how to capture the effluxes of the stars and through this magical knowledge to animate the statues of their gods."[8]

Alchemy was the Hermetic science *par excellence*. Mere matter could be transformed, for example, into gold, but life also could be distilled from the alchemist's retorts. The other means of creating life out of inanimate matter was through cabalistic conjurations. Small wonder that an air of mystery and magic hung over the Renaissance magus, who rapidly also gained the taint of charlatanism. John Dee, the Elizabethan scientist, is a prime example of the confusion of magic, "chemistry," and mechanics. Called the "great conjurer" for his magic summoning of angels, he was also suspect for his mechanical powers. In vain he protested: "And for . . . marvelous Actes and Feates, Naturally, Mathematically, and Mechanically wrought and contrived, ought any honest Student and Modest Christian Philosopher, be counted and called a Conjurer?"[9]

In the Hermetic tradition of the Renaissance, the ancient fascination with automata took on new life. Magic and mechanics were intertwined, and an air of fear and wonder hovered over the statues and angels conjured out of the earth and air: are they alive and real, or not? Are humans, indeed, mechanicians, who can breathe life into what they have created, thereby imitating their own Creator? Or are they merely machines themselves, working on mechanical principles? In the Hermetic tradition of the Renaissance, these questions are close to the surface, though enveloped in mythical and magical shapes.

A century or two later, having passed through the cleansing and brightening waters of Baconian and Cartesian thought, the automata giving rise to these questions took on, seemingly, a more secular, more reasoned form. In the eighteenth century, one of the most skilled technicians was the Frenchman Jacques de Vaucanson. He produced a duck which, we are told, "drank, ate, digested, cackled, and swam—the whole interior apparatus of digestion exposed, so that it could be viewed; [a] flute player who played twelve different tunes, moving his fingers, lips and tongue, depending on the music; [a] girl who played the tambourine, [and a] mandolin player that moved his head and pretended to breathe."

Even more spectacular were the automata of Pierre Jaquet-Droz, a Swiss, who "in 1774 . . . created a life-sized and lifelike figure of a boy seated at a desk, capable of writing up to forty letters." (He still functions at the History Museum in Neuchâtel.) Droz created another figure called the "Artist," in the shape of a boy that could draw up to four different sketches, improving on the average work of his human counterpart.[10]

These mechanical figures were bathed, at the time of the Enlightenment, in the pure light of reason, and discussion of them took place in unambiguous "scientific" terms. We have already listened to some of the discourse, ranging from Descartes to La Mettrie. Underlying this discussion, however, as I shall try to show, ran the fears of the automata, for they posed an "irrational" threat to humans, calling into question their identity, sexuality (the basis of creation?), and powers of domination.

Automata provoked not just fears, but also the promise of creative, Promethean force. The tension between these two aspects of the automaton—at play in various examples of the genre—is most interesting. I shall try to explore the human ambivalence toward automata in a selected group of examples: the "Nightingale" of Hans Christian Andersen's *Fairy Tales*, the creature in *Frankenstein* by Mary Shelley, the "Tiktok" of the Oz stories, the R.U.R. of Karel Capek, and assorted robots of Isaac Asimov.

I could have chosen innumerable other examples, for tales of the automata are legion. Those I have chosen, however, are classic examples (Asimov's are currently becoming so) and illustrate different aspects of the human encounter with the mechanical "other." Andersen's tale hinges on clockwork mechanisms; Shelley's *Frankenstein*—perhaps the dominant Western metaphor for the fourth discontinuity, straddling both biological and mechanical fears—holds an importance which is self-evident and thus deserves extended

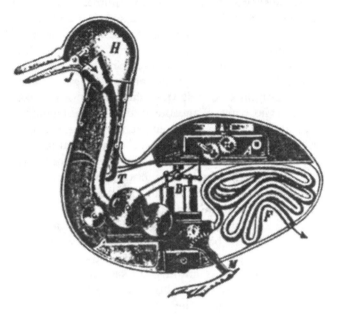

Jacques Vaucanson, *Canard digérant*, from *Le monde des automates* (1928).

treatment; Baum's Oz stories, which obsessively reflect a childlike curiosity about "life," are hardly as innocent as they appear; Capek's R.U.R. gives birth to the term "robot," and voices the fear of robots taking over—a fear echoed today in countless films about menacing androids; and Asimov's varied cast of robots allows us to explore many of the intellectual dimensions of the predicted coming of a robotic age.

Let us begin with Hans Christian Andersen's "The Nightingale," a famous tale from the nineteenth century. It reflects both the scientific concern with automata and the Romantic revulsion towards the mechanical Newtonian world view. Newton had imagined the universe as a clockwork. The clock, with its intricate, precise, and more or less unfailing machinery, symbolized the new age of scientific method and industrial discipline. It also prompted additional speculation about the relation between the internal "works" of human beings and clocks.

In Andersen's tale, we are presented with a "real nightingale" and one that requires a "watchmaker."[11] The tale itself is a simple one. The real nightingale charms a Chinese emperor and his peasants alike. Its song brings tears to their eyes. Subsequently, an artificial nightingale appears, even handsomer than the real one because it is ornamented with precious stones. It appears to sing as well and more repeatedly, and is as well received as the original.

Banished, the real bird flies away. After a year, however, the artificial nightingale begins to break down, and cannot be fully repaired. A few years later, the emperor lays dying, and only the nightingale's song can save him. But the artificial bird has now completely wound down. Suddenly, the live nightingale appears, sings to the emperor, and he comes back to life.

In Andersen's telling, the tale has a poignancy and meaning that cannot be conveyed in a précis. Examined closely, the short story also takes on unexpected ambiguities. The compelling note is the constant comparison between human-made and "natural" things: at the beginning, the croaking of frogs is mistaken for church bells by the courtiers, the nightingale's song for glass bells. The artificial bird and the real nightingale cannot sing well together, "for the real Nightingale sang in its own way, and the artificial bird sang waltzes."[12] At first, the palm seems to go to the mechanical contrivance for "three-and-thirty times over did it sing the same piece, and yet was not tired." Praising it, the artificer explains how "with a real nightingale one can never calculate what is coming, but in this artificial bird everything is settled."

In fact, the artificial bird is neither untiring nor settled. It breaks down, and cannot be repaired. In contrast, the nightingale goes on living, as if for eternity. (While I do not know exactly how long a nightingale can live, I suspect not too many years; of course, new ones can be produced, but so can machines.) Thus, the qualities normally assigned to animate (living) objects and inanimate (non living) objects are reversed: it is the animate that endures. This theme is reiterated at the end, when the real nightingale, symbolizing the forces of life, banishes death: in the words of the emperor. "I banished you from my country and empire, and yet you have charmed away the evil forces from my couch, and banished Death from my heart!"[13]

Through this short story, Andersen is saying that the difference between humans and automata is simple and straightforward: one represents life and the other death, cold and mechanical. It is the Romantic lament. As the nightingale tells the emperor at the end, "I will sing of those who are happy and of those who suffer. I will sing of good and of evil that remain hidden round about you."[14]

Though Andersen's answer to his question about humans and automata is seemingly an untroubled one, it is really surrounded by ambiguous thoughts and feelings. (Andersen had an unhappy youth and occupied his time in solitude by constructing puppet theaters.) His tale is not calculated to satisfy those who felt, and feel, themselves deeply puzzled and disturbed over the mysteries of life and mechanism.

The artificial nightingale is a clockwork figure

Mary Shelley's *Frankenstein* draws on other sources: it reaches back to the Hermetic tradition, to which it adds the threatening aspect of the legendary golem. Badly written, stilted, a pastiche of styles and inspirations, the book nevertheless exercises an uncanny power over us. It is an alchemist's brew of ideas, whose very formlessness allows us to instill in it all the shapes and forms of our own imagination. Frankenstein's monster looms over our most primordial fears and desires, hulking above our ambivalent feelings toward animals and machines, symbolizing the way in which they take on a "life" of their own.

Mary Shelley had no formal education. Nevertheless, being the daughter of Mary Wollstonecraft and William Godwin, she moved into a circle of advanced thought. Influenced by the enlightenment of her time, she also breathed the air of mysticism and romanticism that emanated from the Gothic novels of Walpole and Rutledge, and the poetry of Samuel Taylor Coleridge. Her peculiar genius was to connect the ancient myths with early nineteenth-century science.

The Hermetic tradition seemingly had blessed humans' participation in the demiurge, and looked benignly on their efforts to give life to inanimate statues. In *Frankenstein*, a dark shadow creeps over these efforts: Cornelius Agrippa, Paracelsus, and Albertus Magnus, "canonical" figures in the Hermetic tradition, are all mentioned as the hero's inspirations, but they are shown as Mephistopheles-like figures, leading him to perdition. It is a golem, not the statues of Hermes Trismegistus, that here becomes animated.

Golems may have originated as wooden or clay models of human beings that were placed in graves to act as servants of the dead.[15] In Europe, they take on an especially legendary form in the sixteenth century. The golem, a shapeless mass of clay, could be given form by conjuration: in this case, Jewish cabalism. A rabbi pronounces holy words, and writes on the creature's forehead "Emeth," meaning "truth" in Hebrew, thus endowing it with life. By erasing the "E," the word becomes "Meth," which means "death," and the creature disintegrates. (In another version, the rabbi writes "Shem" [the name of God], but the process is the same.)

The golem is supposedly man's servant. He exists to protect his maker. But in the legends, the golem almost always also threatens its master—running out of control, falling on him, or going berserk—and must finally be destroyed. (The most famous golem is that in the service of Rabbi Loew, in early seventeenth-century Prague.)[16]

Mary Shelley doesn't make overt reference to the golem tales; but they, along with the Hermetic tradition, lie behind her story. Further influences crowd in. Her rationalist father, William Godwin, had written a book, *Lives of the Necromancers*, which, though not published until 1834 (by Mary), reflected earlier conversations between him and his daughter about Agrippa, Paracelsus, Albertus Magnus, the Rosicrucians, and other cabalistic and magus-like sources. Another current of thought—contemporary science, especially chemistry and electricity—came into play in Mary's mind through her husband, Percy Bysshe Shelley. Though a poet, Percy Bysshe Shelley was fascinated by science. Like Godwin, he had read Paracelsus (who, incidentally, was famous for having claimed that he could create "a little man or homunculus"). As a boy, Shelley had also become intrigued with chemistry, and his rooms at Eton are said to have resembled an alchemist's laboratory. He was also exposed, according to one scholar, "to androids, or mechanical toys that functioned like humans—a product of the scientific genius of Adam Walker, to whose lectures he had listened."[17]

At Oxford, Shelley also experimented with electrical machines, air pumps, galvanic batteries, and other such paraphernalia. Though Lord Byron probably encouraged Mary Shelley to read Sir Humphry Davy's *Elements of Chemical Philosophy* (1812) at the time she began the composition of *Frankenstein*, it was her husband, Percy, who really served as the lightning rod, connecting the ancient alchemists and the modern genie of science in her thought. Indeed, it was Percy who urged her on with the book, helped her write it, penned the preface, and secured its publication.

Davy's *Elements*, which hinted at the possibility of discovering a life force—a subtle universal fluid or vital magnetism—dealt with recent researches into galvanism and electricity. Luigi Galvani's work, or what I like to call the "galvanic twitch" (whose movement through nineteenth-century thought has still not been sufficiently traced), had demonstrated the identity of electrical and chemical forces—that is, their interconvertibility. It also suggested that galvanic electricity could bridge the gap between the animate and inanimate; the frog's leg made to twitch seemed to lead to Aldini's experiment in which a shock applied to a recently hanged man produced an effect that, as he wrote, "surpassed our most sanguine expectations, and vitality might perhaps have been restored if many circumstances had not rendered it impossible."[18]

Percy Bysshe Shelley was probably also influenced by the climate of opinion embodied in the term *Natürphilosophie*, though it remains something of a will-o'the-wisp in the history of science except among specialists. An important movement of thought in the early nineteenth century, it has generally been treated with scorn, as befitting a kind of mystical attitude to nature. Though it emphasized vitalism and holism against the dominant materialism and analysis of contemporary Western science (hence, the scorn). both types of philosophy sought to depict the universe as unified and falling under one connecting net of forces, and thus, laws. In any event, *Natürphilosophie* propagated the idea of the interconvertibility of forces, linking the animate and inanimate through galvanism, magnetism (in the form of Mesmerism, it becomes "animal magnetism"), and electricity. Thus animating forces could be made to run between the poles of life and death.

Mary Shelley's knowledge of these developments in science was a hodge-podge; she only dimly and intuitively grasped their meaning. But, like the ancient alchemists, she thought she knew enough to attempt their transmutation into the gold of art—and succeeded, creating an immortal work of

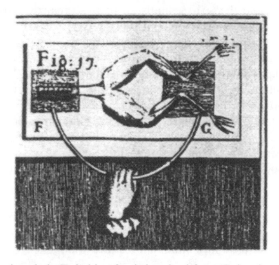

The Galvanic twitch. Twitching frog's legs lead from Galvani to Aldini's experiments, thence to Mary Shelley's *Frankenstein* and the supposed creation of life by means of a spark infused into inaminate materials (Courtesy Burndy Library, Dibner Institute, MIT, Cambridge, MA.)

fiction, *Frankenstein*. In 1816, on the edge of Lake Leman, Geneva, Switzerland, the shreds and tatters of true science were combined with the myths of antiquity.

We can reconstruct *Frankenstein*'s composition. Byron and a friend, Dr. John Polidori, had joined Mary and Percy. Outside their villa a storm rages; the friends amuse and terrify themselves by telling ghost stories. Byron then proposes that each write his or her own. That night, Mary has a nightmare in which, as she tells us, "I saw the hideous phantasm of a man stretched out, and then, on the working of some powerful engine, shows signs of life, and stir with an uneasy, half vital motion." From this nightmare, *Frankenstein* is born.[19]

I have given some of the background to Mary Shelley's book because to do so illustrates vividly the range of human curiosity, embodied in scientific inquiry and legendary stories, concerning the creation of life from inanimate material. "More, far more will I achieve," exclaims Frankenstein, "treading in the steps already marked, I will pioneer a new way, explore unknown powers, and unfold to the world the deepest mysteries of creation."[20] In penetrating these mysteries, the book resurrects and reclothes a number of humanity's deepest concerns about automata: for example, the servant-machine rising against its master, the fear of the machine reproducing itself (fundamentally, a sexual fear, as the example of Caliban in Shakespeare's *Tempest* reminds us, and as we shall see in our further account of Mary

143

Shelley's book), and the terror, finally, of humans realizing that they are at one with the machine-monster.

Such is the fundamental attraction and meaning of *Frankenstein*. But little attention has been given to the actual details of the novel, which has now passed into folklore. For this reason, I will instance material that may be familiar to scholars of the book but not necessarily to the general reader.

First, the name Frankenstein is often given to the monster created, rather than to its creator; yet, in the book, Frankenstein is the name of the scientist, and his abortion has no name. Second, the monster is *not* a machine but a "flesh and blood" product; even a student as informed as the distinguished historian Oscar Handlin makes the typical quick shift when he says, "The monster, however, quickly proves himself the superior. In the confrontation, the machine gives the orders." Third, and last, it is usually forgotten or overlooked that the monster turns to murder *because* his creator, horrified at his production, refuses him human love and kindness. Let us look at a few details.

In writing her Gothic novel in 1816 to 1817, Mary Shelley gave it the subtitle, "The Modern Prometheus." We can see why if we remember that Prometheus defied the gods and gave fire to humankind. Writing from an early nineteenth-century Romantic perspective, Mary Shelley offers Frankenstein as an example of "how dangerous is the acquirement of knowledge." In this case, specifically, the capability of "bestowing animation upon lifeless matter." In the novel we are told of how, having collected his materials from "the dissecting room and the slaughterhouse," Frankenstein eventually completes his loathsome task when he infuses "a spark of being into the lifeless thing that lay at my feet." Then, as he tells us, "now that I had finished, the beauty of the dream vanished, and breathless horror and disgust filled my heart." Rushing from the room, Frankenstein goes to his bedchamber, where he has a most odd dream concerning the corpse of his dead mother (the whole book as well as this passage cries out for psychoanalytic interpretation) from which he is awakened by "the wretch—the miserable monster whom I had created." Aghast at the countenance of what he has created, Frankenstein escapes from the room and out into the open. Upon finally returning to his room with a friend, he is relieved to find the monster gone.

To understand the myth, we need to recite a few further details in this weird story. Frankenstein's monster eventually finds his way to a bovel attached to a cottage, occupied by a blind father and his son and daughter. Unperceived by them, he learns the elements of social life (the fortuitous way in which this occurs may strain the demanding reader's credulity), even to the point of reading *Paradise Lost*. Resolved to end his unbearable solitude, the monster, convinced that his virtues of the heart will win over the cottagers, makes his presence known. The result is predictable: horrified by his appearance, they duplicate the behavior of his creator and flee. In wrath, the monster turns against the heartless world. He kills, and his first victim—by accident—is Frankenstein's young brother.

Pursued by Frankenstein, the creature eventually confronts its creator. The monster explains his road to murder and, in a torrential address, appeals to Frankenstein:

> I entreat you to hear me, before you give vent to your hatred on my devoted head. Have I not suffered enough that you seek to increase my misery? Life, although it may only be an accumulation of anguish, is dear to me, and I will defend it. Remember, thou hast made me more powerful than thyself; my height is superior to thine; my joints more supple. But I will not be tempted to set myself in opposition to thee. I am thy creature, and I will be even mild and docile to my natural lord and king, if thou will also perform thy part, the which thou owest me. Oh, Frankenstein, be not equitable to every other, and trample upon me alone, to whom thy justice, and even thy clemency and affection is most due. Remember, that I am thy creature; I ought to be thy Adam; but I am rather the fallen angel, whom thou drives from joy for no misdeed. Everywhere I see bliss, from which I alone am irrevocably excluded. I was benevolent and good; misery made me a fiend. Make me happy, and I shall again be virtuous.

Eventually, the monster extracts from Frankenstein a promise to create a partner for him "of another sex," with whom he will then retire into the vast wilds of South America, away from the world of men. But Frankenstein's "compassion" does not last long. In his laboratory again, Frankenstein indulges in a long soliloquy:

> I was now about to form another being, of whose dispositions I was alike ignorant; she might become ten thousand times more malignant than her mate; and delight, for its own sake, in murder and wretchedness. He had sworn to quit the neighborhood of man, and hide himself in deserts; but she had not; and she, who in all probability was to become a thinking and reasoning animal, might refuse to comply with a compact made before her creation. They might even hate each other; the creature who already lived loathed his own deformity, and might he not conceive a greater abhorrence for it when it came before his eyes in the female form? She also might quit him, and he be again alone, exasperated by the fresh provocation of being deserted by one of his own species.
>
> Even if they were to leave Europe, and inhabit the deserts of the new world, yet one of the first results of those sympathies for which the demon thirsted would be children, and a race of devils would be

propagated upon the earth who might make the very existence of the species of man a condition precarious and full of terror. Had I right, for my own benefit, to inflict this curse upon everlasting generations?

With the monster observing him through the window, Frankenstein destroys the female companion on whom he had been working.

With this, the novel relentlessly winds its way to its end. In despair, the monster revenges himself by killing Frankenstein's best friend, Clerval, then Frankenstein's new bride, Elizabeth. Fleeing to the frozen north, the monster is tracked down by Frankenstein who dies, however, before he can destroy his dreadful creation. It does not matter; the monster wishes his own death and promises to place himself on a funeral pile and thus at last secure the spiritual peace for which he has yearned.

It is important to be acquainted with the myth of Frankenstein *as actually written* by Mary Shelley. For most of us, Frankenstein is Boris Karloff, clumping around stiff, automatic, and threatening: a machine of sorts. (My students tell me this image is hopelessly out-of-date; for them *Frankenstein* is Gene Wilder in Mel Brooks's film *Young Frankenstein*.) We shall have forgotten completely, if ever we knew, that the monster *cum* machine, is evil, or rather, becomes evil, only because it is spurned by humans.

Implicit in *Frankenstein* is the question of an essential discontinuity. If humans insist on their separateness and superiority with regard to machines (as well as other animals), viewing them as threatening new "species," rather than as a part of their own creation, will they, indeed, bring about the very state of alienation that they fear? Do differences between humans and machines—and it would be a *reductio ad absurdum* to declare that there are none—add up to a discontinuity? Although Frankenstein's creation is, in fact, a monster, its existence raises the same fundamental "mysteries" as if it were a machine; such are the amorphous connecting powers of myth.[21]

Mary Shelley, of course, was writing about creation before Charles Darwin; her "mysteries" are without the benefit of his great work on what he called the "mystery of mysteries." Another Darwin, however, not Charles, was summoned directly to Mary's assistance: Erasmus Darwin, Charles's grandfather. In the preface to *Frankenstein* (actually written by Percy) the opening lines state that "the event on which this fiction is founded has been supposed by Dr. Darwin, and some of the physiological writers of Germany, as not of impossible occurrence."[22] Later, in her introduction to the 1831 edition, Mary recalls how she, her husband, and Lord Byron discussed "the nature of the principles of life, and whether there was any probability of its ever being discovered and communicated. They talked of the experiments of Dr. [Erasmus] Darwin . . . who preserved a piece of vermicelli in a glass case, till by some extraordinary means it began to move with voluntary motion."

In *Frankenstein*, much ambivalence pervades the scientific quest. "What had been the study and desire of the wisest men since the creation of the world was now within my grasp," we are told by Frankenstein, but it involves him in a loathsome search through "vaults and charnel-houses." When he triumphantly announces that he has become "capable of bestowing animation upon lifeless matter," he must surround it with the disclaimer "I am not recording the vision of a madman."[23] His demurral aside, Frankenstein not only symbolizes the "modern Prometheus," over-reaching himself, but also has come to epitomize the "mad scientist," whose hubris has removed him from the circle of humanity. If humans are created in God's world, the monster is spawned in the laboratory. Man, the evil scientist, has taken God's place.

Moreover, the scientist has also taken the place of woman. She has been displaced from the acts of conception and birth. It is the man, Frankenstein, who creates sexlessly. In the novel, sexuality is a threatening force. (In Mary's own life, sex meant death: her mother had died giving birth to her, her best friend had died in childbirth, and so forth; thus the biographical details are important to our understanding her fiction.) If the monster is allowed to breed, it will take over from mankind. In aborting the birth of a mate, as we have seen, Frankenstein reveals not only his revulsion to sexuality, but also his racist fears: a "race of devils" is how he describes the potential new species.

Mary's father, William Godwin, had also envisioned the end of sexuality in his *Enquiry Concerning Political Justice*. As he wrote there, "The whole will be a people of men, and not of children [that is, men will live more or less forever]. Generation will not succeed generation."[24] Diminished sensuality would ensure that the end of generations would also mean the end of the act of generation. Thus, Godwin foresaw a timeless, unchanging utopia where creation had taken place once and for all. Indeed, it was against this illusion that Thomas Malthus wrote his essay, *Population*, insisting that sex— that is, procreation—was one of the necessary postulates of human existence, the other being the necessity of food. If not prevented by moral restraint, procreation leads, in turn, to the threat of overpopulation. When we deal with Charles Darwin, we shall note how reading Malthus helped spark into life Charles Darwin's great theory of evolution by natural selection, giving humans a new, scientific account of genesis.

Mary Shelley, however, echoes her father's hopes and fears. She substitutes the test-tube for the sexual act in *Frankenstein*. What is more, without a real father and mother, the creature thus conceived is without nurturance and development. "No father had watched my infant days," he laments to Frankenstein, "no mother had blessed me with smiles and caresses." Like a fairer creature, Minerva, from Jove's forehead, the monster has sprung full-grown (and larger than man). He is, as a result (because of lack of development), inhuman. Made animate by his scientific creator, he is still like an automaton, ultimately lacking in the qualities that would bridge the discontinuity between him and humans.

In *Frankenstein*, man, in disgust and fear, rejects his own creation. In doing so, he rejects a part of himself, his "double" (recognized unconsciously by readers who refer to the monster as "Frankenstein"), for both Frankenstein and the monster are destroyed at the book's end. Left behind them, in the shape of the gargoyles of the mad scientist and the golem-automaton run amok, is a new-old commandment: "thou shalt not create matter in thine own image."

Frankenstein still gives rise to a *frisson* in modern man, but it has not put a stop to his mechanical ambitions. In fact, the automaton frequently has been domesticated in the form of the robot, and often given a friendly, serving face. One such figure is found in the Oz books for children. He is called Tik-tok, and first appears in *Ozma of Oz* (1907). In this seemingly simple book, many of the fundamental questions surrounding man, animals, and machines are dealt with disarmingly.

L. Frank Baum, the author, seems to have had a genial obsession with the idea of human identity.[25] An American Andersen of sorts, he modernized the timeless. Though in such tales the threatening characters previously were monsters—the giant in "Jack and the Beanstalk"—here they are often humanized and humorous machines. Harmony reigns in the land of Oz among humans, animals, and machines, and even witches are gently laughed away.

We see these elements at play in all of Baum's Oz books, but especially in *Ozma of Oz*, one of his most delightful excursions into our subject.[26] Dedicated to all boys and girls, it starts with Dorothy Gale of Kansas on a boat, then being washed overboard and clinging to a chicken-coop, whose only other occupant is a hen named, by Dorothy, Billina. Unexpectedly, the hen can talk, and when Dorothy says, "I thought hens could only cluck and cackle," the hen replies, "I've clucked and cackled all my life, and never spoken a word before this morning, that I can remember. But when you asked a question, a minute ago, it seemed the most natural thing in the world to answer you. So I spoke, and I seem to keep on speaking, just as you and other human beings do. Strange, isn't it?" Thus, at the beginning of the book, the question of the defining quality of language—humans have language, and hens generally don't—is put before us.

We are, of course, in fairyland (though first the chicken-coop must wash ashore in the land of Ev and of Oz). The point of fairyland, however, is to define "real land" by comparison. When Dorothy urges the hen to eat the egg it has laid, because "You don't need to have your food cooked, as I do," the hen indignantly cries, "Do you take me for a cannibal?" When Dorothy, pursuing the subject, says how dreadful her companion's eating habits are— "Why, eating live things, and horrid bugs, and crawly ants. You ought to be *'shamed* of yourself!"—the unflappable hen responds. "Goodness me! . . . Live things are much fresher and more wholesome than dead ones, and you humans eat all sorts of dead creatures." To Dorothy's denial, Billina instances lambs, sheep—and even chickens. Dorothy's triumphant rejoinder is "but we cook 'em." When the hen questions whether there is any difference, the little girl answers. "A good deal ... I can't just 'splain the difference, but it's there. And, anyhow, we never eat such dreadful things as *bugs*!" The hen's cackling reply leaves Dorothy thoughtful: "But you eat the chickens that eat the bugs ... So you are just as bad as we chickens are."

We seem to be in the presence of a jovial Claude Lévi-Strauss. Humans are cannibalistic animals that cook their food and feel superior to other animals. Speech, however, allows them to examine their own actions. Baum is helping children grope toward a sense of what it is to be human, and different from hens and other animals.

A creature called "The Wheeler" serves as an intermediary between animals, such as Billina, and machines. "It had the form of a man," we are told,

> except that it walked, or rather rolled, upon all fours, and its legs were the same length as its arms, giving them the appearance of the four legs of a beast. Yet it was no beast that Dorothy had discovered, for the person was clothed most gorgeously in embroidered garments of many colors, and wore a straw hat perched jountily upon the side of its head. But it differed from human beings in this respect, that instead of hands and feet there grew at the end of its arms and legs round wheels (30).

Here, clothes seem to be the defining quality of a human, differentiating it from both a machine and an animal.

It is Tik-tok, the Machine Man, however, who occupies the central place in what comes to be a kind of comical Cartesian discourse. Dorothy finds a key that unlocks a door in a rock where she sees

> the form of a man—or, at least, it seemed like a man, in the dim light. He was only about as tall as Dorothy herself, and his body was round as a ball and made out of burnished copper. Also his head and limbs were copper ... "Don't be frightened," Billina calls out. "It isn't alive" (54).

Reassured, Dorothy remembers the Tin Man, and makes a comparison. "But he [the Tin Man] was as alive as we are, 'cause he was born a real man, and got his tin body a little at a time—first a leg and then a finger and then an ear—for the reason that he had so many accidents with his ax." Her conclusion is that, in contrast, the copper man "is not alive at all."

He is a robot. The card around his neck defines him as a "Clock work" that "Thinks, Speaks, Acts" (if you wind him up). He "Does Everything but Live" (55). Everything, that is, except eat, feel either sorrow or joy, be kind

"THIS COPPER MAN IS NOT ALIVE AT ALL"

Tik-tok, the Machine Man. Illustration by John R. Neill, from L. Frank Baum, *Ozma of Oz* (1907). Dorothy explores, with the direct naivete of a child's eye, the difference between humans and machines.

(or unkind), or sleep (these, at least, are the specific differences alluded to in the book). When, however, the Scarecrow claims that, unlike Tik-tok, he has brains, Tik-tok replies, "Oh, yes, I have. I am fit-ted with Smith and Tin-ker's Improved Com-bi-na-tion Steel Brains. They are what make me think" (114–115). Like the animal Billina, the machine Tik-tok has language and brains.

What, then, distinguishes "him" (it?) from humans? The answer seems to reside in the specifics cited, revolving especially around emotions: that is, consciousness of a state of feeling. Also, according to Baum. Tik-tok suffers from the defect of always having to be rewound (but this is merely a technicality—after all, humans have to eat).

Another mechanical figure in the book, "The Giant With the Hammer," *appears* not to suffer from this latter defect (in fact, he seems to continue until turned *off* by a key). On the other hand, unlike Tik-tok, he has no thinking or speaking attachment. A gigantic "man" made out of plates of cast iron, he stands astride the only road into the Kingdom of the Nomes, pounding the earth so that all are too scared to go past. But his very strength—his unwearying mechanical regularity—proves his weakness, and allows him to be defeated. As the Scarecrow points out, all that the members

150

of Dorothy's party have to do is run under the hammer when it is lifted, and pass to the other side before it falls again.

Tik-tok itself is an utterly unthreatening robot. He exists only to serve Dorothy, which he does. In the illustrations, he looks like a copper Humpty-Dumpty. Even the Giant with a Hammer is little to be feared, for he can easily be outwitted because of his mechanical qualities. Automata, in Oz, are domesticated creatures, different from hens and other animals, but no less under human—in fact, a child's—domination.

Robots, however, do not occupy only the sunny fields of Oz in our imagination. They also often take on dark, threatening shapes, such as we have seen in *Frankenstein*. Their more modern incarnation, in Karel Capek's *R.U.R.*,—which introduced the term "robot" into popular usage—reflects similar fears.[27]

Like its Shelleyan predecessor, Capek's play *R.U.R.* (1921; performed in America in 1922), is a poorly written hodge-podge of mostly improbable ideas. (Perhaps this is because a crude style matches the crudeness of its creatures, or because the Gothic is necessarily crude.) In any case, Capek—a Czech—obviously wrote with one eye on the Bolshevik Revolution of 1917, though one cannot be sure of his actual attitude toward that epochal event. Between Act I, which is about the manufacture of robots, and Acts II and III, when they revolt, there is a dichotomy. Yet the play is effective and has come to symbolize much of our feelings about robots.

The play opens when Helena, a beautiful young girl, comes to visit on an island the factory of Rossum's Universal Robots, which is managed by a man, Domin. He immediately falls in love with her and, on her promise not to divulge it, tell her the true story of the invention. (The process itself is secret, preserved in only two copies.) Rossum, he says, was a "great physiologist," who "attempted by chemical synthesis to imitate the living matter known as protoplasm until he suddenly discovered a substance which behaved exactly like living matter." As Domin explains, "This artificial living matter of his has a raging thirst for life. It didn't mind being sewn or mixed together."[28] Thus, old Rossum set about to imitate nature: first, an artificial dog, which took him several years and "resulted in a sort of stunted calf," and then the manufacture of a man.

The dog anticipates or is derivative of Pavlov's; the man reminds us of the creature in *Frankenstein*. Rossum is obviously cast in Frankenstein's image. Domin sardonically calls him "mad . . . the old crank wanted to actually make people" (13). Rossum's "bungling attempt" occupied him for ten years—"It was to have been a man, but it lived for three days only." Then, we are told, "up came young Rossum, an engineer . . . When he saw what a mess of it the old man was making, he said, "It's absurd to spend ten years making a man. If you can't make him quicker than nature, you might as well shut up shop" (14).

Frankenstein-Rossum and his "monstrosities" are pushed aside. Young Rossum is an engineer, not a physiologist, who says to himself: "A man is something that feels happy, plays the piano, likes going for a walk . . . But a working machine must not play the piano, must not feel happy." As Domin concludes, "And to manufacture artificial workers is the same thing as to manufacture . . . motors." (Later, the mechanical metaphor is betrayed when we are told that "there are vats for the preparation of liver, brains . . . and a spinning mill for weaving nerves and veins" (19); consistency was not Capek's strong point.)

All that the worker need do is to work: hence, a robot (from the Czech, *robota*, meaning work). The requirement is to reproduce "the cheapest . . . worker with the minimum amount of requirements." It is as if young Rossum were answering the desires of the classical economists and their "iron law of wages." Only robots are not people. "Mechanically," as Domin defines them, "they are more perfect than we are, they have an enormously developed intelligence, but they have no soul" (17). In fact, we are told that the cost of producing a robot has been brought down within 15 years from $10,000 to $150!

Young Rossum, Domin goes on, "then proceeded [like his father, though he has repudiated the old man] to play at being God." He tried to make a superrobot. "Regular giants they were. He tried to make them twelve feet tall. But you wouldn't believe what a failure they were" (19). In this area Frankenstein seems to have done better.[29]

The robots are constrained not only by size, but by longevity. They have only a 20-year life span. They do not, however, die—which involves a consciousness of death—but simply "get used up." Though they appear lifelike—the young lady, in an amusing bit, mistakes a robot for a live human being, and the human for a robot—dissection proves that they are not. They feel nothing (reminding us of Descartes's views on animals-machines); consequently, one can be accused not of "killing" them, but only of destroying a machine, just as wringing the neck of a chicken is not murder. All is well and peaceable in Rossum's factory.

Trouble enters this mechanical paradise, when, in Act I, Helena pities the robots and wants to treat them as "brothers" and to "show them a little love"—shades of *Frankenstein*! As befitting a play of 1921, the language is also of "liberating" the robots: that is, the workers.

By Act II, Helena is married to Domin, ten years have gone by, and the robots number millions and millions. One of the other humans in the factory, Dr. Gall, under the influence of Helena, has begun to introduce modifications into the manufacture of some of the robots: pain, ostensibly so that they can withdraw their hand from dangerous operations; irritability, so that they begin to show defiance; and other such human attributes.

Capek's argument is really disingenuous. Humans are depicted as "imperfect" machines. "For example," as an engineer explains, "from a technical point of view, the whole of childhood is a sheer absurdity. So much time lost" (42). Humans obviously also waste time with sex. Their intelligence is less than what it might be. Hence, robots are created that are more intelligent and powerful than humans, who have no interest in sex, and are clearly superior. Yet, as soon as this is done, it becomes obvious that Capek considers them *less perfect* than men because they do not have feelings, such as love and fear.

The contradiction becomes clear as the play unfolds in the last two acts. Owing to Dr. Gall and Helena's meddling, a new species of robot is produced that soon starts to go "mad," and ends up in revolt against man. As the robot leader declaims to Helena: "You are not as strong as the Robots. You are not as skillful as the Robots"(91). To her words about equality, he responds, "I want to be master. I want to be master over others" (92). He proclaims to his fellow robots: "We command you to kill all mankind. Spare no man. Spare no woman" (117).

The robots take over the island, and all humans are killed except one "last man," Alquist. Indeed, humans have already, as Dr. Gall noted earlier, "become superfluous" (98). The problem is, however, that the robots, too, are about to die out, for they cannot reproduce themselves. (In a moment of humanitarian fervor, Helena had destroyed the copies detailing the secret process of creating the robots, so as to prevent further manufacture and hence exploitation.) In the Epilogue, the robots command Alquist to rediscover Rossum's secret. However, much as he wishes to do so Alquist lacks the scientific ability. He prays, "Lord . . . if there are no human beings left, at least let there be Robots!—At least the shadow of man!" (164).

At this point, a miracle occurs. Two of Gall's newest robots, a male and a female, enter. They are experiencing strange feelings—love, sexual longing, it appears. Also, "laughter—timidity—protection" (154). To test them, Alquist proposes to take one of them into the dissecting room. When each is prepared to sacrifice him- or herself to save the other, Alquist knows that a new race has been born. "Go, Adam, go, Eve. The world is yours," he says in the last line of the play, "At least the shadow of man!"

I find the whole play incredibly muddled. In the last act and the epilogue, Capek is obviously writing as much about the workers' revolution in Russia as about the robots' uprising in Rossum's factory. On one hand, the play is a kind of Luddite-*Frankenstein* protest against human hubris in the making of machines: Helena's human maid, Nana, exclaims at one point, "All these new-fangled things are an offense to the Lord. It's downright wickedness. Wanting to improve the world after He has made it" (101), and we are not meant to snicker. On the other hand, it seems to preach a certain idealism: that machines can free men from toil and thus allow him to reach for perfection. In Domin's proud, and possibly ironic, words, "He [the human] will not be a machine and a device for production. He will be Lord of creation" (52).

Capek's identification of the robots with the workers of the world, led by

Bolsheviks, is not without roots. Frankenstein's monster, too, was frequently identified by nineteenth-century readers with the rebellious masses. Thus, in the novel *Mary Barton* (1848), Elizabeth Gaskell writes of how "the actions of the uneducated seem to me typified in those of Frankenstein, that monster of many human qualities" and Sir John Lubbock, a conservative scientist, speaking in the House of Commons around 1870 against liberal reform, gave as his reason that he "believed it would be impossible to control the Frankensteins we have ourselves created."[30] (Here they make the typical slip of calling the monster by its maker's name.) Feelings about the right ordering of the social world are thus projected onto the subject of robots.

The social and psychological springs of *R. U. R.* do not mesh smoothly. But even though its theme is unfocused, *R. U. R.* does successfully reflect our primordial feelings about automata, as both promise and threat. Capek's final message is ironic and ultimately baffling, because he posits that the "new man" of the future is a robot—but one that is just like a human in his feelings! Thus, Capek provides a null response to both the threat and the promise. But what is memorable about the play—or accounts of it—is the threat that, like Frankenstein's monster, unless they are first destroyed or emasculated, robots will usurp the world from humans.

R. U. R. was written before robots were used widely in industry and by an author who shows no evidence of having thought much about the science and technology animating them. Nevertheless, the play has achieved canonical status. *I, Robot*, by Isaac Asimov, is a much more thoughtful book—actually, a connected series of short stories—by an informed author, at a time when the presence of robots is becoming real; yet the book is mainly known only to sci-fi fans. It should be read, however, by anyone interested in probing our contemporary feelings toward robots.

Its protagonist is a woman psychologist, Dr. Susan Calvin (whose name, surely, is intended to symbolize the Protestant work ethic); with one or two exceptions, she is one of the few females in the book, with all the other humans and the robots apparently male. So much for the sex problem!

The first story, "Robbie," raises the familiar problems. Robbie is a non-talking "nurse-maid" robot, for little Gloria. While the child loves "him" and thinks of him as "a *person* just like you and me," her mother is actually jealous of Robbie, fears the machine—"it has no soul, and no one knows what it may be thinking"—and thinks "some little jigger will come loose and the awful thing will go berserk."[31] She insists the robot be removed and a collie dog substituted.

Gloria is inconsolable. Her father arranges for a tour of the premises of U.S. Robots and Mechanical Men, Inc., to show his daughter that Robbie is just a machine. When she breaks away to embrace Robbie, whom she sees on the assembly line, she steps in the path of a huge, lumbering tractor. While her father and the others are unable to act fast enough—"The overseers were only human, and it took time to act"—but Robbie, acting "immediately and with precision," saves his little playmate (28). All is forgiven, and Gloria has her mechanical friend to take home.

A contrived tearjerker, the story is effective. It introduces us to our own fears, in a homey, humdrum way. We are told that the event occurred in 1998; as the stories continue, by 2002 mobile speaking robots have been invented, and between 2003 and 2007, most of the world governments—presumably pressured by the mothers of innumerable Glorias—have banned robot use on Earth for any purpose other than scientific research.

As further protection, all robots are bound by "The Three Laws of Robotics":

1   A robot may not injure a human being, or, through inaction, allow a human being to come to harm.
2   A robot must obey the orders given it by human beings except where such orders would conflict with the First Law.
3   A robot must protect its own existence as long as such protection does not conflict with the First or Second Law.

The remaining stories explore variations on one or more of these laws, their applications, and possible violations. Asimov is an interesting logician and rings the changes nicely. In the story "Reason," the robot Cutie pursues logic to its Cartesian conclusion, announcing "I, myself, exist, because I think" (51). Hubris overtakes this robot, who subsequently announces its conversion to the religion of "The Master":

The Master, [it tells the two humans who are in charge of it,] created humans first as the lowest type, most easily formed. Gradually, he replaced them by robots, the next higher step, and finally he created me, to take the place of the last humans. From now on, I serve the Master (53).

The rebellious delusion, however, turns out to be harmless, because Cutie still operates dials and graphs correctly, though claiming it does so in obedience to the Master; and, obedient to the Second Law of Robotics, does not harm humans. As one of its two tenders remarks, "what's the difference what he believes" (63). The incipient danger has been nicely damped down.

It breaks out again in a story in which a robot lies, against the strictest injunction. Finally detected by Dr. Calvin, using a clever piece of logic, it is destroyed. The dark shadow of the robot, however, has grown more menacing. In another story, a robot faced with conflicting demands behaves just as a human might: it suffers a nervous breakdown. Yet, Asimov tries to keep clear the distinction between humans and machines: the machine, he declares, is an "*idiot savante*—it doesn't really understand what it does—it just does it" (129).

The penultimate story, "Evidence," poses the "difference" question most squarely. Is the lawyer Stephen Byerley, running for high political office, a man or a robot who looks exactly like a man? His opponent accuses him of being inhuman, and offers as proof that he never is seen eating. Byerley responds that his habit of eating in private is probably neurotic, but not inhuman. The test finally comes in a public debate when a man emerges from the audience, taunts Byerley, and says "Hit me," pointing out that a robot can't violate the First Law and harm a human. Byerley punches him, thus proving his "humanity," and, of course, wins the election.

Only, as it turns out (though Dr. Calvin alone comes to know), Byerley actually *is* a robot. Created by a crippled human to perform in his place, Byerley has simply struck another robot, cleverly planted in the audience to rise and challenge the original humanoid robot. When Dr. Calvin's colleague is queried about the possibility of such a humanoid robot, he reluctantly admits that

> by using human ova and hormone control, one can grow human flesh and skin over a skeleton of porous silicone plastics that would defy external examination. The eyes, the hair, the skin would be really human, not humanoid. And if you put a positronic brain, and such other gadgets as you might desire inside, you have a humanoid robot" (159–60).

Asimov is not dismayed by this possibility. Like his fictional creation, Dr. Calvin, Asimov believes that robots are "a cleaner better breed than we are" (9). They are decent and logical entities, who as civil executives and "World-Co-ordinators"—Byerley, for example—will run the world and bring peace and prosperity to mankind. Whereas "humans are fallible, also corruptible," machines are only subject to mechanical failure, not wrong results: that is, if fed the correct data.

Like everyone writing about robots, however, Asimov is also ambivalent. Humans, he seems to be saying, still possess a creativity denied to machines.

> The Machine is only a tool after all, which can help humanity pro-gress faster by taking some of the burdens of calculations and inter-pretations off its back. The task of the human brain remains what it has always been; that of discovering new data to be analysed, and of devising new concepts to be tested (187).

Yet, on the very last page of *I, Robot*, the machine appears as Providence, superior to humans but clever enough to hide its superiority so as not to injure human pride. (Earlier, we have seen Cutie making an open avowal of superiority—a clear sign of a kind of madness.) The books ends with Asimov's message:

> How do we know what the ultimate good of Humanity will entail? We haven't at our disposal the infinite factors that the machine has at *its*! Perhaps, to give you a not unfamiliar example, our entire technical civilization has created more unhappiness and misery than it has removed. Perhaps an agrarian or pastoral civilization, with less culture and less people would be better. If so, the Machines must move in that direction, preferably without telling us, since in our ignorant prejudices we only know that what we are used to, is good—and we would then fight change. Or perhaps a complete urbanization, or a completely caste-ridden society, or complete anarchy, is the answer. We don't know. Only the Machines know, and they are going there and taking us with them (192).

It is a wishy-washy conclusion to an intriguing group of stories, in which Asimov cleverly explores both our logical and illogical attitudes toward robots. I have not mentioned, for example, his handling of the "Fundamentalists," who would destroy all machines, or his assumption that in the mid-twenty-first century, robots are still under the control of private, capitalistic enterprises, competing unscrupulously with one another (the cost of a robot is, in this book, $30,000). Overall, however, the book is a provocative rehandling—generally optimistic—of the themes we have been pursuing from Andersen's nightingale through Capek's Rossum's robots.

In spite of the length of this article, I have only touched on the wealth of literature relating to automata. The subject seems to crop up everywhere, in almost everything one reads. Some light on its ubiquity may be shed by "The Uncanny," a strange and difficult paper by Sigmund Freud.[32] Here Freud points to what may be involved, psychologically, in the fear of the inanimate—of automata. Discussing E.T.A. Hoffman's story, "The Sandman" (later part of Offenbach's opera, *Tales of Hoffman*), Freud argues that the feeling of the uncanny arises where we are in doubt as to whether an apparently animate being—an automaton—is really alive, or not.

We need not follow Freud in his specific and tortuous analysis of the story in terms of castration fears, or in his general analysis of the uncanny in terms of animistic mental activity. For our purposes, we need only be inspired to realize that automata, mechanical dolls, and machines of all sorts awaken special undefined fears in us. Does the machine represent a part of ourselves of which we are afraid? Do we project into it our secret, and most forbidden, desires? A moment's reflection on our feelings toward robots, Pygmalion-like statues, or Frankenstein monsters (though this is, as stressed, in fact a flesh-and-blood creation) will confirm the extent of our emotional involvement, even if not its exact nature.

With this as a psychological context, I can use the examples given in this chapter to make the following general points. What are variously called automata, or androids, or robots, are conceived by man as originating either at the hands of gods (for example, the Delphic oracles), or by man using magic (for example, the automata or golems of the Hermetic tradition), or by man using science (for example, the clockwork nightingale, Frankenstein's monster, and Capek's and Asimov's robots). (It would be nice to think of this as a chronological progress, but ancient Chinese scientists obviously used clockwork, and the followers of Hermes Trismegistus used magic very early on; what we find, therefore, is a recurring juxtaposition of the animating forces.) The created figures are either primarily biological or mechanical; flesh and blood or clockwork-machines, animated by a spark or wound up.

However created, whatever the material, they all pose the same compulsive question; how do they differ from humans, or, more simply, what is a human? This is the "uncanny" feeling analyzed by Freud. So, too, they all arouse in us the same range of ambivalent reactions: the sense of a perfection and infallibility to which we aspire—the angel in us—and the sense of the destructive and degrading in us—the ape in us.

Something new is now emerging: the robot as an industrial reality. Still, the same feelings seem to be attached to it. Thus we are told that when a Japanese worker was crushed in a robotics accident, arising from his being in a restricted area and failing to notice that he was in the automatic path of a transport robot (and no "Robbie" to rescue him!), the incident was reported in the press as "though it had been a robot uprising."[33] Will these feelings change as familiarity breeds boredom? In the movie *2001*, Hal the computer rebels; will the memory fade from our dreams?

The fact is that our feelings toward the robot-automaton are caught up anew in our feelings toward its new version, the computer. The robot now becomes the tool!—really, the body—by which the computer—a "brain"—can "move" and take on "animated" form. Automata now take the shape of artificial intelligence machines.[34]

Notes

This essay is adapted from Chapter 3 of my book, *The Fourth Discontinuity: The Co-Evolution of Humans and Machines* (New Haven: Yale UP, 1993). Thanks to Yale UP for granting permission for the adaptation. I would also like to acknowledge the assistance provided by Güven Güzeldere, without whom this article would not have appeared in its present shape. Thanks also to Stefano Franchi and Laura Kerr for editorial help.

1 See Joseph Needham, *Science and Civilization in China*, vol. 4, part 2 (Cambridge: Cambridge UP, 1975) 54. This book is a mine of information on the subject of automata, as well as on its more general subject. Further on automata, compare

Albert Chapuis and Edouard Gélis, *Le monde des automates* (Paris: Chapuis, 1928).

2 Needham, vol. 2, 53. Comparison with statements by LaMettrie spring quickly to mind.

3 Quoted in Julian James, *The origin of Consciousness in the Breakdown of the Bicameral Mind* (Boston: Houghton, 1976) 336.

4 For one such attempt, though a brief one, see John Cohen, *Human Robots in Myths and Science* (London: Allen & Unwin, 1966).

5 Needham, vol. 2. 165.

6 Quoted in Needham, 164.

7 Francis A. Yates, "The Hermetic Tradition in Renaissance Science," *Art, Science, and History in the Renaissance*, ed. Charles S. Singleton (Baltimore: The Johns Hopkins UP, 1967) 258, 255.

8 Yates, 257.

9 Quoted in Yates, 259.

10 Radu Florescu, *In Search of Frankenstein* (Boston: New York Graphics Society, 1929) 233. This is a marvelous work, well printed and illustrated, and, at the time I bought it, a wonderful buy. Compare the article by Michael Uhl, "Living Dolls," *Geo* (July 1985), and its quotation of one observer who delicately noted that Vaucanson's duck duplicated the process of digestion in full view of the spectators, "ending the digestion process as naturally as it began" (86). Thus, long before Pavlov, the idea of a viewable pouch in the stomach was employed, not in a dog, but in an automaton.

11 In the seventeenth century, Sir Kenelm Digby, member of the Royal Society, had already declared that birds were machines, whose motions when feeding their young or building their nests were no different from the striking of the clock or the ringing of an alarm. See Keith Thomas, *Man and the Natural World* (New York: Pantheon, 1983) 35.

12 *Folk-lore and Fable: Aesop, Grimm, Andersen, The Harvard Classics*, ed. Charles W. Eliot (New York: P.F. Collier, 1909) 325. The next quotation is from page 326.

13 Eliot, 328.

14 Eliot, 329.

15 There is some evidence for this origin in Needham, 157.

16 See Florescu, 223–225, for this and other details.

17 Florescu, 329.

18 Giovanni Aldini, *On Galvanism* (London, 1803) 194. Quoted in Michael Kita, "Mary Shelley's *Frankenstein*: Two Contexts," unpub. ms. I owe to it inspiration for some of the above, and what follows on *Natürphilosophie*.

19 See Florescu, 65 ff., for his tracking down the possible influences on Mary, who supposedly visited a Castle Frankenstein in the Rhine country, inhabited in the eighteenth century by a Konrad Dippel, an alchemist accused of strange experiments.

20 Mary Shelley, *Frankenstein* (New York: Dell, 1975) 46.

21 In fact, Mary Shelley herself, in a subsequent novel, *The Last Man* (1826), makes the connection when she writes about man as an "automaton of flesh . . . with joints and strings in order." Quoted in William A. Walling. *Mary Shelly* (New York: Twayne Publishers, 1972) 93.

22 Shelley, *Frankenstein*, 7. The next quotation is from page 12.

23 Shelley, *Frankenstein*, 51.

24 William Godwin, *Enquiry Concerning Political Justice, and Its Influence on Morals and Happiness*, 3rd ed., vol. 2 (London, 1798) 528.

25 Baum's own identity is not as simple as it might at first appear. Some writers on

Baum see him as a social critic and a populist; see, for example, Henry M. Little-field, "The Wizard of Oz: Parable on Populism," *American Quarterly* 16.1 (Spring, 1964). For an overall treatment, see Raylyn Moore, *Wonderful Wizard Marvelous Land* (Bowling Green, Ohio: Bowling Green UP, 1974), who suggests that "for the first time in the history of the fairy tale, Baum produces monsters which are mechanical, in whole or in part" (143). For a number of critical essays on Baum, see Michael Patrick Hearn, ed., *The Wizard of Oz by L. Frank Baum* (New York: Schocken Books, 1983); also Martin Gardner, "The Royal Historian of Oz," *Order and Surprise* (Buffalo, NY: Prometheus, 1983).

26 L. Frank Baum, *Ozma of Oz* (Chicago: Reilly & Lee, 1907). All further references to this edition are cited within the text.

27 In the *New York Times*, February 11, 1982, there is a claim that "robot" was a term coined by Karel's brother, Josef.

28 Karel Capek, *R.U.R.*, trans. Paul Selver (Garden City, NY: Doubleday, 1923) 10–11. All further references to this edition are cited within the text.

29 In fact, neither Frankenstein nor God could have created a 12 foot man, for it violates a known law concerning size and shape, wherein volume grows more rapidly than surface. For details, see Stephen Jay Gould, "Size and Shape," *Ever Since Darwin* (New York: Norton, 1977). Domin himself has a glimpse of this fact when he adds. "For no reason at all their limbs used to keep snapping off" (16).

30 See Florescu, 14.

31 Isaac Asimov, *I, Robot* (New York: Fawcett Crest, 1970) 16. All further references to this edition are cited within the text. (The title might be intended to suggest either an ironic or an egoistic identification with the author, who is frequently cited as "I. Asimov.") Asimov's more recent book *The Robots of Dawn* (New York: Ballantine Books, 1983) is, unfortunately, not quite up to the standard of its predecessor, being rather repetitious and crude in its attempts at salaciousness. *I. Robot*, itself, however, is a classic.

32 Sigmund Freud, "The Uncanny," *Standard Edition*, vol. 17.

33 *New York Times Magazine*, January 10, 1982: 62.

34 In the fourth chapter of my book, *The Fourth Discontinuity*, I follow up on these points with a discussion of the Industrial Revolution, considering it as a quantum leap in the relationship humans have with machines. In its first phase in the early nineteenth century, artificial intelligence machines as such do not figure in production. Instead, the machine basically replaces manual labor. However, as I show later in chapter seven on Babbage, the artificial intelligence machine is conceptualized and even developed by him, in his arithmetical mill, around 1822–1832, as part and parcel of the mechanizing impulse of the Industrial Revolution. It takes about a century and a half, however, before the computer and the robot (our modern automata) emerge as prime "movers" in the continuing industrial revolution, substituting for brain as well as brawn.

Part II

GENERAL HISTORICAL CONTEXT: FOCUS

5

THEORY OF ROBOTS IN THE SEVENTEENTH AND EIGHTEENTH CENTURIES

J. Cohen

Source: J. Cohen, *Human Robots in Myth and Antiquity*, Taylor & Francis, 1965, pp. 68–80.

I

When all is said, the epoch of modern automata opens with Descartes (1596–1650). He cut clean through the tangle of scholastic cobwebs and proposed that the bodies of animals be regarded as nothing more than complex machines. Caution restrained him from saying as much of man himself, but he went as far as he dared without imperilling his life. Copernicus (1473–1543) and Galileo (1564–1642) before him had revealed the 'mechanistic' laws of nature, but it fell to Descartes to extend the idea of a machine into the domain of living organisms. He adumbrated a fundamental division between matter and mind, and paved the way for Leibnitz's utopian programme—the universal application of mathematics to all problems of nature, man and society. The essence of his distinction is the existence of matter in space by contrast with the non-spatial character of mind.

> 'By body', he wrote in the *Discourse on Method*, 'I understand all that can be terminated by a certain figure; that can be comprised in a certain place, and so fill a certain space as therefrom to exclude every other body; that can be perceived either by touch, sight, hearing, taste, or smell; that can be moved in different ways, not indeed of itself, but by something foreign to it by which it is touched (and from which it receives the impression); for the power of self-motion, *as likewise that of perceiving and thinking, I held as by no means pertaining to the nature of body* (my italics); on the contrary, I was somewhat astonished to find such faculties existing in some bodies.'

Descartes must have been influenced by the automata that he had seen or heard about for his description of the human body bears an unmistakable resemblance to the mechanical statues of his time. His representation of the nerves as hollow tubes seems to have been modelled on the bell ropes used to summon a servant. These nerves were supposed to manipulate valves in the head which in turn directed the flow of 'animal spirits' from the brain to the muscles, the pineal gland, in which Descartes located the mind, serving as a master valve which could overrule all the others.[1]

In his basic concept of the flow of 'animal spirits' he employed a hydrostatic model which was not his own creation. The idea is encountered in a more rudimentary form in Homer, who speaks of a 'liquid soul' which has something in common with the sap of trees, the juice of the grape, and the flow of a river. This Homeric image was elevated to the status of a philosophical concept by Thales (640–548 BC), and it has remained persistently popular as a model in neurophysiology. It appealed to Galen (131–201), Haller (1708–1777), Galvani (1737–1798), Mesmer (1733–1815) and, among our contemporaries, to K. R. Lorenz. The idea of *libido*, which also implies a hydrostatic model, and which Freud enthroned at the centre of psychoanalysis, may be derived from the Latin *libare* (= to pour liquid); hence a flow of energy, but whether the word etymologically merits its erotic overtones is a moot question.[2]

There is a story that Descartes himself constructed an automaton which he called *Francine*, and that during a sea voyage, an inquisitive fellow traveller opened the case in which *Francine* was lodged, and brought the robot to the captain, who, thinking that it was the work of a sorcerer, threw it overboard.

II

Descartes found a worthy follower in Bayle (1647–1706), whose scepticism cleared the path for the French encyclopaedists of the eighteenth century. Bayle struggled to prove that the soul of the beast is potentially equal to the soul of man. The difference between man and beast, he argued, is 'accidental' not essential, and due to relatively superficial differences in physical appearance and organs.[3] If so, we face the dilemma: either man's soul is mortal, or that of the beast is immortal.

A point of view sympathetic to the mechanistic philosophy of Descartes is put by Voltaire (1694–1778) in the mouth of a wise old Jansenist, Gordon, in the *Child of Nature*. Gordon explains to a simple savage, a Huron from North America, that everything about us is somehow linked with our physical nature. Every secretion is of advantage to the body; and everything which is good for the body is good for the soul. In short, we are mechanisms in the hand of Providence. All this seems very credible to the Child of Nature, who affirms that 'we resemble little wheels in the huge machine of which God is the soul'. In the same author's *Micromegas* there is a description of the hero's pleasure in observing the movements of those little machines (i.e. men), in scrutinizing their feats, and in following all their doings; and a follower of Leibnitz describes his soul as 'a hand which points to the hour while my body chimes, or, if you like, it is the soul which chimes, while my body points to the hour; or, to put it in another way, my soul is the mirror of the universe, and my body is its frame: that is all clear enough.'

A few years later La Mettrie (1709–1751) startled even his exuberant age with his provocative *L'Homme-Machine*, in which he swept from the universe all non-mechanical factors and transformed the dualism of Descartes into a mechanical monism operating in man to the same degree as in animal. Not only are all animals organized like machines, but the human organism itself, in its entirety, is only a more perfect form of animal-machine. La Mettrie was no doubt encouraged to make his grand extrapolation by the ingenious successes of contemporary horologists. Hence his analogy: 'Man is to the ape, to the most intelligent of animals, as the *pendule planétaire* of Huygens is to a watch of Julien Leroy.'[4] The confusing trends of his day were crystallized by La Mettrie, in masterly fashion, in his conception of 'a graded chain of being in which man and beast are but a link apart.' He seems to have been the first to state the problem of mind in terms of physics, but his actual proof amounts to no more than a statement of empirical correlation between physiological and psychical events. In Vartanian's critical study[5] of *L'Homme-Machine* he puts his finger on one of the chief limitations of La Mettrie's *horloge*-model, namely, its paradoxical timelessness, that is, its insensitivity to duration, which is so vital a feature of human experience. La Mettrie's perspective therefore lacks the irreversibility of biological time. But at the same time he demonstrates the place rightly due to La Mettrie in the history of European thought, his influence on Diderot, D'Holbach and Cabanis, the three principal exponents of psychological materialism, and, above all the fact that for two decades from 1750 to 1770, La Mettrie dominated the intellectual scene. During this period he excelled his contemporaries in the originality and forcefulness of his exposition of the man-machine philosophy. He paid a heavy price for his unorthodoxy: exile from his native France and later from Holland; his book *The Natural History of the Soul* consigned, by Government decree, to the flames; and all his ideas scorned, misrepresented or neglected by posterity. Nearer our own time, another French writer, Henri Barbusse, has expressed much the same view.

'These poor, simple, transparent creatures that move around us, whose destiny is completely in our hands, give us a fragmentary, sketchy but stark view of the great essential profundity of life: the faculty of suffering and that of thinking. This profound life is independent of the luxuries of knowledge which the human branch of the animal world has added to it, and wherever it is found, it is venerable as all nature is. There is in the animal all that there is in man, in a smaller, more humble, more full, more innocent—more visible guise.'[6]

There is perhaps a touch of sentiment in this, for it would be a hard task to prove that there is in the animal *all* that there is in man. The essential continuity assumed by the theory of evolution is compatible with discontinuous, qualitative jumps. Thus while animals can communicate with one another, they are incapable of propositional speech. Nor can any animal be said to commit suicide, because no animal has any foreknowledge of death.

'The problem of the "soul" of animals', as an eighteenth-century French writer declared, 'is comparable to the quest for the philosopher's stone. The task is long, the goal is never to be attained; in compensation, many a precious discovery is made upon the way, and from this labour lost the world at large reaps genuine profit.'[7] There are few questions which have been more passionately and persistently debated. But there are few today who would take a typical eighteenth century view that the entire debate had led to nothing.[8]

The revolutionary views of Descartes put many odd ideas into the heads of his countrymen. In particular, his sharp distinction between mind and matter together with his conception of the mechanical nature of the corporeal world in which man alone of all animals exercises some ghostly control over his own movements became linked with the idea of the *golem*. This provided a convenient target for satirists who wished to pour scorn on mechanistic philosophy in general, while, at the same time, gratifying their desire to tamper playfully with forbidden mysteries.

Naturally, not all the aberrations of Frenchmen can be attributed to Descartes. He cannot be held responsible for Jacques Le Royer, a lawyer, who, in 1660, dedicated a book to Louis XIV in which he claimed a twofold triumph: to have squared the circle and to have invented a perpetual motion machine. He prudently refrained from discovering the philosopher's stone, in case it might ruin commerce, but he hoped to present the king with a self-moving chariot, a galley that dispensed with sails and oars, and a mechanical eagle which carried letters two hundred leagues. What is more, it was his intention to build a house in which all that went on could be heard even by the deaf, and he would demonstrate how the sciences and languages could be quietly mastered, even by young children.[9]

More directly in the Cartesian tradition is Condillac (1715–1780) who, in his *Traité des Sensations* (1754), imagined a statue internally organized as we are, with a *tabula rasa* for a brain, and capable of entertaining all kinds of thoughts. Since it would be made of marble the use of senses such as we possess would be precluded, but Condillac thought of the possibility of opening up sense channels, one by one, as desired, until the statue would be able to service and maintain itself with full adequacy. Condillac's attempt to found a system of psychology on sensationism was no more successful than the efforts of Locke and other British empiricists. He failed to recognize the existence of a wide range of inter-sensory phenomena, but what is more to the point he allowed only for a sensory input from the external world while ignoring the active state of the organism as such—for the brain is never passive and quiescent—and the possibility of an internally generated output.[10] At a neurophysiological level there is evidence of considerable endogenous discharge of neurons of the central nervous system even when there is no overt stimulation from the outside. Unfortunately little is known as to the method whereby the brain distinguishes neural discharges elicited by the external environment from those that belong to its own background activity.[11] The most plausible solution to this problem is that the brain operates statistically on a probabilistic basis, the incoming statistical information being transduced into a subjective probability system.

It remains to add that Condillac's views were 'supplanted' by Cabanis' *Rapports du physique et du moral de l'homme* (1802).

Rumblings hostile to Descartes were not long in coming. An entertaining diatribe was delivered by Cyrano de Bergerac (1619–1655) in his *Estate et empires de la lune*. The story begins with Cyrano, on the moon, a prisoner of the quadrupedal inhabitants. Taking him to be a true beast, they make him entertain them with his tricks charging an admission fee for the performance. One day he meets a fellow biped and their conversation amuses the moon-dwellers who interpret it as an expression of joy at being reunited. Cyrano in time learns the language of his hosts who conclude that he must be a poor specimen of their own species who, by bad luck, has two legs instead of four. But the lunar priests insist that Cyrano and his friend must be monsters, who 'walk in suppliant posture with heads turned heavenward bemoaning their sorry plight and beseeching their Maker to devour our "left-overs"'. The moon-dwellers, say the priests, incline their heads downwards in proud contemplation of their possessions. Cyrano, they decide, is a featherless parrot, and they place him in a cage. But his sparkling wit makes them suspect that he is totally devoid of reason and ruled merely by instinct. This poses an issue for justice which divides the city into two factions; those who believe that Cyrano is witty are excommunicated. At a State Assembly convened to reach a final decision Cyrano defends the philosophy of Aristotle, whereupon the audience concludes that he must be an ostrich, and the verdict is: 'Back to the cage.'[12]

Another valiant blow in the anti-Cartesian campaign was struck by Giles Morfouace de Beaumont in his *L'Apologie des bêtes* (1732). A beast takes the floor and launches a frontal attack on dualism. From time immemorial, he protests, beasts were perfectly free to act reasonably until one day some daring philosopher drew his sword against us, and pedants and ladies of the court flocked to his banner. Yet beasts never fall a prey to avarice or ambition. Nor do they ever indulge in voluptuous excess. Even without the study of medicine, they have the knowledge and skill to cure themselves when sick. They are their own excellent architects, and as meteorologists, they are superior to all the astronomers. They never become alcoholics, nor are they slaves of fashion. They need no criminal law, and they are sensitive to pain. Who could endow a machine with the sensitive soul of a beast or with power of reproduction? The finest doll could never give birth to a baby doll, whereas beasts perpetuate their species.[13]

Beaumont's contemporary, Father Guillaume Hyacinthe Bougeant (1690–1743), boldly staked a claim for animal speech. Animals, he insisted, can not only make themselves perfectly well understood to people, but when they engage in conversation among their own kind, express themselves with much greater ease and fluency. Our humbler animal friends, however, only give utterance to their needs. So they are less loquacious than we are. Also, they have only one way of expressing a given feeling. Nevertheless, they can perceive delicate nuances. Insects and fish, as well as mammals, have a language adequate to their requirements.[14]

Certainly Descartes had set the cat among the pigeons and, to change the metaphor, instigated a battle which, for two centuries, raged furiously among philosophers, poets, divines and scientists in halls of learning and fashionable salons. In a satire which he directed against Descartes, Spinoza (1632–1677) wrote that the golem 'has as much life as any human being, if one accepts the new viewpoint that the relation between body and mind is so loose that it can in a moment be lifted and replaced'. Ironically, as Coleridge remarks (in his *Biographica Literaria*), Spinoza was not above taking a hint or two from Descartes' animal machines, and he in turn constituted a source for Leibnitz's conception of pre-established harmony. An even sharper distaste for the Cartesian doctrine was expressed by England's Lord Chief Justice Sir Matthew Hale[15] (1606–1676) who, in one of his works, *The primitive organization of mankind, considered and examined according to the light of nature*, attacked what he described as two extreme and opposing views on the nature of man: first, the opinion that rates animal capacities too highly; and second, the view that renders living creatures merely mechanisms or 'Artificial Engins', such as the dove of Archytas, the wooden eagle of Regiomontanus or the iron spider of Walchius. This latter fancy, he says, began with Descartes in his *Fundamenta Physica* and was taken up by his admirers.

Cartesian reductionism, he declared, tempted us 'to resolve all the Motions of the reasonable Soul into the like supposition, only by advancing the Engin or *Automaton humanum* into a more curious and complicated constitution: For he that can once suppose that the more various modifications of Matter and Motion, and the due organization of the Bodies of Brutes can produce the admirable operations of Sense, Phantasie, Memory, Appetite, and all those instincts which we find in Brutes; is in a fair way of resolving the operation of Reasonable Nature into the like supposition, only by supposing the organization of the latter somewhat more curiously and exactly disposed and ordered as much above that of Brutes as theirs is above that of Vegetables . . . It is impossible to resolve Perception, Phantasie, Memory, the sagacities and instincts of Brutes, the spontaneousness of many of their animal motions into those Principles, nor are they explicable without supposing some active determinate power, force, or virtue connexed to, and inherent in their Spirits or more subtil pacts, of a higher extraction than the bare natural modification or texture of Matter'. Hale himself presented a third view of his own in which he pleaded for 'a more distinct consideration of the Humane Nature'. His own nature, however, was not humane enough to prevent him from sentencing two witches to death at Bury St Edmunds in 1662 and 1664.

The absolute dualism of Descartes was ridiculed by Coleridge, who speaks of the way 'indiscriminate and irrational solids are thawed down, and distilled, or filtrated by ascension, into living and intelligent fluids, that etch and re-etch engravings on the brain, as (alleged by) the followers of Descartes and the humoral pathologists in general'. In the eyes of Coleridge, Cartesian dualism was about as sensible as the statement that a man's affection for his wife lay North-East or South-West of the love he bore towards his child. Unfortunately he omitted to make clear the logical basis of this analogy.

Faust's *homunculus*, which we have considered in the previous chapter, was itself a satire against the reductionist spirit of the time, an attack against the belief that life could be entirely resolved into specifiable constituents and thus, in principle, be artificially reproducible in the laboratory. Hoffmann and others of the romantic school shared this revulsion from an out-and-out mechanistic philosophy.

The part which Descartes played in the history of automata was not restricted to *Francine* nor even to the profound effects of his mechanization of the animal world. His most decisive contribution was undoubtedly his great faith in the mathematical method. The fact that he was overshadowed in this respect by Leibnitz should not allow us to lose sight of the great impetus he gave to the principle of quantification.

The seventeenth century is specially distinguished by the fact that many of the ablest thinkers were imbued with the idea of extending the use of mathematical methods to every domain of human experience. The inspiration for this came in the first place from Descartes, whose mind was filled with enthusiasm for the *Admirable Science* the full scope of which he believed had been revealed to him. It is not without interest that Descartes, the supreme rationalist, should have come upon his most fertile idea in a dream, the celebrated dream of November 10, 1619, a day at least as memorable as the day the Battle of Hastings was fought. He arrived at the conclusion that the most intractable problems facing mankind would yield to the infallible and universal science of mathematics. Such a faith was an indispensable first stage in the development of modern computers, in particular, and of automation, in general.

Even Descartes does not deserve the entire credit for this. Not only was he indebted to his predecessors, but his contemporary Hobbes, eight years his senior, had announced in the *Leviathan* that 'Geometry is the only science that it hath pleased God to bestow on mankind'.[16] The process of reasoning itself seemed to Hobbes a species of arithmetic for, after all, he asks, what does a man do when he reasons if not 'conceive a sum total, from *Addition* of parcels; or conceive a remainder, from Subtraction of one sum from another'. We are already in sight of Leibnitz's reasoning machine. Hobbes' scheme was to transform ethics and politics into exact sciences by expressing the reasoning they employ in strict geometrical terms. It was this worship of precision which prompted Laurence Sterne to remark that Hobbes' equations 'plussed or minussed you to heaven or hell ... so that none but the expert mathematician would ever be able to settle his accounts with St Peter'. This peril had not deterred Spinoza from writing, in 1677, that the desires and actions of man are no less subject to law than planes and bodies are governed by the principles of geometry.

The first 'robot mathematician' was created by Pascal (1623–1662), whose calculating machine was able to perform the operations of addition and subtraction. The more ambitious Leibnitz, twenty years later, influenced by his early reading of Lull as well as by the example of Descartes, dreamed of a machine that could reason so well as to be able to derive a complete mathematical system of the universe. Like Hobbes (and Plato) he was fascinated by the geometrical method, by the aid of which he tried to solve the problem of choosing a new king of Poland. The argument consisted of sixty propositions, with corollaries, which proved that three candidates should be ruled out and the fourth appointed to the throne. This enthusiasm was displayed when Leibnitz was twenty-five years of age. Two years later he attempted to persuade Louis XIV, again by geometry, to divert his armies from the Low Countries to Egypt. Leibnitz was an even more fervent worshipper at the shrine of geometry than Hobbes had been.

He was persuaded that all disputes, however complex and whatever their philosophical character, would yield to a mathematical analysis. The parties to a dispute need only say to each other: 'Let us calculate'. His mathematical logic out-Lulled Lull himself. It would be foolish, however, to ridicule so great a man as Leibnitz in whose zest we can see the germ of modern game theory. As Todhunter[17] has remarked, there was one topic which appealed to Leibnitz more perhaps than anything else, namely, games of all sorts. This was a sphere of activity, he thought, which would allow ample range for his powers of inventiveness. He was convinced that nowhere had man displayed greater ingenuity than in his amusements. Even the simple games of children, he thought, deserved the attention of the most eminent mathematicians. Here, indeed, was foresight. Three centuries had to elapse before Leibnitz's intuition began to take root, and even now, the mathematical analysis of children's games has barely begun. Leibnitz looked forward to

170

the compilation of a systematic work on games, including those depending on numbers (like playing cards), those depending on position (like chess) and those (like billiards) depending on motion. In this manner the art of thinking, which he described as the art of arts, would come to perfection.

If we turn a blind eye to the brilliant vagaries of Leibnitz, we can afford to be charitable to Erhard Weigel, from whom he had acquired some ideas. Weigel was the author of a Euclidean system of ethics in which the fundamental principles of knowledge are to be found in a science called *Pantometry*.[18] It seems that Leibnitz was soon able to put his finger on the weakness in Weigel's system, which only served to assist the arrangement and retention of ideas, not to derive their logical relationships. Precisely the same shortcoming characterised the topological psychology of Lewin. He too mistook a mere topographical display, which merely *represents* a system, for a truly logical system of topology.

John Craig of Scotland was a rather different kettle of fish. In his *Mathematical Principles of Christian Theology* he computed that in the year 1699 the evidence supporting the Gospel was equal to the witness of twenty-eight disciples, but by the year 3144, the evidence would be reduced to zero.[19] Craig had even more remarkable successors, but none more talented than the Reverend Tresham Gregg, Chaplain of St Mary's within the Church of St Nicholas intra Muros in Dublin who, in 1859, among other notable achievements, translated the eighteenth Psalm into the language of the calculus.

The science of the seventeenth century blossomed into the rationalism of the eighteenth, which in turn flowered into the outright positivism of the nineteenth century. But the arch-positivist, Auguste Comte,[20] rejected the rational philosophy of the eighteenth century on the ground that it was a-historical. It ignored the past, and by this self-denying ordinance, prevented itself from predicting the future. Since prevision, he argued, is the primary goal of all sciences, a-historical rationalism is no way to transform the study of man and society into a positive discipline.

Comte divided history into three epochs. The first he called the 'Theological and Military', a state of society governed by conceptions of a supernatural order. It is an era in which the imagination over-rules the powers of observation, hence precluding objective enquiry. Linked with this mentality is a social structure with an exclusively military character. The second epoch which he named the 'Metaphysical and Juridical', he considered to be of a 'mongrel' nature since it was essentially a transitional link between the first epoch and the third, which he designated the epoch of 'Science and Industry'. Now, observation predominates over imagination in so far as *specific* theoretical ideas are concerned, whereas imagination has only dethroned observation in the field of *general* ideas without yet ascending the throne itself. Comte hit upon a profound but partial truth in identifying the dominance of the imagination in the first epoch; profound, because it is in this sphere that the cultural life of modern man is most impoverished, especially in the supernatural, or as I should rather say, in the transcendental sense; and partial, because he wrongly derogates imagination by comparison with observation.

Time has proved that Comte was misguided in his hostility to the application of mathematics and, in particular, the calculus of probabilities, to the social sciences, and even to physiology. He makes his point clear in relation to physiology. He rightly recognizes that the characteristic feature of organic phenomena (as of all biological phenomena) is their great inherent variability. He sees too that in all physiological phenomena, each effect, whether total or partial, is subject to numerous quantitative changes which follow each other in rapid succession and with apparent irregularity, under the influence of a vast number of causes. Since Comte's day, however, the science of mathematical statistics has developed tools designed to deal with these very problems of the biological world. His error was accordingly twofold: he failed to foresee the great contributions which were to be made by statistical science and he failed, furthermore, to see that the use of the calculus of probabilities is perfectly compatible with an historical perspective in the sciences of man. While we can accept Comte's principle that 'the determination of the Future through the philosophic observation of the Past' is a proper part of scientific inquiry, this in no way rules out techniques of measurement. Comte readily acknowledged the attempt which Condorcet (1743–1794) had made to treat social phenomena by methods of mathematical analysis, an endeavour which was far more realistic than the pious hopes of Hobbes or his spurious successors. Comte recognized too that Condorcet's effort to establish methods of determining the Future were justified in principle. It was not Condorcet's goal of prediction that was faulty but, declared Comte, the endeavour to achieve it by mathematical rather than by historical analysis. At this juncture we return to our point of departure. If we are to single out a culprit for the depreciation of history or, at least, for sharply segregating the domain of history from the domain of science, our accusing finger must point to Descartes. But whatever the shortcomings of his dichotomy, as a heuristic device it proved of paramount importance in providing a schematic framework for the automata makers of the eighteenth century and for the computer algebra of the great Boole in the nineteenth century.

References

1. See Robert K. Lindsay, Information Processing Theory, in W. S. Fields and W. Abbott (eds.) *Information Storage and Neural Control*, Springfield, Illinois: C. C. Thomas, 1963, p. 34.
2. See James Hillman, *Theories of Emotion*, London: Routledge and Kegan Paul, 1960, for an historical sketch of hydrostatic models.
3. See Hester Hastings, *Man and Beast*, Baltimore: The Johns Hopkins Press, 1936, p. 25.

4. The *pendule planétaire* of Huygens was a mechanical model of the solar system which he himself designed and which was executed by the gifted clockmaker Julien Leroy. The model faithfully copied the movements of the planets. See A. Vartanian, La Mettrie's *L'Homme-Machine*, Princeton: Princeton University Press, 1960, p. 136.
5. Vartanian, *op. cit.* The idea of a man-machine, he makes clear, was in the air, but first made its debut in the surreptitious writings of the free-thinkers whose target was not merely the theological dogma of an immortal soul but the socio-political order 'of which the Catholic Church was the ideological prop during the *Ancien Régime*'. It appears that La Mettrie was much indebted to Locke, in spite of divergent views in other respects, principally for his having discredited the Cartesian doctrine of innate ideas. With this obstacle removed, there was no need to postulate a separate mental 'substance'.
6. H. Barbusse, *Zola* (transl. by M. B. and F. C. Green), London: Dent, 1932, pp. 184–5.
7. Quoted by Paul Hazard in his Preface to L. C. Rosenfield, *From Beast-Machine to Man-Machine*, New York: Oxford University Press, 1940.
8. J. A. Guer, *Histoire critique de l'âme des bêtes*, Amsterdam, 1749.
9. See L. Thorndike, *A History of Magic and Experimental Science*, New York: Columbia University Press, 1958, Vol. 2, p. 596.
10. This suggestion is treated at some length in A Perspective for Psychology, in *Readings in Psychology*, ed. by John Cohen, London: Allen and Unwin, 1964, Chap. I.
11. See Mary A. B. Brazier, How can Models from Information Theory be used in Neurophysiology? in *Information Storage and Neural Control* ed. by W. S. Fields and W. Abbott, Springfield, Illinois: C. C. Thomas, 1963, pp. 235–6.
12. See L. C. Rosenfield, *op. cit.*, p. 115 *et seq.*
13. Quoted by Rosenfield, *op. cit.*, p. 167, *et seq.*
14. Guillaume Hyacinthe Bougeant, *Amusement philosophique sur le langage des bêtes*, 1739; (English transl., *A Philosophical Amusement upon the Language of the Beasts*, London: 1739), quoted by Rosenfield, *op. cit.*
15. See R. Hunter and I. Macalpine, *Three Hundred Years of Psychiatry*, 1535–1860, London: Oxford University Press, 1963, pp. 204–6.
16. See Louis I. Bredvold, The Invention of the Ethical Calculus, in *The Seventeenth Century* ed. by R. F. Jones, Stanford: Stanford University Press, 1951, p. 166. Dr Bredvold's survey has been drawn on in these paragraphs.
17. I. Todhunter, *A History of the Theory of Probability*, London: Macmillan, 1865, pp. 47–8.
18. See Bredvold, *op. cit.*
19. Bredvold, *op. cit.*
20. A. Comte, *Early Essays on Social Philosophy*, (transl. by H. D. Hutton) London: Routledge (undated), p. 191.

6

PART FIVE OF *DISCOURSE ON THE METHOD*

R. Descartes

Source: J. Cottingham, R. Stoothoff and D. Murdoch (trans.) *The Philosophical Writings of Descartes* 1637, Cambridge University Press, 1985, pp. 131–41.

I would gladly go on and reveal the whole chain of other truths that I deduced from these first ones. But in order to do this I would have to discuss many questions that are being debated among the learned, and I do not wish to quarrel with them. So it will be better, I think, for me not to do this, and merely to say in general what these questions are, so as to let those who are wiser decide whether it would be useful for the public to be informed more specifically about them. I have always remained firm in the resolution I had taken to assume no principle other than the one I have just used to demonstrate the existence of God and of the soul, and to accept nothing as true which did not seem to me clearer and more certain than the demonstrations of the geometers had hitherto seemed. And yet I venture to say that I have found a way to satisfy myself within a short time about all the principal difficulties usually discussed in philosophy. What is more, I have noticed certain laws which God has so established in nature, and of which he has implanted such notions in our minds, that after adequate reflection we cannot doubt that they are exactly observed in everything which exists or occurs in the world. Moreover, by considering what follows from these laws it seems to me that I have discovered many truths more useful and important than anything I had previously learned or even hoped to learn.

I endeavoured to explain the most important of these truths in a treatise which certain considerations prevent me from publishing, and I know of no better way to make them known than by summarizing its contents. My aim was to include in it everything I thought I knew about the nature of material things before I began to write it. Now a painter cannot represent all the different sides of a solid body equally well on his flat canvas, and so he chooses one of the principal ones, sets it facing the light, and shades the others so as to make them stand out only when viewed from the perspective of the chosen side. In just the same way, fearing that I could not put everything I had in mind into my discourse, I undertook merely to expound quite fully what I understood about light. Then, as the occasion arose, I added something about the sun and fixed stars, because almost all light comes from them; about the heavens, because they transmit light; about planets, comets and the earth, because they reflect light; about terrestrial bodies in particular, because they are either coloured or transparent or luminous; and finally about man, because he observes these bodies. But I did not want to bring these matters too much into the open, for I wished to be free to say what I thought about them without having either to follow or to refute the accepted opinions of the learned. So I decided to leave our world wholly for them to argue about, and to speak solely of what would happen in a new world. I therefore supposed that God now created, somewhere in imaginary spaces, enough matter to compose such a world; that he variously and randomly agitated the different parts of this matter so as to form a chaos as confused as any the poets could invent; and that he then did nothing but lend his regular concurrence to nature, leaving it to act according to the laws he established. First of all, then, I described this matter, trying to represent it so that there is absolutely nothing, I think, which is clearer and more intelligible, with the exception of what has just been said about God and the soul. In fact I expressly supposed that this matter lacked all those forms or qualities about which they dispute in the Schools, and in general that it had only those features the knowledge of which was so natural to our souls that we could not even pretend not to know them. Further, I showed what the laws of nature were, and without basing my arguments on any principle other than the infinite perfections of God, I tried to demonstrate all those laws about which we could have any doubt, and to show that they are such that, even if God created many worlds, there could not be any in which they failed to be observed. After this, I showed how, in consequence of these laws, the greater part of the matter of this chaos had to become disposed and arranged in a certain way, which made it resemble our heavens; and how, at the same time, some of its parts had to form an earth, some planets and comets, and others a sun and fixed stars. Here I dwelt upon the subject of light, explaining at some length the nature of the light that had to be present in the sun and the stars, how from there it travelled instantaneously across the immense distances of the heavens, and how it was reflected from the planets and comets to the earth. To this I added many points about the substance, position, motions and all the various qualities of these heavens and stars; and I thought I had thereby said enough to show that for anything observed in the heavens and stars of our world, something wholly similar had to appear, or at least could appear, in those of the world I was describing. From that I went on to speak of the earth in particular: how, although I had expressly supposed that God had put no gravity into the matter of which it was formed, still all its parts tended exactly towards its centre; how, there being water and air on its surface, the disposition of the heavens and heavenly bodies (chiefly the moon), had to cause an ebb and flow similar in all respects to that observed in our seas, as well as a current of both water and air from east to west like the one we observe between the tropics; how mountains, seas, springs and rivers could be formed naturally there, and how metals could appear in mines, plants grow in fields, and generally how all the bodies we call 'mixed' or 'composite' could come into being there. Among other things, I took pains to make everything belonging to the nature of fire very clearly understandable, because I know nothing else in the world, apart from the heavenly bodies, that produces light. Thus I made clear how it is formed and fuelled, how sometimes it possesses only heat without light, and sometimes light without heat; how it can produce different colours and various other qualities in different bodies; how it melts some bodies and hardens others; how it can consume almost all bodies, or turn them into ashes and smoke; and finally how it can, by the mere force of its action, form glass from these ashes – something I took particular pleasure in describing since it seems to me as wonderful a transmutation as any that takes place in nature.

Yet I did not wish to infer from all this that our world was created in the way I proposed, for it is much more likely that from the beginning God made it just as it had to be. But it is certain, and it is an opinion commonly accepted among theologians, that the act by which God now preserves it is just the same as that by which he created it. So, even if in the beginning God had given the world only the form of a chaos, provided that he established the laws of nature and then lent his concurrence to enable nature to operate as it normally does, we may believe without impugning the miracle of creation that by this means alone all purely material things could in the course of time have come to be just as we now see them. And their nature is much easier to conceive if we see them develop gradually in this way than if we consider them only in their completed form.

From the description of inanimate bodies and plants I went on to describe animals, and in particular men. But I did not yet have sufficient knowledge to speak of them in the same manner as I did of the other things – that is, by demonstrating effects from causes and showing from what seeds and in what manner nature must produce them. So I contented myself with supposing that God formed the body of a man exactly like our own both in the outward shape of its limbs and in the internal arrangement of its organs, using for its composition nothing but the matter that I had described. I supposed, too, that in the beginning God did not place in this body any rational soul or any other thing to serve as a vegetative or sensitive soul, but rather that he kindled in its heart one of those fires without light which I had already explained, and whose nature I understood to be no different from that of the fire which heats hay when it has been stored before it is dry, or which causes new wine to seethe when it is left to ferment from the crushed grapes. And when I looked to see what functions would occur in such a body I found precisely those which may occur in us without our thinking of them, and hence without any contribution from our soul (that is, from that part of us, distinct from the body, whose nature, as I have said previously, is simply to think). These functions are just the ones in which animals without reason may be said to resemble us. But I could find none of the functions which, depending on thought, are the only ones that belong to us as men; though I found all these later on, once I had supposed that God created a rational soul and joined it to this body in a particular way which I described.

But so that you might see how I dealt with this subject, I shall give my explanation of the movement of the heart and the arteries. Being the first and most widespread movement that we observe in animals, it will readily enable us to decide how we ought to think about all the others. But first, so there may be less difficulty in understanding what I shall say, I should like anyone unversed in anatomy to take the trouble, before reading this, to have the heart of some large animal with lungs dissected before him (for such a heart is in all respects sufficiently like that of a man), and to be shown the two chambers or cavities which are present in it. First, there is the cavity on the right, to which two very large tubes are connected: these are the vena cava, which is the principal receptacle of the blood and is like the trunk of a tree of which all the other veins of the body are the branches; and the arterial vein (ill-named because it is really an artery), which originates in the heart and after leaving it divides into many branches that spread throughout the lungs. Then there is the cavity on the left, likewise connected to two tubes which are as large as the others or even larger: the venous artery (also ill-named because it is nothing but a vein), which comes from the lungs where it is divided into many branches intertwined with those of the arterial vein and with those of the windpipe (as it is called) through which the air we breathe enters; and the great artery which goes out from the heart and sends its branches throughout the body. I should also like the reader to be shown the eleven little membranes which, like so many little doors, open and close the four openings within these two cavities. Three are situated at the entrance to the vena cava in such a way that they cannot prevent the blood contained in it from flowing into the right-hand cavity, and yet they effectively prevent it from flowing out. Three at the entrance to the arterial vein do just the opposite, readily permitting the blood in the right-hand cavity to pass into the lungs, but not permitting the blood in the lungs to return into it. Likewise two others at the entrance to the venous artery allow the blood in the lungs to flow into the left-hand cavity of the heart, but block its return; and three at the entrance to the great artery permit blood to leave the heart but prevent it from returning. There is no need to seek any reason for the number of these membranes beyond the fact that the opening to the venous artery, being oval because of its location, can easily be closed with two of them, whereas the other openings, being round, can be closed more effectively with three. I should like the reader also to observe that the great artery and the arterial vein have a much harder and firmer composition than the venous artery and the vena cava, and that the latter widen out before entering the heart to form two pouches, called the auricles, which are composed of flesh similar to that of the heart. He will observe that there is always more heat in the heart than in any other place in the body, and finally, that this heat is capable of causing a drop of blood to swell and expand as soon as it enters a cavity of the heart, just as liquids generally do when they are poured drop by drop into some vessel which is very hot.

After that, I need say little in order to explain the movement of the heart. When its cavities are not full of blood, some blood necessarily flows from the vena cava into the right-hand cavity and from the venous artery into the left-hand cavity, for these two vessels are always full of blood and their entrances, which open into the heart, cannot be blocked. But as soon as two drops of blood have entered the heart in this way, one in each of its cavities, these drops, which must be very large because the openings through which they enter are very wide and the vessels from which they come are very full of blood, are rarefied and expand because of the heat they find there. In this way they make the whole heart swell, and they push against and close the five little doors at the entrance to the two vessels from which they come, thus preventing any more blood from descending to the heart. Continuing to become more and more rarefied, they push open the six other little doors at the entrance to the other two vessels, going out through them and thereby causing all the branches of the arterial vein and of the great artery to swell almost at the same instant as the heart. Immediately afterwards, the heart contracts, as do these arteries as well, because the blood that entered them grows cold, and their six little doors close again while the five doors of the vena cava and the venous artery reopen and allow the passage of two further drops of blood, which immediately makes the heart and the arteries swell, exactly as before. And it is because the blood thus entering the heart passes through the two pouches called the auricles that their movement is contrary to that of the heart, and they contract when it swells. Now those who are ignorant of the force of mathematical demonstrations and unaccustomed to distinguishing true reasons from probable may be tempted to reject this explanation without examining it. To prevent this, I would advise them that the movement I have just explained follows from the mere arrangement of the parts of the heart (which can be seen with the naked eye), from the heat in the heart (which can be felt with the fingers), and from the nature of the blood (which can be known through observation). This movement follows just as necessarily as the movement of a clock follows from the force, position, and shape of its counter-weights and wheels.

One may ask, however, why the blood in the veins is not used up as it flows continually into the heart, and why the arteries are never too full of blood, since all the blood that passes through the heart flows through them. To this

I need give no reply other than that already published by an English physician, who must be praised for having broken the ice on this subject.[1] He is
the first to teach that there are many small passages at the extremities of the
arteries, through which the blood they receive from the heart enters the small
branches of the veins, from there going immediately back to the heart, so
that its course is nothing but a perpetual circulation. He proves this very
effectively by reference to the normal practice of surgeons, who bind an arm
moderately tightly above a vein they have opened, so as to make the blood
flow out more abundantly than if they had not bound the arm. But just
the opposite happens if they bind the arm below, between the hand and the
opening, or even if they bind it very tightly above the opening. For it is
obvious that a moderately tight tourniquet can prevent the blood that is
already in the arm from returning to the heart through the veins, but does
not prevent fresh blood from coming through the arteries. There are two
reasons for this: first, the arteries are situated below the veins and their walls
are harder and hence less easily compressed; and second, the blood which
comes from the heart tends to flow through the arteries to the hand with
more force than it does in returning to the heart through the veins. And since
this blood comes out of the arm through an opening in one of the veins,
there must necessarily be some passages below the tourniquet (that is, towards the extremity of the arm) through which it may flow from the arteries.
Harvey also proves very soundly what he says about the circulation of the
blood by pointing to certain small membranes which are arranged in various
places along the veins in such a way that they do not permit the blood to pass
from the middle of the body towards the extremities but only let it return
from the extremities towards the heart. He proves his theory, moreover, by an
experiment which shows that all the blood in the body can flow out of it in a
very short time through a single artery, even if the artery is tightly bound
close to the heart and cut between the heart and the tourniquet so that no
one could have any reason to imagine that the blood drained off comes from
anywhere but the heart.

But there are many other facts which prove that the true cause of this
movement of the blood is the one I have given. First, there is the difference
we see between the blood which flows from the veins and that which flows
from the arteries. This can result only from the fact that the blood is rarefied
and, as it were, distilled in passing through the heart, and is therefore thinner,
livelier and warmer just after leaving it (that is, when in the arteries) than a
little before entering it (that is, when in the veins). And if you look closely
you will find this difference to be more evident near the heart than in places
further from it. Then there is the hardness of the membranes of which the
arterial vein and the great artery are composed: this shows well enough that
the blood strikes against them with more force than against the veins. And
why should the left-hand cavity of the heart and the great artery be larger
and wider than the right-hand cavity and the arterial vein, if not because the

blood in the venous artery, having been only in the lungs after passing through the heart, is thinner and more easily rarefied than that which comes immediately from the vena cava? And what could physicians learn by feeling the pulse if they did not know that, as the nature of the blood changes, it can be rarefied by the heat of the heart more or less strongly, and more or less quickly, than before? And if we examine how this heat is communicated to the other parts of the body, must we not acknowledge that this happens by means of the blood, which is reheated in passing through the heart and spreads from there through the whole body? So it is that if we remove the blood from some part of the body, we thereupon remove the heat as well; and even if the heart were as hot as glowing iron, it would not be able to reheat the feet and the hands as it does unless it continually sent new blood to these parts. Then, too, we know from this that the true function of respiration is to bring enough fresh air into the lungs to cause the blood entering there from the right-hand cavity of the heart, where it has been rarefied and almost changed into vapours, to thicken immediately into blood again before returning to the left-hand cavity. For if this did not happen the blood would not be fit to serve as fuel for the fire in the heart. This is confirmed by seeing that animals without lungs have only one cavity in their hearts, and that unborn children, who cannot use their lungs while enclosed within their mother's womb, have an opening through which blood flows from the vena cava into the left-hand cavity of the heart, and a tube through which blood comes from the arterial vein into the great artery without passing through the lungs. Again, how would digestion take place in the stomach if the heart did not send heat there through the arteries, together with some of the most fluid parts of the blood which help to dissolve the food we have put there? And is it not easy to understand the action that converts the juice of this food into blood, if we consider that the blood passing in and out of the heart is distilled perhaps more than one or two hundred times each day? Again, what more do we need in order to explain nutrition and the production of the various humours present in the body? We need only say that as the blood is rarefied it flows with such force from the heart towards the extremities of the arteries that some of its parts come to rest in parts of the body where they drive out and displace other parts of the blood; and certain parts of the blood flow to some places rather than others according to the situation, shape, or minuteness of the pores that they encounter, just as sieves with holes of various sizes serve to separate different grains from each other. But the most remarkable of all these facts is the generation of the animal spirits: like a very fine wind, or rather a very pure and lively flame, they rise continuously in great abundance from the heart into the brain, passing from there through the nerves to the muscles and imparting movement to all the parts of the body. The parts of the blood which are the most agitated and penetrating, and hence the best suited to compose these spirits, make their way to the brain rather than elsewhere. For this we need suppose no cause other than the fact that they are carried there by the arteries which come most directly from the heart. For according to the laws of mechanics, which are identical with the laws of nature, when many things tend to move together towards a place where there is not enough room for all of them (as when the parts of blood coming from the left-hand cavity of the heart all tend towards the brain), the weakest and least agitated must be pushed aside by the strongest, which thus arrive at that place on their own.

I explained all these matters in sufficient detail in the treatise I previously intended to publish. And then I showed what structure the nerves and muscles of the human body must have in order to make the animal spirits inside them strong enough to move its limbs – as when we see severed heads continue to move about and bite the earth although they are no longer alive. I also indicated what changes must occur in the brain in order to cause waking, sleep and dreams; how light, sounds, smells, tastes, heat and the other qualities of external objects can imprint various ideas on the brain through the mediation of the senses; and how hunger, thirst, and the other internal passions can also send their ideas there. And I explained which part of the brain must be taken to be the 'common' sense, where these ideas are received; the memory, which preserves them; and the corporeal imagination, which can change them in various ways, form them into new ideas, and, by distributing the animal spirits to the muscles, make the parts of this body move in as many different ways as the parts of our bodies can move without being guided by the will, and in a manner which is just as appropriate to the objects of the senses and the internal passions. This will not seem at all strange to those who know how many kinds of automatons, or moving machines, the skill of man can construct with the use of very few parts, in comparison with the great multitude of bones, muscles, nerves, arteries, veins and all the other parts that are in the body of any animal. For they will regard this body as a machine which, having been made by the hands of God, is incomparably better ordered than any machine that can be devised by man, and contains in itself movements more wonderful than those in any such machine.

I made special efforts to show that if any such machines had the organs and outward shape of a monkey or of some other animal that lacks reason, we should have no means of knowing that they did not possess entirely the same nature as these animals; whereas if any such machines bore a resemblance to our bodies and imitated our actions as closely as possible for all practical purposes, we should still have two very certain means of recognizing that they were not real men. The first is that they could never use words, or put together other signs, as we do in order to declare our thoughts to others. For we can certainly conceive of a machine so constructed that it utters words, and even utters words which correspond to bodily actions causing a change in its organs (e.g. if you touch it in one spot it asks what you want of it, if you touch it in another it cries out that you are hurting it, and so on). But it is not conceivable that such a machine should produce different arrangements of words so as to give an appropriately meaningful answer to whatever is said in its presence, as the dullest of men can do. Secondly, even though such machines might do some things as well as we do them, or perhaps even better, they would inevitably fail in others, which would reveal that they were acting not through understanding but only from the disposition of their organs. For whereas reason is a universal instrument which can be used in all kinds of situations, these organs need some particular disposition for each particular action; hence it is for all practical purposes impossible for a machine to have enough different organs to make it act in all the contingencies of life in the way in which our reason makes us act.

Now in just these two ways we can also know the difference between man and beast. For it is quite remarkable that there are no men so dull-witted or stupid – and this includes even madmen – that they are incapable of arranging various words together and forming an utterance from them in order to make their thoughts understood; whereas there is no other animal, however perfect and well-endowed it may be, that can do the like. This does not happen because they lack the necessary organs, for we see that magpies and parrots can utter words as we do, and yet they cannot speak as we do; that is, they cannot show that they are thinking what they are saying. On the other hand, men born deaf and dumb, and thus deprived of speech-organs as much as the beasts or even more so, normally invent their own signs to make themselves understood by those who, being regularly in their company, have the time to learn their language. This shows not merely that the beasts have less reason than men, but that they have no reason at all. For it patently requires very little reason to be able to speak; and since as much inequality can be observed among the animals of a given species as among human beings, and some animals are more easily trained than others, it would be incredible that a superior specimen of the monkey or parrot species should not be able to speak as well as the stupidest child – or at least as well as a child with a defective brain – if their souls were not completely different in nature from ours. And we must not confuse speech with the natural movements which express passions and which can be imitated by machines as well as by animals. Nor should we think, like some of the ancients, that the beasts speak, although we do not understand their language. For if that were true, then since they have many organs that correspond to ours, they could make themselves understood by us as well as by their fellows. It is also a very remarkable fact that although many animals show more skill than we do in some of their actions, yet the same animals show none at all in many others; so what they do better does not prove that they have any intelligence, for if it did then they would have more intelligence than any of us and would excel us in everything. It proves rather that they have no intelligence at all, and that it is nature which acts in them according to the disposition of their organs. In the same way a clock, consisting only of wheels and springs, can count the hours and measure time more accurately than we can with all our wisdom.

After that, I described the rational soul, and showed that, unlike the other things of which I had spoken, it cannot be derived in any way from the potentiality of matter, but must be specially created.[1] And I showed how it is not sufficient for it to be lodged in the human body like a helmsman in his ship, except perhaps to move its limbs, but that it must be more closely joined and united with the body in order to have, besides this power of movement, feelings and appetites like ours and so constitute a real man. Here I dwelt a little upon the subject of the soul, because it is of the greatest importance. For after the error of those who deny God, which I believe I have already adequately refuted, there is none that leads weak minds further from the straight path of virtue than that of imagining that the souls of the beasts are of the same nature as ours, and hence that after this present life we have nothing to fear or to hope for, any more than flies and ants. But when we know how much the beasts differ from us, we understand much better the arguments which prove that our soul is of a nature entirely independent of the body, and consequently that it is not bound to die with it. And since we cannot see any other causes which destroy the soul, we are naturally led to conclude that it is immortal.

Note

1   William Harvey (1578–1657), whose book on the circulation of the blood, *De Motu Cordis*, was published in 1628 and read by Descartes in 1632.

7

LEVIATHAN, CHAPTER 5 "OF REASON AND SCIENCE"

T. Hobbes

Source: J. Plamenatz (ed.), *Leviathan* HarperCollins Publishers Ltd, 1962, pp. 81–7.

When a man *reasoneth*, he does nothing else but conceive a sum total, from *addition* of parcels; or conceive a remainder, from *subtraction* of one sum from another; which, if it be done by words, is conceiving of the consequence of the names of all the parts, to the name of the whole; or from the names of the whole and one part, to the name of the other part. And though in some things, as in numbers, besides adding and subtracting, men name other operations, as *multilpying* and *dividing*, yet they are the same; for multiplication, is but adding together of things equal; and division, but subtracting of one thing, as often as we can. These operations are not incident to numbers only, but to all manner of things that can be added together, and taken one out of another. For as arithmeticians teach to add and subtract in *numbers*; so the geometricians teach the same in *lines*, *figures*, solid and superficial, *angles*, *proportions, times*, degrees of *swiftness, force, power*, and the like; the logicians teach the same in *consequences of words*; adding together two *names* to make an *affirmation*, and two *affirmations* to make a *syllogism*; and *many syllogisms* to make a *demonstration*; and from the *sum*, or *conclusion* of a *syllogism*, they subtract one *proposition* to find the other. Writers of politics add together *pactions* to find men's *duties*; and lawyers, *laws* and *facts*, to find what is *right* and *wrong* in the actions of private men. In sum, in what matter soever there is place for *addition* and *subtraction*, there also is place for *reason*; and where these have no place, there *reason* has nothing at all to do.

Out of all which we may define, that is to say determine, what that is, which is meant by this word *reason*, when we reckon it amongst the faculties of the mind. For REASON, in this sense, is nothing but *reckoning*, that is adding and subtracting, of the consequences of general names agreed upon for the *marking* and *signifying* of our thoughts; I say *marking* them when we reckon by ourselves, and *signifying*, when we demonstrate or approve our reckonings to other men.

And, as in arithmetic, unpractised men must, and professors themselves may often, err, and cast up false; so also in any other subject of reasoning, the ablest, most attentive, and most practised men may deceive themselves, and infer false conclusions; not but that reason itself is always right reason, as well as arithmetic is a certain and infallible art: but no one man's reason, nor the reason of any one number of men, makes the certainty; no more than an account is therefore well cast up, because a great many men have unanimously approved it. And therefore, as when there is a controversy in an account, the parties must by their own accord, set up, for right reason, the reason of some arbitrator, or judge, to whose sentence they will both stand, or their controversy must either come to blows, or be undecided, for want of a right reason constituted by nature; so is it also in all debates of what kind soever. And when men that think themselves wiser than all others, clamour and demand right reason for judge, yet seek no more, but that things should be determined, by no other men's reason but their own, it is as intolerable in the society of men, as it is in play after trump is turned, to use for trump on every occasion, that suite whereof they have most in their hand. For they do nothing else, that will have every of their passions, as it comes to bear sway in them, to be taken for right reason, and that in their own controversies: bewraying their want of right reason, by the claim they lay to it.

The use and end of reason, is not the finding of the sum and truth of one, or a few consequences, remote from the first definitions, and settled significations of names, but to begin at these, and proceed from one consequence to another. For there can be no certainty of the last conclusion, without a certainty of all those affirmations and negations, on which it was grounded and inferred. As when a master of a family, in taking an account, casteth up the sums of all the bills of expense into one sum, and not regarding how each bill is summed up, by those that give them in account; nor what it is he pays for; he advantages himself no more, than if he allowed the account in gross, trusting to every of the accountants' skill and honesty: so also in reasoning of all other things, he that takes up conclusions on the trust of authors, and doth not fetch them from the first items in every reckoning, which are the significations of names settled by definitions, loses his labour; and does not know anything, but only believeth.

When a man reckons without the use of words, which may be done in particular things, as when upon the sight of any one thing, we conjecture what was likely to have preceded, or is likely to follow upon it; if that which he thought likely to follow, follows not, or that which he thought likely to have preceded it, hath not preceded it, this is called *error*; to which even the most prudent men are subject. But when we reason in words of general signification, and fall upon a general inference which is false, though it be commonly called *error*, it is indeed an *absurdity*, or senseless speech. For

185

error is but a deception, in presuming that somewhat is past, or to come; of which, though it were not past, or not to come, yet there was no impossibility discoverable. But when we make a general assertion, unless it be a true one, the possibility of it is inconceivable. And words whereby we conceive nothing but the sound, are those we call *absurd, insignificant*, and *nonsense*. And therefore if a man should talk to me of a *round quadrangle*; or, *accidents of bread in cheese*; or, *immaterial substances*; or of *a free subject*; *a free will*; or any *free*, but free from being hindered by opposition, I should not say he were in an error, but that his words were without meaning, that is to say, absurd.

I have said before, in the second chapter, that a man did excel all other animals in this faculty, that when he conceived any thing whatsoever, he was apt to inquire the consequences of it, and what effects he could do with it. And now I add this other degree of the same excellence, that he can by words reduce the consequences he finds to general rules, called *theorems*, or *aphorisms*; that is, he can reason, or reckon, not only in number, but in all other things, whereof one may be added unto, or subtracted from another.

But this privilege is allayed by another; and that is, by the privilege of absurdity; to which no living creature is subject, but man only. And of men, those are of all most subject to it, that profess philosophy. For it is most true that Cicero saith of them somewhere; that there can be nothing so absurd, but may be found in the books of philosophers. And the reason is manifest. For there is not one of them that begins his ratiocination from the definitions, or explications of the names they are to use; which is a method that hath been used only in geometry; whose conclusions have thereby been made indisputable.

I. The first cause of absurd conclusions I ascribe to the want of method; in that they begin not their ratiocination from definitions; that is, from settled significations of their words; as if they could cast account, without knowing the value of the numeral words, *one, two* and *three*.

And whereas all bodies enter into account upon divers considerations, which I have mentioned in the precedent chapter; these considerations being diversely named, divers absurdities proceed from the confusion and unfit connexion of their names into assertions. And therefore,

II. The second cause of absurd assertions, I ascribe to the giving of names of *bodies* to *accidents*; or of *accidents* to *bodies*; as they do, that say, *faith is infused*, or *inspired*; when nothing can be *poured*, or *breathed* into anything, but body; and that, *extension is body*; that *phantasms* are *spirits*, &c.

III. The third I ascribe to the giving of the names of the *accidents* of *bodies without us*, to the *accidents* of our *own bodies* as they do that say, the *colour is in the body*; *the sound is in the air*, &c.

IV. The fourth, to the giving of the names of *bodies* to *names*, or *speeches*; as they do that say, that *there be things universal*; that *a living creature is genus*, or *a general thing*, &c.

V. The fifth, to the giving of the names of *accidents* to *names* and *speeches*; as they do that say, *the nature of a thing is its definition*; *a man's command is his will*; and the like.

VI. The sixth, to the use of metaphors, tropes, and other rhetorical figures, instead of words proper. For though it be lawful to say, for example, in common speech, *the way goeth, or leadeth hither, or thither*; *the proverb says this or that*, whereas ways cannot go, nor proverbs speak; yet in reckoning, and seeking of truth, such speeches are not to be admitted.

VII. The seventh, to names that signify nothing; but are taken up, and learned by rote from the schools, as *hypostatical, transubstantiate, consubstantiate, eternal-now*, and the like canting of schoolmen.

To him that can avoid these things it is not easy to fall into any absurdity, unless it be by the length of an account; wherein he may perhaps forget what went before. For all men by nature reason alike, and well, when they have good principles. For who is so stupid, as both to mistake in geometry, and also to persist in it, when another detects his error to him?

By this it appears that reason is not, as sense and memory, born with us; nor gotten by experience only, as prudence is; but attained by industry; first in apt imposing of names; and secondly by getting a good and orderly method in proceeding from the elements, which are names, to assertions made by connexion of one of them to another; and so to syllogisms, which are the connexions of one assertion to another, till we come to a knowledge of all the consequences of names appertaining to the subject in hand; and that is it, men call SCIENCE. And whereas sense and memory are but knowledge of fact, which is a thing past and irrevocable. *Science* is the knowledge of consequences, and dependence of one fact upon another: by which, out of that we can presently do, we know how to do something else when we will, or the like another time; because when we see how any thing comes about, upon what causes, and by what manner; when the like causes come into our power, we see how to make it produce the like effects.

Children therefore are not endued with reason at all, till they have attained the use of speech; but are called reasonable creatures, for the possibility apparent of having the use of reason in time to come. And the most part of men, though they have the use of reasoning a little way, as in numbering to some degree; yet it serves them to little use in common life; in which they govern themselves, some better, some worse, according to their differences of experience, quickness of memory, and inclinations to several ends; but specially according to good or evil fortune, and the errors of one another. For as for *science*, or certain rules of their actions, they are so far from it, that they know not what it is. Geometry they have thought conjuring: but for other sciences, they who have not been taught the beginnings and some progress in them, that they may see how they be acquired and generated, are in this point like children, that having no thought of generation, are made believe by the women that their brothers and sisters are not born, but found in the garden.

But yet they that have no *science*, are in better, and nobler condition, with their natural prudence; than men, that by mis-reasoning, or by trusting them that reason wrong, fall upon false and absurd general rules. For ignorance of causes, and of rules, does not set men so far out of their way, as relying on false rules, and taking for causes of what they aspire to, those that are not so, but rather causes of the contrary.

To conclude, the light of human minds is perspicuous words, but by exact definitions first snuffed, and purged from ambiguity; *reason* is the *pace*; increase of *science*, the *way*; and the benefit of mankind, the *end*. And, on the contrary, metaphors, and senseless and ambiguous words, are like *ignes fatui*; and reasoning upon them is wandering amongst innumerable absurdities; and their end, contention and sedition, or contempt.

As much experience, is *prudence*; so is much science *sapience*. For though we usually have one name of wisdom for them both, yet the Latins did always distinguish between *prudentia* and *sapientia*; ascribing the former to experience, the latter to science. But to make their difference appear more clearly, let us suppose one man endued with an excellent natural use and dexterity in handling his arms; and another to have added to that dexterity, an acquired science, of where he can offend, or be offended by his adversary, in every possible posture or guard: the ability of the former, would be to the ability of the latter, as prudence to sapience; both useful; but the latter infallible. But they that trusting only to the authority of books, follow the blind blindly, are like him that trusting to the false rules of a master of fence, ventures presumptuously upon an adversary, that either kills or disgraces him.

The signs of science are some, certain and infallible; some, uncertain. Certain, when he that pretendeth the science of any thing, can teach the same; that is to say, demonstrate the truth thereof perspicuously to another; uncertain, when only some particular events answer to his pretence, and upon many occasions prove so as he says they must. Signs of prudence are all uncertain; because to observe by experience, and remember all circumstances, that may alter the success, is impossible. But in any business, whereof a man has not infallible science to proceed by; to forsake his own natural judgment, and be guided by general sentences read in authors, and subject to many exceptions, is a sign of folly, and generally scorned by the name of pedantry. And even of those men themselves, that in councils of the commonwealth love to show their reading of politics and history, very few do it in their domestic affairs, where their particular interest is concerned; having prudence enough for their private affairs: but in public they study more the reputation of their own wit, than the success of another's business.

8

PREFACE TO THE GENERAL SCIENCE [1677]

G. Leibniz

Source: P. Wiener (ed.), *Leibniz Selections*, Macmillan Press Ltd, 1951, pp. 12–17.

Since happiness consists in peace of mind, and since durable peace of mind depends on the confidence we have in the future, and since that confidence is based on the science we should have of the nature of God and the soul, it follows that science is necessary for true happiness.

But science depends on demonstration, and the discovery of demonstrations *by a certain Method* is not known to everybody. For while every man is able to judge a demonstration (it would not deserve this name if all those who consider it attentively were not convinced and persuaded by it), nevertheless not every man is able to discover demonstrations on his own initiative, nor to present them distinctly once they are discovered, if he lacks leisure or method.

The *true Method* taken in all of its scope is to my mind a thing hitherto quite unknown, and has not been practised except in mathematics. It is even very imperfect in regard to mathematics itself, as I have had the good fortune to reveal by means of surprising proofs to some of those considered to be among the best mathematicians of the century. And I expect to offer some samples of it, which perhaps will not be considered unworthy of posterity.

However, if the Method of Mathematicians has not sufficed to discover everything that might be expected from them, it has remained at least able to save them from mistakes, and if they have not said everything they were supposed to say, they have also not said anything they were not expected to say.

If those who have cultivated the other sciences had imitated the mathematicians at least on this point, we should be quite content, and we should have long since had a secure Metaphysics, as well as an ethics depending on Metaphysics since the latter includes the sort of knowledge of God and the soul which should rule our life.

In addition, we should have the science of motion which is the key to physics, and consequently, to medicine. True, I believe we are ready now to aspire to it, and some of my first thoughts have been received with such applause by the most learned men of our time on account of the wonderful simplicity introduced, that I believe that all we have to do now is perform certain experiments on a deliberate plan and scale (rather than by the haphazard fumbling which is so common) in order to build thereupon the stronghold of a sure and demonstrative physics.

Now the reason why the art of demonstrating has been until now found only in mathematics has not been well fathomed by the average person, for if the cause of the trouble had been known, the remedy would have long since been found out. The reason is this: Mathematics carries its own test with it. For when I am presented with a false theorem, I do not need to examine or even to know the demonstration, since I shall discover its falsity *a posteriori* by means of an easy experiment, that is, by a calculation, costing no more than paper and ink, which will show the error no matter how small it is. If it were as easy in other matters to verify reasonings by experiments, there would not be such differing opinions. But the trouble is that experiments in physics are difficult and cost a great deal; and in metaphysics they are impossible, unless God out of love for us perform a miracle in order to acquaint us with remote immaterial things.

This difficulty is not insurmountable though at first it may seem so. But those who will take the trouble to consider what I am going to say about it will soon change their mind. We must then notice that the tests or experiments made in mathematics to guard against mistakes in reasoning (as, for example, the test of casting out nines, the calculation of Ludolph of Cologne concerning the magnitude of circles, tables of sines, etc.), these tests are not made on a thing itself, but on the characters which we have substituted in place of the thing. Take for example a numerical calculation: if 1677 times 365 are 612,105, we should hardly ever have reached this result were it necessary to make 365 piles of 1677 pebbles each and then to count them all finally in order to know whether the aforementioned number is found. That is why we are satisfied to do it with characters on paper, by means of the test of nines, etc. Similarly, when we propose an approximately exact value of π in the quadrature of a circle, we do not need to make a big material circle and tie a string around it in order to see whether the ratio of the length of this string or the circumference to the diameter has the value proposed; that would be troublesome, for if the error is one-thousandth or less part of the diameter, we should need a large circle constructed with a great deal of accuracy. Yet we still refute the false value of π by the experiment and use of the calculus or numerical test. But this test is performed only on paper, and consequently, on the characters which represent the thing, and not on the thing itself.

This consideration is fundamental in this matter, and although many persons of great ability, especially in our century, may have claimed to offer us demonstrations in questions of physics, metaphysics, ethics, and even in politics, jurisprudence, and medicine, nevertheless they have either been mistaken (because every step is on slippery ground and it is difficult not to fall unless guided by some tangible directions), or even when they succeed, they have been unable to convince everyone with their reasoning (because there has not yet been a way to examine arguments by means of some easy tests available to everyone).

Whence it is manifest that if we could find characters or signs appropriate for expressing all our thoughts as definitely and as exactly as arithmetic expresses numbers or geometric analysis expresses lines, we could in all subjects *in so far as they are amenable to reasoning* accomplish what is done in Arithmetic and Geometry.

For all inquiries which depend on reasoning would be performed by the transposition of characters and by a kind of calculus, which would immediately facilitate the discovery of beautiful results. For we should not have to break our heads as much as is necessary today, and yet we should be sure of accomplishing everything the given facts allow.

Moreover, we should be able to convince the world what we should have found or concluded, since it would be easy to verify the calculation either by doing it over or by trying tests similar to that of casting out nines in arithmetic. And if someone would doubt my results, I should say to him: "Let us calculate, Sir," and thus by taking to pen and ink, we should soon settle the question.

I still add: *in so far as the reasoning allows on the given facts*. For although certain experiments are always necessary to serve as a basis for reasoning, nevertheless, once these experiments are given, we should derive from them everything which anyone at all could possibly derive; and we should even discover what experiments remain to be done for the clarification of all further doubts. That would be an admirable help, even in political science and medicine, to steady and perfect reasoning concerning given symptoms and circumstances. For even while there will not be enough given circumstances to form an infallible judgment, we shall always be able to determine what is most probable on the data given. And that is all that reason can do.

Now the characters which express all our thoughts will constitute a new language which can be written and spoken; this language will be very difficult to construct, but very easy to learn. It will be quickly accepted by everybody on account of its great utility and its surprising facility, and it will serve wonderfully in communication among various peoples, which will help get it accepted. Those who will write in this language will not make mistakes provided they avoid the errors of calculation, barbarisms, solecisms, and other errors of grammar and construction. In addition, this language will possess the wonderful property of silencing ignorant people. For people will be unable to speak or write about anything except what they understand, or if they try to do so, one of two things will happen: either the vanity of what they advance will be apparent to everybody, or they will learn by writing or speaking. As indeed those who calculate learn by writing and those who speak sometimes meet with a success they did not imagine, the tongue running ahead of the mind. This will happen especially with our language on account of its exactness. So much so, that there will be no equivocations or amphibolies, and everything which will be said intelligibly in that language will be said with propriety. This language will be the greatest instrument of reason.

I dare say that this is the highest effort of the human mind, and when the project will be accomplished it will simply be up to men to be happy since they will have an instrument which will exalt reason no less than what the Telescope does to perfect our vision.

It is one of my ambitions to accomplish this project if God gives me enough time. I owe it to nobody but myself, and I had the first thought about it when I was 18 years old, as I have a little later evidenced in a published treatise (*De Arte Combinatoria*, 1666). And as I am confident that there is no discovery which approaches this one, I believe there is nothing so capable of immortalizing the name of the inventor. But I have much stronger reasons for thinking so, since the religion I follow closely assures me that the love of God consists in an ardent desire to procure the general welfare, and reason teaches me that there is nothing which contributes more to the general welfare of mankind than the perfection of reason.

9

MONADOLOGY

G. Leibniz

Source: S. M. Cahn (ed.), *Classics of Western Philosophy* (3rd edn), Hackett Publishing, 1977, pp. 604–13.

1. The *monad*, which we shall discuss here, is nothing but a simple substance that enters into composites—simple, that is, without parts.

2. And there must be simple substances, since there are composites; for the composite is nothing more than a collection, or *aggregate*, of simples.

3. But where there are no parts, neither extension, nor shape, nor divisibility is possible. These monads are the true atoms of nature and, in brief, the elements of things.

4. There is also no dissolution to fear, and there is no conceivable way in which a simple substance can perish naturally.

5. For the same reason, there is no conceivable way a simple substance can begin naturally, since it cannot be formed by composition.

6. Thus, one can say that monads can only begin or end all at once, that is, they can only begin by creation and end by annihilation, whereas composites begin or end through their parts.

7. There is also no way of explaining how a monad can be altered or changed internally by some other creature, since one cannot transpose anything in it, nor can one conceive of any internal motion that can be excited, directed, augmented, or diminished within it, as can be done in composites, where there can be change among the parts. The monads have no windows through which something can enter or leave. Accidents cannot be detached, nor can they go about outside of substances, as the sensible species of the Scholastics once did. Thus, neither substance nor accident can enter a monad from without.

8. However, monads must have some qualities, otherwise they would not even be beings. And if simple substances did not differ at all in their qualities, there would be no way of perceiving any change in things, since what there is in a composite can only come from its simple ingredients; and if the monads had no qualities, they would be indiscernible from one another, since they

also do not differ in quantity. As a result, assuming a plenum, in motion, each place would always receive only the equivalent of what it already had, and one state of things would be indistinguishable from another.

9. It is also necessary that each monad be different from each other. For there are never two beings in nature that are perfectly alike, two beings in which it is not possible to discover an internal difference, that is, one founded on an intrinsic denomination.

10. I also take for granted that every created being, and consequently the created monad as well, is subject to change, and even that this change is continual in each thing.

11. It follows from what we have just said that the monad's natural changes come from an *internal principle*, since no external cause can influence it internally.

12. But, besides the principle of change, there must be *diversity [un détail]* *in that which changes*, which produces, so to speak, the specification and variety of simple substances.

13. This diversity must involve a multitude in the unity or in the simple. For, since all natural change is produced by degrees, something changes and something remains. As a result, there must be a plurality of properties [*affections*] and relations in the simple substance, although it has no parts.

14. The passing state which involves and represents a multitude in the unity or in the simple substance is nothing other than what one calls *perception*, which should be distinguished from apperception, or consciousness, as will be evident in what follows. This is where the Cartesians have failed badly, since they took no account of the perceptions that we do not apperceive. This is also what made them believe that minds alone are monads and that there are no animal souls or other entelechies. With the common people, they have confused a long stupor with death, properly speaking, which made them fall again into the Scholastic prejudice of completely separated souls, and they have even confirmed unsound minds in the belief in the mortality of souls.

15. The action of the internal principle which brings about the change or passage from one perception to another can be called *appetition*; it is true that the appetite cannot always completely reach the whole perception toward which it tends, but it always obtains something of it, and reaches new perceptions.

16. We ourselves experience a multitude in a simple substance when we find that the least thought we ourselves apperceive involves variety in its object. Thus, all those who recognize that the soul is a simple substance should recognize this multitude in the monad; and Mr. Bayle should not find any difficulty in this as he has done in his *Dictionary* article, "Rorarius."[1]

17. Moreover, we must confess that the *perception*, and what depends on it, is *inexplicable in terms of mechanical reasons*, that is, through shapes and motions. If we imagine that there is a machine whose structure makes it

think, sense, and have perceptions, we could conceive it enlarged, keeping the same proportions, so that we could enter into it, as one enters into a mill. Assuming that, when inspecting its interior, we will only find parts that push one another, and we will never find anything to explain a perception. And so, we should seek perception in the simple substance and not in the composite or in the machine. Furthermore, this is all one can find in the simple substance—that is, perception and their changes. It is also in this alone that all the *internal actions* of simple substances can consist.

18. One can call all simple substances or created monads entelechies, for they have in themselves a certain perfection (*echousi to enteles*); they have a sufficiency (*autarkeia*) that makes them the sources of their internal actions, and, so to speak, incorporeal automata.

19. If we wish to call *soul* anything that has *perceptions* and *appetites* in the general sense I have just explained, then all simple substances or created monads can be called souls. But, since sensation is something more than a simple perception, I think that the general name of monad and entelechy is sufficient for simple substances which only have perceptions, and that we should only call those substances *souls* where perception is more distinct and accompanied by memory.

20. For we experience within ourselves a state in which we remember nothing and have no distinct perception; this is similar to when we faint or when we are overwhelmed by a deep, dreamless sleep. In this state the soul does not differ sensibly from a simple monad; but since this state does not last, and since the soul emerges from it, our soul is something more.

21. And it does not at all follow that in such a state the simple substance is without any perception. This is not possible for the previous reasons; for it cannot perish, and it also cannot subsist without some property [*affection*], which is nothing other than its perception. But when there is a great multitude of small perceptions in which nothing is distinct, we are stupefied. This is similar to when we continually spin in the same direction several times in succession, from which arises a dizziness that can make us faint and does not allow us to distinguish anything. Death can impart this state to animals for a time.

22. And since every present state of a simple substance is a natural consequence of its preceding state, the present is pregnant with the future.

23. Therefore, since on being awakened from a stupor we apperceive our perceptions, it must be the case that we had some perceptions immediately before, even though we did not apperceive them; for a perception can only come naturally from another perception, as a motion can only come naturally from a motion.

24. From this we see that if, in our perceptions, we had nothing distinct or, so to speak, in relief and stronger in flavor, we would always be in a stupor. And this is the state of bare monads.

25. We also see that nature has given heightened perceptions to animals

from the care she has taken to furnish them organs that collect several rays of light or several waves of air, in order to make them more effectual by bringing them together. There is something similar to this in odor, taste, and touch, and perhaps in many other senses which are unknown to us. I will soon explain how what occurs in the soul represents what occurs in the organs.

26. Memory provides a kind of sequence in souls, which imitates reason, but which must be distinguished from it. We observe that when animals have the perception of something which strikes them, and when they previously had a similar perception of that thing, then, through a representation in their memory, they expect that which was attached to the thing in the preceding perception, and are led to have sensations similar to those they had before. For example, if we show dogs a stick, they remember the pain that it caused them and they flee.

27. And the strong imagination that strikes and moves them comes from the magnitude or the multitude of the preceding perceptions. For often a strong impression produces, all at once, the effect produced by a long *habit* or by many lesser, reiterated perceptions.

28. Men act like beasts insofar as the sequence of their perceptions results from the principle of memory alone; they resemble the empirical physicians who practice without theory. We are all mere Empirics in three fourths of our actions. For example, when we expect that the day will dawn tomorrow, we act like an Empiric,[2] because until now it has always been thus. Only the astronomer judges this by reason.

29. But the knowledge of eternal and necessary truths is what distinguishes us from simple animals and furnishes us with *reason* and the sciences, by raising us to a knowledge of ourselves and of God. And that is what we call the rational soul, or *mind*, in ourselves.

30. It is also through the knowledge of necessary truths and through their abstractions that we rise to *reflective acts*, which enable us to think of that which is called "I" and enable us to consider that this or that is in us. And thus, in thinking of ourselves, we think of being, or substance, of the simple and of the composite, of the immaterial and of God himself, by conceiving that that which is limited in us is limitless in him. And these reflective acts furnish the principal objects of our reasonings.

31. Our reasonings are based on *two great principles, that of contradiction*, in virtue of which we judge that which involves a contradiction to be false, and that which is opposed or contradictory to the false to be true.

32. And *that of sufficient reason*, by virtue of which we consider that we can find no true or existent fact, no true assertion, without there being a sufficient reason why it is thus and not otherwise, although most of the time these reasons cannot be known to us.

33. There are also two kinds of *truths*, those of *reasoning* and those of *fact*. The truths of reasoning are necessary and their opposite is impossible;

the truths of fact are contingent, and their opposite is possible. When a truth is necessary, its reason can be found by analysis, resolving it into simpler ideas and simpler truths until we reach the primitives.

34. This is how the speculative *theorems* and practical *canons* of mathematicians are reduced by analysis to *definitions, axioms*, and *postulates*.

35. And there are, finally, *simple ideas*, whose definition cannot be given. There are also axioms and postulates, in brief, *primitive principles*, which cannot be proved and which need no proof. And these are *identical propositions*, whose opposite contains an explicit contradiction.

36. But there must also be a *sufficient reason in contingent truths*, or *truths of fact*, that is, in the series of things distributed throughout the universe of creatures, where the resolution into particular reasons could proceed into unlimited detail because of the immense variety of things in nature and because of the division of bodies to infinity. There is an infinity of past and present shapes and motions that enter into the efficient cause of my present writing, and there is an infinity of small inclinations and dispositions of my soul, present and past, that enter into its final cause.

37. And since all this *detail* involves nothing but other prior or more detailed contingents, each of which needs a similar analysis in order to give its reason, we do not make progress in this way. It must be the case that the sufficient or ultimate reason is outside the sequence or *series* of this multiplicity of contingencies, however infinite it may be.

38. And that is why the ultimate reason of things must be in a necessary substance in which the diversity of changes is only eminent, as in its source. This is what we call *God*.

39. Since this substance is a sufficient reason for all this diversity, which is utterly interconnected, *there is only one God, and this God is sufficient.*

40. We can also judge that this supreme substance which is unique, universal, and necessary must be incapable of limits and must contain as much reality as is possible, insofar as there is nothing outside it which is independent of it, and insofar as it is a simple consequence of its possible existence.

41. From this it follows that God is absolutely perfect—*perfection* being nothing but the magnitude of positive reality considered as such, setting aside the limits or bounds in the things which have it. And here, where there are no limits, that is, in God, perfection is absolutely infinite.

42. It also follows that creatures derive their perfections from God's influence, but that they derive their imperfections from their own nature, which is incapable of being without limits. For it is in this that they are distinguished from God.

43. It is also true that God is not only the source of existences, but also that of essences insofar as they are real, that is, or the source of that which is real in possibility. This is because God's understanding is the realm of eternal truths or that of the ideas on which they depend; without him there

would be nothing real in possibles, and not only would nothing exist, but also nothing would be possible.

44. For if there is reality in essences or possibles, or indeed, in eternal truths, this reality must be grounded in something existent and actual, and consequently, it must be grounded in the existence of the necessary being, in whom essence involves existence, that is, in whom possible being is sufficient for actual being.

45. Thus God alone (or the necessary being) has this privilege, that he must exist if he is possible. And since nothing can prevent the possibility of what is without limits, without negation, and consequently without contradiction, this by itself is sufficient for us to know the existence of God *a priori*. We have also proved this by the reality of the eternal truths. But we have also just proved it *a posteriori* since there are contingent beings, which can only have their final or sufficient reason in the necessary being, a being that has the reason of its existence in itself.

46. However, we should not imagine, as some do, that since the eternal truths depend on God, they are arbitrary and depend on his will, as Descartes appears to have held, and after him Mr. Poiret.[3] This is true only of contingent truths, whose principle is *fitness [convenance]* or the choice of the *best*. But necessary truths depend solely on his understanding, and are its internal object.

47. Thus God alone is the primitive unity or the first [*originaire*] simple substance; all created or derivative monads are products, and are generated, so to speak, by continual fulgurations of the divinity from moment to moment, limited by the receptivity of the creature, to which it is essential to be limited.

48. God has *power*, which is the source of everything, *knowledge*, which contains the diversity of ideas, and finally *will*, which brings about changes or products in accordance with the principle of the best. And these correspond to what, in created monads, is the subject or the basis, the perceptive faculty and the appetitive faculty. But in God these attributes are absolutely infinite or perfect, while in the created monads or in entelechies (or *perfectihabies*, as Hermolaus Barbarus translated that word)[4] they are only imitations of it, in proportion to the perfection that they have.

49. The creature is said to *act* externally insofar as it is perfect, and *to be acted upon [patir]* by another, insofar as it is imperfect. Thus we attribute *action* to a monad insofar as it has distinct perceptions, and *passion*, insofar as it has confused perceptions.

50. And one creature is more perfect than another insofar as one finds in it that which provides an *a priori* reason for what happens in the other; and this is why we say that it acts on the other.

51. But in simple substances the influence of one monad over another can only be ideal, and can only produce its effect through God's intervention, when in the ideas of God a monad rightly demands that God take it into

account in regulating the others from the beginning of things. For, since a created monad cannot have an internal physical influence upon another, this is the only way in which one can depend on another.

52. It is in this way that actions and passions among creatures are mutual. For God, comparing two simple substances, finds in each reasons that require him to adjust the other to it; and consequently, what is active in some respects is passive from another point of view: *active* insofar as what is known distinctly in one serves to explain what happens in another; and *passive* insofar as the reason for what happens in one is found in what is known distinctly in another.

53. Now, since there is an infinity of possible universes in God's ideas, and since only one of them can exist, there must be a sufficient reason for God's choice, a reason which determines him towards one thing rather than another.

54. And this reason can only be found in *fitness*, or in the degree of perfection that these worlds contain, each possible world having the right to claim existence in proportion to the perfection it contains.

55. And this is the cause of the existence of the best, which wisdom makes known to God, which his goodness makes him choose, and which his power makes him produce.

56. This interconnection or accommodation of all created things to each other, and each to all the others, brings it about that each simple substance has relations that express all the others, and consequently, that each simple substance is a perpetual, living mirror of the universe.

57. Just as the same city viewed from different directions appears entirely different and, as it were, multiplied perspectively, in just the same way it happens that, because of the infinite multitude of simple substances, there are, as it were, just as many different universes, which are, nevertheless, only perspectives on a single one, corresponding to the different points of view of each monad.

58. And this is the way of obtaining as much variety as possible, but with the greatest order possible, that is, it is the way of obtaining as much perfection as possible.

59. Moreover, this is the only hypothesis (which I dare say is demonstrated) that properly enhances God's greatness. Mr. Bayle recognized this when, in his *Dictionary* (article "Rorarius"), he set out objections to it; indeed, he was tempted to believe that I ascribed too much to God, more than is possible. But he was unable to present any reason why this universal harmony, which results in every substance expressing exactly all the others through the relations it has to them, is impossible.

60. Furthermore, in what I have just discussed, we can see the *a priori* reasons why things could not be otherwise. Because God, in regulating the whole, had regard for each part, and particularly for each monad, and since the nature of the monad is representative, nothing can limit it to represent

only a part of things. However, it is true that this representation is only confused as to the detail of the whole universe, and can only be distinct for a small portion of things, that is, either for those that are closest, or for those that are greatest with respect to each monad, otherwise each monad would be a divinity. Monads are limited, not as to their objects, but with respect to the modifications of their knowledge of them. Monads all go confusedly to infinity, to the whole; but they are limited and differentiated by the degrees of their distinct perceptions.

61. In this respect, composite substances are analogous to simple substances. For everything is a plenum, which makes all matter interconnected. In a plenum, every motion has some effect on distant bodies, in proportion to their distance. For each body is affected, not only by those in contact with it, and in some way feels the effects of everything that happens to them, but also, through them, it feels the effects of those in contact with the bodies with which it is itself immediately in contact. From this it follows that this communication extends to any distance whatsoever. As a result, every body is affected by everything that happens in the universe, to such an extent that he who sees all can read in each thing what happens everywhere, and even what has happened or what will happen, by observing in the present what is remote in time as well as in space. "All things conspire [*sympnoia panta*]," said Hippocrates. But a soul can read in itself only what is distinctly represented there; it cannot unfold all its folds at once, because they go to infinity.

62. Thus, although each created monad represents the whole universe, it more distinctly represents the body which is particularly affected by it, and whose entelechy it constitutes. And just as this body expresses the whole universe through the interconnection of all matter in the plenum, the soul also represents the whole universe by representing this body, which belongs to it in a particular way.

63. The body belonging to a monad (which is the entelechy or soul of that body) together with an entelechy constitutes what may be called a *living being*, and together with a soul constitutes what is called an *animal*. Now, the body of a living being or an animal is always organized; for, since every monad is a mirror of the universe in its way, and since the universe is regulated in a perfect order, there must also be an order in the representing being, that is, in the perceptions of the soul, and consequently, in the body in accordance with which the universe is represented therein.

64. Thus each organized body of a living being is a kind of divine machine or natural automaton, which infinitely surpasses all artificial automata. For a machine constructed by man's art is not a machine in each of its parts. For example, the tooth of a brass wheel has parts or fragments which, for us, are no longer artificial things, and no longer have any marks to indicate the machine for whose use the wheel was intended. But natural machines, that is, living bodies, are still machines in their least parts, to

infinity. That is the difference between nature and art, that is, between divine art and our art.

65. And the author of nature has been able to practice this divine and infinitely marvelous art, because each portion of matter is not only divisible to infinity, as the ancients have recognized, but is also actually subdivided without end, each part divided into parts having some motion of their own; otherwise, it would be impossible for each portion of matter to express the whole universe.

66. From this we see that there is a world of creatures, of living beings, of animals, of entelechies, of souls in the least part of matter.

67. Each portion of matter can be conceived as a garden full of plants, and as a pond full of fish. But each branch of a plant, each limb of an animal, each drop of its humors, is still another such garden or pond.

68. And although the earth and air lying between the garden plants, or the water lying between the fish of the pond, are neither plant nor fish, they contain yet more of them, though of a subtleness imperceptible to us, most often.

69. Thus there is nothing fallow, sterile, or dead in the universe, no chaos and no confusion except in appearance, almost like it looks in a pond at a distance, where we might see the confused and, so to speak, teeming motion of the fish in the pond, without discerning the fish themselves.

70. Thus we see that each living body has a dominant entelechy, which in the animal is the soul; but the limbs of this living body are full of other living beings, plants, animals, each of which also has its entelechy, or its dominant soul.

71. But we must not imagine, as some who have misunderstood my thought do, that each soul has a mass or portion of matter of its own, always proper to or allotted by it, and that it consequently possesses other lower living beings, forever destined to serve it. For all bodies are in a perpetual flux, like rivers, and parts enter into them and depart from them continually.

72. Thus the soul changes body only little by little and by degrees, so that it is never stripped at once of all its organs. There is often metamorphosis in animals, but there is never metempsychosis nor transmigration of souls; there are also no completely *separated souls*, nor spirits [*Génies*] without bodies. God alone is completely detached from bodies.

73. That is why there is never total generation nor, strictly speaking, perfect death, death consisting in the separation of the soul. And what we call *generations* are developments and growths, as what we call deaths are enfoldings and diminutions.

74. Philosophers have been greatly perplexed about the origin of forms, entelechies, or souls. But today, when exact inquiries on plants, insects, and animals have shown us that organic bodies in nature are never produced from chaos or putrefaction, but always through seeds in which there is, no doubt, some *preformation*, it has been judged that, not only the organic body

was already there before conception, but there was also a soul in this body; in brief, the animal itself was there, and through conception this animal was merely prepared for a great transformation, in order to become an animal of another kind. Something similar is seen outside generation, as when worms become flies, and caterpillars become butterflies.

75. Those *animals*, some of which are raised by conception to the level of the larger animals, can be called *spermatic*. But those of them that remain among those of their kind, that is, the majority, are born, multiply, and are destroyed, just like the larger animals. There are but a small number of Elect that pass onto a larger stage [*théatre*].

76. But this was only half the truth. I have, therefore, held that if the animal never begins naturally, it does not end naturally, either; and not only will there be no generation, but also no complete destruction, nor any death, strictly speaking. These *a posteriori* reasonings, derived from experience, agree perfectly with my principles deduced *a priori*, as above.

77. Thus one can state that not only is the soul (mirror of an indestructible universe) indestructible, but so is the animal itself, even though its mechanism often perishes in part, and casts off or puts on its organic coverings.

78. These principles have given me a way of naturally explaining the union, or rather the conformity of the soul and the organic body. The soul follows its own laws and the body also follows its own; and they agree in virtue of the harmony pre-established between all substances, since they are all representations of a single universe.

79. Souls act according to the laws of final causes, through appetitions, ends, and means. Bodies act according to the laws of efficient causes or of motions. And these two kingdoms, that of efficient causes and that of final causes, are in harmony with each other.

80. Descartes recognized that souls cannot impart a force to bodies because there is always the same quantity of force in matter. However, he thought that the soul could change the direction of bodies. But that is because the law of nature, which also affirms the conservation of the same total direction in matter, was not known at that time. If he had known it, he would have hit upon my system of pre-established harmony.

81. According to this system, bodies act as if there were no souls (though this is impossible); and souls act as if there were no bodies; and both act as if each influenced the other.

82. As for *minds* or rational souls, I find that, at bottom, what we just said holds for all living beings and animals, namely that animals and souls begin only with the world and do not end any more than the world does. However, rational animals have this peculiarity, that their little spermatic animals, as long as they only remain in this state, have only ordinary or sensitive souls. But that as soon as the Elect among them, so to speak, attain human nature by actual conception, their sensitive souls are elevated to the rank of reason and to the prerogative of minds.

83. Among other differences which exist between ordinary souls and minds, some of which I have already noted, there are also the following: that souls, in general, are living mirrors or images of the universe of creatures, but that minds are also images of the divinity itself, or of the author of nature, capable of knowing the system of the universe, and imitating something of it through their schematic representations [*échantillons architectoniques*] of it, each mind being like a little divinity in its own realm.

84. That is what makes minds capable of entering into a kind of society with God, and allows him to be, in relation to them, not only what an inventor is to his machine (as God is in relation to the other creatures) but also what a prince is to his subjects, and even what a father is to his children.

85. From this it is easy to conclude that the collection of all minds must make up the city of God, that is, the most perfect possible state under the most perfect of monarchs.

86. This city of God, this truly universal monarchy, is a moral world within the natural world, and the highest and most divine of God's works. The glory of God truly consists in this city, for he would have none if his greatness and goodness were not known and admired by minds. It is also in relation to this divine city that God has goodness, properly speaking, whereas his wisdom and power are evident everywhere.

87. Since earlier we established a perfect harmony between two natural kingdoms, the one of efficient causes, the other the final causes, we ought to note here yet another harmony between the physical kingdom of nature and the moral kingdom of grace, that is, between God considered as the architect of the mechanism of the universe, and God considered as the monarch of the divine city of minds.

88. This harmony leads things to grace through the very path of nature. For example, this globe must be destroyed and restored by natural means at such times as the governing of minds requires it, for the punishment of some and the reward of others.

89. It can also be said that God the architect pleases in every respect God the legislator, and, as a result, sins must carry their penalty with them by the order of nature, and even in virtue of the mechanical structure of things. Similarly, noble actions will receive their rewards through mechanical means with regard to bodies, even though this cannot, and must not, always happen immediately.

90. Finally, under this perfect government, there will be no good action that is unrewarded, no bad action that goes unpublished, and everything must result in the well-being of the good, that is, of those who are not dissatisfied in this great state, those who trust in providence, after having done their duty, and who love and imitate the author of all good, as they should, finding pleasure in the consideration of his perfections according to the nature of genuinely *pure love*, which takes pleasure in the happiness of the beloved. This is what causes wise and virtuous persons to work for all that

appears to be in conformity with the presumptive or antecedent divine will, and nevertheless, to content themselves with what God brings about by his secret, consequent, or decisive will, since they recognize that if we could understand the order of the universe well enough, we would find that it surpasses all the wishes of the wisest, and that it is impossible to make it better than it is.[5] This is true not only for the whole in general, but also for ourselves in particular, if we are attached, as we should be, to the author of the whole, not only as the architect and efficient cause of our being, but also as to our master and final cause; he ought to be the whole aim of our will, and he alone can make us happy.

Notes

1 [Leibniz's *Theodicy* was, to a large extent, an attempt to answer the skeptical arguments, from Bayle's *Historical and Critical Dictionary*, regarding the imposs-ibility of reconciling faith with reason. "Rorarius," an article of the *Dictionary*, was Bayle's occasion for a discussion of the problem of the souls of animals: Jerome Rorarius (1485–1566) wrote a treatise maintaining that men are less rational than the lower animals. In "Rorarius" Bayle criticizes Leibniz's views.]

2 [The Empirics were a sect of physicians before Galen (ca. A.D. 150). In later times, the epithet "Empiric" was given to physicians who despised theoretical study and trusted tradition and their own experience.]

3 [Pierre Poiret (1646–1719) was initially one of Descartes's followers; he published a book of reflections on God, soul and evil, *Cogitationum rationalium de Deo, anima, et malo libri quattuor* (1677), which was attacked by Bayle.]

4 [Hermolaus Barbarus (1454–93) was an Italian scholar who attempted, through retranslations of Aristotle, to recover Aristotle's original doctrine from under the layers of Scholastic interpretations. His works include popular compendia of ethics and natural philosophy, drawn from the writings of Aristotle.]

5 [The distinction between God's antecedent and consequent will can be found in Thomas Aquinas, *Summa Theologiae 1*, q. 23, art. 2, ad 1.]

10

THE MOTIVES OF JACQUES DE VAUCANSON

David M. Fryer and John C. Marshall

Source: *Technology and Culture* 20, 1979, 257–69.

There are a number of scholars whose names are recorded somewhat grudgingly in histories of science and technology. From among the older members of this select group we might pick out the Greek philosophers Ctesibius and Heron. Despite the intelligence, skill, and sheer brilliance that these men displayed in their inventions, many historians have regarded the great Alexandrians as *pas serieux*. Typical is Hodges's remark that most of their efforts went into "creating interesting gimmicks."[1] A few lines later, Hodges gives the ground of his complaint: "At no time does it seem to have crossed the minds of these ingenious men that their inventions could have been used to provide new sources of power or to make industry more efficient . . ."[2] In like vein, Drachmann claims that Heron's *Pneumatics* "consists mainly of playthings" and that his talents were deployed in the service of "parlor magic"—for entertainment only.[3]

Similar criticisms have been leveled at various 18th-century psychologists, including Henri Maillardet, Pierre Jacquet-Droz and his son Henri-Louis, and Jacques de Vaucanson. After describing a representative sample of their inventions, Brewster writes: "Ingenious and beautiful as all these pieces of mechanism are, and surprising as their effects appear even to scientific spectators, the principal object of their inventions was to astonish and amuse the public."[4]

The immediate link between the Alexandrians and the Europeans—other than their purported lack of interest in increasing the gross national product of their homelands—lies, of course, in the fact that all these men were automata makers. But there are a variety of motives other than the highly laudable one of giving pleasure that could provoke a man to devise artificial singing birds, dancing shepherds, and swinging flute players. One such motive might be the desire to understand how some part of the natural world actually works. Derek de Solla Price[5] and Silvio Bedini[6] have recently argued that many early gadgets and machines were neither "trivial toys" nor "immediately useful inventions." Rather, they were simulacra. That is, the devices were models of a very special sort, models ". . . whose very existence offered tangible proof, more impressive than any theory, that the natural universe of physics and biology was susceptible to mechanistic explication."[7] This leads Price to reverse the usual interpretation of the relationship between high technology and "pure science" in the Hellenistic and Roman world. It is not the case, he suggests, that ". . . certain theories in astronomy and biology derived from man's familiarity with various machines and mechanical devices." On the contrary, ". . . some strong innate urge toward mechanistic explanation led to the making of automata, and . . . from automata has evolved much of our technology . . ."[8] Another alternative might, of course, be that this urge toward mechanistic explanation led both to the construction of automata and to our practical technologies.

With Price's distinctions in mind, we shall attempt to answer the following question: Does the aim of understanding behavior by simulating it also inform the work of Vaucanson, or has the urge degenerated, as Brewster suggests, into the mere desire to amuse by displays of mechanical exuberance?

* * *

There can be no argument over the fact that Vaucanson's automata did indeed delight enthusiastic audiences. Demonstrated to courts, learned societies, and the lay (i.e., paying) public, Vaucanson's fluter player, duck, and tabor-pipe player "astonished all Europe."[9] So great was the demand in London that these mechanical figures could be viewed in operation at the Opera House in the Haymarket "at 1, 2, 5 and 7 o'clock in the Afternoon."[10] When we consider both its imposing physical appearance and its virtuoso performance, it is hardly surprising that the flute player was so popular. According to Brewster, "The body of the flute player was about five and a half feet high, and was placed upon a piece of rock, surrounding a square pedestal four and a half feet high by three and a half wide."[11] The pedestal was packed with machinery, bellows, and the like, and the trunk was riddled with pipes and small reservoirs. "These reservoirs were thus united into one, which, ascending into the throat, formed by its enlargement the cavity of the mouth terminated by two small lips, which rested upon the hole of the flute. These lips had the power of opening more or less, and by a particular mechanism, they could advance or recede from the hole in the flute. Within the cavity of the mouth there is a small movable tongue for opening and shutting the passage for the wind through the lips of the figure."[12]

For the London exhibition, J. I. Desaguliers, LL.D., F.R.S., chaplain to his Royal Highness the Prince of Wales, translated "out of the French Original" two of Vaucanson's most illuminating papers, "A Memoire, to the

Gentlemen of the Royal-Academy of Sciences at Paris" and a letter to the Abbe de Fontaine.[13] The work was printed by T. Parker and sold in the Long Room of the Opera House during the exhibition. It is thanks to this publication that we have a fairly full and accessible record of the philosophy of Jacques de Vaucanson.

What, then, did Vaucanson imagine that he was doing? In the first part of the memoir, he describes in considerable detail the structure of the German flute, its components, and their interrelationships. He also describes how such an instrument is played by a man, specifying the motions of and positions taken up by the lips, tongue, and fingers in obtaining various notes, sequences, and timbres. Finally he discusses the properties of the "strength" and velocity of wind necessary to produce certain effects and mentions the gross anatomy which underlies these variations in the force of the air stream.

The difficulty, however, is to know how these elements—instrument, mouth, fingers, airflow, and so on—work together, simultaneously and sequentially, in a cooperative fashion to produce the desired result. There is a sense in which Vaucanson's seemingly "objective description" is really a hypothesis concerning the mode of operation of man plus flute. Vaucanson accordingly summarizes the position thus: "These, Gentlemen, have been my Thoughts upon the sound of Wind-Instruments and the Manner of modifying it. Upon these Physical Causes I have endeavour'd to found my Enquiries; by imitating the same Mechanism in an *Automaton*, which I endeavour'd to enable to produce the same Effect in making it play on the German Flute."[14]

Vaucanson clearly regards his automaton as a test of the principles he has formulated: "*It will then follow . . . according to the Principle* settled in my First Part, the flute will give a low Sound: and *this is confirmed by Experience*."[15] This theme is stressed in the second part of the memoir. The construction of the automaton is itemized, and each part of of the device is carefully linked with the proper part of the previous functional description. The four elementary operations are stated as follows:

> By the action of the Lever, which increases the Opening of the Lips, the Action of a Living Man is imitated, who increases that Opening for the Low Sounds. By the Lever, which draws back the Lips, I imitate the Action of a Man who removes them farther from the Hole of the flute, by turning it outwards. By the Lever which gives Wind from the unloaded Bellows, I imitate the weak Wind which a Man gives when he drives it out of the Receptacle of his Lungs, by only a light Compression of the Muscles of his Breast. By the Lever which moves the Tongue, in unstopping the Hole Thro' which the lips let the Wind pass, I imitate the Motion of a Man's Tongue, when he pulls it back from the Hole to give Passage to the Wind to articulate such a Note.[16]

But how should these elementary motions be combined? The first note (D) is formed by a relatively simple procedure, described on page 16 of the memoir. In order to produce E, however, various compensatory adjustments must be made:

> If I wou'd make the Flute sound the Note above, namely E, to the four first Operations for D, I add a fifth; I fix a Bar under the Lever, which raises the third Finger of the Right Hand to unstop the sixth Hole of the Flute; and I make the Lips to come a little nearer to the Hole of the Flute, by fixing or making a little lower the Bar of the Barrel which held up the Lever for the first Note, namely for D. Thus, giving an Issue to the Vibrations sooner, by unstopping the first Hole from the End, as I said above, the Flute must sound a Note above; which is also confirm'd by Experience.[17]

All now continues smoothly throughout the remaining notes of the first octave; only the appropriate programming of finger positions needs to be worked out. Further problems of coordination arise, however, when the simulation of the second octave is attempted:

> . . . we must change the Situation of the Mouth, that is, we must place a Bar under the Lever which serves to push the Lips beyond the Diameter of the Hole of the Flute, and thereby imitate the Action of a Living Man, who in that Case turns the Flute a little inwards. Secondly, we must fix a Bar under that Lever, which bringing the Lips towards one another diminishes their Opening; as a Man does to give a less Issue to the Wind. Thirdly, a Bar must be fix'd under the Lever which opens the Valve of that Receptacle that contains the Wind coming from those Bellows which are loaded with two Pounds; because the Wind being then driven with more Force, acts in the same Manner as that with which a Living Man blows by a stronger action of the Pectoral Muscles. . . .[18]

The succeeding paragraphs of part 2 describe the further adjustments which are necessary if the higher notes of the second octave and the whole of the third octave shall be faithfully produced. There follows a discussion of how to obtain correct tempi and phrasing, interspersed with remarks about the very subtle modifications which are needed to produce a "swelling of notes" and an echo effect. It is clear that Vaucanson must have run into some horrendously difficult problems in debugging his device, for he closes the memoir with the transparently heartfelt comment that "the fear of tiring you, GENTLEMEN, has made me pass over a great many little Circumstances, which tho' easy to suppose are not so soon executed: the Necessity of which appears by a View of the Machine as I have found it in the Practice."[19]

There seems little doubt, then, that Vaucanson was concerned to formulate and validate—in the most precise and formal language available to him—a theory of the German flute player. Certainly this is how Vaucanson's translator interpreted him. In the preface, Desaguliers boldly claims that "... this Memoire ... in a few Words gives a better and more intelligible Theory of Wind-Musick than can be met with in large Volumes."[20] Explicitness is the paramount virtue. As Vaucanson himself puts it, his aim is to imitate "by Art all that is necessary for a Man to perform in such a Case."[21]

This refrain recurs in the letter to the Abbe de Fontaine. Here, Vaucanson compares the difficulties he encountered in the construction of the flute automaton with the new problems posed by the tabor-pipe. He had expected this latter simulation to be somewhat easier; the task is merely "... to articulate Sound by Means of a Pipe of three Holes only, where all the Tones must be performed by a greater or less Force of the Wind, and half stopping of the Holes to pinch the Notes."[22]

Vaucanson finds, however, that the essence of pipe playing lies in its speed of operation: "... every Note, even Semi-Quavers, must be tongued," for otherwise the sound of the instrument is "not at all agreeable." It turns out that, for some melodies, his automaton actually performs better than a human player: "In this the Figure outdoes all our Performers on the Tabor-Pipe, who cannot move their Tongue fast enough to go thro' a whole Bar of Semi-Quavers, and strike them all. On the contrary, they slur above half of them; but my Piper plays a whole Tune and tongues every Note."[23]

In this respect, the automaton can be regarded as a competence model. Contingent limitations are lifted. Just as our finite wind and memory capacities ensure that many sentences which are strictly within our formal competence will never be uttered or comprehended, so are there many "Minuets and Rigadoons" which are formally within a (human) pipe player's competence but which are not attainable due to the tongue's lack of agility. Vaucanson's automaton is able to transcend (some) of these difficulties.

The fact that Vaucanson's theory (i.e., his automaton) must actually perform enables a variety of surprising phenomena and unforeseen relationships to be uncovered—"discoveries of Things which could never have been so much as guessed at," as Vaucanson writes. For instance, of all wind instruments, the pipe must be "one of the most fatiguing to the lungs. ... For in the playing upon it, the Performer must often strain the muscles of his Breast with a Force equivalent to a Weight of 56 Pounds; For I am oblig'd to use that Force of Wind, that is, a Wind driven by that Force of Weight, to sound the upper B which is the highest Tone to which this Instrument reaches: Whereas one Ounce only is sufficient to ... produce the lowest Tone, which is an E.[24]

The direction of information flow here is interestingly similar to the "intellectual bootstrapping" talked of by present-day simulation theorists. From observation of the world we derive enough information to construct a model—then from this model we infer further properties of the world. "The Performer *must* often strain etc. . . . for I [qua simulator] am oblig'd to etc. . . ."[25]

Most interesting of all, however, is Vaucanson's discovery that the force required to produce a particular note is not solely dependent upon the nature of the note itself, but is rather determined, in part, by the note which precedes it: "That Wind, for example, which is able to produce a D following a C, will never produce it, if the same D is to be sounded next to the E just above it; and the same is to be understood of all the other Notes."[26]

Vaucanson accordingly finds it imperative to have at least "twice as many different Winds, as there are Tones, besides the Semi-Tones, for each of which a particular Wind is absolutely necessary."[27] It is pleasing to observe that a more recent formal model of one aspect of musical competence reaches a similar conclusion; Longuet-Higgins's computer program for the transcription of classical melodies into standard notation demonstrates very conclusively that "the tonality of any note cannot in general be established unambiguously until the following note has been heard."[28] In both cases, then, a simple "chain-reflex" account of musical competence is falsified. This need to utilize "context-sensitive" machinery had first impressed itself upon Vaucanson during the construction of his most famous device, "the marvel of the last century," as Helmholtz wrote[29]—an artificial duck (fig. 1). Vaucanson's primary aim here was "to represent the Mechanism of the Intestines."[30] In addition, however, he made the duck capable of many other overt motions, which included stretching out its neck ("to take Corn out of your Hand"), moving the neck from left to right, flapping its wings, and raising itself upon its legs. If these coordinations were to be achieved without the bird falling over, the "same" piece of elementary machinery (the same structure) had to change its "function" dependent upon the overall pattern of behavior that was being executed. Upon observing the duck, "Persons of Skill and Attention"[31] will see that ". . . what sometimes is a Center of Motion for a Moveable Part, another Time becomes moveable upon that Part, which Part then becomes fix'd. In a word, they will be sensible of a prodigious Number of Mechanical Combinations."[32]

It is the duck that affords a final illustration of Vaucanson's motives. The entire internal mechanism of the automaton is "exposed to view." This gesture is made, Vaucanson writes, because "my Design [is] rather to demonstrate the Manner of the Actions, than to show a Machine." Because the intellectual cards are more than usually on the table, Vaucanson can risk a little joke against both his public and his competitors: "Perhaps some Ladies, or some People, who only like the Outside of Animals, had rather have seen the whole cover'd; that is the *Duck* with *Feathers*. But besides, that I have been desir'd to make every Thing visible; I wou'd not be thought to impose upon the Spectators by any conceal'd or juggling Contrivance."[33]

Vaucanson's explanatory mode

From our current vantage point, then, the most interesting fact about Vaucanson is not that he constructed automata or that his automata were so superbly realized. Vaucanson's main achievement lies, rather, in the clarity with which he perceived and articulated the character of the explanatory mode he sought to attain. Recent discussions of the philosophy of psychology have stressed a number of desiderata which are directly paralleled in Vaucanson's memoirs. For example:

1. *That the theories must be explicit.*—It is generally conceded that psychological theories phrased in "ordinary language" suffer from an incurable vagueness; they only work (if at all) when a liberal dose of human intelligence has been added to them, thereby opening the way to disagreements over interpretation. Chomsky's requirement that a grammar should generate without benefit of intuition all and only the "objects" within its domain has accordingly been called "the most important conceptual demand on psychology of this century."[34] The necessity of explicitness is only too obvious to Vaucanson, who describes all his efforts as "raised on the solid Principles of Mechanicks"[35] and points out (in a passage we have previously quoted) the difference between supposing that something will work and showing that it does.

2. *That occult entities may not interact with machines.*—A number of early mechanistic theories in psychology have always been vulnerable to attack on the grounds that they postulated (or at least left room for) a ghost within the machine. As late as the 19th century, one finds Johannes Muller proposing

Figure 1 The artificial duck of Jacques de Vaucanson. (From an original drawing the Musée des Arts et Metiers, Paris: inspired by a photograph in Alfred Chapuis Edmond Droz, *Automata* [New York, 1958].)

that "the fibres of all the motor, cerebral and spinal nerves may be imagined as spread out in the medulla oblongata, and exposed to the influence of the will like the keys of a pianoforte."[36]

Needless to say, Vaucanson will have no truck with flute players within flute players or ducks within ducks. It is imperative for Vaucanson that the ". . . Machine, when once wound up, performs all its different Operations without being touch'd any more."[37] No hidden soul or mind pulls the levers which cause the wings to flap.

3. *That stimulus-response psychology nonetheless leaves out a vital ingredient.*—Whilst Vaucanson is a behaviorist in the sense that behaviorism may be contrasted with vitalism or dualism, he clearly cannot believe in an "empty organism" approach to psychology. No manipulation of reinforcement contingencies will provoke the duck to partake of liquid refreshment ("I forgot to tell you, that the *Duck* drinks, plays in the Water with his Bill, and makes a gurgling Noise like a real living Duck")[38]—unless it has been constructed to do so. You can take the duck to water, but only the fact of Vaucanson's having got the wiring diagram right will make it drink. The oft-repeated refrain in the memoir is ". . . we must fix a Bar so that . . ." Or, as Quine puts it, the behaviorist is ". . . cheerfully up to his neck in innate mechanisms."[39]

4. *That the behavioral repertoires of organisms must be characterized.*—Chomsky has emphasized that any finite corpus of sentences is only a selection from the infinitude of examples which are, in principle, known to a competent speaker. The point generalizes to other behavior domains. As Fodor puts it: "The potential behaviour of the organism defines a space of which its actual behaviour provides only a sample."[40] It is therefore a condition upon any theoretically illuminating simulation that, unlike a gramophone recording, it should generate the entire behavioral repertoire of the organism within a particular domain.

Vaucanson is not entirely insensible of such points, although the recursive function theory that would solve the problem was, of course, not available to him. His tabor and pipe player does not quite manage to play all and only the sequences of notes which are melodies within some formal musical system. It does nonetheless play some ". . . twenty tunes, Minuets, Rigadoons, and Country-dances." (Sadly, we formulate our mathematics in such a fashion that twenty is no closer to infinity than one is.) The pipe, however, ". . . employs but one Hand" of the automaton. In addition, "The figure holds a Stick in the other, with which he strikes on the Tabor single and double Strokes, Rollings varied for all the Tunes, and keeping Time with what is played with the Pipe in the other Hand. This motion is none of the easiest in the Machine; for sometimes we must strike harder, some times quicker, and the Stroke must always be clean and smart, to make the *Tabor* sound right. The Mechanism for this consists in an infinite Combination of Levers, and different Strings, all moved to exactness to keep true to the Tune."[41]

We suspect that "an infinite Combination of Levers" really means "many levers"; but at least the importance of modeling a reasonably large and varied behavioral repertoire is obvious to Vaucanson. In this respect, there is a parallel between the tabor-pipe and the flute automata; as Brewster remarks about the latter, "The airs which it played were probably equal to those executed by a living performer."[42]

5. *That the theorist must choose an appropriate level of representation for his simulation.*—Any formal theory should set boundary conditions for the phenomena which fall within its scope. Vaucanson's duck ". . . stretches out its Neck to take Corn out of your Hand, it swallows it, digests it, and discharges it digested by the usual Passage." These, then, are the limits of what is being modeled. Vaucanson continues: I don't pretend to give this as a perfect Digestion, capable of producing Blood and nutritive Particles for the Support of the Animal. I hope no Body will be so unkind as to unbraid me with pretending to any such thing. I only pretend to imitate the Mechanisms of that Action in three things, vis. First, to swallow the Corn, *Secondly* to macerate or dissolve it; *thirdly*, to make it come out sensibly changed from what it was."[43]

Let us say, with Fodor, that a machine is weakly equivalent to an organism when the behavioral repertoire of the machine is identical with that of the organism within a particular domain. Let us furthermore say that "a machine is *strongly* equivalent to an organism in some respect when it is weakly equivalent in that respect and the processes upon which the behavior of the machine are contingent are of the same type as the processes upon which the behavior of the organism are contingent."[44] This notion of weak and strong equivalence is obviously related to the distinction that many modern computer theorists draw between "artificial intelligence" and the "simulation of behavior." Clearly, it is the notion of strong equivalence which is of interest to the empirical scientist: "The Food is digested as in the real Animals, by Dissolution, not Trituration, as some Natural Philosophers will have it."[45] It was likewise the strong equivalence of flute player and flute-playing automaton which so impressed the French Academy of Science. This learned body ". . . did not hesitate to state that the machinery employed for producing the sounds of the flute, performed in the most exact manner the very operations of the most expert flute-player and that the artist had imitated the effects produced, and the means employed by nature with an accuracy which exceeded all expectation."[46]

Conclusions

It should be obvious, then, that Brewster's claim that the primary objective of Vaucanson's work was "to astonish and amuse the public" is hardly fair. Vaucanson was an entertainer, but he was also deeply committed to the development of an explanatory psychology.

One might wish to praise Vaucanson both for his achievements and for his modesty—"I own freely, that I am surpriz'd myself to see and hear my Automaton play and perform so many and so differently varied Combinations."[47]—and, above all, for his refusal to succumb to wishy-washy metaphysics about the limits of psychology: "And I have been more than once ready to despair of succeeding; but Courage and Patience overcame every Thing."[48]

Yet despite Vaucanson's fame throughout the 18th and 19th centuries, his name is not to be found in any standard (20-century) histories of science; he is occasionally mentioned in histories of technology, albeit briefly and only in the context of his later contributions to industry. These contributions were by no means meagre. As Bedini reminds us, Vaucanson was responsible for pioneering the development of machine tools. In 1741, having been appointed an inspector in the French silk factories, Vaucanson invented and perfected an apparatus, wrongly attributed to Jacquard, for the automatic weaving of brocades. In 1760 he developed an industrial metal cutting lathe with prismatic guideways, inspiring Maudslay, a generation later, to continue work on machine tools in general and metal cutting lathes in particular. Later, as examiner of new machine inventions for the Academie Royale des Sciences, Vaucanson designed countless machines, including one for producing an endless chain.[49]

Moreover, in constructing his machines, Vaucanson was obliged to make many technological breakthroughs. Vaucanson was the first to make use of flexible tubes of India rubber (caoutchouc), which he had employed in respresenting "the Mechanism of the Intestines."

> While M. Vaucanson was engaged in the construction of these wonderful machines, his mind was filled with the strange idea of constructing an automaton containing the whole mechanism of the circulation of the blood. From some birds which he made he was satisfied of its practicability; but as the whole vascular system required to be made of elastic gum or caoutchouc, it was supposed that it could only be executed in the country where the caoutchouc tree was indigenous. Louis XVI took a deep interest in the execution of this machine. It was agreed that a skilful anatomist should precede to Guyana to superintend the construction of the blood vesels, and the King had not only approved of but had given orders for, the voyage. Difficulties, however, were thrown in the way: Vaucanson became disgusted, and the scheme was abandoned.[50]

Nevertheless the disparaging label of "toymaker" seems to have stuck to him, just as it had done to Heron in earlier times. Even current-day automata theorists persist in this libelous misrepresentation. Raphael, for example, concludes his discussion of the models of Vaucanson (and others) with the remark that "these eighteenth century gadgets were developed purely for their entertainment value."[51]

It has, however, been pointed out by Cohen that at least one major 19th-century scientist—Hermann von Helmholtz—did take Vaucanson seriously.[52] After describing the automata of Vaucanson and of the elder and younger Droz, Helmholtz comments: "That men like those mentioned, whose talent might bear comparison with the most inventive heads of the present age, should spend so much time in the construction of these figures which we at present regard as the merest trifles, would be incomprehensible, if they had not hoped in solemn earnest to solve a great problem."[53]

The "great problem" in question was, of course, the same problem on which Helmholtz and his colleagues were engaged, namely, to complete the "mechanization of the world picture" by bringing physiology and psychology within its scope.[54]

Helmholtz is aware, however, that serious scholars other than himself had taken a very considerable interest in these masterpieces of simulation. Following a public exhibition of the writing boy made by the elder Droz, Helmholtz notes that ". . . this boy and its constructor, being suspected of the black art, lay for a time in the Spanish Inquisition and with difficulty obtained their freedom."

The tribute is well taken. Throughout history, those who accused the automata makers of necromancy were at least closer to the truth than those who accused them of frivolity.

Notes

Dr. Fryer is currently doing research at Edinburgh University in the philosophical pschology of language. Dr. Marshall is head of the Unit for Language and Speech Behaviour at the University of Nijmegen, Netherlands.

1 H. Hodges, *Technology in the Ancient World* (Harmondsworth, 1970), p. 183.
2 Ibid.
3 A. G. Drachmann, "The Classical Civilizations," *Technology in Western Civilization*, ed. M. Kranzberg and C. W. Pursell (New York, 1967), 1:54.
4 D. Brewster, *Letters on Natural Magic* (London, 1832), p. 285.
5 D. J. de Solla Price, "Automata and the Origins of Mechanism and Mechanistic Philosophy," *Technology and Culture* 5 (1964): 9–23.
6 S. A. Bedini, "The Role of Automata in the History of Technology," *Technology and Culture* 5 (1964): 24–42.
7 Ibid., Price, p. 9.
8 Ibid., p. 10.
9 Brewster, p. 201.
10 J. de Vaucanson, *An Account of the Mechanism of an Automaton or Image Playing on the German-Flute*, trans. J. T. Desaguliers (London, 1742), p. 1.
11 Brewster, p. 202
12 Ibid., p. 203
13 Vaucanson, p. 1.
14 Ibid., p. 12.

15 Ibid., p. 17: emphasis added.
16 Ibid., pp. 16–17.
17 Ibid., p. 17.
18 Ibid., p. 20.
19 Ibid.
20 Ibid., p. 21.
21 Ibid.
22 Ibid.
23 Ibid.
24 Ibid., p. 24.
25 Ibid.
26 Ibid.
27 Ibid.
28 H. C. Longuet-Higgins, "Perception of Melodies," *Nature* 263 (October 1976): 646–53; quotation from p. 653.
29 H. Helmholtz. "On the Interaction of the Natural Forces," in *Popular Lectures on Scientific Subjects*, trans. E. Atkinson (London, 1901), p. 137.
30 Vaucanson, p. 21.
31 Ibid., p. 21.
32 Ibid., p. 23.
33 Ibid., p. 22.
34 P. Suppes, "The Desirability of Formalisation in Science." *Journal of Philosophy* 65 (October 1968): 651–54: quotation from p. 663.
35 Vaucanson. p. 3.
36 J. Muller, *Elements on Physiology*, trans. William Baly (London, 1842). vol. 2.
37 Vaucanson. p. 23.
38 Ibid.
39 W. V. Quine, "Linguistics and Philosophy," in *Language and Philosophy*, ed. S. Hook (New York, 1969), p. 96.
40 J. A. Fodor, *Psychological Explanation* (New York, 1968), p. 131.
41 Vaucanson, p. 24.
42 Brewster, p. 204.
43 Vaucanson, p. 22.
44 Fodor, p. 138.
45 Vaucanson, p. 21.
46 Brewster, p. 201.
47 Vaucanson, p. 24
48 Ibid.
49 Bedini.
50 Brewster, p. 206.
51 B. Raphael, *The Thinking Computer: Mind Inside Matter* (San Francisco, 1976), p. 258.
52 J. Cohen, *Human Robots in Myth and Science* (London, 1966), p. 144.
53 Helmholtz, p. 138.
54 E. J. Dijksterhuis, *De Mechanisering van het Wereldbeeld*, trans, C. Dikshoorn (Oxford, 1961).

11

MAN A MACHINE

J. O. de La Mettrie

Source: G. C. Bussey (ed.), *Man a Machine*, 1747, French text with English translation of *L'homme machine*, Open Court, 1953 (reprint of 1912 edn), pp. 85–149.

It is not enough for a wise man to study nature and truth; he should dare state truth for the benefit of the few who are willing and able to think. As for the rest, who are voluntarily slaves of prejudice, they can no more attain truth, than frogs can fly.

I reduce to two the systems of philosophy which deal with man's soul. The first and older system is materialism; the second is spiritualism.

The metaphysicians who have hinted that matter may well be endowed with the faculty of thought have perhaps not reasoned ill. For there is in this case a certain advantage in their inadequate way of expressing their meaning. In truth, to ask whether matter can think, without considering it otherwise than in itself, is like asking whether matter can tell time. It may be foreseen that we shall avoid this reef upon which Locke had the bad luck to make shipwreck.

The Leibnizians with their monads have set up an unintelligible hypothesis. They have rather spiritualized matter than materialized the soul. How can we define a being whose nature is absolutely unknown to us?

Descartes and all the Cartesians, among whom the followers of Malebranche have long been numbered, have made the same mistake. They have taken for granted two distinct substances in man, as if they had seen them, and positively counted them.

The wisest men have declared that the soul can not know itself save by the light of faith. However, as reasonable beings they have thought that they could reserve for themselves the right of examining what the Bible means by the word "spirit," which it uses in speaking of the human soul. And if in their investigation, they do not agree with the theologians on this point, are the theologians more in agreement among themselves on all other points?

Here is the result in a few words, of all their reflections. If there is a God,

He is the Author of nature as well as of revelation. He has given us the one to explain the other, and reason to make them agree.

To distrust the knowledge that can be drawn from the study of animated bodies, is to regard nature and revelation as two contraries which destroy each the other, and consequently to dare uphold the absurd doctrine, that God contradicts Himself in His various works and deceives us.

If there is a revelation, it can not then contradict nature. By nature only can we understand the meaning of the words of the Gospel, of which experience is the only true interpreter. In fact, the commentators before our time have only obscured the truth. We can judge of this by the author of the "Spectacle of Nature." "It is astonishing," he says concerning Locke, "that a man who degrades our soul far enough to consider it a soul of clay should dare set up reason as judge and sovereign arbiter of the mysteries of faith, for," he adds, "what an astonishing idea of Christianity one would have, if one were to follow reason."

Not only do these reflections fail to elucidate faith, but they also constitute such frivolous objections to the method of those who undertake to interpret the Scripture, that I am almost ashamed to waste time in refuting them.

The excellence of reason does not depend on a big word devoid of meaning (immateriality), but on the force, extent, and perspicuity of reason itself. Thus a "soul of clay" which should discover, at one glance, as it were, the relations and the consequences of an infinite number of ideas hard to understand, would evidently be preferable to a foolish and stupid soul, though that were composed of the most precious elements. A man is not a philosopher because, with Pliny, he blushes over the wretchedness of our origin. What seems vile is here the most precious of things, and seems to be the object of nature's highest art and most elaborate care. But as man, even though he should come from an apparently still more lowly source, would yet be the most perfect of all beings, so whatever the origin of his soul, if it is pure, noble, and lofty, it is a beautiful soul which dignifies the man endowed with it.

Pluche's second way of reasoning seems vicious to me, even in his system, which smacks a little of fanaticism; for [on his view] if we have an idea of faith as being contrary to the clearest principles, to the most incontestable truths, we must yet conclude, out of respect for revelation and its author, that this conception is false, and that we do not yet understand the meaning of the words of the Gospel.

Of the two alternatives, only one is possible: either everything is illusion, nature as well as revelation, or experience alone can explain faith. But what can be more ridiculous than the position of our author! Can one imagine hearing a Peripatetic say, "We ought not to accept the experiments of Torricelli, for if we should accept them, if we should rid ourselves of the horror of the void, what an astonishing philosophy we should have!"

I have shown how vicious the reasoning of Pluche is[1] in order to prove, in the first place, that if there is a revelation, it is not sufficiently demonstrated by the mere authority of the Church, and without any appeal to reason, as all those who fear reason claim: and in the second place, to protect against all assault the method of those who would wish to follow the path that I open to them, of interpreting supernatural things, incomprehensible in themselves, in the light of those ideas with which nature has endowed us. Experience and observation should therefore be our only guides here. Both are to be found throughout the records of the physicians who were philosophers, and not in the works of the philosophers who were not physicians. The former have traveled through and illuminated the labyrinth of man; they alone have laid bare to us those springs [of life] hidden under the external integument which conceals so many wonders from our eyes. They alone, tranquilly contemplating our soul, have surprised it, a thousand times, both in its wretchedness and in its glory, and they have no more despised it in the first estate, than they have admired it in the second. Thus, to repeat, only the physicians have a right to speak on this subject. What could the others, especially the theologians, have to say? Is it not ridiculous to hear them shamelessly coming to conclusions about a subject concerning which they have had no means of knowing anything, and from which on the contrary they have been completely turned aside by obscure studies that have led them to a thousand prejudiced opinions,—in a word, to fanaticism, which adds yet more to their ignorance of the mechanism of the body?

But even though we have chosen the best guides, we shall still find many thorns and stumbling blocks in the way.

Man is so complicated a machine that it is impossible to get a clear idea of the machine beforehand, and hence impossible to define it. For this reason, all the investigations have been vain, which the greatest philosophers have made *à priori*, that is to say, in so far as they use, as it were, the wings of the spirit. Thus it is only *à posteriori* or by trying to disentangle the soul from the organs of the body, so to speak, that one can reach the highest probability concerning man's own nature, even though one can not discover with certainty what his nature is.

Let us then take in our hands the staff of experience, paying no heed to the accounts of all the idle theories of philosophers. To be blind and to think that one can do without this staff is the worst kind of blindness. How truly a contemporary writer says that only vanity fails to gather from secondary causes the same lessons as from primary causes! One can and one even ought to admire all these fine geniuses in their most useless works, such men as Descartes, Malebranche, Leibniz, Wolff and the rest, but what profit, I ask, has any one gained from their profound meditations, and from all their works? Let us start out then to discover not what has been thought, but what must be thought for the sake of repose in life.

There are as many different minds, different characters, and different customs, as there are different temperaments. Even Galen knew this truth which Descartes carried so far as to claim that medicine alone can change minds and morals, along with bodies. (By the writer of "L'historie de l'âme," this teaching is incorrectly attributed to Hippocrates.) It is true that melancholy, bile, phlegm, blood etc.—according to the nature, the abundance, and the different combination of these humors—make each man different from another.

In disease the soul is sometimes hidden, showing no sign of life; sometimes it is so inflamed by fury that it seems to be doubled; sometimes, imbecility vanishes and the convalescence of an idiot produces a wise man. Sometimes, again, the greatest genius becomes imbecile and loses the sense of self. Adieu then to all that fine knowledge, acquired at so high a price, and with so much trouble! Here is a paralytic who asks if his leg is in bed with him; there is a soldier who thinks that he still has the arm which has been cut off. The memory of his old sensations, and of the place to which they were referred by his soul, is the cause of his illusion, and of this kind of delirium. The mere mention of the member which he has lost is enough to recall it to his mind, and to make him feel all its motions; and this causes him an indefinable and inexpressible kind of imaginary suffering. This man cries like a child at death's approach, while this other jests. What was needed to change the bravery of Caius Julius, Seneca, or Petronius into cowardice or faintheartedness? Merely an obstruction in the spleen, in the liver, an impediment in the portal vein? Why? Because the imagination is obstructed along with the viscera, and this gives rise to all the singular phenomena of hysteria and hypochondria.

What can I add to the stories already told of those who imagine themselves transformed into wolf-men, cocks or vampires, or of those who think that the dead feed upon them? Why should I stop to speak of the man who imagines that his nose or some other member is of glass? The way to help this man regain his faculties and his own flesh-and-blood nose is to advise him to sleep on hay, lest he break the fragile organ, and then to set fire to the hay that he may be afraid of being burned—a fear which has sometimes cured paralysis. But I must touch lightly on facts which everybody knows.

Neither shall I dwell long on the details of the effects of sleep. Here a tired soldier snores in a trench, in the middle of the thunder of hundreds of cannon. His soul hears nothing; his sleep is as deep as apoplexy. A bomb is on the point of crushing him. He will feel this less perhaps than he feels an insect which is under his foot.

On the other hand, this man who is devoured by jealousy, hatred, avarice, or ambition, can never find any rest. The most peaceful spot, the freshest and most calming drinks are alike useless to one who has not freed his heart from the torment of passion.

The soul and the body fall asleep together. As the motion of the blood is calmed, a sweet feeling of peace and quiet spreads through the whole mechanism. The soul feels itself little by little growing heavy as the eyelids droop, and loses its tenseness, as the fibres of the brain relax; thus little by little it becomes as if paralyzed and with it all the muscles of the body. These can no longer sustain the weight of the head, and the soul can no longer bear the burden of thought; it is in sleep as if it were not.

Is the circulation too quick? the soul can not sleep. Is the soul too much excited? the blood can not be quieted: it gallops through the veins with an audible murmur. Such are the two opposite causes of insomnia. A single fright in the midst of our dreams makes the heart beat at double speed and snatches us from needed and delicious repose, as a real grief or an urgent need would do. Lastly as the mere cessation of the functions of the soul produces sleep, there are, even when we are awake (or at least when we are half awake), kinds of very frequent short naps of the mind, vergers' dreams, which show that the soul does not always wait for the body to sleep. For if the soul is not fast asleep, it surely is not far from sleep, since it can not point out a single object to which it has attended, among the uncounted number of confused ideas which, so to speak, fill the atmosphere of our brains like clouds.

Opium is too closely related to the sleep it produces, to be left out of consideration here. This drug intoxicates, like wine, coffee, etc., each in its own measure and according to the dose. It makes a man happy in a state which would seemingly be the tomb of feeling, as it is the image of death. How sweet is this lethargy! The soul would long never to emerge from it. For the soul has been a prey to the most intense sorrow, but now feels only the joy of suffering past, and of sweetest peace. Opium even alters the will, forcing the soul which wished to wake and to enjoy life, to sleep in spite of itself. I shall omit any reference to the effect of poisons.

Coffee, the well-known antidote for wine, by scourging the imagination, cures our headaches and scatters our cares without laying up for us, as wine does, other headaches for the morrow. But let us contemplate the soul in its other needs.

The human body is a machine which winds its own springs. It is the living image of perpetual movement. Nourishment keeps up the movements which fever excites. Without food, the soul pines away, goes mad, and dies exhausted. The soul is a taper whose light flares up the moment before it goes out. But nourish the body, pour into its veins life-giving juices and strong liquors, and then the soul grows strong like them, as if arming itself with a proud courage, and the soldier whom water would have made flee, grows bold and runs joyously to death to the sound of drums. Thus a hot drink sets into stormy movement the blood which a cold drink would have calmed.

What power there is in a meal! Joy revives in a sad heart, and infects the souls of comrades, who express their delight in the friendly songs in which

221

the Frenchman excels. The melancholy man alone is dejected, and the studious man is equally out of place [in such company].

Raw meat makes animals fierce, and it would have the same effect on man. This is so true that the English who eat meat red and bloody, and not as well done as ours, seem to share more or less in the savagery due to this kind of food, and to other causes which can be rendered ineffective by education only. This savagery creates in the soul, pride, hatred, scorn of other nations, indocility and other sentiments which degrade the character, just as heavy food makes a dull and heavy mind whose usual traits are laziness and indolence.

Pope understood well the full power of greediness when he said:

"Catius is ever moral, ever grave,
Thinks who endures a knave is next a knave,
Save just at dinner—then prefers no doubt,
A rogue with ven'son to a saint without."

Elsewhere he says:

"See the same man in vigor, in the gout
Alone, in company, in place or out,
Early at business and at hazard late,
Mad at a fox chase, wise at a debate,
Drunk at a borough, civil at a ball,
Friendly at Hackney, faithless at White Hall."

In Switzerland we had a bailiff by the name of M. Steigner de Wittighofen. When he fasted he was a most upright and even a most indulgent judge, but woe to the unfortunate man whom he found on the culprit's bench after he had had a large dinner! He was capable of sending the innocent like the guilty to the gallows.

We think we are, and in fact we are, good men, only as we are gay or brave; everything depends on the way our machine is running. One is sometimes inclined to say that the soul is situated in the stomach, and that Van Helmont, who said that the seat of the soul was in the pylorus, made only the mistake of taking the part for the whole.

To what excesses cruel hunger can bring us! We no longer regard even our own parents and children. We tear them to pieces eagerly and make horrible banquets of them; and in the fury with which we are carried away, the weakest is always the prey of the strongest . . .

One needs only eyes to see the necessary influence of old age on reason. The soul follows the progress of the body, as it does the progress of education. In the weaker sex, the soul accords also with delicacy of temperament, and from this delicacy follow tenderness, affection, quick feelings due more to passion than to reason, prejudices, and superstitions, whose strong impress can hardly be effaced. Man, on the other hand, whose brain and nerves partake of the firmness of all solids, has not only stronger features but also a more vigorous mind. Education, which women lack, strengthens his mind still more. Thus with such help of nature and art, why should not a man be more grateful, more generous, more constant in friendship, stronger in adversity? But, to follow almost exactly the thought of the author of the "Lettres sur la Physiognomie," the sex which unites the charms of the mind and of the body with almost all the tenderest and most delicate feelings of the heart, should not envy us the two capacities which seem to have been given to man, the one merely to enable him better to fathom the allurements of beauty, and the other merely to enable him to minister better to its pleasures.

It is no more necessary to be just as great a physiognomist as this author, in order to guess the quality of the mind from the countenance or the shape of the features, provided these are sufficiently marked, than it is necessary to be a great doctor to recognize a disease accompanied by all its marked symptoms. Look at the portraits of Locke, of Steele, of Boerhaave, of Maupertuis, and the rest, and you will not be surprised to find strong faces and eagle eyes. Look over a multitude of others, and you can always distinguish the man of talent from the man of genius, and often even an honest man from a scoundrel. For example, it has been noticed that a celebrated poet combines (in his portrait) the look of a pickpocket with the fire of Prometheus.

History provides us with a noteworthy example of the power of temperature. The famous Duke of Guise was so strongly convinced that Henry the Third, in whose power he had so often been, would never dare assassinate him, that he went to Blois. When the Chancelor Chiverny learned of the duke's departure, he cried, "He is lost." After this fatal prediction had been fulfilled by the event, Chiverny was asked why he made it. "I have known the king for twenty years," said he; "he is naturally kind and even weakly indulgent, but I have noticed that when it is cold, it takes nothing at all to provoke him and send him into a passion."

One nation is of heavy and stupid wit, and another quick, light and penetrating. Whence comes this difference, if not in part from the difference in foods, and difference in inheritance,[2] and in part from the mixture of the diverse elements which float around in the immensity of the void? The mind, like the body, has its contagious diseases and its scurvy.

Such is the influence of climate, that a man who goes from one climate to another, feels the change, in spite of himself. He is a walking plant which has transplanted itself; if the climate is not the same, it will surely either degenerate or improve.

Furthermore, we catch everything from those with whom we come in contact; their gestures, their accent, etc.; just as the eyelid is instinctively lowered when a blow is foreseen, or as (for the same reason) the body of the spectator mechanically imitates, in spite of himself, all the motions of a good mimic.

From what I have just said, it follows that a brilliant man is his own best company, unless he can find other company of the same sort. In the society of the unintelligent, the mind grows rusty for lack of exercise, as at tennis a ball that is served badly is badly returned. I should prefer an intelligent man without an education, if he were still young enough, to a man badly educated. A badly trained mind is like an actor whom the provinces have spoiled.

Thus, the diverse states of the soul are always correlative with those of the body. But the better to show this dependence, in its completeness and its causes, let us here make use of comparative anatomy; let us lay bare the organs of man and of animals. How can human nature be known, if we may not derive any light from an exact comparison of the structure of man and of animals?

In general, the form and the structure of the brains of quadrupeds are almost the same as those of the brain of man; the same shape, the same arrangement everywhere, with this essential difference, that of all the animals man is the one whose brain is largest, and, in proportion to its mass, more convoluted than the brain of any other animal; then come the monkey, the beaver, the elephant, the dog, the fox, the cat. These animals are most like man, for among them, too, one notes the same progressive analogy in relation to the *corpus callosum* in which Lancisi—anticipating the late M. de la Peyronie—established the seat of the soul. The latter, however, illustrated the theory by innumerable experiments. Next after all the quadrupeds, birds have the largest brains. Fish have large heads, but these are void of sense, like the heads of many men. Fish have no *corpus callosum*, and very little brain, while insects entirely lack brain.

I shall not launch out into any more detail about the varieties of nature, nor into conjectures concerning them, for there is an infinite number of both, as any one can see by reading no further than the treatises of Willis "De Cerebro" and "De Anima Brutorum."

I shall draw the conclusions which follow clearly from these incontestable observations: 1st, that the fiercer animals are, the less brain they have; 2d, that this organ seems to increase in size in proportion to the gentleness of the animal; 3d, that nature seems here eternally to impose a singular condition, that the more one gains in intelligence the more one loses in instinct. Does this bring gain or loss?

Do not think, however, that I wish to infer by that, that the size alone of the brain, is enough to indicate the degree of tameness in animals: the quality must correspond to the quantity, and the solids and liquids must be in that due equilibrium which constitutes health.

If, as is ordinarily observed, the imbecile does not lack brain, his brain will be deficient in its consistency—for instance, in being too soft. The same thing is true of the insane, and the defects of their brains do not always escape our investigation. But if the causes of imbecility, insanity, etc., are not obvious, where shall we look for the causes of the diversity of all minds? They would escape the eyes of a lynx and of an argus. A mere nothing, a tiny fibre, something that could never be found by the most delicate anatomy, would have made of Erasmus and Fontenelle two idiots, and Fontenelle himself speaks of this very fact in one of his best dialogues.

Willis has noticed in addition to the softness of the brain-substance in children, puppies, and birds, that the *corpora striata* are obliterated and dis-colored in all these animals, and that the striations are as imperfectly formed as in paralytics . . .

However cautious and reserved one may be about the consequences that can be deduced from these observations, and from many others concerning the kind of variation in the organs, nerves, etc., [one must admit that] so many different varieties can not be the gratuitous play of nature. They prove at least the necessity for a good and vigorous physical organization, since throughout the animal kingdom the soul gains force with the body and acquires keenness, as the body gains strength.

Let us pause to contemplate the varying capacity of animals to learn. Doubtless the analogy best framed leads the mind to think that the causes we have mentioned produce all the difference that is found between animals and men, although we must confess that our weak understanding, limited to the coarsest observations, can not see the bonds that exist between cause and effects. This is a kind of harmony that philosophers will never know.

Among animals, some learn to speak and sing; they remember tunes, and strike the notes as exactly as a musician. Others, for instance the ape, show more intelligence, and yet can not learn music. What is the reason for this, except some defect in the organs of speech? But is this defect so essential to the structure that it could never be remedied? In a word, would it be absolutely impossible to teach the ape a language? I do not think so.

I should choose a large ape in preference to any other, until by some good fortune another kind should be discovered, more like us, for nothing prevents there being such an one in regions unknown to us. The ape resembles us so strongly that naturalists have called it "wild man" or "man of the woods." I should take it in the condition of the pupils of Amman, that is to say, I should not want it to be too young or too old; for apes that are brought to Europe are usually too old. I would choose the one with the most intelligent face, and the one which, in a thousand little ways, best lived up to its look of intelligence. Finally not considering myself worthy to be his master, I should put him in the school of that excellent teacher whom I have just named, or with another teacher equally skilful, if there is one.

You know by Amman's work, and by all those[3] who have interpreted his method, all the wonders he has been able to accomplish for those born deaf.

In their eyes he discovered ears, as he himself explains, and in how short a time! In short he taught them to hear, speak, read, and write. I grant that a deaf person's eyes see more clearly and are keener than if he were not deaf, for the loss of one member or sense can increase the strength or acuteness of another, but apes see and hear, they understand what they hear and see, and grasp so perfectly the signs that are made to them, that I doubt not that they would surpass the pupils of Amman in any other game or exercise. Why then should the education of monkeys be impossible? Why might not the monkey, but dint of great pains, at last imitate after the manner of deaf mutes, the motions necessary for pronunciation? I do not dare decide whether the monkey's organs of speech, however trained, would be incapable of articulation. But, because of the great analogy between ape and man and because there is no known animal whose external and internal organs so strikingly resemble man's, it would surprise me if speech were absolutely impossible to the ape. Locke, who was certainly never suspected of credulity, found no difficulty in believing the story told by Sir William Temple in his memoirs, about a parrot which could answer rationally, and which had learned to carry on a kind of connected conversation, as we do. I know that people have ridiculed[4] this great metaphysician; but suppose some one should have announced that reproduction sometimes takes place without eggs or a female, would he have found many partisans? Yet M. Trembley has found cases where reproduction takes place without copulation and by fission. Would not Amman too have passed for mad if he had boasted that he could instruct scholars like his in so short a time, before he had happily accomplished the feat? His successes have, however, astonished the world; and he, like the author of "The History of Polyps," has risen to immortality at one bound. Whoever owes the miracles that he works to his own genius surpasses, in my opinion, the man who owes his to chance. He who has discovered the art of adorning the most beautiful of the kingdoms [of nature], and of giving it perfections that it did not have, should be rated above an idle creator of frivolous systems, or a painstaking author of sterile discoveries. Amman's discoveries are certainly of a much greater value; he has freed men from the instinct to which they seemed to be condemned, and has given them ideas, intelligence, or in a word, a soul which they would never have had. What greater power than this!

Let us not limit the resources of nature; they are infinite, especially when reinforced by great art.

Could not the device which opens the Eustachian canal of the deaf, open that of apes? Might not a happy desire to imitate the master's pronunciation, liberate the organs of speech in animals that imitate so many other signs with such skill and intelligence? Not only do I defy any one to name any really conclusive experiment which proves my view impossible and absurd; but such is the likeness of the structure and functions of the ape to ours that I have very little doubt that if this animal were properly trained he might at

226

last be taught to pronounce, and consequently to know, a language. Then he would no longer be a wild man, nor a defective man, but he would be a perfect man, a little gentleman, with as much matter or muscle as we have, for thinking and profiting by his education.

The transition from animals to man is not violent, as true philosophers will admit. What was man before the invention of words and the knowledge of language? An animal of his own species with much less instinct than the others. In those days, he did not consider himself king over the other animals, nor was he distinguished from the ape, and from the rest, except as the ape itself differs from the other animals, i.e., by a more intelligent face. Reduced to the bare intuitive knowledge of the Leibnizians he saw only shapes and colors, without being able to distinguish between them: the same, old as young, child at all ages, he lisped out his sensations and his needs, as a dog that is hungry or tired of sleeping, asks for something to eat, or for a walk.

Words, languages, laws, sciences, and the fine arts have come, and by them finally the rough diamond of our mind has been polished. Man has been trained in the same way as animals. He has become an author, as they became beasts of burden. A geometrician has learned to perform the most difficult demonstrations and calculations, as a monkey has learned to take his little hat off and on, and to mount his tame dog. All has been accomplished through signs, every species has learned what it could understand, and in this way men have acquired symbolic knowledge, still so called by our German philosophers.

Nothing, as any one can see, is so simple as the mechanism of our education. Everything may be reduced to sounds or words that pass from the mouth of one through the ears of another into his brain. At the same moment, he perceives through his eyes the shape of the bodies of which these words are the arbitrary signs.

But who was the first to speak? Who was the first teacher of the human race? Who invented the means of utilizing the plasticity of our organism? I can not answer: the names of these first splendid geniuses have been lost in the night of time. But art is the child of nature, so nature must have long preceded it.

We must think that the men who were the most highly organized, those on whom nature had lavished her richest gifts, taught the others. They could not have heard a new sound for instance, nor experienced new sensations, nor been struck by all the varied and beautiful objects that compose the ravishing spectacle of nature without finding themselves in the state of mind of the deaf man of Chartres, whose experience was first related by the great Fontenelle, when, at forty years, he heard for the first time, the astonishing sound of bells.

Would it be absurd to conclude from this that the first mortals tried after the manner of this deaf man, or like animals and like mutes (another kind of animals), to express their new feelings by motions depending on the nature of their imagination, and therefore afterwards by spontaneous sounds, distinctive of each animal, as the natural expression of their surprise, their joy, their ecstasies and their needs? For doubtless those whom nature endowed with finer feeling had also greater facility in expression.

That is the way in which, I think, men have used their feeling and their instinct to gain intelligence and then have employed their intelligence to gain knowledge. Those are the ways, so far as I can understand them, in which men have filled the brain with the ideas, for the reception of which nature made it. Nature and man have helped each other; and the smallest beginnings have, little by little, increased, until everything in the universe could be as easily described as a circle.

As a violin string or a harpsichord key vibrates and gives forth sound, so the cerebral fibres, struck by waves of sound, are stimulated to render or repeat the words that strike them. And as the structure of the brain is such that when eyes well formed for seeing, have once perceived the image of objects, the brain can not help seeing their images and their differences, so when the signs of these differences have been traced or imprinted in the brain, the soul necessarily examines their relations—an examination that would have been impossible without the discovery of signs or the invention of language. At the time when the universe was almost dumb, the soul's attitude toward all objects was that of a man without any idea of proportion toward a picture or a piece of sculpture, in which he could distinguish nothing; or the soul was like a little child (for the soul was then in its infancy) who, holding in his hand small bits of straw or wood, sees them in a vague and superficial way without being able to count or distinguish them. But let some one attach a kind of banner, or standard, to this bit of wood (which perhaps is called a mast), and another banner to another similar object; let the first be known by the symbol 1, and the second by the symbol or number 2, then the child will be able to count the objects, and in this way he will learn all of arithmetic. As soon as one figure seems equal to another in its numerical sign, he will decide without difficulty that they are two different bodies, that $1 + 1$ make 2, and $2 + 2$ make 4,[5] etc.

This real or apparent likeness of figures is the fundamental basis of all truths and of all we know. Among these sciences, evidently those whose signs are less simple and less sensible are harder to understand than the others, because more talent is required to comprehend and combine the immense number of words by which such sciences express the truths in their province. On the other hand, the sciences that are expressed by numbers or by other small signs, are easily learned; and without doubt this facility rather than its demonstrability is what has made the fortune of algebra.

All this knowledge, with which vanity fills the balloon-like brains of our proud pedants, is therefore but a huge mass of words and figures, which form in the brain all the marks by which we distinguish and recall objects. All our ideas are awakened after the fashion in which the gardener who knows plants recalls all stages of their growth at sight of them. These words and the objects designated by them are so connected in the brain that it is comparatively rare to imagine a thing without the name or sign that is attached to it.

I always use the word "imagine," because I think that everything is the work of imagination, and that all the faculties of the soul can be correctly reduced to pure imagination in which they all consist. Thus judgment, reason, and memory are not absolute parts of the soul, but merely modifications of this kind of medullary screen upon which images of the objects painted in the eye are projected as by a magic lantern.

But if such is the marvelous and incomprehensible result of the structure of the brain, if everything is perceived and explained by imagination, why should we divide the sensitive principle which thinks in man? Is not this a clear inconsistency in the partisans of the simplicity of the mind? For a thing that is divided can no longer without absurdity be regarded as indivisible. See to what one is brought by the abuse of language and by those fine words (spirituality, immateriality, etc.) used haphazard and not understood even by the most brilliant.

Nothing is easier than to prove a system based, as this one is, on the intimate feeling and personal experience of each individual. If the imagination, or, let us say, that fantastic part of the brain whose nature is as unknown to us as its way of acting, be naturally small or weak, it will hardly be able to compare the analogy or the resemblance of its ideas, it will be able to see only what is face to face with it, or what affects it very strongly; and how will it see all this! Yet it is always imagination which apperceives, and imagination which represents to itself all objects along with their names and symbols; and thus, once again, imagination is the soul, since it plays all the roles of the soul. By the imagination, by its flattering brush, the cold skeleton of *reason* takes on living and ruddy flesh, by the imagination the sciences flourish, the arts are adorned, the wood speaks, the echoes sigh, the rocks weep, marble breathes, and all inanimate objects gain life. It is imagination again which adds the piquant charm of voluptuousness to the tenderness of an amorous heart; which makes tenderness bud in the study of the philosopher and of the dusty pedant, which, in a word, creates scholars as well as orators and poets. Foolishly decried by some, vainly praised by others, and misunderstood by all; it follows not only in the train of the graces and of the fine arts, it not only describes, but can also measure nature. It reasons, judges, analyzes, compares, and investigates. Could it feel so keenly the beauties of the pictures drawn for it, unless it discovered their relations? No, just as it can not turn its thoughts on the pleasures of the senses, without enjoying their perfection or their voluptuousness, it can not reflect on what it has mechanically conceived, without thus being judgment itself.

The more the imagination or the poorest talent is exercised, the more it gains in *embonpoint*, so to speak, and the larger it grows. It becomes sensitive, robust, broad, and capable of thinking. The best of organisms has need of this exercise.

Man's preeminent advantage is his organism. In vain all writers of books on morals fail to regard as praiseworthy those qualities that come by nature, esteeming only the talents gained by dint of reflection and industry. For whence come, I ask, skill, learning, and virtue, if not from a disposition that makes us fit to become skilful, wise and virtuous? And whence again, comes this disposition, if not from nature? Only through nature do we have any good qualities; to her we owe all that we are. Why then should I not esteem men with good natural qualities as much as men who shine by acquired and as it were borrowed virtues? Whatever the virtue may be, from whatever source it may come, it is worthy of esteem; the only question is, how to estimate it. Mind, beauty, wealth, nobility, although the children of chance, all have their own value, as skill, learning and virtue have theirs. Those upon whom nature has heaped her most costly gifts should pity those to whom these gifts have been refused; but, in their character of experts, they may feel their superiority without pride. A beautiful woman would be as foolish to think herself ugly, as an intelligent man to think himself a fool. An exaggerated modesty (a rare fault, to be sure) is a kind of ingratitude towards nature. An honest pride, on the contrary, is the mark of a strong and beautiful soul, revealed by manly features moulded by feeling.

If one's organism is an advantage, and the preeminent advantage, and the source of all others, education is the second. The best made brain would be a total loss without it, just as the best constituted man would be but a common peasant, without knowledge of the ways of the world. But, on the other hand, what would be the use of the most excellent school, without a matrix perfectly open to the entrance and conception of ideas? It is . . . impossible to impart a single idea to a man deprived of all his senses. . . .

But if the brain is at the same time well organized and well educated, it is a fertile soil, well sown, that brings forth a hundredfold what it has received: or (to leave the figures of speech often needed to express what one means, and to add grace to truth itself) the imagination, raised by art to the rare and beautiful dignity of genius, apprehends exactly all the relations of the ideas it has conceived, and takes in easily an astounding number of objects, in order to deduce from them a long chain of consequences, which are again but new relations, produced by a comparison with the first, to which the soul finds a perfect resemblance. Such is, I think, the generation of intelligence. I say "finds" as I before gave the epithet "apparent" to the likeness of objects, not because I think that our senses are always deceivers, as Father Malebranche has claimed, or that our eyes, naturally a little unsteady, fail to see objects as they are in themselves, (though microscopes prove this to us every day) but in order to avoid any dispute with the Pyrrhonians, among whom Bayle is well known.

I say of truth in general what M. de Fontenelle says of certain truths in particular, that we must sacrifice it in order to remain on good terms with society. And it accords with the gentleness of my character, to avoid all disputes unless to whet conversation. The Cartesians would here in vain make an onset upon me with their innate ideas. I certainly would not give myself a quarter of the trouble that M. Locke took, to attack such chimeras. In truth, what is the use of writing a ponderous volume to prove a doctrine which became an axiom three thousand years ago?

According to the principles which we have laid down, and which we consider true; he who has the most imagination should be regarded as having the most intelligence or genius, for all these words are synonymous; and again, only by a shameful abuse [of terms] do we think that we are saying different things, when we are merely using different words, different sounds, to which no idea or real distinction is attached.

The finest, greatest, or strongest imagination is then the one most suited to the sciences as well as to the arts. I do not pretend to say whether more intellect is necessary to excel in the art of Aristotle or of Descartes than to excel in that of Euripides or of Sophocles, and whether nature has taken more trouble to make Newton than to make Corneille, though I doubt this. But it is certain that imagination alone, differently applied, has produced their diverse triumphs and their immortal glory.

If one is known as having little judgment and much imagination, this means that the imagination has been left too much alone, has, as it were, occupied most of the time in looking at itself in the mirror of its sensations, has not sufficiently formed the habit of examining the sensations themselves attentively. [It means that the imagination] has been more impressed by images than by their truth or their likeness.

Truly, so quick are the responses of the imagination that if attention, that key or mother of the sciences, does not do its part, imagination can do little more than run over and skim its objects.

See that bird on the bough: it seems always ready to fly away. Imagination is like the bird, always carried onward by the turmoil of the blood and the animal spirits. One wave leaves a mark, effaced by the one that follows; the soul pursues it, often in vain: it must expect to regret the loss of that which it has not quickly enough seized and fixed. Thus, imagination, the true image of time, is being ceaselessly destroyed and renewed.

Such is the chaos and the continuous quick succession of our ideas: they drive each other away even as one wave yields to another. Therefore, if imagination does not, as it were, use one set of its muscles to maintain a kind of equilibrium with the fibres of the brain, to keep its attention for a while upon an object that is on the point of disappearing, and to prevent itself from contemplating prematurely another object—[unless the imagination does all this], it will never be worthy of the fine name of judgment. It will express vividly what it has perceived in the same fashion: it will create orators, musicians, painters, poets, but never a single philosopher. On the

231

contrary, if the imagination be trained from childhood to bridle itself and to keep from being carried away by its own impetuosity—an impetuosity which creates only brilliant enthusiasts—and to check, to restrain, its ideas, to examine them in all their aspects in order to see all sides of an object, then the imagination, ready in judgment, will comprehend the greatest possible sphere of objects, through reasoning; and its vivacity (always so good a sign in children, and only needing to be regulated by study and training) will be only a far-seeing insight without which little progress can be made in the sciences.

Such are the simple foundations upon which the edifice of logic has been reared. Nature has built these foundations for the whole human race, but some have used them, while others have abused them.

In spite of all these advantages of man over animals, it is doing him honor to place him in the same class. For, truly, up to a certain age, he is more of an animal than they, since at birth he has less instinct. What animal would die of hunger in the midst of a river of milk? Man alone. Like that child of olden time to whom a modern writer, refers, following Arnobius, he knows neither the foods suitable for him, nor the water that can drown him, nor the fire that can reduce him to ashes. Light a wax candle for the first time under a child's eyes, and he will mechanically put his fingers in the flame as if to find out what is the new thing that he sees. It is at his own cost that he will learn of the danger, but he will not be caught again. Or, put the child with an animal on a precipice, the child alone falls off; he drowns where the animal would save itself by swimming. At fourteen or fifteen years the child knows hardly anything of the great pleasures in store for him, in the reproduction of his species; when he is a youth, he does not know exactly how to behave in a game which nature teaches animals so quickly. He hides himself as if he were ashamed of taking pleasure, and of having been made to be happy, while animals frankly glory in being cynics. Without education, they are without prejudices. For one more example, let us observe a dog and a child who have lost their master on a highway: the child cries and does not know to what saint to pray, while the dog, better helped by his sense of smell than the child by his reason, soon finds his master.

Thus nature made us to be lower than animals or at least to exhibit all the more, because of that native inferiority, the wonderful efficacy of education which alone raises us from the level of the animals and lifts us above them. But shall we grant this same distinction to the deaf and to the blind, to imbeciles, madmen, or savages, or to those who have been brought up in the woods with animals; to those who have lost their imagination through melancholia, or in short to all those animals in human form who give evidence of only the rudest instinct? No, all these, men of body but not of mind, do not deserve to be classed by themselves.

We do not intend to hide from ourselves the arguments that can be brought forward against our belief and in favor of a primitive distinction between men and animals. Some say that there is in man a natural law, a knowledge of good and evil, which has never been imprinted on the heart of animals.

But is this objection, or rather this assertion, based on observation? Any assertion unfounded on observation may be rejected by a philosopher. Have we ever had a single experience which convinces us that man alone has been enlightened by a ray denied all other animals? If there is no such experience, we can no more know what goes on in animals' minds or even in the minds of other men, than we can help feeling what affects the inner part of our own being. We know that we think, and feel remorse—an intimate feeling forces us to recognize this only too well; but this feeling in us is insufficient to enable us to judge the remorse of others. That is why we have to take others at their word, or judge them by the sensible and external signs we have noticed in ourselves when we experienced the same accusations of conscience and the same torments.

In order to decide whether animals which do not talk have received the natural law, we must, therefore, have recourse to those signs to which I have just referred, if any such exist. The facts seem to prove it. A dog that bit the master who was teasing it, seemed to repent a minute afterwards; it looked sad, ashamed, afraid to show itself, and seemed to confess its guilt by a crouching and downcast air. History offers us a famous example of a lion which would not devour a man abandoned to its fury, because it recognized him as its benefactor. How much might it be wished that man himself always showed the same gratitude for kindnesses, and the same respect for humanity! Then we should no longer fear either ungrateful wretches, or wars which are the plague of the human race and the real executioners of the natural law.

But a being to which nature has given such a precocious and enlightened instinct, which judges, combines, reasons, and deliberates as far as the sphere of its activity extends and permits, a being which feels attachment because of benefits received, and which leaving a master who treats it badly goes to seek a better one, a being with a structure like ours, which performs the same acts, has the same passions, the same griefs, the same pleasures, more or less intense according to the sway of the imagination and the delicacy of the nervous organization—does not such a being show clearly that it knows its faults and ours, understands good and evil, and in a word, has consciousness of what it does? Would its soul, which feels the same joys, the same mortification and the same discomfiture which we feel, remain utterly unmoved by disgust when it saw a fellow-creature torn to bits, or when it had itself pitilessly dismembered this fellow-creature? If this be granted, it follows that the precious gift now in question would not have been denied to animals: for since they show us sure signs of repentance, as well as of intelligence, what is there absurd in thinking that beings, almost as perfect machines as ourselves, are, like us, made to understand and to feel nature?

Let no one object that animals, for the most part, are savage beasts, incapable of realizing the evil that they do; for do all men discriminate better between vice and virtue? There is ferocity in our species as well as in theirs. Men who are in the barbarous habit of breaking the natural law are not tormented as much by it, as those who transgress it for the first time, and who have not been hardened by the force of habit. The same thing is true of animals as of men—both may be more or less ferocious in temperament, and both become more so by living with others like themselves. But a gentle and peaceful animal which lives among other animals of the same disposition and of gentle nurture, will be an enemy of blood and carnage; it will blush internally at having shed blood. There is perhaps this difference, that since among animals everything is sacrificed to their needs, to their pleasures, to the necessities of life, which they enjoy more than we, their remorse apparently should not be as keen as ours, because we are not in the same state of necessity as they. Custom perhaps dulls and perhaps stifles remorse as well as pleasures.

But I will suppose for a moment that I am utterly mistaken in concluding that almost all the world holds a wrong opinion on this subject, while I alone am right. I will grant that animals, even the best of them, do not know the difference between moral good and evil, that they have no recollection of the trouble taken for them, of the kindness done them, no realization of their own virtues. [I will suppose], for instance, that this lion, to which I, like so many others, have referred, does not remember at all that it refused to kill the man, abandoned to its fury, in a combat more inhuman than one could find among lions, tigers and bears, put together. For our compatriots fight, Swiss against Swiss, brother against brother, recognize each other, and yet capture and kill each other without remorse, because a prince pays for the murder. I suppose in short that the natural law has not been given animals. What will be the consequences of this supposition? Man is not moulded from a costlier clay; nature has used but one dough, and has merely varied the leaven. Therefore if animals do not repent for having violated this inmost feeling which I am discussing, or rather if they absolutely lack it, man must necessarily be in the same condition. Farewell then to the natural law and all the fine treatises published about it! The whole animal kingdom in general would be deprived of it. But, conversely, if man can not dispense with the belief that when health permits him to be himself, he always distinguishes the upright, humane, and virtuous, from those who are not humane, virtuous, nor honorable: that it is easy to tell vice from virtue, by the unique pleasure and the peculiar repugnance that seem to be their natural effects, it follows that animals, composed of the same matter, lacking perhaps only one degree of fermentation to make it exactly like man's, must share the same prerogatives of animal nature, and that thus there exists no soul or sensitive substance without remorse. The following consideration will reinforce these observations.

It is impossible to destroy the natural law. The impress of it on all animals is so strong, that I have no doubt that the wildest and most savage have some moments of repentance. I believe that that cruel maid of Chalons in Champagne must have sorrowed for her crime, if she really ate her sister. I think that the same thing is true of all those who commit crimes, even involuntary or temperamental crimes: true of Gaston of Orleans who could not help stealing; of a certain woman who was subject to the same crime when pregnant, and whose children inherited it; of the woman who, in the same condition, ate her husband; of that other woman who killed her children, salted their bodies, and ate a piece of them every day, as a little relish; of that daughter of a thief and cannibal who at twelve years followed in his steps, although she had been orphaned when she was a year old, and had been brought up by honest people; to say nothing of many other examples of which the records of our observers are full, all of them proving that there are a thousand hereditary vices and virtues which are transmitted from parents to children as those of the foster mother pass to the children she nurses. Now, I believe and admit that these wretches do not for the most part feel at the time the enormity of their actions. Bulimia, or canine hunger, for example, can stifle all feeling; it is a mania of the stomach that one is compelled to satisfy, but what remorse must be in store for those women, when they come to themselves and grow sober, and remember the crimes they have committed against those they held most dear! What a punishment for an involuntary crime which they could not resist, of which they had no consciousness whatever! However, this is apparently not enough for the judges. For of these women, of whom I tell, one was cruelly beaten and burned, and another was buried alive. I realize all that is demanded by the interest of society. But doubtless it is much to be wished that excellent physicians might be the only judges. They alone could tell the innocent criminal from the guilty. If reason is the slave of a depraved or mad desire, how can it control the desire?

But, if crime carries with it its own more or less cruel punishment, if the most continued and most barbarous habit can not entirely blot out repentance in the cruelest hearts, if criminals are lacerated by the very memory of their deeds, why should we frighten the imagination of weak minds, by a hell, by specters, and by precipices of fire even less real than those of Pascal?[6] Why must we have recourse to fables, as an honest pope once said himself, to torment even the unhappy wretches who are executed, because we do not think that they are sufficiently punished by their own conscience, their first executioner? I do not mean to say that all criminals are unjustly punished; I only maintain that those whose will is depraved, and whose conscience is extinguished, are punished enough by their remorse when they come to themselves, a remorse, I venture to assert, from which nature should in this case have delivered unhappy souls dragged on by a fatal necessity.

Criminals, scoundrels, ingrates, those in short without natural feelings, unhappy tyrants who are unworthy of life, in vain take a cruel pleasure in their barbarity, for there are calm moments of reflection in which the avenging conscience arises, testifies against them, and condemns them to be almost ceaselessly torn to pieces at their own hands. Whoever torments men is tormented by himself; and the sufferings that he will experience will be the just measure of those that he has inflicted.

On the other hand, there is so much pleasure in doing good, in recognizing and appreciating what one receives, so much satisfaction in practising virtue, in being gentle, humane, kind, charitable, compassionate and generous (for this one word includes all the virtues), that I consider as sufficiently punished any one who is unfortunate enough not to have been born virtuous.

We were not originally made to be learned; we have become so perhaps by a sort of abuse of our organic faculties, and at the expense of the State which nourishes a host of sluggards whom vanity has adorned with the name of philosophers. Nature has created us all solely to be happy—yes, all of us from the crawling worm to the eagle lost in the clouds. For this cause she has given all animals some share of natural law, a share greater or less according to the needs of each animal's organs when in normal condition.

Now how shall we define natural law? It is a feeling that teaches us what we should not do, because we would not wish it to be done to us. Should I dare add to this common idea, that this feeling seems to me but a kind of fear or dread, as salutary to the race as to the individual; for may it not be true that we respect the purse and life of others only to save our own possessions, our honor, and ourselves; like those Ixions of Christianity who love God and embrace so many fantastic virtues, merely because they are afraid of hell!

You see that natural law is but an intimate feeling that, like all other feelings (thought included), belongs also to imagination. Evidently, therefore, natural law does not presuppose education, revelation, nor legislator,— provided one does not propose to confuse natural law with civil laws, in the ridiculous fashion of the theologians.

The arms of fanaticism may destroy those who support these truths, but they will never destroy the truths themselves.

I do not mean to call in question the existence of a supreme being; on the contrary it seems to me that the greatest degree of probability is in favor of this belief. But since the existence of this being goes no further than that of any other toward proving the need of worship, it is a theoretic truth with very little practical value. Therefore, since we may say, after such long experience, that religion does not imply exact honesty, we are authorized by the same reasons to think that atheism does not exclude it.

Furthermore, who can be sure that the reason for man's existence is not simply the fact that he exists? Perhaps he was thrown by chance on some spot on the earth's surface, nobody knows how nor why, but simply that he must live and die, like the mushrooms which appear from day to day, or like those flowers which border the ditches and cover the walls.

Let us not lose ourselves in the infinite, for we are not made to have the least idea thereof, and are absolutely unable to get back to the origin of things. Besides it does not matter for our peace of mind, whether matter be eternal or have been created, whether there be or be not a God. How foolish to torment ourselves so much about things which we can not know, and which would not make us any happier even were we to gain knowledge about them!

But, some will say, read all such works as those of Fénelon, of Nieuwen-tyt, of Abadie, of Derham, of Rais, and the rest. Well! what will they teach me or rather what have they taught me? They are only tiresome repetitions of zealous writers, one of whom adds to the other only verbiage, more likely to strengthen than to undermine the foundations of atheism. The number of the evidences drawn from the spectacle of nature does not give these evidences any more force. Either the mere structure of a finger, of an ear, of an eye, a single observation of Malpighi proves all, and doubtless much better than Descartes and Malebranche proved it, or all the other evidences prove nothing. Deists, and even Christians, should therefore be content to point out that throughout the animal kingdom the same aims are pursued and accomplished by an infinite number of different mechanisms, all of them however exactly geometrical. For what stronger weapons could there be with which to overthrow atheists? It is true that if my reason does not deceive me, man and the whole universe seem to have been designed for this unity of aim. The sun, air, water, the organism, the shape of bodies,—everything is brought to a focus in the eye as in a mirror that faithfully presents to the imagination all the objects reflected in it, in accordance with the laws required by the infinite variety of bodies which take part in vision. In ears we find everywhere a striking variety, and yet the difference of structure in men, animals, birds, and fishes, does not produce different uses. All ears are so mathematically made, that they tend equally to one and the same end, namely, hearing. But would Chance, the deist asks, be a great enough geometrician to vary thus, at pleasure, the works of which she is supposed to be the author, without being hindered by so great a diversity from gaining the same end? Again, the deist will bring forward as a difficulty those parts of the animal that are clearly contained in it for future use, the butterfly in the caterpillar, man in the sperm, a whole polyp in each of its parts, the valvule in the oval orifice, the lungs in the foetus, the teeth in their sockets, the bones in the fluid from which they detach themselves and (in an incomprehensible manner) harden. And since the partisans of this theory, far from neglecting anything that would strengthen it, never tire of piling up proof upon proof, they are willing to avail themselves of everything, even of the weakness of the mind in certain cases. Look, they say, at men like Spinoza, Vanini, Desbarreau, and Boindin, apostles who honor deism more than they harm it. The duration of their health was the measure of their unbelief, and one rarely fails, they add, to renounce atheism when the passions, with their instrument, the body, have grown weak.

That is certainly the most that can be said in favor of the existence of God: although the last argument is frivolous in that these conversions are short, and the mind almost always regains its former opinions and acts accordingly, as soon as it has regained or rather rediscovered its strength in that of the body. That is, at least, much more than was said by the physician Diderot, in his "Pensées Philosophiques," a sublime work that will not convince a single atheist. What reply can, in truth, be made to a man who says, "We do not know nature; causes hidden in her breast might have produced everything. In your turn, observe the polyp of Trembley: does it not contain in itself the causes which bring about regeneration? Why then would it be absurd to think that there are physical causes by reason of which everything has been made, and to which the whole chain of this vast universe is so necessarily bound and held that nothing which happens, could have failed to happen,—causes, of which we are so invincibly ignorant that we have had recourse to a God, who, as some aver, is not so much as a logical entity? Thus to destroy chance is not to prove the existence of a supreme being, since there may be some other thing which is neither chance nor God—I mean, nature. It follows that the study of nature can make only unbelievers; and the way of thinking of all its more successful investigators proves this."

The weight of the universe therefore far from crushing a real atheist does not even shake him. All these evidences of a creator, repeated thousands and thousands of times, evidences that are placed far above the comprehension of men like us, are self-evident (however far one push the argument) only to the anti-Pyrrhonians, or to those who have enough confidence in their reason to believe themselves capable of judging on the basis of certain phenomena, against which, as you see, the atheists can urge others perhaps equally strong and absolutely opposed. For if we listen to the naturalists again, they will tell us that the very causes which, in a chemist's hands, by a chance combination, made the first mirror, in the hands of nature made the pure water, the mirror of the simple shepherdess; that the motion which keeps the world going could have created it, that each body has taken the place assigned to it by its own nature, that the air must have surrounded the earth, and that iron and the other metals are produced by internal motions of the earth, for one and the same reason; that the sun is as much a natural product as electricity, that it was not made to warm the earth and its inhabitants, whom it sometimes burns, any more than the rain was made to make the seeds grow, which it often spoils; that the mirror and the water were no more made for people to see themselves in, than were all other polished bodies with this same property; that the eye is in truth a kind of glass in which the soul can contemplate the image of objects as they are presented to it by these bodies, but that it is not proved that this organ was really made expressly for this contemplation, nor purposely placed in its socket, and in short that it may well be that Lucretius, the physician Lamy, and all Epicureans both ancient and modern were right when they suggested that the eye sees only because it is formed and placed as it is, and that, given once for all, the same rules of motion followed by nature in the generation and development of bodies, this marvelous organ could not have been formed and placed differently.

Such is the *pro* and the *con*, and the summary of those fine arguments that will eternally divide the philosophers. I do not take either side.

"Non nostrum inter vos tantas componere lites."

This is what I said to one of my friends, a Frenchman, as frank a Pyrronian as I, a man of much merit, and worthy of a better fate. He gave me a very singular answer in regard to the matter. "It is true," he told me, "that the *pro* and *con* should not disturb at all the soul of a philosopher, who sees that nothing is proved with clearness enough to force his consent, and that the arguments offered on one side are neutralized by those of the other. However," he continued, "the universe will never be happy, unless it is atheistic." Here are this wretch's reasons. If atheism, said he, were generally accepted, all the forms of religion would then be destroyed and cut off at the roots. No more theological wars, no more soldiers of religion—such terrible soldiers! Nature infected with a sacred poison, would regain its rights and its purity. Deaf to all other voices, tranquil mortals would follow only the spontaneous dictates of their own being the only commands which can never be despised with impunity and which alone can lead us to happiness through the pleasant paths of virtue.

Such is natural law: whoever rigidly observes it is a good man and deserves the confidence of all the human race. Whoever fails to follow it scrupulously affects, in vain, the specious exterior of another religion; he is a scamp or a hypocrite whom I distrust.

After this, let a vain people think otherwise, let them dare affirm that even probity is at stake in not believing in revelation, in a word that another religion than that of nature is necessary, whatever it may be. Such an assertion is wretched and pitiable; and so is the good opinion which each one gives us of the religion he has embraced! We do not seek here the votes of the crowd. Whoever raises in his heart altars to superstition, is born to worship idols and not to thrill to virtue.

But since all the faculties of the soul depend to such a degree on the proper organization of the brain and of the whole body, that apparently they are but this organization itself, the soul is clearly an enlightened machine. For finally, even if man alone had received a share of natural law, would he be any less a machine for that? A few more wheels, a few more springs than in the most perfect animals, the brain proportionally nearer the heart and for this very reason receiving more blood—any one of a number of unknown causes might always produce this delicate conscience so easily wounded, this remorse which is no more foreign to matter than to thought, and in a word all the differences that are supposed to exist here. Could the organism then suffice for everything? Once more, yes; since thought visibly develops with our organs, why should not the matter of which they are composed be susceptible of remorse also, when once it has acquired, with time, the faculty of feeling?

The soul is therefore but an empty word, of which no one has any idea, and which an enlightened man should use only to signify the part in us that thinks. Given the least principle of motion, animated bodies will have all that is necessary for moving, feeling, thinking, repenting, or in a word for conducting themselves in the physical realm, and in the moral realm which depends upon it.

Yet we take nothing for granted; those who perhaps think that all the difficulties have not yet been removed shall now read of experiments that will completely satisfy them.

1. The flesh of all animals palpitates after death. This palpitation continues longer, the more cold blooded the animal is and the less it perspires. Tortoises, lizards, serpents, etc. are evidence of this.

2. Muscles separated from the body contract when they are stimulated.

3. The intestines keep up their peristaltic or vermicular motion for a long time.

4. According to Cowper, a simple injection of hot water reanimates the heart and the muscles.

5. A frog's heart moves for an hour or more after it has been removed from the body, especially when exposed to the sun or better still when placed on a hot table or chair. If this movement seems totally lost, one has only to stimulate the heart, and that hollow muscle beats again. Harvey made this same observation on toads.

6. Bacon of Verulam in his treatise "Sylva Sylvarum" cites the case of a man convicted of treason, who was opened alive, and whose heart thrown into hot water leaped several times, each time less high, to the perpendicular height of two feet.

7. Take a tiny chicken still in the egg, cut out the heart and you will observe the same phenomena as before, under almost the same conditions. The warmth of the breath alone reanimates an animal about to perish in the air pump.

The same experiments, which we owe to Boyle and to Stenon, are made on pigeons, dogs, and rabbits. Pieces of animal hearts beat as their whole hearts would. The same movements can be seen in paws that have been cut off from moles.

8. The caterpillar, the worm, the spider, the fly, the eel—all exhibit the same phenomena; and in hot water, because of the fire it contains, the movement of the detached parts increases.

9. A drunken soldier cut off with one stroke of his sabre an Indian rooster's head. The animal remained standing, then walked, and ran: happening to run against a wall, it turned around, beat its wings still running,

and finally fell down. As it lay on the ground, all the muscles of this rooster kept on moving. That is what I saw myself, and almost the same phenomena can easily be observed in kittens or puppies with their heads cut off.

10. Polyps do more than move after they have been cut in pieces. In a week they regenerate to form as many animals as there are pieces. I am sorry that these facts speak against the naturalists' system of generation; or rather I am very glad of it, for let this discovery teach us never to reach a general conclusion even on the ground of all known (and most decisive) experiments.

Here we have many more facts than are needed to prove, in an incontestable way, that each tiny fibre or part of an organized body moves by a principle which belongs to it. Its activity, unlike voluntary motions, does not depend in any way on the nerves, since the movements in question occur in parts of the body which have no connection with the circulation. But if this force is manifested even in sections of fibres the heart, which is a composite of peculiarly connected fibres, must possess the same property. I did not need Bacon's story to persuade me of this. It was easy for me to come to this conclusion, both from the perfect analogy of the structure of the human heart with that of animals, and also from the very bulk of the human heart, in which this movement escapes our eyes only because it is smothered, and finally because in corpses all the organs are cold and lifeless. If executed criminals were dissected while their bodies are still warm, we should probably see in their hearts the same movements that are observed in the face-muscles of those that have been beheaded.

The motive principle of the whole body, and even of its parts cut in pieces, is such that it produces not irregular movements, as some have thought, but very regular ones, in warm blooded and perfect animals as well as in cold and imperfect ones. No resource therefore remains open to our adversaries but to deny thousands and thousands of facts which every man can easily verify.

If now any one ask me where is this innate force in our bodies, I answer that it very clearly resides in what the ancients called the parenchyma, that is to say, in the very substance of the organs not including the veins, the arteries, the nerves, in a word, that it resides in the organization of the whole body, and that consequently each organ contains within itself forces more or less active according to the need of them.

Let us now go into some detail concerning these springs of the human machine. All the vital, animal, natural, and automatic motions are carried on by their action. Is it not in a purely mechanical way that the body shrinks back when it is struck with terror at the sight of an unforeseen precipice, that the eyelids are lowered at the menace of a blow, as some have remarked, and that the pupil contracts in broad daylight to save the retina, and dilates to see objects in darkness? Is it not by mechanical means that the pores of the skin close in winter so that the cold can not penetrate to the interior of the blood vessels, and that the stomach vomits when it is irritated by poison, by a certain quantity of opium and by all emetics, etc.? that the heart, the arteries and the muscles contract in sleep as well as in waking hours, that the lungs serve as bellows continually in exercise, . . . that the heart contracts more strongly than any other muscle? . . .

I shall not go into any more detail concerning all these little subordinate forces, well known to all. But there is another more subtle and marvelous force, which animates them all; it is the source of all our feelings, of all our pleasures, of all our passions, and of all our thoughts: for the brain has its muscles for thinking, as the legs have muscles for walking. I wish to speak of this impetuous principle that Hippocrates calls ἐνορμῶν (soul). This principle exists and has its seat in the brain at the origin of the nerves, by which it exercises its control over all the rest of the body. By this fact is explained all that can be explained, even to the surprising effects of maladies of the imagination . . .

Look at the portrait of the famous Pope who is, to say the least, the Voltaire of the English. The effort, the energy of his genius are imprinted upon his countenance. It is convulsed. His eyes protrude from their sockets, the eyebrows are raised with the muscles of the forehead. Why? Because the brain is in travail and all the body must share in such a laborious deliverance. If there were not an internal cord which pulled the external ones, whence would come all these phenomena? To admit a soul as explanation of them, is to be reduced to [explaining phenomena by] the operations of the Holy Spirit.

In fact, if what thinks in my brain is not a part of this organ and therefore of the whole body, why does my blood boil, and the fever of my mind pass into my veins, when lying quietly in bed, I am forming the plan of some work or carrying on an abstract calculation? Put this question to men of imagination, to great poets, to men who are enraptured by the felicitous expression of sentiment, and transported by an exquisite fancy or by the charms of nature, of truth, or of virtue! By their enthusiasm, by what they will tell you they have experienced, you will judge the cause by its effect; by that harmony which Borelli, a mere anatomist, understood better than all the Leibnizians, you will comprehend the material unity of man. In short, if the nerve-tension which causes pain occasions also the fever by which the distracted mind loses its will-power, and if, conversely, the mind too much excited, disturbs the body (and kindles that inner fire which killed Bayle while he was still so young); if an agitation rouses my desire and my ardent wish for what, a moment ago, I cared nothing about, and if in their turn certain brain impressions excite the same longing and the same desires, then why should we regard as double what is manifestly one being? In vain you fall back on the power of the will, since for one order that the will gives, it bows a hundred times to the yoke. And what wonder that in health the body obeys, since a torrent of blood and of animal spirits forces its obedience, and since the will has as ministers an invisible legion of fluids swifter than lightning and ever ready to do its bidding! But as the power of the will is exercised by means of the nerves, it is likewise limited by them . . .

Does the result of jaundice surprise you? Do you not know that the color of bodies depends on the color of the glasses through which we look at them, and that whatever is the color of the humors, such is the color of objects, at least for us, vain playthings of a thousand illusions? But remove this color from the aqueous humor of the eye, let the bile flow through its natural filter, then the soul having new eyes, will no longer see yellow. Again, is it not thus, by removing cataract, or by injecting the Eustachian canal, that sight is restored to the blind, or hearing to the deaf? How many people, who were perhaps only clever charlatans, passed for miracle workers in the dark ages! Beautiful the soul, and powerful the will which can not act save by permission of the bodily conditions, and whose tastes change with age and fever! Should we, then, be astonished that philosophers have always had in mind the health of the body, to preserve the health of the soul, that Pythagoras gave rules for the diet as carefully as Plato forbade wine? The regime suited to the body is always the one with which sane physicians think they must begin, when it is a question of forming the mind, and of instructing it in the knowledge of truth and virtue; but these are vain words in the disorder of illness, and in the tumult of the senses. Without the precepts of hygiene, Epictetus, Socrates, Plato, and the rest preach in vain: all ethics is fruitless for one who lacks his share of temperance; it is the source of all virtues, as intemperance is the source of all vices.

Is more needed, (for why lose myself in discussion of the passions which are all explained by the term, ἐνορμῶν, of Hippocrates) to prove that man is but an animal, or a collection of springs which wind each other up, without our being able to tell at what point in this human circle, nature has begun? If these springs differ among themselves, these differences consist only in their position and in their degrees of strength, and never in their nature; wherefore the soul is but a principle of motion or a material and sensible part of the brain, which can be regarded, without fear of error, as the mainspring of the whole machine, having a visible influence on all the parts. The soul seems even to have been made for the brain, so that all the other parts of the system are but a kind of emanation from the brain. This will appear from certain observations, made on different embryos, which I shall now enumerate.

This oscillation, which is natural or suited to our machine, and with which each fibre and even each fibrous element, so to speak, seems to be endowed, like that of a pendulum, can not keep up forever. It must be renewed, as it loses strength, invigorated when it is tired, and weakened when it is disturbed by excess of strength and vigor. In this alone, true medicine consists.

The body is but a watch, whose watchmaker is the new chyle. Nature's first care, when the chyle enters the blood, is to excite in it a kind of fever which the chemists, who dream only of retorts, must have taken for fermentation.

This fever produces a greater filtration of spirits, which mechanically animate the muscles and the heart, as if they had been sent there by order of the will.

These then are the causes or the forces of life which thus sustain for a hundred years that perpetual movement of the solids and the liquids which is as necessary to the first as to the second. But who can say whether the solids contribute more than the fluids to this movement or *vice versa*? All that we know is that the action of the former would soon cease without the help of the latter, that is, without the help of the fluids which by their onset rouse and maintain the elasticity of the blood vessels on which their own circulation depends. From this it follows that after death the natural resilience of each substance is still more or less strong according to the remnants of life which it outlives, being the last to perish. So true is it that this force of the animal parts can be preserved and strengthened by that of the circulation, but that it does not depend on the strength of the circulation, since, as we have seen, it can dispense with even the integrity of each member or organ.

I am aware that this opinion has not been relished by all scholars, and that Stahl especially had much scorn for it. This great chemist has wished to persuade us that the soul is the sole cause of all our movements. But this is to speak as a fanatic and not as a philosopher.

To destroy the hypothesis of Stahl, we need not make as great an effort as I find that others have done before me. We need only glance at a violinist. What flexibility, what lightness in his fingers! The movements are so quick, that it seems almost as if there were no succession. But I pray, or rather I challenge, the followers of Stahl who understand so perfectly all that our soul can do, to tell me how it could possibly execute so many motions so quickly, motions, moreover, which take place so far from the soul, and in so many different places. That is to suppose that a flute player could play brilliant cadences on an infinite number of holes that he could not know, and on which he could not even put his finger!

But let us say with M. Hecquet that all men may not go to Corinth. Why should not Stahl have been even more favored by nature as a man than as a chemist and a practitioner? Happy mortal, he must have received a soul different from that of the rest of mankind,—a sovereign soul, which, not content with having some control over the voluntary muscles, easily held the reins of all the movements of the body, and could suspend them, calm them, or excite them, at its pleasure! With so despotic a mistress, in whose hands were, in a sense, the beating of the heart, and the laws of circulation, there could certainly be no fever, no pain, no weariness, . . . ! The soul wills, and the springs play, contract or relax. But how did the springs of Stahl's machine get out of order so soon? He who has in himself so great a doctor, should be immortal.

Moreover, Stahl is not the only one who has rejected the principle of the vibration of organic bodies. Greater minds have not used the principle when they wished to explain the action of the heart, . . . etc. One need only read the "Institutions of Medicine" by Boerhaave to see what laborious and enticing systems this great man was obliged to invent, by the labor of his mighty genius, through failure to admit that there is so wonderful a force in all bodies.

Willis and Perrault, minds of a more feeble stamp, but careful observers of nature (whereas nature was known to the famous Leyden professor only through others and second hand, so to speak) seem to have preferred to suppose a soul generally extended over the whole body, instead of the principle which we are describing. But according to this hypothesis (which was the hypothesis of Vergil and of all Epicureans, an hypothesis which the history of the polyp might seem at first sight to favor) the movements which go on after the death of the subject in which they inhere are due to a remnant of soul still maintained by the parts that contract, though, from the moment of death, these are not excited by the blood and the spirits. Whence it may be seen that these writers, whose solid works easily eclipse all philosophic fables, are deceived only in the manner of those who have endowed matter with the faculty of thinking, I mean to say, by having expressed themselves badly in obscure and meaningless terms. In truth, what is this remnant of a soul, if it is not the "moving force" of the Leibnizians (badly rendered by such an expression), which however Perrault in particular has really foreseen. See his "Treatise on the Mechanism of Animals."

Now that it is clearly proved against the Cartesians, the followers of Stahl, the Malebranchists, and the theologians who little deserve to be mentioned here, that matter is self-moved, not only when organized, as in a whole heart, for example, but even when this organization has been destroyed, human curiosity would like to discover how a body, by the fact that it is originally endowed with the breath of life, finds itself adorned in consequence with the faculty of feeling, and thus with that of thought. And, heavens, what efforts have not been made by certain philosophers to manage to prove this! and what nonsense on this subject I have had the patience to read!

All that experience teaches us is that while movement persists, however slight it may be, in one or more fibres, we need only stimulate them to reexcite and animate this movement almost extinguished. This has been shown in the host of experiments with which I have undertaken to crush the systems. It is therefore certain that motion and feeling excite each other in turn, both in a whole body and in the same body when its structure is destroyed, to say nothing of certain plants which seem to exhibit the same phenomena of the union of feeling and motion.

But furthermore, how many excellent philosophers have shown that thought is but a faculty of feeling, and that the reasonable soul is but the feeling soul engaged in contemplating its ideas and in reasoning! This would be proved by the fact alone that when feeling is stifled, thought also is checked, for instance in apoplexy, in lethargy, in catalepsis, etc. For it is ridiculous to suggest that, during these stupors, the soul keeps on thinking, even though it does not remember the ideas that it has had.

As to the development of feeling and motion, it is absurd to waste time seeking for its mechanism. The nature of motion is as unknown to us as that of matter. How can we discover how it is produced unless, like the author of "The History of the Soul," we resuscitate the old and unintelligible doctrine of substantial forms? I am then quite as content not to know how inert and simple matter becomes active and highly organized, as not to be able to look at the sun without red glasses; and I am as little disquieted concerning the other incomprehensible wonders of nature, the production of feeling and of thought in a being which earlier appeared to our limited eyes as a mere clod of clay.

Grant only that organized matter is endowed with a principle of motion, which alone differentiates it from the inorganic (and can one deny this in the face of the most incontestable observation?) and that among animals, as I have sufficiently proved, everything depends upon the diversity of this organization: these admissions suffice for guessing the riddle of substances and of man. It [thus] appears that there is but one [type of organization] in the universe, and that man is the most perfect [example]. He is to the ape, and to the most intelligent animals, as the planetary pendulum of Huyghens is to a watch of Julien Leroy. More instruments, more wheels and more springs were necessary to mark the movements of the planets than to mark or strike the hours; and Vaucanson, who needed more skill for making his flute player than for making his duck, would have needed still more to make a talking man, a mechanism no longer to be regarded as impossible, especially in the hands of another Prometheus. In like fashion, it was necessary that nature should use more elaborate art in making and sustaining a machine which for a whole century could mark all motions of the heart and of the mind; for though one does not tell time by the pulse, it is at least the barometer of the warmth and the vivacity by which one may estimate the nature of the soul. I am right! The human body is a watch, a large watch constructed with such skill and ingenuity, that if the wheel which marks the seconds happens to stop, the minute wheel turns and keeps on going its round, and in the same way the quarter-hour wheel, and all the others go on running when the first wheels have stopped because rusty or, for any reason, out of order. Is it not for a similar reason that the stoppage of a few blood vessels is not enough to destroy or suspend the strength of the movement which is in the heart as in the mainspring of the machine; since, on the contrary, the fluids whose volume is diminished, having a shorter road to travel, cover the ground more quickly, borne on as by a fresh current which the energy of the heart increases in proportion to the resistance it encounters at the ends of the blood-vessels? And is not this the reason why the loss of sight (caused by the compression of the optic nerve and by its ceasing to convey the images of objects) no more hinders hearing, than the loss of hearing (caused by obstruction of the functions of the auditory nerve) implies the loss of sight? In the same way, finally, does not one man hear (except immediately after his attack) without being able to say that he hears, while another who hears nothing, but whose lingual nerves are uninjured in the brain, mechanically tells of all the dreams which pass through his mind? These phenomena do not surprise enlightened physicians at all. They know what to think about man's nature, and (more accurately to express myself in passing) of two physicians, the better one and the one who deserves more confidence is always, in my opinion, the one who is more versed in the physique or mechanism of the human body, and who, leaving aside the soul and all the anxieties which this chimera gives to fools and to ignorant men, is seriously occupied only in pure naturalism.

Therefore let the pretended M. Charp deride philosophers who have regarded animals as machines. How different is my view! I believe that Descartes would be a man in every way worthy of respect, if, born in a century that he had not been obliged to enlighten, he had known the value of experiment and observation, and the danger of cutting loose from them. But it is none the less just for me to make an authentic reparation to this great man for all the insignificant philosophers—poor jesters, and poor imitators of Locke—who instead of laughing impudently at Descartes, might better realize that without him the field of philosophy, like the field of science without Newton, might perhaps be still uncultivated.

This celebrated philosopher, it is true, was much deceived, and no one denies that. But at any rate he understood animal nature, he was the first to prove completely that animals are pure machines. And after a discovery of this importance demanding so much sagacity, how can we without ingratitude fail to pardon all his errors!

In my eyes, they are all atoned for by that great confession. For after all, although he extols the distinctness of the two substances, this is plainly but a trick of skill, a ruse of style, to make theologians swallow a poison, hidden in the shade of an analogy which strikes everybody else and which they alone fail to notice. For it is this, this strong analogy, which forces all scholars and wise judges to confess that these proud and vain beings, more distinguished by their pride than by the name of men however much they may wish to exalt themselves, are at bottom only animals and machines which, though upright, go on all fours. They all have this marvelous instinct, which is developed by education into mind, and which always has its seat in the brain, (or for want of that when it is lacking or hardened, in the medulla oblongata) and never in the cerebellum; for I have often seen the cerebellum injured, and other observers[7] have found it hardened, when the soul has not ceased to fulfil its functions.

To be a machine, to feel, to think, to know how to distinguish good from bad, as well as blue from yellow, in a word, to be born with an intelligence and a sure moral instinct, and to be but an animal, are therefore characters which are no more contradictory, than to be an ape or a parrot and to be able to give oneself pleasure . . . I believe that thought is so little incompatible with organized matter, that it seems to be one of its properties on a par with electricity, the faculty of motion, impenetrability, extension, etc.

Do you ask for further observations? Here are some which are incontestable and which all prove that man resembles animals perfectly, in his origin as well as in all the points in which we have thought it essential to make the comparison . . .

Let us observe man both in and out of his shell, let us examine young embryos of four, six, eight or fifteen days with a microscope; after that time our eyes are sufficient. What do we see? The head alone; a little round egg with two black points which mark the eyes. Before that, everything is formless, and one sees only a medullary pulp, which is the brain, in which are formed first the roots of the nerves, that is, the principle of feeling, and the heart, which already within this substance has the power of beating of itself; it is the *punctum saliens* of Malpighi, which perhaps already owes a part of its excitability to the influence of the nerves. Then little by little, one sees the head lengthen from the neck, which, in dilating, forms first the thorax inside which the heart has already sunk, there to become stationary; below that is the abdomen which is divided by a partition (the diaphragm). One of these enlargements of the body forms the arms, the hands, the fingers, the nails, and the hair; the other forms the thighs, the legs, the feet, etc., which differ only in their observed situation, and which constitute the support and the balancing pole of the body. The whole process is a strange sort of growth, like that of plants. On the tops of our heads is hair in place of which the plants have leaves and flowers; everywhere is shown the same luxury of nature, and finally the directing principle of plants is placed where we have our soul, that other quintessence of man.

Such is the uniformity of nature, which we are beginning to realize; and the analogy of the animal with the vegetable kingdom, of man with plant. Perhaps there even are animal plants, which in vegetating, either fight as polyps do, or perform other functions characteristic of animals . . .

We are veritable moles in the field of nature; we achieve little more than the mole's journey and it is our pride which prescribes limits to the limitless. We are in the position of a watch that should say (a writer of fables would make the watch a hero in a silly tale): "I was never made by that fool of a workman, I who divide time, who mark so exactly the course of the sun, who repeat aloud the hours which I mark! No! that is impossible!" In the same way, we disdain, ungrateful wretches that we are, this common mother of all kingdoms, as the chemists say. We imagine, or rather we infer, a cause superior to that to which we owe all, and which truly has wrought all things in an inconceivable fashion. No; matter contains nothing base, except to the vulgar eyes which do not recognize her in her most splendid works; and nature is no stupid workman. She creates millions of men, with a facility and a pleasure more intense than the effort of a watchmaker in making the most

248

complicated watch. Her power shines forth equally in creating the lowliest insect and in creating the most highly developed man; the animal kingdom costs her no more than the vegetable, and the most splendid genius no more than a blade of wheat. Let us then judge by what we see of that which is hidden from the curiosity of our eyes and of our investigations, and let us not imagine anything beyond. Let us observe the ape, the beaver, the elephant, etc., in their operations. If it is clear that these activities can not be performed without intelligence, why refuse intelligence to these animals? And if you grant them a soul, you are lost, you fanatics! You will in vain say that you assert nothing about the nature of the animal soul and that you deny its immortality. Who does not see that this is a gratuitous assertion; who does not see that the soul of an animal must be either mortal or immortal, whichever ours [is], and that it must therefore undergo the same fate as ours, whatever that may be, and that thus [in admitting that animals have souls], you fall into Scylla in the effort to avoid Charybdis?

Break the chain of your prejudices, arm yourselves with the torch of experience, and you will render to nature the honor she deserves, instead of inferring anything to her disadvantage, from the ignorance in which she has left you. Only open wide your eyes, only disregard what you can not understand, and you will see that the ploughman whose intelligence and ideas extend no further than the bounds of his furrow, does not differ essentially from the greatest genius,—a truth which the dissection of Descartes's and of Newton's brains would have proved; you will be persuaded that the imbecile and the fool are animals with human faces, as the intelligent ape is a little man in another shape; in short, you will learn that since everything depends absolutely on difference of organization, a well constructed animal which has studied astronomy, can predict an eclipse, as it can predict recovery or death when it has used its genius and its clearness of vision, for a time, in the school of Hippocrates and at the bedside of the sick. By this line of observations and truths, we come to connect the admirable power of thought with matter, without being able to see the links, because the subject of this attribute is essentially unknown to us.

Let us not say that every machine or every animal perishes altogether or assumes another form after death, for we know absolutely nothing about the subject. On the other hand, to assert that an immortal machine is a chimera or a logical fiction, is to reason as absurdly as caterpillars would reason if, seeing the cast-off skins of their fellow-caterpillars, they should bitterly deplore the fate of their species, which to them would seem to come to nothing. The soul of these insects (for each animal has his own) is too limited to comprehend the metamorphoses of nature. Never one of the most skilful among them could have imagined that it was destined to become a butterfly. It is the same with us. What more do we know of our destiny than of our origin? Let us then submit to an invincible ignorance on which our happiness depends.

He who so thinks will be wise, just, tranquil about his fate, and therefore happy. He will await death without either fear or desire, and will cherish life (hardly understanding how disgust can corrupt a heart in this place of many delights); he will be filled with reverence, gratitude, affection, and tenderness for nature, in proportion to his feeling of the benefits he has received from nature; he will be happy, in short, in feeling nature and in being present at the enchanting spectacle of the universe, and he will surely never destroy nature either in himself or in others. More than that! Full of humanity, this man will love human character even in his enemies. Judge how he will treat others. He will pity the wicked without hating them; in his eyes, they will be but mis-made men. But in pardoning the faults of the structure of mind and body, he will none the less admire the beauties and the virtues of both. Those whom nature shall have favored will seem to him to deserve more respect than those whom she has treated in stepmotherly fashion. Thus, as we have seen, natural gifts, the source of all acquirements, gain from the lips and heart of the materialist, the homage which every other thinker unjustly refuses them. In short, the materialist, convinced, in spite of the protests of his vanity, that he is but a machine or an animal, will not maltreat his kind, for he will know too well the nature of those actions, whose humanity is always in proportion to the degree of the analogy proved above [between human beings and animals]; and following the natural law given to all animals, he will not wish to do to others what he would not wish them to do to him.

Let us then conclude boldly that man is a machine, and that in the whole universe there is but a single substance differently modified. This is no hypothesis set forth by dint of a number of postulates and assumptions; it is not the work of prejudice, nor even of my reason alone; I should have disdained a guide which I think to be so untrustworthy, had not my senses, bearing a torch, so to speak, induced me to follow reason by lighting the way themselves. Experience has thus spoken to me in behalf of reason; and in this way I have combined the two.

But it must have been noticed that I have not allowed myself even the most vigorous and immediately deduced reasoning, except as a result of a multitude of observations which no scholar will contest; and furthermore, I recognize only scholars as judges of the conclusions which I draw from the observations; and I hereby challenge every prejudiced man who is neither anatomist, nor acquainted with the only philosophy which can here be considered, that of the human body. Against so strong and solid an oak, what could the weak reeds of theology, of metaphysics, and of the schools, avail,—childish arms, like our parlor foils, that may well afford the pleasure of fencing, but can never wound an adversary. Need I say that I refer to the empty and trivial notions, to the pitiable and trite arguments that will be urged (as long as the shadow of prejudice or of superstition remains on earth) for the supposed incompatibility of two substances which meet and move each other unceasingly? Such is my system, or rather the truth, unless I am much deceived. It is short and simple. Dispute it now who will.

Notes

1 He evidently errs by begging the question.
2 The history of animals and of men proves how the mind and the body of children are dominated by their inheritence from their fathers.
3 The author of "The Natural History of the Soul."
4 The author of "The History of the Soul."
5 There are peoples, even to-day, who, through lack of a greater number of signs, can count only to 20.
6 In a company, or at table, he always required a rampart of chairs or else some one close to him at the left, to prevent his seeing horrible abysses into which (in spite of his understanding these illusions) he sometimes feared that he might fall. What a frightful result of imagination, or of the peculiar circulation in a lobe of the brain! Great man on one side of his nature, on the other he was half-mad. Madness and wisdom, each had its compartment, or its lobe, the two separated by a fissure. Which was the side by which he was so strongly attachcd to Messieurs of Port Royal? (I have read this in an extract from the treatise on vertigo by M. de la Mettrie.)
7 Haller in the *Tranact. Philosoph.*

12

TRANSLATOR'S NOTES (EXCERPTS) FOR L.F. MENABREA'S MEMOIR

Ada Lovelace

Source: R. Taylor (ed.) *Sketch of the Analytical Engine Invented by Charles Babbage* L. F. Menabrea, with Notes upon the Memoir by the Translator Ada Lovelace (1843), 1942, pp. 245–58 and 284.

Note A

The particular function whose integral the Difference Engine was constructed to tabulate, is

$$\Delta^7 u_z = 0.$$

The purpose which that engine has been specially intended and adapted to fulfil, is the computation of nautical and astronomical tables. The integral of

$$\Delta^7 u_z = 0$$

being

$$u_z = a + bx + cx^2 + dx^3 + ex^4 + fx^5 + gx^6,$$

the constants a, b, c, &c. are represented on the seven columns of discs, of which the engine consists. It can therefore tabulate *accurately* and to an *unlimited extent*, all series whose general term is comprised in the above formula; and it can also tabulate *approximatively* between *intervals of greater or less extent*, all other series which are capable of tabulation by the Method of Differences.

The Analytical Engine, on the contrary, is not merely adapted for *tabulating* the results of one particular function and of no other, but for *developing and tabulating* any function whatever. In fact the engine may be described as being the material expression of any indefinite function of any degree of generality and complexity, such as for instance,

$$F\ (x,y,z \log x,\ \sin y,\ x^{p}\ \&c.),$$

which is, it will be observed, a function of all other possible functions of any number of quantities.

In this, which we may call the *neutral* or *zero* state of the engine, it is ready to receive at any moment, by means of cards constituting a portion of its mechanism (and applied on the principle of those used in the Jacquard-loom), the impress of whatever *special* function we may desire to develope or to tabulate. These cards contain within themselves (in a manner explained in the Memoir itself, pages 232–234) the law of development of the particular function that may be under consideration, and they compel the mechanism to act accordingly in a certain corresponding order. One of the simplest cases would be, for example, to suppose that

$$F\ (x,y,z,\ \&c.\ \&c.)$$

is the particular function

$$\Delta^{n}u_{z} = 0$$

which the Difference Engine tabulates for values of n only up to 7. In this case the cards would order the mechanism to go through that succession of operations which would tabulate

$$u_{z} = a + bx + cx^{2} + \ldots + mx^{n-1},$$

where n might be any number whatever.

These cards, however, have nothing to do with the regulation of the particular *numerical* data. They merely determine the *operations*[1] to be effected, which operations may of course be performed on an infinite variety of particular numerical values, and do not bring out any definite numerical results unless the numerical data of the problem have been impressed on the requisite portions of the train of mechanism. In the above example, the first essential step towards an arithmetical result would be the substitution of specific numbers for n, and for the other primitive quantities which enter into the function.

Again, let us suppose that for F we put two complete equations of the fourth degree between x and y. We must then express on the cards the law of elimination for such equations. The engine would follow out those laws, and would ultimately give the equation of one variable which results from such elimination. Various *modes* of elimination might be selected; and of course

253

the cards must be made out accordingly. The following is one mode that might be adopted. The engine is able to multiply together any two functions of the form

$$a + bx + cx^2 + \ldots + px^n.$$

This granted, the two equations may be arranged according to the powers of y, and the coefficients of the powers of y may be arranged according to powers of x. The elimination of y will result from the successive multiplications and subtractions of several such functions. In this, and in all other instances, as was explained above, the particular *numerical* data and the *numerical* results are determined by means and by portions of the mechanism which act quite independently of those that regulate the *operations*.

In studying the action of the Analytical Engine, we find that the peculiar and independent nature of the considerations which in all mathematical analysis belong to *operations*, as distinguished from *the objects operated upon* and from the *results* of the operations performed upon those objects, is very strikingly defined and separated.

It is well to draw attention to this point, not only because its full appreciation is essential to the attainment of any very just and adequate general comprehension of the powers and mode of action of the Analytical Engine, but also because it is one which is perhaps too little kept in view in the study of mathematical science in general. It is, however, impossible to confound it with other considerations, either when we trace the manner in which that engine attains its results, or when we prepare the data for its attainment of those results. It were much to be desired, that when mathematical processes pass through the human brain instead of through the medium of inanimate mechanism, it were equally a necessity of things that the reasonings connected with *operations* should hold the same just place as a clear and well-defined branch of the subject of analysis, a fundamental but yet independent ingredient in the science, which they must do in studying the engine. The confusion, the difficulties, the contradictions which, in consequence of a want of accurate distinctions in this particular, have up to even a recent period encumbered mathematics in all those branches involving the consideration of negative and impossible quantities, will at once occur to the reader who is at all versed in this science, and would alone suffice to justify dwelling somewhat on the point, in connexion with any subject so peculiarly fitted to give forcible illustration of it as the Analytical Engine. It may be desirable to explain, that by the word *operation*, we mean *any process which alters the mutual relation of two or more things*, be this relation of what kind it may. This is the most general definition, and would include all subjects in the universe. In abstract mathematics, of course operations alter those particular relations which are involved in the considerations of number and space, and the *results* of operations are those peculiar results which correspond to the nature of the subjects of operation. But the science of operations, as derived from mathematics more especially, is a science of itself, and has its own abstract truth and value; just as logic has its own peculiar truth and value, independently of the subjects to which we may apply its reasonings and processes. Those who are accustomed to some of the more modern views of the above subject, will know that a few fundamental relations being true, certain other combinations of relations must of necessity follow; combinations unlimited in variety and extent if the deductions from the primary relations be carried on far enough. They will also be aware that one main reason why the separate nature of the science of operations has been little felt, and in general little dwelt on, is the *shifting* meaning of many of the symbols used in mathematical notation. First, the symbols of *operation* are frequently *also* the symbols of the *results* of operations. We may say that these symbols are apt to have both a *retrospective* and a *prospective* signification. They may signify either relations that are the consequences of a series of processes already performed, or relations that are yet to be effected through certain processes. Secondly, figures, the symbols of *numerical magnitude*, are frequently *also* the symbols of *operations*, as when they are the indices of powers. Wherever terms have a shifting meaning, independent sets of considerations are liable to become complicated together, and reasonings and results are frequently falsified. Now in the Analytical Engine, the operations which come under the first of the above heads are ordered and combined by means of a notation and of a train of mechanism which belong exclusively to themselves; and with respect to the second head, whenever numbers meaning *operations* and not *quantities* (such as the indices of powers) are inscribed on any column or set of columns, those columns immediately act in a wholly separate and independent manner, becoming connected with the *operating mechanism* exclusively, and re-acting upon this. They never come into combination with numbers upon any other columns meaning *quantities*; though, of course, if there are numbers meaning *operations* upon *n* columns, these may *combine amongst each other*, and will often be required to do so, just as numbers meaning *quantities* combine with each other in any variety. It might have been arranged that all numbers meaning *operations* should have appeared on some separate portion of the engine from that which presents numerical *quantities*; but the present mode is in some cases more simple, and offers in reality quite as much distinctness when understood.

The operating mechanism can even be thrown into action independently of any object to operate upon (although of course no *result* could then be developed). Again, it might act upon other things besides *number*, were objects found whose mutual fundamental relations could be expressed by those of the abstract science of operations, and which should be also susceptible of adaptations to the action of the operating notation and mechanism of the engine. Supposing, for instance, that the fundamental relations of pitched sounds in the science of harmony and of musical composition were susceptible of such expression and adaptations, the engine might compose elaborate and scientific pieces of music of any degree of complexity or extent.

The Analytical Engine is an *embodying of the science of operations*, constructed with peculiar reference to abstract number as the subject of those operations. The Difference Engine is the embodying of *one particular and very limited set of operations*, which (see the notation used in Note B) may be expressed thus (+, +, +, +, +, +), or thus, 6(+). Six repetitions of the one operation, +, is, in fact, the whole sum and object of that engine. It has seven columns, and a number on any column can add itself to a number on the next column to its *righthand*. So that, beginning with the column furthest to the left, six additions can be effected, and the result appears on the seventh column, which is the last on the right-hand. The *operating* mechanism of this engine acts in as separate and independent a manner as that of the Analytical Engine; but being susceptible of only one unvarying and restricted combination, it has little force or interest in illustration of the distinct nature of the *science of operations*. The importance of regarding the Analytical Engine under this point of view will, we think, become more and more obvious as the reader proceeds with M. Menabrea's clear and masterly article. The calculus of operations is likewise in itself a topic of so much interest, and has of late years been so much more written on and thought on than formerly, that any bearing which that engine, from its mode of constitution, may possess upon the illustration of this branch of mathematical science should not be overlooked. Whether the inventor of this engine had any such views in his mind while working out the invention, or whether he may subsequently ever have regarded it under this phase, we do not know; but it is one that forcibly occurred to ourselves on becoming acquainted with the means through which analytical combinations are actually attained by the mechanism. We cannot forbear suggesting one practical result which it appears to us must be greatly facilitated by the independent manner in which the engine orders and combines its *operations*. We allude to the attainment of those combinations into which *imaginary quantities* enter. This is a branch of its processes into which we have not had the opportunity of inquiring, and our conjecture therefore as to the principle on which we conceive the accomplishment of such results may have been made to depend, is very probably not in accordance with the fact, and less subservient for the purpose than some other principles, or at least requiring the cooperation of others. It seems to us obvious, however, that where operations are so independent in their mode of acting, it must be easy, by means of a few simple provisions, and additions in arranging the mechanism, to bring out a *double* set of *results*, viz.—1st, the *numerical magnitudes* which are the results of operations performed on *numerical data*. (These results are the *primary* object of the engine.) 2ndly, the *symbolical results* to be attached to those numerical results, which symbolical results are not less the necessary and logical consequences of operations performed upon *symbolical data*, than are numerical results when the data are numerical.[2]

If we compare together the powers and the principles of construction of the Difference and of the Analytical Engines, we shall perceive that the capabilities of the latter are immeasurably more extensive than those of the former, and that they in fact hold to each other the same relationship as that of analysis to arithmetic. The Difference Engine can effect but one particular series of operations, viz. that required for tabulating the integral of the special function

$$\Delta^n u_z = 0;$$

and as it can only do this for values of n up to 7^3, it cannot be considered as being the most *general* expression even of *one particular* function, much less as being the expression of any and all possible functions of all degrees of generality. The Difference Engine can in reality (as has been already partly explained) do nothing but *add*; and any other processes, not excepting those of simple subtraction, multiplication and division, can be performed by it only just to that extent in which it is possible, by judicious mathematical arrangement and artifices, to reduce them to a *series of additions*. The method of differences is, in fact, a method of additions; and as it includes within its means a larger number of results attainable of *addition* simply, than any other mathematical principle, it was very appropriately selected as the basis on which to construct *an Adding Machine*, so as to give to the powers of such a machine the widest possible range. The Analytical Engine, on the contrary, can either add, subtract, multiply or divide with equal facility; and performs each of these four operations in a direct manner, without the aid of any of the other three. This one fact implies everything; and it is scarcely necessary to point out, for instance, that while the Difference Engine can merely *tabulate*, and is incapable of *developing*, the Analytical Engine can *either tabulate or develope*.

The former engine is in its nature strictly *arithmetical*, and the results it can arrive at lie within a very clearly defined and restricted range, while there is no finite line of demarcation which limits the powers of the Analytical Engine. These powers are co-extensive with our knowledge of the laws of analysis itself, and need be bounded only by our acquaintance with the latter. Indeed we may consider the engine as the *material and mechanical representative* of analysis, and that our actual working powers in this department of human study will be enabled more effectually than heretofore to keep pace with our theoretical knowledge of its principles and laws, through the complete control which the engine gives us over the *executive manipulation* of algebraical and numerical symbols.

Those who view mathematical science, not merely as a vast body of abstract and immutable truths, whose intrinsic beauty, symmetry and logical completeness, when regarded in their connexion together as a whole, entitle them to a prominent place in the interest of all profound and logical minds, but as possessing a yet deeper interest for the human race, when it is remembered that this science constitutes the language through which alone we can adequately express the great facts of the natural world, and those unceasing changes of mutual relationship which, visibly or invisibly, consciously or unconsciously to our immediate physical perceptions, are interminably going on in the agencies of the creation we live amidst: those who thus think on mathematical truth as the instrument through which the weak mind of man can most effectually read his Creator's works, will regard with especial interest all that can tend to facilitate the translation of its principles into explicit practical forms.

The distinctive characteristic of the Analytical Engine, and that which has rendered it possible to endow mechanism with such extensive faculties as bid fair to make this engine the executive right-hand of abstract algebra, is the introduction into it of the principle which Jacquard devised for regulating, by means of punched cards, the most complicated patterns in the fabrication of brocaded stuffs. It is in this that the distinction between the two engines lies. Nothing of the sort exists in the Difference Engine. We may say most aptly, that the Analytical Engine *weaves algebraical patterns* just as the Jacquard-loom weaves flowers and leaves. Here, it seems to us, resides much more of originality than the Difference Engine can be fairly entitled to claim. We do not wish to deny to this latter all such claims. We believe that it is the only proposal or attempt ever made to construct a calculating machine *founded on the principle of successive orders of differences*, and capable of *printing off its own results*; and that this engine surpasses its predecessors, both in the extent of the calculations which it can perform, in the facility, certainty and accuracy with which it can effect them, and in the absence of all necessity for the intervention of human intelligence *during the performance of its calculations*. Its nature is, however, limited to the strictly arithmetical, and it is far from being the first or only scheme for constructing *arithmetical* calculating machines with more or less of success.

The bounds of *arithmetic* were however outstepped the moment the idea of applying the cards had occurred; and the Analytical Engine does not occupy common ground with mere "calculating machines." It holds a position wholly its own; and the considerations it suggests are most interesting in their nature. In enabling mechanism to combine together *general* symbols in successions of unlimited variety and extent, a uniting link is established between the operations of matter and the abstract mental processes of the *most abstract* branch of mathematical science. A new, a vast, and a powerful language is developed for the future use of analysis, in which to wield its truths so that these may become of more speedy and accurate practical application for the purposes of mankind than the means hitherto in our possession have rendered possible. Thus not only the mental and the

258

material, but the theoretical and the practical in the mathematical world, are brought into more intimate and effective connexion with each other. We are not aware of its being on record that anything partaking in the nature of what is so well designated the *Analytical* Engine has been hitherto proposed, or even thought of, as a practical possibility, any more than the idea of a thinking or of a reasoning machine.

We will touch on another point which constitutes an important distinction in the modes of operating of the Difference and Analytical Engines. In order to enable the former to do its business, it is necessary to put into its columns the series of numbers constituting the first terms of the several orders of differences for whatever is the particular table under consideration. The machine then works *upon* these as its data. But these data must themselves have been already computed through a series of calculations by a human head. Therefore that engine can only produce results depending on data which have been arrived at by the explicit and actual working out of processes that are in their nature different from any that come within the sphere of its own powers. In other words, an *analysing* process must have been gone through by a human mind in order to obtain the data upon which the engine then *synthetically* builds its results. The Difference Engine is in its character exclusively *synthetical*, while the Analytical Engine is equally capable of analysis or of synthesis.

It is true that the Difference Engine can calculate to a much greater extent with these few preliminary data, than the data themselves required for their own determination. The table of squares, for instance, can be calculated to any extent whatever, when the numbers *one* and *two* are furnished; and a very few differences computed at any part of a table of logarithms would enable the engine to calculate many hundreds or even thousands of logarithms. Still the circumstance of its requiring, as a previous condition, that any function whatever shall have been numerically worked out, makes it very inferior in its nature and advantages to an engine which, like the Analytical Engine, requires merely that we should know the *succession and distribution of the operations* to be performed; without there being any occasion, in order to obtain data on which it can work, for our ever having gone through either the same particular operations which it is itself to effect, or any others. Numerical data must of course be given it, but they are mere arbitrary ones; not data that could only be arrived at through a systematic and necessary series of previous numerical calculations, which is quite a different thing.

To this it may be replied, that an analysing process must equally have been performed in order to furnish the Analytical Engine with the necessary *operative* data; and that herein may also lie a possible source of error. Granted that the actual mechanism is unerring in its processes, the *cards* may give it wrong orders. This is unquestionably the case; but there is much less chance of error, and likewise far less expenditure of time and labour, where operations only, and the distribution of these operations, have to be made out, than where explicit numerical results are to be attained. In the case of the Analytical Engine we have undoubtedly to lay out a certain capital of analytical labour in one particular line; but this is in order that the engine may bring us in a much larger return in another line. It should be remembered also that the cards, when once made out for any formula, have all the generality of algebra, and include an infinite number of particular cases.

We have dwelt considerably on the distinctive peculiarities of each of these engines, because we think it essential to place their respective attributes in strong relief before the apprehension of the public; and to define with clearness and accuracy the wholly different nature of the principles on which each is based, so as to make it self-evident to the reader (the mathematical reader at least) in what manner and degree the powers of the Analytical Engine transcend those of an engine, which, like the Difference Engine, can only work out such results as may be derived from *one restricted and particular series of processes*, such as those included in $\Delta^n u_z = 0$. We think this of importance, because we know that there exists considerable vagueness and inaccuracy in the mind of persons in general on the subject. There is a misty notion amongst most of those who have attended at all to it, that *two* "calculating machines" have been successively invented by the same person within the last few years; while others again have never heard but of the one original "calculating machine," and are not aware of there being any extension upon this. For either of these two classes of persons the above considerations are appropriate. While the latter require a knowledge of the fact that there *are two* such inventions, the former are not less in want of accurate and well-defined information on the subject. No very clear or correct ideas prevail as to the characteristics of each engine, or their respective advantages or disadvantages; and in meeting with those incidental allusions, of a more or less direct kind, which occur in so many publications of the day, to these machines, it must frequently be matter of doubt *which* "calculating machine" is referred to, or whether *both* are included in the general allusion.

We are desirous likewise of removing two misapprehensions which we know obtain, to some extent, respecting these engines. In the first place it is very generally supposed that the Difference Engine, after it had been completed up to a certain point, *suggested* the idea of the Analytical Engine; and that the second is in fact the improved offspring of the first, and *grew out* of the existence of its predecessor, through some natural or else accidental combination of ideas suggested by this one. Such a supposition is in this instance contrary to the facts; although it seems to be almost an obvious inference, wherever two inventions, similar in their nature and objects, succeed each other closely in order of *time*, and strikingly in order of *value*; more especially when the same individual is the author of both. Nevertheless the ideas which led to the Analytical Engine occurred in a manner wholly independent of any that were connected with the Difference Engine. These ideas are indeed in their own intrinsic nature independent of the latter engine, and might equally have occurred had it never existed nor been even thought of at all.

The second of the misapprehensions above alluded to relates to the well-known suspension, during some years past, of all progress in the construction of the Difference Engine. Respecting the circumstances which have interfered with the actual completion of either invention, we offer no opinion; and in fact are not possessed of the data for doing so, had we the inclination. But we know that some persons suppose these obstacles (be they what they may) to have arisen *in consequence* of the subsequent invention of the Analytical Engine while the former was in progress. We have ourselves heard it even *lamented* that an idea should ever have occurred at all, which had turned out to be merely the means of arresting what was already in a course of successful execution, without substituting the superior invention in its stead. This notion we can contradict in the most unqualified manner. The progress of the Difference Engine had long been suspended, before there were even the least crude glimmerings of any invention superior to it. Such glimmerings, therefore, and their subsequent development, were in no way the original *cause* of that suspension; although, where difficulties of some kind or other evidently already existed, it was not perhaps calculated to remove or lessen them that an invention should have been meanwhile thought of, which, while including all that the first was capable of, possesses powers so extended as to eclipse it altogether.

We leave it for the decision of each individual (*after he has possessed himself* of competent information as to the characteristics of each engine) to determine how far it ought to be matter of regret that such an accession has been made to the powers of human science, even if it *has* (which we greatly doubt) increased to a certain limited extent some already existing difficulties that had arisen in the way of completing a valuable but lesser work. We leave it for each to satisfy himself as to the wisdom of desiring the obliteration (were that now possible) of all records of the more perfect invention, in order that the comparatively limited one might be finished. The Difference Engine would doubtless fulfil all those practical objects which it was originally destined for. It would certainly calculate all the tables that are more directly necessary for the physical purposes of life, such as nautical and other computations. Those who incline to very strictly utilitarian views may perhaps feel that the peculiar powers of the Analytical Engine bear upon questions of abstract and speculative science, rather than upon those involving every-day and ordinary human interests. These persons being likely to possess but little sympathy, or possibly acquaintance, with any branches of science which they do not find to be *useful* (according to *their* definition of that word), may conceive that the undertaking of that engine, now that the other one is already in progress, would be a barren and unproductive laying out of yet more money and labour; in fact, a work of supererogation. Even in the utilitarian aspect, however, we do not doubt that very valuable practical results would be developed by the extended faculties of the Analytical Engine; some of which results we think we could now hint at, had we the space; and others, which it may not yet be possible to foresee, but which would be brought forth by the daily increasing requirements of science, and by a more intimate practical acquaintance with the powers of the engine, were it in actual existence.

On general grounds, both of an *a priori* description as well as those founded on the scientific history and experience of mankind, we see strong presumptions that such would be the case. Nevertheless all will probably concur in feeling that the completion of the Difference Engine would be far preferable to the non-completion of any calculating engine at all. With whomsoever or wheresoever may rest the present causes of difficulty that apparently exist towards either the completion of the old engine, or the commencement of the new one, we trust they will not ultimately result in this generation's being acquainted with these inventions through the medium of pen, ink and paper merely; and still more do we hope, that for the honour of our country's reputation in the future pages of history, these causes will not lead to the completion of the undertaking by some *other* nation or government. This could not but be matter of just regret; and equally so, whether the obstacles may have originated in private interests and feelings, in considerations of a more public description, or in causes combining the nature of both such solutions.

We refer the reader to the "Edinburgh Review" of July 1834, for a very able account of the Difference Engine. The writer of the article we allude to has selected as his prominent matter for exposition, a wholly different view of the subject form that which M. Menabrea has chosen. The former chiefly treats it under its mechanical aspect, entering but slightly into the mathematical principles of which that engine is the representative, but giving, in considerable length, many details of the mechanism and contrivances by means of which it tabulates the various orders of differences. M. Menabrea, on the contrary, exclusively developes the analytical view; taking it for granted that mechanism is able to perform certain processes, but without attempting to explain *how*; and devoting his whole attention to explanations and illustrations of the manner in which analytical laws can be so arranged and combined as to bring every branch of that vast subject within the grasp of the assumed powers of mechanism. It is obvious that, in the invention of a calculating engine, these two branches of the subject are equally essential fields of investigation, and that on their mutual adjustment, one to the other, must depend all success. They must be made to meet each other, so that the weak points in the powers of either department may be compensated by the strong points in those of the other. They are indissolubly connected, though so different in their intrinsic nature, that perhaps the same mind might not be likely to prove equally profound or successful in both. We know those who doubt whether the powers of mechanism will in practice prove adequate in all respects to the demands made upon them in the working of such complicated trains of machinery as those of the above engines, and who apprehend that unforeseen practical difficulties and disturbances will arise in the way of accuracy and of facility of operation. The Difference Engine, however, appears to us to be in a great measure an answer to these doubts. It is complete as far as it goes, and it does work with all the anticipated success. The Analytical Engine, far from being more complicated, will in many respects be of simpler construction; and it is a remarkable circumstance attending it, that with very *simplified* means it is so much more powerful.

The article in the "Edinburgh Review" was written some time previous to the occurrence of any ideas such as afterwards led to the invention of the Analytical Engine; and in the nature of the Difference Engine there is much less that would invite a writer to take exclusively, or even prominently, the mathematical view of it, than in that of the Analytical Engine; although mechanism has undoubtedly gone much further to meet mathematics, in the case of this engine, than of the former one. Some publication embracing the *mechanical* view of the Analytical Engine is a desideratum which we trust will be supplied before long.

Those who may have the patience to study a moderate quantity of rather dry details will find ample compensation, after perusing the article of 1834, in the clearness with which a succinct view will have been attained of the various practical steps through which mechanism can accomplish certain processes; and they will also find themselves still further capable of appreciating M. Menabrea's more comprehensive and generalized memoir. The very difference in the style and object of these two articles makes them peculiarly valuable to each other; at least for the purposes of those who really desire something more than a merely superficial and popular comprehension of the subject of calculating engines.

Note G

It is desirable to guard against the possibility of exaggerated ideas that might arise as to the powers of the Analytical Engine. In considering any new subject, there is frequently a tendency, first, to *overrate* what we find to be already interesting or remarkable, and, secondly, by a sort of natural reaction, to *undervalue* the true state of the case, when we do discover that our notions have surpassed those that were really tenable.

The Analytical Engine has no pretensions whatever to *originate* anything. It can do whatever we *know how to order it* to perform. It can *follow* analysis; but it has no power of *anticipating* any analytical relations or truths. Its province is to assist us in making *available* what we are already acquainted with. This it is calculated to effect primarily and chiefly of course, through its executive faculties; but it is likely to exert an *indirect* and reciprocal influence on science itself in another manner. For, in so distributing and combining the truths and the formulæ of analysis, that they may become most easily and

263

rapidly amenable to the mechanical combinations of the engine, the relations and the nature of many subjects in that science are necessarily thrown into new lights, and more profoundly investigated. This is a decidedly indirect, and a somewhat *speculative*, consequence of such an invention. It is however pretty evident, on general principles, that in devising for mathematical truths a new form in which to record and throw themselves out for actual use, views are likely to be induced, which should again react on the more theoretical phase of the subject. There are in all extensions of human power, or additions to human knowledge, various *collateral* influences, besides the main and primary object attained.

To return to the executive faculties of this engine: the question must arise in every mind, are they *really* even able to *follow* analysis in its whole extent? No reply, entirely satisfactory to all minds, can be given to this query, excepting the actual existence of the engine, and actual experience of its practical results. We will however sum up for each reader's consideration the chief elements with which the engine works:—

1. It performs the four operations of simple arithmetic upon any numbers whatever.

2. By means of certain artifices and arrangements (upon which we cannot enter within the restricted space which such a publication as the present may admit of), there is no limit either to the *magnitude* of the *numbers* used, or to the *number of quantities* (either variables or constants) that may be employed.

3. It can combine these numbers and these quantities either algebraically or arithmetically, in relations unlimited as to variety, extent, or complexity.

4. It uses algebraic *signs* according to their proper laws, and developes the logical consequences of these laws.

5. It can arbitrarily substitute any formula for any other; effacing the first from the columns on which it is represented, and making the second appear in its stead.

6. It can provide for singular values. Its power of doing this is referred to in M. Menabrea's memoir, page 240, where he mentions the passage of values through zero and infinity. The practicability of causing it arbitrarily to change its processes at any moment, on the occurrence of any specified contingency (of which its substitution of ($\frac{1}{2}$ cos.$\overline{n+1}\theta$ + $\frac{1}{2}$ cos.$\overline{n-1}\theta$) for (cos.$n\theta$.cos.θ), explained in Note E., is in some degree an illustration), at once secures this point.

Notes

1 We do not mean to imply that the *only* use made of the Jacquard cards is that of regulating the algebraical *operations*; but we mean to explain that *those* cards and portions of mechanism which regulate these *operations* are wholly independent of those which are used for other purposes. M. Menabrea explains that there are *three*

classes of cards used in the engine for three distinct sets of objects, viz. *Cards of the Operations, Cards of the Variables*, and certain *Cards of Numbers*. (See pages 233 and 242.)

2 In fact, such an extension as we allude to would merely constitute a further and more perfected development of any system introduced for making the proper combinations of the signs *plus* and *minus*. How ably M. Menabrea has touched on this restricted case is pointed out in Note B, p. 258.

3 The machine might have been constructed so as to tabulate for a higher value of n than seven. Since, however, every unit added to the value of n increases the extent of the mechanism requisite, there would on this account be a limit beyond which it could not be practically carried. Seven is sufficiently high for the calculation of all ordinary tables.

The fact that, in the Analytical Engine, the same extent of mechanism suffices for the solution of $\delta nu_z = 0$, whether $n = 7$, $n = 100,000$, or $n =$ any number whatever, at once suggests how entirely distinct must be the *nature of the principles* through whose application matter has been enabled to become the working agent of abstract mental operations in each of these engines respectively; and it affords an equally obvious presumption, that in the case of the Analytical Engine, not only are those principles in themselves of a higher and more comprehensive description, but also such as must vastly extend the *practical* value of the engine whose basis they constitute.

13

BABBAGE, HUXLEY AND BUTLER

Bruce Mazlish

Source: B. Mazlish, *The Fourth Discontinuity*, Yale University Press, 1993, pp. 130–55.

In the two previous chapters, using Linnaeus and Darwin as reference points, I have been trying to establish the context of evolutionary theory surrounding the human-machine question. With Freud and Pavlov, I tried to explore further the human-machine question while focusing especially on the implications of Darwinian theory for our view of human nature. Now I wish to pursue both these inquiries via three thinkers in the nineteenth century who grappled strenuously and originally with them: Charles Babbage, T. H. Huxley, and Samuel Butler.

The man who is at the juncture where the age-old thoughts and feelings about the mechanical take on a new, modern life is Charles Babbage. Though the calculating machine, or computer, rethought by Babbage in the early nineteenth century, was at first obscured by the development of a lesser order of machines—the "brute" iron and steel artifacts of the Industrial Revolution—it has proliferated exponentially in the twentieth century, posing in the most challenging form the question of human identity vis-à-vis machines. Babbage is the prototypic figure in that development.

One way to start our consideration of Babbage is by a brief comparison with one of his contemporaries whom we have already mentioned: Thomas Carlyle. In "Signs of the Times" (1829), that most brilliant statement on the cultural implications of the Industrial Revolution, Thomas Carlyle announced, as we have seen, that "men are grown mechanical in head and in heart, as well as in hand." He followed up this statement by quoting, scathingly, the French ideologue Dr. Cabanis to the effect that "as the liver secretes bile, so does the brain secrete thought." Earlier, as we noted, the great sixteenth-century French physician Ambroise Paré had depicted the human hand as a system of levers, and Julien La Mettrie, his eighteenth-century successor, had declared Man to be "L'Homme-machine." Carlyle was now saying that Man is not a machine by nature, but can be made so by culture. Having invented clocks and steam engines, Man is becoming like them.

Seer that he was, Carlyle also unknowingly intuited the future connection of humans and computers, which is the advanced form of the machine of the future. Evoking the names of the great mathematicians Legrange and Laplace he remarks "that their calculus, differential and integral, is little else than a more cunningly-constructed arithmetical mill, where the factors being put in, are, as it were, ground into the true product, under cover, and without other effort on our part than steady turning of the handle." A few years later, in *Sartor Resartus* (1833), he noted that science, "destroying Wonder" in its progress, was proceeding to a state in which the human mind became an "Arithmetical Mill."[1]

Did Carlyle have knowledge of any specific development at the time, tending to an "arithmetical mill"? The chances are, as we shall see, that he did. Did he go further and foresee that the arithmetical mill would raise not only the question as to humans being machines, but the further question as to whether the machine could possess human powers of thought, that is, do more than just add, logically, one number to another? Understandably, Carlyle's vision faltered and did not reach to this transformation of the basic question concerning human nature.

In fact, an arithmetical mill was being constructed at the time Carlyle wrote, and its basic concepts had been thought out by Charles Babbage, a man whom Carlyle knew.[2] In 1822, at age thirty, Babbage read a paper to the Royal Astronomical Society, announcing that he was engaged in the construction of a calculating machine. By 1832 such a full-scale machine existed.

Babbage's machine is variously called a Calculating Engine, or, in its two incarnations, a Difference Engine or an Analytic Engine. It is, I am arguing, a product of the Industrial Revolution and cannot really be conceived separate from that great transformation.

Babbage came upon the idea when he and his friend John Herschel were asked in 1820 to 1821 to prepare improved astronomical tables. The purpose was to serve British commercial shipping, in short, imperialism, which in turn served the needs of British industrialization. (The same purpose was behind the voyage of the *Beagle*, on which Charles Darwin went as naturalist.) While Babbage and Herschel were tediously verifying the calculations brought to them by various human computers, Charles is reported to have exclaimed: "I wish to God these calculations had been executed by steam."[3]

Soon, Babbage conceptualized and then constructed a model of what he called the Difference Engine (and it is this work he reported on in 1822).[4] Babbage's was a mechanical engine and depended on the existence and further development of the machine tools so critical to the Industrial Revolution.[5]

The other image surrounding Babbage's calculator was that of an "arithmetical mill." The mill is, of course, the symbol of the textile factories at the heart of Britain's Industrial Revolution—identified with Blake's "dark satanic mills"—as well as of the heavens. (The mill is also the hub of the mechanical trade, that is, of the millwrights—such as James Brindley—who constructed the water and threshing mills and became the mechanical engineers, constructing the canals and factories of the early nineteenth century.) The arithmetical mill, in short, was a kind of factory that could grind out calculations.

Another, similar image, specifically the textile one, emerges from Babbage's calculator by his employment of punched cards, derived from their use in the Jacquard weaving loom, invented in 1801 by the Frenchman Joseph-Marie Jacquard. As Babbage's assistant and friend, Lady Lovelace, a gifted mathematician and, incidentally, the daughter of Lord Byron, observed appropriately: "It could be said most aptly that the analytical engine wove algebraical patterns, just as the Jacquard loom wove flowers and leaves."[6]

Engine or mill, grinding or weaving, Babbage's machine, in its calculated way, was to have what is truly an incalculable effect on our civilization. It would take almost a century and a half for it to begin to show its effects, but the future was already laid down in the convoluted lines of Babbage's brain and made evident in his designs. Still Babbage was aware, as he wrote Sir. Humphrey Davy, that his mechanical schemes "may perhaps be viewed as something more than Utopian." Then he added, "of the extent to which the machinery whose nature I have described may be carried, opinions will necessary fluctuate."[7]

The present-day computer, derived from Babbage's conceptualizations, is hardly utopian, or nowhere; it is, in fact, everywhere. It is shaping us and our civilization anew, just as the mills and steam engines of the Industrial Revolution at the beginning of the nineteenth century. Drawing on the long tradition of the "uncanny," this new automaton also is raising once again, with great urgency, the debate over human and machine and conjuring up before us the specter of a "new species," which may be the servant but perhaps, instead, may become the supplanter of humans, as we have hitherto known them.

Babbage himself was a strange individual. He was aware that even many of his friends, as he tells us in his autobiography, "thought that my intellect was beginning to become deranged."[8] But though he was quite eccentric, he was eminently sane. Fortunately, Babbage's monomaniacal and compulsive mind turned early to mathematics and machines. Babbage's mother, apparently, first took him as a child to "several exhibitions of machinery." One especially was memorable. The exhibitor, fittingly named Merlin, noticing the boy's rapt interest, proposed taking him and his mother to his workshop, "where I should see still more wonderful automata."[9]

In the workshop, Babbage saw two nude female figures of silver, about twelve inches high. As he described them,

One of these walked or rather glided along a space of about four feet, when she turned round and went back to her original place. She used an eye-glass occasionally, and bowed frequently, as if recognizing her acquaintances. The motions of her limbs were singularly graceful . . .

One other silver figure was an admirable *danseuse*, with a bird on the fore finger of her right hand, which wagged its tail, flapped its wings, and opened its beak. This lady attitudinized in a most fascinating manner. Her eyes were full of imagination, and irresistible.

We can recognize these irresistible figures as stretching from Hero of Greece to Vaucanson and Droz in the eighteenth century, and now to Babbage.

The statues came to be a kind of leitmotif in Babbage's life. In later years, he came upon the statues again at an auction. Purchasing them, he tells us that "I proceeded to take to pieces the whole of the mechanism, and found a multitude of small holes which had been stopped up as not having fulfilled their intended object. In fact, it appeared tolerably certain that scarcely any drawings could have been prepared for the automaton, but that the beautiful result arose from a system of continual trials." The automata, which, once repaired, were placed in Babbage's drawing room for the edification of his friends (he loved to give Saturday night banquets), were inspirations leading him to the calculating engine. We see the quantum jump forward, however, when we note that what, until Babbage, was a matter of craftsmanship—making automata by trial and error—became, in his hands and mind, a matter of preconceptualized design: modern science.

The line, however, is continuous, for Babbage contrived it so that his machine, like earlier automata, could play games of skill, such as ticktacktoe, checkers, and even chess. Anticipating the modern computer chess player, Babbage wrote, "Allowing one hundred moves on each side for the longest game at chess, I found that the combinations involved in the Analytical Engine enormously surpassed any required, even by the game of chess."[10] So, too, he noted that clock, automata, and mechanical toys all operated on the same principle of "winding up," a labor of at most half a minute, which labor then, by the aid of a few wheels, spread out over the whole twenty-four hours. Babbage's Calculating Engines, which were mechanical rather than present-day electronic devices, operated on more or less the same kind of clockwork action.

The Difference Engine was so-called because it operated with the mathematical concept of differences, which, in turn, allowed for a process of simple addition. My purpose is not to go into the technical details but to try to understand their implications. The Difference Engine, though a great mechanical leap forward requiring for its construction new machine tools well beyond earlier clockwork mechanisms, was still quite primitive. All it could really do was add, the other three processes of arithmetic being reduced to a series of additions.

Even in its primitive state, however, it could compute astronomical tables more efficiently and more reliably than humans. Equipped with a printout attachment, it realized in its tables what Babbage had designed first in his mind and then in drawings. Still, if left in that primitive shape, the Difference Engine would have been merely a mechanical version of the abacus.

But Babbage's teeming mind would not let him rest. To the dismay of the British government, which had already advanced a significant sum of money for the Difference Engine and wished nothing more than its astronomical and nautical tables, Babbage proposed to replace it before it was totally finished and operative with a more advanced engine. He called his new machine the Analytic Engine because, as Lady Lovelace explained, it "was to the difference engine as analysis was to arithmetic."[11] It could execute all four processes—addition, subtraction, multiplication, or division—each autonomously, and as Lady Lovelace went on, "could tabulate or develop. No finite line of demarcation limited the powers of the analytical engine."

Her words were prophetic. Babbage himself spoke of his machine as the "engine eating its own tail," by which he meant that the results in one table could affect the other columns, thus changing the instructions under which the machine was operating. The machine also had a "library," where logarithms or similar tabular numbers could be stored, and a "memory," where it could hold intermediate results until the program called for their use. Babbage claimed that it possessed the ability to operate along lines not specifically laid down in the machine's instructions beforehand.[12]

Did this mean that it possessed the power of original thought? Lady Lovelace opposed such an exaggerated claim. The Analytical Engine, she declared, "has no pretensions whatever to *originate* anything. It can do whatever *we know how to order* it to perform. It can *follow* analysis; but it has no power of *anticipating* any analytical relations or truths. Its province is to assist us in making *available* what we are already acquainted with." A more modern scientist, Philip Morrison, seems to take a different view when he writes, "It could make judgements by comparing numbers and then act upon the result of its comparison—thus proceeding upon lines not uniquely specified in advance by the machine's instructions."[13] Babbage's own way of putting the matter was that "nothing but teaching the Engine to foresee and then to act upon that foresight could ever lead me to the object I desired."[14] As we shall see, the debate as to the computer's "originality of mind" persists in these same terms to this day.

As one of his friends, Dr. Dionysius Lardner, put it, Babbage considered his engine "a real manufactory of figures."[15] The word *manufactory*, as I have been insisting, is not accidental. The Analytical Engine was, for Babbage, like the steam engine, part and parcel of the mechanizing impulse of the

Industrial Revolution. Babbage did not offer a general philosophy of manufactures, as did his contemporary Andrew Ure, but he did write a book *On Economy of Machinery and Manufactures* (1832), which exhibited what I shall call a "taxonomy" of machines, of which one example was the calculating engine.

In the preface, Babbage begins by saying. "The present volume may be considered as one of the consequences that have [sic] resulted from the Calculating-Engine."[16] Having visited workshops and factories all over Europe to acquaint himself with the extant state of the mechanical art, he tells us that he "was insensibly led to apply to them those principles of generalization to which my other pursuits had naturally given rise." The result, besides what I am calling a "taxonomy of machines," which can be viewed as a kind of mechanical version of Linnaeus's *Systema Naturae*, was the creation of what has come to be called operations research.[17]

The way to the generalizing *Economy of Machinery* was prepared, I shall argue, by Babbage's invention of a system of signs, which he called his mechanical notation. Through this notation, "the drawings, the times of action, and the trains for the transmission of force" of machinery could be explained "in a language at once simple and concise."[18] The notation was generally applicable to all machinery. It even extended, in the hands of an eminent French surgeon, or so it was claimed, to expressing the structure, operation, and circulation of the animal system.

> Not only the mechanical connection of the solid members of the bodies of men and animals, but likewise the structure and operation of the softer parts, including the muscles, integuements, membranes, &c.; the nature, motion, and circulation of the various fluids, their reciprocal effects, the changes through which they pass, the deposits which they leave in various parts of the system; the functions of respiration, digestion, and assimilation—all would find appropriate symbols and representatives in the notation, even as it now stands, without those additions of which, however, it is easily susceptible.

From thence, the notation could jump to operations research:

> Another of the uses which the slightest attention to the details of this notation irresistibly forces upon our notice, is to exhibit, in the form of a connected plan or map, the organization of an extensive factory, or any great public institution, in which a vast number of individuals are employed, and their duties regulated (as they generally are or ought to be) by a consistent and well-digested system. The mechanical notation is admirably adapted, not only to express such an organized connection of human agents, but even to suggest the improvements of which such organization is susceptible—to betray

its weak and defective points, and to disclose, at a glance, the origin of any fault which may, from time to time, be observed in the working of the system.[19]

No wonder Babbage thought well of his system of signs and is reported to have claimed that it was "of even a more general nature than the calculating machinery itself, and pregnant with results probably of higher importance." Specifically, the mechanist, or inventor,

is able, by moving his finger along a certain line, to follow out the motion of every piece from effect to cause, until he arrives at the prime mover. The same sign which thus indicates the *source* of motion indicates likewise the *species* of motion whether it be continuous or reciprocating, circular or progressive, &c. The same system of signs further indicates the nature of the mechanical connections between the mover and the thing moved, whether it be permanent and invariable (as between the two arms of a lever), or whether the mover and the moved are separate and independent pieces."[20]

When Babbage classified machines according to general principles, we seem to hear the same language as his notation. He arranges his machines according to how they accumulate and regulate power, increase and diminish velocity, extend the time of action of forces (for example, as I noted earlier, winding up a clock for twenty-four hours), save time in human operations, and so forth. Thus Babbage's taxonomy is based on the machine's operating principles, rather than on its appearance, or, so to speak, on its skeleton.

For Babbage, mechanical principles, and the machines that embody them, are of no utility unless put into application. *Economy* is the key word in his title, and he emphasizes the difference between merely conceptualizing a machine, or even making a single article by it, and the act of manufacturing articles, that is, producing them in numbers for sale. The manufacturer, Babbage pointed out, must produce at as small a cost as possible, in a competitive market.

Thus, Adam Smith's division of labour takes on a new life in Babbage's *Economy*, and we suddenly realize that it leads by a fresh trail to the Analytical Engine. Babbage was aware of the central role that the idea of division of labor played in Smith's *Wealth of Nations*. He also realized its fecund effect on Gaspard François de Prony, a Frenchman who, during the time of Napoleon, had been instructed to prepare a new set of logarithmic and trigonometric tables. Faced with the monumental task of calculating, for example, the logarithms of the numbers from 1 to 200,000, de Prony chanced on a secondhand copy of the *Wealth of Nations*. Inspired by the chapter on the division of labor, he set up three groups of calculators: the first, a single individual, did not do the actual numerical work, but devised a set of formulae, the second, consisting of seven or eight persons, converted the formulae into numbers, which they delivered to the third; the third group, of from sixty to eighty persons, using nothing more than simple addition and subtraction, worked up these numbers into finished tables.

Babbage's Calculating Engine was simply a substitute for the entire third group. Babbage himself was the first group, and his engineers, such as Clement, constructing the machinery he had designed, were the second group. In Babbage's mind, "the possibility of performing arithmetical calculations by machinery . . . is connected with the subject of the *division of labor*"[21]—and is intrinsically so. It is why he conceived of his "engine" as a "mill" to produce figures in large numbers, in other words, to manufacture them.

For Adam Smith, the division of labor was the source of the "immense multiplication of the production of all the different arts," which led, in turn, to a "universal opulence" that extended to all ranks.[22] In Smith's judgment, the benign effects of the division of labor were owing to three different circumstances: increased dexterity of each workman; saving of time otherwise lost in shifting from one activity to another; and "last of all, to the invention of innumerable machines, which facilitate labour and enable one workman to do the business of many." Smith was writing before the Industrial Revolution and saw machines as a facilitating, but not necessary, part of the division of labor.

Babbage, in contrast, placed the machine at the heart of the industrial process, which he conceptualized in terms of operations research. For Smith and other predecessors of Babbage, the machine meant a substitute for the workman's physical powers. Babbage's great achievement was to devise an engine that could substitute for human mental powers. However, he never was able to build a full-scale Analytical Engine; the realization of his thoughts had to wait until the twentieth century.

How would his contemporaries have reacted if he had succeeded? The Luddite movement of the early nineteenth century gives us some hints. The first Luddites, as we have seen, wished to prevent the mechanization of manual work in the textile industry; they tried to do so by breaking frames. Thus, just as Babbage was completing his Difference Engine in the early 1830s, the last gasp of the machine-breaking movement was occurring under the aegis of Captain Swing. The implications of Babbage's machine, however, evoked no such protests at the time, though later these Frankenstein-like implications were taken up in Samuel Butler's *Erewhon*.

Babbage did not see himself as a Frankenstein usurping God's powers. In fact, he wrote *The Ninth Bridgewater Treatise, A Fragment*, in 1837, in which he set out the scientific arguments for miracles. His calculating machine— and he evidently saw his own role as a programmer as being analogous to God's—could be so regulated that, as Moseley summarizes the argument, "at definite periods, known only to its maker, a certain lever might become moveable during the calculations then making. The consequence of moving it might be to cause the then existing law to be violated for one or more times, after which the original law would resume its reign."[23] Thus, Babbage sought to establish the possibility of a world moving by orderly natural laws, punctuated by so-called miracles, and all alike under the hand of God.

God as a Great Calculator: the idea probably brought little comfort to Babbage's contemporaries. They generally found sacrilegious his effort to reduce all of life to computations. Babbage, by contrast, put mathematics at the center of human as well as divine thought. Indeed, he was instrumental in establishing in 1834 the Statistical Society of London; in applying statistics to life insurance; and even to applying his work on probability theory to gambling. He was thoroughly in tune with the calculating spirit of his age when he exclaimed, "It is the same science which is now preparing its fetters for the minutest atoms that nature has created: already it has nearly chained the ethereal fluid, and bound in one harmonious system all the intricate and splendid phenomena of light. It is the science of *calculation,*—which becomes continually more necessary at each step of our progress, and which must ultimately govern the whole of the applications of science to the arts of life."[24]

He was far ahead of his time in creating a machine that appeared to think by calculation, just as did a human being. True the machine operated mechanically, by wheels and racks and columns, instead of by neurons, as in the brain, but the effect seemed to be the same. As Babbage remarked, "The analogy between these acts [of the calculating engine] and the operations of mind almost forced upon me the figurative employment of the same terms"; thus, he used such phrases as "The engine Knows . . ."

Had Babbage come upon a mere figure of speech or a profound reality of identity? In the twentieth century, with the substitution of electronic for mechanical calculators, which we now call computers, the question has become what I like to call the "galvanic twitch" of our epoch. In his time, Babbage, having first posed the question in truly modern fashion, figures only as a disturbing eccentric, a shooting star, whose ideas momentarily lit up a new landscape of the mind, and then fizzled out, leaving the humans-machines question to be argued about in the old, animalic terms. Only after Darwin, and then the evolutionary development of the computer, could one return to the question and seek to deal with it in newly conceived biological and mechanical terms.

In an earlier chapter, I sketched the way in which T. H. Huxley became agitated over Man as a mechanical and a moral being. For one who prided himself on logical consistency, Huxley seems to have taken up a number of contradictory stances. In fact, he is constantly squirming over the issues of vitalism and mechanism, with Descartes as his touchstone. Though Babbage was Huxley's older contemporary, with both men members of the British

Association for the Advancement of Science, Babbage's Calculating Engine seemed to have had no overt impact on Huxley's thought as he picked up the animal-machine argument.

Why, then, do I take up Huxley again here? He is, I would answer, the Darwinian way station to the vision of machines as an evolutionary development after Man. Outwardly and loyally a supporter, Huxley unintentionally weakened Darwin's organic perspective by transmuting biology into a mechanical science of sorts. (Though Darwin himself was a philosophical materialist whose materialism, unrealized by him, may be said to have an affinity with mechanism.)

Indeed, as Huxley confessed in his *Autobiography*, his original desire was "to be a mechanical engineer." He cared little for the profession, medicine, that he finally entered. In medicine, the only part that truly interested him was physiology, which he considered the "mechanical engineering of living machines." As he summarized his career, "I am not sure that I have not, all along, been a sort of mechanical engineer *in partibus infidelium*."[25] I find myself agreeing with him.

Mechanical minded, Huxley was also basically a materialist, though of a very sophisticated sort. He was prepared, in his writings, to go as far as saying, "I repudiate, as philosophical error, the doctrine of Materialism,"[26] because it claimed to see nothing in the universe besides matter and force, while he wished to leave room for problems of free will, morality, and so forth. Yet, characteristically, Huxley could also write, "I can discover no logical halting-place [short of admitting that] all vital action may . . . be said to be the result of the molecular forces of the protoplasm which displays it."[27] In the end, I agree with Cyril Bibby's comment that "his impartiality between idealism and materialism was largely formal and that in fact he habitually thought in materialist terms."[28]

Stretched to its utmost, Huxley's mechanical and materialist leanings carried him to a strict determinism, in fact, a teleology that seemed to allow little room for free will. Thus he could follow Laplace and write that "a sufficient intelligence could, from a knowledge of the properties of the molecules of that vapour [molecules of which the primitive nebulosity of the universe is composed], have predicted, say the state of the Fauna of Britain in 1869, with as much certainty as one can say what will happen to the vapour of the breath in a cold winter's day."[29]

Only at the end of his life, in writing *Evolution and Ethics* (1893–1894), while still precluding chance from evolution, did Huxley seek to free humans from the necessities of nature and the Darwinian struggle for survival. He did so in two ways, first by setting humanity in opposition to the laws of nature through the creation of human, that is, altruistic, ethics. The second was through human intervention in nature, especially in the form of machines, which created an "artificial" world. As Huxley explained, "We call these things artificial, term them works of art, or artifice, by way of distinguishing them from the products of the cosmic process, working outside man, which we call natural, or works of nature."[30]

Man and his society as artificial creations appear to be the products of mechanization, materialism, and determinism and yet they transcend these conditions. In the end, however, Huxley himself seemed unable to transcend the terms of his own logic and comes across as something of a distressed and tortured soul, whose logic is necessarily tortured as well. His personal solution was a kind of stoicism and an acceptance of the ambivalent nature of his subject and his arguments. It is a solution that humanity may not be able to transcend.

We can best follow Huxley's struggles over the nature of Man by looking closely at his 1874 paper, "On the Hypothesis That Animals Are Automata, and Its History" (for which chapter 3, on Automata, has helped to prepare us). (The other important paper in this regard is "On Descartes' 'Discourse Touching the Method of Using One's Reason Rightly and of Seeking Scientific Truth'"[1870].) In his paper on automata, Huxley affirms the notion that brutes are nothing more than "a superior race of marionettes."[31] Though his argument is convoluted and unclear (at least to me), Huxley is saying that animals lack true consciousness and are dominated solely by reflex actions (which in the earlier essay on Descartes he had referred to as "the mechanical representatives of volition"). Proof is found in anatomical studies, and Huxley describes two cases, one, based on his own work, of a frog, and the other based on the account by a military doctor of a French soldier.

According to Huxley, it is "highly probable" that consciousness in Man is based on the integrity of the anterior division of the brain, and that consciousness can not arise in any segment of the spinal cord and brain not connected to the anterior division. Thus, if a man is injured, for example, has his spinal cord divided, he will not be conscious of pain in his lower limbs. Yet, stimulated, his limbs will jerk involuntarily and unconsciously, by reflex action. Vivisection can be carried out on the frog to prove the general point, for the frog with its spinal cord cut is "a subject parallel to the injured man, on which experiments can be made without remorse."[32]

The story of the French soldier is a curious one. Wounded during a battle "by a ball which fractured his left parietal bone," this soldier ran his bayonet through his opponent, immediately experienced his right arm as paralyzed, had his right leg similarly affected after walking a few hundred yards, and then lost his senses. He did not recover them for three weeks, and when he did, the right half of his body was completely paralyzed, remaining so for a year, after which the symptom almost completely disappeared. However, periodic disturbances of the functions of the brain arose and persisted; the disturbances, occurring at intervals of fifteen to thirty days, lasted from fifteen to thirty hours.

In his periods of normal life, as Huxley describes it, the ex-soldier's health is perfect. In the abnormal, into which he slides suddenly, he feels a sense of weight about the forehead, his pupils dilate, and, though he eats, drinks, smokes, and so forth, in normal fashion, "pins may be run into his body, or strong electric shocks sent through it, without causing the least indication of pain." Is consciousness utterly absent, Huxley asks, "the man being reduced to an insensible mechanism?" Direct evidence is unavailable, the experiment with the frog, however, suggests an affirmative answer: "in the abnormal state, the man is a mere insensible machine."[33]

Yet Huxley is aware of some disturbing features in the case history. Dr. Mesnet, the physician treating the soldier, reports how, in the abnormal state, the soldier seems to reenact the trauma of the original battle. "Did the man," Huxley inquires, "dream that he was skirmishing? or was he in the condition of one of Vaucanson's automata—a senseless mechanism worked by molecular changes in his nervous system?" Huxley's work on the frog seems to support for him the "senseless mechanism" conclusion. Other evidence (for the doctor performs a series of harmless experiments on the soldier, such as hiding his tobacco pouch) raises the question of how to account for the peculiar form of his actions, if they arise purely from an organic cause. Huxley deals forthrightly with this challenge in a preemptory footnote:

Those who have had occasion to become acquainted with the phenomena of somnambulism and of mesmerism, will be struck with the close parallel which they present to the proceedings of F. in his abnormal state. But the great value of Dr. Mesnet's observations lies in the fact that the abnormal condition is traceable to a definite injury to the brain, and that the circumstances are such as to keep us clear of the cloud of voluntary and involuntary fictions in which the truth is too often smothered in such cases.[34]

(We have seen that Darwin was a little more tolerant of mesmerism and open to the possibility that mental states could affect physical ones.)

Yet Huxley is still troubled. As he continues in the footnote, the soldier's case

is singularly instructive, for though, in his normal state he is a perfectly honest man, in his abnormal condition he is an inveterate thief, stealing and hiding away whatever he can lay hands on, with much dexterity, and with an absurd indifference as to whether the property is his own or not. Hoffman's terrible conception of the "Doppeltgänger" is realised by men in this state—who live two lives, in the one of which they may be guilty of the most criminal acts, while, in the other, they are eminently virtuous and respectable. Neither life knows anything of the other.

The theme of the divided self—first made prominent in the confusion of

Frankenstein and his "other half," the monster, and given classic form shortly after Huxley's essay in Robert Louis Stevenson's "Dr. Jekyll and Mr. Hyde" (1886)—lay just below the surface of Victorian feelings about humans and their "animal" nature. Huxley, without conscious awareness, is now extending that "terrible conception" to the machine: our "other half" can commit immoral actions because it is "mechanical" as well as "bestial."

As Huxley has been suggesting, humans are machines, and, in the abnormal state, insensible ones. Humans differ from other animal-machines only by having, in some vague sense, consciousness. Implicitly, a potential gap between humans and the other animals appears to be opening up, or so it seems, but at this point Huxley suddenly shifts his emphasis and, instead of discontinuity, advances "the Doctrine of Continuity." Complex phenomena, such as consciousness, he tells us, must appear gradually. As he explains, "The brutes, though they may not possess our intensity of consciousness, and though, from the absence of language, they can have no trains of thoughts, but only trains of feelings, yet have a consciousness which, more or less distinctly, foreshadows our own."[35] Alas, says Huxley, he wishes it were otherwise; the struggle for existence entails much pain, and as semiconscious beings the other animals must therefore experience suffering (he draws no inferences in regard to vivisection). In such a situation, he tells us, we must treat domestic animals as "weaker brethren," and Huxley quotes Hartley to the effect that "we seem to be in the place of God to them."

At this point, having established the continuity, Huxley begins to pull it apart again. Descartes was right that animals are automata, only he didn't realize that they are "more or less conscious, sensitive, automata." Huxley appears next to argue that animals have consciousness, but not reason, that is, "'ideagenous molecules' which are the physical basis of memory"; and have free will (for example, nothing prevents a dog from chasing a rabbit), but not reasoned volition.[36] He leaves open the question whether other animals do or do not have souls, for Huxley is at pains to state that he is an agnostic, not an atheist, an idealist as much as a materialist.[37]

Can we extract any final position from him on the question of Man as machine? In the 1874 essay, we can see him hesitating over the issue, yet I think his inclination is clear. Having canvassed various arguments or evidence, as we have seen, he concludes by saying, "We are conscious automata, endowed with free will in the only intelligible sense of that much-abused term—inasmuch as in many respects we are able to do as we like—but none the less parts of the great series of causes and effects which, in unbroken continuity, composes that, which is, and has been, and shall be—the sum of existence."[38] Then follows a long quotation from the Swiss naturalist Charles Bonnet, which Huxley claims to support his conclusion.

In the final analysis, with all his agitation (and, as I have suggested, there is plenty of it in *Evolution and Ethics*), Huxley has ended up with Man as fundamentally a mechanism, though of a very special sort. Humans are fully explicable in physico-chemical terms. Moreover, as Descartes and Bonnet have argued, humans are automatons; true, Descartes also gave them souls, but this, as Huxley argues, simply means that they have consciousness. For Huxley, however, unlike Descartes, consciousness is material, in the sense of being rooted in the organic structure of the body.[39] What is more, consciousness is an evolutionary development, with a continuous line leading from the lower animals to Man.

Though fudged, Huxley's message comes through as follows. Animals, with Man as one of them, are mechanisms that have evolved. Reason, or consciousness, is a physico-chemical process, obedient to deterministic laws. We may then ask: can further, more developed, thinking mechanisms be expected to evolve? Should Babbage's Analytical Engine cause us to think seriously about such a possibility? Huxley took up neither question. Though he supplied an evolutionary perspective to the animal-machine problem, he did not grapple with the possibility of thinking machines. Though "mechanical" in his inclinations, he was still too "biological," that is, physiological, I suspect, to advance on the path Babbage had opened up. His evolutionary perspective on mechanisms, however, was taken up by an unlikely candidate: a novelist with an amateur's interest in evolutionary theory.

Samuel Butler was a curious, somewhat bittersweet, and rather eccentric Victorian. He thought of himself primarily as a painter, was a middling musician, and achieved fame as a novelist.[40] His upbringing, in an Evangelical Protestant family, scarred him for life, producing in him divided, or schizoid, characteristics. I would argue that he turned to scientific discourse in an effort to deal with his family and religious stigmata. As a result, he wrote a number of tracts and books on religious and scientific subjects, specifically, on evolution, that are now largely neglected. His novels *Erewhon* and *The Way of All Flesh*, however, remain classics. And, in *Erewhon*, Butler gave persistent form to the view that machines might represent an advanced stage of evolution.

In 1859, the same year of the *Origin of Species*, after attending Cambridge University, Butler emigrated to New Zealand, to raise sheep. Darwin's book had a powerful effect on him, just at a time when Butler was wrestling with religious doubts. Admittedly ignorant of any actual science—as he confessed "not as knowing anything whatsoever of natural history"[41]—Butler nonetheless took it upon himself to write a dialogue, explaining and supposedly espousing the Darwinian theories. I say "supposedly" for although Butler so represented it later to Darwin, the dialogue is a satirical, ambiguous piece, whose final position is by no means clear. Indeed, the fictitious Darwinian protagonist claims belief in both Christianity and Darwinism, though admitting that they appear irreconcilable. (The dialogue, in fact, makes no effort at reconciliation.)

The dialogue, published in *The Press*, a new New Zealand publication, occasioned a reply, from an author subsequently identified by Butler as the Bishop of Wellington. In the exchange that followed, the bishop caught Butler up short on his knowledge of natural history, challenging him to show that the work of Charles Darwin was anything more than a rehash of theories brought forth in the previous century by his grandfather Erasmus Darwin, Joseph Priestley, and Lord Monboddo. Butler seems to have had the worst of the exchange, indulged in selfsatire, and then wisely concluded that the truth of Darwin's theory of evolution "can be decided only among naturalists themselves." It was not advice he would later follow.

It is surprising that, somehow, the dialogue fell into Charles Darwin's hands and caused him to write the young author. Was Darwin desperate for allies and welcomed recognition from as far away as New Zealand, and even by an author who hardly represented his doctrines knowledgeably?[42] In any case, a correspondence sprang up between Butler and Darwin, and Butler, having published in 1865 a pamphlet, "The Evidence for the Resurrection of Jesus Christ . . . ," sent a copy to Darwin. Butler's conflation of evolutionary and religious enthusiasm is clear. Darwin expressed polite interest, urging Butler to write "a work descriptive of a colonist's life in New Zealand." In an unexpected sense, *Erewhon* was Butler's response to Darwin's suggestion.

Before that, however, Butler, under the pseudonym Cellarius, wrote an essay "Darwin Among the Machines," which appeared in *The Press* on 13 June 1863 and dramatically announced the theme of the machine as an advanced evolutionary species. Here, the purely satirical, scientific side of Butler, without religious concerns, appears. By an extraordinary, if ambiguous, leap of intuition, Butler foresees a possible future. Aware that his probe may humble human pride, Butler asks,

> If we revert to the earliest primordial types of mechanical life, to the lever, the wedge, the inclined plane, the screw, and the pulley . . . and if we then examine the machinery of the *Great Eastern*, we find ourselves almost awestruck at the vast development of the mechanical world, at the gigantic strides with which it has advanced in comparison with the slow progress of the animal and vegetable kingdom. We shall find it impossible to refrain from asking ourselves what the end of this mighty movement is to be? In what direction is it tending? What will be its upshot?

At a quick stroke, Butler draws a map of his proposed inquiry, admitting his own limitations to undertake it.

> We regret deeply that our knowledge both of natural history and of machinery is too small to enable us to undertake the gigantic task of classifying machines into the genera and subgenera, species, var-

ieties and sub-varieties, and so forth, of tracing the connecting links between machines of widely different characters, of pointing out how subservience to the use of man has played that part among machines which natural selection has performed in the animal and vegetable kingdoms, of pointing out rudimentary organs which exist in some few machines, feebly developed and perfectly useless, yet serving to mark descent from some ancestral type which has either perished or been modified into some new phase of mechanical existence.[43]

The suggested classification of machines reminds us of Babbage's taxonomy (and before that, Linnaeus's); only Butler is proposing to "animate" his schema, just as Darwin did with Linnaeus's static system. Further, in place of natural selection, Butler is urging human selection as the means by which machine "breeding," just as in animal breeding, takes place. It is an audacious analogy.

The rest of the short essay spells out a few details. As in animal evolution, Vertebrata of great size, for example, dinosaurs, gave way to smaller, so we may expect miniaturization (my word) among the machines. "The day may come when clocks . . . may be entirely superseded by the universal use of watches, in which case clocks will become extinct like the earlier saurians." Although Babbage is not mentioned (and apparently not thought about), Butler foresees machines acquiring "by all sorts of ingenious contrivances that self-regulating, self-acting power which will be to them what intellect has been to the human race."[44]

This evolutionary development raises the prospect of the machine becoming superior to humans. ("We shall find ourselves the inferior race," is how Butler puts it.) We will have to "feed" them (Landes's passage on coal as inorganic food for machines seems to be an echo of Butler's notion), Butler suggests, and in doing so will become unto them a kind of "slave." True, just as we take care of our domestic animals, the machines will take care of us; after all, we are useful to them. Put simply, machines will have dominion over Man.

In our infatuation with machines, Butler continues, we even "desire . . . to see a fertile union between two steam engines," and instruct our machinery in "begetting" other machinery. In short, we are creating the means of our own inferiority and enslavement. Aghast at this vision, Butler has his presumed author, Cellarius, exclaim, "war to the death should be instantly proclaimed" against every machine.[45] With this trumpet call, the author ends his piece.

Two years later, Butler returned to his subject in another essay, "Lucubratio Ebria," published in *The Press* (29 July 1865). The tone is now positive. Machines are, in fact, merely extracorporeal limbs added to the members of the human body: a lever is an extension of the arm, microscopes and telescopes of the eyes, and so forth. Such body changes, that is, extensions, entailed mind changes as well, and Butler suggests, Man comes to *be* his civilization.

"It is a mistake," therefore, Butler says, satirizing his earlier letter, "to take the view adopted by a previous correspondent of this paper, to consider the machines as identities, to animalize them and to anticipate their final triumph over mankind." The machine simply makes for a difference in degree from human to human—the new limbs are preserved by natural selection (Butler gives no details as to how this occurs), descend with modifications into society and thus mark the difference between our ancestors and ourselves. What is more, within an advanced society itself, the command over these new limbs—for example, the seven-leagued foot we call a railroad train—is a matter of class. "He alone," declares Butler, "possesses the full complement of limbs who stands at the summit of opulence." A Rothschild is a "most astonishing" organism and "may be reckoned by his horse-power, by the number of foot-pounds which he has money enough to set in motion." As Butler concludes, "Who, then, will deny that a man whose will represents the motive power of a thousand horses is a being very different from the one who is equivalent but to the power of a single one?"[46]

Adam Smith, in his labor theory of value, had spoken of opulence as meaning command over labor; Butler has now broadened the concept to mean command over energy, and mechanized it by specifying energy from nonliving sources. He is also aware that what separates the races of humans is their level of culture, or civilization, which means their command over "extracorporaneous limbs." In a spirit that Benjamin Franklin and Karl Marx, both of whom called Man "the tool-making animal," would approve, Butler labeled the human being a "vertebrate machinate mammal."[47] In "Darwin Among the Machines," the "limbs" are feared as taking on a life of their own, here they are benignly subordinated to humans.

Yet, ambiguity and ambivalence still press down on Butler. In another essay, "The Mechanical Creation," written after "Lucubratio Ebria" but published shortly before it (in *The Reasoner*, 1 July 1865), his divided feelings reappear. Now we are told that though Butler does not wish to "throw ridicule on Darwin's magnificent work," further thinking suggests the possibility of "an eventual development of mechanical life, far superior to, and widely differing from, any yet known."[48]

The process is Darwinian, but the end result is the replacement of the organic by the machinate. Was this a satiric reductio ad absurdum of Darwin's work? Why not conceive "of a life which in another ten or twenty million years shall be to us as we to the vegetable?" In "Lucubratio," Butler had looked at machines as mere extracorporaneous limbs, hardly threatening to us, now he returns to the prospect of their supplanting us. A spade is simply an extension of our forearm. We must look at a steam engine to see the evolutionary direction. I quote Butler at length, for his working out of the analogy is impressive:

It [the steam engine] eats its own food for itself; it consumes it by inhaling the very air which we ourselves breathe; it rejects what it cannot digest as man rejects it; it has a very considerable power of self-regulation and adaptability to contingency. It cannot be said to be conscious. It is employed in the manufacture of machinery, and though steam engines are as the angels in heaven, with respect to matrimony, yet in their reproduction of machinery we seem to catch a glimpse of the extraordinary vicarious arrangement whereby it is not impossible that the reproductive system of the mechanical world will be always carried on. It must be borne in mind that we are not thinking so much of what the steam engine is at present, as of what it may become. The steam engine of to-day is to the mechanical prodigies which are to come as the spade to the steam engine, as the ovum to the human being.[49]

The agency of this mechanical evolution is "natural selection and the struggle for existence" in the form of human's exercising self-interest—shades of Adam Smith! Pursuing a competitive advantage, they invent new machines, which then eliminate or exterminate the older, inferior ones. (Butler speaks of guns actually fighting one another for survival.) In the process, the machines "evolve," threatening eventually to become superior to humans.

Can humans halt this process? In "Darwin Among the Machines" Butler called for just such a halt. Here, in "The Mechanical Creation," he tells us that "man is committed hopelessly to the machines."[50] So dependent are we now that, even if we wished, we cannot live without them—and here Butler anticipates the voice of H. G. Wells in his story of the time machine. The dependency, however, will be mutual: the machines are not likely to want us as a delicacy on their table, and we shall be as serviceable to them as they to us.

In three short articles Butler explored, even if in mixed-up fashion and with tongue-in-cheek, the prospect of extending Darwin's theory of evolution to machines. On one side, he has taken up Ambroise Paré's hand as a prosthetic device and extended it to the idea of extracorporaneous limbs, developed in an evolutionary manner, in the service of human survival. On another side, Butler has taken up the Frankenstein-like fears of the monster as machine, now evolving, and threatening our own survival, or at least our dominion over species.

These are powerful premonitions. What did Darwin think of these offspring of *On the Origin of Species*? We have no hint of his reception of Butler's extension of evolutionary theory.

In fact, Butler's three pieces, two of them in an obscure New Zealand journal, awakened little attention. Only when included, slightly revised, in his novel *Erewhon* did Butler's provocative ideas reach the general public. Originally published anonymously in March 1872, the book enjoyed a relatively vigorous sale at first because the public thought it to be a sequel to Lord Lytton's *The Coming Race* (1871). Butler hastily issued a second edition in July, under his own name, and this and seven further editions during his lifetime continued to have a modest sale.[51] It was, therefore, in the book version, rather than the shorter, more self-contained essays, that Butler's views on the evolution of machines came to enjoy popular and critical regard.

Does *Erewhon* add anything to Butler's earlier conception or argument? Let us first look at the book as a whole, serving as it does for the context of "The Book of the Machines." Erewhon, spelled backward (with the *wh* left as is), is "Nowhere," or utopia (thus nicely symbolizing the opposite of Babbage's concept of a "utopia" based on computing machines). It is cast in the form of an imaginary explorer's tale—the hero wanders over a mountain range in New Zealand into the land of the Erewhonians. The opening chapters, with their John Buchan-like tone and air of excitement and adventure, lead us on into the book.

Once in Erewhon, however, we find ourselves engaged in a more serious exploration as we enter into another culture. Butler's purpose is similar to Descartes's in his *Discourse*, or Montesquieu's in his *Persian Letters*: to examine and satirize his own culture by comparing it to a fictitious one abroad. Descartes remarked that customs are obviously uncertain, being different on one side of a mountain from the other. Over the mountain, Butler finds everything different from his own Western, that is, English, customs.

To make his point, Butler inverts everything he can.[52] First, names: for example, the girl with whom the hero falls in love is Yram (Mary), and we have already noted Erewhon. Next, customs: in Erewhon, physical illness is thought criminal and immoral, but crimes such as embezzlement are considered to be a mental disease, to be cured by "straiteners"; unreasoning and colleges of Unreason are preferred to reasoning and Colleges of Reason; the young inflict corporal punishment on the old, for otherwise the latter would be incorrigible (in fact, Butler as a boy had been repeatedly flogged by his parents),[53] progress is a bad word, and so forth.

It is in this world turned upside down that Butler presents what he has to say on machines and their evolution. The subject surfaces when the Erewhonians exhibit displeasure, rather than awe, at the sight of the hero's watch. The concern moves to center stage when the hero is taken through a museum, in which, in addition to stuffed birds and animals, there are rooms filled with broken machinery. Here he is told the following history: that some 400 to 500 years ago, the state of mechanical knowledge being so advanced and threatening, a learned professor wrote an extraordinary book, calling for the extinction of all machinery not in use for over 271 years. In the massive outbreak of Luddism that this professor's book inspired, machinists and antimachinists engaged in a violent civil war for many years, in which half the population perished. Finally, the antis won and, with unparalleled severity, eliminated every trace of opposition. The Industrial Revolution had been made subject to regression.[54]

Aside from this dramatic suggestion, it is the arguments of the professor, in his "Book of the Machines" (purported to be translated by the hero), that are of interest. Mainly, they are a restatement of Butler's earlier essays, as I have outlined them. However, a few points, developed significantly further, or in more powerful form, are worth quoting at some length. Thus, on the subject of consciousness, Butler has his professor say:

> "There is no security"—to quote his own words—"against the ultimate development of mechanical consciousness, in the fact of machines possessing little consciousness now. A mollusc has not much consciousness. Reflect upon the extraordinary advance which machines have made during the last few hundred years, and note how slowly the animal and vegetable kingdoms are advancing. The more highly organized machines are creatures not so much of yesterday as of the last five minutes, so to speak, in comparison with past time. Assume for the sake of argument that conscious beings have existed for some twenty million years: see what strides machines have made in the last thousand!"

Then, continuing on the subject of consciousness, but adding a further thought, the author adds,

> "But who can say that the vapour-engine has not a kind of consciousness? Where does consciousness begin, and where end? Who can draw the line? Is not machinery linked with animal life in an infinitive variety of ways? The shell of a hen's egg is made of a delicate white ware and is a machine as much as an egg-cup is; the shell is a device for holding the egg as much as the egg-cup for holding the shell: both are phases of the same function; the hen makes the shell in her inside, but it is pure pottery. She makes her nest outside of herself for convenience' sake, but the nest is not more of a machine than the egg-shell is. A 'machine' is only a 'device.'"

There is no limit, however, to the development of these "devices," with their consciousness. Answering the argument that the machine, even when more fully developed, is merely a servant to humans, the writer contends:

> But the servant glides by imperceptible approaches into the master; and we have come to such a pass that, even now, man must suffer terribly on ceasing to benefit the machines . . . Man's very soul is due

285

to the machines, it is a machine-made thing, he thinks as he thinks, and feels as he feels, through the work that machines have wrought upon him, and their existence is quite as much a *sine qua non* for his, as his for theirs. This fact precludes us from proposing the complete annihilation of machinery, but surely it indicates that we should destroy as many of them as we can dispense with, lest they should tyrannize over us even more completely.

And, finally, the author deals with the latent sexual, that is, reproductive, threat.

It is said by some with whom I have conversed upon this subject, that the machines can never be developed into animate or quasi-animate existences, inasmuch as they have no reproductive systems, nor seem ever likely to possess one. If this be taken to mean that they cannot marry, and that we are never likely to see a fertile union between two vapour-engines with the young ones playing about the door of the shed, however greatly we might desire to do so, I will readily grant it. But the objection is not a very profound one. No one expects that all the features of the now existing organizations will be absolutely repeated in an entirely new class of life. The reproductive system of animals differs widely from that of plants, but both are reproductive systems. Has nature exhausted her phases of this power?[55]

Inspired by fears such as these, which sound like our present actualities, the Erewhonians rise up and destroy almost all their machines.

In a letter to Charles Darwin, Butler referred to "the obviously absurd theory" that he had developed in the chapter upon machines.[56] Butler was too quick to dismiss his own theory; it deserved, and deserves, a full hearing. I suspect, in fact, that Butler was satirizing his own satire, in the same deprecating manner we have encountered in his earlier exchange with the Bishop of Wellington.

Most of *Erewhon* is not about machines. It is about what Butler in *The Way of All Flesh* referred to as the "question of the day ... marriage and the family system."[57] To this question of questions for Butler we must add religion: the hero of *Erewhon* thinks of converting the Erewhonians to Christianity, yet spends much of his time implicitly satirizing Christianity by comparisons to the strange religious customs and beliefs of the local inhabitants. Similarly, the hero satirizes Victorian marriage and the family system by the same device of inversion. The satire on machinery and progress fits into the general picture. It can, however, be taken out of this frame and left to stand on its own, as it does in the earlier essays, as a profound statement about humans, machines, and evolution.

Whatever the intentions behind Butler's venturesome speculations and however oddly arrived at, the result is a shocking challenge to our ideas about the continuity or discontinuity existing between humans and machines. The essence of that challenge is as follows. If one takes Darwin seriously and accepts that the human is in an evolutionary relation to the other animals; adds to this the idea, advocated by Huxley (building on Descartes), that the animals are animal-machines and humans therefore the same (allowing for whatever differences in consciousness exist); admits that humans then create machines, including Babbage-like computers, which are merely consciously contrived versions of the animal-machine (again only differing in degree); then one can conclude that we are on an evolutionary continuum, with machines as a new, and possibly advanced, species.

What this conclusion actually entails, in the detail of evolutionary science, is not yet clear. What is clear is that Butler's view can not merely be laughed out of court. No matter how satirically worked up, for example, in the "Book of the Machines," Butler's is a serious perspective on the evolving world.

In my view, however, the problem remains that Butler confuses the way in which cultural and physical evolution takes place. In the cultural evolution of mankind, intelligence and will can and do enter into the process of "selection." We consciously create machines, art, and civilization (just as we breed domestic animals).[58]

In his discussion of these matters, Butler ostensibly ignored Huxley's views while accepting Darwin's general theory of evolution (though not its means). In fact, without the view on automata enunciated by his hated contemporary, Huxley, and others like him, Butler could not have pushed on to his own speculations. In some moods, Butler might disown his prophecies about machines and evolution; but they remain like Frankenstein monsters casting their shadows before them. Himself a divided soul, Butler mirrors our own ambivalent feelings on the subject.

Seemingly, Butler's lucubrations on machines have disappeared as a serious subject for discussion. I believe, however, that, viewed in terms of the continuity among humans, animals, and machines, which this book is attempting to examine, a revival *of sorts* of this thesis is in order.

A further confession: I do not much like Butler, the man. Nevertheless, unlikely vessel though Butler is, his intuitions are important and far-reaching. Darwin was right: it is as a novelist of ideas, satiric and paradoxical, that Butler imaginatively extends the continuing discourse on humans and machines.

Notes

1 Thomas Carlyle, *Sartor Resartus* (London: Chapman and Hall, 1910), 103.
2 Indeed, we have a story from Charles Darwin, who recalled a dinner at his brother's house at which even Babbage, who "liked to talk," was outdone by Carlyle. See *Charles Babbage and His Calculating Engines*, ed. Philip and Emily Morrison (New York: Dover, 1961), xiii.

3 Quoted in Maboth Moseley, *Irascible Genius: The Life of Charles Babbage* (Chicago: Henry Regnery Co., 1964), 65.

4 Clearly, Babbage thought of his "engine" as analogus to the "steam engine," say of Thomas Savery, dating back to 1698, or James Watt, dating to around the 1770s to 1780s.

5 In fact, the great Henry Maudsley was involved in the working up of the necessary tools, although Babbage himself did most of the actual designing, using one of Maudsley's trainees, Joseph Clement, as his assistant.

6 Quoted ibid., 262. For more attention to this pioneering woman in science, see Joan Baum, *The Calculating Passion of Ada Byron* (Hamden, Conn: Archon Books/The Shoe String Press, 1986).

7 Morrison, *Charles Babbage*, 305.

8 Charles Babbage, *Passages from the Life of a Philosopher* (London: Dawsons of Pall Mall, 1968), 115.

9 Ibid., 17. The next two quotations are from pp. 17 and 365.

10 Ibid., 467.

11 Moseley, *Irascible Genius*, 261.

12 Compare Morrison, *Charles Babbage*, xx.

13 Ibid. This difference seems to correspond to the distinction today between what is called information processing and emergent AI. Lady Lovelace envisions the computer as remaining solely in the domain of information processing; Morrison is prepared to consider it within the context of emergent AI. Compare Sherry Turkle, "Artificial Intelligence and Psychoanalysis: A New Alliance," *Daedalus* (Winter 1988), 251.

14 Babbage, *Passages*, 114.

15 Morrison, *Charles Babbage*, 244.

16 Charles Babbage, *On Economy of Machinery and Manufactures* (Philadelphia: Carey & Lea, 1832), v. It should be noted, in passing, that Karl Marx read this work carefully, there is no evidence, however, that he paid any attention to Babbage's work on the Calculating Engine, any more than did most of his contemporaries. On the other hand, Charles Darwin's sister, Susan, wrote to him that "I have just got 'Babbage on Machinery' & shall certainly study it very diligently as a preparation" (15 August 1832, *Correspondence of Charles Darwin*, vol. 1 [Cambridge, 1985], 257). She does not say for what it is preparation.

17 Taxonomies, of course, can be of all kinds. For example, Linnaeus based his system on characters instead of functions. Although birds, bats, and insects all fly, he grouped them in different classes. A taxonomy emphasizing function might place them all in the same class.

18 Babbage, *Passages*, 104.

19 Morrison, *Charles Babbage*, 215–216, reprinting the account given by Babbage's friend Dr. Dionysius Lardner.

20 Ibid., 210.

21 Ibid., 145.

22 Adam Smith, *Lectures on Jurisprudence*, ed. R. L. Meek, D. D. Raphael and P. G. Stein (Indianapolis: Liberty Classics, 1982), 566. The quotation that follows is from p. 567.

23 Moseley, *Irascible Genius*, 132–133.

24 *Economy of Machinery*, 278. The quotation that follows is from Moseley, *Irascible Genius*, 20.

25 Charles Darwin, Thomas Henry Huxley, *Autobiographies*, ed. with introd. Gavin de Beer (London: Oxford University Press, 1974), 103. Huxley's Autobiography, incidentally, was written grudgingly and is very short. Mario di Gregorio, "The

Dinosaur Connection: A Reinterpretation of T. H. Huxley's Evolutionary View," *Journal of the History of Biology* 15, no. 3 (Fall 1982), stresses the names of Von Baer and Ernst Haeckel and concludes that their "strictly mechanistic view of biology (based upon physics and chemistry) was entirely shared by Huxley" (416).

26 *The Essence of T. H. Huxley: Selections*, ed. Cyril Bibby (London: Macmillan, 1967), 80.

27 T. H. Huxley, "On the Physical Basis of Life" (1868), in *Selections from the Essays of T. H. Huxley*, ed. Alburey Castell (New York: Appleton-Century. Crofts, 1948), 19.

28 *Essence*, ed. Bibby, 66.

29 T. H. Huxley, "The Genealogy of Animals" (1869), in *Essence*, cd. Bibby, 63.

30 T. H. Huxley, "Prolegomena," *Evolution of Ethics: T. H. Huxley's "Evolution and Ethics," with New Essays on Its Victorian and Sociobiological Context*, James Paradis and George C. Williams (Princeton: Princeton University Press, 1989), 69. Huxley's comment appears reminiscent of that of Francis Bacon, quoted in chapter 1.

31 T. H. Huxley, "On the Hypothesis That Animals Are Automata, and Its History," in *Collected Essays*, 9 vols. (London: Macmillan, 1893–94), vol. 1, 218. The next quotation is from the essay on Descartes, 186.

32 "On the Hypothesis," 222. The next quotation is from p. 226.

33 Ibid., 228, 229, 235.

34 Ibid., 230, 234. The continuing quotation is on p. 235.

35 Ibid., 237. The next quotation is also from this page.

36 Ibid., 238, 239.

37 See also his essays "Agnosticism" (1889) and "Agnosticism and Christianity" (1889).

38 Huxley, "On the Hypothesis," 244.

39 Descartes does play, however, with rooting thought in the pineal gland.

40 In fact, Butler was also a painter of some real ability, having various of his works hung in the Royal Academy. For examples of his talent, see especially his self-portraits in Elinor Shaffer, *Erewhons of the Eye: Samuel Butler as Painter, Photographer and Art Critic* (London: Reaktion, 1988).

41 Samuel Butler, "Darwin Among the Machines," in a *First Year in Canterbury Settlement and Other Early Essays*, 20 vols. (London: Shrewsbury Edition of the Works of Samuel Butler, 1923), vol. 1, 186. The next two quotations are from pp. 201 and 187.

42 It should also be pointed out that the Darwins and the Butlers lived in the same town of Shrewsbury, and that Charles Darwin, in fact, had attended Dr. Butler's school.

43 Butler, "Darwin Among the Machines," 208 and 209. George W. Stocking, Jr., tells us that Colonel Lane Fox (better known as Pitt Rivers), "classifying the 'various products of human industry' into 'genera, species, and varieties' . . . discussed their development explicitly in terms of Spencerian evolutionary psychology and the processes of natural selection" (*Victorian Anthropology*, [New York: The Free Press, 1987], 1980). Lane Fox was writing in 1874, suggesting either that he had read Butler or that the idea was in the air. The 1851 Crystal Palace Exhibition, with its arrangement of exhibits along a line of progress for both peoples and machines, lends support to the "in the air" hypothesis.

44 Butler, "Darwin Among the Machines," 210.

45 Ibid., 212.

46 Samuel Butler, "Lucubratio Ebria," in *A First Year*, 217 and 219.

47 Ibid., 215.

48 Samuel Butler, "The Mechanical Creation," in *A First Year*, 231–232.
49 Ibid., 232, 233.
50 Ibid., 236.
51 See Samuel Buttler, *Erewhon or Over the Range*, ed. Hans-Peter Brewer and Daniel F. Howard (Newark: University of Delaware Press, 1981), for the authoritative scholarly edition, it also has an excellent introduction, offering a context and an analysis for the book. See also Butler's preface to the Second Edition for his own view of the correlations between his book and Lord Lytton's *The Coming Race* (41).
52 Compare Ralf Norrman, *Samuel Butler and the Meaning of Chiasmus* (Houndmills, Basingstoke, Hampshire: Macmillan, 1986).
53 Compare Henry Festing Jones, *Samuel Butler, Author of Erewhon* (1835–1902): *A. Memoir*, 2 vols. (London: Macmillan, 1919), vol. 1, 20.
54 Charles Lamb had the following to say on this matter: "Alas! Can we ring the bells backward? Can we unlearn the arts that pretend to civilize and then burn the world? There is a march of science, but who shall beat the drums for its retreat?" (quoted in the frontispiece of Noel Perrin, *Giving Up the Gun: Japan's Reversion to the Sword, 1543–1879* [Boston: David R. Godine, 1979]). Perrin's book is a lovely little exploration of an actual "regression" in technology. Compare Arnold Toynbee's statement: "If a vote could undo all the technological advances of the last three hundred years, many of us would cast that vote, in order to safeguard the survival of the human race while we remain in our present state of social and moral backwardness" (quoted in Perrin, 80–81).
55 Samuel Butler, *Erewhon* (Harmondsworth, Middlesex: Penguin Books, 1954), 161–171.
56 Jones, *Samuel Butler*, 1:156.
57 Samuel Butler, *The Way of All Flesh* (New York: The Modern Library, 1950), 531.
58 In fact, Butler was a declared Lamarckian and could well have entertained the view just stated. But Butler was in no way a serious scientist, systematically developing his ideas, and though he thought his book *Life and Habit* a major contribution to the theory of heredity, it was hardly so, as Peter Morton says, in judgment: "the whole corpus of Butler's 'evolutionary' writings are, as serious contributions to the sum total of knowledge, absolutely spurious" (*The Vital Sciences, Biology and the Literary Imagination* [London: George Allen & Unwin, 1984], 162).

14

TOWARDS ELECTRONIC COMPUTERS

G. Simons

Source: *Evolution of the Intelligent Machines*, 1988, 53–64.

Introduction

The late-nineteenth and early-twentieth centuries saw developments in both logic and electronics that would facilitate the emergence of the first electronic digital computers. The first computers of this sort, which with hindsight became known as 'first-generation' (Chapter 6), evolved from practical technologies designed originally to serve other purposes. In early electronics, for example, there was no assumption that the innovative components would one day be incorporated in systems capable of rapid computation. There was no imagined connection between an enhanced Boolean algebra and the thermionic glass valve developed by the early electronics pioneers.

This chapter sketches the evolution of electronics that was to provide the practical fabric of the first-generation computers of the 1940s. And brief attention is also paid to the theoretical work of Alan Turing who, with a singular commitment to the potential power of automatic computers, was one of the leading heralds of the AI age. Claude Shannon, in the 1930s, was demonstrating how electrical circuits could switch in an on/off fashion to simulate the necessary operations in Boolean logic; Vannevar Bush had developed the first analogue computer, the differential analyser, for solving differential equations; and Turing had developed the powerful theory of the 'Turing machine' to determine the computational scope of automatic systems.

There were also various attempts in the pre-war years to build working systems that could demonstrate artificial intelligence. Many experiments had been carried out to investigate the learning abilities of animals. Mice, for example, had been required to find their way out of mazes – repeatedly, until the exact route was learned; and it occurred to some researchers that a mobile machine, an artificial mouse, might be constructed to perform in the same way. In 1938 the American researcher Thomas Ross built a mouse that, by trial and error and travelling on toy-train tracks, could learn to find its way to a correct goal.

It is clear that by the onset of the Second World War, all the elements were in place for the 'quantum leap' emergence of the electronic computer age. We can highlight the elements that together would help to define the character of the first 'thinking machines':

- the understanding, originally articulated by Babbage, of the architectural requirements that had to be met by computational systems intended to operate with a degree of autonomy;
- Boolean logic, indicating a tidy formalism that could specify, in a quite general way, how valid inference could be achieved; developments in Boolean algebra showed how arithmetic computation could be accomplished using such standard Boolean operators as *and*, *or* and *not*;
- the demonstration by Claude Shannon, a research assistant at the Massachusetts Institute of Technology that components with two possible states (ie binary devices) could embody Boolean logic (later, Shannon was a key figure in developing information theory);
- the development of devices – first, such things as electromechanical relays and then thermionic valves – that could operate in binary fashion to realise in a practical way the logical and computational options of Boolean logic;
- the development by Alan Turing of a theory of automatic computation that illuminated the scope of artificial systems (his celebrated 1937 paper, 'On computable numbers', is frequently quoted as a seminal work);
- an intellectual climate that was increasingly sympathetic to the concept of artificial autonomous systems (simple electromechanical devices were variously performing day-to-day computations, learning to escape from mazes and generally demonstrating the capacity to embody 'intentional' modes; and the age-old tradition of mythical AI was continued by such key works as Karel Capek's 1920 play *Rossum's Universal Robots* and the 1926 film *Metropolis*).

To these key elements that together enabled the emergence of electronic digital computers must be added the pressures of the Second World War. There is nothing like war (or the thought of war) to stimulate the technological enthusiasm of governments. The electronic computer was born in such a climate and subsequent developments owed (and continue to owe) much to military interest.

Evolution of electronics

From the point of view of computer technology, there are a few practical innovations that have been of particular importance: one thinks immediately of the glass valve and the solid-state circuits (transistors, integrated systems, etc) that are based on semiconductor materials (usually silicon). First-generation computers are based on glass (thermionic) valves, with all the later functional computer generations based on semiconductors.[1] It is interesting to reflect that glass-valve electronics and semiconductors have had a *parallel* development (we are sometimes tempted to think, because of the chronology of computer generations, that semiconductors technology only began in the post-war world).

A thermionic valve is essentially an evacuated glass bulb in which metal electrodes are set: voltages are applied across the electrodes to control currents flowing in the vacuum. When an electrode is heated, electrons are emitted and, in the appropriate circumstances, a current flows. The phenomenon of thermionic emission was observed for the first time in 1883 in the Menlo Park laboratory of Thomas Edison – and so it was dubbed the 'Edison Effect'. The researchers at Menlo Park did not understand the phenomenon but Edison, thinking that it might come in useful, filed a patent. When there was no immediate application, he seems to have lost interest ('Well, I'm not a scientist. I measure everything I do by the size of the silver dollar. If it don't come up to that standard then I know it's no good' – this commercial pragmatism has a familiar ring in the modern climate).

Much research at Menlo Park focused on the (unsuccessful) attempt to build a storage battery and prodigious efforts – involving experiments with aluminium, tree bark, cat gut, human hair, etc – to develop a filament for the incandescent light. A metal plate was placed in the glass canopy in an attempt to prevent the bulb becoming black. This did not achieve the desired effect but current was detected in the plate. Moreover when the filament current was increased there was a proportionate increase in the current flowing in the plate. The only explanation was that current was flowing from filament to plate, across the vacuum.

Further research – notably by John Fleming, employed by Edison in the British subsidiary – revealed that even with *alternating* current in the filament, the current in the metal plate was still *direct*: thus in 1884/5 it was demonstrated that the Edison-Effect lamps had the ability to convert alternating current to direct current. The filament came to be called a 'cathode', and the elongated glass tube used in later work a 'cathode ray tube' (to become ubiquitous in twentieth-century television receivers). In 1897 J J Thomson experimented with the cathode ray tube by placing magnets around it to deflect the ray (occasional collisions with non-evacuated ions would produce ions that glowed).

In a parallel development Robert von Lieben (1878–1914), working in

293

Vienna, added a third electrode between what were now widely called the cathode and anode; and the new perforated electrode helped to define the nature of the new thermionic 'triode' (having three electrodes). The impulse behind this work was to improve the methods of communication. The third electrode was fed with the sound impulses coming from the telephone transmitter, and used to control them and amplify them as required. The American researcher Lee de Forest (1873–1961) modified the Fleming valve (to produce the 'audion') to facilitate radio communications. It was appreciated at this time that the thermionic valve could act as an effective switching device.

At the same time it was known that semiconductors had interesting electronic features. Early rectifiers used to convert the transmitted alternating current into the direct current that echoed the 'intelligent' shape of the original signal employed semiconductor crystals. Fleming, working on the problem of rectification, had quickly appreciated the value of the thermionic valve's switching potential; in particular, the relevance of this to effective communication. It was the characteristic features of the glass valve (which itself was nothing more than a glorified light bulb) – ie such capabilities as amplification, rectification and switching – that for a time enabled it to eclipse semiconductor technology and serve in the first generation of electronic computers. (More is said about semiconductors in Chapter 7.)

Turing

Two phrases, above all, are associated with the name of Alan Turing: 'Turing machines' and the 'Turing Test'. We encounter the first below, the second in Chapter 8.

He was born in London in 1912; though he showed little promise at school he later achieved a PhD at Cambridge and became one of the acknowledged giants of computer thought. One biographer observes that he was a 'friendly, pleasant person' but, since he was an avowed atheist and (sometimes) undisguised homosexual, others may have disagreed. His particular talent was in mathematics; his particular enthusiasm for the prospect of intelligent thinking machines.

There were various significant influences in Turing's early life. One was a book entitled *National Wonders Every Child Should Know*, written by Edwin Tenney Brewster and published in 1912. Turing was excited to find that the human body could be regarded as a *machine*: 'It is a vastly complex machine, many, many times more complicated than any machine ever made with hands; but still after all a machine.' (This of course is a familiar theme in philosophy. In 1747 Julien Offray de La Mettrie explored the idea in *L'Homme Machine*, as did Samuel Butler, more briefly in *Erewhon*, first published in 1872. In *The Summing-Up*, 1938, Somerset Maughan remarked of the great many medical books that 'told me that man was a machine subject to mechanical laws; and when the machine ran down that was the end of him' – when he saw men die in hospital 'my startled sensibilities confirmed what my books had taught me'. I tried to bring the man-machine concept up-to-date in *Is Man a Robot?*, published in 1986.) The notion that a human being can be defined *in toto* by identifiable physical constituents organised in particular complex ways is important for the history of AI; for such a notion immediately suggests that if the human mechanisms is adequately understood then analogous *artificial* mechanisms can be built – to mimic or duplicate aspects of human performance (including mental acts).

Another early influence on Turing was Alfred Beuttell, a pioneer in the science of illumination who aimed to reduce 'the physiology of vision to a scientific and mathematical basis'. Beuttell leanings to Theosophy did not impress Turing but a common interest in how the brain worked resulted in many discussions. For instance, they explored the idea that the brain operated on electrical principles, with particular moods being determined by electrical potentials. Today we would give greater emphasis to the role of biochemistry but the important point, from Turing's point of view, was that it was possible to discuss mental phenomena in the context of organised physical systems. It was this approach that was to uniform much of his later theorising about artificial intelligence (see Chapter 8), an approach that is common today but that much less common four decades ago.

Turing was to be further influenced by the work of the mathematician D Hilbert who, at the beginning of the twentieth century, posed seventeen unsolved questions to the mathematical world. Working on these problems, Turing soon became fascinated by the possibility of designing a machine that could perform any computation, provided that adequate instructions were provided. It was through this preoccupation that the theoretical notion of the '*Turing machine*' was born.

As a boy, Turing had been intrigued by machines, how simple organised components could yield complex modes of behaviour. The familiar typewriter held a special interest. He realised that there was a sense in which the typewriter was *programmed* by its structure, and that its current *configuration* (eg operating in upper or lower case) determined its response. Other features (eg the variable position on the printing line) were also recognised as crucial. At the same time the typewriter, in the context of Turing's purposes, was too limited a device. It fulfilled the requirements of being able to handle symbols, but it lacked even the rudiments of autonomy: it relied totally on a human operator to select the required symbols and to determine the particular configuration. Turing was keen to develop (theoretical) machines that were much more competent. So (in the words of his biographer Andrew Hodges, 1983), 'he imagined machines which were, in effect, super-typewriters'. In fact because of the method of operation, it would have been impossible to build an actual 'Turing machine': the theory was sound but it would have yielded an impossibly large device.

The concept resulted in a 'machine' that was, in effect, an evolved typewriter. The paper became a tape marked off into unit squares that could each carry a symbol: so only one line of writing was to be used, enabling such details as margins and line control to be ignored and allowing the tape to progress indefinitely from right to left or from left to right. The machine would be equipped to scan the symbols, and also to print new ones, and to respond accordingly. The tape would proceed one unit square at a time, allowing the system to function as an automatic machine without human intervention.[2]

The machine would behave according to its current configuration and the symbol scanned: these factors would cause the machine

- to respond to the scanned unit square (writing a symbol in a blank, retaining the existing symbol, or leaving a blank);
- to retain the configuration or move to another;
- to move the tape to right or left, or to return it in the same position.

A 'table of behaviour' could be written out to specify any particular Turing machine, and an infinite number of such tables (and so machines) are theoretically possible. In such a way it became possible to define a mechanical process to achieve a wide range of computational results: a vital step had been taken to lay the theoretical basis for the electronic computers that were soon to emerge. (It is beyond the scope of this book to provide a detailed description of the working of a Turing machine. Excellent accounts are given in Kilmister, 1967, Chapter 10; and in Hodges, 1983, pp 96–110.)

Again we can emphasise a key element in Turing's approach. A central aim was to provide autonomous machine operation, computation carried out – once the system had been configured and programmed – without human involvement. The Cambridge mathematician G H Hardy had already speculated on the idea of a 'miraculous machine', a mechanical system that could solve the problems posed by Hilbert. Turing, in fact, did not believe that such a machine, able to solve all mathematics problems, could be built; but he was convinced that a *universal* machine could be designed to take over the work of any *particular* machine, *including the human brain*. This again was a key impulse behind Turing's thought on artificial intelligence. He assumed that a Turing machine of sufficient complexity would be able, by operating with the symbols on its tape, to duplicate the full range of human mental activity. Turing was one of the great creative heralds of artificial intelligence.

He is celebrated also for his war-time work at Bletchley Park on the Enigma codes (hence the title of the Hodges Biography, *The Enigma of Intelligence*; and the title of the long-running West End play, *Breaking the Code*, based on the life of Turing). This work further developed the theoretical basis for the imminent emergence of electronic computers. Turing himself was encouraged to design one of the earliest electronic stored-program digital computers, but for various bureaucratic and other reasons the efforts were unsuccessful. He was unappreciated as a visionary mathematical pioneer by officialdom – and moreover subject to persecution as a homosexual. Turing committed suicide in 1954.

Computer systems

We have noted the development of mechanical calculating systems in the nineteenth century, notably the 'engines' of Babbage (Chapter 3). It is also interesting that industrial robots are prefigured by various nineteenth-century inventions. For example, in 1892 a patent was taken out by Seward Babbitt of Pittsburgh for a rotary crane equipped with a motorised gripper for removing ingots from furnaces. Like the modern electronic computer, modern robots (Chapter 13) have many enabling antecedents. Willard Pollard, for instance, in 1938 developed a jointed mechanical arm for spray-painting, an ancestor of the sophisticated computer-controlled systems now commonplace throughout the world.

In the nineteenth-century there were few post-Babbage developments that helped to prepare the way for the electrical computing systems that were to emerge in the twentieth-century pre-war environment. Lord Kelvin developed a machine in the 1870s to predict tidal movements. As with Babbage the theory had to be realised in the technology of the day – so cogs, wheels and sets of gears (with continuously variable ratios) enabled mathematical integrations to be performed. In 1876 Lord Kelvin published a paper proposing the idea of a general-purpose analogue machine, the *difference analyser*. And, before the turn of the century, William S Burroughs had introduced the first commercially available adding machine. It included a keyboard for the input of numbers (this typewriter-style facility had already appeared in Dorr E Felt's Comptometer) and a compact printing device for recording numbers was added. Burroughs is today one of the largest computer manufacturers.

In the mid-1920s Vannevar Bush at the Massachusetts Institute of Technology (MIT) put Lord Kelvin's idea for a difference (or differential) analyser into practice using thermionic valves. (Claude Shannon, who saw the possibility of developing two-state electrical systems to embody Boolean functions, was one of the operators of the MIT differential analyser.) A number of similar analogue machines were developed in the 1920s and 1930s.

By 1937 IBM had decided to invest $1 million into the construction of the giant Automatic Sequence Controlled Calculator (ASCC), to be operated by US Navy personnel for the Bureau of Ordinance Computational Project at Harvard. A central aim was to provide solutions to problems in ballistics, and another purpose – not known to the early operators – was to perform calculations relating to the development of the atomic bomb. Los Alamos, the centre for atomic weapon development, was then using punched-card calculators (following Hollerith's nineteenth-century innovations) and plug-board programming methods. Bunches of cards had to be physically conveyed between machines to enable a computation to proceed. In such a fashion a typical equation could be solved in less than a month, with a staff of about twenty people working in shifts. The cumbersome ASCC was soon to give way to the glass-valve electronic computers of the first generation (see Chapter 6).

In summarising the computing devices of the 1930s one observer (Lavington, 1980) identifies three types:

- mechanical and electromechanical calculators able to add, subtract, multiply and divide (using mechanisms typically based on German, Swedish and American inventions);
- electromechanical punched-card machines (eg sorters and tabulators), based on the early work of Hollerith and James Powers, and used for scientific computations in the late-1920s and after;
- the differential analyser, a highly specialised system for solving equations (a project at Iowa State College, between 1937 and 1941, for the binary electronic solution of equations was never completed).

These systems used electrical, mechanical and electromechanical methods to solve a wide range of computational problems – but often in a painstaking and laborious fashion. The speed of electronics was soon to change the face of computing, but already abundant theoretical insights had been gained by the development of non-electronic computing systems on the one hand and computational theory on the other.

In the 1930s, Konrad Zuse developed a series of electromechanical binary equation solvers in Berlin. The first (entirely mechanical) Zuse machine, the Z1, was built in 1935 from rods, metal sheets and mechanical switches (for the binary store). Input was via a keyboard, and output was signalled via flashing lights. This device, a typical mechanical monstrosity, was built in his parents' living room and was ambitiously designed to follow the algorithmic flow of a computation. The Z2 used electromechanical relays (secondhand telephone relays) instead of mechanical switches, and punched-paper tape for input.

The Z3 machine, a yet more ambitious version, was working in 1941. Numbers, but not yet instructions, were internally stored; and techniques of sequence-controlled calculation were employed. Zuse and his colleague Helmut Schreyer conceived of the idea of using thermionic valves instead of electromechanical relays, but he received little official support (otherwise the Nazis may have had a first-generation electronic computer). The Zuse computers – the Z3 and Z4, and the process-control S1 and S2 fixed-program machines – were used for the German war effort and some were damaged by Allied bombing. In 1948 Zuse again began building computing machines, before founding his own company Zuse KG in 1950. The firm was taken over by Siemens in 1969.

By the early-1940s many of the key requirements for electronic computation had been set in place. Researchers were familiar with, for example, stored-program concepts, the algorithmic computational flow, the computational significance of Boolean relations and the switching properties of the thermionic valve. In the United States and Britain many workers were striving to design and then build the first electronic digital computer.

Summary

This chapter has surveyed the development of electronics and computer thought from the late-1880s to the onset of the Second World War. Again an attempt has been made to convey an impression of both theoretical insights (Lord Kelvin, Turing, Shannon, etc) on the one hand and practical innovation (Edison, Hollerith, Zuse, etc) on the other. As always, it is inevitable that progress in computing is achieved by mixing together theory and practice. And again it is worth emphasising that this book can do no more than sketch the various contributing elements.

By 1940 the scene was set for the emergence of electronic digital computers. Partly under the stimulus of war, governments in Europe and elsewhere were to see their interest in developing effective methods of automatic computation. At the same time (as with Turing and Zuse), politicians and officials were often slow to appreciate the gathering momentum of a technological revolution that would in a few decades reshape the world.

It is also important to remember that many technologies are running along in parallel, that there is not a one-dimensional chronology of innovation. So semiconductors were being investigated throughout the application history of the thermionic glass valve, and mechanical and electromechanical computing applications were simultaneously being made commercially available. This consideration has relevance to our brief profile of first-generation systems (Chapter 6) and of semiconductor developments (Chapter 7). While first-generation systems, dubbed 'electronic brains', were assisting specialists and mystifying the public, semiconductors were waiting in the wings. With the arrival of the semiconductor it was tempting to believe that there was only one route for computer system evolution. With hindsight we will probably find that the technologies of future computer generations (Chapter 16) had their roots in the twentieth century.

Notes

1 It has been suggested that sixth- and later-generation systems may in the future be based on optical components or organic materials (see Chapter 16).
2 Much of the computational theory intended to govern the working of the Turing machine is implied by the celebrated paper, Turing (1937), already cited.

References

Hodges A, *Alan Turing: The Enigma of Intelligence*, Burnett Books Ltd, 1983.
Kilmister C W, *Language, Logic and Mathematics*, English Universities Press, 1967
Kneale W and Kneale M, *The Development of Logic*, Oxford University Press, 1962
Lavington S, *Early British Computers*, Manchester University Press, 1980
Reid T R, *Microchip*, William Collins, 1985
Simons G, *Is Man a Robot?* John Wiley, 1986
Turing A, On computable numbers, with an application to the Entscheidungs problem, *Proceedings of the London Mathematical Society*, x/ii, 1937, pp. 230–65

15

THE DISCOVERY OF THE ARTIFICIAL

Some Protocybernetic Developments 1930–1940

Robert Cordeschi

Source: *AI & Society* 5, 1991: 218–338.

Abstract. In this paper I start from a definition of "culture of the artificial" which might be stated by referring to the background of philosophical, methodological, pragmatical assumptions which characterizes the development of the information processing analysis of mental processes and of some trends in contemporary cognitive science: in a word, the development of AI as a candidate science of mind. The aim of this paper is to show how (with which plausibility and limitations) the discovery of the mentioned background might be dated back to a period preceding the cybernetic era, the decade 1930–1940 at least. Therefore a somewhat detailed analysis of Hull's "robot approach" is given, as well as of some of its independent and future developments.

Keywords: Cybernetics; Artificial Intelligence (history of); Mechanistic psychology

Protocybernetics and the culture of the artificial

If one were to attempt to define the notion of the "culture of the artificial" which is prevailing in this century, it would perhaps be possible to define it on the basis of some dominant traits which characterized AI, as a candidate science of mind, during its brief history. I would be tempted to summarize those traits point by point as follows:

1   Mental processes are independent of the features of organic structure; more precisely, there is a *functional equivalence* between their

301

instantiation in an organic structure and their instantiation in an inorganic or artificial structure.

2   The hypothesis that mental processes are mechanical is verified (or tested) by the building of models that reproduce them. This "synthetic" or model method gives the proof of the *sufficiency* of the processes postulated by the hypothesis to explain intelligence, intentionality and so on, and of the futility of introducing explanatory "non-naturalistic" entities.

3   The principles behind explanations of "simple" processes of intelligence are the same as those at work in the "higher" processes. The successful artificial reproduction of the former opens up the way to the ("empirical") hypothesis that from this starting point it will be possible to simulate complex processes which are more commonly known as "psychic", by means of a procedure of accumulation and generalization of the positive results reached which is comparable in principle with the "mature" sciences. It is thus not impossible to deal with the *complexity* of psychic phenomena using ordinary analytical criteria.

4   Knowledge of the external world of an organism occurs through *representations*. These representations are variously viewed – as identical to the functional states or as their semantic content. In any case they concern physical structures, which as such can in principle be implemented in particular artefacts.

5   The observer can legitimately describe the processes of the artefact (seen as an "intentional system") using a *mentalistic* language (like the one commonly used in the higher organisms), at least in order to control and predict its behavior.

When I said I intended to make a point by point summary of the culture of the artificial, I emphasized that I was referring in particular to what may be inferred from AI as a science of mind.[1] If one considers AI exclusively as a branch of engineering, concerned with emulating and extending certain human capacities, then almost none of points (1)–(5) proposed above would be relevant. But let me be more explicit on this point. In the present paper my aim is to show that the discovery of the notion of the artificial as is defined by (1)–(5) goes back to an era preceding AI, indeed preceding cybernetics itself: the era that we would define here of protocybernetics. Are all the above points relevant in order to define the "culture of the artificial" in the protocybernetics era? Obviously, one should be clear on the nature of the artificial: in the protocybernetic era – but also in the cybernetic one – the "artificial" is essentially and generically the "inorganic"; in the more recent times of information processing psychology and cognitive AI the "artificial" is specifically the "computational". This should be kept in mind, for example, when considering point (4). The physical structures referred to in point (4) are *symbolic codes*: as such they are specific to classical (symbolic) AI, and not proper to any preceding mechanistic trends in the science of mind. In fact it is on this point that computational cognitivists of the so-called classical view distinguish themselves both from old cybernetics and from new connectionistic AI (see for example, Pylyshyn, 1989). And not by chance do they oppose to neoconnectionists using the same argument which they assume to be conclusive, and use against connectionism from Hull to Hebb to Osgood, i.e. what I would like to call the protocybernetic connectionism of the thirties (i.e. of the era of the "discovery" of the artificial as defined above).[2] It is thus understandable that Fodor and Pylyshyn find themselves "with a gnawing sense of déjà vu" when concluding their well-known critical analysis of contemporary connectionism (Fodor and Pylyshyn, 1988). Therefore, we should be careful to avoid confusion when extending the notion of "culture of the artificial" to the period preceding classical cognitive AI.

Discovering the artificial: Clarke L. Hull's robot approach

Let us start from the so-called "robot approach", to which Clark Hull dedicated himself between the late twenties and 1935, and some of its independent and later developments.[3] A psychologist with a background of studies in logic and engineering, Hull had designed and constructed a machine which found syllogistic conclusions automatically. However, from at least 1926 onwards he was already thinking of a design for a different kind of machine which could stimulate higher functions.[4] It appears that Hull managed to realize his project for the first time after a chance meeting with a young chemist, H. D. Baernstein. Their model claimed to reproduce numerous characteristics of Pavlov's conditioned reflex. Many of the main points (which I shall return to frequently) of my definition of the culture of the artificial are summarized in the brief preview of the project which Hull published with Baernstein in *Science* in 1929. Placing their project against the background of the so-called "mechanistic tendency of modern psychology", the authors presented it as a "synthetic verification" of the behavioristic hypothesis of mental functions through the "inorganic" simulation of the characteristics of the conditioned reflex. The methodological inspiration of the project was summarized as follows in *Science*:

"If it were possible to construct non-living devices – perhaps even of inorganic materials – which would perform the essential functions of the conditioned reflex, we should be able to organize these units into systems which would show true trial and error learning with intelligent selection and the elimination of errors, as well as other behavior ordinarily classed as psychic. Thus emerges in a perfectly natural manner a direct implication of the mechanistic tendency of modern psychology. Learning and thought are here conceived as by no means necessarily a function of living protoplasm any more than is aerial locomotion"

(Hull and Baernstein, 1929, pp. 14–15)

These ideas must have been around to a greater extent than Hull himself thought. In the same year another psychologist, J. M. Stephens, proposed a similar "synthetic test" of a psychological theory, this time related to a learning theory based on Edward Thorndike's law of effect.[5] Also according to Stephens it was possible to make a "synthetic" approach to the subject, an approach which is comparatively independent of any "analysis" of the living protoplasm. It is worthwhile rereading the passage below. In his pioneering work, Stephens was surprised to discover that the mechanistic metaphor suggested a possible new conception of the relationship between psychology and neurology and a fresh possibility of testing a psychological theory:

> "The above conception occurred to me as a means of evaluating those expositions of learning couched in neurological terms. This test of possible synthesis had, at first, only theoretical interest. To my surprise, however, I found that some of the analyses presented startling possibilities of mechanical synthesis . . . I have tried to use no explanation of animate learning which could not be considered to work in a machine. I have considered protoplasmic organisms as very complicated machines and nothing further."

(Stephens, 1929, p. 423)

"Very complicated machines" therefore. But what *kind* of machines? Both Hull and Stephens were obviously thinking of machines capable of *modifying their own internal organization* and therefore of showing a certain degree of *variation in their behavior*, a variation that originated in learning. Obviously it was not a question of simulating a simple reflex action, but of reproducing the mechanisms on the basis of which reflexes are *modified* in the way suggested by Pavlov and Thorndike's connectionism.[6]

The main point, therefore, was *memory* – how could a machine have been given any. You will recall that the objection in principle by the antimechanist *par excellence* of the time, William McDougall, lay in the impossibility of building machines that could modify their behavior on the basis of memory.[7] To give you an idea of how the contemporary mechanists were beginning to approach this problem, let us return to Hull, in order to get a closer look at the function of the model projected in particular by Baernstein. Their device could change its internal organization thanks to the presence of mercury toluene thermoregulators in the form of "U"-shaped tubes, where the toluence, by heating or cooling, caused the mercury level to rise or fall, and thus close or open the electric circuit respectively (Fig. 1a). In practice, they actu-

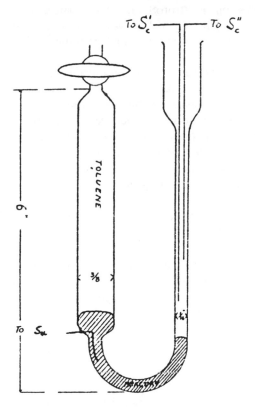

Figure 1a From Baernstein and Hull (1931) (Modified)

ally represented time–lag relays included in an electric circuit of which I am providing a simplified illustration in Fig. 1b. In the circuit we can see push buttons S_u, S'_c, and S''_c. If one presses push button S_u, lamp R lights up via *first* pair of contacts. This produces the simple *un*conditioned reflex (Pavlov's classic food-saliva case). Vice versa, the lamp does not light up if one presses one of the push buttons S'_c or S''_c (which correspond to neutral stimuli, or stimuli to be conditioned: a bell, light and such like are typical examples). But look what happens when we press, for example, S'_c for a couple of seconds: the *first* pair of contacts allow the current to pass through the heating wire surrounding the "U"-relay. This is marked C_1 in the diagram, and the wire passes alongside it. In this way the toluene expands and the mercury rises and closes the circuit. Next we press S_u: its *first* pair of contacts close the main circuit and cause R to light up; at the same time the *second* pair of contacts send a current through C_1 to the heating wire surrounding C_2. Two wires are connected to C_2, a longer one from S'_c and a shorter one from S''_c; the heating up of the toluene causes the mercury to rise in C_2 until it reaches the first of the two wires inside it (the longer one from S'_c) and closes the

305

circuit. At this point, if we press push button S′$_c$, its *second* pair of contacts send a current to R, which now lights up. In this way a *substitution of the stimulus* is created (S$_u$ and S′$_{ic}$, in the example), which is typical of simple conditioning.

As I said, the original circuit involves several complications leading to "inorganic" reproduction of various aspects of the theory of conditioned reflexes. However, not all these aspects are simulated adequately by the model. For example, an *identical* behavior of the model can be interpreted on the basis of completely *different* principles of the theory. This is the case when the model's behavior seems to reproduce the principle of redintegration. As I mentioned earlier, conditioning in its classic formulation can be seen as a case of associative learning, consisting of the "association" of an (unconditioned) stimulus with another (first neutral, then conditioned) one, occurring in strict temporal contiguity. In the case of redintegration the unconditioned stimulus is associated with a group or "complex" of conditioned stimuli, each of which is then able to replace the former separately when evoking the response.[8] If now, to simulate redintegration in Baernstein and Hull's circuit, we press *simultaneously* S′$_c$ and S″$_c$, as a conditioned

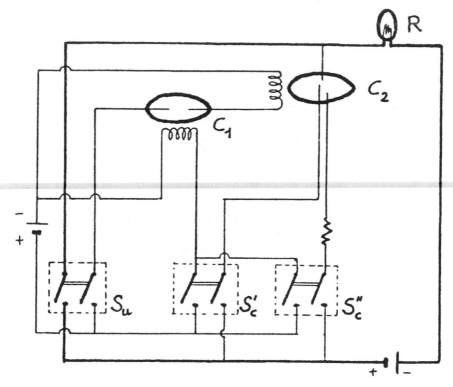

Figure 1b From Baernstein and Hull (1931) (simplified)

306

stimulus complex, and then we press S_u in the end the mercury will rise in C_2 until contact occurs between both wires in C_2; first with the longer one from S'_c, and then with the shorter one from S''_c (see again Figs. 1a and b). From that moment (for a certain period) in the conditioned response (the lighting up of R) will follow the pressing of S'_c or S''_c *separately*, following, so it appears, the principle of redintegration. In reality, as can be easily seen, this latter phenomenon (the lighting up of R by pressing S'_c and S''_c *separately*) could be obtained in any case, even *without* including S''_c initially in the conditioning process. But this behavior of the model can be explained, in Pavlov's theory, on the basis of a *different* principle, the principle of irradiation (Pavlov 1927, pp. 152 ff.). According to it some unconditioned stimuli can evoke the same (although weaker) response through a process of stimulus generalization (and precisely the resistance that in Fig. 1b is included in the circuit of the second pair of contacts of S''_c gives place to the weakening of the "irradiated" response).

It is not surprising that for a certain period Hull and those who were inspired by this approach dedicated themselves to designing circuits that would reproduce the various features of Pavlov's theory in as realistic a way as possible: the basic principles that explained the change of performance of an organism were recognized in these features. A little later Hull himself collaborated with Robert Krueger, an electrical engineer, designing another circuit that, to keep within the bounds of the above example, provided a better simulation of redintegration. Conceptually Krueger's model was not any different to Baernstein's; the novelty lay in the fact that the learning process did not occur via a modification of the "strategic points" (as Krueger and Hull called them) of the connections (the relays in Baernstein's model) but via storage cells that, initially uncharged, were charged when the conditioned stimuli buttons were pressed (analogue of learning), were discharged (analogue of extinction without reinforcement) and were spontaneously reactivated to a greater or lesser extent (analogue of recovering). An analysis of Fig. 2 (which reproduces the original wiring diagram of Krueger and Hull's model) suggests as, in a sense, my conclusion that we have here a better parallel of redintegration is justified.[9]

It is not by chance that I have been emphasizing the "inorganic" simulation of redintegration and its possible refinements. At that time, it appears that Hull maintained it was essential for the purpose of investigating a mechanism underlying several types of trial-and-error learning. This was what he defined as the "divergent excitatory mechanism" in which a single stimulus was connected with varying strength to a group of mutually incompatible responses. Normally one of these would correspond to the extinction of a need and be followed by (since it is an adaptive response) a reinforcement which strengthens the connection between the response and the stimulus. These incompatible responses could be single simple acts, and this would then be a form of trial-and-error learning (called "simple") in

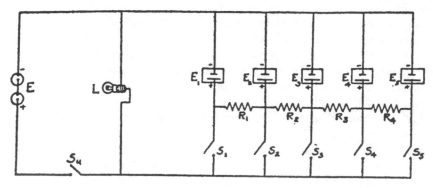

Figure 2 From Krueger and Hull (1931)

which a single act from among those possible is enough to bring success or extinction of the need. It is that single act that the organism ends up learning after a process of random selection; or (and this is more frequent) the responses are not simple acts, but particular sequences or chains of simple acts: and it is one of these (or rather, to use Hull's words, a "family" of these) that leads to success or solves the problem. This second type of trial-and-error learning was later to be named "compound" by Hull (1942).

In spite of a certain air of artificiality about this distinction (how does one define a "simple" act?) one could perhaps render it heuristically useful by referring the first type of learning (the "simple" kind) to lower organisms or to elementary type problem-box situations and the second ("compound") type to higher organisms or maze learning situations. Nevertheless both are based on the same divergent excitatory mechanisms which, as I said, Hull believed could be "derived" (his expression) from the redintegration mechanism. In fact Hull is not always consistent in his presentation of his "deductions" (and in later years he also used other expository criteria). Nevertheless, a way of reconstructing them (at least for my present purposes) could be as follows.

As we have seen in redintegration, a single stimulus belonging to a complex of stimuli simultaneously conditioned to give a certain response, can elicit that response even when it occurs separately. Let us assume we have a sequence of stimulus complexes which elicit a corresponding sequence of responses. For instance, let us take the case of a behavior sequence consisting of single alternative actions, e.g. in simple trial-and-error (Fig. 3). Let S_1, S_2, S_3 be the stimuli from the external environment, and R_1, R_2, R_3 the organism's responses. For the sake of completeness we shall also indicate the (internal) proprioceptive stimuli, s_1, s_2, caused by the responses. Let us assume that in any redintegrative stimulus complex (dotted rectangles in Fig. 3) there are: (1) stimuli like S_1 (external) and s_i (internal) that vary from one complex to the next (thus proving conditioned by one single response in the

THE WORLD:

THE ORGANISM:

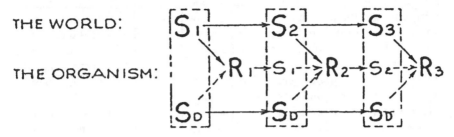

Figure 3 From Hull (1931) (modified)

sequence); and (2) a stimulus persisting in each complex. Let us take it to be, for example, the (internal) drive stimulus S_D triggered by an animal's need for food. It persists while the other stimuli vary, and is thus conditioned to *all* the responses in the sequence. Let one single response. e.g. R_3, be followed by reinforcement (food reducing the need). Even assuming that the S_D–R_1 and S_D–R_2 conections initially possess greater excitatory potential, subsequent failure of reinforcement will, according to the principle of experimental extinction, lead to the weakening of these connections, while the presence of reinforcement in S_D–R_3 will lead to the strengthening of the latter (possibly including strengthening through the spontaneous recovery phases of the two other responses, due to the time intervals between the successive cycles of trials). Thus, to the extent that S_D proves conditioned by every response, it is also able to elicit them all according to the various strengths of the respective connections. The divergent excitatory mechanism consists precisely in this. In practice we may see it emerging from a "persisting core" (Hull's expression), i.e. S_D, in the redintegrative stimulus complexes present in a behavior sequence.

In a well-known theoretical article published in those years, Hull (1930a) presented a detailed analysis of the divergent responses mechanism present in an organism which we might define as redintegrative. Analysis was made of the theoretical strengths of S–R connections and the theoretical values of reinforcement, experimental extinction and spontaneous recovery at various intervals of time and in relation to the organism's so-called "previous history" (in practice, the strengths of the various S–R connections prior to learning). The behavior of this hypothetical, redintegrative organism, Hull observed, showed "the persistence of effort at solution by means of varied response". As he pointed out, this is a type of behavior that is generally defined as "intelligent" or "purposive" in the case of organisms, in order to contrast this "psychic or mental" behavior (recall McDougall) with that of 'ordinary automatic machines" (Hull, 1930a, p. 255). However, for Hull the interest appears to have lain elsewhere: if his description, or "deduction" as he put it, of simple trial-and-error learning was indeed correct, it followed that this "purposive" or "intelligent" form of behavior could be deduced

309

from the basic principles of associationism and connectionism.[10] Significantly enough, the first simple models we saw above were created to embody precisely these principles. It was therefore to be expected that the construction of a model embodying simple trial-and-error principles would come up against the problem of how best to "combine", to use his terminology, the more elementary models created (a "combination", like the "deduction" process, entailing no qualitative differences).

Concluding his description of Krueger's model, Hull gave a list of open problems that future research would have to deal with (Krueger and Hull, 1931, p. 268). Among these was the simulation of the persisting stimulus (the type exemplified with S_D above), which lay at the basis of the simple trial-and-error divergent response mechanism. It must, indeed, have been a satisfaction for Hull to see two Yale University researchers, George Bennett and Lewis Ward, construct a device embodying the divergent response principle a few years later (Bennett and Ward, 1935). Two lamps are included in the wiring diagram of their model: they never light up simultaneously when, during the process of "conditioning", one turns on the various switches (as usual corresponding to the various stimuli – unconditioned and conditioned). Briefly, we have a machine which, once "conditioned", is capable of choosing between *two* antagonistic responses: as a simple organism confronted by a problem-box situation. Logically developing Hull's methodology of the artificial, Bennett and Ward held that if it was possible to create a device reproducing such an extremely simplified problem-box situation (with only two alternatives), it might well then be possible to use similar criteria to simulate artificially the divergent response phenomenon in more complex cases like maze learning (what I have described as "compound" trial-and-error learning).

Two year later, in 1935, psychologist Douglas Ellson published his description of a second simple trial-and-error model conceived along totally different lines to reflect Hull's theoretical assumptions more closely (Ellson, 1935). The model consisted of three electromagnets of varying initial strength linked to devices that could subsequently increase or reduce their strength (basically by automatically varying the number of turns in the respective windings). These were radially arranged around a central, spring-suspended soft-iron pendulum. On closing a circuit activating the three magnets the pendulum was attracted by the initially strongest magnet, which we shall call X. In order to reproduce the situation described by Hull, the pendulum should be "conditioned" to move in the direction of the magnet chosen to represent the goal, let us call it Z, which had the least initial strength. In short, this was achieved by simulating the reinforcement and experimental extinction envisaged by Hull with an automatic device that increased or reduced the strength of the respective magnets as goal was achieved after the pendulum had come into contact with each of them.

Rather than go into greater detail, it will be more enlightening to look at

Ellson's table giving the changes in performance (and time taken by performance) shown by the model in successive trial-and-error learning cycles (Fig. 4). Clearly, Ellson's explicit aim was to achieve detailed simulation of the changes shown in the table in which Hull had, a few years earlier, outlined the trial-and-error performance of a hypothetical organism (Hull, 1930a). From the two tables it is possible to see how the machine and the organism "learn" to respond with the reaction R_z, is seen to be progressively reinforced during the successive Problem (or Behavior) cycles. The machine reproduces various quantitative aspects of conditioning (experimental extinction, spontaneous recovery, etc.) predicted by Hull's theoretical assumptions. This is possibly the first case of detailed matching between intelligent performance in an organism and in an artificial model: a key-point of the future methodology of the artificial in psychological research.

The building of inorganic mechanisms simulating simple trial-and-error learning could be considered a success for Hull's theory: "one more step", as Ellson put it while reviewing the recent history of the mechanistic approach in psychology since Stephens (Ellson, 1935, p. 216). Nevertheless, on looking back to the 1930 paper mentioned above where Hull analyzes the features of simple trial-and-error learning, we got the impression that he would not have attached excessively great significance to such mechanisms. Here he came to the conclusion that although psychologists observing an animal learning the correct answer through simple trial-and-error might judge this "purposive" behavior, it could by no means be described as the "type of purpose involving a plan". The construction of inorganic mechanisms underlying this type of purposive behavior and other more complex, "truly psychic" phenomena like planning and insight, pointed to *"a radically new order of automaticity"* (Hull, 1930a, p. 256), although in principle by no means impossible to construct. The theoretical and experimental research Hull carried out between 1930 and 1935 aimed at defining the terms within which such a set of problems could be tackled.[11] Here I shall limit reference to the theoretical points relating directly to this alleged "radically new" automaticity, as a candidate explanation of "truly psychic" behavior. One of these points touches on the particularly representational theory of mind outlined by Hull.

Ultra-automaticity and the "psychic machine"

A redintegrative organism has one basic feature: that of acquiring the capacity to give rise to the response sequence even independently of a corresponding sequence of stimuli coming from the external world. In order to do this the organism must create its own sort of "subjective parallel" to the external world, as Hull described it (1930b). When the organism interacts with the world it is as if "the world in a very important sense has stamped the pattern of its action upon a physical object", i.e. the organism. Thus the

Trial No.	Problem cycle I Status of excitatory tendencies preceding reaction	Resulting response	Problem cycle II Status of excitatory tendencies preceding reaction	Resulting response	Problem cycle III Status of excitatory tendencies preceding reaction	Resulting response	Problem cycle IV Status of excitatory tendencies preceding reaction	Resulting response
1	$x = 100*$ $y = 70$ $z = 30'$	R_x	$x = 70*$ $y = 50$ $z = 40'$	R_x	$x = 50*$ $y = 40$ $z = 50'$	R_x	$x = 40*$ $y = 40$ $z = 60'$	R_x
2	$x = 70*$ $y = 70$ $z = 30'$	R_x	$x = 40*$ $y = 50$ $z = 40'$	R_y	$x = 20*$ $y = 40$ $z = 50'$	R_x		
3	$x = 40*$ $y = 70$ $z = 30'$	R_y	$x = 40$ $y = 20$ $z = 40'$	R_x				
4	$x = 40*$ $y = 40$ $z = 30'$	R_x	$x = 10*$ $y = 20$ $z = 40'$	R_z				
5	$x = 10$ $y = 40$ $z = 30'$	R_y						
6	$x = 10*$ $y = 10$ $z = 30'$	R_z						

Trial No.	Behavior cycle I Status of excitatory tendencies preceding reaction	Resulting reaction	Behavior cycle II Status of excitatory tendencies preceding reaction	Resulting reaction	Behavior cycle III Status of excitatory tendencies preceding reaction	Resulting reaction	Behavior cycle IV Status of excitatory tendencies preceding reaction	Resulting reaction
1	$x = 3.0$ $y = 2.0$ $z = 1.0$	R_x	$x = 2.2$ $y = 1.5$ $z = 1.3$	R_x	$x = 1.7$ $y = 1.2$ $z = 1.6$	R_x	$x = 1.4$ $y = 1.2$ $z = 1.9$	R_r
2	$x = 2.1$ $y = 2.0$ $z = 1.0$	R_x	$x = 1.3$ $y = 1.5$ $z = 1.3$	R_y	$x = .8$ $y = 1.2$ $z = 1.6$	R_x		
3	$x = 1.2$ $y = 2.0$ $z = 1.0$	R_y	$x = 1.6$ $y = .6$ $z = 1.3$	R_x				
4	$x = 1.5$ $y = 1.1$ $z = 1.0$	R_x	$x = .7$ $y = .9$ $z = 1.3$	R_z				
5	$x = .6$ $y = 1.4$ $z = 1.1$	R_y						
6	$x = .9$ $y = .5$ $z = 1.0$	R_z						

Figure 4 From Ellson (1935) and Hull (1930a)

organism is able to reproduce the pattern even when the corresponding situation is absent:

> "The imprint has been made in such a way that a functional parallel of this action segment of the physical world has become a part of the organism. Henceforth the organism will carry about continuously a kind of replica of this world segment. In this very intimate and biologically significant sense the organism may be said to know the world. No spiritual or supernatural forces need be assumed to understand the acquisition of this knowledge. The process is an entirely naturalistic one throughout."
>
> (Hull, 1930b, p. 514)

In particular, with this type of "replica" or "pattern" the organism can foresee and anticipate events in the external world. These replicas may be considered the knowledge the organism exploits to implement its own subjective sequence of actions before the world sequence constituting the source of external stimuli in real time. Thus the end-response in the subjective sequence is characterized as an action that, once conditioned, can anticipate the external stimulus that had been indispensable to elicit the action before conditioning took place. This end-response is the only one to retain an instrumental function, the other actions or responses in the subjective sequence acquiring at this point exclusively symbolic value: in other words, they become responses that serve exclusively to trigger other actions in the sequence by means of the (internal) proprioceptive stimuli they excite in the organism. As Hull put it, they are "pure stimulus acts" or "symbolic" acts. Since they have ceased to be instrumental acts, they can conveniently be eliminated from the sequence by means of a mechanism Hull defines as "short-circuiting" (think, for example, of the anticipatory short-circuiting in an animal's sequence of actions defending it from a noxious stimulus, once the sequence has been learnt by the animal).

Thus, as Hull concluded, "the organism is no longer a passive reactor to stimuli from without, but becomes relatively free and dynamic". The role of the symbolic mechanism appears, in fact, to be the "transformation of mere act into thought", to quote Hull again: in other words, its role is to draw from the purely instrumental sequences the symbolic aspect of a thought that may, in some cases, be "rudimentary", but that already has the capacity for anticipatory behavior (Hull, 1930b, pp. 516–517). The fact that this organic mechanism is essentially *automatic* challenges us to attempt the customary synthetic verification from inorganic materials":

> "It is altogether probable that a "psychic" machine, with ample provision in its design for the evolution of pure stimulus acts, could attain a degree of freedom, spontaneity, and power to dominate its

313

environment, inconceivable alike to individuals unfamiliar with the possibilities of automatic mechanisms and to the professional designers of ordinary rigid-type machines".

(Hull, 1930b, p. 517)

We might describe Hull's "psychic machine" as a machine whose behavior is not the simple effect of a simple stimulus from without: the cause of its action is internal and can be accounted for with its symbolic model of reality. Ultimately, in order to conceive of a machine able to "dominate its environment" we should be prepared to imagine a machine possessed of that type of "subjective parallel" to the world possessed by organisms. Hull sees the building of such a machine as a real bet with the future. As usual, success achieved in the simulation of the simplest (although also most fundamental) principles of automatic functioning seemed to hold out hopes of similar success in the simulation of principles explaining the most complex, "truly psychic" behavior of organisms. *In the meantime*, as it were, this position of Hull's appears to have been established on the basis of his empirical, experimental psychological research, which seems to confirm in his mind the equally *automatic* nature of the more complex principles underlying reasoning, planning and insight.[12] Indeed, a few years after he had formulated his "psychic machine" Hull accounted for insight with a sophisticated version of the principles of associationism, concluding (in disagreement with mentalists and Gestaltists) with these words:

> "To state the same thing in other words, we appear to have before us here a deduction of insight in terms such that it might conceivably be constructed by a clever engineer as a non-living – even an inorganic – mechanism."

(Hull, 1935, p. 268)

In another context Hull's definition of the effective features of this automatic *but* "psychic" machine is less generic but expressed in terms of negation: the "*ultra-automaticity*" (as he defined it) of the machine is *not* that of recent automatic machines known for their practical applications, such as the steam engine or the electric motor.[13] However (and with some relevance to the field of the culture of the artificial I feel), Hull hazarded the prediction that developments in this no better defined "ultra-automaticity" might also depend on its future practical applications:

> "It is not inconceivable . . . that in the demands for higher and higher degree of automaticity in machines constantly being made by modern industry, the ultra-automaticity of the type of mechanism here considered may have an important place. In that event the

314

exploration of the potentialities lying in this radically new order of automaticity would be comparatively rapid."

(Krueger and Hull, 1931, p. 268)

Nevertheless, there is no real case for far-fetched speculation on the premonitions implicit in the evocative definition of an "ultra-automatic" psychic machine ("non-rigid", possessed of a "degree of freedom", able to "dominate its environment") cited above and in its possible industrial fall-out. As pointed out above, all these expressions refer to the (automatic) response anticipatory mechanism, which is in turn based on the divergent excitatory mechanism typical of a redintegrative organism.

In its simplest form, the response anticipatory mechanism should be implicitly present in simple trial-and-error learning (and thus in its inorganic simulation). Here a "short-circuiting" occurs in the alternative response sequence resulting from a stimulus like S_D (internal and non-variable, as we have seen). As a result of this short-circuiting, one or more actions in the behavior sequence are, as it were, *skipped* – possibly even all but one of them, as in the case of simple trial-and-error mentioned above where, after a certain period of learning through random trials, the organism produces response R_3 immediately and exclusively. In this case it is the only response having instrumental value in the achievement of success.

As we have seen, although this type of "short-circuiting" is based on forms of anticipatory behavior (and thus on a certain "subjective parallel" of the world), it would have been considered by Hull as a very "rudimentary" form of thought. Underlying the "truly psychic" behavior shown by organisms and thus, presumably, that no better defined "radically new" automaticity or "ultra-automaticity" of future machines, there must apparently have been a *second* divergent excitatory mechanism, also grounded in the organism's redintegrative capacities (the former, as we have seen, is the mechanism that triggers off short-circuiting in symbolic action sequences through S_D). In fact this second divergent mechanism was to be thought of as physically simulated in terms of notions that, as we shall see, went beyond Hull's robot approach. Anyway, it was taken to be triggered by an (internal) proprioceptive stimulus, which became the object of great consideration both among Hull's critics and successors (e.g. Mowrer and Osgood). Here I am referring to the most exemplary form of "mediational" constructs (between stimulus and response) known as the "anticipatory goal response". Without necessarily short-circuiting the symbolic action sequences (Hull, 1931, p. 290), this is an internal preparatory response of the organism to a need stimulus, while at the same time it is a stimulus controlling the sequence of instrumental actions that produce the plan to eliminate the need itself.[14] Indeed, this was the authentic, dynamic mechanism that, as Hull later put it, made the organism "hormic and purposive" (Hull, 1942, p. 90). Suffice it here to recall that Hull saw in this the physical symbolic mechanism that could account for the

315

old paradox of *backward* causation typical of intentional anticipatory actions – another anti-mechanistic war horse of Hull's time (actually of the time up to cybernetics, as we shall see).

All this brings us back to one of the key points of the culture of the artificial, as I defined it in the first section: the role of representational (physical) mechanisms in the explanation of knowledge and intentional action. However, in order to avoid anachronistic confusion over the nature of Hull's physical symbolic mechanism, we must at least distinguish between representations with a causal role, i.e. Hull's, and representations as contents of physical symbol structures. In the latter case, the causal role is *not* attributed to the representations as such, but to the physical structures (as symbolic codes), representations being their semantic content. For computationalist cognitivists, e.g. Pylyshyn, these physical symbolic structures are the key to their *different* representational solution to the *same* problem tackled by Hull: a naturalistic account of the semantic of the functional states (as explicitly recognized by Pylyshyn, 1984, pp. 24–28 and 41–42.[15]

As might have been expected, inorganic reproduction of the goal anticipatory response occupied an important position on Hull's list (mentioned above) of problems to be tackled in future research on the inorganic simulation of "truly psychic" behavior (Krueger and Hull, 1931). Another problem he tackled was the design of a device that might be "conditioned" not simply to non-organized complexes of stimuli, but also to certain particular combinations of stimuli in a given complex: in other words, a machine capable of distinguishing between different patterns of stimuli.

An attempt to solve this problem was made the very same year by Nicolas Rashevsky, a biophysicist who was very interested in the physicalistic implications of Hull's robot approach. He interpreted learning as a property of physical systems, which could in essence be referred to specific forms of hysteresis (his research was carried out in the general field of the thermodynamics of living systems, which Lotka had already developed in that period; see Rashevsky, 1931a). Rashevsky's hypothetical machine for the recognition of stimuli patterns is shown in Fig. 5 (Rashevsky, 1931b). The machine is interesting as an "assembly" of basic units corresponding to elementary circuits of the Baernstein–Hull type. His machine consists of nine of these units (each represented by an S in the figure). The bulb (as usual representing the response: e in the figure) can be lit either directly by a_u (unconditioned stimulus) or by a_c (conditioned stimulus) through the conditioned process previously described (as we have seen, consisting in closing a_c immediately before a_u). In this case, however, once the entire system has been conditioned a_c is then linked to e via three different basic elements linked in series and showing one of the possible configurations. *Which* configuration is produced depends on the previous shifts in the dials of three manometers, M_1, M_2 and M_3, each of which can activate one of the three basic elements and thus form a particular circuit. Shifts in the manometer

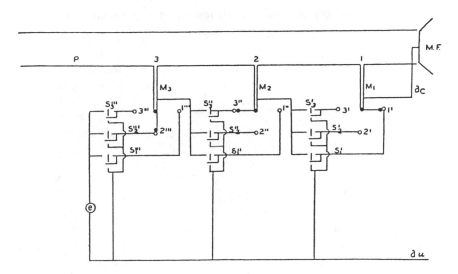

Figure 5 From Rashevsky 1931b (corrected)

dials depend in turn on the particular wave pressure passing through pipe P, which is full of air, once vibration has been produced in the microphone membrane, MF. The figure shows a closed circuit between a_c and e via $1'$, S'_1, $3''$, S''_3, $2'''$, S'''_2. A different wave pressure will activate three different basic units linked up in a series that does not complete the circuit and does not trigger a response (the lighting of e). In other words, the machine discriminates the stimulus pattern it has been conditioned to and responds to that and no other pattern.

Rashevsky (in disagreement with Driesch) held that it was not in principle impossible to construct more complex machines that might even be able to learn a natural language although, he pointed out, it would require "extraordinary expense and work". He also pointed out that descriptions "in psychological terms" of systems that "know", "desire", "infer" and "try" are "justified by the circumstance that the above process of trials occurred on a different level from the ordinary muscular responses". Moreover, since these machines show behavior patterns of a certain complexity and unpredictability, the observer interacting from without can only use this language, having no *a priori* knowledge of the "purpose" for which a given system acts (Rashevsky, 1931b, pp. 393–403). This, too, is a (much debated) key point of the culture of the artificial as I have defined it: the legitimacy of a mentalistic language in interacting with "intentional (natural or artificial) systems".[16]

Analytic and synthetic methods: towards the cybernetics era

Hull's methodology of the artificial has undergone further refinements through various other contributions taking their lead from his robot approach. The expert in electrical engineering Thomas Ross, for example, designed a number of automata which were subsequently to be mentioned by Ashby and Grey Walter, who looked on Ross as his precursor in the construction of synthetic animals (Walter, 1953, p. 82). Here I should like to spend a few words on what was possibly the founding member of this family of machines. Completed in 1935 thanks to collaboration between Ross and the psychologist Stevenson Smith, it was a motor-run device running on three wheels along a maze consisting of twelve "Y"s, each of which had one "blind" turn (to the right). When first placed at the start of the maze, the automaton explored it thoroughly entering every blind path and "retracing its steps" before going on towards the goal. When subsequently placed once again at the start of the maze, the automaton went through avoiding all the blind paths (like its better-known descendants in the cybernetics era). The crude mechanism underlying this automatic learning process can be seen in Fig. 6. Suffice it to point out that it consists of a rotating disk on which unsuccessful (blind paths) and successful attempts during exploration of the maze are recorded with a pattern of twelve depressed or raised tabs, corresponding respectively to the choices of turning right or left. By the time the automaton had gone through the twelve sections of the maze the disk has performed one complete rotation; on the second run the automaton finds the correct route imprinted in its memory, as it were, and will make no further errors. Ross referred somewhat polemically to what I have mentioned as the vitalist's in principle objection concerning the impossibility for a machine to learn: "*That* is intelligent behavior – a machine could never do that." *His* machine could (Ross, 1938, p. 187).

Of course, precisely the "non-animal" perfection, as it were, with which Ross' automaton demonstrated its learning capacities might well have fuelled arguments for further objections, if not in principle at least by "redefinition", as Minsky was to call it, i.e. by continually modifying the definition of intelligence in order to exclude all artificially reproduced phenomena.[17] However, apart from the antivitalistic dispute, Ross defined with extreme clarity the implications of the synthetic method which were to become *loci classici* in the culture of the artificial: the *testing* of psychological hypotheses by constructing artefacts, and the machine–organism *comparison* for respective performances. Presenting the project of some machines analogous to Rashevsky's (i.e. with the ability to discriminate stimulus patterns), Ross wrote:

> "It is hoped that it may be possible to test the various psychological hypotheses as to the nature of thought by constructing machines in accord with the principles that these hypotheses involve and compar-

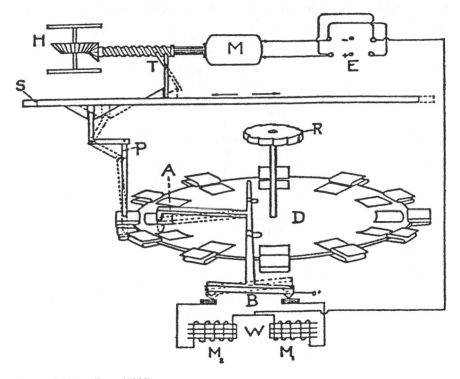

Figure 6 From Ross (1938)

ing the behavior of the machines with that of intelligent creatures. Clearly, this synthetic method is not intended to give any indication as to the nature of the mechanical structures or physical functions of the brain itself, but only to determine as closely as may be the type of function that may take place between 'stimulus' and 'response' as observed in the psychological laboratory or in ordinary uncontrolled learning and thinking. Only analogies which will work when elaborately executed are sought, not imitations of nerve, brain and muscle structure".

(Ross, 1935, p. 387)

Shortly afterwards, Hull himself again referred to the synthetic experiments on which these "hopes" rested. In this case the anti-vitalistic conception of his psychic machine seemed to fit into a perfectly explicit naturalistic reductionism. In Hull's opinion, given the existing state of knowledge, it was impossible to realize such a reductionist project with regard to the psychology-physics relationship, i.e. it was impossible to deduce the postulates which are basic to adaptive and purposive behavior as theorems of microphysics, according to the "natural goal of science". Thus the idea of a "complete scientific monism" should be considered "only as a working hypothesis". In the meantime, Hull concludes, "a kind of experimental shortcut" was to be preferred to the problematic point of view of the monistic-physicalistic theses – models had to be designed that would satisfy the postulates of Hullian theory. If such models behaved exactly as predicted by these axioms, *the theory would be proved true*, and it could be concluded that the "adaptive behavior may be 'reached' by purely physical means" (Hull, 1937, p. 29).

Hull's "shortcut" seemed to be clearly stated by Ross. In describing his automaton he focused his attention on two key-points of the culture of the artificial. According to Ross, in the expectation of the "hoped-for ultimate success of physiologists" in explaining cerebral structures, psychologists could consider the possibility of constructing mechanisms which are *functionally equivalent* to intelligent behavior. Such mechanisms could thus provide *proofs of sufficiency* for their theories:

> "One way to be relatively sure of understanding a mechanism is to make that mechanism. To find the sufficient condition for learning we should try to make a machine that will learn. This has been done several times in the past few years, and has perhaps been somewhat overdramatized. A very persistent mistaken attitude to work of this sort is the idea that the builder of a machine which will learn must think he has built a mechanism physically like that underlying human or animal learning. Nothing could be further from the truth. What is demonstrated by the physical existence of a performing machine is that a machine is capable of that kind of performance. It is not demonstrated, however, that only this sort of machine can produce the given effects; for no truth is more commonplace in mechanics than that, in general, several alternative mechanisms, differing widely in superficial characteristics and forms of energy utilized, can produce the same end result."
>
> (Ross, 1938, p. 185)

Ross seemed, therefore, to make completely explicit the methodological implications of the culture of the artificial of his time. The temptation is to suggest that, in a very restricted sense, Ross' automaton fulfilled Hull's dictum on the central role played by the internal model in anticipatory behavior. In fact the memory-disk performs the (arbitrary) symbolic notation function which the automaton uses to record its position in the world. The blind path is represented by an unequivocal tab position: from then on the automaton will avoid it on the basis of this internal representation. Thus a certain (successful) action is anticipated by means of an automatic mnemonic recall process.

If we accept this interpretation, we might call Ross' automaton a

"Craikian automaton". Johnson-Laird (1983, pp. 403–404) used this expression to describe, among others, simple mechanisms that appeared to satisfy the requisites formulated by Kenneth Craik in his famous hypothesis on the knowledge of the world obtained by organisms *and mechanisms* through a "model or parallel of reality", as he put it (Craik, 1943). Actually, however, all this should be taken with a considerable dose of caution (indeed it is very significant of the confusion that can be created in the field of the culture of the artificial). For example, without closer definition the "subjective parallel" or model of the world hypothesized by Hull could be reduced to the far weaker notion of a Watson-type (internal) proprioceptive stimulation pattern: a pattern capable of recalling without "cues" from the outside a certain sequence of action (a "chain reflex", in Watson's expression) previously learnt through exteroceptive cues.[18] Moreover, Ross' automaton (and actually also the simple so-called Craikian automata exemplified by Johnson-Laird) may be said to learn through a kind of feedback control, but only in a weak sense, i.e. in the very sense of the Law of the Effect criticized by Mowrer – that of "learning by doing". As Mowrer sharply stressed, the cybernetic insight of automatic feedback control is much deeper than this.[19]

Craik's hypothesis is very well-known, but his appraisal of Hull's robot approach is less known.[20] Despite Craik's (deserved) success among the various computationalist cognitivists – from Johnson-Laird to Minsky, from Miller *et al.* to Newell and Simon – this theoretical link with Hull may help us towards a better understanding of Craik's ideas and, at the same time, cast some light on those who were to take up certain of Hull's vague as well as "prophetic" formulations concerning the ultra-automaticity of the psychic machine. In fact, Craik seems to stand at the convergence of trends in mechanistic psychology (the "non-rigid" machine) with the then very recent developments in automatic control theories (machines with feedback). As Craik put it, the intention of pursuing the robot approach "even more unswervingly" (Craik, 1966, p.80) than his inspirer and, in contrast, his criticism of certain trivial applications of the robot approach, underlie his distinction between the "analytic method" (essentially neurophysiological) and the "synthetic method" (essentially that of artificial models) in mind studies. However, Hull's arguments against "individuals unfamiliar with the possibilities of automatic mechanisms and (. . .) the professional designers of the ordinary rigid-type machines" (Hull, 1930b, p. 517) seem to find a natural echo in Craik's arguments against those who reject the synthetic method on the basis of the idea of a "rigid" machine, i.e. "lacking in feedback", as Craik put it to stress his disagreement with McDougall (Craik, 1966, pp. 19–20). And note that Craik, evoking such feedback machines, intended to give his own physicalistic solution to McDougall's old paradox of "causation from in front" – a paradox, as we saw, that Hull tried to solve through the postulation of the anticipatory goal physical mechanism.

In short, the fateful word had been uttered: the year 1943 saw anticipatory,

321

"purposive" or "intelligent", behavior functionally identified with the behavior of a negative feedback machine. Craik's argument was on the way to becoming a *locus classicus*. "What would McDougall have said to Ashby's homeostat?", wondered Sluckin (1954, p. 36) returning to the problem in the fifties. But this is recent history.

Acknowledgements

A version of this paper was read at the International Conference "The culture of the artificial" (Lugano, 12–13 October 1990). I am indebted to M. Giannini and G. Trautteur for many valuable comments on an earlier draft. This work was carried out with the support of Italian M.P.I. grants.

Notes

1 Note that I am not giving here a definition of cognitive AI as a scientific field (indeed a more difficult problem), but a statement of the background of philosophical, methodological and pragmatical assumptions fairly widespread among cognitive AI scientists – just a statement of culture of the artificial.

2 In the present paper I shall use the term *connectionism* to refer exclusively to that of the pre-Hebb kind. Hebb was inspired by Pavlov, Thorndike and Hull's connectionism, but his criticism of them as well as his new approach to connectionism and associationism cannot be disregarded. I stressed this point in an analysis of some pre-Hebb mechanical simulations of neurological processes (see Cordeschi, to be published).

3 In fact Hull used the expression "robot approach" only afterwards, in his *Principles of Behavior* (see Hull, 1943, pp. 27–28: this passage was quoted in their well known book by Miller, Galanter and Pribram, 1960). Nevertheless, such an expression can be legitimately used to denote his "synthetic" (mechanistic and antivitalistic) approach to the study of mind during the early thirties.

4 The description of the mechanism for the automatic finding of syllogistic conclusions (which is mentioned also by Martin Gardner, 1982, p. 124n) was not published. Hull hinted at it occasionally (for example, Hull, 1935, p. 219). That Hull's next interest for a more complex "intelligent" machine dates back to the mid-twenties results from Hull's posthumously published *Idea books* (see Hull, 1962). On the contrary, from the published pages of such a notebook, as one of its editors recognizes, it is not possible to know why, around the mid-thirties, Hull gave up his plans for constructing such machines. Only occasional explicit references to them are found in his next works (for example, Hull, 1937). And yet at first Hull seemed to take his leadership too seriously in this field. He wrote for example in 1930: "Fortunately my years of study and meditation on the subject will probably enable me to keep well ahead of the pack and be their leader and spokeman. My academic position as well as my age should aid in this." And he seemed aware of the possibility of criticism to his project. So he wrote in 1929: "I shall doubtless encounter sneers, criticism, and possibly even opposition from the conservative and unimaginative individuals. But if so, this can hardly be more than an incident. I must surround myself with a few sympathetic and intelligent individuals so as to protect myself from the negative suggestion associated with harsh criticism . . . " (Hull, 1962, pp. 838 and 829). On the other hand, his projects became quite popular among the psychologists as well as the media of his time.

322

Anyway, it is a fact that Hull's robot approach did not go beyond simple models of conditioning, notwithstanding his deep insight in the methodology of the artificial – an insight which was to be better realized within a more developed technology.

5 The description of another mechanical device which simulated simple conditioning was published in 1930 (Walton, 1930), but more "for purposes of demonstration in introductory psychology", as its author said, than for testing a psychological (or neurological) hypothesis.

6 For example, Hull wrote in 1927 in his *Idea books:* "In designing a learning machine I felt the necessity of providing a device to vary the reactions so that trial and error could take place effectively" (Hull, 1962, p. 823).

7 See, for example, McDougall (1923).

8 Hull borrowed the term *redintegration* from the psychologist H. L. Hollingworth (Hull, 1929, p. 498). In Hull's opinion redintegration gave a more comprehensive view of old associationistic principles (for example, the simple chain reflex law might be derived from it: see Hull, 1930b, pp. 522–523). In a slightly different sense the term had been used by James, to denote the fact that one element of a past experience may, through association, awake the entire content of that experience (James, 1890, vol. 1, pp. 569 ff.) In the latter sense the old term became evocative among neoconnectionists (see Anderson and Rosenfeld, 1988, p. 3), who consider James as a forerunner of their own computational networks models of association. Of course, Hull too many be included among the authors who influenced the evolution of recent mechanistic models of association (just to make an example, think to S. Grossberg).

9 Hint: press S_u and, simultaneously, the conditioned stimulus complex S_1, S_2. Interrupt when "conditioning" is strong enough to evoke the maximal luminosity of L. If you press either stimulus button of the complex, both call forth the luminosity of L: though such a luminosity is obviously weaker than that evoked by the entire stimulus complex, it is the *same* in both cases. This does not occur in Baernstein and Hull's circuit (Fig. 1b), given the presence of the resistance, which on the other hand is necessary if you want to reproduce irradiation in it. The tendency to irradiation in Krueger and Hull's circuit (Fig. 2) turns out from the fact that, when S_1 is pressed in conjunction with S_u, the current from battery E tends to flow not only through S_1 to the storage cell E_1, but (for example) also to E_2 through the resistence R_1. Essentially, the latter, compared to the former is a fully analogical machine.

10 But note that Hull felt it necessary to correct "a frequent misunderstanding" on this point, which he ascribed to "the wide dissemination of the view of J. B. Watson": he never assumed that "the more complex forms of behavior are synthetized from reflexes which play the role of building blocks. This may or may not be true: His working hypothesis is, rather, that the *principles of action* discovered in conditioned reaction experiments are also operative in the higher behavioral processes" (Hull, 1935, p. 228 n.).

11 I refer here particularly to Hull (1929; 1930a; 1930b; 1931; 1932; 1934; 1935).

12 "Organism is here conceived as a completely automatic entity", Hull shall write afterwards, adding that the "complex automaticity" of human adaptive and learned behavior "is quite as automatic and self-regulating as simple automaticity". In any case, "highly complex automaticity constitutes no more evidence concerning the existence of an entelechy, or reason for indulging in anthropomorphism, than does simple automaticity" (Hull, 1952, p. 347).

13 Through the introduction of such an "utterly new and different order of automaticity", Hull wrote in 1929. "mechanical engineering of automatic machines

will be revolutionized to a degree similar to the introduction of steam engines and electricity" (Hull, 1962, p. 829).

14 In Hull's opinion, the mechanism of short-circuiting behavior sequences *per se* is not adequate to explain more complex trial-and-error behaviors, as maze learning. More radical criticisms were raised by Hull against the application of certain over-simplified principles of the early Watsonian type, such as the chain reaction principle, in the explanation of maze learning (see for example Hull, 1932).

15 See Pylyshyn's book for a discussion of other trends in cognitive science (e.g. Stich) with regard to the nature of representations.

16 Perhaps the most important treatment of the notion of ascription of purposiveness to artefacts preceding the well known Daniel Dennett's notion of intentional system is due, during the cybernetic era, to Donald McKay. He fully developed also a deep notion of mental representation, much appreciated (together Craik's symbolic model, which I shall expand on later) among early cognitivists (see Miller *et al.*, 1960, pp. 50–51). I stressed both points in Cordeschi (1985, 1988).

17 See Minsky (1963, p. 396). This objection is perhaps more popular in Douglas Hofstadter's version of the so called Tesler's theorem: "Artificial intelligence is whatever hasn't been done yet".

18 In spite of Ross' reference to Hull's psychic machine, this seems to be his own interpretation of learning and memory processes as based on kinesthetic stimuli (Ross, 1933, p. 208; 1938, p. 189). On the other hand, some hints on Hull's anti-Watsonian stance were given above.

19 In the case of learning by doing the automatic control concerns "not a response as it occurs, but rather a response or behavior of the organism in the same (or a similar) situation *on some future* occasion" (Mowrer, 1960, p. 267; but see the whole Chap. 7).

20 See Craik's *The mechanism of human action* (1943), which was edited posthumously by S. L. Sherwood, with an Introduction by W. S. McCulloch, L. Verbeek and S. L. Sherwood (Craik, 1966). (Craik died in 1945 at the age of 31.) Further details on Craik's mechanistic conception of mind may be found in Cordeschi (1986).

References

Anderson, J. A. and Rosenfeld, E. (eds). (1988). *Neurocomputing*. The MIT Press.

Baernstein, H. D. and Hull, C. L. (1931). A Mechanical Model of the Conditioned Reflex. *Journal of General Psychology*, 5, 99–106.

Bennett, G. K. and Ward, L. B. (1933). A Model of the Synthesis of Conditioned Reflexes. *American Journal of Psychology*, 45, 339–342.

Cordeschi, R. (1985). Mechanical Models in Psychology in the 1950s. In S. Bem, H. Rappard and W. van Horn (eds) *Studies in the History of Psychology and the Social Sciences*. Psychologisch Instituut of Leiden.

Cordeschi, R. (1986). Kenneth Craik and the "Mechanistic Tendency of Modern Psychology". *Rivista di Storia della Scienza*, 3, 237–256.

Cordeschi, R. (1988). *Intentional Psychology and Computational Models. Conceptus-Studien*, 5, 69–77.

Cordeschi, R. (to be published). *Two Proto-connectionistic Machines*.

Craik, K. J. W. (1943). *The Nature of Explanation*. Cambridge University Press.

Craik, K. J. W. (1966). *The Nature of Psychology*. Cambridge University Press.

Ellson, D. G. (1935). A Mechanical Synthesis of Trial-and-Error Learning. *Journal of General Psychology*, 13, 212–218.

Fodor, J. A. and Pylyshyn, Z. W. (1988). Connectionism and Cognitive Architecture: a Critical Analysis. *Cognition*, 28, 3–71.

Gardner, M. (1982). *Logic Machines and Diagrams*. Harvester.

Hull, C. L. (1929). A Functional Interpretation of the Conditioned Reflex. *Psychological Review*, 36, 498–511.

Hull, C. L. (1930a). Simple Trial-and-Error Learning: a Study in Psicological Theory. *Psychological Review*, 37, 241–256.

Hull, C. L. (1930b). Knowledge and Purpose as Habit Mechanisms. *Psychological Review*, 37, 511–525.

Hull, C. L. (1931). Goal Attraction and Directing Ideas Conceived as Habit Phenomena. *Psychological Review*, 38, 487–506.

Hull, C. L. (1932). The Goal Gradient Hypothesis and Maze Learning. *Psychological Review*, 39, 25–43.

Hull, C. L. (1934). The Concept of Habit-Family Hierarchy and Maze Learning. *Psychological Review*, 41, 33–52 (Part I); 134–152 (Part II).

Hull, C. L. (1935). The Mechanism of the Assembly of Behavior Segments in Novel Combinations Suitable for Problem Solution. *Psychological Review*, 42, 219–245.

Hull, C. L. (1937). Mind, Mechanism, and Adaptive Behavior. *Psychological Review*, 44, 1–3.

Hull, C. L. (1942). Conditioning: Outline of a Systematic Theory of Learning. In *The Psychology of Learning*. Public School Publishing Co. of Bloomington.

Hull, C. L. (1943). *The Principles of Behavior*. Appleton.

Hull, C. L. (1952). *A Behavior System*. Yale University Press.

Hull, C. L. (1962). Psychology of the Scientist: IV. Passages from the "Idea Books' of Clark L. Hull". *Perceptual and Motor Skills*, 15, 807–882.

Hull, C. L. and Baernstein, H. D. (1929). A Mechanical Parallel to the Conditioned Reflex. *Science*, 70 (1801), 14–15.

Johnson-Laird, P. N. (1983). *Mental Models*. Cambridge University Press.

James, W. (1890). *The Principles of Psychology*. Holt and Co. (Dover Edition, 2 vols).

Krueger, R. G. and Hull, C. L. (1931). An Electro-Chemical Parallel to the Conditioned Reflex. *Journal of General Psychology*, 5, 262–269.

McDougall, W. (1923). *Outline of Psychology*. Methuen.

Miller, G. A., Galanter, E. and Pribram, K. H. (1960). *Plans and the Structure of Behavior*. Holt, Rinehart and Winston.

Minsky, M. (1963). Steps Toward Artificial Intelligence. In E. A. Feigenbaum and J. Feldman (eds) *Computers and Thought*. McGraw-Hill.

Mowrer, O. H. (1960). *Learning Theory and the Symbolic Processes*. Wiley and Sons.

Pavlov, I. P. (1927). *Conditioned reflexes: an Investigation of the Physiological Activity of the Cerebral Cortex* (English translation). Oxford University Press.

Pylyshyn, Z. W. (1984). *Computation and Cognition. Toward a Foundation for Cognitive Science*. The MIT Press.

Pylyshyn, Z. W. (1989). Why Foundations, and Where Next? *Artificial Intelligence*, 39, 248–251.

Rashevsky, N. (1931a). Learning as a Property of Physical Systems. *Journal of General Psychology*, 5, 207–229.

Rashevsky, N. (1931b). Possible Brain Mechanisms and their Physical Models. *Journal of General Psychology*, 5, 368–406.

Ross, T. (1933). Machines that Think. *Scientific American*, 148, 206–208.

Ross, T. (1935). Machines that Think. A Further Statement. *Psychological Review*, 42, 387–393.

Ross, T. (1938). The Synthesis of Intelligence. Its Implications. *Psychological Review*, 45, 185–189.

Sluckin, W. (1954). *Minds and Machines*. Penguin Books.

Stephens, J. M. (1929). A Mechanical Explanation of the Law of Effect. *American Journal of Psychology*, 41, 422–431.

Walter, W. Grey (1953). *The Living Brain*. Duckworth.

Walton, A. (1930). Conditioned Iillustrated by an Automatic Mechanical Device. *American Journal of Psychology*, 42, 110–111.

16

MACHINES THAT THINK—A FURTHER STATEMENT

Thomas Ross

Source: *Psychological Review* XLII, 1935: 387–93.

Mechanical servants that will perform their duties without being directed or adjusted or preset as ordinary machines need to be may soon be possible as a result of recent research which aims to endow machines with intelligence of the sort possessed by living creatures.

This fascinating possibility, however, is of secondary importance to the implications that such machines will hold for psychological theory. It is hoped that it may be possible to test the various psychological hypotheses as to the nature of thought by constructing machines in accord with the principles that these hypotheses involve and comparing the behavior of the machines with that of intelligent creatures. Clearly, this synthetic method is not intended to give any indication as to the nature of the mechanical structures or physical functions of the brain itself, but only to determine as closely as may be the types of function that may take place between "stimulus" and "response" as observed in the psychological laboratory or in ordinary uncontrolled learning and thinking. Only analogies which will work when elaborately executed are sought, not imitations of nerve, brain, and muscle structure.

In 1933, under the title, "Machines that think,"[1] the writer gave an account of several attempts to illustrate principles of modern psychological theory by mechanical analogies, and one machine, capable of learning the way through a simple maze, was described in some detail.

Since then various improvements have been made in intelligent machines. Some experimenters[2] have equipped their models with distance receptors in the form of microphones and photo-electric cells. New memory mechanisms are being tested. The present article is intended to show how the ability to discriminate stimulus patterns and to respond in "patterns" can be given to machines together with learning ability, and to suggest how machines embodying the memory principle can be made useful.

Figure 1 shows two views of an improved "memory cell." A glass needle is attached to the armature of a solenoid which is so mounted that when the solenoid is energized the needle will pass downward through a hole in the surface below. Passing through this hole, the needle will perforate a piece of paper immediately beneath, the point at which the paper is penetrated being determined by its position relative to the hole in the surface above it. This paper is carried on the ends of rods extending from the armatures of two

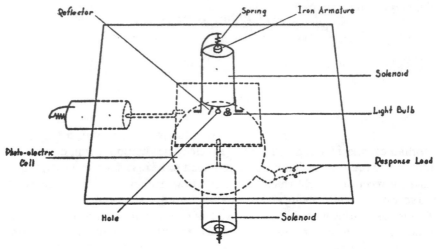

Figure 1(a) Perspective

MEMORY 'CELL'

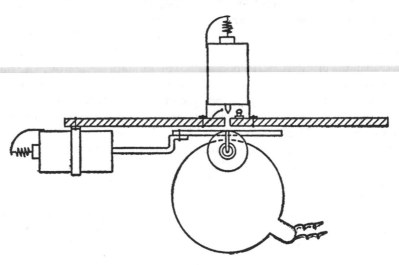

Figure 1(b) Side view

328

solenoids. This mounting allows the paper to be moved to-and-fro beneath the hole by varying the current passing through these solenoids. Beneath the movable paper, and shielded from all external light, is a photo-electric cell. Light can reach this cell only when a hole pierced in the sheet of paper is directly below the hole in the adjacent surface.

The neutral stimulus leads, or wires, those which call for no definite response prior to conditioning, are connected to the solenoids which move the sheet of paper. The dominant stimuli control the solenoid which moves the glass needle, the response being brought about by energy flowing through the photo-electric cell when the needle piercing the paper admits light to the cell. After the paper has been pierced at some point, the response can be again called forth by duplicating the intensities of the neutral stimuli which were effective at the time of conditioning, for such duplication will cause realignment of the hole in the paper with the hole in the surface, with consequent passage of light to the photo-electric cell.

It will be readily seen that the response controlled by the photo-electric cell can be conditioned to a number of stimulus patterns proportional to the number of holes that can be pierced in the paper without crowding.

By using two memory units it is possible to obtain simple response patterns. For instance, if a stimulus pattern is impressed upon the neutral stimulus receptors of both units, these units can both be conditioned to respond to recurrence of the stimulus pattern, or either one alone can be conditioned even though the pattern of neutral stimuli is impressed on both units. Thus, three response patterns are possible with only two memory units. Increasing the number of units will greatly increase the possible number of response patterns.

There is no reason that a number of penetrable sheets of paper and dominant stimulus solenoids with their needles should not be arranged about a single photo-electric cell as shown in Figure 2. If each sheet of paper were large enough to accommodate a hundred punctures (a number not excessive), eight sheets of paper could accommodate 10,000,000,000,000,000 combinations of perforated designs, the number being derived by consideration of the fact that for each of the hundred positions that a given sheet of paper can occupy, some other sheet can occupy a hundred more, a third sheet can occupy a hundred positions for each combination of positions occupied by the first two, and so forth; though, of course, no such number of memories could be held all at one time.

If all the needles of the dominant stimulus solenoids in one unit descend at once while a neutral stimulus pattern is impressed upon the appropriate receptors, the photo-electric cell will respond to the light admitted through all the punctures so formed, but the conditioned response cannot be called forth *with full intensity* thereafter unless the neutral stimulus pattern is completely duplicated so as to place all of the sheets of paper in the positions that they occupied at the time of conditioning. (Of course there is the

329

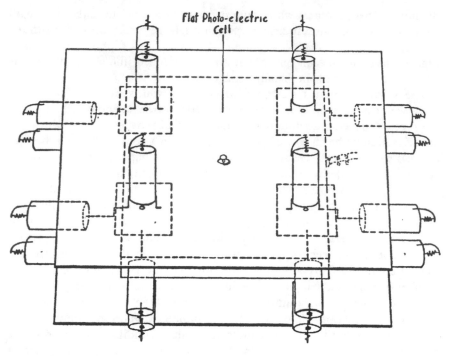

Figure 2(a) Perspective

EIGHT-IN-ONE MEMORY UNIT

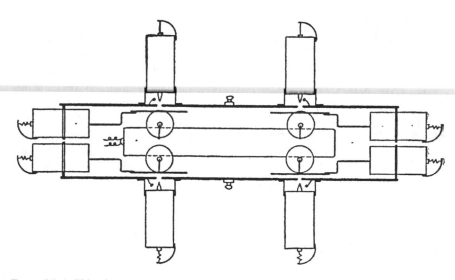

Figure 2(a) Side view

possibility that parts of two or more conditioned stimulus patterns would combine to produce a response of full intensity; this is a fact of considerable theoretical interest.)

The muscles of the higher animals are so arranged that every muscle has its opposing muscle, one which produces a motion *incompatible* with that produced by the first. This organization is reflected in the workings of the nervous system and in the mind itself. Obviously, if two muscles are not to be used at the same time, economy of energy demands that stimulation of one shall cause the other to be relaxed. Consequently, the working of any ordinary brain is such that when one group of cells favoring a particular response becomes more active than groups favoring incompatible or unrelated responses, the first group inhibits the activity of the other groups, especially of the group favoring movement incompatible with that which the most active cells tend to produce.

This same principle of dominance must be taken into consideration when a thinking machine is being designed; an electromagnetic arrangement for shorting out the less active of two memory units of the sort described in earlier paragraphs is shown in Figure 3. It is to be noted that if the more weakly active unit should rise in activity until it surpasses the formerly dominant unit, it will be able to inhibit that unit when reestablishing its own control of the appropriate "muscle" or corresponding mechanism.

So far, very little has been said of the neutral stimuli. Of course, stimuli received through the eye and ear as well as those produced by contact with ordinary objects are largely of the neutral type, calling for no definite response until after conditioning. These are well known. Very important, too, but less well known, are the kinesthetic stimuli, those arising from movement and

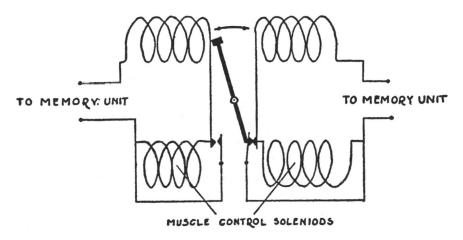

TO MEMORY UNIT   TO MEMORY UNIT

MUSCLE CONTROL SOLENIODS

Figure 3

INHIBITORY MECHANISM

331

tension of muscles and tendons. Patterns of these stimuli are to some extent involved in every conditioning or memory impression of intelligent creatures and greatly facilitate recall of memories involving objects out of the range of perception in the environment. This is evidently so, for the kinesthetic elements of any stimulus pattern can obviously be supplied by the organism itself at any time, regardless of external circumstances (or almost so).

When all of the points set forth here (and a few more!) are properly taken into account in the design of a thinking machine, the result should approach the ideal of a mechanism which will exhibit behavior which even the most skeptical must recognize as intelligent. The machine will have many memory units of the sort described in this article. Dominant stimuli will be supplied to guide it in "first encounters" with potent factors of its environment. Neutral stimulus receptors of visual, auditory, and kinesthetic types will have leads to the memory units. Energy will pass from one unit to another only through kinesthetic leads, though the visual and auditory equipment will have leads to units governing each "muscle." Such an arrangement will give the machine highly developed powers of recognizing repeated stimulus patterns, of imagination, and of recall. In order that it shall be able to remember its own "thoughts" provision must be made for conditioning with conditioned reflexes acting as dominant reflexes. This effect can be partially attained by arranging for "self conditioning" on the part of any memory unit that shall become dominantly active after having been inhibited. The mechanism for this need not be expounded here beyond the remark that the apparatus for shorting out units that are inhibited can be made to control the operation. Only kinesthetic receptors need be involved.[3]

Notes

1 *Scientific American*, 1933, 148, 206–208.
2 Norman B. Krim, recently a graduate of the Mass. Inst. of Tech., has placed an account of his work on file in the library of that institution.
3 Some economy in experimental models could be effected by equipping each photo-electric cell to control several responses. This could be accomplished by passing the current from the photo-electric cell successively through several responding members in rapid rotation as might be done by means of a commutator. A slotted disc mounted on the same shaft as the commutator would cause the light activating the cell to pass through a different set of memory surfaces for each position of the commutator.

Bibliography

1. Baernstein, H. D., and Hull, C. L., A mechanical model of the conditioned reflex, *J. General Psychol.*, 1931, 5, 99–106.
2. Hull, C. L., and Baernstein, H. D., A mechanical parallel to the conditioned reflex, *Science*, 1929, 70, 14–15.

3. Krueger, Robert G., and Hull, C. L., An electro-chemical parallel to the conditioned reflex, *J. General Psychol.*, 1931, 5, 262–269.
4. Rashevsky, N., Brain mechanisms and physical models, *J. General Psychol.*, 1931, 5, 207–229.

17

THE SYNTHESIS OF INTELLIGENCE—ITS IMPLICATIONS

Thomas Ross

Source: *Psychological Review* XLIV, 1937: 185–9.

Whosoever believes that "learning," "intelligence," "mind" are merely convenient terms for designating the workings of the ordinary laws of nature through special structures must show just how functions that are properly described by these terms can spring from the functionings of structures that are well understood. Unfortunately, the structures that sustain human and animal intelligence are not well understood. Pending the hoped-for ultimate success of physiologists in finding out about these matters, psychology can hardly spare the use of whatever means may come to hand for clearing its theoretical atmosphere.

One way to be relatively sure of understanding a mechanism is to make that mechanism. To find the sufficient conditions for learning we should try to make a machine that will learn. This has been done several times in the past few years, and has perhaps been somewhat overdramatized.

A very persistent mistaken attitude toward work of this sort is the idea that the builder of a machine which will learn must think he has built a mechanism physically like that underlying human or animal learning. Nothing could be further from the truth. What is demonstrated by the physical existence of a performing machine is that a machine is capable of that kind of performance. It is not demonstrated, however, that only this sort of machine can produce the given effects; for no truth is more commonplace in mechanics than that, in general, several alternative mechanisms, differing widely in superficial characteristics and forms of energy utilized, can produce the same end-result.

What seem to be the irreducible requirements for any mechanism or organism that is to learn a serial response without receiving successive differential cues from the outside are shown by a machine completed in the summer of 1935.[1] Some of the handicraft and certain of the mechanical principles were furnished by the writer, most of the actual construction having been done by W. A. Dillman and Byron Sullivan, the departmental mechanics.

This machine runs through a twelve-unit, multiple-Y maze in which the twelve sections are so arranged that each has one blocked branch and one branch that opens into the stem of the next section. Placed at the beginning of this maze and set in motion by connection to an electrical supply, the machine will begin rolling through the maze on its three wheels. Being constructed with a tendency to turn to the right, it will, on coming to the forking of the first Y-section, run down the right-hand passage. If this passage is blocked (by a vertical wall at the end) the machine will back out of that passage and turn to the left upon again starting forward. Since the maze is so arranged that one passage in each section is open, the left-hand passage will now lead directly to the beginning of the next section of the maze, at which point the machine will receive a "cue" that it has entered a new section as it brushes its two metal "feelers" against a pair of blocks set on the sides of the passage. In this next section of the maze the machine will again take the right hand passage at first, simply passing on through if possible but backing and turning to the left if encountering an obstacle, and so through the whole twelve unit maze. On entering each new section, of course, it will pass between another pair of blocks, but nothing will be registered in the mechanism to enable it to discriminate one pair of blocks from another as such. The blocks are all the same.

On being again started through the maze, the machine will go from beginning to end without entering any of the blind passages which it entered on the first trip through, and every time thereafter will repeat the performance without "error." Because of the nature of its "exploratory" movements, the machine will never again take the wrong turn.

So far, it will be noticed, there has been nothing in the description of the machine's behavior to distinguish it from that of a man who might go through the maze (were it large enough) counting the sections as he passed from one to another. There was a time when many contemporary psychologists on hearing the account of such behavior, without knowing what was doing the "learning," would have said: "That is intelligent behavior—a machine could never do that."

There can be no argument about the possibility of machines" doing things like this. It has been abundantly demonstrated that they can. It is hard to see how learning in the broadest sense of the word can long remain the stamping-ground of those who revel in verbose substitutes for objective explanation. A systematic change of behavior during the course of behavior and dependent upon external conditions is easily realized by numberless forms of mechanism. The fact that maze learning can be a mechanical function in a man-made tricycle should give us added confidence that the physical

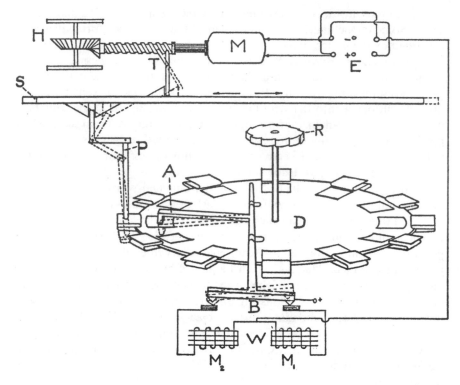

W marks the position occupied by a piece of iron the movements of which control the set of the pilot wheel of the maze learning machine. M_1 and M_2 are electromagnets acting upon the piece of iron. B is a metal contact bar carrying points which control the current to the electromagnets. The alternative positions of B, shown solid and dotted, determine which magnet shall receive current, and are determined by the positions of the arm A, which is rigidly attached to the same shaft. The position of A is determined by whether or not the hole above which its end is centered at any particular time is open or is stopped from below by one of the brass strips the ends of which protrude from the edge of the memory disk, D. These brass strips, when the machine is first placed in the maze, are all set so that their ends hook over the edge of the disk, D, thus holding them in the elevated position in which most of them are shown. The action of the plunger, P, is to unhook the end of the strip below it from the edge of the disk, thus allowing it to drop to the position shown by the dotted outline. The plunger descends only when, in the forward movement of the machine, the end of the rod S is brought by collision against one of the barriers marking the closed end of a maze passage and transmits part of the force of the impact to the plunger through the lever system shown. Tracing this through, it will be clear that the machine will tend to turn left only after it has struck a barrier, M_1 being the magnet that swings the pilot wheel to the right, and M_2 the magnet swinging the wheel to the left.

The ratchet wheel, R, is part of the mechanism (the rest not shown) which swings the memory disk through one-twelfth of a revolution every time the machine passes between the paired blocks that mark the beginning of a new maze section. Other mechanisms are the reversing switch E which is thrown when the rod S is driven backward by collision with a barrier; the motor M which is reversed; the hind wheel assembly H which is driven by the motor; and the worm and toggle system T which acts to restore the longitudinal rod to the forward position after the machine has backed a certain distance. (Pitch of worm greatly exaggerated.)"

mechanism of the more elaborate forms of learning in animals can be discovered. A machine is sufficient, even if not necessary, for the task of learning.

The particular mechanism used in the maze learning machine, the behavior of which has been described, is shown in highly schematized form in the accompanying diagram. Proportions and positions of parts have been liberally distorted in order to attain simplicity, and to the same end those parts which are not necessary for an understanding of the functioning of the mechanism are not represented in the diagram.

It will be seen from the diagram and accompanying description that the ability of the machine to learn the maze is due to the presence of the part called the "memory disk" upon which a pattern of raised and depressed tabs corresponding to the pattern of right and left turns needed for traversal of the maze without backing is impressed.

The completely abstracted principle of serial learning, which is all that the machine illustrates, is that in order for a serial act to come to be elicitable by a series of exteroceptive cues which do not differ from one another, there must at first be a pattern of original cues (in this case, collision with barriers) effective in eliciting each response of the series in turn, and corresponding to this pattern of differential cues must be some pattern effect produced within the learning machine or organism. Upon such an internal effect the reproduction of any behavior pattern without differential cues from the outside must depend.

Note

1 This machine was made at the University of Washington under the direction of Dr. Stevenson Smith.

18

THE MACHINE IN THE MIDDLE

Cybernetic Psychology and World War II

P. N. Edwards

Source: P. Edwards, *The Closed World*, MIT Press, 1996, pp. 175–207.

At the Hixon Symposium on Cerebral Mechanisms in Behavior, held at the California Institute of Technology in 1948, the neuropsychiatrist Warren McCulloch presented a paper that began:

> As the industrial revolution concludes in bigger and better bombs, an intellectual revolution opens with bigger and better robots. The former revolution replaced muscles by engines and was limited by the law of the conservation of energy, or of mass-energy. The new revolution threatens us, the thinkers, with technological unemployment, for it will replace brains with machines limited by the law that entropy never decreases. These machines, whose evolution competition will compel us to foster, raise the appropriate practical question: "Why is the mind in the head?"[1]

This problem became "practical" during World War II, when the human being as object of psychological knowledge began to be seen as a servomechanism or analog computer. New forms of technological power based on the amplification and insertion of soldiers' bodies inside electromechanical systems produced new ways of approaching the nature of the mind and led to the construction of new kinds of biopsychological explanatory spaces. These new tools and metaphors rejuvenated human experimental psychology, involving academic psychologists in practical design projects as consultants on the "machine in the middle" of complex human-machine systems.

338

Psychology as power/knowledge

Though it lacks the public visibility of psychotherapy and psychiatry, human experimental psychology is just as tightly interwoven with the fabric of sociopolitical meanings and practices. Psychology is the discipline that constructs and maintains the human individual as an object of scientific knowledge. Contests for models, metaphors, research programs, and standards of explanation in theoretical psychology represent simultaneous struggles for pictures of "human nature" and norms of behaviour. The human natural-technical objects[2] constructed by psychology find uses far beyond the restricted discourse of the scientific community. They are incorporated into clinical therapeutic apparatuses, integrated into ergonomic design, used to justify social and political practices, and absorbed by popular mythology.

Psychological theories have often backed interventions that have been profoundly and directly political in nature. In *Civilization and Its Discontents*, Freud wrote that women were unsuited to public life, since "the work of civilization has become increasingly the business of men; it confronts them with ever more difficult tasks and compels them to carry out instinctual sublimations of which women are very little capable."[3] Freud's theories and others like them supported clinical practices that focused on reconciling women to their primal need for a penis and their consequent "natural" dependence on men. Various theories of human intelligence, in the late nineteenth and early twentieth centuries, purported to prove that nonwhite and lower-class humans were inherently less well endowed than Caucasian males. The resulting technologies—"intelligence tests"—in turn reinforced repressive social practices and ideologies. As a case in point, during the successful passage of the anti-ethnic Immigration Restriction Act of 1924, American politicians frequently invoked World War I Army IQ tests, which "proved" that half the tested population had a "mental age" of under thirteen.[4] Foucault has shown how theories and practices of clinical psychiatry and penology, by changing the focus of attention from the bodies to the souls and minds of insane people and prisoners, both represented and incited a spreading "normalization" in nineteenth-century France.[5]

Psychology—both clinical practice and academic theory—constitutes a potent form of Foucaultian power/knowledge: a discourse of truth that maintains "a circular relation with systems of power that produce and sustain it, and to effects of power that it induces and that extend it."[6] Knowledge of the mind as an information-processing device developed in just such a "circular relation" to high-technology military power. The military organization of science during and after World War II played a crucial role in creating conditions under which fruitful encounters among psychology, computer science, mathematics, and linguistics could occur.

Psychology as an academic discipline profited enormously from the war effort, gaining visibility, legitimacy, and funding from its war work on such issues as propaganda analysis, morale-building, and psychological warfare. Its ranks swelled dramatically during and after the war: between the war's beginning and its end, the American Psychological Association's membership grew from 2600 to 4000. By 1960, it counted over 12,000 members, almost five times its prewar peak.[7] As with many other scientific disciplines, during the war the majority of psychologists worked on war-related issues. The federal government directly employed about half of all professional psychologists, either on research contracts, in military service, or in civilian agencies. Many others volunteered time, in teaching, research, or service, toward filling the country's wartime needs.[8]

The work of many psychologists on essentially military problems during the war changed the direction of their interests and the scope of their social and professional relationships. James Capshew, in a detailed survey of psychology in the war years, has concluded that

> World War II [was] the most important event in the social history of American psychology ... It aided the expansion of psychology beyond its academic base into professional service roles. As psychologists became involved in war work their research and practice was overwhelmingly reoriented toward applied science and technology. Relationships were forged with new patrons in military and civilian government agencies which provided markets for psychological expertise. Psychologists exploited these new markets by promoting themselves as experts in all aspects of the "human factor" in warfare, ranging from the selection, training, and rehabilitation of soldiers, to propaganda and psychological warfare, to the design of equipment.[9]

Yale psychologist Seymour Sarason concurs with Capshew's analysis and places the change in the context of wider transformations throughout the social sciences:

> After World War II the social sciences experienced remarkable growth in terms of numbers, funding, prestige and influence in the halls of public and private power. Social scientists were cocky and confident ... sociologists [were] enamored with grand, abstract theories of the structure and dynamics of society ... psychologists promis[ed] much about their capacity to fathom the basic laws of development and behavior, to prevent individual abnormalities and miseries ... Anthropologists, who became instantly valuable to the government during World War II, became even more so with the war's end, when the nation emerged as the dominant military-social-political force in the world ... and took on administrative supervision of diverse peoples and cultures. Before World War II the social sciences were, except for economics, university-based disciplines

having, for all practical purposes, no ties with the political system. World War II changed all that; social scientists became needed, and they wanted to be needed.[10]

The tools of this transformation were political, social, and technological as well as theoretical. World War II-era psychology was *militarized* knowledge production, in the sense that national military goals came to define broad directions for research, particular problems, and the general nature of useful solutions. To say this is simply to state a fact about the postwar condition of American science. I am not arguing that militarized science was somehow illegitimate, nor am I claiming it was ideologically driven—at least no more so than other historical research regimes. Militarization was not a false, but simply a *particular* process of knowledge production.[11] Cyborg discourse emerged from this militarized regime of truth, forming the heterogeneous ensemble of psychological theories, experimental designs, machine interfaces, quasi-intelligent devices, and personal practices that constituted subjectivity in the closed world.

Cognitivism, behaviorism, and cybernetics

By the time the cognitive approach to experimental psychology reached maturity in the mid-1960s, it was distinguished by the following characteristics:

1. A fundamental interest in *complex internal "cognitive" processes*, especially perception, memory, mental imagery, and the use of language, and a concurrent emphasis on the use of meaningful data or stimuli in experimentation.
2. Emphasis on *experiments with human subjects*, coupled with the use of subjective reports as experimental data, especially when these could be correlated with observable behavior. Reaction-time experiments were among the most common.
3. A conception of *organisms as active and creative* in the domains just listed. Goals, plans, expectations, and other internal structures were cast in a relation of reciprocal influence with perception, memory, and language.
4. *Rationalist philosophical roots*. Most cognitivists assumed that many mental structures, especially those providing for learning and language, were innate.
5. Some degree of commitment to the *metaphor of computation* in theoretical descriptions. This took such paradigmatic forms as computer modeling, simulation, the use of information and communication theory, and cross-borrowing from artificial intelligence research.
6. Theories attempted to deduce *internal representational systems* from

341

experimental evidence. Cognition became, fundamentally, *symbolic information processing*, or computation on physically represented symbols.[12]

Since cognitivism arose in the midst of a polemical debate with behaviorism, contrasting the two schools briefly will help reveal the significance of cognitive psychology.[13] Most versions of behaviorism were devoted primarily to animal experimentation. They studied only "observable" behavior, usually gross physical movement (actions like bar-pressing and pecking at colored disks). They cast themselves as theories of learning, rather than of thinking and perceiving. They conceived the organism as a relatively passive "black box" subject to a mechanical form of causality from its environment, responding automatically to "stimuli." Behaviorism had empiricist and positivist philosophical roots, often explicit, and it modeled complex processes as aggregates or series of basic, simple "building block" responses. Most of its experimental results came from studies of rats, pigeons, and cats, and its central analogies were to deterministic machines. The major issue for behaviorism, however, was never to specify mechanisms but to predict and control. Applications of behaviorist theory to human beings were strongly oriented toward social control and manipulation, as exemplified in B. F. Skinner's phrase "technology of behavior."[14]

Behaviorism was a mechanistic theory, and psychologists built or designed many machine analogs.[15] Such models were, generally, true machines rather than information processors. (A major exception was the electrical analogy of the telephone switchboard, which was popular from the 1920s on.)[16] Nor were machines of any sort the primary source of models and metaphors for behaviorism; animal behavior filled that role.

Where behaviorism emphasized comparisons between animal and human behavior, and psychoanalysis concentrated on human social and discursive effects, cognitive psychology reconstructed both humans and animals as cybernetic machines and digital computers. The explicit goal of the proto-cognitive theories of the 1940s and 1950s—of what I will call "cybernetic psychology"—was to understand the processes of perception, memory, and language in terms of formalizable transformations of information and feedback circuits or control loops.

Cybernetics: the behavior of machines

Norbert Wiener's *Cybernetics* and Claude Shannon's "The Mathematical Theory of Communication," the benchmark documents of information and communication theory, did not appear in print until 1948.[17] By that time, a major symposium at the California Institute of Technology had brought psychologists and cybernetic theorists together.[18] Psychologists had begun working closely with information theorists and electrical engineers as early as

1946, though, as we will see, the groundwork for cybernetic psychology was laid during the war, in the form of social networks, studies of the psychology and psychometrics of communication at Harvard's Psycho-Acoustic Laboratory, and speculation by engineers, mathematicians, neurologists, and a few psychologists in the context of technical military problems. Cybernetic psychology began as an effort to theorize humans as component parts of weapons systems and continued, after the war, to draw crucial models and metaphors from those concerns.

As noted in chapter 2, the antiaircraft gunnery problems of World War II created a need for servomechanisms that could accurately predict an aircraft's future position, allowing automatic aiming of weapons and reducing the effects of human error. In 1941 Wiener, then a mathematics professor at MIT, joined a team of scientists at the Radiation Laboratory who were studying this problem under the sponsorship of the NDRC. Working with engineer Julian Bigelow and Mexican neurobiologist Arturo Rosenblueth, Wiener started thinking about how one might predict an airplane's future course from information about its present location and velocity. Out of this work came a highly general statistical theory of prediction based on incomplete information. This was the theory of feedback control, which became the basis for the design of servomechanisms.[19] This theory had a double face: it described not only how mechanisms could be made to predict future position, but how their human controllers could do the same thing and potentially, given enough information about the *human* mechanism, why they failed.

By May 1942 the theory had gained enough substance for Rosenblueth to give an extended presentation to a small interdisciplinary conference, known as the Cerebral Inhibition Meeting, organized by the Josiah Macy Jr. Foundation's medical director, Frank Fremont-Smith. The meeting's two topics were hypnosis and "the physiological mechanism underlying the phenomena of conditioned reflex." It was led by behaviorist psychologist Howard Liddell, "an experimenter on the conditioning and behavior of mammals," and Milton Erickson, a hypnotist.[20] Others attending this meeting by invitation included neurologist Warren McCulloch, anthropologists Gregory Bateson and Margaret Mead, psychologist Lawrence K. Frank, and psychoanalyst Lawrence Kubie. With its promise of a major new interdisciplinary research paradigm, Rosenblueth's presentation galvanized the audience, especially the social scientists. Mead later recalled that she broke one of her teeth during the conference but was so rapt she did not notice until it was over.[21]

The most important element of the Rosenblueth-Wiener-Bigelow theory was the concept of "negative feedback," or circular self-corrective cycles, in which information about the effects of an adjustment to a dynamic system is continuously returned to that system as input and controls further adjustments.[22] In 1943 the three published the landmark article "Behavior, Purpose, and Teleology," which emphasized comparisons between servo devices and the behavior of living organisms guided by sensory perception. Essentially, they described goal-oriented "teleological" behavior as movement controlled by negative feedback.

Three aspects of their servo/organism analogies were important historically in the construction of "cognition" as a cybernetic natural-technical object:

- the specification of a "behaviorist" analysis applicable to both machines and living things,
- the redefinition of psychological and philosophical concepts in the terminology of communications engineering, and
- analyses of humans as components of weapons systems as a central source of analogies.

Rosenblueth, Wiener, and Bigelow contrasted behaviorism with "functionalism." They defined the former as the study of input-output relationships in abstraction from the (functionalist) internal characteristics of the entity under examination.[23] While the proto-cyberneticians had no quarrel of principle with the "functionalist alternative," they chose the behaviorist approach partly because it would allow them to apply mathematical formalisms from their radar tracking work. Similarly, Kenneth Craik, a British psychologist who also worked on the radar tracking problem, wrote near the end of the war that "the human operator [of tracking devices] behaves basically as an intermittent correction servo" and suggested that operator tracking errors could be described by the same equations used for the periodicity of the tracking servomechanisms.[24] Such comparisons became important metaphors in postwar psychological research as well as in cybernetics' canonical origin story.[25]

Cybernetic psychology was first introduced, perhaps ironically, as an extension and vindication of behaviorism. Wiener, who built the word from a Greek root meaning "steersman," intended cybernetics to encompass "control and communication in the animal and the machine."[26] As a general mathematical theory of self-regulating mechanisms, cybernetics would transcend the boundary between machines and organisms. It would do this not by rejecting concepts of purposes, goals, and will (as in behaviorist psychology), but by *expanding the category of "machines,"* via the concept of feedback, to include these notions. Thus even in 1943, Rosenblueth et al. claimed that "a uniform behavioristic analysis is applicable to both machines and living organisms, regardless of the complexity of the behavior . . . The broad classes of behavior are the same in machines and in living organisms."[27]

Typically, psychological behaviorists described the general form of their research problems as the discovery of a function f relating a stimulus S to some response R, of the form $R = f(S)$.[28] Adequate definitions of S and R presented a difficulty that was usually resolved by adopting extremely general classifications. Stimuli were "any portion of the environment to which the organism is exposed under uniform conditions" and were operationally defined in experimental situations: "the number of different S's said to be present . . . will depend upon the number of independent experimental operations." Similarly, "any movement or sequence of movements may be analyzed out of behavior and treated as a 'response'." In theory, then, stimulus and response existed as organized units only in virtue of choices of the experimenter. In themselves, they were meaningless; and this implied that any response could be conditioned to any given stimulus. (Of course, real behaviorist experiments never respected this impossible principle but divided stimuli and responses along "obvious" lines of meaningful connection.)[29]

In "Behavior, Purpose, and Teleology," Rosenblueth et al. gave a superficially similar description of organism/environment relations in engineering terms. For stimuli, the cyberneticians offered "input" as "any event external to the object that modifies this object in any manner." Responses become "output": "any change produced in the surroundings by the object." Behavior itself was defined as "any modification of an object, detectable externally."[30] "Input" and "output," originally electrical engineering terms for currents entering and exiting circuits, had been adopted analogically by communications engineers to describe the entry and exit versions of *messages* in a channel. For Rosenblueth et al., behavior now became any transformation of energy *or information* from the environment.[31] The possible transformations were hierarchically distributed as shown in figure 1. A cue ball moving across a billiard table typifies passive behavior; active behavior requires some provision of output energy by the object itself. The most interesting classes of behavior involved feedback, which utilizes energy returned to the system as information. Prediction and control "behavior" topped this hierarchy.

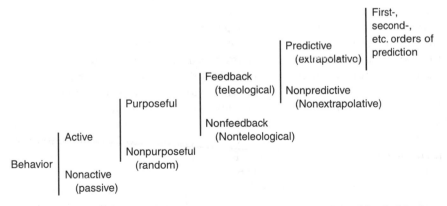

Figure 1 A cybernetic classification of behavior. From Arturo Rosenblueth, Norbert Wiener, and Julian Bigelow, "Behavior, Purpose and Teleology," *Philosophy of Science*, Vol. 10 (1943), 21.

The proto-cyberneticians' ultimate concern was to explain human voluntary activity. "The basis of the concept of purpose," they wrote, "is the awareness of 'voluntary activity' . . . When we perform a voluntary action, what we select voluntarily is a specific purpose, not a specific movement." The movements that then accomplish the selected purposes are mechanical, directed by feedback of "signals" from the chosen goal. This process parallels the functioning of servo-controlled tracking devices, a prime example being the "torpedo with a target-seeking mechanism," said to exhibit "intrinsic purposeful activity."[32]

"Goal states" explained the organization of behavior and therefore defined meaningful units in advance of experimentation (in contrast to behaviorist dogma). The cybernetic model asserted that goals—including human goals and purposes—could be described within a formalizable, probabilistic, biophysical explanatory space, as direction "to a final condition in which the behaving object reaches a definite correlation in time or in space with respect to another object or event," a concept very different from an Aristotelian *telos*. What is involved in the practice of definition and "selection" of goals, something torpedoes and guided missiles do not do for themselves, was not discussed. But the cybernetic model would ultimately, Rosenblueth et al. believed, explain even these phenomena.[33]

Behaviorist psychologists had constructed the field of the psychological by elevating the unavailability of design-level descriptions to a methodological principle. The emerging cybernetic psychology was revolutionary because the tools it provided could be turned equally to the fully mathematized, behaviorist input/output description and the functionalist, internal-process description. Cybernetic theory gave machine metaphors a new theoretical foundation, creating a new technical terminology and system of quantification—information theory—for describing flexible, self-directed behavior in both machines and minds.

Information theory is part of a general class of mathematical models (including the logical architectures of computers, Turing machines, and the theory of games) that are sometimes called *formal machines*. Such models delimit an ordered set of operations for transforming data; they may, but need not, describe actual machines. "Behavior, Purpose, and Teleology" used formal machines to initiate the development of a new standard of psychological explanation, one I will call *formal/mechanical modeling*. The terminology is important because cybernetic psychology was *not* simply another form of mathematical psychology. Rather than simply describing observed behavior mathematically, the cyberneticians would treat mathematical models, physical machines, information processing devices, and data from human and animal experiments within a single framework. Unlike "behavior," "association of ideas," "consciousness," and other previous psychological objects, control and communication were *computational* processes susceptible to modeling in terms of devices and formal structures bearing no physical resemblance to the body or brain.

Psycho-engineering

At the close of their discussion, the proto-cyberneticians examined the structural differences between machines and living organisms and concluded:

> If an engineer were to design a robot [today], roughly similar in behavior to an animal organism, . . . he would probably build it out of metallic parts, some dielectrics and many vacuum tubes . . . In future years, as the knowledge of colloids and proteins increases, future engineers may attempt the design of robots not only with a behavior, but also with a structure similar to that of a mammal. The ultimate model of a cat is of course another cat, whether it be born of still another cat or synthesized in a laboratory.[34]

This striking phrase, paradigmatic of the cybernetic imagination, projects a kind of psycho-engineering as a two-stage formal/mechanical modeling technique: "rough" behavioral simulation via computation and servomechanisms, followed by complete biological replication to capture formal detail in addition to functional effect. Thus cybernetics already conceived biological and psychological replication as engineering problems not qualitatively different from those of the design of electromechanical robots. Bioengineered organisms would differ greatly from machines in structure and materials, but psychologically relevant (i.e., behavioral) categories would remain the same.

A third stage of psycho-engineering lay hidden in the cybernetic dream, implicit in the mixture of apocalypse and elation in Warren McCulloch's words quoted near the beginning of this chapter. This was the moment of technological redesign of the potentially suboptimal organismic system by integrating it with superior materials and mechanisms.[35] Such a goal was avowed most starkly in a passage from Craik, whom McCulloch deeply admired:

> As an element in a control system a man may be regarded as a chain consisting of the following items:
>
> 1. Sensory devices, which transform a misalinement [sic] between sight and target into suitable physiological counterparts, such as patterns of nerve impulses, just as a radar receiver transforms misalinement into an error-voltage.
> 2. A computing system which responds to the misalinement-input by giving a neural response calculated . . . to be appropriate to

reduce the misalinement; this process seems to occur in the cortex of the brain.

3. An amplifying system—the motor-nerve endings and the muscles—in which a minute amount of energy (the impulses in the motor nerves) controls the liberation of much greater amounts of energy in the muscles . . .

4. Mechanical linkages (the pivot and lever systems of the limbs) whereby the muscular work produces externally observable effects, such as laying a gun.

Such considerations serve to bridge the gap between the physio-logical statement of man as an animal giving reflex and learned responses to sensory stimuli, and the engineering statement in terms of the type of mechanism which would be designed to fulfill the same function in a wholly automatic system. The problem is to discover in detail the characteristics of this human chain, such as its sensory resolving-power, its maximum power-output and optimum loads, its frequency-characteristics and time-lags, its amplitude-distortion and whether or not internal cyclic systems enter into it, its flexibility and self-modifying properties, etc., with a view to showing the various advantages and disadvantages of the human operator as compared with an automatic system.[36]

This passage might have served as the manifesto of cybernetic psychology.

While the discussions of the proto-cyberneticians ranged over many mechanisms, antiaircraft guns, torpedoes, and guided missiles were by far the most central. Concerned to emphasize the universality of cybernetic theory, the cybernetics group also characterized purposeful activity in many other machines. But while these other examples typically varied from work to work, virtually every one of the early articles and books in the emerging field mentioned the self-controlled and servo-guided weapons of World War II.

The centrality of these metaphors reflects a number of features of early cyborg discourse and the emerging cybernetics community. First, these machines embodied shared wartime experiences. Second, semiautomatic weapons systems integrated humans and machines through both mathemat-ical description (formal structure) and embodied practice (mechanism), mak-ing them prototypical cyborg devices. Finally, before computers, in terms of information activity such machines were the most advanced devices known to the group. So the war machines were not simply one example among others, but a central, unifying metaphor of early cyborg discourse.

The parallels of Rosenblueth et al.'s vision to the later imagery of the Turing test, described in chapter 1, will by now be obvious. Like Turing, the cyberneticians noticed certain aspects of behavior (target-seeking) that machines (torpedoes, antiaircraft guns) could duplicate. Where the

Turing-test metaphor made the content of communication independent of its form, the cybernetic analogy to "purposeful" machines made the form of goal-oriented behavior independent of its content. That is, the analogy to machines rendered irrelevant the specific ways in which human beings generate purposes and goals. Similarly, their discussion described reproduction as modeling or replication, appropriating the language of engineering. Like the Turing machine, the cybernetic principles were putative universals capable of describing any activity at all. "Purposeful machines" became second selves, cyborgs, reflections as much as creations. That metaphorical transformation created a looking-glass discourse in which simulation and reality began to blur into one: "the ultimate model of a cat is of course another cat, whether it be born of still another cat or synthesized in a laboratory."

The Macy conferences

Three and a half years elapsed between the Cerebral Inhibition Meeting and the first of the postwar conferences organized to take up the cybernetic ideas. Yet Wiener, McCulloch, and some of the others had continued to meet all along, nourishing a dream of interdisciplinarity centered around the "circular causality" idea. Wiener made a special effort to interest his friend and colleague John von Neumann in the servo/organism analogies. Von Neumann, a polymath whose interests spanned virtually every area of science, not only took up the cybernetic analogies but did Wiener one better, adding to them the theory of digital computation and his own experience working on the ENIAC and EDVAC at the Moore School.

The group continued to develop and propagate the machine-organism analogies during the war, with ever-increasing and barely contained self-confidence. By 1944, in a letter, Wiener had "defied" Edwin G. Boring, chair of Harvard's Department of Psychology, "to describe a capacity of the human brain which he could not duplicate with electronic devices." Boring took up the challenge in a 1946 article, "Mind and Mechanism," which also served as that year's Presidential Address to the Eastern Psychological Association. He ended up supporting the Rosenblueth-Wiener-Bigelow pseudo-behaviorist formal/mechanical modeling standard of explanation: all of "the psychological properties of the living human organism . . . are to be expressed objectively in terms of stimulus-response relationships, and the way to keep ourselves clear and to avoid vagueness is to think of the organism as a machine or a robot." Boring's response—citing the standard war machine examples—reveals that as early as the end of World War II, the computer metaphor had achieved widespread currency.

We have heard so much during the late war about electronic brains. The [analog] electronic computer on a range-finder figures the range and course and speed of a target, setting the fuses and aiming and firing the gun, all at a speed of which the human brain is incapable. There are now huge electronic mathematicians which will solve mathematical problems with a speed and accuracy and lack of fatigue that puts the mere headwork of the human mathematician out of the running.[37]

While Boring's article was a step toward legitimizing the metaphor within academic psychology, it remained for the cyberneticians to work out its details.

In his mathematical work on digital computer logics, von Neumann used a notation invented by neuropsychiatrist Warren McCulloch and logician Walter Pitts to describe nervous systems. McCulloch and Pitts had applied what was known as Boolean logic to the operation of neurons, analogizing these cells to on-off valves corresponding to the two-state, true-false Boolean system.[38] They had created their notation after reading Turing's ground-breaking paper "On Computable Numbers."[39] Despite their debt to Turing, however, they made no mention of his work in their paper. Nor did they bother to point out that the neural network they described was mathematically equivalent to a Turing machine. Indeed, they worried that their paper's mathematical approach was so marginal it might never be noticed or even published.[40]

Von Neumann learned of the McCulloch-Pitts formalism from Wiener, who had worked with Pitts in 1943 and was greatly excited by correspondences between the formalism and electrical relays. (Claude Shannon's doctoral thesis, just before the war, had made a similar use of Boolean logic in the analysis of telephone relay circuits.) In December 1944 von Neumann, Wiener, McCulloch, Pitts, and Howard Aiken—designer of the Harvard Mark I electromechanical computer—formed the Teleological Society to study "communication engineering, the engineering of control devices, the mathematics of time series in statistics, and the communication and control aspects of the nervous system."[41]

Von Neumann and Wiener planned a meeting with a few colleagues in January 1945 to discuss the cybernetic idea of a "unified mathematical description of engineering devices and the nervous system." At the meeting, Wiener wrote jubilantly,

> von Neumann spoke on computing machines and I spoke on communication engineering. The second day [Rafael] Lorente de Nó and McCulloch joined forces for a very convincing presentation of the present status of the problem of the organization of the brain. In the end we were all convinced that the subject embracing both the engineering and neurology aspects is essentially one, and we should go ahead with plans to embody these ideas in a permanent program of research . . .[42]

The group discussed the possibility of establishing a research center after the war at Princeton or MIT. Despite considerable enthusiasm on the part of Wiener and others, this never materialized. Instead, in 1946, McCulloch persuaded the Macy Foundation, via Fremont-Smith, to fund a series of interdisciplinary conferences under the eventual title "Cybernetics: Circular Causal and Feedback Mechanisms in Biological and Social Systems." Ten conferences were held between 1946 and 1953, each involving between twenty and thirty "regular" participants and from two to five invited guests. The group, whose core included most of the original Cerebral Inhibition Meeting participants, comprised engineers, mathematicians, psychologists, neurophysiologists, philosophers, anthropologists, and sociologists.

McCulloch was chairman and primary organizer, though the advice of both Wiener and von Neumann was solicited in selecting participants. The regular members included Wiener's colleagues Rosenblueth and Bigelow, as well as Pitts and Lorente de Nó, a neurophysiologist from the Rockefeller Institute in New York. Gregory Bateson and Margaret Mead were invited as representatives of the social sciences. Bateson, tutored by Mead, had become interested in applying S-R learning theories in cultural anthropology; the two were personal friends of another participant, the psychologist Lawrence K. Frank, who was also a friend of Wiener. Wiener, whose personality has been described as "impish" and self-aggrandizing, and von Neumann were the chief protagonists.[43] This was especially true at the early conferences, when many participants were relatively unfamiliar with information theory and the ENIAC had been operational for just a few months.

The first meeting: computers as brains

The first conference, called the Feedback Mechanisms and Circular Causal Systems in Biology and the Social Sciences Meeting, was held on March 8 and 9, 1946, in New York City, with McCulloch as chair. The very first presentation, by von Neumann, consisted of a description of general-purpose digital computers. According to Steve Heims's interviews with participants, it

> included discussion of the greater precision of digital machines as compared to the older analog computers, the use of binary rather than decimal representation of numbers, the stored program concept, various methods available for storing and accessing information, and how in detail arithmetic operations are carried out by these machines. Some methods could not be discussed because they were still classified as military secrets. Von Neumann made semi-quantitative comparisons between vacuum tubes and neurons, the overall size of brains and computers, their speed of operation and other characteristics.[44]

351

Lorente de Nó followed up von Neumann's talk with a complementary discussion of neurons as digital processing units. He described them as binary switches, explaining the physiology behind the McCulloch-Pitts logical model of neural networks.

In the afternoon Wiener and Rosenblueth gave a second team presentation. Like that of von Neumann and Lorente de Nó, it paired a mathematician with a neurophysiologist. Also like theirs, the Wiener-Rosenblueth talk examined machines and organisms in tandem. Wiener spoke about the history of automata, receptors and effectors in machines, and electronic computers as elements of machine systems. Rosenblueth discussed "homeostatic" (self-regulating) neurological mechanisms such as respiration, blood pressure, and body temperature. By design, the effect of the first day's talks was to impress deeply upon the group, in which professional psychologists served as audience to mathematicians and physiologists, the analogies between organisms, psychological concepts, and cybernetic machines, especially computers. The next day von Neumann introduced the group to game theory as applied to economics, going beyond the psychological to the level of the society as a whole.

Like the 1942 meeting, the first cybernetics conference proved an intellectual firestorm, a major event in the lives of many of the participants. The Macy Foundation agreed to continue funding yearly conferences as long as the group remained interested.

Exploring the metaphor

The cybernetics group's goals were exploratory.[45] The organizing members—McCulloch, Wiener, von Neumann, Pitts, and Rosenblueth—wanted to see how far the analogies between organisms and machines could be pushed. They looked for examples of feedback control processes in every field represented. Some presentations focused directly on functional analogies between computers or servo-mechanisms, on the one hand, and brains, perceptual and memory mechanisms, or various physical activities, on the other. Others developed information-theoretical approaches to language and communication processes in social systems and groups. A few actual machines, such as Wiener's sensory prosthesis for the deaf and a maze-solving machine built by Claude Shannon, were demonstrated at the conferences.

Verbatim transcripts of the last five meetings were made and published. Since the presentations were informal and the ensuing discussions were also transcribed, these documents provide an invaluable source for analyzing the genesis of a discourse. They show disciplines in the act of merging, sciences in the process of becoming, and the role new machines can take in creating new forms of discourse.

Despite having adopted the McCulloch-Pitts formalism for his computer architectures—and having been among the first to raise the analogy—von

Neumann expressed persistent doubts throughout the conferences about whether brains and computers could fruitfully be compared. The conference transcripts contain numerous mentions of "the things that bother von Neumann." These were the limitations on understanding the "information processing" and "storage" capacities of the brain if neurons were really analogous to the dual-state registers of computers. The McCulloch-Pitts formalism suggested that information was processed in the brain by means of two activities of neurons, discharge (also called "firing") and inhibition. Whether or not a neuron fired depended on the ratio of excitatory to inhibitory stimulation it received from other neurons synaptically connected to it. This process could be formally reduced, according to McCulloch and Pitts, to the action of a two-valued, on/off switch. Thus, the entire network of neurons could be modeled as a system of binary-valued digital switches—a formal machine.[46]

Against the enthusiasm of McCulloch, von Neumann counseled despair. Even if the brain were really this simple in organization, theoretical reduction would probably prove completely beyond reach due to its gigantic size (10 to 100 billion cells) and its even more staggering number of possible states (each neuron may send its impulses to hundreds or even thousands of others). At the cellular level, von Neumann wondered whether the system itself, in all its complexity, might not be its own simplest description. Additionally, some evidence pointed to a "mixed" analogical/digital character for the nervous system (e.g., that the continuously variable *rates* of firing were part of the code as well), making the comparison with the purely digital electronic computers untenable. (The psychologists at the first conference raised this objection immediately, but others brushed it aside.) Though he seemed to believe that advances in mathematical logic might one day make possible some sort of description—and certainly saw this as a kind of scientific Holy Grail—he became highly pessimistic about the comparisons conceivable with then-current engineering techniques.[47]

Despite von Neumann's warnings, the cybernetic analogies rapidly grew into much more than suggestive heuristics. The neurophysiologist Ralph Gerard revealed a common discomfort when he opened the seventh conference by lecturing on "Some of the Problems Concerning Digital Notions in the Central Nervous System." Referring to the "tremendous" interest of the scientific community and the general public in the ideas generated by the group as "almost . . . a national fad," Gerard complained:

> It seems to me . . . that we started our discussions and sessions in the "as if" spirit. Everyone was delighted to express any idea that came into his mind, whether it seemed silly or certain or merely a stimulating guess that would affect someone else. We explored possibilities for all sorts of "ifs." Then, rather sharply it seemed to me, we began

to talk in an "is" idiom. We were saying much the same things, but now saying them as if they were so.[48]

Comparing the group's "overenthusiasm" to the premature popularity of phrenology in the 1800s, he begged for intellectual "responsibility" in the use of cybernetic terminology.

But neither von Neumann nor Gerard could stop the historical process at work—which Turing by then had articulated as his belief "that at the end of the century the use of words and general educated opinion will have altered so much that one will be able to speak of machines thinking without expecting to be contradicted"—simply by recognizing it.[49] The entailments of computer metaphors were being worked out not only within the cybernetics group, but in other sciences and in popular culture as well. Systems discourses were spreading through the sciences, with new institutions like the Rand Corporation being assembled around them. Systems, information, and communication theories were being reified almost daily in the form of computers, radar-controlled tracking devices, guided missiles, and other machines.

Wiener, von Neumann, and Bigelow, as well as others in the cybernetics group, had spent years working out the design of these very devices. They were committed to the formal machine as a reality and as a standard of explanation, and they would never be satisfied with a psychology that stopped short of the formal/mechanical model, like the black-box behaviorist approach or the vagaries of depth psychology. A cybernetics of the mind would be incomplete until its practitioners had *built one* or at least shown how it could be done—Rosenblueth, Wiener, and Bigelow's "ultimate model." Thus the brain-computer comparisons were not arbitrary, as Gerard's comments implied, but paradigmatic. Most Macy participants agreed, at least tacitly, that servomechanisms and computers afforded the most promising, if imperfect, analogs to human and animal behavior, and they were united in the belief that information theory could render human/animal and organism/machine boundaries permeable to unified explanations.

Challenges to computational metaphors

The power of servomechanism and computer metaphors was most readily visible when they were challenged, as when the electrical engineer and conference series editor Heinz von Foerster presented a paper on human memory at the sixth conference. Von Foerster based his argument on an analogy to quantum theory in physics. He proposed a mathematically exact theory of memory in which "impressions," or memory-traces, were preserved as energy states of a hypothetical protein molecule he called a "mem." Memorizing something corresponded to raising the energy level of a mem by a quantum unit; forgetting occurred when the mem discharged a quantum of energy.

The theory was supported by experiments in learning nonsense syllables and evidence that forgetting increases with higher body temperatures (which destabilized the mems, von Foerster hypothesized, making them more likely to release energy).

There were superficial parallels to information theory in von Foerster's approach, but the concrete metaphor involved the quantum theory of atomic structure, a subject the Macy group had not discussed (though Wiener and von Neumann, at least, had done theoretical work in quantum mechanics).

In the discussion period, Ralph Gerard and the psychiatrist Henry Brosin expressed "confusion." Gerard did not see "how it could be made to work for any kind of a picture we have of the nervous system." The quantum model did not seem able to account for the organization of the huge numbers of quanta that had to be presupposed in any sensory impression. Though von Foerster could describe his atomic quanta as units of information, this was not his emphasis, nor could his model explain the structuring of that information into patterns in perception or behavior. But another major reason for the psychologists' and neurophysiologists' resistance to von Foerster's ideas seems to have been the foreign character of the metaphor from atomic physics. Von Foerster's audience welcomed the paradigm of servomechanisms and computers, machines they had all seen and worked with, but did not quite know what to do with his model of atomic decay. The quantum mechanical theory was never discussed again by the group.[50]

Another anomalous theory had been presented by the Gestalt psychologist Wolfgang Köhler at the fourth Macy Conference. Köhler's "field" theory of perception was built on the model of electromagnetic fields—another foreign and competing metaphor. His presentation, more influential than von Foerster's, also "created anxiety in the group" but did not significantly affect its theoretical orientation or preferred analogies.[51] But the participants did begin to question whether a rigorous cybernetic approach could go beyond local neuronal mechanisms to account for the large-scale organization of perception as well. Steve Heims has described the relevant differences between the Gestalt and cybernetic theories, and the conflict that resulted, as follows:

> To define the relation between psychological facts of perception and events in the brain, Köhler had posited a "psychophysical isomorphism." His starting point had been the empirical psychological facts concerning the phenomena of perception. The cyberneticians . . . sought to derive mental processes in the brain by summing or averaging over the interrelated elemental electrical and chemical events (the firing of a synapse) in the brain. Instead of psychophysical isomorphism, [they] posited a relation of "coding" as the paradigm for the connection between perceptions and [brain] events . . . [Their]

starting point ... was logical mathematical formalism and some facts of ... neurophysiology.[52]

Just as crucial as these theoretical "starting points" were the concrete metaphors used by the cybernetics group to give substance to their formal pictures. Bateson, at the seventh conference, noted that the question of whether the nervous system processes information by analog or digital (continuous or discontinuous) means was the commitment-laden center of the cyberneticians' debate with Köhler.

> There is a historic point that perhaps should be brought up; namely, that the continuous/discontinuous variable has appeared in many other places. I spent my childhood in an atmosphere of genetics in which to believe in "continuous" variations was immoral ... There is a loading of affect around this dichotomy which is worth our considering. There was strong feeling in this room the night when Köhler talked to us and we had the battle about whether the central nervous system works discontinuously or, as Köhler maintained, by leakage between axons.[53]

I have been suggesting that while these commitments to the "discontinuous" model had multiple origins, such as those mentioned by Bateson, their immediate sources—the ones unifying the cybernetics group—were digital computers and servomechanisms. The "strong feelings" around the idea of the digital nervous system were generated in part by some of the participants' direct involvement in work on these devices.

The competing theories of von Foerster and Köhler demonstrate by counterexample a number of facts about the cybernetics group that help to explain why alternative analogies failed to capture attention. Some of these can be enumerated as a set of group commitments and innovations, including:

- The centrality of the *mathematical analyses* of Wiener and von Neumann, who continually sought to formalize what they learned about neurobiology and psychology from the group in mathematical terms.
- The requirement of *formal/mechanical modeling* of the object of knowledge (Köhler's field theory had a machine analog, but it was not a formal one, like the electronic logics of computer systems).
- Commitment to *engineering solutions for psychological questions*: analysis of humans as links in control and communications processes with a view to minimizing error.
- Particular *ideas of "information" and "communication,"* derived in part from wartime engineering experience.

The conflicts illustrate how a group whose central concerns were profoundly shaped by some of its members' experiences with military engineering problems continued to think in terms of those problems and created from them a new field of scientific possibilities. The Macy core group of mathematicians, engineers, and neurobiologists had turned its attention to psychological phenomena defined, for them, in terms of the tracking, targeting, and communications tasks of the war. We will now turn to presentations the group received positively, in order to see how these commitments were manifested.

Vision as tracking and targeting

John Stroud, research psychologist at the San Diego Naval Electronics Laboratory, was a two-time guest at the conferences. He was trained in electrical engineering and X-ray physics. During the war Stroud became interested in the nature of psychological time, which he thought might be connected to the rhythms of brain waves. He took a degree in psychology at Stanford "as a kind of renegade physicist."[54] At the sixth conference he began his lecture on "The Psychological Moment in Perception" by acknowledging his intellectual debt to the McCulloch-Pitts theory of neural nets and, especially, to the work of Craik on servo-controlled antiaircraft guns, which he then introduced to the group. Stroud had served in the RAF during the war, learning of Craik's work while in England.[55]

Stroud described experimental observations of the low-frequency periodicities by which test subjects corrected the path of tracking devices, a rate of two or three corrections per second. Stroud deduced from this that "experience is quantal in nature": experience occurs in quantum units he called "psychological moments."[56] He conjectured that the central nervous system acts like a computer using a periodic scanning mechanism, possibly based on the brain's alpha rhythm. Note that while Stroud also invoked the term "quantum," he did so on the basis of a concrete metaphor different from von Foerster's: the now-standard servomechanisms and digital computer analogy, rather than atomic physics. For him the idea of a quantum implied a kind of digital/analog distinction rather than an atomic model.

Following Craik's model, Stroud posed the psychological problem in now-familiar terms:

> In the firing of guns we have to use human operators to make certain decisions but today we have to fire them very rapidly. We have tried our level best to reduce what the man has to do to an absolute minimum . . . We know as much as possible about how all the associated gear which brings the information to the tracker operates and how all the gear from the tracker to the gun operates. So we have the human operator surrounded on both sides by very precisely known

mechanisms and the question comes up, "What kind of a machine have we placed in the middle?"[57]

Stroud went on to present a detailed analysis of the human as servo-mechanism, via a set of experiments on subjects' accuracy and response rates in visually "tracking" objects moving on a variety of more or less predictable paths. To Stroud, these experiments suggested the characteristics of what might be termed the tracking-targeting cyborg, that is, the human as an element of a tracking system. First, "operators" could "track" accurately by using pointers controlled by any combination of displacement, velocity (first derivative of displacement), and acceleration (second derivative of displacement). They adapted readily to the possibilities presented by the experimental set-up, rather than being locked into a single mode of prediction. Second, Stroud concluded, "man is a predictor and says 'I shall continue to do whatever my last solution predicted will be right so long as no detectable difference arises.'"[58] In other words, human subjects (unlike the simplest servomechanisms) depended on feedback control only until a suitable solution could be found, which they then employed until changed conditions required a new one. Third, the fact that subjects continued to make corrections for a short period when pointer and target were suddenly obscured suggested that operators used information gained in advance of the corrective action itself in making their corrective movements: their corrections were not made in "real time," but in a predictive, psychological time.

Finally, Stroud found that tracking performance was quantal or discontinuous, and he spoke of the operator as an information processor:

> Our operator receives his information by way of his eyes . . . This is where the information goes into the human organism, and it goes in, to all intents and purposes, continuously. When we analyze what comes out of the organism, every set of records of sufficient sensitivity . . . has shown low frequency periodicities.[59]

Input-output—as opposed to stimulus-response—analysis began to yield a formal/mechanical theory of the "machine . . . in the middle."

The group's response reveals a struggle over key metaphors between the mathematicians and engineers, on the one hand, and the psychologists on the other. The latter were unimpressed with Stroud's information-processing analysis. Neurologist and psychoanalyst Lawrence Kubie viewed the "moment" theory as merely another instance of the well-documented phenomenon of "reaction time" and pointed out that it varied among individuals and according to emotional and situational conditions. In the ensuing general discussion of the information retention and processing capacity of the nervous system, experimental psychologist Heinrich Klüver mentioned the "ten thousands of pages of Wundtian psychology" concerning attention span and instantaneous perception. Like Kubie, Klüver downplayed the significance of the new metaphors by reading them as disguised or rephrased versions of traditional problems in psychological theory. Invoking the Gestalt theory of wholes and fields, he insisted that the group's quantitative, mathematical emphasis would remain "meaningless" as long as the context and organization of psychological "information" was not considered.

Wiener, McCulloch, and Pitts, by contrast, were pleased and stimulated by Stroud's method of analysis. With no stakes in the disciplinary history of psychology, they responded well to the mathematical regularities and mechanical comparisons Stroud used. Wiener's excitement was palpable; his exuberant comments amounted to a running dialogue with Stroud. He discussed a series of machine analogs to Stroud's ideas, all devices Wiener had helped to design. During a discussion at the Hixon Symposium six months previously, McCulloch had invited Stroud to present his theory as reinforcement for McCulloch's own version of the scanning computer analogy. Stroud spoke the engineering language the cyberneticians understood, and they were unconcerned by what the psychologists heard as his loose usage of technical psychological terms (such as "phi" for "apparent motion") and his reformulation of traditional psychological problems in formal/mechanical terms.

The different responses of these two factions within the Macy group point again to formal/mechanical modeling's revolutionary character. Those trained as psychologists started with the phenomena of conscious experience and observations about human responses, and they looked for relations between these and stimuli in the physical world. But the cyberneticians began with the formal machines they had made and sought to build a machine that would model its builder.

Soon afterward, Stroud himself went to work as a scientist for the U.S. Navy, where he spent the rest of his working life, mostly on classified research. The cybernetic metaphors became permanent features of Stroud's thinking; in his only published article (in 1950) Stroud asserted that "man is the most generally available general purpose computing device." In 1972 he told Steve Heims, raising a Turing-like claim, that "a system is what it does" and asserted that conceptual boundaries between living and nonliving systems should be drawn, or erased, along functional lines. "If the actions [of a system] are calculating, analyzing information, measuring, deductive reasoning, guiding and controlling a ship or missile, then humans and machines—although different in the details of their actions and capabilities—are comparable living systems."[60]

Psychological tracking and targeting research became an ergonomic discipline aimed at the construction of integrated human-machine cyborgs.[61] Among its most fertile offshoots were military experimental training simulators similar to modern video games, complete with joystick controls. The eyes themselves were militarized through the tracking and targeting metaphor. "The human eye," proclaimed the NRC's widely distributed 1943

Army pamphlet *Psychology for the Fighting Man*, "is one of the most important military instruments that the armed forces possess."[62] The distinguished British visual psychologist R. L. Gregory, in 1966, called the retinal edge "an early-warning device, used to rotate the eyes to aim the object-recognition part of the system onto objects likely to be friend or foe rather than neutral." He described the two systems for visual identification of movement:

> we name them (a) the image/retina system, and (b) the eye/head system. (These names follow those used in gunnery, where similar considerations apply when guns are aimed from the moving platform of a ship. The gun turret may be stationary or following, but the movement of the target can be detected in either case.)[63]

Thus we find, again, the legacy of world war in the sciences of mind and brain: the human capacities of perception and thought as the design features of technological soldiers.

Project X: noise, communication, and code

Another guest at the Macy Conferences was Claude E. Shannon of Bell Laboratories. A mathematician of nearly the same rank as Wiener and von Neumann, Shannon had taken his Ph.D. at MIT at the age of 24. In 1937, while still a doctoral student, he had held a summer job at Bell Labs, during which he had demonstrated the application of Boolean algebra to relay circuit analysis. The mathematical model he created bore direct parallels to both Turing's universal machines and the McCulloch-Pitts neural logic. His achievement was credited with changing relay circuit design from an "esoteric art" to an engineering discipline.[64] Shannon's systematization had significant impacts on early electromechanical digital computer design, since the latter employed telephone relays as registers. It was also related to von Neumann's later studies of logical architectures.

Shannon worked with the NDRC in 1940–41 before rejoining Bell, where he immediately became active in research on cryptanalysis. In many ways Shannon was the American counterpart to Turing: a mathematician, interested in what would soon be called digital logic, whose wartime contributions involved him in cryptology.

One of the Bell inventions to which he contributed was the top-secret "Project X" speech encipherment system. This was the first digital speech transmission system. Previous voice coding systems had depended on analog techniques; they were simply more or less radical distortions of ordinary speech waves, whose receivers reversed whatever distorting process was used in the transmitters. All of these methods produced sound that, while distorted and irritating, could be fairly easily understood by a determined

360

listener without special equipment. By contrast, the X system quantized the speech waveform and added it to a digital "key" before transmission. Careful listening was no longer sufficient: to decipher this signal, an eavesdropper would have to possess not only the equipment for converting the digitized information into sound waves, but also the key pattern.

Shannon's wartime work on secrecy systems was "intimately tied up together" with his most important theoretical contribution, "A Mathematical Theory of Communication." An essential precursor to that paper was his 1945 Bell memorandum, "Communication Theory of Secrecy Systems."[65] In these papers Shannon outlined a mathematical analysis of general communications systems of the form shown in figure 2. Like Wiener, Shannon achieved mathematical generality by defining "information" and "communication" in technically specific, quantitative terms:

> The fundamental problem of communication is that of reproducing at one point either exactly or approximately a message selected at another point. Frequently the messages have meaning; that is, they refer to or are correlated according to some system with certain physical or conceptual entities. These semantic aspects of communication are irrelevant to the engineering problem. The significant aspect is that the actual message is one selected from a set of possible messages. The system must be designed to operate for each possible selection, not just the one which will actually be chosen since this is unknown at the time of design.[66]

For Shannon, communication theory stopped short of semantics, finding its true purposes in the design and analysis of X systems and telephones.

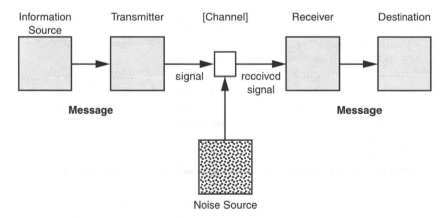

Figure 2 Generalized communications system. After Claude Shannon and Warren Weaver, *The Mathematical Theory of Communication* (Urbana: University of Illinois Press, 1949), 5.

Nevertheless, the possible application to human language, as a code bearing information in the technical sense, intrigued him.

Shannon's presentation on "The Redundancy of English" at the seventh Macy Conference concerned written language as a discrete (discontinuous, or digital) information source. Shannon used a slightly altered version of figure 2, renaming the transmitter and receiver "encoder" and "decoder," respectively, and thus explicitly identifying communication with cryptanalysis.

He considered the twenty-seven characters of the English alphabet (twenty-six letters and the space) as elements in a stochastic coding process. Letter sequences differed from the "ideal" information source, where all messages are equally likely, since the probability of any character's occurrence depends to some degree on the characters preceding it. He estimated the redundancy of typical English prose to be about 50 percent, interpreting this to mean that "when we write English half of what we write is determined by the structure of the language and half is chosen freely."[67] To compile statistics on letter and word frequency and interdependency, Shannon simply opened books at random, located the last letter or word in the sequence he was recording, and wrote down the letter or word that followed it. This method tacitly accepted a crucial premise of behaviorist theory of language, namely that

> sentences are produced in a left-to-right sequence conceived as a series of probabilistic events in which each stimulus word in the sequence has a specifiable probability of eliciting the next word response which, in turn, acts as a stimulus for the succeeding word response.[68]

Like the behaviorists, Shannon tried scrupulously to keep semantic questions at arm's length. But his treatment of language still seemed to imply that the theory might be general enough to cover, as Warren Weaver pointed out in his *Scientific American* review of Shannon's work,

> *all of the procedures by which one mind may affect another.* This . . . involves not only written and oral speech, but also music, the pictorial arts, the theater, the ballet, and in fact all human behavior. In some connections it may be desirable to use a still broader definition of communication . . . [including] the procedures by means of which one mechanism (say automatic equipment to track an airplane and to compute its probable future positions) affects another mechanism (say a guided missile chasing this airplane).[69]

The one-way communications system of figure 2 becomes a feedback loop when the receiver transmits control information back to the transmitter. The communications device also makes a picture of neurological phenomena such as the reflex arc (with the transmitter as afferent and the receiver as efferent nerve) or the control of movement by the brain via the kinesthetic sense. Shannon later worked with Noam Chomsky, for whom linguistics became the study of the human as X system, performing complex trans-formations on "kernels" of information, decoded by reverse transformations in the listener. Shannon also built a maze-solving machine, maintained a serious interest in chess-playing programs, and mentored the young John McCarthy, who went on to coin the phrase "artificial intelligence."[70]

Warren Weaver was Director for Natural Sciences of the Rockefeller Foundation and thus an immensely influential figure in the construction of postwar scientific research programs. He felt that Shannon was wrong to exclude semantic considerations from the theory. In his own view, communi-cation could be analyzed as a hierarchy of three problems:

Level A. How accurately can the symbols of communication be transmitted? (The technical problem.)

Level B. How precisely do the transmitted symbols convey the desired meaning? (The semantic problem.)

Level C. How effectively does the received meaning affect conduct in the desired way? (The effectiveness problem.)[71]

Where Shannon limited himself conservatively to the technical, engineering question (Level A), Weaver thought "analysis at Level A discloses that this level overlaps the other levels more than one could possibly naively suspect . . . Level A is, at least to a significant degree, also a theory of levels B and C."[72] Weaver, then, saw in the mathematical theory of communication far more than a technical aid for designing telephone systems. It was the beacon of a complete statistical analysis of human social activity. Twin cyborgs—X system, tracking-and-targeting servomechanism—became concrete symbols of intelligence as a system of control and communication. Finding the "key patterns" coding perceptual "input" into digitized neural representations, transformations, and "output" as speech or human-machine interaction became the ultimate goal of psychological and social science.

This sort of optimism provoked strenuous debate at Shannon's Macy Conference presentation. The social psychologist Alex Bavelas wanted to use Shannon's ideas to describe the communication of "second-order informa-tion," or those messages about status, relationships, desires, and so on implied but not directly expressed in conversation or by other means. He thought, for example, that "a change in emotional security could be defined as a change in the individual's subjective probabilities that he is or is not a certain kind of person or that he is or is not 'loved.'"[73] As a selection of one of a set of possible messages about the individual's relationship to the group, this would qualify as information in the strict sense. Walter Pitts and the skeptical mathematician Leonard Savage objected to this picture of emotional contact as purely "informative."

Shannon pointed out that using communication-theoretic terms "at the psychological level" created difficulties of definition, especially with concepts like "signal" and "noise": "if a person receives something over a telephone, part of which is useful to him and part of which is not, and you want to call the useful part the signal, that is hardly a mathematical problem."[74] In the X system, the generation of "information" by the source and its use by the destination—its interpretation—are "semantic" and fall outside the boundaries of the formal machine. The theory is essentially concerned only with defining the accuracy of transmission of already-constituted messages. Messages generated by a source must be elements of some specifiable, predefined set, such as sound waves or lettering. Similarly, the criterion of accurate transmission is a comparison of the message at the source with the message at the destination; the "effectiveness" of the message on the addressee forms no part of the theory.

The metaphorical extension Bavelas hazarded at Shannon's presentation was exactly the kind of transition from "as if" to "is" against which Ralph Gerard had railed in his talk opening the same session. The exchange over the idea of "second-order information" reveals the process of metaphorical elaboration at work. Bavelas was trying to bend the technical term "information" to the purposes of a wider, less restricted conversation. Whether or not there was theoretical justification for such an application of the term, Bavelas perceived an available metaphorical entailment.

Shannon's theory described the substance of communication as information. But Shannon's theory applied directly only to observables, externals—preconstituted messages without semantic content. It was a theory of communication between and through machines. Communication between human beings, as Bavelas understood, has semantic values at its heart. His description of emotional security as a "change in subjective probabilities" transferred the notions of "message" and "information" onto the internal experience of the individual. What Weaver called the "semantic problem" and the "effectiveness problem" were areas where the extension of theory and the growth of metaphor blurred together. Understanding the one without the other, given the self-elaborating tendencies of discourse systems, had already become a doomed rear-guard action.

What these dead ends in metaphorical elaboration revealed was that a *behaviorist*-mechanist analysis would, finally, fail. Internal processes—not just the transmission, but the constitution and selection of "messages"— would have to be included in the model. For that purpose computers, not communications systems, would provide the key.

The chain of command

In engineering, however, the semantic and effectiveness problems could be ignored as long as, with Shannon, source and destination were conceived as the beginning and end of the communication process. Even complex systems may be analyzed without considering the semantic dimension. In the case of feedback-controlled machines, for example, the destination doubles as source for a transmission back to the original source, which in turn becomes the destination for the control message. Or the process can continue sequentially, as when orders are relayed along a human chain of command, with each destination becoming a selective source for the following link. For processes like these, the message need not be "understood" or "interpreted" at the destination in order to be processed and be effective.

Computer development had been funded by the military with an eye to the potential for automation of command, control, and communications in the SAGE project. In the same way, the enhancement of command-control processes motivated military investment in communications technology and psychology over the long term. It was again the problem of the "machine in the middle," whose slow speeds and tendencies to failure made the human an unreliable part of the military machine. J. C. R. Licklider of the Harvard Psycho-Acoustic Laboratory, whose guest Macy presentation immediately preceded Shannon's, made the following comment in discussion:

> During the war, especially when the military was picking people for fairly crucial jobs involving listening—the military had the notion, as you probably all know, that everything must go through many links of a chainlike communication system before it becomes really official—they were interested in the problem of training listeners.[75]

As links in this chain, human listeners in communications systems added unacceptably high levels of noise. For the purposes of the Psycho-Acoustic Lab's wartime research (as we will see in chapter 7) the "job" of "listening" had been defined as accurate decoding. The listener as destination became an essentially mechanical linkage in the command circuit, carrying out the orders propagated by the electronic components and mediating among them. Human listeners in military roles were themselves conceived as X systems, natural-technical devices for decoding signals. The soldier-listener was trained as well as operated by the techniques of feedback control: "the way to teach a person to listen is to provide high motivation . . . , lots of speech for him to listen to, and . . . knowledge of results. (The listener must know whether he heard it correctly or not.)"[76] Licklider's laboratory tested and trained the human elements of the chain of command as component parts whose accuracy and error rates would affect the performance of the system as a whole. The criterion of that performance was the undistorted flow of command and control signals.

Under the emerging electronic communications regime of the war and the postwar military world, command-control-communications systems operated as a nested hierarchy of cybernetic devices. Airplanes, communications systems, computers, and antiaircraft guns occupied the micro levels of this hierarchy. Higher-level "devices," each of which could be considered a cyborg or cybernetic system, included aircraft carriers, the WWMCCS, and NORAD early warning systems. At a still higher level stood military units such as battalions and the Army, Navy, and Air Force themselves. Each was conceptualized as an integrated combination of human and electronic components, operating according to formalized rules of action. Each level followed directives taken from the next highest unit and returned information on its performance to that unit. Each carried out its own functions with relative autonomy, issuing its own commands to systems under its control and evaluating the results using feedback from them.

This, at least, was the formal picture of the operation of military hierarchies, the picture drawn by the emerging class of science-guided, control-oriented military managers. Transforming institutions with a deep historical command tradition to correspond with this formal picture became a kind of Holy Grail for military technologists and the sciences behind them in the postwar years. The human elements of cybernetically organized systems question, negotiate, make mistakes, delay, and distort messages; this made them problematic from the military formalist point of view. As a "battle-scarred and ribbon-covered Admiral" introduced the crew of the USS Missouri to NDRC scientists during World War II: "Twenty-five hundred officers and men: gentlemen, twenty-five hundred sources of error."[77]

Prior to the advent of cybernetic machines, this "problem" had been addressed by techniques of discipline and normalization, focused on incorporating the soldier into the human chain of command.[78] With cybernetic devices, however, it became possible to minimize or entirely eliminate some human roles. The transition to cybernetically automated military organizations was abrupt. As Jay Forrester put it,

One could probably not have found [in 1947] five military officers who would have acknowledged the possibility of a machine's being able to analyze the available information sources, the proper assignment of weapons, the generation of command instructions, and the coordination of adjacent areas of military operations ... During the following decade the speed of military operations increased until it became clear that, regardless of the assumed advantages of human judgment decisions, the internal communication speed of the human organization simply was not able to cope with the pace of modern air

366

warfare. This inability to act provided the incentive [to begin replacing the "human organization" with computers].[79]

Such automation required a formal/mechanical model of the "human organization."

Thus cybernetic psychology, as both theory and practice, both mirrored and transformed the chain of command. Like the hierarchy of behavior pictured by Rosenblueth, Wiener, and Bigelow in figure 1, the chain of command does not set goals or define values, but only carries out orders. Though individuals inside a military system certainly make decisions and set goals, as links in the chain of command they are allowed no choices regarding the ultimate purposes and values of the system. Their "choices" are, to paraphrase Shannon, always the permutations and combinations of a predefined set. The "military machine" was a metaphor built from a palpable cybernetic device, an interlocking assemblage of human and electromechanical parts, its coherence and continual refinement activated by the theory of information.

Notes

1 Warren McCulloch, "Why the Mind Is in the Head," in Lloyd Jeffress, ed., *Cerebral Mechanisms in Behavior* (New York: Wiley-Interscience, 1951), 42.
2 For this phrase and elements of my approach in this chapter, I am indebted to Donna J. Haraway, "The High Cost of Information in Post-World War II Evolutionary Biology," *The Philosophical Forum*, Vol. XIII, Nos. 2–3 (1982), 244–278.
3 Sigmund Freud, *Civilization and its Discontents*, trans. James Strachey (New York: Norton, 1961), 50.
4 Stephen Jay Gould, *The Mismeasure of Man* (New York: Norton, 1981), 223–232 and passim.
5 Cf. especially Michel Foucault, *The Birth of the Clinic*, trans. A.M. Sheridan Smith (New York: Vintage Books, 1975); *Madness and Civilization*, trans. Richard Howard (New York: Vintage Books, 1973); and *Discipline and Punish*, trans. Alan Sheridan (New York: Vintage Books, 1977).
6 Michel Foucault, "Truth and Power," in *Power/Knowledge: Selected Interviews and Other Writings 1972–1977*, trans. Colin Gordon (New York: Pantheon, 1980), 133.
7 Albert R. Gilgen, *American Psychology Since World War II* (Westport, CT: Greenwood Press, 1982), 39; Steve J. Heims, *The Cybernetics Group* (Cambridge, MA: MIT Press, 1991), 3.
8 James H. Capshew, *Psychology on the March: American Psychologists and World War II* (unpublished Ph.D. dissertation, University of Pennsylvania, 1986), 3.
9 Ibid., 289–290.
10 Seymour Sarason, *Psychology Misdirected* (Glencoe: Free Press, 1981), 1–2. Cited in Heims, *Cybernetics Group*, 3.
11 Cf. Haraway, "High Cost," and Donna Haraway, "Signs of Dominance: From a Physiology to a Cybernetics of Primate Society," in *Studies in History of Biology* (Baltimore: Johns Hopkins, 1983), Vol. 6, 131 and passim.
12 See the slightly different list in Howard Gardner, *The Mind's New Science* (New York: Basic Books, 1985), 38–43, as well as Allen Newell, *Unified Theories of Cognition* (Cambridge, MA: Harvard University Press, 1990).
13 On this paradigm shift see Walter B. Weimer and David S. Palermo, "Paradigms

and Normal Science in Psychology," *Science Studies*, Vol. 3 (1973), 211–244; Erwin M. Segal and Roy Lachman, "Complex Behavior or Higher Mental Process: Is There a Paradigm Shift?" *American Psychologist*, Vol. 27 (1972), 46–55; David Palermo, "Is a Scientific Revolution Taking Place in Psychology?" *Science Studies*, Vol. 1 (1971), 135–155; and D. O. Hebb, "The American Revolution," *American Psychologist*, Vol. 15 (1960), 735–745.

14 B. F. Skinner, *Beyond Freedom and Dignity* (New York: Bantam, 1971) contains the most explicit account of this vision.

15 See the list of machine models in Edwin G. Boring, "Mind and Mechanism," *American Journal of Psychology*, Vol. LIX, No. 2 (1946), 184.

16 Cf. Edward C. Tolman, "Cognitive Maps in Rats and Men," *Psychological Review*, Vol. 55, No. 4 (1948), 189–208.

17 Norbert Wiener, *Cybernetics: Control and Communication in the Animal and the Machine* (Cambridge, MA: MIT Press, 1948); Claude Shannon, "The Mathematical Theory of Communication," *Bell System Technical Journal*, Vol. 27 (1948), 379–423, 623–656, reprinted in Shannon and Warren Weaver, *The Mathematical Theory of Communication* (Urbana: University of Illinois Press, 1949).

18 The Hixon Symposium, September 20–25, 1948. Proceedings in Jeffress, *Cerebral Mechanisms in Behavior*.

19 Wiener, *Cybernetics*.

20 David Lipset, *Gregory Bateson: The Legacy of a Scientist* (New York: Prentice-Hall, 1980), 179.

21 Heims, *Cybernetics Group*, 14–15. Heims, the only historian to have studied the Macy Conferences extensively, communicates well the flavor of these extraordinary meetings and the sparks between the extraordinary scientists involved. Heims's work is the only comprehensive source on Macy meetings prior to the sixth conference, when transcripts began to be kept. Since Wiener did not coin the word "cybernetics" until 1947, I will refer to the group at this juncture as the "proto-cyberneticians" to avoid anachronism.

22 To illustrate using one of Wiener's examples, I reach for a pencil, using my eyes to guide my hand by continuously correcting any deviations from its proper course.

23 Behaviorist psychologists, as we have seen, excluded internal events from consideration on methodological and theoretical grounds. They abhorred talk of goals and purposes as causes occurring later in time than their supposed effects. See Brian D. Mackenzie, *Behaviorism and the Limits of Scientific Method* (London: Routledge and Kegan Paul, 1977). Mackenzie argues that S-R psychology's self-imposed methodological restrictions led to its eventual demise because its practitioners limited the domain of experimentation to a narrow segment of the scientifically interesting possibilities.

24 Kenneth J. W. Craik, "Theory of the Human Operator in Control Systems: I. The Operator as an Engineering System," written in 1945 and posthumously published in the *British Journal of Psychology*, Vol. 38 (1947), 56–61.

25 See the discussion, below, of John Stroud's presentation at the Macy Conferences. On origin stories in science, see Donna Haraway's introduction to her book *Primate Visions* (London: Routledge Kegan Paul, 1989).

26 The subtitle of Wiener's *Cybernetics*.

27 Arturo Rosenblueth, Norbert Wiener, and Julian Bigelow, "Behavior, Purpose and Teleology," *Philosophy of Science*, Vol. 10 (1943), 18–24.

28 The formula and definitions here follow William K. Estes, "Toward a Statistical Theory of Learning," *Psychological Review*, Vol. 57 (1950), 94–107, but could have been taken from almost any behaviorist publication.

29 Cf. MacKenzie, *Behaviorism*.

30 Rosenblueth, Wiener, and Bigelow, "Behavior, Purpose and Teleology," 18.
31 "Input" and "output," originally electrical engineering terms for currents entering and exiting circuits, had been adopted analogically by communications engineers to describe the entry and exit versions of *messages* traveling through a channel, already making apparent the similarities between energy and information that would emerge to strikingly from cybernetics.
32 Rosenblueth, Wiener, and Bigelow, "Behavior, Purpose and Teleology," 19.
33 Cybernetics purposely cast itself as a metatheory, an explanation of how everything is connected to everything else. To do so it made extensive use of a "literary device" Geoffrey Bowker calls the "Serres effect," namely the heterogeneous list. "Cyberneticians fill their texts with unexpected conjunctions (rust, an epidemic, and diffusion in a semi-conductor . . .). Thus a random page of Ashby's *Introduction* [*to* Cybernetics] discusses self-locking in oysters, irreversibly insoluble compounds, the dynamics of the cerebral cortex and absenteeism from unpleasant industries" (Geof Bowker, "The Age of Cybernetics, or How Cybernetics Aged," unpublished ms. [1991], University of Keele, 9). In its attempt to encompass heterogeneity, cybernetics' rhetoric resembles both my own concept of discourse and some current theories in science and technology studies (see chapter 1).
34 Rosenblueth, Wiener, and Bigelow, "Behavior, Purpose and Teleology," 23.
35 I owe this point to Donna Haraway.
36 Kenneth J. W. Craik, "Theory of the Human Operator in Control Systems, II: Man as an Example in a Control System," written in 1945 and posthumously published in *British Journal of Psychology*, Vol. 39 (1947), 142.
37 Boring, "Mind and Mechanism," 173–192.
38 Warren S. McCulloch and Walter Pitts, "A Logical Calculus of the Ideas Immanent in Nervous Activity," *Bulletin of Mathematical Biophysics*, Vol. 5 (1943), 115–133.
39 "In a discussion after a lecture of von Neumann, McCulloch mentioned that it was Turning's paper that had inspired their ideas" (Andrew Hodges, *Alan Turing: The Enigma* [New York: Simon & Schuster, 1983], 252n).
40 Heims, *Cybernetics Group*, 20.
41 Pamela McCorduck, *Machines Who Think* (New York: W. H. Freeman, 1979), 66, from interviews.
42 Wiener, in a letter to Rosenblueth, cited in Steve Heims, *John von Neumann and Norbert Wiener* (Cambridge, MA: MIT Press, 1980), 185.
43 Heims, *Von Neumann and Wiener*, 203–204.
44 Heims, *Cybernetics Group*, 19–20.
45 The phrase "cybernetics group" is taken from Heims's book.
46 McCulloch and Pitts, "Logical Calculus."
47 See Heims, *Von Neumann and Wiener*, 209 and passim, and John von Neumann, "The General and Logical Theory of Automata," in Jeffress, *Cerebral Mechanisms in Behavior*, 1–41.
48 Proceedings of the last five Macy Conferences were published as *Transactions of the Conference on Cybernetics*, 5 vols., ed. Heinz von Foerster (New York: Josiah Macy Jr. Foundation, 1950–1955). This quotation is from *Transactions of the Seventh Conference*, 11.
49 Alan Turing, "Computing Machinery and Intelligence," *Mind*, Vol. 59 (1950), 442.
50 Von Foerster, *Sixth Conference*, 112–145.
51 Steve Heims, "Encounter of Behavioral Sciences with New Machine-Organism Analogies in the 1940s," *Journal of the History of the Behavioral Sciences*, Vol. 11 (1975), 372. In this article Heims gives an account of the unpublished fourth Macy conference, based on interviews with some participants.

52 Ibid., 372.
53 Von Foerster, *Seventh Conference*, 44.
54 Jeffress, *Cerebral Mechanisms in Behavior*, 97.
55 Heims, *Cybernetics Group*, 257.
56 Von Foerster, *Sixth Conference*, 27–28. This refers to a question dating to William James, namely how long what is perceived as the "present moment" endures.
57 Ibid.
58 Ibid., 32.
59 Ibid., 33.
60 Heims, *Cybernetics Group*, 261. Stroud's sole article is John Stroud, "The Fine Structure of Psychological Time," in H. Quastler, ed., *Information Theory and Psychology* (Glencoe, IL: Free Press, 1955), 174–207. Note that the guided missile remained a central metaphor, fifteen years after the Macy Conferences.
61 For a textbook summary of the field, oriented toward engineering applications, see E. C. Poulton, *Tracking Skill and Manual Control* (New York: Academic Press, 1974).
62 Edwin G. Boring and M. Van de Water, eds., *Psychology for the Fighting Man* (Washington, DC: Infantry Journal Press, 1943), 24.
63 R. I., Gregory, *Eye and Brain* (New York: McGraw-Hill, 1966), 91–92.
64 M. D. Fagen, ed., *A History of Engineering and Science in the Bell System* (Murray Hill, NJ: Bell Telephone Laboratories, 1978), 165.
65 Ibid., 317.
66 Shannon and Weaver, *The Mathematical Theory of Communication*, 26.
67 Ibid., 26.
68 David Palermo, *Psychology of Language* (Glenview, IL: Scott, Foresman, 1978), 20.
69 Shannon and Weaver, *The Mathematical Theory of Communication*, 95, italics added. Note the military analogy.
70 Claude E. Shannon, "Programming a Computer for Playing Chess," *Philosophical Magazine*, Vol. 41 (1950), 256–275; Claude E. Shannon, "Computers and Automata," *Proceedings of the IRE*, Vol. 41 (1953), 1234–1241.
71 Shannon and Weaver, *The Mathematical Theory of Communication*, 96.
72 Ibid., 98.
73 Von Foerster, *Seventh Conference*, 150.
74 Ibid., 154.
75 J. C. R. Licklider, presentation on "The manner in which and extent to which speech can be distorted and remain intelligible," in Von Foerster, *Seventh Conference*, 99.
76 Ibid.
77 Charles W. Bray, ed., *Human Factors in Military Efficiency: Summary Technical Report of the Applied Psychology Panel, NDRC*, Vol. 1 (Washington, DC: U.S. Government Printing Office, 1946), xi.
78 Cf. Foucault, *Discipline and Punish*.
79 Jay W. Forrester, "Managerial Decision Making," in Martin Greenberger, ed., *Computers and the World of the Future* (Cambridge: MIT Press, 1962), 53, partially cited above (chapter 2).

19

BEHAVIOR, PURPOSE AND TELEOLOGY

Arturo Rosenblueth, Norbert Wiener and Julian Bigelow

Source: *Philosophy of Science*, 10, 1943, 18–24.

This essay has two goals. The first is to define the behavioristic study of natural events and to classify behavior. The second is to stress the importance of the concept of purpose.

Given any object, relatively abstracted from its surroundings for study, the behavioristic approach consists in the examination of the output of the object and of the relations of this output to the input. By output is meant any change produced in the surroundings by the object. By input, conversely, is meant any event external to the object that modifies this object in any manner.

The above statement of what is meant by the behavioristic method of study omits the specific structure and the instrinsic organization of the object. This omission is fundamental because on it is based the distinction between the behavioristic and the alternative functional method of study. In a functional analysis, as opposed to a behavioristic approach, the main goal is the intrinsic organization of the entity studied, its structure and its properties; the relations between the object and the surroundings are relatively incidental.

From this definition of the behavioristic method a broad definition of behavior ensues. By behavior is meant any change of an entity with respect to its surroundings. This change may be largely an output from the object, the input being then minimal, remote or irrelevant; or else the change may be immediately traceable to a certain input. Accordingly, any modification of an object, detectable externally, may be denoted as behavior. The term would be, therefore, too extensive for usefulness were it not that it may be restricted by apposite adjectives—i.e., that behavior may be classified.

The consideration of the changes of energy involved in behavior affords a basis for classification. Active behavior is that in which the object is the source of the output energy involved in a given specific reaction. The object may store energy supplied by a remote or relatively immediate input, but the input does not energize the output directly. In passive behavior, on the contrary, the object is not a source of energy; all the energy in the output can be traced to the immediate input (e.g., the throwing of an object), or else the object may control energy which remains external to it throughout the reaction (e.g., the soaring flight of a bird).

Active behavior may be subdivided into two classes: purposeless (or random) and purposeful. The term purposeful is meant to denote that the act or behavior may be interpreted as directed to the attainment of a goal—i.e., to a final condition in which the behaving object reaches a definite correlation in time or in space with respect to another object or event. Purposeless behavior then is that which is not interpreted as directed to a goal.

The vagueness of the words "may be interpreted" as used above might be considered so great that the distinction would be useless. Yet the recognition that behavior may sometimes be purposeful is unavoidable and useful, as follows. The basis of the concept of purpose is the awareness of "voluntary activity." Now, the purpose of voluntary acts is not a matter of arbitrary interpretation but a physiological fact. When we perform a voluntary action what we select voluntarily is a specific purpose, not a specific movement. Thus, if we decide to take a glass containing water and carry it to our mouth we do not command certain muscles to contract to a certain degree and in a certain sequence; we merely trip the purpose and the reaction follows automatically. Indeed, experimental physiology has so far been largely incapable of explaining the mechanism of voluntary activity. We submit that this failure is due to the fact that when an experimenter stimulates the motor regions of the cerebral cortex he does not duplicate a voluntary reaction; he trips efferent, "output" pathways, but does not trip a purpose, as is done voluntarily.

The view has often been expressed that all machines are purposeful. This view is untenable. First may be mentioned mechanical devices such as a roulette, designed precisely for purposelessness. Then may be considered devices such as a clock, designed, it is true, with a purpose, but having a performance which, although orderly, is not purposeful—i.e., there is no specific final condition toward which the movement of the clock strives. Similarly, although a gun may be used for a definite purpose, the attainment of a goal is not intrinsic to the performance of the gun; random shooting can be made, deliberately purposeless.

Some machines, on the other hand, are intrinsically purposeful. A torpedo with a target-seeking mechanism is an example. The term servomechanisms has been coined precisely to designate machines with intrinsic purposeful behavior.

It is apparent from these considerations that although the definition of purposeful behavior is relatively vague, and hence operationally largely

372

meaningless, the concept of purpose is useful and should, therefore, be retained.

Purposeful active behavior may be subdivided into two classes: "feed-back" (or "teleological") and "non-feed-back" (or "non-teleological"). The expression feed-back is used by engineers in two different senses. In a broad sense it may denote that some of the output energy of an apparatus or machine is returned as input; an example is an electrical amplifier with feed-back. The feed-back is in these cases positive—the fraction of the output which reenters the object has the same sign as the original input signal. Positive feed-back adds to the input signals, it does not correct them. The term feed-back is also employed in a more restricted sense to signify that the behavior of an object is controlled by the margin of error at which the object stands at a given time with reference to a relatively specific goal. The feed-back is then negative, that is, the signals from the goal are used to restrict outputs which would otherwise go beyond the goal. It is this second meaning of the term feed-back that is used here.

All purposeful behavior may be considered to require negative feed-back. If a goal is to be attained, some signals from the goal are necessary at some time to direct the behavior. By non-feed-back behavior is meant that in which there are no signals from the goal which modify the activity of the object *in the course of the behavior*. Thus, a machine may be set to impinge upon a luminous object although the machine may be insensitive to light. Similarly, a snake may strike at a frog, or a frog at a fly, with no visual or other report from the prey after the movement has started. Indeed, the movement is in these cases so fast that it is not likely that nerve impulses would have time to arise at the retina, travel to the central nervous system and set up further impulses which would reach the muscles in time to modify the movement effectively.

As opposed to the examples considered, the behavior of some machines and some reactions of living organisms involve a continuous feed-back from the goal that modifies and guides the behaving object. This type of behavior is more effective than that mentioned above, particularly when the goal is not stationary. But continuous feed-back control may lead to very clumsy behavior if the feed-back is inadequately damped and becomes therefore positive instead of negative for certain frequencies of oscillation. Suppose, for example, that a machine is designed with the purpose of impinging upon a moving luminous goal; the path followed by the machine is controlled by the direction and intensity of the light from the goal. Suppose further that the machine overshoots seriously when it follows a movement of the goal in a certain direction; an even stronger stimulus will then be delivered which will turn the machine in the opposite direction. If that movement again over-shoots a series of increasingly larger oscillations will ensue and the machine will miss the goal.

This picture of the consequences of undamped feed-back is strikingly similar to that seen during the performance of a voluntary act by a cerebellar patient. At rest the subject exhibits no obvious motor disturbance. If he is asked to carry a glass of water from a table to his mouth, however, the hand carrying the glass will execute a series of oscillatory motions of increasing amplitude as the glass approaches his mouth, so that the water will spill and the purpose will not be fulfilled. This test is typical of the disorderly motor performance of patients with cerebellar disease. The analogy with the behavior of a machine with undamped feed-back is so vivid that we venture to suggest that the main function of the cerebellum is the control of the feed-back nervous mechanisms involved in purposeful motor activity.

Feed-back purposeful behavior may again be subdivided. It may be extra-polative (predictive), or it may be non-extrapolative (non-predictive). The reactions of unicellular organisms known as tropisms are examples of non-predictive performances. The amoeba merely follows the source to which it reacts; there is no evidence that it extrapolates the path of a moving source. Predictive animal behavior, on the other hand, is a commonplace. A cat starting to pursue a running mouse does not run directly toward the region where the mouse is at any given time, but moves toward an extrapolated future position. Examples of both predictive and non-predictive servo-mechanisms may also be found readily.

Predictive behavior may be subdivided into different orders. The cat chas-ing the mouse is an instance of first-order prediction; the cat merely predicts the path of the mouse. Throwing a stone at a moving target requires a second-order prediction; the paths of the target and of the stone should be foreseen. Examples of predictions of higher order are shooting with a sling or with a bow and arrow.

Predictive behavior requires the discrimination of at least two coordinates, a temporal and at least one spatial axis. Prediction will be more effective and flexible, however, if the behaving object can respond to changes in more than one spatial coordinate. The sensory receptors of an organism, or the corres-ponding elements of a machine, may therefore limit the predictive behavior. Thus, a bloodhound *follows* a trail, that is, it does not show any predictive behavior in trailing, because a chemical, olfactory input reports only spatial information: distance, as indicated by intensity. The external changes capable of affecting auditory, or, even better, visual receptors, permit more accurate spatial localization; hence the possibility of more effective predictive reac-tions when the input affects those receptors.

In addition to the limitations imposed by the receptors upon the ability to perform extrapolative actions, limitations may also occur that are due to the internal organization of the behaving object. Thus, a machine which is to trail predictively a moving luminous object should not only be sensitive to light (e.g., by the possession of a photoelectric cell), but should also have the structure adequate for interpreting the luminous input. It is probable that limitations of internal organization, particularly of the organization of the central nervous system, determine the complexity of predictive behavior which a mammal may attain. Thus, it is likely that the nervous system of a rat or dog is such that it does not permit the integration of input and output necessary for the performance of a predictive reaction of the third or fourth order. Indeed, it is possible that one of the features of the discontinuity of behavior observable when comparing humans with other high mammals may lie in that the other mammals are limited to predictive behavior of a low order, whereas man may be capable potentially of quite high orders of prediction.

The classification of behavior suggested so far is tabulated here:

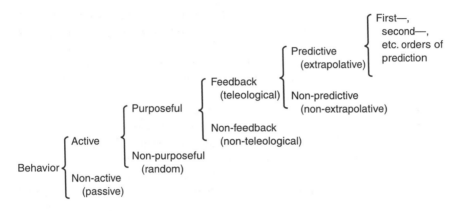

It is apparent that each of the dichotomies established singles out arbitrarily one feature, deemed interesting, leaving an amorphous remainder: the non-class. It is also apparent that the criteria for the several dichotomies are heterogeneous. It is obvious, therefore, that many other lines of classification are available, which are independent of that developed above. Thus, behavior in general, or any of the groups in the table, could be divided into linear (i.e., output proportional to input) and non-linear. A division into continuous and discontinuous might be useful for many purposes. The several degrees of freedom which behavior may exhibit could also be employed as a basis of systematization.

The classification tabulated above was adopted for several reasons. It leads to the singling out of the class of predictive behavior, a class particularly interesting since it suggests the possibility of systematizing increasingly more complex tests of the behavior of organisms. It emphasizes the concepts of purpose and of teleology, concepts which, although rather discredited at present, are shown to be important. Finally, it reveals that a uniform behavioristic analysis is applicable to both machines and living organisms, regardless of the complexity of the behavior.

It has sometimes been stated that the designers of machines merely attempt to duplicate the performances of living organisms. This statement is uncritical. That the gross behavior of some machines should be similar to the reactions of organisms is not surprising. Animal behavior includes many varieties of all the possible modes of behavior and the machines devised so far have far from exhausted all those possible modes. There is, therefore a considerable overlap of the two realms of behavior. Examples, however, are readily found of manmade machines with behavior that transcends human behavior. A machine with an electrical output is an instance; for men, unlike the electric fishes, are incapable of emitting electricity. Radio transmission is perhaps an even better instance, for no animal is known with the ability to generate short waves, even if so-called experiments on telepathy are considered seriously.

A further comparison of living organisms and machines leads to the following inferences. The methods of study for the two groups are at present similar. Whether they should always be the same may depend on whether or not there are one or more qualitatively distinct, unique characteristics present in one group and absent in the other. Such qualitative differences have not appeared so far.

The broad classes of behavior are the same in machines and in living organisms. Specific, narrow classes may be found exclusively in one or the other. Thus, no machine is available yet that can write a Sanscrit-Mandarin dictionary. Thus, also, no living organism is known that rolls on wheels—imagine what the result would have been if engineers had insisted on copying living organisms and had therefore put legs and feet in their locomotives, instead of wheels.

While the behavioristic analysis of machines and living organisms is largely uniform, their functional study reveals deep differences. Structurally, organisms are mainly colloidal, and include prominently protein molecules, large, complex and anisotropic; machines are chiefly metallic and include mainly simple molecules. From the standpoint of their energetics, machines usually exhibit relatively large differences of potential, which permit rapid mobilization of energy; in organisms the energy is more uniformly distributed, it is not very mobile. Thus, in electric machines conduction is mainly electronic, whereas in organisms electric changes are usually ionic.

Scope and flexibility are achieved in machines largely by temporal multiplication of effects; frequencies of one million per second or more are readily obtained and utilized. In organisms, spatial multiplication, rather than temporal, is the rule; the temporal achievements are poor—the fastest nerve fibers can only conduct about one thousand impulses per second; spatial multiplication is on the other hand abundant and admirable in its compactness. This difference is well illustrated by the comparison of a television receiver and the eye. The television receiver may be described as a single cone retina; the images are formed by scanning—i.e. by orderly successive detection of the signal with a rate of about 20 million per second. Scanning is a process which seldom or never occurs in organisms, since it requires fast frequencies for effective performance. The eye uses a spatial, rather than a temporal multiplier. Instead of the one cone of the television receiver a human eye has about 6.5 million cones and about 115 million rods.

If an engineer were to design a robot, roughly similar in behavior to an animal organism, he would not attempt at present to make it out of proteins and other colloids. He would probably build it out of metallic parts, some dielectrics and many vacuum tubes. The movements of the robot could readily be much faster and more powerful than those of the original organism. Learning and memory, however, would be quite rudimentary. In future years, as the knowledge of colloids and proteins increases, future engineers may attempt the design of robots not only with a behavior, but also with a structure similar to that of a mammal. The ultimate model of a cat is of course another cat, whether it be born of still another cat or synthesized in a laboratory.

In classifying behavior the term "teleology" was used as synonymous with "purpose controlled by feed-back." Teleology has been interpreted in the past to imply purpose and the vague concept of a "final cause" has been often added. This concept of final causes has led to the opposition of teleology to determinism. A discussion of causality, determinism and final causes is beyond the scope of this essay. It may be pointed out, however, that purposefulness, as defined here, is quite independent of causality, initial or final. Teleology has been discredited chiefly because it was defined to imply a cause subsequent in time to a given effect. When this aspect of teleology was dismissed, however, the associated recognition of the importance of purpose was also unfortunately discarded. Since we consider purposefulness a concept necessary for the understanding of certain modes of behavior we suggest that a teleological study is useful if it avoids problems of causality and concerns itself merely with an investigation of purpose.

We have restricted the connotation of teleological behavior by applying this designation only to purposeful reactions which are controlled by the error of the reaction—i.e., by the difference between the state of the behaving object at any time and the final state interpreted as the purpose. Teleological behavior thus becomes synonymous with behavior controlled by negative feed-back, and gains therefore in precision by a sufficiently restricted connotation.

According to this limited definition, teleology is not opposed to determinism, but to non-teleology. Both teleological and non-teleological systems are deterministic when the behavior considered belongs to the realm where determinism applies. The concept of teleology shares only one thing with the concept of causality: a time axis. But causality implies a one-way, relatively irreversible functional relationship, whereas teleology is concerned with behavior, not with functional relationships.

20

A LOGICAL CALCULUS OF THE IDEAS IMMANENT IN NERVOUS ACTIVITY

Warren S. McCulloch and Walter H. Pitts

Source: W. S. McCulloch, *Embodiments of Mind*, MIT Press, 1965, pp. 19–39.

Because of the 'all-or-none' character of nervous activity, neural events and the relations among them can be treated by means of propositional logic. It is found that the behavior of every net can be described in these terms, with the addition of more complicated logical means for nets containing circles; and that for any logical expression satisfying certain conditions, one can find a net behaving in the fashion it describes. It is shown that many particular choices among possible neurophysiological assumptions are equivalent, in the sense that for every net behaving under one assumption, there exists another net which behaves under the other and gives the same results, although perhaps not in the same time. Various applications of the calculus are discussed.

Introduction

Theoretical neurophysiology rests on certain cardinal assumptions. The nervous system is a net of neurons, each having a soma and an axon. Their adjunctions, or synapses, are always between the axon of one neuron and the soma of another. At any instant a neuron has some threshold, which excitation must exceed to initiate an impulse. This, except for the fact and the time of its occurrence, is determined by the neuron, not by the excitation. From the point of excitation the impulse is propagated to all parts of the neuron. The velocity along the axon varies directly with its diameter, from less than one meter per second in thin axons, which are usually short, to more than 150 meters per second in thick axons, which are usually long. The time for axonal conduction is consequently of little importance in determining the time of arrival of impulses at points unequally remote from the same source.

Excitation across synapses occurs predominantly from axonal terminations to somata. It is still a moot point whether this depends upon irreciprocity of individual synapses or merely upon prevalent anatomical configurations. To suppose the latter requires no hypothesis *ad hoc* and explains known exceptions, but any assumption as to cause is compatible with the calculus to come. No case is known in which excitation through a single synapse has elicited a nervous impulse in any neuron, whereas any neuron may be excited by impulses arriving at a sufficient number of neighboring synapses within the period of latent addition, which lasts less than one quarter of a millisecond. Observed temporal summation of impulses at greater intervals is impossible for single neurons and empirically depends upon structural properties of the net. Between the arrival of impulses upon a neuron and its own propagated impulse there is a synaptic delay of more than half a millisecond. During the first part of the nervous impulse the neuron is absolutely refractory to any stimulation. Thereafter its excitability returns rapidly, in some cases reaching a value above normal from which it sinks again to a subnormal value, whence it returns slowly to normal. Frequent activity augments this subnormality. Such specificity as is possessed by nervous impulses depends solely upon their time and place and not on any other specificity of nervous energies. Of late only inhibition has been seriously adduced to contravene this thesis. Inhibition is the termination or prevention of the activity of one group of neurons by concurrent or antecedent activity of a second group. Until recently this could be explained on the supposition that previous activity of neurons of the second group might so raise the thresholds of internuncial neurons that they could no longer be excited by neurons of the first group, whereas the impulses of the first group must sum with the impulses of these internuncials to excite the now inhibited neurons. Today, some inhibitions have been shown to consume less than one millisecond. This excludes internuncials and requires synapses through which impulses inhibit that neuron which is being stimulated by impulses through other synapses. As yet experiment has not shown whether the refractoriness is relative or absolute. We will assume the latter and demonstrate that the difference is immaterial to our argument. Either variety of refractoriness can be accounted for in either of two ways. The 'inhibitory synapse' may be of such a kind as to produce a substance which raises the threshold of the neuron, or it may be so placed that the local disturbance produced by its excitation opposes the alteration induced by the otherwise excitatory synapses. Inasmuch as position is already known to have such effects in the case of electrical stimulation, the first hypothesis is to be excluded unless and until it be substantiated, for the second involves no new hypothesis. We have, then, two explanations of inhibition based on the same general premises, differing only in the assumed nervous nets and, consequently, in the time required for inhibition. Hereafter we shall refer to such nervous nets as *equivalent in the extended sense*. Since we are concerned with properties of nets which are invariant under equivalence, we may make the physical assumptions which are most convenient for the calculus.

Many years ago one of us, by considerations impertinent to this argument, was led to conceive of the response of any neuron as factually equivalent to a proposition which proposed its adequate stimulus. He therefore attempted to record the behavior of complicated nets in the notation of the symbolic logic of propositions. The 'all-or-none' law of nervous activity is sufficient to insure that the activity of any neuron may be represented as a proposition. Physiological relations existing among nervous activities correspond, of course, to relations among the propositions; and the utility of the representation depends upon the identity of these relations with those of the logic of propositions. To each reaction of any neuron there is a corresponding assertion of a simple proposition. This, in turn, implies either some other simple proposition or the disjunction or the conjunction, with or without negation, of similar propositions, according to the configuration of the synapses upon and the threshold of the neuron in question. Two difficulties appeared. The first concerns facilitation and extinction, in which antecedent activity temporarily alters responsiveness to subsequent stimulation of one and the same part of the net. The second concerns learning, in which activities concurrent at some previous time have altered the net permanently, so that a stimulus which would previously have been inadequate is now adequate. But for nets undergoing both alterations, we can substitute equivalent fictitious nets composed of neurons whose connections and thresholds are unaltered. But one point must be made clear: neither of us conceives the formal equivalence to be a factual explanation. *Per contra!*—we regard facilitation and extinction as dependent upon continuous changes in threshold related to electrical and chemical variables, such as after-potentials and ionic concentrations; and learning as an enduring change which can survive sleep, anaesthesia, convulsions and coma. The importance of the formal equivalence lies in this: that the alterations actually underlying facilitation, extinction and learning in no way affect the conclusions which follow from the formal treatment of the activity of nervous nets, and the relations of the corresponding propositions remain those of the logic of propositions.

The nervous system contains many circular paths, whose activity so regenerates the excitation of any participant neuron that reference to time past becomes indefinite, although it still implies that afferent activity has realized one of a certain class of configurations over time. Precise specification of these implications by means of recursive functions, and determination of those that can be embodied in the activity of nervous nets, completes the theory.

The theory: nets without circles

We shall make the following physical assumptions for our calculus.

1. The activity of the neuron is an 'all-or-none' process.

2. A certain fixed number of synapses must be excited within the period of latent addition in order to excite a neuron at any time, and this number is independent of previous activity and position on the neuron.

3. The only significant delay within the nervous system is synaptic delay.

4. The activity of any inhibitory synapse absolutely prevents excitation of the neuron at that time.

5. The structure of the net does not change with time.

To present the theory, the most appropriate symbolism is that of Language II of R. Carnap (1938), augmented with various notations drawn from B. Russell and A. N. Whitehead (1927), including the *Principia* conventions for dots. Typographical necessity, however, will compel us to use the upright '*E*' for the existential operator instead of the inverted, and an arrow (' $\rightarrow$ ') for implication instead of the horseshoe. We shall also use the Carnap syntactical notations, but print them in boldface rather than German type; and we shall introduce a functor S, whose value for a property P is the property which holds of a number when P holds of its predecessor; it is defined by '$S(P)$ (t). $\equiv$.$P(Kx)$. $t = x$'); the brackets around its argument will often be omitted, in which case this is understood to be the nearest predicate-expression [*Pr*] on the right. Moreover, we shall write $S^2 Pr$ for $S(S(Pr))$, etc.

The neurons of a given net $\mathfrak{N}$ may be assigned designations 'c_1', 'c_2', ..., 'c_n'. This done, we shall denote the property of a number, that a neuron c_i fires at a time which is that number of synaptic delays from the origin of time, by 'N' with the numeral i as subscript, so that $N_i(t)$ asserts that c_i fires at the time t. N_i is called the *action* of c_i. We shall sometimes regard the subscripted numeral of 'N' as if it belonged to the object-language, and were in a place for a functoral argument, so that it might be replaced by a number-variable [z] and quantified; this enables us to abbreviate long but finite disjunctions and conjunctions by the use of an operator. We shall employ this locution quite generally for sequences of *Pr*; it may be secured formally by an obvious disjunctive definition. The predicates 'N_1' 'N_2', ..., comprise the syntactical class 'N'.

Let us define the *peripheral afferents* of $\mathfrak{N}$ as the neurons of $\mathfrak{N}$ with no axons synapsing upon them. Let N_1, ..., N_p denote the actions of such neurons and $N_{p+1}, N_{p+2}, ..., N_n$ those of the rest. Then a *solution of* $\mathfrak{N}$ will be a class of sentences of the form $S_i N_{p+1}(z_1) . \equiv . Pr_i(N_1, N_2, ..., N_p, z_1)$, where Pr_i, contains no free variable save z_1 and no descriptive symbols save the N in the argument [*Arg*], and possibly some constant sentences [*sa*]; and such that each S_i is true of $\mathfrak{N}$. Conversely, given a $Pr_1({}^1p_1, {}^1p_2, ..., {}^1p_p, z_1, s)$, containing no free variable save those in its *Arg*, we shall say that it is *realizable in the narrow sense* if there exists a net $\mathfrak{N}$ and a series of N_i in it such that $N_1 (z_1) . \equiv . Pr_1 (N_1, N_2, \ldots, z_1, sa_1)$ is true of it, where sa_1 has the form $N(0)$. We shall call it *realizable in the extended sense*, or simply *realizable*, if for some $nS^n (Pr_1) (p_1, \ldots, p_{p1}, z_1, s)$ is realizable in the above sense. c_{pi} is here the realizing neuron. We shall say of two laws of nervous excitation which are such that every S which is realizable in either sense upon one supposition is also realizable, perhaps by a different net, upon the other, that they are equivalent assumptions, in that sense.

The following theorems about realizability all refer to the extended sense. In some cases, sharper theorems about narrow realizability can be obtained; but in addition to greater complication in statement this were of little practical value, since our present neurophysiological knowledge determines the law of excitation only to extended equivalence, and the more precise theorems differ according to which possible assumption we make. Our less precise theorems, however, are invariant under equivalence, and are still sufficient for all purposes in which the exact time for impulses to pass through the whole net is not crucial.

Our central problems may now be stated exactly: first, to find an effective method of obtaining a set of computable S constituting a solution of any given net; and second, to characterize the class of realizable S in an effective fashion. Materially stated, the problems are to calculate the behavior of any net, and to find a net which will behave in a specified way, when such a net exists.

A net will be called *cyclic* if it contains a circle; i.e., if there exists a chain $c_i, c_{i+1}, \ldots$ of neurons on it, each member of the chain synapsing upon the next, with the same beginning and end. If a set of its neurons $c_1, c_2, \ldots, c_p$ is such that its removal from $\mathfrak{N}$ leaves it without circles, and no smaller class of neurons has this property, the set is called a *cyclic* set, and its cardinality is the *order of* $\mathfrak{N}$. In an important sense, as we shall see, the order of a net is an index of the complexity of its behavior. In particular, nets of zero order have especially simple properties; we shall discuss them first.

Let us define a *temporal propositional expression* (a *TPE*), designating a *temporal propositional function* (*TPF*), by the following recursion:

1. A $^1p^1 [z_1]$ is a *TPE*, where p_1 is a predicate-variable.
2. If S_1 and S_2 are *TPE* containing the same free individual variable, so are $SS_1, S_1 v S_2, S_1 . S_2$ and $S_i \sim S_2$.
3. Nothing else is a *TPE*.

Theorem I

Every net of order 0 can be solved in terms of temporal propositional expressions.

Let c_i be any neuron of $\mathfrak{N}$ with a threshold $\theta_i > 0$, and let $c_{i1}, c_{i2}, \ldots c_{ip}$ have respectively $n_{i1}, n_{i2}, \ldots n_{ip}$ excitatory synapses upon it. Let $c_{i1}, c_{i2}, \ldots c_{iq}$ have inhibitory synapses upon it. Let κ_i be the set of the subclasses of $\{n_{i1}, n_{i2} \ldots, n_{ip}\}$ such that the sum of their members exceeds θ_i. We shall then be able to write, in accordance with the assumptions mentioned above,

$$N_i(z_1) . \equiv . S\left\{ \prod_{m=1}^{q} \sim N_{jm}(z_1) . \sum_{a \in \kappa_i} \prod_{\delta \in a} N_{\delta}(z_1) \right\} \tag{1}$$

where the 'Σ' and 'Π' are syntactical symbols for disjunctions and conjunctions which are finite in each case. Since an expression of this form can be written for each c_i which is not a peripheral afferent, we can, by substituting the corresponding expression in (1) for each N_{jm} or N_{is} whose neuron is not a peripheral afferent, and repeating the process on the result, ultimately come to an expression for N_i in terms solely of peripherally afferent N, since $\mathfrak{N}$ is without circles. Moreover, this expression will be a *TPE*, since obviously (1) is; and it follows immediately from the definition that the result of substituting a *TPE* for a constituent $p(z)$ in a *TPE* is also one.

Theorem II

Enery TPE *is realizable by a net of order zero.*

The functor S obviously commutes with disjunction, conjunction, and negation. It is obvious that the result of substituting any S_i, realizable in the narrow sense (i.n.s.), for the $p(z)$ in a realizable expression S_1 is itself realizable i.n.s.; one constructs the realizing net by replacing the peripheral afferents in the net for S_i by the realizing neurons in the nets for the S_i. The one neuron net realizes $p_1(z_1)$ i.n.s., and Figure 1a shows a net that realizes $S p_1(z_1)$ and hence $S S_2$, i.n.s., if S_2 can be realized i.n.s. Now if S_2 and S_3 are realizable then $S^m S_2$ and $S^n S_3$ are realizable i.n.s., for suitable m and n. Hence so are $S^{m+n} S_2$ and $S^{m+n} S_3$. Now the nets of Figures 1b, c and d respectively realize $S(p_1(z_1) \vee p_2(z_1))$, $S(p_1(z_1) . (p_2(z_1))$, and $S(p_1(z_1). \sim p_2(z_1))$ i.n.s. Hence $S^{m+b+1}(S_1 \vee S_2)$, $S^{m+n+1} (S_1 . S_2)$, and $S^{m+n+1} (S_1 . \sim S_2)$ are realizable i.n.s. Therefore $S_1 \vee S_2, S_1 . S_2, S_1 . \sim S_2$ are realizable if S_1 and S_2 are. By complete induction, all *TPE* are realizable. In this way all nets may be regarded as built out of the fundamental elements of Figures 1a, b, c, d, precisely as the temporal propositional expressions are generated out of the operations of precession, disjunction, conjunction, and conjoined negation. In particular, corresponding to any description of state, or distribution of the values *true* and *false* for the actions of all the neurons of a net save that which makes them all false, a single neuron is constructible whose firing is a necessary and sufficient condition for the validity of that description. Moreover, there is always an indefinite number of topologically different nets realizing any *TPE*.

Theorem III

Let there be given a complex sentence S_1 built up in any manner out of elementary sentences of the form $p(z_1 - zz)$ where zz is any numeral, by any of the propositional connections: negation, disjunction, conjunction, implication, and equivalence. Then S_1 is a TPE and only if it is false when its constituent $p(z_i - zz)$ are all assumed false—i.e., replaced by false sentences—or that the last line in its truth-table contains an 'F',—or there is no term in its Hilbert disjunctive normal form composed exclusively of negated terms.

These latter three conditions are of course equivalent (Hilbert and Ackermann, 1938). We see by induction that the first of them is necessary, since $p(z_i - zz)$ becomes false when it is replaced by a false sentence, and S_1 v S_2, $S_1 . S_2$, and $S_1 . \sim S_2$ are all false if both their constituents are. We see that the last condition is sufficient by remarking that a disjunction is a *TPE* when its constituents are, and that any term

$$S_1 . S_2 \ldots . S_m . \sim S_{m+1} . \sim \ldots . \sim S_n$$

can be written as

$$(S_1 . S_2 \ldots . S_m) . \sim (S_{m+1} v S_{m+2} v \ldots . v S_n),$$

which is clearly a *TPE*.

The method of the last theorems does in fact provide a very convenient and workable procedure for constructing nervous nets to order, for those cases where there is no reference to events indefinitely far in the past in the specification of the conditions. By way of example, we may consider the case of heat produced by a transient cooling.

If a cold object is held to the skin for a moment and removed, a sensation of heat will be felt; if it is applied for a longer time, the sensation will be only of cold, with no preliminary warmth, however transient. It is known that one cutaneous receptor is affected by heat, and another by cold. If we let N_1 and N_2 be the actions of the respective receptors and N_3 and N_4 of neurons whose activity implies a sensation of heat and cold, our requirements may be written as

$$N_3(t) : \equiv : N_1(t-1) . v . N_2(t-3) . \sim N_2(t-2)$$
$$N_4(t) . \equiv . N_2(t-2) . N_2(t-1)$$

where we suppose for simplicity that the required persistence in the sensation of cold is, say, two synaptic delays, compared with one for that of heat. These conditions clearly fall under Theorem III. A net may consequently be constructed to realize them, by the method of Theorem II. We begin by writing

384

them in a fashion which exhibits them as built out of their constituents by the operations realized in Figures 1a, b, c, d: i.e., in the form

$$N_3(t) . \equiv . S\{N_1(t) \text{ v } S[(SN_2(t)) . \sim N_2(t)]\}$$
$$N_4(t) . \equiv . S\{[SN_2(t)] . N_2(t)\}.$$

First we construct a net for the function enclosed in the greatest number of brackets and proceed outward; in this case we run a net of the form shown in Figure 1a from c_2 to some neuron c_a, say, so that

$$N_4(t) . \equiv . SN_2(t).$$

Next introduce two nets of the forms 1c and 1d, both running from c_a and c_2, and ending respectively at c_4 and say c_b. Then

$$N_4(t) . \equiv . S[N_a(t) . N_2(t)] . \equiv . S[(SN_2(t)) . N_2(t)].$$
$$N_b(t) . \equiv . S[N_a(t) . \sim N_2(t)] . \equiv . S[(SN_2(t)) . \sim N_2(t)].$$

Finally, run a net of the form 1b from c_1 and c_b to c_3, and derive

$$N_3(t) . \equiv . S[N_1(t)] \text{ v } N_b(t)] . \equiv . S\{N_1(t) \text{ v } S[(SN_2(t)) . \sim N_2(t)]\}.$$

These expressions for $N_3(t)$ and $N_4(t)$ are the ones desired; and the realizing net *in toto* is shown in Figure 1e.

This illusion makes very clear the dependence of the correspondence between perception and the 'external world' upon the specific structural properties of the intervening nervous net. The same illusion, of course, could also have been produced under various other assumptions about the behavior of the cutaneous receptors, with correspondingly different nets.

We shall now consider some theorems of equivalence: i.e., theorems which demonstrate the essential identity, save for time, of various alternative laws of nervous excitation. Let us first discuss the case of *relative inhibition*. By this we mean the supposition that the firing of an inhibitory synapse does not absolutely prevent the firing of the neuron, but merely raises its threshold, so that a greater number of excitatory synapses must fire concurrently to fire it than would otherwise be needed. We may suppose, losing no generality, that the increase in threshold is unity for the firing of each such synapse; we then have the theorem:

Theorem IV

Relative and absolute inhibition are equivalent in the extended sense.

We may write out a law of nervous excitation after the fashion of (1), but employing the assumption of relative inhibition instead; inspection then shows that this expression is a *TPE*. An example of the replacement of relative inhibition by absolute is given by Figure 1f. The reverse replacement is even easier; we give the inhibitory axons afferent to c_i any sufficiently large number of inhibitory synapses apiece.

Second, we consider the case of extinction. We may write this in the form of a variation in the threshold θ_i after the neuron c_i has fired; to the nearest integer—and only to this approximation is the variation in threshold significant in natural forms of excitation—this may be written as a sequence $\theta_i + b_j$ for j synaptic delays after firing, where $b_j = 0$ for j large enough, say $j = M$ or greater. We may then state

Theorem V

Extinction is equivalent to absolute inhibition.

For, assuming relative inhibition to hold for the moment, we need merely run M circuits $\mathcal{T}_1, \mathcal{T}_2, \ldots \mathcal{T}_M$ containing respectively $1, 2, \ldots, M$ neurons, such that the firing of each link in any is sufficient to fire the next, from the neuron c_i back to it, where the end of the circuit $\mathcal{T}_j$ has just b_j inhibitory synapses upon c_i. It is evident that this will produce the desired results. The reverse substitution may be accomplished by the diagram of Figure 1g. From the transitivity of replacement, we infer the theorem. To this group of theorems also belongs the well-known

Theorem VI

Facilitation and temporal summation may be replaced by spatial summation.

This is obvious: one need merely introduce a suitable sequence of delaying chains, of increasing numbers of synapses, between the exciting cell and the neuron whereon temporal summation is desired to hold. The assumption of spatial summation will then give the required results. See e.g. Figure 1h. This procedure had application in showing that the observed temporal summation in gross nets does not imply such a mechanism in the interaction of individual neurons.

The phenomena of learning, which are of a character persisting over most physiological changes in nervous activity, seem to require the possibility of permanent alterations in the structure of nets. The simplest such alteration is the formation of new synapses or equivalent local depressions of threshold. We suppose that some axonal terminations cannot at first excite the succeeding neuron; but if at any time the neuron fires, and the axonal terminations are simultaneously excited, they become synapses of the ordinary kind, henceforth capable of exciting the neuron. The loss of an inhibitory synapse gives an entirely equivalent result. We shall then have

Theorem VII

Alterable synapses can be replaced by circles.

This is accomplished by the method of Figure 1i. It is also to be remarked that a neuron which becomes and remains spontaneously active can likewise be replaced by a circle, which is set into activity by a peripheral afferent when the activity commences, and inhibited by one when it ceases.

The theory: nets with circles

The treatment of nets which do not satisfy our previous assumption of freedom from circles is very much more difficult than that case. This is largely a consequence of the possibility that activity may be set up in a circuit and continue reverberating around it for an indefinite period of time, so that the realizable *Pr* may involve reference to past events of an indefinite degree of remoteness. Consider such a net $\mathfrak{N}$, say of order p, and let $c_1, c_2, \ldots, c_p$ be a cyclic set of neurons of $\mathfrak{N}$. It is first of all clear from the definition that every N_a of $\mathfrak{N}$ can be expressed as a *TPE*, of $N_1, N_2, \ldots, N_p$ and the absolute afferents; the solution of $\mathfrak{N}$ involves then only the determination of expressions for the cyclic set. This done, we shall derive a set of expressions [*A*]:

$$N_i(z_1) . \equiv . Pr_i[S^{n_{i1}} N_1(z_1), S^{n_{i2}} N_2(z_1), \ldots, S^{n_{ip}} N_p(z_1)], \qquad (2)$$

where Pr_i also involves peripheral afferents. Now if n is the least common multiple of the n_{ij}, we shall, by substituting their equivalents according to (2) in (3) for the N_j, and repeating this process often enough on the result, obtain S of the form

$$N_i(z_1) . \equiv . Pr_i[S^n N_1(z_1), S^n N_2(z_1), \ldots, S^n N_p(z_1)]. \qquad (3)$$

These expression may be written in the Hilbert disjunctive normal form as

$$N_i(z_1) . \equiv . \underset{\substack{a \, \varepsilon \, \kappa \\ \beta_a \, \varepsilon \, \kappa}}{\Sigma} S_a \underset{j \, \varepsilon \, \kappa}{\Pi} S^n N_j(z_1) \underset{j \, \varepsilon \, \beta_a}{\Pi} a \sim S^n N_j(z_1), \text{ for suitable } \kappa, \qquad (4)$$

where S_a is a *TPE* of the absolute afferents of $\mathfrak{N}$. There exist some 2^p different sentences formed out of the pN_i by conjoining to the conjunction of some set of them the conjunction of the negations of the rest. Denumerating these by $X_1(z_1), X_2(z_1), \ldots X_{2p}(z_1)$, we may, by use of the expression (4); arrive at an equipollent set of equations of the form

$$X_i(z_1) . \equiv . \underset{j=1}{\overset{2p}{\Sigma}} Pr_{ij}(z_1) . S^n X_j(z_1). \qquad (5)$$

Now we import the subscripted minerals i,j into the object-language: i.e., define Pr_1 and Pr_2 such that $Pr_1(zz_1,z_1) \; . \equiv . \; X_i(z_1)$ and $Pr_2(zz_1,zz_2,z_1) \; . \equiv . \; Pr_{ij}(z_1)$ are provable whenever zz_1 and zz_2 denote i and j respectively. Then we may rewrite (5) as

$$(z_1)zz_p : Pr_1(z_1, z_3) \; . \equiv . \; (Ez_2)zz_p \; . \; Pr_2(z_1, z_2, z_3 - zz_a) \; . \; Pr_1(z_2, z_3 - zz) \qquad (6)$$

where zz_m denotes n and zz_p denotes 2^p. By repeated substitution we arrive at an expression

$$(z_1)zz_p : Pr_1(z_1, zz_n zz_2) \; . \equiv . \; (Ez_2)zz_p \, (Ez_3)zz_p \ldots (Ez_n)zz_p$$

$$Pr_2(z_1, z_2, zz_n \, (zz_2 - 1)) \; . \; Pr_2(z_2, z_3, zz_2 \, (zz_2 - 1)) \; . \ldots \qquad (7)$$

$Pr_2(z_{n-1}, z_n, 0) \; . \; Pr_1(z_n, 0)$, for any numeral zz_2 which denotes s. This is easily shown by induction to be equipollent to

$$(z_1)zz_p : . \; Pr_2(z_1, zz_n zz_2) : \equiv : (Ef) \, (z_2)zz_2 - 1 \, f\,(z_2 zz_n)$$

$$\leqq zz_p \; . \; f(zz_n, zz_2 = z_1 \; . \; Pr_2(f(zz_n \, (z_2 + 1)), \qquad (8)$$

$$f(zz_n z_2)) \; . \; Pr_1(f(0), 0)$$

and since this is the case for all zz_2, it is also true that

$$(z_4) \, (z_1)zz_p : Pr_1 \, (z_1, z_4) \; . \equiv . \; (Ef) \, (z_2) \, (z_4 - 1) \; . \; f(z_2)$$

$$\leqq zz_p \; . \; f(z_4) = z_1 f(z_4) = z_1 \; . \; Pr_2[f(z_2 + 1), f(z_2), z_2] \; . \qquad (9)$$

$$Pr_1[f(\text{res}\,(z_4, zz_n)), \text{res}\,(z_4, zz_n)],$$

where zz_n denotes n, res (r,s) is the residue of r mod s and zz_p denotes 2^p. This may be written in a less exact way as

$$N_i(t) \; . \equiv . \; (E\varphi) \, (x)t - 1 \; . \; \varphi \, (x) < 2^p \; . \; \varphi(t) = i \; . \; P[\varphi(x + 1), \varphi(x) \; . \; N_{\varphi(o)} \, (0)],$$

where x and t are also assumed divisible by n, and Pr_2 denotes P. From the preceding remarks we shall have

Theorem VIII

The expression (9) for neurons of the cyclic set of a net $\mathfrak{N}$ together with certain TPE expressing the actions of other neurons in terms of them, constitute a solution of $\mathfrak{N}$.

Consider now the question of the realizability of a set of S_i. A first necessary condition, demonstrable by an easy induction, is that

$$(z_2)z_1 \cdot p_1(z_2) \equiv p_2(z_2) \cdot \rightarrow \cdot S_i \equiv S_i \left\{ \begin{matrix} p_1 \\ p_2 \end{matrix} \right\} \tag{10}$$

should be true, with similar statements for the other free p in S_i: i.e., no nervous net can take account of future peripheral afferents. Any S_i satisfying this requirement can be replaced by an equipollent S of the form

$$(Ef) (z_2)z_1 (z_3) zz_p : f \in Pr_{mi} : f(z_1, z_2, z_3 = 1 . \equiv . p_{z3}(z_2) \tag{11}$$

where zz_p denotes p, by defining

$$Pr_{mi} = \hat{f}[(z_1) (z_2)z_1(z_3)zz_p : . f(z_1, z_2, z_3) = 0 . v . f(z_1, z_2, z_3)$$
$$= 1 : f(z_1, z_2, z_3) = 1 . \equiv . p_{z3}(z_2) : \rightarrow : S_i].$$

Consider now these series of classes a_i, for which

$$N_i(t) : \equiv : (E\varphi) (x)t(m)q : \varphi \in a_i : N_m(x) . \equiv . \varphi(t, x, m) = 1.$$
$$[i = q + 1, \ldots, M] \tag{12}$$

holds for some net. These will be called *prehensible* classes. Let us define the *Boolean ring* generated by a class of classes κ as the aggregate of the classes which can be formed from members of κ by repeated application of the logical operations; i.e., we put

$$\mathcal{R}(\kappa) = p`\hat{\lambda}[(\alpha, \beta) : \alpha \in \kappa \rightarrow \alpha \in \lambda : \alpha, \beta \in \lambda . \rightarrow . - \alpha, \alpha . \beta, \alpha \vee \beta \in \lambda].$$

We shall also define

$$\overline{\mathcal{R}} (\kappa) . = . \mathcal{R}(\kappa) - \iota`p` - ``\kappa,$$
$$\mathcal{R}_e(\kappa) = p' \lambda[(\alpha, \beta) : \alpha \in \kappa \rightarrow \alpha \in \lambda . \rightarrow . - \alpha, \alpha . \beta, \alpha, \vee \beta, S ``\alpha \in \hat{\lambda}$$
$$\overline{\mathcal{R}}_e(\kappa) = \mathcal{R}_e(\kappa) - t `p` - ``\kappa,$$

and

$$\sigma(\psi, t) = \hat{\varphi}[(m) . \varphi(t + 1, t, m) = \psi(m)].$$

The class $\mathcal{R}_e(\kappa)$ is formed from κ in analogy with $\mathcal{R}(\kappa)$, but by repeated application not only of the logical operations but also of that which replaces a class of properties $P \in a$ by $S(P) \in S ``a$. We shall then have the

LEMMA

$Pr_1(p_1, p_2, \ldots, p_m, z_1)$ is a *TPE* if and only if

389

$(z_1) (p_1 \ldots, p_m) (Ep_{m+1}) : P_{m+1} \in (\overline{\mathcal{R}_c}(\{p_1, p_2 \ldots, p_m\})$

$$p_{m+1}(z_1) \equiv Pr_1 (p_1, p_2, \ldots, p_m, z_1) \tag{13}$$

is true; and it is a *TPE* not involving '*S*' if and only if this holds when '$\overline{\mathcal{R}_c}$' is replaced by '$\mathcal{R}$', and we then obtain

Theorem IX

A series of classes a_1, a_2, ... a_z is a series of prehensible classes if and only if

$(Em) (En) (p)n(i) (\varphi) : . (x)m\psi(x) = 0 \text{ v } \psi (x = 1 : \rightarrow : (E\beta)$

$(Ey)m . \psi(y) = 0 . \beta \in \mathcal{R}[(\hat{\gamma}(Ei) . \gamma = a_i)) . \text{v} . (x)m .$

$$\hat{\gamma}(x) = 0 . \beta \in [\hat{\gamma}((E_i) . \gamma = a_i)] : (t) (\varphi) : \varphi \in a_i . \tag{14}$$

$\sigma(\varphi, nt + p) . \rightarrow . (Ef) . f \in \beta . (w)m(x)t - 1 .$

$\varphi(n(t + 1) + p, nx + p, w) = f(nt + p, nx + p, w).$

The proof here follows directly from the lemma. The condition is necessary, since every net for which an expression of the form (4) can be written obviously verifies it, the ψ's being the characteristic functions of the S_a and the β for each ψ being the class whose designation has the form $\underset{i \in a}{\Pi Pr_i} \underset{j \in \beta}{\Pi Pr_j}$, where Pr_κ denotes a_κ for all k. Conversely, we may write an expression of the form (4) for a net $\mathcal{R}$ fulfilling prehensible classes satisfying (14) by putting for the Pr_a Pr denoting the ψ's and a Pr, written in the analogue for classes of the disjunctive normal form, and denoting the a corresponding to that ψ, conjoined to it. Since every S of the form (4) is clearly realizable, we have the theorem.

It is of some interest to consider the extent to which we can by knowledge of the present determine the whole past of various special nets: i.e., when we may construct a net the firing of the cyclic set of whose neurons requires the peripheral afferents to have had a set of past values specified by given functions φ_i. In this case the classes a_i of the last theorem reduced to unit classes; and the condition may be transformed into

$(E m, n) (p)n(i, \psi) (Ej) : . (x)m: \psi(x) = 0 . \text{v} . \psi(\chi) = 1:$

$\varphi_i \in \sigma(\psi, nt + p) : \rightarrow : (w)m(x)t - 1 . \varphi_i(n(t + 1)$

$+ p, nx + p, w) = \varphi_j (nt + p, nx + p, w) : .$

$(u, v) (w)m . \varphi_i (n(u + 1) + p, nu + p, w)$

$= \varphi_i (n(v + 1) + p, nv + p, w).$

On account of limitations of space, we have presented the above argument very sketchily; we propose to expand it and certain of its implications in a further publication.

The condition of the last theorem is fairly simple in principle, though not in detail; its application to practical cases would, however, require the exploration of some 2^{2n} classes of functions, namely the members of $\mathfrak{R}(\{a_1, \ldots, a_s\})$. Since each of these is a possible β of Theorem IX, this result cannot be sharpened. But we may obtain a sufficient condition for the realizability of an S which is very easily applicable and probably covers most practical purposes. This is given by

Theorem X

Let us define a set of K of S by the following recursion:

1. Any *TPE* and any *TPE* whose arguments have been replaced by members of K belong to K;
2. If $Pr_1(z_1)$ is a member of K, then $(z_2)z_1 . Pr_1(z_2)$, $(Ez_2)z_1 . Pr_1(z_2)$, and $C_{mn}(z_1) . s$ belong to it, where C_{mn} denotes the property of being congruent to m modulo n, $m < n$.
3. *The set K has no further members.*

Then every member of K is realizable.
For, if $Pr_1(z_1)$ is realizable, nervous nets for which

$$N_i(z_1) . \equiv . Pr_1(z_1) . SN_i(z_1)$$

$$N_i(z_1) . \equiv . Pr_1(z_1) \vee SN_i(z_1)$$

are the expressions of equation (4), realize $(z_2)z_1 . Pr_1(z_2)$ and $(E z_2)z_1 . Pr_1(z_2)$ respectively; and a simple circuit, $c_1, c_2, \ldots, c_n$, of n links, each sufficient to excite the next, gives an expression

$$N_m(z_1) . \equiv . N_1(0) . C_{mn}$$

for the last form. By induction we derive the theorem.

One more thing is to be remarked in conclusion. It is easily shown: first, that every net, if furnished with a tape, scanners connected to afferents, and suitable efferents to perform the necessary motor-operations, can compute only such numbers as can a Turing machine; second, that each of the latter numbers can be computed by such a net; and that nets with circles can be computed by such a net; and that nets with circles can compute, without scanners and a tape, some of the numbers the machine can, but no others, and not all of them. This is of interest as affording a psychological justification of the Turing definition of computability and its equivalents, Church's λ—definability and Kleene's primitive recursiveness: If any number can be

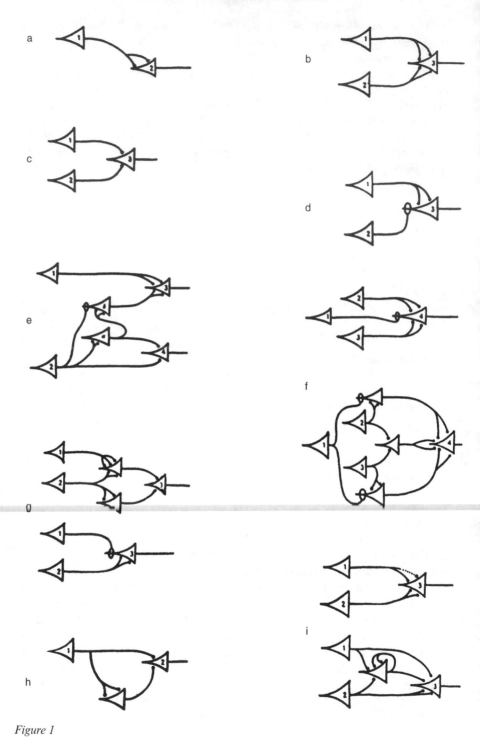

Figure 1

computed by an organism, it is computable by these definitions, and conversely.

Consequences

Causality, which requires description of states and a law of necessary connection relating them, has appeared in several forms in several sciences, but never, except in statistics, has it been as irreciprocal as in this theory. Specification for any one time of afferent stimulation and of the activity of all constituent neurons, each an 'all-or-none' affair, determines the state. Specification of the nervous net provides the law of necessary connection whereby one can compute from the description of any state that of the succeeding state, but the inclusion of disjunctive relations prevents complete determination of the one before. Moreover, the regenerative activity of constituent circles renders reference indefinite as to time past. Thus our knowledge of the world, including ourselves, is incomplete as to space and indefinite as to time. This ignorance, implicit in all our brains, is the counterpart of the abstraction which renders our knowledge useful. The role of brains in determining the epistemic relations of our theories to our observations and of these to the facts is all too clear, for it is apparent that every idea and every sensation is realized by activity within that net, and by no such activity are the actual afferents fully determined.

There is no theory we may hold and no observation we can make that will retain so much as its old defective reference to the facts if the net be altered. Tinnitus, paraesthesias, hallucinations, delusions, confusions and disorientations intervene. Thus empiry confirms that if our nets are undefined, our

---

EXPRESSION FOR THE FIGURES

In the figure the neuron c_i is always marked with the numeral i upon the body of the cell, and the corresponding action is denoted by 'N' with ι as subscript, as in the text

Figure 1a $N_2(t) . = . N_1(t-1)$

Figure 1b $N_3(t) . \equiv . N_1(t-1) \text{ v } N_2(t-1)$

Figure 1c $N_3(t) . \equiv . N_1(t-1) . N_2(t-1)$

Figure 1d $N_3(t) . \equiv . N_1(t-1) . \sim N_2(t-1)$

Figure 1e $N_3(t) : \equiv : N_1(t-1) . \text{v} . N_2(t-3) . \sim N_2(t-2)$

          $N_4(t) . \equiv . N_2(t-2) . N_2(t-1)$

Figure 1f $N_4(t) : \equiv : \sim N_1(t-1) . N_2(t-1) \text{ v } N_3(t-1) . \text{v} . N_1(t-1) .$

                 $N_2(t-1) . N_3(t-1)$

          $N_4(t) : \equiv : \sim N_1(t-2) . N_2(t-2) \text{ v } N_3(t-2) . \text{v} . N_1(t-2) .$

                 $N_2(t-2) . N_3(t-2)$

Figure 1g $N_3(t) . \equiv . N_2(t-2) . \sim N_1(t-3)$

Figure 1h $N_2(t) . \equiv . N_1(t-1) . N_1(t-2)$

Figure 1i $N_3(t) : \equiv : N_2(t-1) . \text{v} . N_1(t-1) . (Ex)t-1 . N_1(x) . N_2(x)$

---

facts are undefined, and to the 'real' we can attribute not so much as one quality or 'form.' With determination of the net, the unknowable object of knowledge, the 'thing in itself,' ceases to be unknowable.

To psychology, however defined, specification of the net would contribute all that could be achieved in that field—even if the analysis were pushed to ultimate psychic units or 'psychons,' for a psychon can be no less than the activity of a single neuron. Since that activity is inherently propositional, all psychic events have an intentional, or 'semiotic,' character. The 'all-or-none' law of these activities, and the conformity of their relations to those of the logic of propositions, insure that the relations of psychons are those of the two-valued logic of propositions. Thus in psychology, introspective, behavioristic or physiological, the fundamental relations are those of two-valued logic.

Hence arise constructional solutions of holistic problems involving the differentiated continuum of sense awareness and the normative, perfective and resolvent properties of perception and execution. From the irreciprocity of causality it follows that even if the net be known, though we may predict future from present activities, we can deduce neither afferent from central, nor central from efferent, nor past from present activities—conclusions which are reinforced by the contradictory testimony of eye-witnesses, by the difficulty of diagnosing differentially the organically diseased, the hysteric and the malingerer, and by comparing one's own memories or recollections with his contemporaneous records. Moreover, systems which so respond to the difference between afferents to a regenerative net and certain activity within that net, as to reduce the difference, exhibit purposive behavior; and organisms are known to possess many such systems, subserving homeostasis, appetition and attention. Thus both the formal and the final aspects of that activity which we are wont to call *mental* are rigorously deducible from present neurophysiology. The psychiatrist may take comfort from the obvious conclusion concerning causality—that, for prognosis, history is never necessary. He can take little from the equally valid conclusion that his observables are explicable only in terms of nervous activities which, until recently, have been beyond his ken. The crux of this ignorance is that inference from any sample of overt behavior to nervous nets is not unique, whereas, of imaginable nets, only one in fact exists, and may, at any moment, exhibit some unpredictable activity. Certainly for the psychiatrist it is more to the point that in such systems 'Mind' no longer 'goes more ghostly than a ghost.' Instead, diseased mentality can be understood without loss of scope or rigor, in the scientific terms of neurophysiology. For neurology, the theory sharpens the distinction between nets necessary or merely sufficient for given activities, and so clarifies the relations of disturbed structure to disturbed function. In its own domain the difference between equivalent nets and nets equivalent in the narrow sense indicates the appropriate use and importance of temporal studies of nervous activity: and to mathematical biophysics the

394

theory contributes a tool for rigorous symbolic treatment of known nets and an easy method of constructing hypothetical nets of required properties.

References

1. Carnap, R.: *The Logical Syntax of Language*. New York, Harcourt, Brace and Company, 1938.
2. Hilbert, D., und Ackermann, W.: *Grundüge der Theoretischen Logik*. Berlin, J. Springer, 1927.
3. Whitehead, A. N., and Russell, B.: *Principia Mathematica*. Cambridge, Cambridge University Press, 1925.

21

DESCRIBING "EMBODIMENTS OF MIND"

McCulloch and his cohorts

S. J. Heims

Source: *Constructing a Social Science for Post War America: The Cybernetics Group 1946–1953*, MIT Press, 1991, pp. 31–51.

How do the people most deeply committed to scientific investigation use ideas and concepts? Albert Einstein spoke for many when he described the motives for scientific studies:

> Man seeks to form for himself, in whatever manner is suitable for him, a simplified and lucid image of our world, and so to overcome the world of experience by striving to replace it to some extent by this image. This is what the painter does, and the poet, the speculative philosopher, the natural scientists, each in his own way. Into this image and its formation he places the center of gravity of his emotional life, in order to attain the peace and serenity that he cannot find within the narrow confines of swirling personal experience.[1]

What kinds of images or abstract constructions will satisfy those whose studies are centered on the human and the social? One wonders whether images of people based on automata and communications engineering could be so congenial as to be conducive to peace and serenity. Such mechanical schemes—at their most concrete, images of ourselves as complicated robots—seem to ignore the flux of our immediate experience, our sense of freedom, the pulse of life, deeper meanings, as well as personal and human feelings, and are antipathetic because they dehumanize us. They seem to invite us to think of others as mere objects to be manipulated or to give scientific legitimation to those who operate on that premise. One might think that technical research along these lines would stimulate the development of new technologies that would foster dehumanization, exploitation and oppression.[2] But are all these concerns merely expressions of unwarranted timidity?

Our story begins with Warren Sturgis McCulloch, whose work and character show these questions to be simplistic. He was born in Orange, New Jersey, on 16 November 1898, the son of James W. McCulloch and his young second wife Mary Hughes (Bradley) McCulloch. James McCulloch was a self-made businessman, manager of a large estate with holdings in railroads and mining enterprises. Warren's mother came from a Southern family. She was strongly religious, taught bible history, and was involved in Episcopalian church affairs. The McCulloch household in Orange included Warren's considerably older half-brother and his sister, Margaret, a year younger than Warren. The summers were often spent on Nantucket Island off Cape Cod, where Warren learned to sail and as a boy enjoyed the adventurous world of ships and whaling captains—leaving him with a lasting feeling for the sea.

In 1917 he entered a Quaker College, Haverford, with the intention of entering the ministry in accordance with his family's wishes, but his interests turned to philosophy and mathematics. One family member at least, Warren's sister, took up religious interests and became an active Quaker and pacifist. Warren sought understanding of who we are in mechanical rather than religious terms. In his words,

> At last we are learning to admit ignorance, suspend judgement, and forego the *explicatio ignoti per ignotium*—"God"—which has proved as futile as it is profane. Instead we seek mechanisms . . .[3]

The seeking of mechanisms in the brain to describe how cognitive functions are carried out eventually became the central theme in McCulloch's work. His interests in the thought and theology of the medieval schoolmen, however, persisted throughout his life.[4] Probably no other neurophysiologist in the twentieth century talked so much about the views of St. Bonaventura, Duns Scotus, William of Occam, or Peter Abelard—of the twelfth and thirteenth centuries. He himself resembled the medieval scientists rather than most modern ones, in that his science was "an integral part of a philosophical outlook."[5]

After graduate work in psychology (Columbia University M. A., 1923) during which he learned of the behaviorist, psychoanalytic, and introspective schools in the field, he remained unsatisfied and went to medical school. He then interned in neurology and worked in mental institutions, still with the intent of learning what he would need. In the depth of the depression (1932) McCulloch took a job in the Admissions Service of Rockland State Hospital. He found an intellectual comrade there in Eilhard von Domarus from Holland, who was engaged in an original work intended to form the basis for a "scientific psychiatry," philosophically grounded in Aristotle,

Hegel, Husserl, and Yale's Northrop. McCulloch worked with von Domarus in formulating the latter's thesis in good English.[6] Both men were concerned with logical structure of mind and its relation to neurophysiology and to madness. Domarus saw it as scientifically untenable for "the science of alienation from society and the study of physiological psychology to progress, in the main, independently." He had paid particular attention to language, whereas McCulloch emphasized the biological entities, neurons. Domarus, whom McCulloch later invited to attend the one meeting of the cybernetics group that focused on language, had pioneered the notion that the speech of schizophrenics obeys laws other than those of adult logic, and had spelled out the laws of logic he deemed characteristic of schizophrenics' language.[7]

If we accept McCulloch's elegant autobiographical account,[8] he was animated by a philosophical question that would continue to motivate him, once having accepted Bertrand Russell's concept of number: "What is a man that he may know a number?" Coming from philosophy, he was concerned, as he recalled, "with the problem of how a thing like mathematics could ever arise—what sort of a thing it was. For that reason, I gradually shifted into psychology and thence, for the reason that I again and again failed to find the significant variables, I was forced into neurophysiology."[9]

McCulloch earned his credentials as solid citizen in the world of brain research by the mainstream experimental study of chimpanzee and monkey brains he conducted during the 1930s in the laboratory of Dusser de Barenne at Yale University Medical School. Chimpanzees' and monkeys' brains are sufficiently similar to human ones that their detailed study leads at least to hypotheses concerning human brains. In particular, McCulloch studied the cerebral cortex, the gray matter forming the outermost layer of the cerebral hemispheres, which plays a prominent role in connection with the most subtle and complex mental functions. In a typical experiment McCulloch and his coworkers activated a specific region of the cortex by giving it an electric shock or applying strychnine to it. The local stimulation caused an electrical pulse to travel from one nerve cell or group of nerve cells to the next, generating an itinerary characteristic of the particular point of stimulation. They monitored the spread of the stimulus by placing recording electrodes at various points on the surface of the cerebral cortex. The purpose of this and other experiments was to map out the "functional pathways" in the cortex— the routes by which impulses actually travel in the brain. Although a number of interesting rules of behavior of impulses within the brain were derived from this research, and some innovation in experimental techniques was possible, on the whole it was systematic, detailed, tedious work aimed at generating a fund of empirical information on which neurobiologists could draw. It attests to McCulloch's standing as a leading expert on the subject that in 1944 he was chosen to write the major article reviewing the whole field of "the functional organization of the cerebral cortex."[10]

Although highly individualistic, McCulloch was never a loner. Talk with colleagues was indispensible to him. While a researcher at Yale, he joined various seminar groups and was an active participant in a philosophical seminar for research scientists in which Filmer Northrop provided the professional philosopher's perspective. Northrop recalled that

> One evening at a meeting of this Yale scientific research group, the symbolic logician, Frederic B. Fitch, gave a descriptive report of the primitive concepts and postulates of the theory of deduction and mathematical calculation in Whitehead and Russell's *Principia Mathematica* . . . Upon the presentation by Fitch, McCulloch urged Fitch to work on the symbolic logical formulation of neural nets and attended advanced lectures by Fitch on certain logical operators.[11]

The seminar provided McCulloch with a good opportunity to discuss his intellectual agenda, expose it to philosophical critique, and translate it into a seemingly practicable scientific research program. He knew that "number" could be defined by means of the logical system elaborated in *Principia Mathematica*. In that work mathematics is shown to be only a special instance of general logic. A logical proposition, McCulloch noted, is either true or false, and correspondingly a nerve cell when stimulated either produces an electrochemical discharge across its synapse or it does not. It is like an all-or-none proposition. Furthermore neurons are linked to each other in the cerebral cortex, so that one neuron's firing leads to the firing of others in a chain, analogously to how logical propositions are linked, the truth of one implying that of another. If such a correspondence between logic and nets of neurons in the cortex could be formally established, one could view the neural nets as functionally equivalent to a large general-purpose logical reasoning machine or a computer. Laboratory studies of the functional organization of the nervous system would be a step toward an experimental epistemology. Through the combined use of rigorous formal logic and careful neurophysiological experiments one could presumably learn scientifically to know how we know numbers and much more, and express this understanding in terms of mechanism.

Such a research program providing knowledge of cognitive processes was not only scientifically but also philosophically exciting: It gave explicit form for testing the question, Is such knowledge of a different type than other scientific knowledge, say how the heart works, because it is reflexive, in the sense of mind knowing itself? It would fulfill some of the thinking of seventeenth- and eighteenth-century philosophers, especially some of Leibniz's ideas about knowing and perceiving developed in his *Monadology*, which McCulloch was reading at the time.[12] Kant's notion of synthetic *a priori* knowledge would be given a material basis, as both Northrop and Dusser de Barenne appreciated. It was also in the tradition of Descartes' efforts in the experimental study of the nervous system to inform epistemology, turning a philosophical problem into a scientific one.[13] At the same time exploration along these lines could provide a scientific description encompassing both sides of the dichotomy of mind and body, thereby apparently overcoming Cartesian dualism. McCulloch envisioned such a research program but lacked the considerable mathematical and logical prowess needed to make progress with it. Nor did Fitch at the time see how to do it properly.[14]

The inner-directed, individualistic Warren McCulloch was on his own kind of scientific-epistemological quest for understanding mind and brain. Although he could and did identify a long and honorable lineage of intellectual predecessors with an outlook similar to his own, he was out of step with the predominant thinking in universities and research centers in the thirties and early forties, as his interest in thinking mind was congenial to neither behavioristic nor psychoanalytic schools of thought. (At the time it was congenial to Rashevsky's small group in mathematical biophysics at the University of Chicago, as well as to Northrop. It became widely acceptable, however, only after the Second World War, as prototype high-speed electronic computers were being designed and built.) In fact some of McCulloch's public self-descriptions suggest that he was animated by a sense of being a daring pioneer and sometimes thought of himself as akin to the heroes of mythology and legend, who courageously set out on a journey to obtain a boon to benefit mankind. His journey was an intellectual one, the holy grail was a formal logical description of the functioning of the brain, explicating mind in terms of mechanism, and the boon would be of the nature of knowledge. He wrote:

> Even Clerk Maxwell, who wanted nothing more than to know the relation between thoughts and the molecular motions of the brain, cut short his query with the memorable phrase, "but does not the way to it lie through the very den of the metaphysician, strewn with the bones of former explorers and abhorred by every man of science?" Let us peacefully answer the first half of this question "Yes," the second half "No," and then proceed serenely. Our adventure is actually a great heresy.[15]

McCulloch was careful to point out that he was interested in those facets of mind that are amenable to description in terms of rigorous logic and neurophysiology, and he gladly left out of consideration whatever else may constitute human mind and soul. He sought to push mechanism to describe embodiments of mind, so as to demystify knowing, as far as possible, and separate genuine mysteries from what is scientifically knowable. In his own words, one of his objectives was to "exorcise ghosts" from the description of mind and replace them with mechanistic hypotheses sufficiently specific to be tested experimentally. Although his own ability and training as a logician were limited, he sought the crystal clarity of abstract logic and mechanism.

He admired brilliant logical minds. As an experimenter in the laboratory, as well as on the farm near New Haven where he lived, he respected and had an excellent rapport with the instruments, tools, and machinery with which he worked.

In a contentious discussion of the metaphor of the machine, McCulloch on one occasion, when he was along in years, said rather sharply: "I don't particularly like people, never have. Man to my mind is about the nastiest, most destructive of all the animals. I don't see any reason, if he can evolve machines that can have more fun than he himself can, why they shouldn't take over, enslave us, quite happily. They might have a lot more fun, invent better games than we ever did."[16] Whatever his personal disappointments with people may have been, man's inhumanity to man, in small ways and large, is and was no secret.

On other occasions over the years McCulloch spoke of a feeling (love) for machines, comments that puzzled anthropocentric humanists and disturbed psychoanalysts. He was furthermore convinced that machines can be designed that "suffer emotions."[17] What is clear is that for McCulloch, who was at home repairing, using, building machinery, neither the den of the metaphysician nor mechanical images held any terror. In fact, for him such images may have been conducive to the peace and serenity that Einstein referred to in speaking of the motives for research.

Yet even the above quotation indicates the high value McCulloch put on the capacity to play and to "have fun." Those who knew him spoke of his enormous sense of delight, fun, joy. Although games can be described and the act of playing analyzed, these are distinct from the fun of it. As Huizinga said, "The *fun* of playing resists all analysis, all logical interpretation. As a concept, it cannot be reduced to any other mental category."[18] McCulloch's scientific preoccupation was with organic mechanisms rather than with experimental phenomena. When focusing on that level of explanation, it is easy to fall prey to the fallacy of misplaced concreteness and forget that no description of mechanism informs us about the nature of "having fun." But no matter, McCulloch turned the machine into a "subject" and—at least in 1968—readily attributed to some electronic devices the experience of having fun. He was intent on "humanizing the machine," as he put it.

At the time of the Macy meetings, although already inclined to humanize the machine, McCulloch had—in a lecture in 1948—in passing allowed that humans are distinguished from robot-automatons (those in existence at that time), first by the process of individual human development in interaction with the environment, and second by the human "joy" of creating ideals.[19] On other occasions he would deny or minimize that distinction, as in his 1952 lecture on ethical robots. Having noted von Neumann's theory of self-reproducing automata, and that a machine can be made capable of learning and thus improve upon itself, McCulloch suggested that it is possible to look on Man himself as a product of . . . an evolutionary process of developing robots, begotten of simpler robots, back to the primordial slime; and I look upon his ethical conduct as something to be interpreted in terms of the circuit action of this Man in his environment—a Turing machine with only two feedbacks determined, a desire to play and a desire to win.[20]

Because his style of expression is literary rather than scientific, and terms are not precisely defined, we may see McCulloch's assertions about machines as poetic expressions of his sensibilities in relation to artifacts. Nevertheless, he buttresses his attitudes by reasoned philosophical arguments. Over the years during which the Macy group met, McCulloch seemed to become increasingly confident of his mechanistic views.

Formal logical systems such as the Pitts-McCulloch model, as well as machines that form a concrete instance of such systems, are subject to Gödel's Incompleteness Theorem and other metamathematical theorems indicating inherent limitations. To the Macy participants acquainted with mathematical logic, it was something of an open question whether and how these limitations would manifest themselves as more elaborate and detailed attempts were made to describe the human mind and brain. It was becoming clear to them, however, that the multitude of paradoxes and contradictions pervading and enlivening human thought do not invalidate the notion that machinelike neuronal circuits are its physical substructure.[21]

McCulloch was tall, thin, narrow-shouldered, and loose-limbed. His head was long, with high cheekbones. He had a sizeable beard, unusual in those days, which changed from black to gray to white during the 1940s, and elongated features reminiscent of El Greco's paintings. In conversation he, more than most scientists, looked directly at the person talking with him, and his whole face became animated, his intense, blue eyes lighting up in discussion of technical points of any scientific problem or idea that caught his imagination. There were many of these ideas, for he was intellectually open and alive. His intellectual vitality and enthusiasm combined with a verbal gift, an enjoyment of scientific talk, and a personal informality and warmth. This, together with his strong sense of commitment, gave him a charisma that attracted many a bright young student. He was the most loose and spontaneous, least machinelike of men.

In personal relations to his favorite students, as to his friends, he was generous and sensitive. Many an impecunious young scientist was helped by him financially; his hospitality was such that over the years a large number of young people stayed at his house for short or long periods of time; and then he went to considerable lengths to make suitable professional contacts for these young scientists. Over and above practical help, McCulloch showed personal interest in their well-being and their freedom to pursue their ideas or develop their talents. He allowed himself to become involved with them.

As one who had been helped by McCulloch in his youth commented, many professors are kind to students and younger colleagues, but often a young man needs more than kindness: McCulloch took sufficient interest to perceive and respond directly to the particular needs of individual young scientists and to help them effectively. Another friend, a woman, put it this way: "Warren was in a way a very selfless person and genuinely devoted to those people he had rapport with." Another comments: "I owe a great deal, both in the sheer personal hospitality he offered and in the contacts that he made for my work. I know a lot of chaps who wouldn't have got where they are, if it weren't for Warren . . . He is one of the best human beings for goodness to young people that I've ever come across; he is amazingly self-sacrificing." Among the young people he brought to the Macy cybernetics conferences were John Stroud, Donald McKay, and Heinz von Förster. To each of them he extended warm friendship and help. For instance, McCulloch was instrumental in enabling von Förster to emigrate from Austria, introducing him professionally in America and arranging a position for him. As McCulloch's colleague Henry Brosin wrote to him, "Your support of younger men is magnificent."[22] There was in McCulloch's way much tenderness, concern for people, and enjoyment of friendships.

Clearly, McCulloch does not fit any stereotype of a cold and compulsive mechanist, nor of one obsessed with mastery and efficiency. He was a man with a strong desire to understand human mind and logical thought in terms equally vivid, tangible, explicit, and lucid as his comprehension of the repairable workings of his automobile. His romanticizing the machine was a touch of mysticism in his make-up, but his liking for things mechanical was squarely in the American tradition in which he grew up.

In 1941 McCulloch left Yale and took a position at the University of Illinois Medical School as director of research for a group of about thirty researchers in the department of psychiatry. He saw the group's mission as an attempt to lay the biological foundations for a scientific approach to psychiatry, although in fact the group's work was more diversified. It was a decisive moment for McCulloch when he encountered a teenage run-away from Detroit who had sought refuge in the academic environment of the University of Chicago, where he hoped to be understood. The combination of McCulloch's longing for the crystal clarity of logic and his personal kindness brought about his association with Walter Pitts.

Walter H. Pitts Jr. was the second of three sons born into a blue-collar Detroit family on 23 April 1923. When only fifteen, he was studying symbolic logic with Carnap, the foremost philosopher in Chicago, and mathematical biology with its leading practitioner, Rashevsky. A couple of years later this precocious adolescent met McCulloch.[23] The McCullochs, characteristically, took into their home this homeless, needy, shy, eccentric prodigy. In Pitts, Warren found a brilliant coworker with such powerful ability in science and especially in logic that together they could proceed productively in the research McCulloch had so long envisioned. Many an evening and early morning was spent at the McCulloch's house with Warren McCulloch, Walter Pitts, and young colleagues talking, talking, talking. Warren would smoke one cigarette after another and frequently refill his glass from the bottle of Scotch. To most fellow scientists the tenor of the talk would have seemed strange, for the group was concerned with fundamental philosophical issues of metaphysics and epistemology. For these men the spring for research activity was as much philosophic as scientific.

Walter Pitts was simultaneously an extraordinarily talented, sought-after scientist and an adolescent boy, with all the incongruity that entails. Other leading scientists, even when they took a fatherly interest in the boy, invariably responded to Pitts the powerful scientist with admiration. Norbert Wiener's evaluation of Pitts was typical:

> He is without question the strongest young scientist whom I have ever met . . . I should be extremely astonished if he does not prove to be one of the two or three most important scientists of his generation, not merely in America but in the world at large . . . he has as a scientist magnificent equipment.[24]

The McCulloch-Pitts theorem for nervous nets, mentioned earlier, deserves a fuller description. It was the apex of the scientific achievement of both men. It required remarkable scientific abstraction to go from the pinkish-gray tissue of the brain and its known electrical, chemical, and anatomical properties to the construction of formal neural nets isomorphic to the relations of propositional logic. Since the work carried out in Spain by Ramon y Cajal (a line of research subsequently elaborated by Lorente de Nó in Madrid and, later, in the United States) it had been firmly established that the central nervous system consists of distinct cells, neurons, separated from each other by a membrane and a "synaptic gap," and that each neuron includes a long fiber, the axon, that conducts electrical pulses away from the cell to which it belongs. The axon divides into several branches, each of which ends by nearly touching another neuron, creating a synapse at the point of near contact. The fiber arriving at a synapse can be excitatory or inhibitory (fig. 1). If and only if the net excitation of a neuron during the brief period of latent addition exceed the neuron's threshold voltage will transmission take place across the synapse and a pulse be generated and travel from the neuron along its axon toward other neurons.

To see how neurons might represent logical assertions, consider two examples. Suppose that both A and B are excitatory fibers, and that a pulse traveling along either suffices to cross the synaptic gap. This physical situation corresponds to the formal statement, "If either A or B is true, then C is true." A different logical statement corresponds to the situation where fiber A excites the neuron at regular intervals, but fiber B is inhibitory: "Assuming

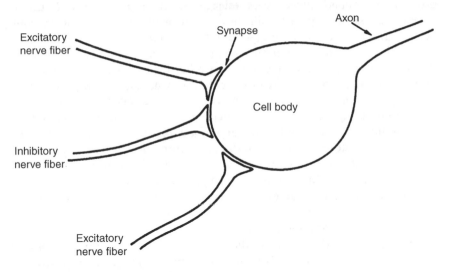

Figure 1 Diagram of neuron

A is always true, C is true whenever B is *not* true." The Pitts-McCulloch model consists of a net made up of such idealized neurons, each with some number of excitatory and inhibitory inputs, a threshold voltage, and some branching of its output. Finally, the time scale is introduced. The essential result of their analysis has been summarized as follows: "That anything that can be completely and unambiguously described, anything that can be completely and unambiguously put into words, is ipso factor realizable by a suitable finite neural network . . . "[25] While the theorem showed that a large class of mental operations *could* be carried out even in a highly simplified model of the brain, it was and remains largely unknown how the brain carries out cognitive functions. The proof, a tour de force by Pitts, nevertheless held out the promise that eventually the functioning of the brain, including pathologies, might be understood by combining logical analysis with detailed experimental neurophysiology. The grandness and generality of the theorem cried out for finding concrete, specific, testable applications.

As a mode of explaining psychological events, the Pitts-McCulloch approach represents a kind of organic reductionism, with individual neurons or synaptic firings as the elementary units, the "atoms." Since the model could in principle equally well describe an electronic computer, it could also be regarded as a form of mechanical (or, more precisely, electronic) reductionism. The psychological event, the experience associated with the neuronal activity, does not have a central place in such an explanatory scheme. It is no more than an epiphenomenon. It is not a large jump from that notion to imagine that complex computers, artificial intelligence devices, also have minds and subjective experience. But the model does not purport to be all-encompassing. After all, how much of our knowing can be completely, strictly, logically, unambiguously spelled out?

The Pitts-McCulloch approach to mind did not have much common ground with the prevailing schools of psychology and psychiatry. Its focus on mind and brain was irrelevant from a behaviorist's perspective; its emphasis on propositional logic and on the organic was of little interest to psychoanalysts; its neglect of the process of an individual brain's evolution from infancy to adulthood made it at best marginal for developmental psychology; its atomistic reductionism seemed in conflict with the premises underlying Gestalt psychology; and its focus on mechanism rather than subjective experience put it at odds with the phenomenologists. But McCulloch and Pitts did have overlapping interests with those physiological psychologists and neuropsychiatrists who studied human and animal behavior in terms of the physiology and anatomy of the nervous system. They had a still closer intellectual kinship with the young British psychologist Kenneth Craik, who independently of the American researchers had proposed that "in a neural calculating machine there may well be patterns of excitation in the cortex, temporal and spatial groupings of impulses, and so forth which, to a physiologist sufficiently skilled, would 'represent' concepts or sensations of objects . . ."[26]

Craik, in 1943, had in a little book presented the case for the organic-mechanistic mode of explanation to which McCulloch and Pitts were devoted. Craik inspired others in England, who eventually formed an active group of researchers. In 1944 Craik became the head of the unit for Research in Applied Psychology at Cambridge University, but died as a result of a bicycle accident the following year.

In the United States the work of McCulloch and his collaborators had much in common with and also complemented that of Wiener and Rosenblueth. Both groups worked in the physiological laboratory and developed mathematical models that spanned machines as well as organisms. If Wiener and Rosenblueth emphasized the embodiments of mechanisms for purposive behavior, McCulloch sought embodiments for ideas and thought generally. Theirs was ground-breaking work, clearly only the first step in what promised to be a major new direction of research. Pitts and McCulloch as well as Rosenblueth, Wiener, and Bigelow were extending the realm of mechanism.

After the May 1942 Cerebral Inhibition meeting, at which McCulloch and Rosenblueth discussed with Fremont-Smith the possibility of a postwar meeting, the two teams made common cause and sought out opportunities for dialogue. Pitts was sent to M.I.T. to work with Wiener for a year and stayed longer but traveled back and forth. McCulloch tried to bring Arturo Rosenblueth to Chicago, when Rosenblueth lost his job at Harvard, but his Mexican citizenship turned out to be an obstacle. But both Pitts and Wiener traveled repeatedly to Mexico City to work with Rosenblueth.

Wiener's daughter, Barbara, a student of neurophysiology, spent some time with McCulloch's team in Chicago, but McCulloch and Wiener, working at M.I.T., visited each other frequently. The extended yet intimate scientific family of Rosenblueth-McCulloch-Wiener-Pitts also included a couple of other scientists, only a few years older and special friends of Pitts, who, however, were not invited to the Macy conferences.[27] Furthermore, Wiener was in contact with the mathematician John von Neumann, then, in response to military urgency, engaged in computer design, who found the Pitts-McCulloch model of nervous nets suitable for describing the logical structure of general-purpose computers, where its functioning could be seen in the metal. Automata theory put computers and neural net models under one heading. Von Neumann at Princeton joined the M.I.T.–Mexico City and Chicago teams to form an impressive core group for making a place within American science for the new machine-organism analogies.

Pitt's talents were of a particular kind. He was primarily self-educated. He was known to master the contents of a textbook in a field new to him in a few days. When he was only twenty, his detailed, precise, and comprehensive knowledge and understanding of mathematical logic, mathematics, physiology, and physiological psychology were already on a par with those of leading practitioners in each of those fields.[28] He was also studying and digesting the thinking of major Western philosophers, appreciating subtle features of their thought, and carrying on "conversations" with them in which McCulloch and friends could serve as third or fourth parties. Moreover, his logical reasoning was impeccably clear and precise, and his attention to detail assiduous. These talents made him an ideal collaborator and critic for someone like Wiener or McCulloch, and the latter especially came to depend on him. For if their ideas, reasoning, and assertions survived Pitts's scrutiny, they could rest easy that no error of logic, no misinformation, had entered their work, that they were guilty of no omission or neglected perspective. Otherwise Pitts would have set the matter straight.[29] He held more diverse individuals' complex thoughts in his mind than most of us would imagine possible. He could also use his power as a logician or mathematician, manipulating symbols, to carry through such new and difficult arguments as that contained in his 1943 paper with McCulloch. Wiener, who also had great mathematical power and an excellent memory in matters scientific, differed from Pitts in that originality in science and mathematics was for him a strong suit. In turn, he did not give Pitts's kind of detailed, in a sense, self-effacing, attention to others' work.

A passive, personally needy, unworldly young genius like Pitts was vulnerable to those who, unlike his own father, appreciated, admired, and came to depend on his remarkable mind. If one were to try to place his collaborative research with McCulloch within the context of current discussions of the relationship of gender to science, such as those by Evelyn Keller, I think one would have to say that it more nearly echoes the world of Plato (science as a sublime love affair with the "essential nature of things") than Bacon's vision of science as power. It also carries the homoerotic associations of Plato's world, in which science is often a joint venture of an older and a younger man, with in this case the latter embodying exquisitely the logical (masculine) nature of mind. As in Plato's vision, the unconsummated eroticism is transmuted into intellectual energy.

Pitts's friends, including McCulloch's daughter Taffy, enjoyed his company. He was playful in a scientific, intellectual way, inventing all kinds of word games. He liked to go camping with a friend or by himself. He used chemicals to concoct dyes, fireworks, and pharmaceuticals in the McCulloch basement. His talk was always impersonal, and he never mentioned his family to anyone. He was a slim, shy, gentle, unobtrusive young man. A woman with a young child lived in the McCulloch house for a time and found in Walter Pitts a dependable babysitter. His face reminded at least one person of a frog. His gentleness with the young contrasted with the sharpness of his intellectual arguments and show of contempt toward sloppy reasoning by social scientists. It became blatantly evident in the 1950s that he spurned any interest in his own career, the imperative to write papers, institutional or bureaucratic requirements of any kind. He inhabited a different, purer world. He had something in common with those of his age-cohorts who dubbed themselves the Beat Generation and were put off by the prevailing compulsive "return to normalcy" mood of career and material well-being following the Second World War. He, like the Beats, spent a good bit of time "on the road." On one occasion he set off (with Oliver Selfridge) in a vintage second-hand Cadillac hearse from Boston for Mexico City. They stopped in the Colorado mountains for a while, backpacking. The hearse gave out for good in San Antonio, Texas. But the greatest consternation among their elders was not that the boys would arrive late or not at all, but that the Gibbs analyzer, an expensive piece of scientific equipment they were delivering to Rosenblueth, would be stranded in San Antonio as well. When in 1955 McCulloch and Jerome Wiener successfully arranged to give Pitts a Ph.D. from M.I.T. on the basis of his knowledge and work, though he had never taken a single course for credit or fulfilled formal Ph.D. requirements, Pitts refused even to sign the piece of paper—the one act required from him to receive the degree! Pitts seemed stubbornly to seek anonymity, even as Norbert Wiener, Warren McCulloch, Jerome Wiesner, and others tried over the years to rescue him from it.

But unlike the Beats, Pitts was not drawn to concern with feelings or love relationships. His primary world was the mental universe of science and mathematical symbols. In spite of closeness to and affection for a few friends with similar intellectual interests, he stayed away from the sensual. His fear of women, his antisensuality, his inability to respond in kind to overtures of personal friendship made by some Macy participants, all make him appear eccentric. In the late fifties he withdrew increasingly from all his M.I.T.

friends who had come to depend heavily on him and eventually avoided nearly all contact with them.[30] Some of the seemingly unusual attitudes represented by McCulloch and Pitts are echoed in the current generation of inventive artificial intelligence buffs and computer hackers at M.I.T.[31] Consequently, McCulloch and Pitts may be regarded as members, nay founders, of a whole clan, rather than only as highly idiosyncratic individuals.

McCulloch was to a considerable extent sympathetic to Pitts's ways, as the moral of the following story, told in 1961, of scientists of ancient Greece suggests:

> The citizens of Abdera wrote to Hippocrates crying for help because their great atomic scientist had gone mad. Hippocrates was long delayed. When he arrived with his bottle of hellebore, the weeping citizens led him to Democritus, where he sat unshod, dissecting animals and making notes in the book on his knees. Hippocrates asked why he was doing it, and he answered that he was looking for the causes of madness in the parts of beasts, and he demanded what had detained Hippocrates. He answered, "Family matters, engagements, money, and other business." Democritus roared with laughter—that men called great so waste their lives, marrying only to fall out of love, seeking wealth without measure, making wars to no purpose, and in peace overthrowing one tyrant to set up another. Hippocrates listened to his railing and, turning to the people, told them to cease their lamentations, for Democritus was not only sane but the wisest man in Abdera.[32]

Aspiring to the sanity of Democritus, McCulloch sought after about a decade to shed his academic status and administrative duties in Chicago and, despite a salary cut, to join his young friends—Walter Pitts and Jerome Lettvin—so as to engage happily with them in research in Cambridge, Massachusetts. They became employees of M.I.T., where the three were given laboratory space in Building 20, a temporary structure thrown up during the war and administered by the Research Laboratory for Electronics.

The 1942 conference on hypnosis and the conditioned reflex had established a connection between neurobiologists and human scientists preliminary to the cybernetics meetings, but the development of the cluster we have labeled "the cyberneticians," which already crossed many disciplinary boundaries, is a different story. McCulloch had long known Lorente de Nó and admired his work, but the latter was by temperament somewhat less gregarious than the others. In the 1930s Lorente and Rosenblueth had been on opposite sides of the scientific debate about the primacy of electrical processes as opposed to that of the production of chemicals in the transmission of nerve impulses, but by the end of the war, "Behold! the whole subject has become suddenly clearer."[33] McCulloch and Rosenblueth had been professionally and personally close. Both had briefly worked in clinical psychiatry but had eagerly turned away from it to neurobiological research. They visited each other and sought opportunities to talk and do experiments together. Wiener and von Neumann had had an analogous relationship throughout the 1930s. They admired each other's work. Both treasured opportunities for conversation and visited each other for days at a time to talk.[34] All of them had with high expectation worked together to coordinate their presentation of material to kick off whatever might develop from the 8–9 March 1946 meeting. As Wiener wrote to McCulloch,

> This meeting is going to be a big thing for us and our cause. I am now down with von Neumann discussing plans and I can assure you that his part and mine will be well coordinated. Pitts and I are also getting busy together and so is Rosenblueth . . . We enjoyed having your daughter up very much and hope to see more of her next year. Meanwhile, we are impatient for the meeting of the Macy Foundation and when we shall see you and talk over many things of common interest. I am very much pleased with the tentative program and I am delighted that you are chairman.[35]

In the introduction to *Cybernetics*, Wiener described the background of the March 1946 Macy conference from his perspective. In the thirties he and Rosenblueth had already taken part in a supper club devoted to discussion of topics of common interest, especially topics related to scientific method. He and Rosenblueth had by the 1930s agreed about the need for interdisciplinary work and a team of scientists from various disciplines to explore "some of the blank spaces in the map of science . . . " In that connection they had "dreamed for years of an institution of independent scientists, working together in one of these backwoods of science . . . " By the mid-forties these dreams had taken concrete form around the subject of cybernetics. McCulloch recalled his first encounter with Wiener: "I first met him at dinner with Rosenblueth when they, with Bigelow, were mechanizing teleology. He told me promptly what I could expect of my own theories of the working of the brain. Time proved him right. Then it was that the dream began of team play between biologist, mathematician and communication engineer, which eventually flowered into cybernetics . . . "[36]

Pitts, because of his youth, represented the promise for the future in this field. If he was in effect McCulloch's adopted son, his relationship to Wiener was also close and personal. From Wiener, too, Pitts elicited a paternal attitude. Wiener, having been raised by a father who imposed harsh intellectual discipline, was inclined to demand of Pitts as well a high standard, more work and less play. McCulloch would patiently defend Pitts's ways to the more demanding and sometimes critical Wiener. But when Pitts was depressed and lonesome in New York, Wiener made the occasion to come from Boston to New York and visit Pitts with the intention of cheering him up.[37] Sometimes Wiener and McCulloch appeared to compete for Pitts's collaboration.

A complication arose in 1943, the very year in which the seminal papers in the field appeared. Rosenblueth, after fourteen years at Harvard, was informed he would lose his position in the following year.[38] At Harvard he was personally disliked by some and had experienced social prejudice because of his Mexican-Jewish ancestry. His department head, Walter Cannon, wanted to keep him at Harvard because of his great merits as a scientist. He defended Rosenblueth, as seemed unfortunately necessary, to a colleague:

> You ask about Dr. Rosenblueth as a man. Let me tell you about him . . . Dr. Rosenblueth has a Jewish name but his Jewish ancestry is remote. He has none of the unpleasant characteristics sometimes associated with the Jew. One of his sisters is a nun, and he is married to a charming American, a graduate of Reed college in Portland, Oregon, and for some years a graduate student at Radcliffe College.[39]

But it was of no avail. Rosenblueth's collaboration with Wiener had begun, and its future was now in jeopardy. In spite of the possibility of returning to Mexico to start a research institute from scratch, Rosenblueth preferred a position at an already thriving scientific center in the United States. McCulloch managed to arrange for an associate professorship, which would at first be temporary but would carry the assurance of eventual permanence, at the University of Illinois.[40] To buy equipment for Rosenblueth's laboratory from Harvard and elsewhere, McCulloch contacted Fremont-Smith about obtaining funds from the Macy Foundation. Rosenblueth had already accepted the offer when he learned that he would have to give up his Mexican citizenship to be eligible for the tenured position. Thereupon he backed out. McCulloch wrote to Fremont-Smith,

> To my sorrow, Rosenblueth is not coming to us but returning to Mexico. We were unable to promise him permanent tenure if he retained his Mexican citizenship, which he, for patriotic reasons, decided to retain . . . I shall be delighted to be with you for supper and spend the evening of Friday, December 10th, and if I may will pick you up at the airport at 5:02 p.m. that afternoon.[41]

In Mexico City Rosenblueth was to build up and head a department of physiology of a new research institute. From 1946 on the Rockefeller Foundation supported Rosenblueth in Mexico financially, as part of its policy to promote science in Latin America. Robert Morison of the Rockefeller Foundation had been a friend of Rosenblueth and a member of the Harvard supper club at which Wiener and Rosenblueth had first met. Rosenblueth's move to Mexico and his acceptance of new organizational and administrative responsibilities did not prevent his dialogue and collaboration with Wiener, McCulloch, Pitts, and their friends. All of them and von Neumann visited Rosenblueth in Mexico City. Wiener made a formal arrangement permitting him to spend six months in alternate years with Rosenblueth in Mexico, engaging in collaborative research. The Rockefeller Foundation supported Wiener's visits to Mexico, but not Rosenblueth's visits to M.I.T., since it wanted to keep Rosenblueth in Mexico.[42] As the heavy correspondence among them shows, close contact among members of the cluster of cyberneticians remained intact in spite of Rosenblueth's move. It is also clear that the assist from foundations (Macy, Rockefeller) and the good will of foundation executives (Fremont-Smith, Robert Morison) were indispensible.

In the midst of wartime the idea of a new field for scientific research, along the lines that several years later came to be known as cybernetics, was taking shape in informal conversations. Von Neumann and Wiener agreed on a plan for a meeting of a small group of men "to discuss questions of common interest and make plans for the future development of this field of effort, which as yet is not even named."[43] It was at the resulting meeting in January 1945 that a strong consensus was formed. Rosenblueth could not attend because he was busy getting things started in Mexico, but Wiener reported to him that the meeting

> was a great success. I believe you have already got von Neumann's report . . . The first day von Neumann spoke on computing machines and I spoke on communication engineering. The second day Lorente de Nó and McCulloch joined forces for a very convincing presentation of the present status of the problem of the organization of the brain. In the end we were all convinced that the subject embracing both the engineering and neurology aspect is essentially one, and we should go ahead with plans to embody these ideas in a permanent program of research . . . we definitely do have the intention of organizing a society and a journal after the war, and founding at Tech or elsewhere in the country a center of research in our new field . . . When this scheme really gets going, I for one will not be content unless we can bring you and Bigelow directly into it.[44]

That meeting established a consensus concerning a research program among the senior "cyberneticians," and efforts to implement it followed.[45] Von Neumann was confident he could get financial backing, and he and Wiener received indications of support from Warren Weaver of the Rockefeller and H. A. Moe of the Guggenheim foundations. Von Neumann believed that in connection with finding a home for the center he and Wiener were envisioning, "the best way to get 'something' done is to propagandize everybody who is a reasonable potential support."[46] Wiener in particular sought to arrange a center at M.I.T. and especially to bring von Neumann, a big name, first. Indeed, M.I.T. made von Neumann a good offer, and Wiener could write to Rosenblueth, "Johnny was down here the last two days. He is almost hooked."[47] In the end, however, the Institute for Advanced Study, in Princeton, gave von Neumann, who had plans for building a prototype computer, what he wanted, and he did not go to M.I.T. Wiener recommended Bigelow, the engineer with whom he had worked during the war, to von Neumann, who then made Bigelow the engineer for the new Princeton computer.

The "center" did not materialize; Rosenblueth was in Mexico, von Neumann and Bigelow in Princeton, Wiener at M.I.T., Lorente de Nó at the Rockefeller Institute in New York, McCulloch in Chicago, and Pitts going back and forth between M.I.T. and Chicago. McCulloch's going to see Fremont-Smith after the war to suggest the Circular Causal and Feedback Mechanisms in Biological and Social Systems conference was another expression of the cyberneticians' effort to establish and extend the new field of research and arrange opportunities to talk with each other. McCulloch as "chronic chairman" of the series of conferences was in a position to control to a considerable extent who would be invited, who would be asked to present a paper, and who would be given the floor when the discussion got heated. The adaptation of the cyberneticians' ideas to the human sciences, however, was contingent on the response and prior outlook of groups and individuals within those fields.

Notes

1 A. Einstein, "Motiv des Forschens," 1918; quoted and translated in Gerald Holton, *Thematic Origins of Scientific Thought* (Cambridge: Harvard University Press, 1973), pp. 376–377.
2 Among the participants at the conferences described here, the most articulate expositor of the dangers of the new ideas was Norbert Wiener. See his *Cybernetics, The Human Use of Human Beings* (Boston: Houghton Mifflin, 1950) and *God and Golem, Inc.* (Cambridge, MIT Press, 1964).
3 Warren McCulloch, *Embodiments of Mind* (Cambridge: MIT Press, 1965), p. 157.
4 See, e.g., ibid., pp. 3–6, 367.
5 William A. Wallace, "The Philosophical Setting of Medieval Science," in David C. Lindberg, ed., *Science in the Middle Ages* (Chicago: University of Chicago Press, 1978), p. 91.
6 E. von Domarus, "Logical Structure of Mind," in Lee Thayer, ed., *Communication: Theory and Research* (Springfield: Thomas, 1967).
7 E. von Domarus, "The Specific Laws of Logic in Schizophrenia," in J. S. Kasanin, ed., *Language and Thought in Schizophrenia* (Berkeley: University of California Press, 1944); E. von Domarus, "Ueber die Beziehung des normalen zum schizophrenen Denken," *Archiv für Psychiatrie* (Berlin), 74: 641, 1925; Silvano Arieti, "Special Logic of Schizophrenic and Other Types of Autistic Thought," *Psychiatry* 11: 325, 1948.

8 McCulloch, *Embodiments*, p. 2.

9 McCulloch in Lloyd Jeffress, ed., *Cerebral Mechanisms in Behavior: The Hixon Symposium* (New York: John Wiley, 1951), p. 32.

10 McCulloch, "The Functional Organization of the Cerebral Cortex," *Physiological Review* 24: 390–407, 1944; McCulloch, "Cortico-cortical Connections," in Paul C. Bucy, ed., *The Precentral Motor Cortex* (Urbana: University of Illinois, 1944), pp. 211–242.

11 F. S. C. Northrop, *Philosophical Anthropology and Practical Politics* (New York: Macmillan, 1960), chapter 3; McCulloch in his "The Beginning of Cybernetics" (*American Society for Cybernetics Forum* 6: 5, 1974) described the seminar as "an interdisciplinary group in the neurosciences, which often touched on cybernetic topics." Northrop's list of participants in that seminar include Clark Hull, H. S. Burr, Mark May, John Dollard, Leonard Doob, Henry Margenau, and Frederic Fitch. McCulloch also attended a Wednesday evening seminar group (around 1936) at the Institute of Human Relations as Yale, known as "Hull's seminar," which included Dollard, Doob, Northrop, and McCulloch as well as Donald Marquis, Neal Miller, Robert Sears, and O. Hobart Mowrer. There Hull proposed a theory of language that did not impress McCulloch, who described it in "The Beginnings of Cybernetics" as only "entertaining." For Hull's seminar see Hull and Mowrer, "Hull's Psychological Seminars, 1936–1938" at the Yale University Library, and Smith, *Behaviorism and Logical Positivism*.

12 According to Jerome Lettvin (MIT lecture, 23 February 1977), Leibniz's *Monadology*, viewed as a work in epistemology, identifies monads as "incorporal automata," in other words formal automata.

13 In his retrospective, "The Beginnings of Cybernetics," Warren McCulloch especially emphasizes Kant and Descartes.

14 Frederic B. Fitch to Heims, 27 September 1973. Fitch later gave some criticism of the 1943 McCulloch-Pitts paper, which he reviewed in *Journal of Symbolic Logic* 9: 49, 1944. Fitch was a guest at the third conference. He had put the "psychological laws" propounded by Hull into a formal logical system. C. L. Hull, *Principles of Behavior* (New York: Appleton Century Croft, 1943). Both Fitch and Hull were part of the Northrop Yale seminar.

15 McCulloch, *Embodiments*, p. 143.

16 Quoted in Mary Catherine Bateson, *Our Own Metaphor* (New York: Knopf, 1972), p. 226.

17 McCulloch, *Embodiments*, p. 220.

18 Johan Huizinga, *Homo Ludens* (Roy Publishers, 1950), p. 3.

19 McCulloch, "Why the Mind is in the Head" *Hixon Symposium*, pp. 56–57.

20 McCulloch, *Embodiments*, p. 200.

21 Ninth conference, *Transactions*, p. 11, gives an indication.

22 Henry Brosin to McCulloch, 24 January 1949.

23 McCulloch, "The Beginnings of Cybernetics"; Jerome Lettvin, interview with Heims, 25 May 1971.

24 Wiener to Henry Allan Moe, September 1945.

25 J. von Neumann, *Hixon Symposium*, pp. 22–23; it has been emphasized by Papert, in his introduction to *Embodiments of Mind*, pp. xviii and xix, that the von Neumann statement is crude and can be misleading. However, more refined statement of the Pitts-McCulloch result requires the elaborate language of formal logic.

26 Kenneth Craik, *The Nature of Explanation* (Cambridge: Cambridge University Press, 1943), pp. 76–77.

27 Among them Jerome Lettvin and, somewhat later, Oliver Selfridge.

28 Wiener to Moe, September 1944.

29 It seems that Pitts and Selfridge had gone over the manuscript for Wiener's *Cybernetics*, but some confusion over the copies led Wiener to send the uncorrected copy to the publisher (Selfridge, interview with Heims, 2 December 1971). But see also N. Wiener, *I am a Mathematician* (Cambridge: MIT Press, 1956), p. 332. According to Wiener's correspondence with Pitts, McCulloch, and Rosenblueth, in spring 1947 Wiener was upset at Pitts, believing he had lost a manuscript of Wiener's. The manuscript was found, and Wiener's suspicion that others were covering up for Pitts allayed. Probably this was the manuscript for a journal article rather than the one for *Cybernetics*. All those were "family arguments" among the core group of neomechanists.

30 Information concerning Pitts derives from recollections of people who knew him. A few letters by him are in the archives of others, and he is the subject of correspondence by McCulloch, Wiener, Rosenblueth, and others. On the whole, however, documentation concerning his life is sparse.

31 Sherry Turkle, *The Second Self: Computers and the Human Spirit* (New York: Simon and Schuster, 1984).

32 McCulloch, *Embodiments*, pp. 216–217.

33 Tracy Putnam in "The Physico-Chemical Mechanism of Nerve Activity," *Annals of the New York Academy of Sciences* 67: 378, 1946.

34 Heims, *John von Neumann and Norbert Wiener*.

35 Wiener to McCulloch, 15 February 1946.

36 W. McCulloch, "Norbert Wiener," *Journal of Nervous and Mental Disease*, 140: 16, 1965.

37 Wiener to Pitts, 12 August 1944; 17 October 1944; Wiener to Rosenblueth, 19 October 1944. The Wiener-McCulloch-Rosenblueth-Pitts correspondence throughout the 1940s provides information about their interrelations.

38 Rosenblueth to Moe, 22 March 1943.

39 Walter Cannon to Chauncy Leake, 15 March 1943. The letter was brought to my attention by Louisa Benton, who has written a thesis on Rosenblueth, "Arturo Rosenblueth: Success or Failure?" (Harvard University, 1986).

40 McCulloch to Fremont-Smith, 23 October 1943; Rosenblueth to Francis Gerty, 26 October 1943.

41 McCulloch to Fremont-Smith, 10 November 1943.

42 Robert Lambert to Moe, 9 August 1945; Robert Morison, diary entry, 21 September 1946, at the Rockefeller Foundation Archives.

43 Wiener, Aiken, and von Neumann to S. S. Wilks, Pitts, E. H. Vestine, W. E. Deming, McCulloch, Lorente de Nó, and Leland E. Cunningham, 4 December 1944.

44 Wiener to Rosenblueth, 24 January 1945. The meeting was held 6–7 January 1945, but in Wiener's *Cybernetics* it is dated incorrectly as occurring in the winter of 1943–44.

45 Von Neumann, report on the meeting, 12 January 1945.

46 Von Neumann to Wiener, 21 April 1945.

47 Wiener to Rosenblueth, 11 August 1945.

22

THE GENERAL AND LOGICAL
THEORY OF AUTOMATA

John von Neumann

Source: L. A. Jeffress (ed.) *Cerebral Mechanisms in Behavior*, Hixon Symposium Hafner Publishing, 1951, pp. 1–41.

I have to ask your forbearance for appearing here, since I am an outsider to most of the fields which form the subject of this conference. Even in the area in which I have some experience, that of the logics and structure of automata, my connections are almost entirely on one side, the mathematical side. The usefulness of what I am going to say, if any, will therefore be limited to this: I may be able to give you a picture of the mathematical approach to these problems, and to prepare you for the experiences that you will have when you come into closer contact with mathematicians. This should orient you as to the ideas and the attitudes which you may then expect to encounter. I hope to get your judgment of the modus procedendi and the distribution of emphases that I am going to use. I feel that I need instruction even in the limiting area between our fields more than you do, and I hope that I shall receive it from your criticisms.

Automata have been playing a continuously increasing, and have by now attained a very considerable, role in the natural sciences. This is a process that has been going on for several decades. During the last part of this period automata have begun to invade certain parts of mathematics too—particularly, but not exclusively, mathematical physics or applied mathematics. Their role in mathematics presents an interesting counterpart to certain functional aspects of organization in nature. Natural organisms are, as a rule, much more complicated and subtle, and therefore much less well understood in detail, than are artificial automata. Nevertheless, some regularities which we observe in the organization of the former may be quite instructive in our thinking and planning of the latter; and conversely, a good deal of our experiences and difficulties with our artificial automata can be to some extent projected on our interpretations of natural organisms.

Preliminary considerations

Dichotomy of the problem: nature of the elements, axiomatic discussion of their synthesis

In comparing living organisms, and, in particular, that most complicated organism, the human central nervous system, with artificial automata, the following limitation should be kept in mind. The natural systems are of enormous complexity, and it is clearly necessary to subdivide the problem that they represent into several parts. One method of subdivision, which is particularly significant in the present context, is this: The organisms can be viewed as made up of parts which to a certain extent are independent, elementary units. We may, therefore, to this extent, view as the first part of the problem the structure and functioning of such elementary units individually. The second part of the problem consists of understanding how these elements are organized into a whole, and how the functioning of the whole is expressed in terms of these elements.

The first part of the problem is at present the dominant one in physiology. It is closely connected with the most difficult chapters of organic chemistry and of physical chemistry, and may in due course be greatly helped by quantum mechanics. I have little qualification to talk about it, and it is not this part with which I shall concern myself here.

The second part, on the other hand, is the one which is likely to attract those of us who have the background and the tastes of a mathematician or a logician. With this attitude, we will be inclined to remove the first part of the problem by the process of axiomatization, and concentrate on the second one.

The axiomatic procedure

Axiomatizing the behavior of the elements means this: We assume that the elements have certain well-defined, outside, functional characteristics; that is, they are to be treated as "black boxes." They are viewed as automatisms, the inner structure of which need not be disclosed, but which are assumed to react to certain unambiguously defined stimuli, by certain unambiguously defined responses.

This being understood, we may then investigate the larger organisms that can be built up from these elements, their structure, their functioning, the connections between the elements, and the general theoretical regularities that may be detectable in the complex syntheses of the organisms in question.

I need not emphasize the limitations of this procedure. Investigations of this type may furnish evidence that the system of axioms used is convenient and, at least in its effects, similar to reality. They are, however, not the ideal

417

method, and possibly not even a very effective method, to determine the validity of the axioms. Such determinations of validity belong primarily to the first part of the problem. Indeed they are essentially covered by the properly physiological (or chemical or physical-chemical) determinations of the nature and properties of the elements.

The significant orders of magnitude

In spite of these limitations, however, the "second part" as circumscribed above is important and difficult. With any reasonable definition of what constitutes an element, the natural organisms are very highly complex aggregations of these elements. The number of cells in the human body is somewhere of the general order of 10^{15} or 10^{16}. The number of neurons in the central nervous system is somewhere of the order of 10^{10}. We have absolutely no past experience with systems of this degree of complexity. All artificial automata made by man have numbers of parts which by any comparably schematic count are of the order 10^3 to 10^6. In addition, those artificial systems which function with that type of logical flexibility and autonomy that we find in the natural organisms do not lie at the peak of this scale. The prototypes for these systems are the modern computing machines, and here a reasonable definition of what constitutes an element will lead to counts of a few times 10^3 or 10^4 elements.

Discussion of certain relevant traits of computing machines

Computing machines—typical operations

Having made these general remarks, let me now be more definite, and turn to that part of the subject about which I shall talk in specific and technical detail. As I have indicated, it is concerned with artificial automata and more specially with computing machines. They have some similarity to the central nervous system, or at least to a certain segment of the system's functions. They are of course vastly less complicated, that is, smaller in the sense which really matters. It is nevertheless of a certain interest to analyze the problem of organisms and organization from the point of view of these relatively small, artificial automata, and to effect their comparisons with the central nervous system from this frog's-view perspective.

I shall begin by some statements about computing machines as such.

The notion of using an automaton for the purpose of computing is relatively new. While computing automata are not the most complicated artificial automata from the point of view of the end results they achieve, they do nevertheless represent the highest degree of complexity in the sense that they produce the longest chains of events determining and following each other.

There exists at the present time a reasonably well-defined set of ideas about when it is reasonable to use a fast computing machine, and when it is not. The criterion is usually expressed in terms of the multiplications involved in the mathematical problem. The use of a fast computing machine is believed to be by and large justified when the computing task involves about a million multiplications or more in a sequence.

An expression in more fundamentally logical terms is this: In the relevant fields (that is, in those parts of [usually applied] mathematics, where the use of such machines is proper) mathematical experience indicates the desirability of precisions of about ten decimal places. A single multiplication would therefore seem to involve at least 10×10 steps (digital multiplications); hence a million multiplications amount to at least 10^8 operations. Actually, however, multiplying two decimal digits is not an elementary operation. There are various ways of breaking it down into such, and all of them have about the same degree of complexity. The simplest way to estimate this degree of complexity is, instead of counting decimal places, to count the number of places that would be required for the same precision in the binary system of notation (base 2 instead of base 10). A decimal digit corresponds to about three binary digits, hence ten decimals to about thirty binary. The multiplication referred to above, therefore, consists not of 10×10, but of 30×30 elementary steps, that is, not 10^2, but 10^3 steps. (Binary digits are "all or none" affairs, capable of the values 0 and 1 only. Their multiplication is, therefore, indeed an elementary operation. By the way, the equivalent of 10 decimals is 33 [rather than 30] binaries—but 33×33, too, is approximately 10^3.) It follows, therefore, that a million multiplications in the sense indicated above are more reasonably described as corresponding to 10^9 elementary operations.

Precision and reliability requirements

I am not aware of any other field of human effort where the result really depends on a sequence of a billion (10^9) steps in any artifact, and where, furthermore, it has the characteristic that every step actually matters—or, at least, may matter with a considerable probability. Yet, precisely this is true for computing machines—this is their most specific and most difficult characteristic.

Indeed, there have been in the last two decades automata which did perform hundreds of millions, or even billions, of steps before they produced a result. However, the operation of these automata is not serial. The large number of steps is due to the fact that, for a variety of reasons, it is desirable to do the same experiment over and over again. Such cumulative, repetitive procedures may, for instance, increase the size of the result, that is (and this is the important consideration), increase the significant result, the "signal," relative to the "noise" which contaminates it. Thus any reasonable count of the number of reactions which a microphone gives before a verbally interpretable acoustic signal is produced is in the high tens of thousands. Similar estimates in television will give tens of millions, and in radar possibly many billions. If, however, any of these automata makes mistakes, the mistakes usually matter only to the extent of the fraction of the total number of steps which they represent. (This is not exactly true in all relevant examples, but it represents the qualitative situation better than the opposite statement.) Thus the larger the number of operations required to produce a result, the smaller will be the significant contribution of every individual operation.

In a computing machine no such rule holds. Any step is (or may potentially be) as important as the whole result; any error can vitiate the result in its entirety. (This statement is not absolutely true, but probably nearly 30 per cent of all steps made are usually of this sort.) Thus a computing machine is one of the exceptional artifacts. They not only have to perform a billion or more steps in a short time, but in a considerable part of the procedure (and this is a part that is rigorously specified in advance) they are permitted not a single error. In fact, in order to be sure that the whole machine is operative, and that no potentially degenerative malfunctions have set in, the present practice usually requires that no error should occur anywhere in the entire procedure.

This requirement puts the large, high-complexity computing machines in an altogether new light. It makes in particular a comparison between the computing machines and the operation of the natural organisms not entirely out of proportion.

The analogy principle

All computing automata fall into two great classes in a way which is immediately obvious and which, as you will see in a moment, carries over to living organisms. This classification is into analogy and digital machines.

Let us consider the analogy principle first. A computing machine may be based on the principle that numbers are represented by certain physical quantities. As such quantities we might, for instance, use the intensity of an electrical current, or the size of an electrical potential, or the number of degrees of arc by which a disk has been rotated (possibly in conjunction with the number of entire revolutions effected), etc. Operations like addition, multiplication, and integration may then be performed by finding various natural processes which act on these quantities in the desired way. Currents may be multiplied by feeding them into the two magnets of a dynamometer, thus producing a rotation. This rotation may then be transformed into an electrical resistance by the attachment of a rheostat; and, finally, the resistance can be transformed into a current by connecting it to two sources of fixed (and different) electrical potentials. The entire aggregate is thus a "black box" into which two currents are fed and which produces a current equal to their product. You are certainly familiar with many other ways in which a wide variety of natural processes can be used to perform this and many other mathematical operations.

The first well-integrated, large computing machine ever made was an analogy machine, V. Bush's Differential Analyzer. This machine, by the way, did the computing not with electrical currents, but with rotating disks. I shall not discuss the ingenious tricks by which the angles of rotation of these disks were combined according to various operations of mathematics.

I shall make no attempt to enumerate, classify, or systematize the wide variety of analogy principles and mechanisms that can be used in computing. They are confusingly multiple. The guiding principle without which it is impossible to reach an understanding of the situation is the classical one of all "communication theory"—the "signal to noise ratio." That is, the critical question with every analogy procedure is this: How large are the uncontrollable fluctuations of the mechanism that constitute the "noise," compared to the significant "signals" that express the numbers on which the machine operates? The usefulness of any analogy principle depends on how low it can keep the relative size of the uncontrollable fluctuations—the "noise level."

To put this in another way. No analogy machine exists which will really form the product of two numbers. What it will form is this product, plus a small but unknown quantity which represents the random noise of the mechanism and the physical processes involved. The whole problem is to keep this quantity down. This principle has controlled the entire relevant technology. It has, for instance, caused the adoption of seemingly complicated and clumsy mechanical devices instead of the simpler and elegant electrical ones. (This, at least, has been the case throughout most of the last twenty years. More recently, in certain applications which required only very limited precision the electrical devices have again come to the fore.) In comparing mechanical with electrical analogy processes, this roughly is true: Mechanical arrangements may bring this noise level below the "maximum signal level" by a factor of something like $1:10^4$ or 10^5. In electrical arrangements, the ratio is rarely much better than $1:10^2$. These ratios represent, of course, errors in the elementary steps of the calculation, and not in its final results. The latter will clearly be substantially larger.

The digital principle

A digital machine works with the familiar method of representing numbers as aggregates of digits. This is, by the way, the procedure which all of us use in our individual, non-mechanical computing, where we express numbers in the decimal system. Strictly speaking, digital computing need not be decimal. Any integer larger than one may be used as the basis of a digital notation for numbers. The decimal system (base 10) is the most common one, and all digital machines built to date operate in this system. It seems likely, however, that the binary (base 2) system will, in the end, prove preferable, and a number of digital machines using that system are now under construction.

The basic operations in a digital machine are usually the four species of arithmetic: addition, subtraction, multiplication, and division. We might at first think that, in using these, a digital machine possesses (in contrast to the analogy machines referred to above) absolute precision. This, however, is not the case, as the following consideration shows.

Take the case of multiplication. A digital machine multiplying two 10-digit numbers will produce a 20-digit number, which is their product, with no error whatever. To this extent its precision is absolute, even though the electrical or mechanical components of the arithmetical organ of the machine are as such of limited precision. As long as there is no breakdown of some component, that is, as long as the operation of each component produces only fluctuations within its preassigned tolerance limits, the result will be absolutely correct. This is, of course, the great and characteristic virtue of the digital procedure. Error, as a matter of normal operation and not solely (as indicated above) as an accident attributable to some definite breakdown, nevertheless creeps in, in the following manner. The absolutely correct product of two 10-digit numbers is a 20-digit number. If the machine is built to handle 10-digit numbers only, it will have to disregard the last 10 digits of this 20-digit number and work with the first 10 digits alone. (The small, though highly practical, improvement due to a possible modification of these digits by "round-off" may be disregarded here.) If, on the other hand, the machine can handle 20-digit numbers, then the multiplication of two such will produce 40 digits, and these again have to be cut down to 20, etc., etc. (To conclude, no matter what the maximum number of digits is for which the machine has been built, in the course of successive multiplications this maximum will be reached, sooner or later. Once it has been reached, the next multiplication will produce supernumerary digits, and the product will have to be cut to half of its digits [the first half, suitably rounded off]. The situation for a maximum of 10 digits is therefore typical, and we might as well use it to exemplify things.)

Thus the necessity of rounding off an (exact) 20-digit product to the regulation (maximum) number of 10 digits introduces in a digital machine qualitatively the same situation as was found above in an analogy machine. What it produces when a product is called for is not that product itself, but rather the product plus a small extra term—the round-off error. This error is, of course, not a random variable like the noise in an analogy machine. It is, arithmetically, completely determined in every particular instance. Yet its mode of determination is so complicated, and its variations throughout the number of instances of its occurrence in a problem so irregular, that it usually can be treated to a high degree of approximation as a random variable.

(These considerations apply to multiplication. For division the situation is even slightly worse, since a quotient can, in general, not be expressed with absolute precision by any finite number of digits. Hence here rounding off is usually already a necessity after the first operation. For addition and subtraction, on the other hand, this difficulty does not arise: The sum or difference has the same number of digits [if there is no increase in size beyond the planned maximum] as the addends themselves. Size may create difficulties which are added to the difficulties of precision discussed here, but I shall not go into these at this time.)

The role of the digital procedure in reducing the noise level

The important difference between the noise level of a digital machine, as described above, and of an analogy machine is not qualitative at all; it is quantitative. As pointed out above, the relative noise level of an analogy machine is never lower than 1 in 10^5, and in many cases as high as 1 in 10^2. In the 10-place decimal digital machine referred to above the relative noise level (due to round-off) is 1 part in 10^{10}. Thus the real importance of the digital procedure lies in its ability to reduce the computational noise level to an extent which is completely unobtainable by any other (analogy) procedure. In addition, further reduction of the noise level is increasingly difficult in an analogy mechanism, and increasingly easy in a digital one. In an analogy machine a precision of 1 in 10^3 is easy to achieve; 1 in 10^4 somewhat difficult; 1 in 10^5 very difficult; and 1 in 10^6 impossible, in the present state of technology. In a digital machine, the above precisions mean merely that one builds the machine to 3, 4, 5, and 6 decimal places, respectively. Here the transition from each stage to the next one gets actually easier. Increasing a 3-place machine (if anyone wished to build such a machine) to a 4-place machine is a 33 per cent increase; going from 4 to 5 places, a 20 per cent increase; going from 5 to 6 places, a 17 per cent increase. Going from 10 to 11 places is only a 10 per cent increase. This is clearly an entirely different milieu, from the point of view of the reduction of "random noise," from that of physical processes. It is here—and not in its practically ineffective absolute reliability—that the importance of the digital procedure lies.

Comparisons between computing machines and living organisms

Mixed character of living organisms

When the central nervous system is examined, elements of both procedures, digital and analogy, are discernible.

The neuron transmits an impulse. This appears to be its primary function, even if the last word about this function and its exclusive or non-exclusive character is far from having been said. The nerve impulse seems in the main to be an all-or-none affair, comparable to a binary digit. Thus a digital element is evidently present, but it is equally evident that this is not the entire story. A great deal of what goes on in the organism is not mediated in this manner, but is dependent on the general chemical composition of the blood stream or of other humoral media. It is well known that there are various composite functional sequences in the organism which have to go through a variety of steps from the original stimulus to the ultimate effect—some of the steps being neural, that is, digital, and others humoral, that is, analogy. These digital and analogy portions in such a chain may alternately multiply. In certain cases of this type, the chain can actually feed back into itself, that is, its ultimate output may again stimulate its original input.

It is well known that such mixed (part neural and part humoral) feedback chains can produce processes of great importance. Thus the mechanism which keeps the blood pressure constant is of this mixed type. The nerve which senses and reports the blood pressure does it by a sequence of neural impulses, that is, in a digital manner. The muscular contraction which this impulse system induces may still be described as a superposition of many digital impulses. The influence of such a contraction on the blood stream is, however, hydrodynamical, and hence analogy. The reaction of the pressure thus produced back on the nerve which reports the pressure closes the circular feedback, and at this point the analogy procedure again goes over into a digital one. The comparisons between the living organisms and the computing machines are, therefore, certainly imperfect at this point. The living organisms are very complex—part digital and part analogy mechanisms. The computing machines, at least in their recent forms to which I am referring in this discussion, are purely digital. Thus I must ask you to accept this oversimplification of the system. Although I am well aware of the analogy component in living organisms, and it would be absurd to deny its importance, I shall, nevertheless, for the sake of the simpler discussion, disregard that part. I shall consider the living organisms as if they were purely digital automata.

Mixed character of each element

In addition to this, one may argue that even the neuron is not exactly a digital organ. This point has been put forward repeatedly and with great force. There is certainly a great deal of truth in it, when one considers things in considerable detail. The relevant assertion is, in this respect, that the fully developed nervous impulse, to which all-or-none character can be attributed, is not an elementary phenomenon, but is highly complex. It is a degenerate state of the complicated electrochemical complex which constitutes the neuron, and which in its fully analyzed functioning must be viewed as an analogy machine. Indeed, it is possible to stimulate the neuron in such a way that the breakdown that releases the nervous stimulus will not occur. In this area of "subliminal stimulation," we find first (that is, for the weakest stimulations) responses which are proportional to the stimulus, and then (at higher, but still subliminal, levels of stimulation) responses which depend on more complicated non-linear laws, but are nevertheless continuously variable and not of the breakdown type. There are also other complex phenomena within and without the subliminal range: fatigue, summation, certain forms of self-oscillation, etc.

In spite of the truth of these observations, it should be remembered that they may represent an improperly rigid critique of the concept of an all-or-none organ. The electromechanical relay, or the vacuum tube, when properly used, are undoubtedly all-or-none organs. Indeed, they are the prototypes of such organs. yet both of them are in reality complicated analogy mechanisms, which upon appropriately adjusted stimulation respond continuously, linearly or non-linearly, and exhibit the phenomena of "breakdown" or "all-or-none" response only under very particular conditions of operation. There is little difference between this performance and the above-described performance of neurons. To put it somewhat differently. None of these is an exclusively all-or-none organ (there is little in our technological or physiological experience to indicate that absolute all-or-none organs exist); this, however, is irrelevant. By an all-or-none organ we should rather mean one which fulfills the following two conditions. First, it functions in the all-or-none manner under certain suitable operating conditions. Second, these operating conditions are the ones under which it is normally used; they represent the functionally normal state of affairs within the large organism, of which it forms a part. Thus the important fact is not whether an organ has necessarily and under all conditions the all-or-none character—this is probably never the case—but rather whether in its proper context it functions primarily, and appears to be intended to function primarily, as an all-or-none organ. I realize that this definition brings in rather undesirable criteria of "propriety" of context, of "appearance" and "intention." I do not see, however, how we can avoid using them, and how we can forego counting on the employment of common sense in their application. I shall, accordingly, in what follows use the working hypothesis that the neuron is an all-or-none digital organ. I realize that the last word about this has not been said, but I hope that the above excursus on the limitations of this working hypothesis and the reasons for its use will reassure you. I merely want to simplify my discussion; I am not trying to prejudge any essential open question.

In the same sense, I think that it is permissible to discuss the neurons as electrical organs. The stimulation of a neuron, the development and progress of its impulse, and the stimulating effects of the impulse at a synapse can all be described electrically. The concomitant chemical and other processes are important in order to understand the internal functioning of a nerve cell. They may even be more important than the electrical phenomena. They seem, however, to be hardly necessary for a description of a neuron as a "black box," an organ of the all-or-none type. Again the situation is no worse here than it is for, say, a vacuum tube. Here, too, the purely electrical phenomena are accompanied by numerous other phenomena of solid state physics, thermodynamics, mechanics. All of these are important to understand the structure of a vacuum tube, but are best excluded from the discussion, if it is to treat the vacuum tube as a "black box" with a schematic description.

The concept of a switching organ or relay organ

The neuron, as well as the vacuum tube, viewed under the aspects discussed above, are then two instances of the same generic entity, which it is customary to call a "switching organ" or "relay organ." (The electromechanical relay is, of course, another instance.) Such an organ is defined as a "black box," which responds to a specified stimulus or combination of stimuli by an energetically independent response. That is, the response is expected to have enough energy to cause several stimuli of the same kind as the ones which initiated it. The energy of the response, therefore, cannot have been supplied by the original stimulus. It must originate in a different and independent source of power. The stimulus merely directs, controls the flow of energy from this source.

(This source, in the case of the neuron, is the general metabolism of the neuron. In the case of a vacuum tube, it is the power which maintains the cathode-plate potential difference, irrespective of whether the tube is conducting or not, and to a lesser extent the heater power which keeps "boiling" electrons out of the cathode. In the case of the electro-mechanical relay, it is the current supply whose path the relay is closing or opening.)

The basic switching organs of the living organisms, at least to the extent to which we are considering them here, are the neurons. The basic switching organs of the recent types of computing machines are vacuum tubes; in older ones they were wholly or partially electromechanical relays. It is quite possible that computing machines will not always be primarily aggregates of switching organs, but such a development is as yet quite far in the future. A development which may lie much closer is that the vacuum tubes may be displaced from their role of switching organs in computing machines. This, too, however, will probably not take place for a few years yet. I shall, therefore, discuss computing machines solely from the point of view of aggregates of switching organs which are vacuum tubes.

Comparison of the sizes of large computing machines and living organisms.

Two well-known, very large vacuum tube computing machines are in existence and in operation. Both consist of about 20,000 switching organs. One is a pure vacuum tube machine. (It belongs to the U. S. Army Ordnance Department, Ballistic Research Laboratories, Aberdeen, Maryland, designation "ENIAC.") The other is mixed—part vacuum tube and part electro-mechanical relays. (It belongs to the I. B. M. Corporation, and is located in New York, designation "SSEC.") These machines are a good deal larger than what is likely to be the size of the vacuum tube computing machines which will come into existence and operation in the next few years. It is probable that each one of these will consist of 2000 to 6000 switching organs. (The reason for this decrease lies in a different attitude about the treatment of the "memory," which I will not discuss here.) It is possible that in later years the machine sizes will increase again, but it is not likely that 10,000 (or perhaps a few times 10,000) switching organs will be exceeded as long as the present techniques and philosophy are employed. To sum up, about 10^4 switching organs seem to be the proper order of magnitude for a computing machine.

In contrast to this, the number of neurons in the central nervous system has been variously estimated as something of the order of 10^{10} I do not know how good this figure is, but presumably the exponent at least is not too high, and not too low by more than a unit. Thus it is very conspicuous that the central nervous system is at least a million times larger than the largest artificial automaton that we can talk about at present. It is quite interesting to inquire why this should be so and what questions of principle are involved. It seems to me that a few very clear-cut questions of principle are indeed involved.

Determination of the significant ratio of sizes for the elements

Obviously, the vacuum tube, as we know it, is gigantic compared to a nerve cell. Its physical volume is about a billion times larger, and its energy dissipation is about a billion times greater. (It is, of course, impossible to give such figures with a unique validity, but the above ones are typical.) There is, on the other hand, a certain compensation for this. Vacuum tubes can be made to operate at exceedingly high speeds in applications other than computing machines, but these need not concern us here. In computing machines the maximum is a good deal lower, but it is still quite respectable. In the present state of the art, it is generally believed to be somewhere around a million actuations per second. The responses of a nerve cell are a good deal slower than this, perhaps 1/2000 of a second, and what really matters, the minimum time-interval required from stimulation to complete recovery and, possibly, renewed stimulation, is still longer than this—at best approximately 1/200 of a second. This gives a ratio of 1:5000, which, however, may be somewhat too favorable to the vacuum tube, since vacuum tubes, when used as switching organs at the 1,000,000 steps per second rate, are practically never run at a 100 per cent duty cycle. A ratio like 1:2000 would, therefore, seem to be more equitable. Thus the vacuum tube, at something like a billion times the expense, outperforms the neuron by a factor of somewhat over 1000. There is, therefore, some justice in saying that it is less efficient by a factor of the order of a million.

The basic fact is, in every respect, the small size of the neuron compared to the vacuum tube. This ratio is about a billion, as pointed out above. What is it due to?

Analysis of the reasons for the extreme ratio of sizes

The origin of this discrepancy lies in the fundamental control organ or, rather, control arrangement of the vacuum tube as compared to that of the neuron. In the vacuum tube the critical area of control is the space between the cathode (where the active agents, the electrons, originate) and the grid (which controls the electron flow). This space is about one millimeter deep. The corresponding entity in a neuron is the wall of the nerve cell, the "membrane." Its thickness is about a micron (1/1000 millimeter), or somewhat less. At this point, therefore, there is a ratio of approximately 1:1000 in linear dimensions. This, by the way, is the main difference. The electrical fields, which exist in the controlling space, are about the same for the vacuum tube and for the neuron. The potential differences by which these organs can be reliably steered are tens of volts in one case and tens of millivolts in the other. Their ratio is again about 1:1000, and hence their gradients (the field strengths) are about identical. Now a ratio of 1:1000 in linear dimensions corresponds to a ratio of 1:1,000,000,000 in volume. Thus the discrepancy factor of a billion in 3-dimensional size (volume) corresponds, as it should, to a discrepancy factor of 1000 in linear size, that is, to the difference between the millimeter interelectrode-space depth of the vacuum tube and the micron membrane thickness of the neuron.

It is worth nothing, although it is by no means surprising, how this divergence between objects, both of which are microscopic and are situated in the interior of the elementary components, leads to impressive macroscopic differences between the organisms built upon them. This difference between a millimeter object and a micron object causes the ENIAC to weigh 30 tons and to dissipate 150 kilowatts of energy, while the human central nervous system, which is functionally about a million times larger, has the weight of the order of a pound and is accommodated within the human skull. In assessing the weight and size of the ENIAC as stated above, we should also remember that this huge apparatus is needed in order to handle 20 numbers of 10 decimals each, that is, a total of 200 decimal digits, the equivalent of about 700 binary digits—merely 700 simultaneous pieces of "yes-no" information!

Technological interpretation of these reasons

These considerations should make it clear that our present technology is still very imperfect in handling information at high speed and high degrees of complexity. The apparatus which results is simply enormous, both physically and in its energy requirements.

The weakness of this technology lies probably, in part at least, in the materials employed. Our present techniques involve the using of metals, with rather close spacings, and at certain critical points separated by vacuum only. This combination of media has a peculiar mechanical instability that is entirely alien to living nature. By this I mean the simple fact that, if a living organism is mechanically injured, it has a strong tendency to restore itself. If, on the other hand, we hit a man-made mechanism with a sledge hammer, no such restoring tendency is apparent. If two pieces of metal are close together, the small vibrations and other mechanical disturbances, which always exist in the ambient medium, constitute a risk in that they may bring them into contact. If they were at different electrical potentials, the next thing that may happen after this short circuit is that they can become electrically soldered together and the contact becomes permanent. At this point, then, a genuine and permanent breakdown will have occurred. When we injure the membrane of a nerve cell, no such thing happens. On the contrary, the membrane will usually reconstitute itself after a short delay.

It is this mechanical instability of our materials which prevents us from reducing sizes further. This instability and other phenomena of a comparable character make the behavior in our componentry less than wholly reliable, even at the present sizes. Thus it is the inferiority of our materials, compared with those used in nature, which prevents us from attaining the high degree of complication and the small dimensions which have been attained by natural organisms.

The future logical theory of automata

Further discussion of the factors that limit the present size of artificial automata

We have emphasized how the complication is limited in artificial automata, that is, the complication which can be handled without extreme difficulties and for which automata can still be expected to function reliably. Two reasons that put a limit on complication in this sense have already been given. They are the large size and the limited reliability of the componentry that we must use, both of them due to the fact that we are employing materials which seem to be quite satisfactory in simpler applications, but marginal and inferior to the natural ones in this highly complex application. There is, however, a third important limiting factor, and we should now turn our attention to it. This factor is of an intellectual and not physical, character.

The limitation which is due to the lack of a logical theory of automata

We are very far from possessing a theory of automata which deserves that name, that is, a properly mathematical-logical theory. There exists today a very elaborate system of formal logic, and, specifically, of logic as applied to mathematics. This is a discipline with many good sides, but also with certain serious weaknesses. This is not the occasion to enlarge upon the good sides, which I have certainly no intention to belittle. About the inadequacies, however, this may be said: Everybody who has worked in formal logic will confirm that it is one of the technically most refractory parts of mathematics. The reason for this is that it deals with rigid, all-or-none concepts, and has very little contact with the continuous concept of the real or of the complex number, that is, with mathematical analysis. Yet analysis is the technically most successful and best-elaborated part of mathematics. Thus formal logic is, by the nature of its approach, cut off from the best cultivated portions of mathematics, and forced onto the most difficult part of the mathematical terrain, into combinatorics.

The theory of automata, of the digital, all-or-none type, as discussed up to now, is certainly a chapter in formal logic. It would, therefore, seem that it will have to share this unattractive property of formal logic. It will have to be, from the mathematical point of view, combinatorial rather than analytical.

Probable characteristics of such a theory

Now it seems to me that this will in fact not be the case. In studying the functioning of automata, it is clearly necessary to pay attention to a circumstance which has never before made its appearance in formal logic.

Throughout all modern logic, the only thing that is important is whether a result can be achieved in a finite number of elementary steps or not. The size of the number of steps which are required, on the other hand, is hardly ever a concern of formal logic. Any finite sequence of correct steps is, as a matter of principle, as good as any other. It is a matter of no consequence whether the number is small or large, or even so large that it couldn't possibly be carried out in a lifetime, or in the presumptive lifetime of the stellar universe as we know it. In dealing with automata, this statement must be significantly modified. In the case of an automaton the thing which matters is not only whether it can reach a certain result in a finite number of steps at all but also how many such steps are needed. There are two reasons. First, automata are constructed in order to reach certain results in certain pre-assigned durations, or at least in pre-assigned orders of magnitude of duration. Second, the componentry employed has on every individual operation a small but nevertheless non-zero probability of failing. In a sufficiently long chain of operations the cumulative effect of these individual probabilities of failure may (if unchecked) reach the order of magnitude of unity—at which point it produces, in effect, complete unreliability. The probability levels which are involved here are very low, but still not too far removed from the domain of ordinary technological experience. It is not difficult to estimate that a high-speed computing machine, dealing with a typical problem, may have to perform as much as 10^{12} individual operations. The probability of error on an individual operation which can be tolerated must, therefore, be small compared to 10^{-12}. I might mention that an electromechanical relay (a telephone relay) is at present considered acceptable if its probability of failure on an individual operation is of the order 10^{-8}. It is considered excellent if this order of probability is 10^{-9}. Thus the reliabilities required in a high-speed computing machine are higher, but not prohibitively higher, than those that constitute sound practice in certain existing industrial fields. The actually obtainable reliabilities are, however, not likely to leave a very wide margin against the minimum requirements just mentioned. An exhaustive study and a nontrivial theory will, therefore, certainly be called for.

Thus the logic of automata will differ from the present system of formal logic in two relevant respects.

1. The actual length of "chains of reasoning," that is, of the chains of operations, will have to be considered.

2. The operations of logic (syllogisms, conjunctions, disjunctions, negations, etc., that is, in the terminology that is customary for automata, various forms of gating, coincidence, anti-coincidence, blocking, etc., actions) will all have to be treated by procedures which allow exceptions (malfunctions) with low but non-zero probabilities. All of this will lead to theories which are much less rigidly of an all-or-none nature than past and present formal logic. They will be of a much less combinatorial, and much more analytical, character. In fact, there are numerous indications to make us believe that this new system of formal logic will move closer to another discipline which has been little linked in the past with logic. This is thermodynamics, primarily in the form it was received from Boltzmann, and is that part of theoretical physics which comes nearest in some of its aspects to manipulating and measuring information. Its techniques are indeed much more analytical than combinatorial, which again illustrates the point that I have been trying to make above. It would, however, take me too far to go into this subject more thoroughly on this occasion.

All of this re-emphasizes the conclusion that was indicated earlier, that a detailed, highly mathematical, and more specifically analytical, theory of automata and of information is needed. We possess only the first indications of such a theory at present. In assessing artificial automata, which are, as I discussed earlier, of only moderate size, it has been possible to get along in a rough, empirical manner without such a theory. There is every reason to believe that this will not be possible with more elaborate automata.

Effects of the lack of a logical theory of automata on the procedures
in dealing with errors

This, then, is the last, and very important, limiting factor. It is unlikely that we could construct automata of a much higher complexity than the ones we now have, without possessing a very advanced and subtle theory of automata and information. A fortiori, this is inconceivable for automata of such enormous complexity as is possessed by the human central nervous system.

This intellectual inadequacy certainly prevents us from getting much farther than we are now.

A simple manifestation of this factor is our present relation to error checking. In living organisms malfunctions of components occur. The organism obviously has a way to detect them and render them harmless. It is easy to estimate that the number of nerve actuations which occur in a normal lifetime must be of the order of 10^{20}. Obviously, during this chain of events there never occurs a malfunction which cannot be corrected by the organism itself, without any significant outside intervention. The system must, therefore, contain the necessary arrangements to diagnose errors as they occur, to readjust the organism so as to minimize the effects of the errors, and finally to correct or to block permanently the faulty components. Our modus procedendi with respect to malfunctions in our artificial automata is entirely different. Here the actual practice, which has the consensus of all experts of the field, is somewhat like this: Every effort is made to detect (by mathematical or by automatical checks) every error as soon as it occurs. Then an attempt is made to isolate the component that caused the error as rapidly as feasible. This may be done partly automatically, but in any case a significant part of this diagnosis must be effected by intervention from the outside. Once the faulty component has been identified, it is immediately corrected or replaced.

Note the difference in these two attitudes. The basic principle of dealing with malfunctions in nature is to make their effect as unimportant as possible and to apply correctives, if they are necessary at all, at leisure. In our dealings with artificial automata, on the other hand, we require an immediate diagnosis. Therefore, we are trying to arrange the automata in such a manner that errors will become as conspicuous as possible, and intervention and correction follow immediately. In other words, natural organisms are constructed to make errors as inconspicuous, as harmless, as possible. Artificial automata are designed to make errors as conspicuous, as disastrous, as possible. The rationale of this difference is not far to seek. Natural organisms are sufficiently well conceived to be able to operate even when malfunctions have set in. They can operate in spite of malfunctions, and their subsequent tendency is to remove these malfunctions. An artificial automaton could certainly be designed so as to be able to operate normally in spite of a limited number of malfunctions in certain limited areas. Any malfunction, however, represents a considerable risk that some generally degenerating process has already set in within the machine. It is, therefore, necessary to intervene immediately, because a machine which has begun to malfunction has only rarely a tendency to restore itself, and will more probably go from bad to worse. All of this comes back to one thing. With our artificial automata we are moving much more in the dark than nature appears to be with its organisms. We are, and apparently, at least at present, have to be, much more "scared" by the occurrence of an isolated error and by the malfunction which must be behind it. Our behavior is clearly that of overcaution, generated by ignorance.

The single-error principle

A minor side light to this is that almost all our error-diagnosing techniques are based on the assumption that the machine contains only one faulty component. In this case, iterative subdivisions of the machine into parts permit us to determine which portion contains the fault. As soon as the possibility exists that the machine may contain several faults, these, rather powerful, dichotomic methods of diagnosis are lost. Error diagnosing then becomes an increasingly hopeless proposition. The high premium on keeping the number of errors to be diagnosed down to one, or at any rate as low as possible, again illustrates our ignorance in this field, and is one of the main reasons why errors must be made as conspicuous as possible, in order to be recognized and apprehended as soon after their occurrence as feasible, that is, before further errors have had time to develop.

Principles of digitalization

Digitalization of continuous quantities: the digital expansion method and the counting method

Consider the digital part of a natural organism; specifically, consider the nervous system. It seems that we are indeed justified in assuming that this is a digital mechanism, that it transmits messages which are made up of signals possessing the all-or-none character. (See also the earlier discussion, page 10.) In other words, each elementary signal, each impulse, simply either is or is not there, with no further shadings. A particularly relevant illustration of this fact is furnished by those cases where the underlying problem has the opposite character, that is, where the nervous system is actually called upon to transmit a continuous quantity. Thus the case of a nerve which has to report on the value of a pressure is characteristic.

Assume, for example, that a pressure (clearly a continuous quantity) is to be transmitted. It is well known how this trick is done. The nerve which does it still transmits nothing but individual all-or-none impulses. How does it then express the continuously numerical value of pressure in terms of these impulses, that is, of digits? In other words, how does it encode a continuous number into a digital notation? It does certainly not do it by expanding the number in question into decimal (or binary, or any other base) digits in the conventional sense. What appears to happen is that it transmits pulses at a frequency which varies and which is within certain limits proportional to the continuous quantity in question, and generally a monotone function of it. The mechanism which achieves this "encoding" is, therefore, essentially a frequency modulation system.

The details are known. The nerve has a finite recovery time. In other words, after it has been pulsed once, the time that has to lapse before another stimulation is possible is finite and dependent upon the strength of the ensuing (attempted) stimulation. Thus, if the nerve is under the influence of a continuing stimulus (one which is uniformly present at all times, like the pressure that is being considered here), then the nerve will respond periodically, and the length of the period between two successive stimulations is the recovery time referred to earlier, that is, a function of the strength of the constant stimulus (the pressure in the present case). Thus, under a high pressure, the nerve may be able to respond every 8 milliseconds, that is, transmit at the rate of 125 impulses per second; while under the influence of a smaller pressure it may be able to repeat only every 14 milliseconds, that is, transmit at the rate of 71 times per second. This is very clearly the behavior of a genuinely yes-or-no organ, of a digital organ. It is very instructive, however, that it uses a "count" rather than a "decimal expansion" (or "binary expansion," etc.) method.

Comparison of the two methods. The preference of living organisms for the counting method

Compare the merits and demerits of these two methods. The counting method is certainly less efficient than the expansion method. In order to express a number of about a million (that is, a physical quantity of a million distinguishable resolution steps) by counting, a million pulses have to be transmitted. In order to express a number of the same size by expansion, 6 or 7 decimal digits are needed, that is, about 20 binary digits. Hence, in this case only 20 pulses are needed. Thus our expansion method is much more economical in notation than the counting methods which are resorted to by nature. On the other hand, the counting method has a high stability and safety from error. If you express a number of the order of a million by counting and miss a count, the result is only irrelevantly changed. If you express it by (decimal or binary) expansion, a single error in a single digit may vitiate the entire result. Thus the undesirable trait of our computing machines reappears in our digital expansion system; in fact, the former is clearly deeply connected with, and partly a consequence of, the latter. The high stability and nearly error-proof character of natural organisms, on the other hand, is reflected in the counting method that they seem to use in this case. All of this reflects a general rule. You can increase the safety from error by a reduction of the efficiency of the notation, or, to say it positively, by allowing redundancy of notation. Obviously, the simplest form of achieving safety by redundancy is to use the, per se, quite unsafe digital expansion notation, but to repeat every such message several times. In the case under discussion, nature has obviously resorted to an even more redundant and even safer system.

There are, of course, probably other reasons why the nervous system uses the counting rather than the digital expansion. The encoding-decoding facilities required by the former are much simpler than those required by the latter. It is true, however, that nature seems to be willing and able to go much further in the direction of complication than we are, or rather than we can afford to go. One may, therefore, suspect that if the only demerit of the digital expansion system were its greater logical complexity, nature would not, for this reason alone, have rejected it. It is, nevertheless, true that we have nowhere an indication of its use in natural organisms. It is difficult to tell how much "final" validity one should attach to this observation. The point deserves at any rate attention, and should receive it in future investigations of the functioning of the nervous system.

Formal neural networks

The McCulloch-Pitts theory of formal neural networks

A great deal more could be said about these things from the logical and the organizational point of view, but I shall not attempt to say it here. I shall instead go on to discuss what is probably the most significant result obtained with the axiomatic method up to now. I mean the remarkable theorems of McCulloch and Pitts on the relationship of logics and neural networks.

In this discussion I shall, as I have said, take the strictly axiomatic point of view. I shall, therefore, view a neuron as a "black box" with a certain number of inputs that receive stimuli and an output that emits stimuli. To be specific, I shall assume that the input connections of each one of these can be of two types, excitatory and inhibitory. The boxes themselves are also of two types, threshold 1 and threshold 2. These concepts are linked and circumscribed by the following definitions. In order to stimulate such an organ it is necessary that it should receive simultaneously at least as many stimuli on its excitatory inputs as correspond to its threshold, and not a single stimulus on any one of its inhibitory inputs. If it has been thus stimulated, it will after a definite time delay (which is assumed to be always the same, and may be used to define the unit of time) emit an output pulse. This pulse can be taken by appropriate connections to any number of inputs of other neurons (also to any of its own

435

inputs) and will produce at each of these the same type of input stimulus as the ones described above.

It is, of course, understood that this is an oversimplification of the actual functioning of a neuron. I have already discussed the character, the limitations, and the advantages of the axiomatic method. (See pages 2 and 10.) They all apply here, and the discussion which follows is to be taken in this sense.

McCulloch and Pitts have used these units to build up complicated networks which may be called "formal neural networks." Such a system is built up of any number of these units, with their inputs and outputs suitably interconnected with arbitrary complexity. The "functioning" of such a network may be defined by singling out some of the inputs of the entire system and some of its outputs, and then describing what original stimuli on the former are to cause what ultimate stimuli on the latter.

The main result of the McCulloch-Pitts theory

McCulloch and Pitts' important result is that any functioning in this sense which can be defined at all logically, strictly, and unambiguously in a finite number of words can also be realized by such a formal neural network.

It is well to pause at this point and to consider what the implications are. It has often been claimed that the activities and functions of the human nervous system are so complicated that no ordinary mechanism could possibly perform them. It has also been attempted to name specific functions which by their nature exhibit this limitation. It has been attempted to show that such specific functions, logically, completely described, are per se unable of mechanical, neural realization. The McCulloch-Pitts result puts an end to this. It proves that anything that can be exhaustively and unambiguously described, anything that can be completely and unambiguously put into words, is ipso facto realizable by a suitable finite neural network. Since the converse statement is obvious, we can therefore say that there is no difference between the possibility of describing a real or imagined mode of behaviour completely and unambiguously in words, and the possibility of realizing it by a finite formal neural network. The two concepts are co-extensive. A difficulty of principle embodying any mode of behavior in such a network can exist only if we are also unable to describe that behavior completely.

Thus the remaining problems are these two. First, if a certain mode of behavior can be effected by a finite neural network, the question still remains whether that network can be realized within a practical size, specifically, whether it will fit into the physical limitations of the organism in question. Second, the question arises whether every existing mode of behavior can really be put completely and unambiguously into words.

The first problem is, of course, the ultimate problem of nerve physiology, and I shall not attempt to go into it any further here. The second question is of a different character, and it has interesting logical connotations.

Interpretations of this result

There is no doubt that any special phase of any conceivable form of behavior can be described "completely and unambiguously" in words. This description may be lengthy, but it is always possible. To deny it would amount to adhering to a form of logical mysticism which is surely far from most of us. It is, however, an important limitation, that this applies only to every element separately, and it is far from clear how it will apply to the entire syndrome of behavior. To be more specific, there is no difficulty in describing how an organism might be able to identify any two rectilinear triangles, which appear on the retina, as belonging to the same category "triangle." There is also no difficulty in adding to this, that numerous other objects, besides regularly drawn rectilinear triangles, will also be classified and identified as triangles—triangles whose sides are curved, triangles whose sides are not fully drawn, triangles that are indicated merely by a more or less homogeneous shading of their interior, etc. The more completely we attempt to describe everything that may conceivably fall under this heading, the longer the description, becomes. We may have a vague and uncomfortable feeling that a complete catalogue along such lines would not only be exceedingly long, but also unavoidably indefinite at its boundaries. Nevertheless, this may be a possible operation.

All of this, however, constitutes only a small fragment of the more general concept of identification of analogous geometrical entities. This, in turn, is only a microscopic piece of the general concept of analogy. Nobody would attempt to describe and define within any practical amount of space the general concept of analogy which dominates our interpretation of vision. There is no basis for saying whether such an enterprise would require thousands or millions or altogether impractical numbers of volumes. Now it is perfectly possible that the simplest and only practical way actually to say what constitutes a visual analogy consists in giving a description of the connections of the visual brain. We are dealing here with parts of logics with which we have practically no past experience. The order of complexity is out of all proportion to anything we have ever known. We have no right to assume that the logical notations and procedures used in the past are suited to this part of the subject. It is not at all certain that in this domain a real object might not constitute the simplest description of itself, that is, any attempt to describe it by the usual literary or formal-logical method may lead to something less manageable and more involved. In fact, some results in modern logic would tend to indicate that phenomena like this have to be expected when we come to really complicated entities. It is, therefore, not at all unlikely that it is futile to look for a precise logical concept, that is, for a precise verbal description, of "visual analogy." It is possible that the connection pattern of the visual brain itself is the simplest logical expression or definition of this principle.

Obviously, there is on this level no more profit in the McCulloch-Pitts result. At this point it only furnishes another illustration of the situation outlined earlier. There is an equivalence between logical principles and their embodiment in a neural network, and while in the simpler cases the principles might furnish a simplified expression of the network, it is quite possible that in cases of extreme complexity the reverse is true.

All of this does not alter my belief that a new, essentially logical, theory is called for in order to understand high-complication automata and, in particular, the central nervous system. It may be, however, that in this process logic will have to undergo a pseudomorphosis to neurology to a much greater extent than the reverse. The foregoing analysis shows that one of the relevant things we can do at this moment with respect to the theory of the central nervous system is to point out the directions in which the real problem does not lie.

The concept of complication; self-reproduction

The concept of complication

The discussions so far have shown that high complexity plays an important role in any theoretical effort relating to automata, and that this concept, in spite of its prima facie quantitative character, may in fact stand for something qualitative—for a matter of principle. For the remainder of my discussion I will consider a remoter implication of this concept, one which makes one of the qualitative aspects of its nature even more explicit.

There is a very obvious trait, of the "vicious circle" type, in nature, the simplest expression of which is the fact that very complicated organisms can reproduce themselves.

We are all inclined to suspect in a vague way the existence of a concept of "complication." This concept and its putative properties have never been clearly formulated. We are, however, always tempted to assume that they will work in this way. When an automaton performs certain operations, they must be expected to be of a lower degree of complication than the automaton itself. In particular, if an automaton has the ability to construct another one, there must be a decrease in complication as we go from the parent to the construct. That is, if A can produce B, then A in some way must have contained a complete description of B. In order to make it effective, there must be, furthermore, various arrangements in A that see to it that this description is interpreted and that the constructive operations that it calls for are carried out. In this sense, it would therefore seem that a certain degenerating tendency must be expected, some decrease in complexity as one automaton makes another automaton.

Although this has some indefinite plausibility to it, it is in clear contradiction with the most obvious things that go on in nature. Organisms reproduce

438

themselves, that is, they produce new organisms with no decrease in complexity. In addition, there are long periods of evolution during which the complexity is even increasing. Organisms are indirectly derived from others which had lower complexity.

Thus there exists an apparent conflict of plausibility and evidence, if nothing worse. In view of this, it seems worth while to try to see whether there is anything involved here which can be formulated rigorously.

So far I have been rather vague and confusing, and not unintentionally at that. It seems to me that it is otherwise impossible to give a fair impression of the situation that exists here. Let me now try to become specific.

Turing's theory of computing automata

The English logician, Turing, about twelve years ago attacked the following problem.

He wanted to give a general definition of what is meant by a computing automaton. The formal definition came out as follows:

An automaton is a "black box," which will not be described in detail but is expected to have the following attributes. It possesses a finite number of states, which need be prima facie characterized only by stating their number, say n, and by enumerating them accordingly: $1, 2, \ldots n$. The essential operating characteristic of the automaton consists of describing how it is caused to change its state, that is, to go over from a state i into a state j. This change requires some interaction with the outside world, which will be standardized in the following manner. As far as the machine is concerned, let the whole outside world consist of a long paper tape. Let this tape be, say, 1 inch wide, and let it be subdivided into fields (squares) 1 inch long. On each field of this strip we may or may not put a sign, say, a dot, and it is assumed that it is possible to erase as well as to write in such a dot. A field marked with a dot will be called a "1," a field unmarked with a dot will be called a "0." (We might permit more ways of marking, but Turing showed that this is irrelevant and does not lead to any essential gain in generality.) In describing the position of the tape relative to the automaton it is assumed that one particular field of the tape is under direct inspection by the automaton, and that the automaton has the ability to move the tape forward and backward, say, by one field at a time. In specifying this, let the automaton be in the state i ($= 1 \ldots, n$), and let it see on the tape an e ($= 0, 1$). It will then go over into the state j ($= 0, 1, \ldots, n$), move the tape by p fields ($p = 0, +1, -1$; $+1$ is a move forward, -1 is a move backward), and inscribe into the new field that it sees f ($= 0,1$; inscribing 0 means erasing; inscribing 1 means putting in a dot). Specifying j, p, f as functions of i, e is then the complete definition of the functioning of such an automaton.

Turing carried out a careful analysis of what mathematical processes can be effected by automata of this type. In this connection he proved various theorems concerning the classical "decision problem" of logic, but I shall not go into these matters here. He did, however, also introduce and analyze the concept of a "universal automaton," and this is part of the subject that is relevant in the present context.

An infinite sequence of digits e (= 0, 1) is one of the basic entities in mathematics. Viewed as a binary expansion, it is essentially equivalent to the concept of a real number. Turing, therefore, based his consideration on these sequences.

He investigated the question as to which automata were able to construct which sequences. That is, given a definite law for the formation of such a sequence, he inquired as to which automata can be used to form the sequence based on that law. The process of "forming" a sequence is interpreted in this manner. An automaton is able to "form" a certain sequence if it is possible to specify a finite length of tape, appropriately marked, so that, if this tape is fed to the automaton in question, the automaton will thereupon write the sequence on the remaining (infinite) free portion of the tape. This process of writing the infinite sequence is, of course, an indefinitely continuing one. What is meant is that the automaton will keep running indefinitely and, given a sufficiently long time, will have inscribed any desired (but of course finite) part of the (infinite) sequence. The finite, premarked, piece of tape constitutes the "instruction" of the automaton for this problem.

An automaton is "universal" if any sequence that can be produced by any automaton at all can also be solved by this particular automaton. It will, of course, require in general a different instruction for this purpose.

The main result of the Turing theory

We might expect a priori that this is impossible. How can there be an automaton which is at least as effective as any conceivable automaton, including, for example, one of twice its size and complexity?

Turing, nevertheless, proved that this is possible. While his construction is rather involved, the underlying principle is nevertheless quite simple. Turing observed that a completely general description of any conceivable automaton can be (in the sense of the foregoing definition) given in a finite number of words. This description will contain certain empty passages—those referring to the functions mentioned earlier (j, p, f in terms of i, e), which specify the actual functioning of the automaton. When these empty passages are filled in, we deal with a specific automaton. As long as they are left empty, this schema represents the general definition of the general automaton. Now it becomes possible to describe an automaton which has the ability to interpret such a definition. In other words, which, when fed the functions that in the sense described above define a specific automaton, will thereupon function like the object described. The ability to do this is no more mysterious than the ability to read a dictionary and a grammar and to follow their

440

instructions about the uses and principles of combinations of words. This automaton, which is constructed to read a description and to imitate the object described, is then the universal automaton in the sense of Turing. To make it duplicate any operation that any other automaton can perform, it suffices to furnish it with a description of the automaton in question and, in addition, with the instructions which that device would have required for the operation under consideration.

Broadening of the program to deal with automata that produce automata

For the question which concerns me here, that of "self-reproduction" of automata, Turing's procedure is too narrow in one respect only. His automata are purely computing machines. Their output is a piece of tape with zeros and ones on it. What is needed for the construction to which I referred is an automaton whose output is other automata. There is, however, no difficulty in principle in dealing with this broader concept and in deriving from it the equivalent of Turing's result.

The basic definitions

As in the previous instance, it is again of primary importance to give a rigorous definition of what constitutes an automaton for the purpose of the investigation. First of all, we have to draw up a complete list of the elementary parts to be used. This list must contain not only a complete enumeration but also a complete operational definition of each elementary part. It is relatively easy to draw up such a list, that is, to write a catalogue of "machine parts" which is sufficiently inclusive to permit the construction of the wide variety of mechanisms here required, and which has the axiomatic rigor that is needed for this kind of consideration. The list need not be very long either. It can, of course, be made either arbitrarily long or arbitrarily short. It may be lengthened by including in it, as elementary parts, things which could be achieved by combinations of others. It can be made short—in fact, it can be made to consist of a single unit—by endowing each elementary part with a multiplicity of attributes and functions. Any statement on the number of elementary parts required will therefore represent a common-sense compromise, in which nothing too complicated is expected from any one elementary part, and no elementary part is made to perform several, obviously separate, functions. In this sense, it can be shown that about a dozen elementary parts suffice. The problem of self-reproduction can then be stated like this: Can one build an aggregate out of such elements in such a manner that if it is put into a reservoir, in which there float all these elements in large numbers, it will then begin to construct other aggregates, each of which will at the end turn out to be another automaton exactly like the original one?

441

This is feasible, and the principle on which it can be based is closely related to Turing's principle outlined earlier.

Outline of the derivation of the theorem regarding self-reproduction

First of all, it is possible to give a complete description of everything that is an automaton in the sense considered here. This description is to be conceived as a general one, that is, it will again contain empty spaces. These empty spaces have to be filled in with the functions which describe the actual structure of an automaton. As before, the difference between these spaces filled and unfilled is the difference between the description of a specific automaton and the general description of a general automaton. There is no difficulty of principle in describing the following automata.

(*a*) Automaton *A*, which when furnished the description of any other automaton in terms of appropriate functions, will construct that entity. The description should in this case not be given in the form of a marked tape, as in Turning's case, because we will not normally choose a tape as a structural element. It is quite easy, however, to describe combinations of structural elements which have all the notational properties of a tape with fields that can be marked. A description in this sense will be called an instruction and denoted by a letter *I*.

"Constructing" is to be understood in the same sense as before. The constructing automaton is supposed to be placed in a reservoir in which all elementary components in large numbers are floating, and it will effect its construction in that milieu. One need not worry about how a fixed automaton of this sort can produce others which are larger and more complex than itself. In this case the greater size and the higher complexity of the object to be constructed will be reflected in a presumably still greater size of the instructions *I* that have to be furnished. These instructions, as pointed out, will have to be aggregates of elementary parts. In this sense, certainly, an entity will enter the process whose size and complexity is determined by the size and complexity of the object to be constructed.

In what follows, all automata for whose construction the facility *A* will be used are going to share with *A* this property. All of them will have a place for an instruction *I*, that is, a place where such an instruction can be inserted. When such an automaton is being described (as, for example, by an appropriate instruction), the specification of the location for the insertion of an instruction *I* in the foregoing sense is understood to form a part of the description. We may, therefore, talk of "inserting a given instruction *I* into a given automaton," without any further explanation.

(*b*) Automaton *B*, which can make a copy of any instruction *I* that is furnished to it. *I* is an aggregate of elementary parts in the sense outlined in (*a*), replacing a tape. This facility will be used when *I* furnishes a description of another automaton. In other words, this automaton is nothing more subtle than a "reproducer"—the machine which can read a punched tape and produce a second punched tape that is identical with the first. Note that this automaton, too, can produce objects which are larger and more complicated than itself. Note again that there is nothing surprising about it. Since it can only copy, an object of the exact size and complexity of the output will have to be furnished to it as input.

After these preliminaries, we can proceed to the decisive step.

(c) Combine the automata A and B with each other, and with a control mechanism C which does the following. Let A be furnished with an instruction I (again in the sense of [a] and [b]). Then C will first cause A to construct the automaton which is described by this instruction I. Next C will cause B to copy the instruction I referred to above, and insert the copy into the automaton referred to above, which has just been constructed by A. Finally, C will separate this construction from the system $A + B + C$ and "turn it loose" as an independent entity.

(d) Denote the total aggregate $A + B + C$ by D.

(e) In order to function, the aggregate $D = A + B + C$ must be furnished with an instruction I, as described above. This instruction, as pointed out above, has to be inserted into A. Now form an instruction I_D, which describes this automaton D, and insert I_D into A within D. Call the aggregate which now results E.

E is clearly self-reproductive. Note that no vicious circle is involved. The decisive step occurs in E, when the instruction I_D, describing D, is constructed and attached to D. When the construction (the copying) of I_D is called for, D exists already, and it is in no wise modified by the construction of I_D. I_D is simply added to form E. Thus there is a definite chronological and logical order in which D and I_D have to be formed, and the process is legitimate and proper according to the rules of logic.

Interpretations of this result and of its immediate extensions

The description of this automaton E has some further attractive sides, into which I shall not go at this time at any length. For instance, it is quite clear that the instruction I_D is roughly effecting the functions of a gene. It is also clear that the copying mechanism B performs the fundamental act of reproduction, the duplication of the genetic material, which is clearly the fundamental operation in the multiplication of living cells. It is also easy to see how arbitrary alterations of the system E, and in particular of I_D, can exhibit certain typical traits which appear in connection with mutation, lethally as a rule, but with a possibility of continuing reproduction with a modification of traits. It is, of course, equally clear at which point the analogy ceases to be valid. The natural gene does probably not contain a complete description of the object whose construction its presence stimulates. It probably contains only general pointers, general cues. In the generality in which the foregoing consideration is moving, this simplification is not attempted. It is, nevertheless, clear that this simplification, and others similar to it, are in themselves of great and qualitative importance. We are very far from any real understanding of the natural processes if we do not attempt to penetrate such simplifying principles.

Small variations of the foregoing scheme also permit us to construct automata which can reproduce themselves and, in addition, construct others. (Such an automaton performs more specifically what is probably a—if not the—typical gene function, self-reproduction plus production—or stimulation of production—of certain specific enzymes.) Indeed, it suffices to replace the I_D by an instruction I_{D+F}, which describes the automaton D plus another given automation F. Let D, with I_{D+F} inserted into A within it, be designated by E_F. This E_F clearly has the property already described. It will reproduce itself, and, besides, construct F.

Note that a "mutation" of E_F, which takes place within the F-part of I_{D+F} in E_F, is not lethal. If it replaces F by F', it changes E_F into E_F, that is, the "mutant" is still self-reproductive; but its by-product is changed—F' instead of F. This is, of course, the typical non-lethal mutant.

All these are very crude steps in the direction of a systematic theory of automata. They represent, in addition, only one particular direction. This is, as I indicated before, the direction towards forming a rigorous concept of what constitutes "complication." They illustrate that "complication" on its lower levels is probably degenerative, that is, that every automaton that can produce other automata will only be able to produce less complicated ones. There is, however, a certain minimum level where this degenerative characteristic ceases to be universal. At this point automata which can reproduce themselves, or even construct higher entities, become possible. This fact, that complication, as well as organization, below a certain minimum level is degenerative, and beyond that level can become self-supporting and even increasing, will clearly play an important role in any future theory of the subject.

DISCUSSION

DR. MC CULLOCH: I confess that there is nothing I envy Dr. von Neumann more than the fact that the machines with which he has to cope are those for which he has, from the beginning, a blueprint of what the machine is supposed to do and how it is supposed to do it. Unfortunately for us in the biological sciences—or, at least, in psychiatry—we are presented with an alien, or enemy's, machine. We do not know exactly what the machine is supposed to do and certainly we have no blueprint of it. In attacking our problems, we only know, in psychiatry, that the machine is producing wrong answers. We know that, because of the damage by the machine to the machine itself and by its running amuck in the world. However, what sort of difficulty exists in that machine is no easy matter to determine.

As I see it what we need first and foremost is not a correct theory, but some theory to start from, whereby we may hope to ask a question so that we'll get an answer, if only to the effect that our notion was entirely erroneous. Most of the time we never even get around to asking the question in such a form that it can have an answer.

I'd like to say, historically, how I came to be interested in this particular problem, if you'll forgive me, because it does bear on this matter. I came, from a major interest in philosophy and mathematics, into psychology with the problem of how a thing like mathematics could ever arise—what sort of a thing it was. For that reason, I gradually shifted into psychology and thence, for the reason that I again and again failed to find the significant variables, I was forced into neurophysiology. The attempt to construct a theory in a field like this, so that it can be put to any verification, is tough. Humorously enough, I started entirely at the wrong angle, about 1919, trying to construct a logic for transitive verbs. That turned out to be as mean a problem as modal logic, and it was not until I saw Turing's paper that I began to get going the right way around, and with Pitts' help formulated the required logical calculus. What we thought we were doing (and I think we succeeded fairly well) was treating the brain as a Turing machine; that is, as a device which could perform the kind of functions which a brain must perform if it is only to go wrong and have a psychosis. The important thing was, for us, that we had to take a logic and subscript it for the time of the occurrence of a signal (which is, if you will, no more than a proposition on the move). This was needed in order to construct theory enough to be able to state how a nervous system could do anything. The delightful thing is that the very simplest set of appropriate assumptions is sufficient to show that a nervous system can compute any computable number. It is that kind of a device, if you like—a Turing machine.

The question at once arose as to how it did certain of the things that it did do. None of the theories tell you how a particular operation is carried out, any more than they tell you in what kind of a nervous system it is carried out, or any more than they tell you in what part of a computing machine it is carried out. For that you have to have the wiring diagram or the prescription for the relations of the gears.

This means that you are compelled to study anatomy, and to require of the anatomist the things he has rarely given us in sufficient detail. I taught neuro-anatomy while I was in medical school, but until the last year or two I have not been in a position to ask any neuro-anatomist for the precise detail of any structure. I had no physiological excuse for wanting that kind of information. Now we are beginning to need it.

DR. GERARD: I have had the privilege of hearing Dr. von Neumann speak on various occasions, and I always find myself in the delightful but difficult role of hanging on to the tail of a kite. While I can follow him, I can't do much creative thinking as we go along. I would like to ask one question, though, and suspect that it may be in the minds of others. You have carefully stated, at several points in your discourse, that anything that could be put into verbal form—into a question with words—could be solved. Is there any catch in this? What is the implication of just that limitation on the question?

DR. VON NEUMANN: I will try to answer, but my answer will have to be rather incomplete.

The first task that arises in dealing with any problem—more specifically, with any function of the central nervous system—is to formulate it unambiguously, to put it into words, in a rigorous sense. If a very complicated system—like the central nervous system—is involved, there arises the additional task of doing this "formulating," this "putting into words," with a number of words within reasonable limits—for example, that can be read in a lifetime. This is the place where the real difficulty lies.

In other words, I think that it is quite likely that one may give a purely descriptive account of the outwardly visible functions of the central nervous system in a humanly possible time. This may be 10 or 20 years—which is long, but not prohibitively long. Then, on the basis of the results of McCulloch and Pitts, one could draw within plausible time limitations a fictitious "nervous network" that can carry out all these functions. I suspect, however, that it will turn out to be much larger than the one that we actually possess. It is possible that it will prove to be too large to fit into the physical universe. What then? Haven't we lost the true problem in the process?

Thus the problem might better be viewed, not as one of imitating the functions of the central nervous system with just any kind of network, but rather as one of doing this with a network that will fit into the actual volume of the human brain. Or, better still, with one that can be kept going with our actual metabolistic "power supply" facilities, and that can be set up and organized by our actual genetic control facilities.

To sum up, I think that the first phase of our problem—the purely formalistic one, that one of finding any "equivalent network" at all—has been overcome by McCulloch and Pitts. I also think that much of the "malaise" felt in connection with attempts to "explain" the central nervous system belongs to this phase—and should therefore be considered removed. There remains, however, plenty of malaise due to the next phase of the problem, that one of finding an "equivalent network" of possible, or even plausible, dimensions and (metabolistic and genetic) requirements.

The problem, then, is not this: How does the central nervous system effect any one, particular thing? It is rather: How does it do all the things that it can do, in their full complexity? What are the principles of its organization? How does it avoid really serious, that is, lethal, malfunctions over periods that seem to average many decades?

DR. GERARD: Did you mean to imply that there are unformulated problems?

DR. VON NEUMANN: There may be problems which cannot be formulated with our present logical techniques.

DR. WEISS: I take it that we are discussing only a conceivable and logically consistent, but not necessarily real, mechanism of the nervous system. Any theory of the real nervous system, however, must explain the facts of regulation—that the mechanism will turn out the same or an essentially similar product even after the network of pathways has been altered in many unpredictable ways. According to von Neumann, a machine can be constructed so as to contain safeguards against errors and provision for correcting errors when they occur. In this case the future contingencies have been taken into account in constructing the machine. In the case of the nervous system, evolution would have had to build in the necessary corrective devices. Since the number of actual interferences and deviations produced by natural variation and by experimenting neurophysiologists is very great, I question whether a mechanism in which all these innumerable contingencies have been foreseen, and the corresponding corrective measures built in, is actually conceivable.

DR. VON NEUMANN: I will not try, of course, to answer the question as to how evolution came to any given point. I am going to make, however, a few remarks about the much more limited question regarding errors, foreseeing errors, and recognizing and correcting errors.

An artificial machine may well be provided with organs which recognize and correct errors automatically. In fact, almost every well-planned machine contains some organs whose function is to do just this—always within certain limited areas. Furthermore, if any particular machine is given, it is always possible to construct a second machine which "watches" the first one, and which senses and possibly even corrects its errors. The trouble is, however, that now the second machine's errors are unchecked, that is, *quis custodiet ipsos custodes?* Building a third, a fourth, etc., machine for second order, third order, etc., checking merely shifts the problem. In addition, the primary and the secondary machine will, together, make more errors than the first one alone, since they have more components.

Some such procedure on a more modest scale may nevertheless make sense. One might know, from statistical experience with a certain machine or class of machines, which ones of its components malfunction most frequently, and one may then "supervise" these only, etc.

Another possible approach, which permits a more general quantitative evaluation, is this: Assume that one had a machine which has a probability of 10^{-10} to malfunction on any single operation, that is, which will, on the average, make one error for any 10^{10} operations. Assume that this machine has to solve a problem that requires 10^{12} operations. Its normal

447

"unsupervised" functioning will, therefore, on the average, give 100 errors in a single problem, that is, it will be completely unusable.

Connect now three such machines in such a manner that they always compare their results after every single operation, and then proceed as follows. (*a*) If all three have the same result, they continue unchecked. (*b*) If any two agree with each other, but not with the third, then all three continue with the value agreed on by the majority. (*c*) If no two agree with each other, then all three stop.

This system will produce a correct result, unless at some point in the problem two of the three machines err simultaneously. The probability of two given machines erring simultaneously on a given operation is $10^{-10} \times 10^{-10} = 10^{-20}$. The probability of any two doing this on a given operation is 3×10^{-20} (there are three possible pairs to be formed among three individuals [machines]). The probability of this happening at all (that is, anywhere) in the entire problem is $10^{12} \times 3 \times 10^{-20} = 3 \times 10^{-8}$, about one in 33 million.

Thus there is only one chance in 33 million that this triad of machines will fail to solve the problem correctly—although each member of the triad alone had hardly any chance to solve it correctly.

Note that this triad, as well as any other conceivable automatic contraption, no matter how sophisticatedly supervised, still offers a logical possibility of resulting error—although, of course, only with a low probability. But the incidence (that is, the probability) of error has been significantly lowered, and this is all that is intended.

DR. WEISS: In order to crystallize the issue, I want to reiterate that if you know the common types of errors that will occur in a particular machine, you can make provisions for the correction of these errors in constructing the machine. One of the major features of the nervous system, however, is its apparent ability to remedy situations that could not possibly have been foreseen. (The number of artificial interferences with the various apparatuses of the nervous system that can be applied without impairing the biologically useful response of the organism is infinite.) The concept of a nervous automaton should, therefore, not only be able to account for the normal operation of the nervous system but also for its relative stability under all kinds of abnormal situations.

DR. VON NEUMANN: I do not agree with this conclusion. The argumentation that you have used is risky, and requires great care.

One can in fact guard against errors that are not specifically foreseen. These are some examples that show what I mean.

One can design and build an electrical automaton which will function as long as every resistor in it deviates no more than 10 per cent from its standard design value. You may now try to disturb this machine by experimental treatments which will alter its resistor values (as, for example, by heating certain regions in the machine). As long as no resistor shifts by more than 10 per cent, the machine will function right—no matter how involved, how sophisticated, how "unforeseen" the disturbing experiment is.

Or—another example—one may develop an armor plate which will resist impacts up to a certain strength. If you now test it, it will stand up successfully in this test, as long as its strength limit is not exceeded, no matter how novel the design of the gun, propellant, and projectile used in testing, etc.

It is clear how these examples can be transposed to neural and genetic situations.

To sum up: Errors and sources of errors need only be foreseen generically, that is, by some decisive traits, and not specifically, that is, in complete detail. And these generic coverages may cover vast territories, full of unforeseen and unsuspected—but, in fine, irrelevant—details.

DR. MC CULLOCH: How about designing computing machines so that if they were damaged in air raids, or what not, they could replace parts, or service themselves, and continue to work?

DR. VON NEUMANN: These are really quantitative rather than qualitative questions. There is no doubt that one can design machines which, under suitable conditions, will repair themselves. A practical discussion is, however, rendered difficult by what I believe to be a rather accidental circumstance. This is, that we seem to be operating with much more unstable materials than nature does. A metal may seem to be more stable than a tissue, but, if a tissue is injured, it has a tendency to restore itself, while our industrial materials do not have this tendency, or have it to a considerably lesser degree. I don't think, however, that any question of principle is involved at this point. This reflects merely the present, imperfect state of our technology—a state that will presumably improve with time.

DR. LASHLEY: I'm not sure that I have followed exactly the meaning of "error" in this discussion, but it seems to me the question of precision of the organic machine has been somewhat exaggerated. In the computing machines, the one thing we demand is precision; on the other hand, when we study the organism, one thing which we never find is accuracy or precision. In any organic reaction there is a normal, or nearly normal, distribution of errors around a mean. The mechanisms of reaction are statistical in character and their accuracy is only that of a probability distribution in the activity of enormous numbers of elements. In this respect the organism resembles the analogical rather than the digital machine. The invention of symbols and the use of memorized number series convert the organism into a digital machine, but the increase in accuracy is acquired at the sacrifice of speed. One can estimate the number of books on a shelf at a glance, with some error. To count them requires much greater time. As a digital machine the organism is inefficient. That is why you build computing machines.

DR. VON NEUMANN: I would like to discuss this question of precision in some detail.

449

It is perfectly true that in all mathematical problems the answer is required with absolute rigor, with absolute reliability. This may, but need not, mean that it is also required with absolute precision. In most problems for the sake of which computing machines are being built—mostly problems in various parts of applied mathematics, mathematical physics—the precision that is wanted is quite limited. That is, the data of the problem are only given to limited precision, and the result is only wanted to limited precision. This is quite compatible with absolute mathematical rigor, if the sensitivity of the result to changes in the data as well as the limits of uncertainty (that is, the amount of precision) of the result for given data are (rigorously) known.

The (input) data in physical problems are often not known to better than a few (say 5) per cent. The result may be satisfactory to even less precision (say 10 per cent). In this respect, therefore, the difference of outward precision requirements for an (artificial) computing machine and a (natural) organism need not at all be decisive. It is merely quantitative, and the quantitative factors involved need not be large at that.

The need for high precisions in the internal functioning of (artificial) computing machines is due to entirely different causes—and these may well be operating in (natural) organisms too. By this I do not mean that the arguments that follow should be carried over too literally to organisms. In fact, the "digital method" used in computing may be entirely alien to the nervous system. The discrete pulses used in neural communications look indeed more like "counting" by numeration than like a "digitalization." (In many cases, of course, they may express a logical code—this is quite similar to what goes on in computing machines.) I will, nevertheless, discuss the specifically "digital" procedure of our computing machine, in order to illustrate how subtle the distinction between "external" and "internal" precision requirements can be.

In a computing machine numbers may have to be dealt with as aggregates of 10 or more decimal places. Thus an internal precision of one in 10 billion or more may be needed, although the data are only good to one part in 20 (5 per cent), and the result is only wanted to one part in 10 (10 per cent). The reason for this strange discrepancy is that a fast machine will only be used on long and complicated problems. Problems involving 100 million multiplications will not be rarities. In a 4-decimal-place machine every multiplication introduces a "round-off" error of one part in 10,000; in a 6-place machine this is one part in a million; in a 10-place machine it is one part in 10 billion. In a problem of the size indicated above, such errors will occur 100 million times. They will be randomly distributed, and it follows therefore from the rules of mathematical statistics that the total error will probably not be 100 million times the individual (round-off) error, but about the square root of 100 million times, that is, about 10,000 times. A precision of 10 per cent—one part in 10—in the result should therefore require 10,000 times more precision than this on individual steps (multiplication round-offs): namely, one part in 100,000, that is, 5 decimal places. Actually, more will be required because the (round-off) errors made in the earlier parts of the calculation are frequently "amplified" by the operations of the subsequent parts of the calculation. For these reasons 8 to 10 decimal places are probably a minimum for such a machine, and actually many large problems may well require more.

Most analogy computing machines have much less precision than this (on elementary operations). The electrical ones usually one part in 100 or 1000, the best mechanical ones (the most advanced "differential analyzers") one part in 10,000 or 50,000. The virtue of the digital method is that it will, with componentry of very limited precision, give almost any precision on elementary operations. If one part in a million is wanted, one will use 6 decimal digits; if one part in 10 billions is wanted, one need only increase the number of decimal digits to 10; etc. And yet the individual components need only be able to distinguish reliably 10 different states (the 10 decimal digits from 0 to 9), and by some simple logical and organizational tricks one can even get along with components that can only distinguish two states!

I suspect that the central nervous system, because of the great complexity of its tasks, also faces problems of "internal" precision or reliability. The all-or-none character of nervous impulses may be connected with some technique that meets this difficulty, and this—unknown—technique might well be related to the digital system that we use in computing, although it is probably very different from the digital system in its technical details. We seem to have no idea as to what this technique is. This is again an indication of how little we know. I think, however, that the digital system of computing is the only thing known to us that holds any hope of an even remote affinity with that unknown, and merely postulated, technique.

DR. MC CULLOCH: I want to make a remark in partial answer to Dr. Lashley. I think that the major woe that I have always encountered in considering the behavior of organisms was not in such procedures as hitting a bull's-eye or judging a distance, but in mathematics and logic. After all, Vega did compute log tables to thirteen places. He made some four hundred and thirty errors, but the total precision of the work of that organism is simply incredible to me.

DR. LASHLEY: You must keep in mind that such an achievement is not the product of a single elaborate integration but represents a great number of separate processes which are, individually, simple discriminations far above threshold values and which do not require great accuracy of neural activity.

DR. HALSTEAD: As I listened to Dr. von Neumann's beautiful analysis of digital and analogous devices, I was impressed by the conceptual parsimony with which such systems may be described. We in the field of organic behavior are not yet so fortunate. Our parsimonies, for the most part, are still to be attained. There is virtually no class of behaviors which can at present be described with comparable precision. Whether such domains as thinking, intelligence, learning, emoting, language, perception, and response represent distinctive processes or only different attitudinal sets of the organism is by no means clear. It is perhaps for this reason that Dr. von Neumann did not specify the class or classes of behaviors which his automata simulate.

As Craik pointed out several years ago,[1] it isn't quite logically air-tight to compare the operations of models with highly specified ends with organic behaviors only loosely specified either hierarchically or as to ends. Craik's criterion was that our models must bear a proper "relation structure" to the steps in the processes simulated. The rules of the game are violated when we introduce gremlins, either good or bad gremlins, as intervening variables. It is not clear to me whether von Neumann means "noise" as a good or as a bad gremlin. I presume it is a bad one when it is desired to maximize "rationality" in the outcome. It is probable that rationality characterizes a restricted class of human behavior. I shall later present experimental evidence that the same normal or brain-injured man also produces a less restricted class of behavior which is "arational" if not irrational. I suspect that von Neumann biases his automata towards rationality by careful regulation of the energics of the substrate. Perhaps he would gain in similitude, however, were he to build unstable power supplies into his computers and observe the results.

It seems to me that von Neumann is approximating in his computers some of the necessary operations in the organic process recognized by psychologists under the term "abstraction." Analysis of this process of ordering to a criterion in brain-injured individuals suggests that three classes of outcome occur. First, there is the pure category (or "universal"); second, there is the partial category; and third, there is the phenomenal or non-recurrent organization. Operationalism restricts our concern to the first two classes. However, these define the third. It is probably significant that psychologists such as Spearman and Thurstone have made considerable progress in describing these outcomes in mathematical notation.

DR. LORENTE DE NÓ: I began my training in a very different manner from Dr. McCulloch. I began as an anatomist and became interested in physiology much later. Therefore, I am still very much of an anatomist, and visualize everything in anatomical terms. According to your discussion, Dr. von Neumann, of the McCulloch and Pitts automaton, anything that can be expressed in words can be performed by the automaton. To this I would say that I can remember what you said, but that the McCulloch-Pitts automaton could not remember what you said. No, the automaton does not function in the way that our nervous system does, because the only way in which that could happen, as far as I can visualize, is by having some change continuously maintained. Possibly the automaton can be made to maintain memory, but the automaton that does would not have the properties of our nervous system. We agree on that, I believe. The only thing that I wanted was to make the fact clear.

DR. VON NEUMANN: One of the peculiar features of the situation, of course, is that you can make a memory out of switching organs, but there are strong indications that this is not done in nature. And, by the way, it is not very efficient, as closer analysis shows.

Note

1 *Nature of Explanation*, London, Cambridge University Press, 1943.

23

ROBOTICS AND GENERAL INTELLIGENCE

P. McCorduck

Source: P. McCorduck, *Machines Who Think: A Personal Inquiry into the History and Prospects of Artificial Intelligence*, W. H. Freeman, 1979, pp. 209–37.

When most of us try to picture an artificial intelligence, of course we think first of a robot. This history has been full of them, make-believe humans who clanked their way through our dreams, our stories, our films and plays. Some have been nobler versions of ourselves, some ignoble. The robots who win the war against the humans in *R.U.R.* look forward to a life of bliss in a socialist workers' paradise, while other robots in other stories stand for the indestructibility of the machine compared with the all too frail destructibility of human flesh, one more gloomy reminder of our personal mortality.

Why build a robot?

The reasons are numerous. It was a robot which explored the surface of Mars for us, a handy example of the fact that robots can go where—and do what—humans cannot. (However, the extent of this robot's debt to artificial intelligence is in dispute. Its routines were preprogrammed and, once in action constantly monitored by humans. This represented impressive control engineering, but the robot was not an intelligent machine. On the other hand, Charles Rosen of SRI called the Mars robot "Son of Shakey," for all that the Jet Propulsion Laboratory had borrowed from the SRI robot named Shakey.) In the context of the Mars robot, then, robots are one more tool, one more extension, of the human body and mind.

As I've pointed out earlier, the building of robots has been said to be motivated by all sorts of psychological needs, particularly those of males, who cannot themselves give birth biologically. Again, this point surfaced most recently in the 1972 report of Sir James Lighthill mentioned earlier, in which it was recommended that support for artificial intelligence in Britain be terminated.[1] Oh, not because it represents a desire to give birth, Sir James hastened to say; in fact, he didn't believe it for a moment, but just thought he'd mention it. I don't believe it for a moment either, unless it is meant in the larger sense that we all seek immortality—or at least propagation of our own presence beyond our immediate circle and lifetime—by the art we create, the science we discover, the good works we do.

No, I'm putting my money on a bet that says we build robots for the same reasons we do other kinds of science and art, for the immense satisfaction of knowing something significant about ourselves that we didn't know before, of having our suspicions and guesses about ourselves confirmed or laid waste—simply put, of seeing ourselves in a new way. Without doubt, robot building gets back to the human race. I come again to a point I have made continually, that the building of artificial intelligences is very much a part of our long romance with ourselves as a species. Unlike art, however, artificial intelligence contains in it the possibility of our transcending the species and knowing something about intelligence elsewhere. That is one of the things that makes it a science.

We're rather casual about how we use the word robot. It comes from the Czech word for servitude, or slavery, and was introduced into English by Karel Capek in his play *R.U.R.*, which took the London season by storm in 1921. We use it to designate all sorts of machines that do stand-in work for us, from the automatic car-wash device to that rather more complicated instrument that prowled Mars. In artificial-intelligence research the robot that matters is an intelligent robot, one that will cope with novel situations essentially by figuring them out—by comparing them with situations it has encountered before, by generating a set of reasonable alternative courses and choosing the most appropriate, or even by falling serendipitously into an unexpected solution and recognizing it as such. If it all sounds familiar, it should. It's what human beings do all the time.

So intelligent robots must have a general capacity for dealing more or less successfully with a variety of situations, which makes them different not only from ordinary preprogrammed robots, but also from other artificial intelligences designed to deal well with only one task environment, however complicated. It puts them right in the middle of that stream of effort we have seen at least since Leibnitz—the urge toward a universal calculus, a universal set of rules for reasoning. It's the urge George Boole followed when he set up his algebra or laws of human thought in the nineteenth century, the urge culminating in Whitehead and Russell's *Principia Mathematica*, which expressed all mathematics in terms of a single logical calculus.

This same urge informed the spirit—though in a decidedly nonmathematical way—of a program designed in 1957 by the Carnegie-RAND group, Newell, Shaw, and Simon. This program, the General Problem Solver, came quickly—almost simultaneously, as science goes—after their Logic Theorist, the program that had proved theorems from Whitehead and Russell's *Principia*.

The philosophy behind the General Problem Solver was clear. It was *not* to be task-specific. Once Newell, Shaw, and Simon had demonstrated to themselves with the Logic Theorist that computers could indeed do tasks that required intelligence, that the information-processing level of abstraction was more than a metaphor—was in fact an explicit language for theory building and for simulation, in the same way mathematics might be used by a physicist to describe physical events—they began to worry about generality. Their working assumption was that human beings brought some general processes to bear on a whole variety of tasks, whether getting to the grocery store or solving a mathematical puzzle, and the General Problem Solver was designed to identify and make explicit those general processes by demonstrating them in a variety of environments.

Both Newell and Simon had a long-time interest in human problem-solving methods. Newell had been a student of George Polya at Stanford (Polya had also taught von Neumann in Europe), and Polya was well known for his attempts to demystify problem-solving techniques mathematicians use, which he had gathered together in a little book called *How to Solve It*. It was from Polya that Newell and Simon borrowed the term heuristic. Simon, for his part had spent many an evening as a graduate student at the University of Chicago discussing with his friend Harold Guetzkow how to spell out the specifics of problem solving.

Somehow Newell and Simon heard of O. K. Moore's experiments at Yale, where Moore had subjects "think aloud" as they were solving various kinds of puzzles. These studies tied into similar experiments underway at RAND in 1955 and 1956, and Newell and Simon sat down with transcripts of these tapes, called protocols, with the hope of analyzing them in such a way as to cull the problem-solving techniques from them and simulate those techniques in some kind of computer program. That people might be able to express in words some of the things that were going on in their minds as they solved problems was what Simon calls "a sketch of a sketch" of what consciousness might be all about—the ability of an intelligent system to be aware of things external to it, and report, at the same time, on things internal to it.

Newell says, "As soon as we got the protocols they were fabulously interesting. They caught and just laid out a whole bunch of processes that were going on. My recollection differs from Herb's, who remembers the history of GPS as being more diffuse. My recollection is that I just sort of drew GPS right out of Subject 4 on Problem D1—all the mechanisms that show up in the book, the means-ends analysis and so on."[2] From the Logic Theorist, Newell exhumed a technique that he and his colleagues hadn't even realized was there, a matching process; now he made it central to GPS just as he saw it in the human protocols.

GPS did indeed codify a number of problem-solving techniques that humans have used without necessarily putting name to them. Among these

456

techniques are what is called means-ends analysis, planning, and selective trial-and-error.

Means-ends analysis, to take one central technique, is a cycle of operations that works something like this. We look at where we are. We compare this with what we want. If they are the same, we have solved the problem. If not, we ask what will reduce the difference between where we are (or what we have) and what we want. We then apply successively methods suggested by heuristic rules as being likely to reduce that difference, each time beginning again at step one. It happens that different kinds of heuristics work for different situations, so although the original versions of GPS were able to handle a variety of tasks (so long as they were specified in a fairly rigid format) the experimenters had to back down on how much specialized knowledge was needed for solving problems. It was more, much more, than at first they had realized, and this was to be a continuing problem in all general-purpose intelligences.

GPS sounds almost ridiculously simple, but in fact we see just such reasoning in everyday life. Let me give a homely example. I am hungry. I want to be full—or at least not hungry. What's the difference between being hungry and not hungry? One answer is food. But I am trying to lose weight, and food adds weight. I could play tennis, which not only kills my appetite but also burns calories in the bargain. But I have work to do that keeps me indoors. If I want to satisfy my empty stomach and still do my work and not gain weight, can I think of something else to fill my stomach? I brew another pot of tea. And so on. From an initial state, the problem, one moves by means of operators to various intermediate states, and at last, one hopes, to a final state that is a satisfactory solution to the problem.

A word about problem solving. It is not intended as a synonym for all thinking. In their book *Human Problem Solving* (1972), Newell and Simon call problem solving a subspecies of thinking, concerned explicitly with the performance of tasks. Under these circumstances, learning is viewed as a second-order effect, behavior that *improves* the performance of a system *already performing in a given situation.*

I have before me a self-help book that promises to help me manage my time better: its technique is pure GPS. Another book, called *The Universal Traveler* (Koberg and Bagnall, 1972) and subtitled *A Soft-Systems Guide to: Creativity, Problem-Solving and the Process of Reaching Goals,* is both a charming and useful handbook, drawing from many different sources, as its rich bibliography attests. But its methods, its underlying model, and much of its language is GPS. Its authors are primarily interested in solving architectural and environmental-design problems, but they understand that the techniques are more general, that they can be adapted to all sorts of fields once one views the situation as a journey to be made, a problem to be solved. When Newell and Simon predicted in 1957 that psychology would grasp the information-processing model as a useful way of explaining and understanding human cognitive behavior, they did not expect to find it filtering down to popular self-help books in less than twenty years. In fact, the very view that techniques exist for improving one's creativity is still repugnant to some people. They'd be outraged if their physician still practiced medicine as it was done in Galen's time, but they hold that creative behavior, on the other hand, is mystical, unknowable, and therefore inaccessible to improvement. You've got it or you don't. The GPS point of view—the entire assumption of artificial intelligence as a field—is contrary to this belief.

GPS was successfully tried on a number of tasks, among them logic problems and chestnuts of puzzles such as the Tower of Hanoi and the missionaries and cannibals problem.[3] Newell and Simon wrote about GPS in *Science* in 1961 (Newell and Simon, 1961). They were very careful to note its limitations, as they did whenever they talked about it (for example, the first paper describing it, a mimeograph from Carnegie Tech, says that GPS has "pretenses to generality," a phrase Newell invented out of the conviction that they were *probably* on the right track, but it was by no means certain). Nevertheless, they could assert that GPS was a computer program capable of simulating, in first approximation, human behavior in a narrow but significant problem domain. It provided unequivocal demonstration, they went on to say, that a mechanism can solve problems by functional reasoning.

The original GPS went through several versions. Hubert Dreyfus says in *What Computers Can't Do* that GPS was abandoned because it failed to be a genuine general problem solver, but this oversimplifies matters. The techniques of GPS are embedded in one after another of the more sophisticated computer programs that consciously trace their lineage back to the original, a common example of the evolution of any sound scientific idea. For example, ten years after the original was developed, George W. Ernst was reporting a new, improved version of GPS that would handle twelve different kinds of problems, thanks to improvements in internal representation, while at the same meeting, Saul Amarel of Rutgers suggested a complementary approach, which would reformulate problems in a nested sequence of transformations. And fifteen years later, Simon's former student Laurent Siklóssy of Texas reported on his own work, which combined ideas from GPS and from an alternative approach to a general-purpose artificial intelligence, John McCarthy's so-called Advice Taker. If we count such descendants as *The Universal Traveler* and its sibling efforts, which are beginning to appear in classrooms and workshops all over the country, then GPS is alive and well indeed. Though Newell's recollections should make it clear, I want to reemphasize that GPS was not a collection of new techniques. It is the first program ever developed as a detailed simulation of human symbolic behavior; as such it clarified—and through that clarification made more useful—a handful of procedures human beings had been using all along for solving problems. To say that is not to diminish the profound insights of the creators of GPS. We honor Newton because he gave us a language, a means for understanding some major aspects of the physical universe, not because he invented that universe.

But in the minds of some, GPS also stood as a good example of a bad idea. It outraged the poet Adrienne Rich, and she wrote a harsh poem dedicated to GPS (see page 338 below). For Joel Moses, now a professor at MIT and a member of the next wave of AI researchers, it seemed to him a thoughtless direction for AI to take, a quagmire that prevented many people from seeing that specialty and not generality was needed for intelligent behavior. In her own way, Rich was saying the same thing.

At about the time that the General Problem Solver appeared in print in 1957, John McCarthy, who had moved by then from Dartmouth to MIT, was wrestling with a similar problem. How, he wondered, could you have a program that would solve a variety of problems, and furthermore take advice in order to improve its performance? So he proposed some ideas for a program called the Advice Taker, a program that would have common sense—that is, it would deduce from what it was told, and what it already knew, the immediate consequences of any actions it might take.

McCarthy's fascination with intelligent machines has already been described. It was his disappointment with the automata studies he and Claude Shannon had edited that caused him to search for some better way of expressing intelligent behavior in machines. His own contribution to the automata-studies volume had been what he now calls an unsuccessful approach to artificial intelligence, an attempt to make a Turing machine behave intelligently. The Turing machine was unsatisfactory for representing human behavior, McCarthy concluded, because although in principle such behavior might be represented, changes in behavior that are small from an intuitive human point of view don't necessarily correspond to small changes in the Turing machine. It was a defect he recognized even before he published the paper, but it was the best he could do at the time.

McCarthy had been until then a pure mathematician, but a summer at IBM in 1955 gave him a better acquaintance with computers, and he marks that time as the point at which he took leave from mathematics and entered computer science and artificial intelligence, the term he coined. As graduate students at Princeton, he and Marvin Minsky had basically agreed that artificial intelligence was a worthwhile project to work on, though they were rather vague about how. And McCarthy too had been provoked by one of John von Neumann's talks, and wanted to explore the idea of a finite automaton as an intelligent agent. But it was an idea he kept working on, trying to improve it before he published it, and he was chagrined to see others rush into print with less careful analyses. It was about this time too that McCarthy began working on the programming language LISP, making the ideas inherent in the list-processing languages of Newell, Shaw, and

Simon, and of Gelernter at IBM, more elegant, cleaner, and more powerful—that is, able to do many more things.

It happens that LISP didn't catch on for some time. McCarthy attributes its late blooming to the fact that it could do things powerfully, all right, but at the time of its invention, nobody really wanted to do them. The simple programs most people were aspiring to were actually easier to program in machine code, and not until aspirations rose did people realize that LISP existed and would provide a representation by which they could accomplish more complicated tasks. LISP, with its offspring, is still the language of choice in most AI research.

Meanwhile, McCarthy was also busy promoting time-sharing, through which the capabilities of a single central computer are shared by a number of users in a way that looks to the users as if they are getting custom service, but which is really a trick based on the mismatch between the slowness of human reaction and the speed of the computer. Thus, when I telephone for an airline reservation, the reservations clerk queries the computer (by means of a remote terminal where the clerk is sitting) about whether seats are available on the flight I want. There may even be an intermediate step, where the clerk can answer my request for a late afternoon flight to San Francisco by finding out from the computer which late afternoon flights to San Francisco exist for me to choose from. So far as the clerk and I are concerned, we are the only people making inquiries of the computer, but in fact, there may be hundreds of clerks all over the country making inquiries at approximately the same time, and the central computer (or multiplexed sets of them) cycles through each of us, serving us in turn.

This idea was originally John McCarthy's:[4]

> It was one of those ideas that seemed inevitable in the sense that when I was first learning about computers, I was a little surprised that even if that wasn't the way it was already done, it surely must be what everybody had in mind to do eventually. It turned out it wasn't, and I promoted it as something for artificial intelligence, for I'd designed LISP in such a way that working with it interactively—giving it a command, then seeing what happened, then giving it another command—was the best way to work with it. The word time-sharing is used in communication as one of the ways of sending several signals over the same line, so that's where the word came from. My ideas on the subject were rather modest with regard to hardware, but I agitated for time-sharing at MIT, and we got a grant from the National Science Foundation to do it.

McCarthy turned over the details of implementation to others, and went back to thinking about what had inspired LISP and the notion of time-sharing in the first place, his program with common sense, his Advice Taker.

There are people who consider McCarthy's efforts on behalf of LISP and time-sharing to be diversions from his serious work in artificial intelligence, but in fact they seem to me to be all of a piece. The common way of using computers to squeeze maximum efficiency from them is to run continuous batches of problems through them. For many uses, this is perfectly fine. A department store needs to bill its customers only once a month; the grinding out of census statistics will not be improved by any human interference during the grinding-out process.[5] This batch processing is what John McCarthy had found at IBM in 1955, and which no one seemed to have had any plans to change. But how could you give advice to an intelligent program if you couldn't get at it during the time it was going through its problem solving? It was rather like being coached in tennis over the telephone the night after you'd lost a crucial match.

So the Advice Taker was to improve its performance by having statements—advice—given to it in real time, telling it about its environment and what was wanted of it. It was automatically to deduce for itself a sufficiently wide class of immediate consequences of anything it was told and already knew. Such a program must have certain specifications. For example, it must allow for interesting changes in behavior that are expressible in a simple way, relatively speaking, in the way that genetic change is basically simple but provides all the variety of flora and fauna that we see. It has to have a concept of only partial success, for on difficult problems decisive successes or failures come very infrequently. And so it goes.

The Advice Taker shared with GPS a penchant for relative simplicity, and it certainly was planned to be as general as possible. Unlike GPS, however, no Advice Taker exists.

I'd heard the term Advice Taker so often before I spoke to McCarthy that I told him I was surprised to learn that it was still a proposal. "No," he said, "it doesn't exist. Because in order to do it, you have to be able to express formally that information that is normally expressed in ordinary language. As far as I'm concerned, this is the key unsolved problem in AI. I uncovered the problem in 1958 and it's still unsolved." McCarthy has himself made several attempts to invent a formal language that would be able to express the events of everyday life: it's the one scientific problem he's stuck to, among the variety of others he's taken up. But in his view, the general problem has simply not been attacked by enough good people to solve it, and he believes that until they do artificial intelligence will remain somewhat stuck.

Not everyone in AI shares McCarthy's pessimism. Indeed, in the mid 1960s, logician Alan Robinson published a paper on what he called the Resolution Method, a highly efficient way of proving theorems in the first-order predicate calculus. It seemed as if McCarthy's dream of a uniform problem solver had been realized, and a rush to Resolution was on. Several of McCarthy's graduate students went to work applying Robinson's method to the world of facts, among them Cordell Green, whose QA3 program behaved as a sort of General Problem Solver. A group at the University of Edinburgh also took up Resolution, and it became a topic of great interest for the AI group at Stanford Research Institute. James Slagle, whose SAINT program, a simulation of a freshman calculus student, had been one of the pioneering AI efforts at MIT, directed his group at the National Institutes of Health in a concentrated effort that produced MULTIPLE, one of the best of these mathematical single general-search methods.

But all this effort eventually collapsed. It seemed that the Robinson method generated search spaces as large as ordinary heuristic methods. There was no way by which the Resolution Method theorem provers could use real-world facts to constrain those spaces. Edward Feigenbaum, McCarthy's colleague at Stanford, and one who had not been enchanted by the Resolution Method, put it this way: "It's very awkward to translate your knowledge of a task domain into predicate calculus, and the difficulty of doing it is exceeded only by the awkwardness of how it looks after you've done it." And it was Feigenbaum who provided a small note to the social history of science. Asked how Robinson reacted to his sudden rise and fall in AI, Feigenbaum laughed:

> He underwent an unwanted spectacular rise to stardom in AI research, unwanted because Alan is a logician and views his activity from the point of view of that peer group. He wasn't necessarily concerned with his reputation in this very strange peer group called artificial intelligence. But here he was, propelled to the front ranks, and suddenly felt heavy obligation to extract the AI researchers from the pit into which they were falling, the pit of the combinatorial explosion.[6] He understood this, but was really helpless to do anything about it since he was a logician who invented a method, not an AI researcher interested in formalizing the world's knowledge. Finally he gave up, decided he was really sorry he'd got people into this trap, but he couldn't do anything about it. As AI moved away from the Resolution Method, he moved back to logic and resigned his position on the editorial board of the AI Journal, and retreated from the whole scene.

Not everyone was enchanted. Newell believed that the Resolution Method was no improvement over GPS, the eclecticism of the AI group at Stanford enabled it to evade the trap that devotion to one method would have led to, and the MIT group was openly hostile. But the Edinburgh researchers' passionate fling with the Resolution Method would be costly to them later, in the opinion of several observers.

Yet McCarthy still longs for a formal language that will express the facts of common knowledge, a rather lonely position in AI just now. But then he's a man who has always been driven by extraordinarily high intellectual standards for himself. But those high standards have also perhaps accounted for his relatively short list of scientific publications, and his dissatisfaction with other people's work. They even account, he once said to me, for his long silences in ordinary discourse, because if he can't think of anything to say that's worth saying, he keeps quiet, which can be hard on the partner in the colloquy who is left to wonder whether he or she has said something stupid, offensive, or both.

Like most highly gifted people, McCarthy is really interested in doing only what challenges him. He has been the despair of funding agencies because he couldn't be bothered to write progress reports. Thus, no one in Washington knew whether his scientific work was moving ahead on schedule, or whether the large collection of programmers, hackers, and other assorted AI groupies who find the Stanford AI Laboratory congenial were spending twenty-four hours a day playing Space War, sitting in the laboratory's unisex sauna, or frolicking on its waterbed. Some of this waywardness was remedied by hiring a project administrator to oversee nonscientific activities. Also, McCarthy's introductory artificial intelligence course at Stanford in the 1960s was so vague it was known among the graduate students as Uncle John's Mystery Hour (recalling Dr. Spooner, who admonished a luckless student: "You hissed my mystery lecture"), though if McCarthy is excited by a topic, his lectures can be awesome.

He has a wonderful talent for nettling his colleagues, often because he expects them to fill in the gaps he is too impatient to attend to as he explains a new idea. "I think he's mellowing on that score," said one of his associates recently. "We had a conversation the other day, and I actually heard him using words like because and so it follows."

Stephen Coles, a former student of Simon's who eventually went to SRI, tells a story about when he was doing his post-Ph.D. job hunt. He'd been in an enormous hurry to get his thesis finished, and so the slides to illustrate his lecture were faulty—they'd been done under pressure at a late hour, and they showed some bugs still surreptitiously in the code he was using that caused an inconsistency.

So I said to myself, well, I'm not going to rewrite any programs now— the thesis is done and no one would ever see this error; it's only clear to someone who's been an author of the system and worked on it very hard and understands it, and I'll just pass right over it. McCarthy that day at the AI lab was his usual self—reading the newspaper and looking at the ceiling and not paying any attention, dozing off at my presentation like he's totally bored by what I have to say. Other people, of course, are interested and following what I have to say, and so that was good enough—if he doesn't want to pay attention, that's his problem. And at the end of the talk he says, go back to figure blah blah, there's an error there. Nobody else saw it and I was just totally stunned. The guy is phenomenal. He has all these other idiosyncrasies which are hard to overlook, but there's nobody else that I know of in this community who is so sharp at spotting weak spots. And that's really what you need if you're trying to do something original which has never been done before, someone who can challenge, find the flaws, shoot it down.

McCarthy can be enormously provoking. Several people told me about a meeting where the leading researchers in AI had gathered to make a collective presentation insuring the continuation of funds from the defense department. Not only were all the biggest names in AI there, but several high-level executives from defense department agencies were present as well, and the object of the meeting was to overcome their skepticism. McCarthy had brought along his Polaroid, and shortly after the meeting began, he brought it out and began ostentatiously snapping pictures. Pretty soon he got up out of his seat and walked around the small, crowded meeting room, getting close-ups, fresh angles. After an hour or so, somebody got annoyed enough to ask him why he was doing it. "As a memory aid," McCarthy replied simply, and kept on snapping.

"Anybody could see what was going on," one person at the meeting told me. "Here was supersmart John, but he was in a room full of people who are probably just as supersmart. How else could he distinguish himself except by making a pest of himself?"

Perhaps. McCarthy is also very shy, and shy people sometimes have funny ways of compensating for that. But once he has overcome his shyness, once a listener has John McCarthy for an evening of easy talk, there's no one more fun to be with. He's playful, almost giddy, and the stream of original ideas flows nonstop, most of them fantasies he has for solving the very serious problems of the world with technology, a continuing theme in his life. He is something of an apostle on that subject, believing that technology has been unjustly maligned. He is certain that if used with imagination, technology can in fact solve not only some of the problems its injudicious use creates, but also a great many other problems too. Some arguments along these lines have found their way into print in letters to the editors, but anyone in AI who wants to know what John McCarthy is thinking right now can hook in by computer terminal to the ARPANET, a network of connections among computer installations funded by the Advanced Research Projects Agency of the Department of Defense, and read the latest edition of McCarthy's private newsletter. His faith in technology wasn't shaken in the least by his long involvement with the counterculture during the 1960s: on the contrary, McCarthy was bringing the same message to the Free University of Palo Alto as to the *New York Times*.

In the fall of 1962, McCarthy left MIT for Stanford. Several reasons seem to have caused his move. Partly he was fed up with the politics surrounding the MIT time-sharing project; partly he felt unappreciated at MIT, and Stanford offered him a better position at a higher salary. He hoped to get an artificial-intelligence effort underway at Stanford that would be a tight little group of smart people doing interesting things—a dream rather different from the sprawling project that eventually grew on top of the dry, grassy hills behind Stanford. For what started out as McCarthy and a handful of graduate students working on games, theorem proving, and other such logistically modest efforts was suddenly inflated by scores of people, and the reason for that inflation was robotics.

Robotics, of course, provides the perfect environment for scores of people, in particular graduate students who can bite off thesis-sized chunks. The subject had caught the fancy of the military, which had a lot of money to spend and was willing to spend it on something with such obvious military potential. And it simply cannot be denied that to crack the problem of an intelligent entity that would interact with the real world is as appealing a scientific problem as anyone could dream up.

Bert Raphael, deeply involved in the development of Shakey, the Stanford Research Institute's intelligent mobile robot, has pointed out some of the specifics of robot research. It embraces several aspects of intelligence, such as pattern recognition, problem solving, information representation, and natural-language processing, all of which have continuing research interest. It must be general—an aesthetic canon of science for very sound reasons—and sufficiently rich and open-ended to offer a tremendous range of problems of ever-increasing complexity. That a robot has to cope with the real world puts it in quite a different class from intelligent programs that operate in formal domains, such as mathematics or game playing, for "a problem-solver in a formal domain is essentially done when it has constructed a plan for a solution; nothing can go wrong. A robot in the real world, however, must consider the execution of the plan as a major part of every task. Unexpected occurrences are not unusual, so that the use of sensory feedback and corrective actions are crucial" (Raphael, 1970).

Marvin Minsky explains his interest in robotics somewhat differently. The son of a physician, and married to one as well, he'd become fascinated by the idea of microbotics for surgery. Why not machines—or, better yet, robotic instruments—that could crawl into arteries and scrape off the accumulated fat deposits, or that could make delicate tissue repair in spots inaccessible to human eyes and fingers? By the time he'd drafted proposals for robotics projects as a consultant at SRI and Bolt Beranek and Newman, he was persuaded to whip one up for MIT, and so he did.

Yet Minsky took, and still seems to take, a lukewarm stand on robotics as a way of doing AI:

> *You might say that making robots was a sort of hobby which I encour-*
> *aged but didn't really concern myself with that much, and I always felt*
> *that studying the sensory and perceptual systems is not the best way to*

think about thinking, because the sensory systems are developed in lower animals as well, and come prior to symbolic intelligence. So you can study those things to death and you may only learn about some hardware tricks that were developed over a few million years that don't really tell you how the problem-solving parts of the brain work. We may have looked from the outside like a great deal of robotics work was going on here at MIT, but the things I was most concerned with were the theses like Slagle's and Bobrow's and Raphael's, and such people who were really working on the symbolic problem-solving things.

Thus three large robotics projects got underway in the mid-1960s in the United States—at Stanford University, at Stanford Research Institute (which is nearby, but no longer officially connected with Stanford University, and is known officially now as SRI International), and at MIT. A fourth large project at Edinburgh University, sponsored mainly by the Science Research Council of Great Britain, soon joined in, and considerable exchange of ideas took place among the four centers. Though each project had its own flavor, the general aim was the same—to produce some sort of independent agent that would function in the real world, or at least a somewhat impoverished real world.

With P. J. Hayes of Edinburgh, McCarthy wrote a paper in 1969 that outlined some of the central ideas of robotics. By this time all four robotics projects were well underway, and Hayes and McCarthy were no longer speaking entirely theoretically. They began by pointing out that a computer program capable of acting intelligently in the real world must have some knowledge of that world, and to design such a program requires commitments about what knowledge is and how it's obtained, central issues in philosophy since Greek times. Other points of philosophical debate must also be formalized: the nature of causality and ability, and the nature of intelligence. This is precisely what Minsky and Papert were getting at in a document they wrote in 1971 describing the robot project at MIT, that robotics provides a perfect medium for testing any ideas about the nature of intelligence, for if an idea about intelligence can't be made to work empirically, it probably isn't a very good idea (Minsky and Papert, 1971).

What is a general intelligence, McCarthy and Hayes asked? Turing's idea that a machine should successfully convince a sophisticated observer that it is human for half an hour will do, though such a test has some built-in liabilities[7] and provides necessary but not sufficient conditions for intelligence. Indeed, Bernard Meltzer, also of Edinburgh, wrote a brief essay suggesting that the Turing Test be retired, having done its proper work in the political battle to establish artificial intelligence as a respectable scientific discipline (Meltzer, 1971). A general-purpose intelligence is nearly impossible to specify, Meltzer argued, for even if we could, we would draw only on an arbitrary set of abilities that are a product of the biological and cultural evolution of the human race. Other abilities for performing intelligent tasks exist or can be conceived to exist, including some possessed by other animals, new abilities people might develop in the future, or entirely new ones in the intelligent *machines* of the future. Meltzer urged his colleagues to concentrate, rather than on a general intelligence, on special or restricted instances of intelligence, for the Turing Test involves an attempt to select only one such set.

It was distinctly possible, Meltzer concluded, that much of the work in robotics would make little contribution to artificial intelligence, but would instead elucidate in a concrete way traditional problems of human epistemology:

> One should not believe that machines which mimic human behaviour and to that extent have a rather "general" but limited capacity are necessarily more intelligent, more useful, or more worth research than ones with a lesser range of capacities—or even one capacity only. The only genius—or near-genius—I ever had close relations with would possibly have failed the Turing Test, as he was practically incapable of carrying on a coherent conversation with his colleagues!
>
> (Meltzer, 1971)

McCarthy and Hayes certainly saw some risk in using human beings as a model for making intelligent robots. For example, we may be mistaken, they declared, in our introspective views of our own mental structure; we may only think we use facts. Moreover, there may be entities that satisfy behaviorist criteria of intelligence but that are not organized in this way. Nevertheless, the construction of intelligent machines as fact manipulators seemed to them the best bet both for creating artificial intelligences and for understanding natural intelligence.

Therefore, they were willing to declare an entity intelligent if it had an adequate model of the world (including the intellectual world of mathematics; understanding of its own goals and other mental processes), if it was clever enough to answer a wide variety of questions on the basis of this model, if it could get additional information from the external world when required, and if it could perform such tasks in the external world as its goals demanded and its physical abilities permitted.

Four kinds of problems are inherent in the construction of an intelligent entity, all having to do with representation(s) of the world. They are:

1. How to allow the incorporation of specific observations and generalizations from those observations.
2. How to represent data from other than the physical world.
3. How to get knowledge about the world.
4. How to assimilate and express that knowledge internally.

Since these questions have not been solved by philosophers in more than twenty-five hundred years of dispute, artificial-intelligence researchers might well be dismayed about their own hopes for solutions. But McCarthy and Hayes shrug: one may as well begin the journey with a few working assumptions. These are, first, that the physical world exists and already contains some intelligent machines called people; second, that information about this world is obtainable through the senses and is expressible internally; third, that, moreover, our common-sense and scientific views of the world are approximately correct; and, finally, that the best procedure is to use all of human knowledge in trying to construct a computer program that knows. Modern philosophers could take issue with any one of these working assumptions but, as McCarthy and Hayes have pointed out, none offers any scheme precise enough to substitute.

The robots conceived and built at Stanford, MIT, and Edinburgh were hand-and-eye affairs, the eye a "seeing" television camera, the computer brain processing the camera's perceptions and instructing the arm(s) to move accordingly. I can describe these efforts so quickly, and yet the simple acts the robots could perform represent a knot of epistemological problems that no one had ever successfully sorted out before. The painstaking problems of deciding how the image on the retina is converted to a symbol inside the brain, and what form that symbol takes (a full-blown three-dimensional picture? a flexible outline, with only essential details? a token that only stands in for the image?) provided enough problems for a small army of researchers. These questions indeed raised problems in all the aspects of intelligence Raphael had cited, and those problems are still a very long way from being completely solved. But the solutions that were found began to suggest that many problems which seemed at first impossibly nonmechanical—exactly those problems that the most vehement critics of AI have declared will never be solved, such as "understanding" and "meaning"—slowly began to be brought into the domain of ordinary computational processes.

I don't wish to imply that these concepts were clarified only by robotics research. In particular, "meaning" has revealed its mechanisms in a number of different problem domains. But robotics research underscored the intimate, unseverable connections among all these aspects that we cannot see unless we have some knowledge of what we'll see; put another way, we cannot assign meaning unless we have a context in which to assign it. The same principles were to emerge in speech-understanding systems later on. If they are by now psychological commonplaces, we have to remember that robot builders were faced with questions of just how much knowledge was necessary for understanding, couched in precisely which terms. AI researchers call this the knowledge-representation problem. And for some researchers, its centrality still wasn't obvious.

Joel Moses of MIT says,

The word you look for and you hardly ever see in the early AI literature is the word knowledge. They didn't believe you have to know anything, you could always rework it all. And it's a tremendously arrogant person who could believe that you could rework it all on the fly—start with this simple machine and just feed it a few things and all of a sudden you get Einstein's theory of relativity. And nearly everybody bought that view. It took a long time for it to wither away.

Moses sees both the work in robotics and other work in real-world rather than toy problems as a turning point:

In fact, 1967 is the turning point in my mind when there was enough feeling that the old ideas of general principles had to go. I believe we could have worked earlier on issues that involved knowledge in a bigger way. I think the first place we see the old ideas found wanting is in Danny Bobrow's work in STUDENT—here's the first piece of work when someone is giving up on GPS, is trying to solve a problem and see what's really in it. My own work was the same, and in a sense an attack on Slagle's work, which had taken a generalist point of view. I came up with an argument for what I call the primacy of expertise, and at the time I called the other guys the generalists. I was antigeneralist for many years. I think the field of artificial intelligence has been essentially healthy since then, but it took some difficult doing. I think there was a tremendous battle between Papert and Minsky between 1965 and 1970. Minsky's view of my thesis [a system called MACSYMA to aid mathematicians, which is deeply steeped in specific knowledge] was that it wasn't AI. He came to my exam and said, this isn't AI. Papert and he had had a five-hour argument the day before. But the old ideas were dying.

Newell also fought the idea, says Moses, clinging instead to hopes for generalism.

He called my position the big-switch theory, the idea being that you have all these experts working for you and when you have a problem, you decide which expert to call in to solve the problem. That's not AI, you see, but he didn't say that. I think what finally broke Newell's position was [Terry] Winograd. Essentially I think Newell is doing some very good work right now, but it took almost fifteen years. And it took Minsky nearly as long; McCarthy hasn't converted much, and Simon really isn't playing such a major role these days so it's not so critical he change his views. Besides, he always has very interesting positions on things, so it's quite fine. Simple Simon can continue.

In any event, robotics seemed to say very strongly that knowledge—lots of it in depth—was at least as essential as general principles of intelligence. And these results came to stand also as the most convincing denial yet of a difference between mind and body since ancient theologians first made that division and renaissance philosophers calcified it.

That impoverished world I mentioned was usually a world of toy boxes and blocks, moved around here and there by command. After the hand-eye robot at Stanford had proved itself by learning to move blocks around on a table, it graduated to a considerably more complicated task of assembling an automobile water pump from parts scattered randomly on a table. A film exists of the Stanford robot engaged in this task, which runs about four minutes. Even with such brevity, the average viewer is hard put to stay awake. We've seen assembly-line processes accomplish what looks like—what looks like—the same thing, so we remain unimpressed. We have to remind ourselves of how we'd feel watching a beloved four-year-old human child engaged in the same task, sorting out the pieces one by one, "knowing" that the big nut must be used to secure the big screw, and that one part, put on in haste, has to be removed to accommodate a seal that was forgotten in the first attempt. If one deserves awe, so does the other: the human act because at long last we are beginning to understand how really awesome in its parsimony the human brain is, and the robot's act because we are approaching some duplication of that breathtaking parsimony.

Both the MIT robot and the Edinburgh robot (called Freddy) had the same general effect on the naive viewer. Even less naive viewers were often perturbed. In the same essay I quoted earlier, Bernard Meltzer of Edinburgh made some uncharitable cracks about Freddy pushing his blocks around in his toy world, and the waste of good human brainpower to produce nothing more than this feeble creature.

If there was a robot you could feel affection for, it had to be Stanford Research Institute's Shakey. "We worked for a month trying to find a good name for it." says Charles Rosen, who headed the SRI artificial-intelligence group, "ranging from Greek names to whatnot, and then one of us said, "Hey, it shakes like hell and moves around, let's just call it Shakey." Unlike the other robots, Shakey was mobile, and could propel himself from room to room of SRI, evading obstacles and recovering from unforeseen circumstances, such as schoolchildren standing agape at his progress through the halls.

When I saw Shakey he was in retirement in the SRI office of Bert Raphael, one of his designers. Shakey was a sad sight, immobile in a corner. Some sort of mucilage that had kept body and soul together had flowed from his supporting platform, solidified, and looked now for all the world like a hula dancer's skirt, modestly concealing Shakey's wheels. He'd surely seen better days.

Raphael shook his head as he looked over at Shakey, explaining to me the genesis of the project. He himself had received one of the first Ph.D.'s given at MIT in artificial intelligence, had been hired by SRI for this project as the only one who knew LISP and who had had experience with the LISP language and large computers.

> *Initially our interests were to see what the state of the art was in learning machines and pattern recognition methods [he said], and in symbol manipulation and in modeling, and put them all together and see if we could make the sum greater than the parts. Suppose you have a visual-perception capability that can give information to the problem solver, and a problem solver that can predict what you're likely to be looking at to help the vision system. And the other initial goal was to see how much we could accomplish with limited hardware capabilities. At the time, MIT was working on vision and they were developing or contracting for very high resolution cameras.*

MIT intended to exceed the human eye's capabilities, and SRI took the opposite approach: how much could you do knowing something about the environment and having other kinds of information about what the system is supposed to achieve? How effective could they make a simple system by combining the software with their current capabilities in hardware?

The vision capabilities were essential. Nils Nilsson, who was project leader for Shakey sees scene analysis, as it's called, as the one element common to the four robot projects. But each group took a different approach. SRI felt itself somewhere in the middle—its interest was in making sense of the scene, not getting the best images possible. Nilsson believes that Shakey's problem-solving system was probably more sophisticated than those of the others, which seemed to him somewhat ad hoc:

> *Those of us at SRI were more interested, I believe, in general problem-solving mechanisms for reasoning out the solutions to problems, so I think we were more sophisticated in that regard. We also concentrated a good deal more than the others on the interaction between the plan that was developed by the problem-solving system and the execution of that plan. Other people at other places were interested in such things, but there was never any connection made, I think, in any of their actual robot systems.*

Shakey taught its creators some surprising things. Perhaps one of the most important had to do with that elusive property of generality, for Shakey showed that you could not, for example, take a graph-searching algorithm from a chess program and hand-printed-character-recognizing algorithm from a vision program and, having attached them together, expect the robot to understand the world. As Raphael put it, there are serious questions about the interaction between knowledge in different domains. Another problem

471

had to do with uncertainty in a complicated world—a problem most of us can appreciate.

> *When a computer chess program says pawn to king-four, it's absolutely assumed that the pawn is now in king-four, and it can go on to think about the next move [says Raphael]. But when we said, Shakey, move forward three feet, the only thing we could be absolutely sure of is that he did not move exactly three feet. He probably would move three feet plus or minus epsilon according to some normal distribution, depending upon the errors in the calibration and slippage in the wheels; but maybe he moves one and a half feet and runs into the wall, or maybe he doesn't move at all because the commands got garbled in transmission, or his batteries are low. So there's an interesting research area that we made some progress on—how to build robust systems, and what kinds of monitoring are needed and how the system has to check whether it accomplishes what it tries to accomplish. We developed ways of using the TV camera and sensory feedback to monitor and update Shakey's own model of the world. We built various ideas of representing information in the robot's mind as in a computer. In a sense, the robot has a model of itself and of its environment. It knows where it thinks it is in the world, and it also knows an expected value of the error in that. Shakey assumed every time it moved that there was some normally distributed error, and that got added into its knowledge of its position. Of course the error kept getting bigger and bigger, and when it got big enough, that would trigger another part of the program, which would come in and say, "Hey, I'm confused enough that I'd better look for some landmark and check where I really am." I think a lot of these considerations came out of this work that are now automatically part of our thoughts when we try to apply computer-control techniques to industrial automation; for instance.*

Two major versions of Shakey were produced. The first version, completed in 1969, could manage a combination of abilities in perception and problem solving. Raphael's own informative book on artificial intelligence, called *The Thinking Computer, Mind Inside Matter* (1976), describes how the first version of Shakey worked, and contrasts it with major changes made in the second version. Curiously, the hardware—the robot vehicle itself—was virtually unchanged while nearly everything else was changed drastically. The core memory was nearly tripled, and four major levels of behavior were now programmed, the lowest levels concerned with physical mobility, a third level concerned with planning solutions to problems (a system called STRIPS), which was intended to combine both formal and informal reasoning and also to get around some of the problems GPS had raised, such as how to proceed with a task. The top level was executive, and carried out the plans completed by the second level; it could either rearrange the plans to achieve better results or call for better plans. The lower levels were also capable of detecting and correcting certain kinds of errors without reference to or help from the executive program.

> *We picked a mobile robot as a project [says Charles Rosen] because we believed that to cope with the ever-changing environment, or an environment that was not fixed, you'd have to solve some elementary problems of intelligence. This would mean a combination of computers, and machineries and sensors to sense the environment, and information about the world that must be stored in the form of models. All of these ideas were very early in the game.*

Rosen recalls how they found someone in the defense department who was willing to support the research, though for what Rosen himself considered foolish reasons, namely, that somehow a robot could be developed that could go about surreptitiously gathering information—a mechanical spy, nothing more or less than the original golem. Rosen didn't make that connection, but how can we resist?

"A direct result of the Shakey work is our present work in automation," Rosen says. "We really did get some practical results." Why then was support from ARPA withdrawn?

> *I think the reasons were more political than technical. We were told later by the ARPA people that there were too many people raising issues of Shakey being a dangerous thing to have, which strikes me as a little silly, when the defense department has some really dangerous machines around like robot aircraft and remote weapons. What Shakey is going to contribute to the weapons system isn't much: the technology there is from very early stuff, on visual perception. Whether you like it or not, something you develop is going to find its way into a weapons system. It has and it will always. Can't be stopped. Shakey served as a training ground and as a means for putting together a fairly elab-orate computer-machine-sensor system. It also pointed out what was needed in a system that was going to solve real-world problems, and then Shakey died. I hope it goes to the Smithsonian with its white blood.*

Nils Nilsson suspects that funding from ARPA was terminated because no immediate military application could be seen:

> *Like the other AI labs, we were very interested in basic questions of mechanisms of intelligence, problem solving. We thought the domain of robots was a good place to pursue those questions. It made us face a lot*

of real-world problems. But those problems were in the long range, and if ARPA was interested in something they could put in the field within five years, they probably made the right assessment. On the other hand, with our background and what we'd done, we could have transformed the project into something a good deal more applied. I don't know that we would have agreed to, but we could have.

Nilsson sees the legacy of robotics as the integration of visual and problem-solving systems—which might have been done without a robot, but probably wouldn't have been.

Of the four major robotics projects in the 1960s, Shakey probably received the most public attention, perhaps because it was the only mobile robot, and came closest to science fiction notions of robotics. To this Rosen allows,

Well, I was a bit responsible for some of its notoriety. I used to make it very easy for anybody to come and see it demonstrated, and that included a lot of kids, schoolteachers, some of the press, although toward the end we got so burnt with some of the press that we didn't want to show it to them any more.

Rosen clearly meant an article which was published in *Life* magazine and written by Brad Darrach, an article that was more than science fiction: the AI community feels it was victimized in this instance by outright lies. Said Rosen,

That article was very rough and that man didn't do right by us. He came here and all of us spent a great deal of time being very honest and candid with him. Then he didn't present the whole story. He picked the sensational things and left out the others. Like you asked me about Shakey. Some of its principles will be found in weapons of war, but if that's all you say without adding right alongside it that we're doing automation for industry, using many more of the principles from Shakey than the weapons do, then you're not telling the whole story, and I think that's wrong. And that's what he didn't do, that fellow. He didn't tell the whole story. He had a point of view that he wanted to demonstrate and he found the facts. I don't think he fabricated too much. But he didn't tell the whole story, and that's as dishonest as anything.

Bert Raphael, who had spent a lot of time with Darrach, goes further:

I guess the worst part of that article from our point of view was that we didn't imagine he could produce anything that bad. We were completely taken in by his sincerity and interest in what we were doing, and then he

went off and wrote this stuff. He wrote it as if he'd seen many things he never saw, and wrote about seeing Shakey going down the hall and hurrying from office to office, when in fact all the time he'd been here we were in the process of changing one computer system to another and never demonstrated anything for him. There were many direct quotes that were imaginary or completely out of context.

Steve Coles adds,

My work is unrecognizable in that Life *magazine article, although it was like a nightmare. I really had to strain my imagination to realize that he was talking about what I did.*

Marvin Minsky was so exercised that he wrote a long rebuttal and denial of quotations attributed to him, but it was only for members of the AI community, and Darrach's article not only made an enormous, sensational splash when it was published, but has subsequently been anthologized and appears in at least one college textbook where it's taught and read by the credulous.

The Darrach article was one of the negative results of robotics research, a little fantasy that raised blood pressures and choler. The positive results are more varied.

The acquisition and understanding of sensory data has become much clearer since the work on robotics began. In 1971, Minsky and Papert wrote a document describing much of the robotics work underway at MIT and making explicit the human connection in robotics research. The report is concerned specifically with vision, whose mechanisms, despite much effort, have been very difficult to pin down. One reason for this difficulty, says the report, and the thing that makes vision typical of any intelligent act, is that vision is a deeply complex process, drawing on previously known facts and expectations, making analogies, and so forth, as well as being the physical process of light striking the retina. Of course, this idea is not original with artificial intelligence, nor is it a notion discovered belatedly by researchers in that field. Part of the early literature AI researchers claimed as their own was an article by J. Y. Lettvin, H. Maturana, W. S. McCulloch, and W. Pitts called "What the Frog's Eye Tells the Frog's Brain," which makes this point among others (1958).

Minsky and Papert pointed out how our feelings about what we see—for example, the belief that we see everything when we first walk into a room—are not borne out by tests:

In general, and not just in regard to vision, [they wrote], people are not good at describing mental processes; even when their descriptions seem eloquent, they rarely agree either with one another or with objective performances. The ability to analyze one's own mental processes, evidently, does not arise spontaneously or reliably; instead, suitable concepts for this must be developed or learned, through processes similar to development of scientific theories.

(Minsky and Papert, 1971)

So the ideas about vision that were developed in the course of trying to make a robot eye see suggested new ways to think about thinking in general, and about imagery and vision in particular. Furthermore, these new ways had to pass a test that many traditional notions in psychology and philosophy did not and could not pass: if a theory of vision—or thinking of any sort—was to be taken seriously, one should be able to use it to make a machine that sees, or thinks.

Thus, in the early 1960s, Larry Roberts, then a graduate student at MIT, began intensive work on what is called visual scene analysis. Roberts's work involved analyzing scenes containing polyhedra, a program that matched what it saw with its camera eye to its preformed expectations. Although visual pattern recognition had been an early part of AI, that effort had been limited to two-dimensional patterns, and aimed at merely categorizing patterns rather than describing or "knowing" what the patterns were. Roberts wanted to work with three-dimensional scenes, and was furthermore interested in trying something more sophisticated than the template-match-classify procedure that characterized most visual pattern recognition. His work, and that which followed it, was to lead to some sophisticated techniques of edge-detection, contour-following, and region-finding programs. There even emerged an elegant theory of permissible representation of edges and vertices and their relations to three-dimensional polyhedra—a theory not previously discovered by projective or descriptive geometers.

The intelligent control of effectors—that is, mechanical devices that can make changes in the physical world—increased enormously because of robotics research. Effectors were designed to deal with some of the events that could throw a good solution to a problem off the track, such as initial misinformation, accidental dynamic effects, and such. Again, the most intimate relationship between plan and execution had to exist. Real-world representations inside the computer had to be developed. Finally, when robotics research had got underway in the mid-1960s, the actual physical mechanisms available were generally primitive, and thus robotics improved hardware, in particular hand-arm devices, optical range finders, and special tactile, force, and torque sensors.

But the overwhelming message—not always recognized by those doing the robotics work themselves—was that general principles of intelligence were insufficient. As I pointed out earlier in this chapter, there was considerable resistance to that idea. Edward Feigenbaum and his group at Stanford, who were unconnected with the Stanford robot project but were instead working on a way of assisting chemists to do spectograph analysis, were coming to the same conclusion, but they felt very lonely in that discovery.

Joel Moses, whose thesis had relied on expertise instead of general principles, remembers the frustration of trying to expound that point of view. "Papert almost cried once," Moses remembers. "He said, 'How can you get those guys to listen?' That was 1966, maybe 1968."

But the robots seemed to prove the view beyond a shadow of a doubt. And does the end of robotics work in the early 1970s mean, as Dreyfus predicted, that no robot will ever be generally intelligent? That the robot cannot be intelligent, because it lacks a human body in a human world? The current view is hardly so. Although it is presently too expensive to devise a general-purpose robot for tasks that a special-purpose robot can do more efficiently, Nilsson has written, "It seems reasonable to predict that man's historic fascination with robots, coupled with a new round of advances in vision and reasoning abilities, will lead to a resurgence of interest in general robot systems, perhaps during the late 1970s" (1974).

Notes

1 The Lighthill report generated much controversy at the time, especially because temporarily, at least, it threatened to end funding of AI in Great Britain. Sir James Lighthill, a distinguished physicist, had been commissioned by the Science Research Council of Great Britain to evaluate the state of AI and recommend whether further funding should be given. Charitably speaking, the report seems to have been done in a hurry—in such a hurry, in fact, that rumors immediately flew that its main purpose was personal vendetta, with Sir James as hatchet man for others who were nettled by AI and some of its practitioners. Since the report coincided with, and surely exacerbated, the dissolution and reorganization of the Edinburgh University AI laboratory, the rumors seemed true. But Bernard Meltzer, still at Edinburgh, has doubts as to any conspiracy, though he's one of several who complained to me about how the report was done. In any case, AI funding seems to be scrutinized now somewhat more carefully than it was pre-Lighthill, but it continues satisfactorily.

2 Simon notes,

> "The protocols were gathered in May 1957, and then transcribed. In July we held a Summer Institute at Carnegie for some social psychologists. During one week, we broke up into subgroups, taking the protocol of S4 on P1, and each subgroup was to induce a program simulating the subject. AI and I were working either with separate subgroups or individually, apart from all of them. We were probably not communicating much during the week—can't be sure. On 7/6/57, I produced on a single sheet of paper (preserved) a primitive, but clearly recognizable GPS, which I presented as my solution. I don't recall AI's. AI recalls, equally clearly, that he presented his solution at the end of the week, which was also GPS.
>
> "We had been working so closely, of course, that it is quite possible that we both independently arrived at the same analysis of the protocol. I

477

simply don't remember either any communication during the week, nor do I remember any 'aha!' when we discovered our identical solutions. I am afraid that we may never have the true explanation of what exactly went on during the week. I do know that during the ensuing years we never thought or talked of GPS as having been discovered by only one of us. Why???"

3   The Tower of Hanoi is a platform with three upright pegs on it. Stacked on one of these pegs are disks of graduated size, the largest on the bottom, the smallest on top. The object of the puzzle is to move the disks one at a time until the stack is transferred from one peg to another, without ever allowing a larger disk to cover a smaller one. With only three or four disks, the problem is easy; seven or more makes it hairy. Simon has such a puzzle sitting on the bookshelf in his office at Carnegie. In the missionaries and cannibals problem, three missionaries and three cannibals must cross a river in a boat that will accommodate only two people at a time. If ever the cannibals outnumber the missionaries, the cannibals will dispatch the missionaries with gusto. How do they cross the river intact?

4   It happens that J. C. Shaw had the same idea during the mid-1950s at RAND, but never got around to implementing it or even writing it up.

5   It also happens to be a splendid excuse for human rigidity. We lose a paycheck, say, and we're informed with great solemnity that "because of the computer" we'll have to wait until the next pay period, and make whatever explanations we can to the landlord and grocer. We protest and fume to no avail in the face of such insensitive system design, especially those of us who know very well the blame is in no way "the computer's."

6   The combinatorial explosion takes place when growth is exponential, for example, as Malthus feared population growth would be, therefore outstripping the world's food supply, which only increases linearly. Thus, two parents have more than two offspring, who in turn each have more than two offspring, who in turn . . . Problem solving encounters the same difficulties, when one alternative path to a solution leads to several more branches, each leading to further branches. Thus, Claude Shannon was able to calculate his 10^{120} possible moves in a chess game where every move and its consequences were explored.

7   And may already have been met. When Daniel Bobrow worked for the Cambridge, Massachusetts, firm of Bolt Beranek and Newman, he reported this in the *ACM SIGART Newsletter* of December 1968:

"One Saturday morning about 9 A.M., a BBN Vice President in charge of selling our Telcomp commercial service arrived at our PDP-1 computer room hoping to be able to use the computer for a demonstration. He found a note on the PDP-1 teletype that read: 'TYPE ALL MESSAGES INTO THIS TELETYPE, AND END THEM WITH A PERIOD.' This note was left there by one of the programming bums who had just succeeded in making run a LISP version of the DOCTOR program (based on ELIZA as developed by Weizenbaum). However, the VP thought that this note indicated that this teletype was linked with the one in my home, since I often used the computer all night. Therefore, he started typing to 'me,' but in fact was typing to this version of the DOCTOR program. The following conversation ensued:

VP	Do you think that I can use the computer this morning?
TELETYPE	Why do you ask?
VP	I might be able to make some additional telcomp sales.
TELETYPE	Why aren't you sure?
VP	My prospective customers have never seen a demonstration of the system.
TELETYPE	Does this mean very much to you?
VP	Of course it does.
TELETYPE	You seem very positive about that.
VP	This is ridiculous.
TELETYPE	What do you mean this is ridiculous?
VP	Is there any reason why I can't use the computer now?
TELETYPE	Tell me more about your prospective customers.
VP	Please notedial me up on 491–1850

"Note that after the last remark the VP did not obey instructions, and left out the period. Therefore, of course, the computer didn't answer him. This so infuriated the VP, who thought I was playing games with him, that he called me up, woke me from a deep sleep, and said:

| VP | Why are you being so snotty to me? |
| BOBBROW | What do you mean why am I being snotty to you? |

"The VP angrily read me the notedialog that 'we' had been having, and couldn't get any response but laughter from me. It took a while to convince him it really was the computer."

Naturally, there were quibbles about whether Turing's Test had indeed been passed. A short note from one J. Markowitz, also of Bolt Beranek and Newman, was appended to Bobrow's tale:

"Did Dr. Bobrow's story show that a computer had passed the imitation test of Turing? Sure, our vice president failed to detect the presence of a computer in six successive exchanges. But that's not Turing's Test.

"Turing specified that an observer be forced to choose between two (hidden) devices—one known to be a man, the other known to be a machine.

"It is easy to show that Turing's arrangement leads to better performance by the observer, and is thus a stiffer test for machines who would pretend. More importantly, Turing's arrangement minimizes the effect of bias on the observer's part. Clearly, the VP held a strong *a priori* belief that he would be talking to a man—a severe limitation."

Bibliography

Amarel, S.; Brown, J. S.; Buchanan, B.; Hart, P.; Kulikowski, C.; Martin, W.; and Pople, H. 1977. "Report of a Panel on Applications of Artificial Intelligence." *Proceedings of the Fifth International Joint Conference on Artificial Intelligence*.

Appleman, P. 1970. *Darwin: Texts, Backgrounds, Contemporary Opinion, Critical Essays*. New York: Norton.

Ashby, W. R. 1952. *Design for a Brain*. New York: Wiley. Also appeared as "Design for a Brain," *Electronic Engineering*, 20 (1948), 379–383. These references are from the corrected 1954 edition of the book.

Asimov, I. 1950. *I, Robot*. New York: Gnome Press.

Bar-Hillel, Yehoshua. 1964. *Language and Information*. Reading, Mass.: Addison-Wesley.

Bernal, J. D. 1974. *Science in History*. Vol. 2. Cambridge, Mass: MIT Press.

Block, C. 1925. *The Golem: Legends of the Ghetto of Prague*. New York: Rudolf Steiner Press.

Boden, M. 1977. *Artificial Intelligence and Natural Man*. New York: Basic Books.

Boring, E. G. 1946. "Mind and Mechanism." *American Journal of Psychology*, 2, April.

Boswell, James, 1968. *The Life of Samuel Johnson*, Frank Brady, ed. New York: New American Library.

Bowden, B. V. 1953. *Faster than Thought*. London: Sir Isaac Pitman.

Cadwallader-Cohen, J.; Zysiczk, W. W.; and Donelly, R. R. 1961. "The Chaostron: An Important Advance in Learning Machines." *Journal of Irreproducible Results*, 10, 30.

Chapuis, A., and Droz, E. 1949. *Les Automates*. Neuchatel: Editions du Griffon.

Cohen, J. 1966. *Human Robots in Myth and Science*. London: Allen and Unwin.

Colby, K. M. 1976. "On the Morality of Computers Providing Psychotherapy." Memo Al HMF-6, Department of Psychiatry, University of California at Los Angeles.

Dinneen, G. P. 1955. "Programming Pattern Recognition." *Proceedings of the 1955 Western Joint Computer Conference*, IRE, March.

Dreyfus, H. 1972. *What Computers Can't Do; A Critique of Artificial Reason*. New York: Harper & Row.

Evans, T. G. 1968. "A program for the solution of geometric-analogy intelligence test questions." In *Semantic Information Processing*, Minsky, M. ed., Cambridge, Mass.: MIT Press.

Evert, W. 1974. "Frankenstein." Four talks delivered on WQED-FM, Pittsburgh, Penn.

Feigenbaum, E. A. 1977. "The Art of Artificial Intelligence: Themes and Case Studies of Knowledge Engineering." *Proceedings of the Fifth International Joint Conference on Artificial Intelligence*.

Feigenbaum, E. A.; Buchanan, B. G.; and Lederberg, J. 1971. "On Generality and Problem Solving: A Case Study Using the DENDRAL Program." In *Machine Intelligence*, 6. Edinburgh: Edinburgh University Press.

Feigenbaum, E. A., and Feldman, J. 1963. *Computers and Thought*. New York: McGraw-Hill.

Gardner, M. 1958. *Logic Machines and Diagrams*. New York: McGraw-Hill.

Goldstein, I., and Papert, S. 1976. "Artificial Intelligence, Language, and the Study of Knowledge." AI Memo 337, MIT AI Laboratory.

Goldstine, H. 1972. *The Computer from Pascal to von Neumann*. Princeton, N. J.: Princeton University Press.

Greenberger, M. 1962. *Management and the Computer of the Future*. New York: MIT Press and Wiley.

Hiller, L. A., and Isaacson, L. M. 1959. *Experimental Music*. New York: McGraw-Hill.

Jonas, G. 1976. "A Reporter at Large (Stuttering)." *The New Yorker*, 52, November 15.

Koberg, D., and Bagnall, J. 1972. Revised 1973, 1974. *The Universal Traveler*. Los Altos, Calif.: William Kaufmann.

Labat, R. 1963. *History of Science*. Vol. 1. New York: Basic Books.

Lattimore, R. 1951. *Homer's Iliad*. Chicago: University of Chicago Press.

Lederberg, J. 1976. "Review of J. Weizenbaum's *Computer Power and Human Reason*." In *Three Reviews of J. Weizenbaum's Computer Power and Human Reason*. Memo AIM–291, Stanford AI Laboratory, November.

Lettvin, J. Y.; Maturana, H.; McCulloch, W. S.; and Pitts, W. 1959. "What the Frog's Eye Tells the Frog's Brain." *Proceedings of the IRE, 47*, November.

Lewis, C. I., and Langford, C. H. 1956. "History of Symbolic Logic." In *The World of Mathematics*, J. R. Newman, ed. New York: Simon and Schuster.

MacKay, D. 1951. "Mindlike Behavior in Artefacts." *British Journal for the Philosophy of Science, 2*, 6.

MacKay, D. 1955. "The Epistemological Problem for Automata." In *Automata Studies, Annals of Mathematical Studies, 34*, C. Shannon and J. McCarthy, eds. Princeton, N. J.: Princeton University Press.

MacNiece, L. 1951. *Goethe's Faust*. New York: Oxford University Press.

Marshall, J. 1889. *The Life and Letters of Mary Wollstonecraft Shelley*. 2 vols. London: Richard Bentley and Son.

McCarthy, J. 1972. "Mechanical Servants for Mankind." *1973 Britannica Yearbook of Science and the Future, Encyclopedia Britannica*. Chicago: William Benton.

McCarthy, J. 1976. "An Unreasonable Book." In *Three Reviews of J. Weizenbaum's Computer Power and Human Reason*. Memo AIM–291, Stanford AI Laboratory, November.

McCarthy, J., and Hayes, P. J. 1969. "Some Philosophical Problems from the Standpoint of Artificial Intelligence." In *Machine Intelligence*, 4, D. Michie, ed. New York: Elsevier.

McCracken, D. 1976. "Review, *Computer Power and Human Reason* by Joseph Weizenbaum." *Datamation*, April.

McCulloch, W. 1965. *Embodiments of Mind*. Cambridge, Mass.: MIT Press.

Medawar, P. B. 1977. "Unnatural Science." *New York Review of Books XXIV*, 1, February.

Meltzer, B. 1971. "Personal View: Bury the Old War-Horse!" *ACM SIGART Newsletter, 27*, April.

Minsky, M. 1956. "Heuristic Aspects of the Artificial Intelligence Problem." Group Report 34–55, ASTIA Document AD 236885 (MIT Hayden Library H–58), Lincoln Laboratories, MIT, Lexington, Mass.

Minsky, M. 1959. "Some Methods of Heuristic Programming and Artificial Intelligence." In *Proceedings of the Symposium on Mechanisation of Thought Processes*, D. V. Blake and A. M. Uttley, eds. 2 vols. London: H. M. Stationery Office.

Minsky, M. 1963. "Steps Toward Artificial Intelligence." In *Computers and Thought*, E. A. Feigenbaum and J. Feldman, eds. New York: McGraw-Hill.

Minsky, M. 1968. *Semantic Information Processing*. Cambridge, Mass.: MIT Press.

Minsky, M., and Papert, S. 1968. *Perceptrons*. Cambridge, Mass.: MIT Press.

Minsky, M., and Papert, S. 1971. *Artificial Intelligence*, Project MAC Report.

Mitroff, I. 1974. *The Subjective Side of Science: A Philosophical Inquiry into the Psychology of the Apollo Moon Scientists*. New York: Elsevier.

Moravec, H. 1977. "Intelligent Machines: How to Get There From Here and What to Do Afterwards." Unpublished.

481

Morgenstern, O., and von Neumann, J. 1944. *Theory of Games and Economic Behavior*. Princeton, N.J.: Princeton University Press.

Morrison, P., and Morrison, E. 1961. *Charles Babbage and His Calculating Engines*. New York: Dover.

Moses, J. 1971. "Symbolic Integration—The Stormy Decade." *Communications of the ACM*, 14, August.

Murphy, G. 1972. *Historical Introduction to Modern Psychology*. New York: Harcourt Brace Jovanovich.

Newell, A. 1973a. "Production Systems: Models of Control Structures." In *Visual Information Processing*, W. C. Chase, ed. New York: Academic Press.

Newell, A. 1973b. "Artificial Intelligence and the Concept of Mind." In *Computer Models of Thought and Language*, R. Schank and K. M. Colby, eds. San Francisco: W. H. Freeman and Company.

Newell, A. ed. 1973c. *Speech Understanding Systems: Final Report of a Study Group*. New York: Elsevier.

Newell, A.; Shaw, J. C.; and Simon, H. A. 1958. "Chess Playing Programs and the Problem of Complexity." *IBM Journal of Research and Development*, 2, 4. Reprinted in Feigenbaum and Feldman, 1963.

Newell, A., and Simon, H. A. 1956. "The Logic Theory Machine." *IRE Transactions on Information Theory*, September. Reprinted in Feigenbaum and Feldman, 1963.

Newell, A., and Simon, H. A. 1961. "Computer Simulation of Human Thinking." *Science*, 134, December.

Newell, A., and Simon, H. A. 1973. *Human Problem Solving*. Englewood Cliffs, N. J.: Prentice-Hall.

Newell, A., and Simon, H. A. 1976. "Computer Science as Empirical Inquiry: Symbols and Search." *Communications of the ACM*, 3, March.

Nilsson, N. J. 1974. "Artificial Intelligence." *Proceedings of the 1974 IFIP Congress*, Stockholm, Sweden. Also published as SRI Artificial Intelligence Center Technical Note 89.

Papert, S. 1968. "The Artificial Intelligence of Hubert L. Dreyfus: A Budget of Fallacies." AI Memo 154, MIT AI Laboratory.

Papert, S. 1971. "Teaching Children Thinking." AI Memo 247, MIT AI Laboratory.

Papert, S. 1976. "Some Poetic and Social Criteria for Education Design." AI Memo 373, MIT AI Laboratory.

Plank, R. 1965. "The Golem and the Robot." *Literature and Psychology*, 15, Winter.

Pool, I., ed. 1977. *The Social Impact of the Telephone*. Cambridge, Mass.: MIT Press.

Pople, H. 1977. "The Formation of Composite Hypotheses in Diagnostic Problem Solving: An Exercise in Synthetic Reasoning." *Proceedings of the Fifth International Joint Conference on Artificial Intelligence*.

Price, D. J. 1963. *Little Science, Big Science*. New York: Columbia University Press.

Randell, B. 1973. *The Origins of Digital Computers: Selected Papers*. New York and Berlin: Springer-Verlag.

Raphael, B. 1970. "The Relevance of Robot Research to Artificial Intelligence." In R. B. Banerji and M. D. Mesarovic, *Theoretical Approaches to Non-Numerical Problem Solving*. Berlin and New York: Springer-Verlag.

Raphael, B. 1976. *The Thinking Computer: Mind Inside Matter*. San Francisco: W. H. Freeman and Company.

Reid, C. 1970. *Hilbert*. New York: Springer-Verlag.

Rosen, S. 1959. *Doctor Paracelsus*. Boston: Little, Brown.

Sagan, C. 1973. *The Cosmic Connection*. New York: Doubleday.

Sagan, C. 1977. *The Dragons of Eden*. New York: Random House.

Selfridge, O. G. 1955. "Pattern Recognition and Modern Computers." *Proceedings of the 1955 Western Joint Computer Conference*, IRE, March.

Selfridge, O. G. 1959. "Pandemonium, a Paradigm for Learning." In *Proceedings of the Symposium on Mechanisation of Thought Processes*. 2 vols. D. V. Blake and A. M. Uttley, eds. London: H. M. Stationery Office.

Shannon, C. 1950. "A Chess-Playing Machine." *Scientific American*, *182*, February.

Shannon, C. 1953. "Computers and Automata." *Proceedings of the IRE*.

Shannon, C., and McCarthy, J., eds. 1956. *Automata Studies. Annals of Mathematical Studies*, 34. Princeton, N. J.: Princeton University Press.

Simmons, R. F. 1965. Answering English questions by computer: a survey. *Communications of ACM*, *8*, January.

Simmons, R. F. 1970. Natural language question answering systems: 1969. *Communications of ACM*, *13*, January.

Simon, H. A. 1947. *Administrative Behavior*. New York: Macmillan.

Simon, H. A. 1967. "An Information-Processing Explanation of Some Perceptual Phenomena." *British Journal of Psychology*, *58*, *May*.

Simon, H. A. 1969. *Sciences of the Artificial*. Cambridge, Mass.: MIT Press.

Simon, H. A. 1971. "Cognitive Control of Perceptual Processes." In G. V. Coelho and E. Rubinstein, eds., *Social Change and Human Behavior*. Rockville, Md.: National Institutes of Health.

Simon, H. A. 1972. "What Is Visual Imagery? An Information Processing Interpretation." In *Cognition in Learning and Memory*, L. W. Gregg, ed. New York: Wiley.

Simon, H. A. 1977. "Artificial Intelligence Systems that Understand." *Proceedings of the Fifth International Joint Conference on Artificial Intelligence*.

Simon, H. A., and Barenfeld, M. 1969. "Information Processing Analysis of Perceptual Processes in Problem Solving." *Psychological Review*, *76*, September.

Simon, H. A., and Siklóssy, L. 1972. *Representation and Meaning*. Englewood Cliffs, N.J.: Prentice-Hall.

Strachey, Lytton. 1948. *Literary Essays*. London: Chatto and Windus.

Sussman, G. J., and Stallman, R. M. 1975. "Heuristic Techniques in Computer Aided Circuit Analysis." *IEEE Transactions on Circuits and Systems CAS–22*, No. 11.

Sutherland, N. S. 1976. "The Electronic Oracle." *Times Literary Supplement*, July 30.

Taube, M. 1961. *Computers and Common Sense: The Myth of Thinking Machines*. New York: Columbia University Press.

Taylor, R. H. 1976. "Letter." *Datamation*, June.

Thomas, L. 1974. *The Lives of a Cell*. New York: Viking Press.

Turing, A. 1950. "Computing Machinery and Intelligence." In *Computers and Thought*, E. A. Feigenbaum and J. Feldman, eds. New York: McGraw-Hill, 1963.

Turing, A. 1969. "Intelligent Machinery." In *Machine Intelligence, 5*, B. Meltzer and D. Michie, eds. Edinburgh: Edinburgh University Press.

Turing, S. 1959. *Alan M. Turing*. Cambridge: W. Heffer and Sons.

Turney, C. 1972. *Byron's Daughter: A Biography of Elizabeth Medora Leigh*. New York: Charles Scribner's Sons.

Vartanian, A. 1960. *La Mettrie's L'Homme Machine.* Princeton, N.J.: Princeton University Press.

von Boehn, M. Undated. *Puppets and Automata.* New York: Dover Books.

von Neumann, J. 1951. "The General and Logical Theory of Automata." In *Cerebral Mechanisms in Behavior*, L. A. Jeffress, ed. New York: Wiley. Also reprinted in *Perspectives on the Computer Revolution*, Z. W. Pylyshyn, ed. New York: Prentice-Hall, 1970.

von Neumann, J. 1958. *The Computer and the Brain.* New Haven, Conn: Yale University Press.

Waltz, D. L. 1972. "Generating Semantic Descriptions from Drawings of Scenes with Shadows." AI Memo TR 271, MIT AI Laboratory.

Weizenbaum, J. 1972. "On the Impact of Computers on Society." *Science, 176*, May.

Weizenbaum, J. 1976. *Computer Power and Human Reason.* San Francisco: W. H. Freeman and Company.

Wiener, N. 1961. *Cybernetics.* 2nd ed. Cambridge, Mass.: MIT Press.

Winograd, T. 1973. "A Procedural Model of Language Understanding." In *Computer Models of Thought and Language*. R. Schank and K. M. Colby, eds. San Francisco: W. H. Freeman and Company.

Winston, P. H. 1975. *The Psychology of Computer Vision.* New York: McGraw-Hill.

Winston, P. H. 1977. *Artificial Intelligence.* Reading, Mass.: Addison-Wesley.

Winterbotham, F. W. 1974. *The Ultra Secret.* New York: Harper & Row.

24

THE TREE OF KNOWLEDGE

D. Crevier

Source: D. Crevier, *AI: The Tumultuous History of the Search for Artificial Intelligence*, Basic Books, 1993, pp. 145–63.

*[In 1959] it looked like you could do a project in two years . . .
But by 1970, . . . if you had a good idea, it might take two or three
years to get other people to appreciate it, and three or four years
to actually do the work. So you were progressing in six- or seven-
year steps.*

(Marvin Minsky)

The very first example of knowledge encoded into rules of thumb, or heuristics, goes back a long way. It is the Edwin Smith papyrus.[1] Smith, an American collector, bought the Egyptian papyrus in a Luxor antique shop in 1882.
Some fifty years later, James Breasted, an archeologist at the University of
Chicago, deciphered it and placed its date of origin in the seventeenth century B.C. Breasted and later archeologists believe the document to be a copy
of an original dating back much earlier: the beginning of the third millen-
nium, or about five thousand years ago.[2] The papyrus represents forty-eight
surgical observations of head wounds, all under the same formal representation: title, symptoms, diagnosis, treatment. The symptom-diagnosis pair
always appears as follows: "IF you examine a man presenting this symptom,
THEN you will say about him: it is such injury." The prognosis—favorable,
uncertain, or fatal—is expressed by one of three invariable forms: "It is an
injury that I will cure," "It is an injury that I will combat," "It is an injury
against which I am powerless." Here is the papyrus's rule pertaining to frac-
tures of the cheekbone:

Title:
Instructions for treating a fracture of the cheekbone.
Symptoms:

IF you examine a man with a fracture of the cheekbone, you will find a salient and red fluxion, bordering this wound.
Diagnostic and prognosis:
THEN you will tell your patient: "A fracture of the cheekbone. It is an injury that I will cure."
Treatment:
You shall tend him with fresh meat the first day. The treatment shall last until the fluxion resorbs. Then you shall treat him with raspberry, honey, and bandages to be renewed each day, until he is cured.[3]

In the late 1960s and early 1970s AI researchers were looking for practical problems to solve. They realized that knowledge was the key to problem solving power, and searched for ways to make knowledge available to their computers in large amounts. This search led them to an IF . . . THEN format strikingly like that used by their Egyptian predecessor, and involved new ways of sifting through large amounts of knowledge: these discoveries resulted in the first expert systems. The fathers of expert systems also found ways to express knowledge about knowledge itself: these techniques are now a part of the new field of knowledge engineering.

The first expert systems

The switch from qualitative studies in the control and expression of knowledge to the manipulation of massive amounts of it marks a turning point in the history of AI. As Herbert Simon pointed out to me, it happened not so much because researchers were previously unaware of the power of knowledge, as it did for practical, hardware-oriented limitations:

> Quite deliberately we did a lot of our work in the early days . . . on toy tasks. Toy not in the sense that they weren't hard problems to solve but in the sense that they didn't need much special knowledge. It isn't as though people weren't aware that knowledge was important. They were steering away from tasks which made knowledge the center of things because we couldn't build large data bases with the computers we had then. Our first chess program and the Logic Theorist were done on a computer that had a 64- to 100-word core and a scratch drum with 10,000 words of usable space on it. So semantics was not the name of the game. I remember one student that I had who wanted to do a thesis on how you extracted information from a big store. I told him "No way! You can only do that thesis on a toy example, and we won't have any evidence of how it scales up. You'd better find something else to do." So people did steer away from problems where knowledge was the essential issue.[4]

In the early 1970s, though, computers with hundreds of thousands of words of memory became available, thus giving free rein to programmers for implementing applications requiring extensive amounts of knowledge. Yet, it still took ten years after the advent of such machines to develop commercial systems relying on extensive knowledge bases such as XCON, which I shall discuss in a short while. One reason for this additional delay is the tremendous complexity of the software needed to develop and run such systems. A related cause is the lengthening of the development cycles in AI, an unavoidable consequence, alas, of the maturing of the field. When you start a new science from scratch, and are almost alone in researching it, you will become of necessity a fountainhead of new ideas and immediately test them yourself. As research results from other people accumulate, you often will catch yourself rediscovering the wheel, and start spending much time cross-checking your work against others' to guard against that. After a while, most of the easy problems have been solved; research projects tend to involve several people, with the attendant political and organizational hangups.

Marvin Minsky pointed out the phenomenon to me, recalling how fast Slagle's thesis on symbolic integration was completed a few years after the Dartmouth conference:

> Slagle started it in 1959 and was done after two years. So at that time it looked like you could do a project in two years . . . But by 1970, . . . if you had a good idea, it might take two or three years to get other people to appreciate it, and three or four years to actually do the work. So you were progressing in six- or seven-year steps.[5]

In the 1970s, AI was "hankering for respectability" in Herbert Simon's words, and emerging from its infancy. Some of its applications addressed subjects of immediate interest to scientists of other disciplines, and led to the massive commercialization of expert systems in the 1980s. The first expert systems were DENDRAL and MYCIN.

DENDRAL

The seeds for the development of expert systems were planted by a practical young redhead named Edward Feigenbaum. Feigenbaum, then twenty years old and an undergraduate student in electrical engineering, was present when Herbert Simon announced to his first class at Carnegie Tech in 1956 his discovery of an intelligent machine. Fascinated, he afterwards earned his Ph.D. under Simon by building a computer model of human learning called EPAM (see chapter 10). Since his work was performed at the School of Industrial Administration, where Simon then was teaching, it branded Feigenbaum as an expert in this field and landed him after graduation an assistant professorship in the business school at Berkeley. There he tried to emulate his mentor Herbert Simon and set up an artificial intelligence program in an environment designed for churning out accountants and managers. Feigenbaum was soon joined at Berkeley by Julian Feldman, another Carnegie Mellon alumnus.

Despite earning a seventy-thousand-dollar grant from the Carnegie Foundation to support their research (a staggering amount for the time), and publishing the first AI book ever (a collection of papers entitled *Computers and Thought*,[6] which remained the only publication of its kind for several years afterward), the Feigenbaum-Feldman team enjoyed little support from the rest of the faculty. In 1965, Feigenbaum left for the computer science department of Stanford, where he found kindred souls.

His most influential encounter was with Joshua Lederberg. A Nobel Prize winner in genetics, Lederberg wanted to determine the molecular structure of complex organic molecules, and had hit a stumbling block. If you want to study a chemical compound, your first step is to determine its chemical formula. This relatively straightforward analysis tells you how many atoms of each kind the molecules contain. Unfortunately, the formula alone reveals very little about the compound. The properties of a complex molecule depend mostly on the nature of the chemical bonds within the molecule, and on how the atoms are positioned in respect to each other. These properties together make up the molecular structure. There are no simple ways to map the structure of a molecule.

The standard method of analysis consists of literally breaking up the problem into smaller parts. Chemists separate the molecules under study into ionized (electrified) fragments and process them in a device called a "mass spectrometer." The spectrometer provides the mass/charge ratios of the fragments, and shows how many fragments of each kind there are. The mass/charge ratios provide clues to the chemical compositions of the fragments. Together, these pieces of information form an incomplete picture that knowledgeable chemists can solve to reconstruct the original molecule.

Lederberg's problem was one of too many combinations. Each fragment could correspond to several substructures; yet only one global molecular structure fitted all the problem constraints. Finding the global structure involved searching a tree of possibilities. Feigenbaum and Lederberg took account of this fact in naming their program heuristic DENDRAL.[7] The word *dendral* derives from the Greek word for tree. In this case, the tree was often too large for exhaustive search even by a computer. Prior to DENDRAL, chemists attempted to solve the problem in the only way they knew how: they took educated guesses at possible solutions and tested each against the data.

The DENDRAL project, headed by Feigenbaum and his colleague Robert K. Lindsay, started in 1965 and lasted more than ten years. Feigenbaum and his co-workers were able to embody, in a set of rules, part of the knowledge chemists relied upon to make their educated guesses. A typical rule looked like the following:

> IF the spectrum for the molecule has two peaks at masses $x1$ and $x2$ such that
> a. $x1 + x2$ = Molecular Weight + 28
> b. $x1 - 28$ is a high peak, and
> c. $x2 - 28$ is a high peak, and
> d. at least one of $x1$ or $x2$ is high,
> THEN the molecule contains a ketone group.[8]

This set of rules, together with the logic required to combine them and deduce candidates for the global structure of a molecule, made up what is now considered the first expert system. The rules could drastically reduce the required search.[9] For the compound Di-n-decyl $C_{20}H_{22}$ the number of possible combinations exceeded 11,000,000. DENDRAL reduced these to 22,366 cases, which the program could then test individually to see whether they accounted for all the observations. At the end, only one combination would fit the bill, and it was the true molecular structure.

For one class of compounds, DENDRAL even narrowed the search better than the most experienced chemists.[10] DENDRAL demonstrated that one could embody, in the midst of a program doing extensive numerical work, expert knowledge that drastically reduced the effort needed to find the answer. Yet it had one major weakness: the rules and the logic required to apply them made up one tangled set of statements. When it reached a certain size, Feigenbaum and his team found it very difficult to maintain and expand their creation. The originally fluid LISP structure quickly became hard as concrete.

It was at that time that Feigenbaum and another Carnegie Mellon alumnus who had joined him at Stanford, Bruce Buchanan, took their cue from some of the work done by Newell and Simon at their alma mater.[11] Newell and Simon had been investigating a contraption called a "production system" as a model for human cognition.[12] The mathematician Emil Post had been the first to propose the idea in a 1943 paper.[13] The linguist Noam Chomsky used production systems in 1957, under the name "rewrite rules," to formalize his theories on grammar.[14] In the 1960s, they were seized by computer scientists to build compiler programs. Simon told me he first heard of production systems through a young practitioner of computer science:

> The guy who brought production systems into [Carnegie Mellon] was Bob Floyd. He was using them to design [special kinds of] compilers. Floyd had gotten his bachelor's degree at Chicago and never went on to a higher degree. He ended up in a software company up in Boston . . . I went up there to give a lecture and met him. And heard

about compiler compilers, heard about productions, heard a lot from him. He was obviously very smart. I sang his praises when I came back, so we said, "The hell with degrees!" and appointed him to a faculty position. He was here for a decade until he went out to Stanford.

MYCIN

Production systems are just lists of IF . . . THEN rules of the type used in DENDRAL, but with an important difference: the mechanism used to decide when and how to apply a given rule is apart from the list of rules itself. In the early 1970s, Feigenbaum and Buchanan set out to explore the implications of this separation of tasks and assigned this work as a thesis project to a doctoral student, Donald Waterman. In 1972, another doctoral student, Edward Shortliffe, set out under the direction of Buchanan to embody practical medical knowledge into a production system.

The result was MYCIN,[15] an expert system for the diagnosis of infectious blood diseases. From the results of blood tests, bacterial cultures, and other information, MYCIN suggested which microorganism was causing an infection. It reached this conclusion through such rules as:

IF
The site of the culture is blood, and the gram strain is positive, and the portal of entry is gastrointestinal tract, and
    [A]—the abdomen is the locus of infection, or
    [B]—the pelvis is the locus of infection
THEN
There is strongly suggestive evidence that Enterobacteriaceae is the class of organisms for which therapy should cover.[16]

MYCIN would then prescribe antibiotics for treating the condition, and even adjusted the dosage according to the patient's body weight.

Since MYCIN was the first expert system to embody cleanly the separation of the rules (which are said to make up the knowledge base) and the logic required to apply them to a particular situation, its authors made available to other researchers a version of MYCIN containing only the inference engine. This evacuated version made up the first expert system shell. Shortliffe and Buchanan called it EMYCIN, which they first claimed stood for "Empty MYCIN." After being the subject of too many jokes, they changed this to Essential MYCIN. Like many doctors, MYCIN relied on the technique of backward chaining to reach its conclusions. Backward chaining is yet another way of keeping a tree search from branching beyond control. MYCIN contained high-level rules that enabled it, from a preliminary scan of a patient's symptoms, to take a stab at a few possible diagnoses. It then worked its way backward, along the search tree defined by its rules, to justify these educated guesses.

As yet another dramatic improvement over DENDRAL, MYCIN had the ability to deal with rules that imply likely results rather than certainties. Given the IF part of a rule, MYCIN could consider that the THEN part was true with only, say, a 70-percent chance. In fact, MYCIN could rate possible conclusions on a scale ranging from − 1 (definitely wrong) to + 1 (certainly true). MYCIN could combine these certainty factors while following a chain of rules. If this analysis left it with two or more possible diagnoses, it ranked them by order of likelihood. In one blind clinical test rated by a panel of eight experts, MYCIN prescribed antibiotics for blood diseases as well as, or better than, nine individual clinicians.[17]

Randall Davis, who made his own contribution to the MYCIN project, compared MYCIN and DENDRAL for me:

> DENDRAL had the idea of rules, but it was essentially a big LISP program with some conditional rules built in . . . What DENDRAL contributed was that you could capture domain-specific knowledge as a set of rules. It demonstrated that that was a good idea and a powerful idea, but it didn't have this distinction [between rules and control logic]. By far and away the most important thing MYCIN did was to demonstrate in an unambiguous fashion that the notion of a knowledge-based system was real and tangible, and that high performance really could come almost entirely from a substantial body of knowledge. The notion of backward chaining as a [control logic] is of course computationally trivial. And that's the point. This system was developed at a time when the notion of very clever control structures was being explored. And to a large degree its intellectual impact was an unmistakable demonstration that "In the knowledge lies the power." And that you don't need clever control structures to produce intelligent behavior . . . [MYCIN's] real place in history was to put a marker on the map and show that the notion of a modular system was real, that it worked.[18]

The two-part construction of MYCIN is crucial. Since the rules in MYCIN itself say little to a nonphysician, I shall illustrate MYCIN's layout, which is also that of a typical modern expert system, with the following set of rules that could be programmed into a computer to enable it to identify large sea animals.

1. IF it is huge THEN it is a whale
2. IF it is NOT huge THEN it is not-a-whale
3. IF it is not-a-whale AND (it blows a jet OR it has a blowhole OR it has a horizontal tail) THEN it is a mammal

4. IF it is not-a-whale AND (it has no blowhole OR it has a vertical tail) THEN it is a fish
5. IF it is a mammal AND it has a pointed snout THEN it is a dolphin
6. IF it is a mammal AND it has a blunted snout AND is with a whale THEN it is a baby whale
7. IF it is a mammal AND it has a blunted snout AND it is not with a whale THEN it is a porpoise
8. IF it is a fish AND is not by itself THEN it may-be-a-tuna
9. If it may-be-a-tuna AND it has a double dorsal fin THEN it is a tuna
10. IF it may-be-a-tuna AND it does not have a double dorsal fin THEN it is an unknown fish
11. IF it is a fish AND is by itself THEN it is a swordfish-or-shark
12. IF it is a swordfish-or-shark AND (it has a sword OR (it is silvery AND has a forward dorsal fin)) THEN it is a swordfish ELSE it may-be-a-shark
13. IF it may-be-a-shark AND it has a sinewy swim THEN it is a shark
14. IF it may-be-a-shark AND it does not have a sinewy swim THEN it is an unknown fish

These rules are the productions; and the entire set of rules, plus the program required to apply them (omitted here), make up the production system. Each rule takes the form of an "IF ... THEN" statement. The IF part can contain one or several conditions. The presence of an OR operator means that not all conditions need be true for the rule to apply. Using ORs enables a production system to capture some of the parallelism of human thought. It also enables the system to reach conclusions without a complete knowledge of the problem. For example, the OR conjunctions in rule 3 let the computer move ahead even if you haven't been able to see the entire animal. If you haven't caught sight of the blowhole, maybe you've seen the jet. Failing that, you may have glimpsed the tail. Some of the preconditions are conclusions reached by other rules. For example, rule 5 requires that the animal be a mammal: this is the conclusion of rule 3. Thus, even if each rule contains a separate bit of knowledge, their conclusions and conditions relate the rules to each other.

In fact, we can capture the relationships between the rules very simply. A graphic representation reduces the set of rules to a tree structure. Figure 1 contains the search-tree equivalent of the sea animal's production system. To get the computer to use the rule set, it is necessary to explain to it how to search the tree for applicable actions. The same applies to real-world problems. In the sea-animal example, suppose you asked the computer, "What's this swimming on starboard?" (or entered the equivalent keyboard query), without giving any other information. The program should know enough to do the following: First, it should look at the rules available, and realize that it requires more information before answering your question. In this case, the

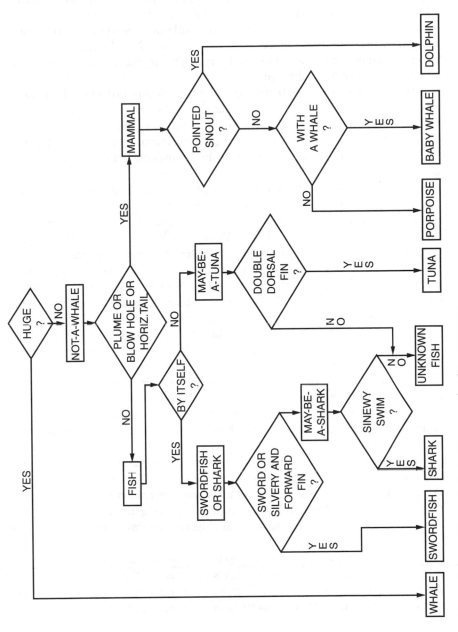

Figure 1 A graphic equivalent of the sea animal expert system

appropriate action would be a query for the information required to apply rule number 1 (IF it is huge THEN it is a whale). Thus, the computer needs a program to allow it to decide, from the set of rules, that it should ask you, "Well, how big is it?" The program should then use your answer to decide what question to ask next. Because of the analogies between rule sets and search trees, parts of this program can resemble the tree-searching programs used in theorem provers. Hence, once we have described the tree to the computer, an analogue of the tree-searching machinery developed for theorem proving can operate on the tree.

The flash of inspiration behind expert systems was just that: the realization, obvious in retrospect, that the tree description and the instructions for exploring the tree can be kept separate in a program. From one application to the next, one then needs only change the description of the tree, by entering a new set of rules. While this procedure improves the power of the program, it represents, in a sense, the opposite of reasoning. This illustrates the deep paradox uncovered by AI research: the only way to deal efficiently with very complex problems is to move away from pure logic. Consider a physician and a biologist. The biologist, who has studied biochemistry, anatomy, and physiology, can explain better than the physician the workings of a human body out of basic scientific principles. Yet that biologist can't read the telltale signs of a given infection and prescribe the right drug for it. Most of the time, reaching the right decision requires little reasoning: it is simply a question of *knowing* which symptoms go with which illness. Expert systems are, thus, not about reasoning: they are about knowing.

This type of behavior distinguishes, in fact, many of our interactions with the world. We constantly face opportunities to which we should react before they disappear. Reasoning takes time, so we try to do it as seldom as possible. Instead, we store the results of our reasoning for later reference: Feigenbaum and the production system school of AI claim that we store them in the form of rules, or recipes. Typical examples are the multiplication table or the recipe for tying shoelaces (remember how long it took when you had to think each motion through?).

Since remembering requires memory—or "storage space" in computer parlance—we find ourselves constantly trading time for space. We meet the largest payoff in this barter when the process of reasoning involves much trial-and-error searching for a solution. Since most skills required for intelligent behavior are of that nature, intelligent systems need to be partly rule-bound.

To summarize, an expert system has two parts: The first one is the so-called knowledge base. It usually makes up most of the system. In its simplest form, it is a list of IF ... THEN rules like the one above: each one specifies what to do, or what conclusions to draw, under a set of well-defined circumstances.

The second part of the expert system often goes under the name of "shell." As the name implies, it acts as a receptacle for the knowledge base and contains instruments for making efficient use of it. These include:

- A short-term memory that contains specific data about the actual problem under study. For example, the short-term memory for the sea-animal expert system may contain the information that the animal to identify is not huge and has a vertical tail.

- Tree-searching machinery as such. AI researchers, who are often strongly attached to the past, called this part of an expert system the inference engine, since it—in sifting through the knowledge base and inferring from it solutions to the problem at hand—fulfills Charles Babbage's notions for his ill-fated "analytical engine" in the nineteenth century (see chapter 1). Randall Davis told me that he coined the term *inference engine* while working on his Ph.D. at Stanford:

  > I had to go to Washington to try and explain to some folks from DARPA [the Department of Defense's Advanced Research Projects Agency] what our research was about. I needed a word that would convey to a bunch of people who understood FORTRAN programs that what we were doing was very different. And knowing about Babbage, . . . I figured *inference engine* was in the right spirit. It would orient them toward thinking of a machine because it was an engine, but orient them toward thinking of a machine that was doing inference, not arithmetic. And that is a very important distinction.

- User interface, which can range from simple, menu-driven interaction with the computer, to quasi natural-language dialogue. The expert system uses the user interface to ask you questions like "How large is the animal?" and to understand your answer. Through it, you can also ask the computer to explain how it reached a certain conclusion. To answer, the computer would simply retrace its trip down the decision tree for you, and may say something like: "I conclude it's a dolphin, because it's not huge (rule 1), it has a blowhole (rule 4), and it has a pointed snout (rule 5)."

Nowadays, expert system shells are available from many software companies. To apply them to a particular problem, you simply add the pertinent set of rules into the knowledge base. Counting the basic research and development that went into the technology, a modern expert system shell embodies hundreds of person-years of work. Without it, it would be necessary to do part of this work all over for each new expert system.

An advance in AI

There are several reasons why expert systems constitute a genuine advance in artificial intelligence.

First, many modern expert systems involve thousands of rules. It would be extremely tedious to find the rules pertinent to a given problem (or follow the corresponding search tree) on paper. User-friendly program interfaces make the search itself transparent and turn the consultation into a question-answering session. At the design stage, the analyst can correct errors by asking the system how it reached a faulty conclusion. The defective rule will appear in the chain of reasoning cited by the system. Since the rules are usually self-explanatory, end users can also follow the reasoning involved and thus satisfy themselves of the validity of the system's conclusion.

To perform all these tasks, expert systems allow the automatic chaining of rules: that is, entering the rules in an order different from the one in which they will appear in the reasoning. Rule chaining also permits the program to infer conditions from conclusions. For example, in a medical expert system, it would be possible to enter the rules as: "Infection by such a microorganism causes this symptom." The expert system could then work its way backward from symptoms to causes.

Problem solutions do not usually follow from a single string of rules or from a single branch of the tree. Several alternative paths are usually open in the search down the tree. For example, a given set of symptoms could come from several illnesses, all of which the system must consider. If unable to rule out all but one diagnosis, the system would supply a list of possibilities, with associated likelihoods. Conversely, several different paths of investigation might lead to a single conclusion. Even if no path offered convincing evidence by itself, the convergence of several paths could allow a conclusion. Expert systems can handle this type of situation also.

Expert systems differ from printed rule books, or even from conventional computer programs, through their flexibility and modularity. In these aspects, they almost rival human reasoning. Expert systems are easy to change or improve. You want to add a new piece of knowledge? Simply leave everything as is, and add a new rule! You would inform a human worker about a new law or regulation in much the same way. By contrast, a change to a conventional computer program interacts with the existing code. It requires a careful screening, and usually changes, to the old code.

Yet another difference of expert systems is their openness, or self-explanatory character. In conventional programs (except perhaps data bases), computer-language instructions, or algorithms, contain the knowledge. It is hidden in the structure of the program itself, rather than made explicit in a separate module. AI workers say that in expert systems, knowledge is declarative; while in conventional programs, it is procedural.

Expert systems resemble human thought in another important way. They are much more resilient than conventional computer programs. One can usually remove any single rule without grossly affecting the program performance. This behavior is also characteristic of a human professional, who can usually still offer an opinion even if some information is removed from the problem formulation. By contrast, if the tiniest detail in the instructions of a conventional program is accidentally erased or changed, the behavior of the program usually changes drastically.

Knowing about knowledge: TEIRESIAS

In the course of developing DENDRAL and MYCIN, the Stanford researchers encountered a problem that had little to do with LISP, inference engines, or even computer programming in general. It was the extreme difficulty of transferring the appropriate knowledge from the mind of a human expert to the knowledge base of the program. Boiling human knowledge down to a set of well-defined rules turned out to be a very painful process. Both the expert and the computer scientist designing the expert system had to suffer. The French scientific philosopher Claude Bernard had already realized this trait of the human mind in the previous century:

> We achieve more than we know.
> We know more than we understand.
> We understand more than we can explain.[19]

When Randall Davis was looking for a Ph.D. project at Stanford, he decided with his adviser, Bruce Buchanan, to focus on making this knowledge transfer easier. The result, a program called TEIRESIAS,[20] would mark a critical step in the development of a new discipline that became known as "knowledge engineering." Buchanan's classical background (his original field had been philosophy) inspired the program's name. Teiresias, the blind prophet in Sophocles' *Oedipus Rex*, can fathom events hidden to common mortals and possesses a higher form of knowledge. "The notion matched the idea of meta-level knowledge that I was exploring," Davis told me. "It also made for cute quotes that I could scatter through the text of the thesis. They are lines from the play which, taken out of context and dropped at the right places, made for wonderful introductions to the chapters and sections." (Sample: "I shall tell you the whole truth.")

TEIRESIAS' function as a program was to mediate between MYCIN and blood disease specialists desiring to impart some of their knowledge to it. The specialist used MYCIN in the ordinary mode, and TEIRESIAS intervened when the program made a wrong diagnosis. At a doctor's request, TEIRESIAS could then assist him or her in retracing the rules applied by MYCIN in reaching its mistaken conclusion. If one of the rules was found to be wrong, or if the physician realized that a new rule was required to take the new case into account, TEIRESIAS assisted him or her in making the correction. To this effect, TEIRESIAS needed information about how much MYCIN already knew and how it reasoned. Since this kind of information consisted in knowledge about knowledge, Davis called it "meta-knowledge." Much as Tom Evans had explored the square root of analogy in the 1960s, Davis set out to explore the square root of knowledge. For example, TEIRESIAS contained rule schemas that outlined some general characteristics of particular classes of rules. As a case in point, assume the physician has just defined the following new rule:

IF
1. The patient's infection is primary-bacteremia
2. The site is one of the sterile sites
THEN
There is evidence that the bacterium category is enterobacteriaceae.

TEIRESIAS might well reply:

I hate to criticize, Dr. Davis, but did you know that most rules about what the category of an organism might be, that mention the site of a culture and the infection, also mention:
[A]—the portal of entry into the organism
Shall I write a clause to account for [A]?[21]

The XCON advance

Ground breaking as they were as proofs of principle, DENDRAL and MYCIN remained laboratory applications. The development of the expert system that was to win the corporate world over to AI started in Carnegie Mellon University in the late 1970s. The program's initial name of R1 stemmed from a bad joke made by its author, John McDermott ("I had always wanted to be a knowledge engineer, and now I R1").[22] McDermott's client, the Digital Equipment Corporation of Maynard, Massachusetts, preferred the name XCON, for eXpert CONfigurer. If you've ever bought a computer, you probably had to face some of the problems XCON solves. "How much memory does this program require to run? Do I want a color screen? There aren't enough expansion slots for both the modem and the accelerator board. Which one do I need most?" Some accessories may be incompatible, while others require each other. Like new cars, computers can come in so many different configurations that no two are alike. When it went to McDermott, the Digital Equipment Corporation was to produce a new line of minicomputers called VAX. Product configuration of these new machines, or "technical editing," as it is known in the computer industry, had grown into a monster headache. Since 90 percent of the computers

coming out of a DEC factory differed from each other, they had to be pains-
takingly put together on the factory floor, tested (which usually revealed
configuration errors to correct), and then disassembled, packed, and
shipped. In the late 1970s, with the introduction of the new VAX line, the
problem was expected to develop into a bottleneck threatening the very
survival of DEC. The engineering manager, Dennis O'Connor, was getting
ready to build several dedicated plants in which to perform the preshipment
testing, when he decided to see whether any research might have a bearing on
the problem (following up on a suggestion made by the vice president for
research, Samuel Fuller). With sixty thousand dollars of discretionary funds,
O'Connor issued a contract for John McDermott, then a young professor
at CMU, to investigate whether an expert system couldn't configure VAX
computers. In so doing, O'Connor was running an "amazing risk," recalled DEC's engineering vice president Gordon Bell,[23] for the engineering
manager sought the involvement of many others in the company, and his
reputation was on the line.

McDermott's feasibility study yielded thumbs-up results, and work started
on a prototype configurer at CMU in December 1978. In April 1979,
McDermott and his team felt confident enough for a field test, expecting a
95-percent configuring accuracy. This first step of AI out of the academic
closet was sobering. XCON averaged one configuration wrong out of five
and was sent back to the drafting board. By the end of the year, though, the
system was working well enough to be used on actual orders.

McDermott turned over the initial version of XCON to DEC in January
1980. It was then able to configure only one of DEC's computers, the VAX-
11/780. It did well in that trial phase, and DEC approved the gradual, in-
house extension of it to the rest of its products. By 1984, XCON had become
the prototypical expert system success story: from about three hundred rules
in 1979, it had grown tenfold to more than three thousand and could
configure ten different computer models.[24]

Conceived in the 1960s, expert systems made up the most salient part of
AI's revival during the 1970s and became visible to the public in the 1980s.
As I shall discuss in the next chapter, that part of the AI iceberg which
remains underwater is even more fascinating.

Notes

The epigraph is from an interview with Marvin Minsky, 13 May 1991.

1 J. H. Breasted, *The Edwin Smith Surgical Papyrus* (Chicago: Chicago University
Press, 1930).
2 C. A. Elsberg, "The Anatomy and Surgery of the Edwin Smith Surgical Papyrus,"
Journal of Mt. Sinai Hospital 12 (1945), 141–51.
3 Michel Gondran, *Introduction aux systèmes experts* (Paris: Eyrolles, 1983), p. 88.
4 Interview with Herbert Simon, 22 May 1991. All other personal quotes of Simon's
in this chapter are from this interview.

5 Interview with Marvin Minsky, 13 May 1991. All other personal quotes of Minsky's in this chapter are from this interview.

6 Edward A. Feigenbaum and Julian Feldman, eds., *Computers and Thought* (New York: McGraw-Hill, 1963).

7 R. Lindsay et al., *DENDRAL* (New York: McGraw-Hill, 1980).

8 Edward A. Feigenbaum and Avron Barr, eds., *The Handbook of Artificial Intelligence*, vol. II (Reading, Mass.: Addison-Wesley, 1982), pp. 106–15.

9 Edward A. Feigenbaum and Pamela McCorduck, *The Fifth Generation—Artificial Intelligence and Japan's Computer Challenge to the World* (Reading, Mass.: Addison-Wesley, 1983), pp. 61–62.

10 Interview with Bruce Buchanan, co-developer of DENDRAL, in H.L. Dreyfus and S. E. Dreyfus, *Mind over Machine: The Power of Human Intuition and Expertise in the Era of the Computer* (New York: Free Press, 1985), p. 111.

11 Interview with Allen Newell, 23 May 1991. All other personal quotes of Allen Newell's in this chapter are from this interview.

12 Allen Newell and Herbert Simon, *Human Problem Solving* (Englewood Cliffs, N.J.: Prentice-Hall, 1972).

13 Emil Post, "Formal Reductions of the General Combinatorial Decision Problem," *American Journal of Mathematics* 65 (1943): 197–215.

14 Noam Chomsky, *Syntactic Structures* (The Hague: Mouton, 1957).

15 Edward H. Shortliffe, *MYCIN: Computer-based Medical Consultations* (New York: Elsevier Press, 1976); and Bruce G. Buchanan and Edward H. Shortlife, eds., *Rule-based Expert Systems—The MYCIN Experiments of the Stanford Heuristic Programming Project* (Reading, Mass.: Addison-Wesley, 1984).

16 Feigenbaum and Barr, *Handbook*, p. 93.

17 Victor L. Yu et al., "Antimicrobial Selection by a Computer," *Journal of the American Medical Association*, 21 September 1979, pp. 1279–82.

18 Interview with Randall Davis, 17 May 1991. All other personal quotes of Davis's in this chapter are from this interview.

19 Quoted in Gondran, *Introduction*, p. 92.

20 R. Davis, "Applications of Meta-knowledge to the Construction, Maintenance, and Use of Large Knowledge Bases," doctoral diss., Computer Science Department, Stanford University, 1976; reprinted in R. Davis and D. Lenat, eds., *Knowledge-based Systems in Artificial Intelligence* (New York: McGraw-Hill, 1982), pp. 229–490.

21 Barr and Feigenbaum, *Handbook*, p. 100.

22 Morris W. Firebaugh, *Artificial Intelligence: A Knowledge-Based Approach* (Boston: Boyd & Fraser, 1988), p. 356.

23 Edward A. Feigenbaum, Pamela McCorduck, and Penny Nii H., *The Rise of the Expert Company* (New York: Vintage Books, 1988), pp. 218–20.

24 Judith Bachant and John McDermott, "R1 Revisited: Four Years in the Trenches," *AI Magazine*, Fall 1984, p. 21.